TIRPITZ
AND THE IMPERIAL GERMAN NAVY

PATRICK J. KELLY

INDIANA UNIVERSITY PRESS

Bloomington & Indianapolis

TIRPITZ

AND THE IMPERIAL GERMAN NAVY

This book is a publication of

Indiana University Press
601 North Morton Street
Bloomington, Indiana 47404-3797 USA

iupress.indiana.edu

Telephone orders   800-842-6796
Fax orders   812-855-7931
Orders by e-mail   iuporder@indiana.edu

∞ The paper used in this publication meets the minimum requirements of the American National Standard for Information Sciences—Permanence of Paper for Printed Library Materials, ANSI Z39.48-1992.

Manufactured in the United States of America

Library of Congress Cataloging-in-Publication Data

Kelly, Patrick J., [date]-
  Tirpitz and the Imperial German Navy / Patrick J. Kelly.
    p. cm.
  Includes bibliographical references and index.
  ISBN 978-0-253-35593-5 (cloth : alk. paper) 1. Tirpitz, Alfred von, 1849–1930.
2. Admirals—Germany—Biography. 3. Germany. Kriegsmarine—History—19th century 4. Germany. Kriegsmarine—History—20th century. 5. Germany—History, Naval—19th century. 6. Germany—History, Naval—20th century. I. Title.
  DD231.T5K45 2011
  359.0092—dc22
  [B]

                         2010035369

1 2 3 4 5   16 15 14 13 12 11

This book is dedicated to my parents, Robert and the late Evelyn Kelly.

CONTENTS

· Acknowledgments   *ix*

· Abbreviations   *xi*

1 Introduction   *1*

2 Tirpitz's Early Life   *14*

3 The Aspirant, 1865–1870   *24*

4 The Young Officer, 1870–1877: A Taste of War   *33*

5 The Creation of the German Torpedo Arm, 1877–1889   *47*

6 Interim, 1889–1891   *69*

7 Oberkommando der Marine, 1892–1895   *81*

8 On the Verge of Power, 1895–1897   *103*

9 Tirpitz Ascendant, 1897–1898   *129*

10 The Second Navy Law, 1899–1900   *166*

· Illustrations   *203*

11 The "Quiet" Years, 1900–1906   *223*

12 Sow the Wind, 1906–1908   *263*

13 The Whirlwind Rises, 1908–1911 293

14 Denouement, 1911–1914 323

15 Tirpitz at War, August 1914–March 1916 375

16 Uncommon Recessional, 1916–1930 410

17 Conclusion 444

· Appendix 467

· Notes 469

· Bibliography 535

· Index 555

ACKNOWLEDGMENTS

In the preparation and writing of this work I owe great thanks to many people and institutions. These include Dr. Dean C. Allard, Bernard Cavalcante, and Harry Reilly of the former U.S. Naval History Office in Washington, D.C.; Robert Hanshew and Chuck Haberlein, photo archivists of its successor organization, the U.S. Naval History and Heritage Command; Robert Wolfe of the U.S. National Archives; the archivists and staffs of the Bundesarchiv-Militärarchiv (Freiburg), particularly the late Dr. Gerd Sandhofer; the Bundesarchiv (Koblenz); the Deutsches Zentralarchiv (Merseburg, now at Potsdam); the Bundesarchiv (Potsdam); the Auswärtiges Amt Archiv (Bonn); the Niedersächsisches Staatsarchiv (Bückeburg); the Landesarchiv (Speyer); and the Militärgeschichtliches Forschungsamt (MGFA) (Freiburg, now at Potsdam), where I was the recipient of encouragement and wise advice from the late Prof. Dr. Wilhelm Deist. The late Professors John Zeender of Catholic University and Thomas Helde of Georgetown University helped greatly in the early stages of this project.

I am very grateful to the late Ambassador Wolf Ulrich von Hassell for his personal account of his grandfather Tirpitz, and to his son, Augustino von Hassell, who gave me untrammeled access to important Tirpitz correspondence and illustrations that are in the possession of the von Hassell family. Dr. Terrell Gottschall kindly provided me with material from the papers of Admiral Otto von Diedrichs. Prof. Dr. Michael Epkenhans, now Research Head of the MGFA, generously shared ideas and documents with me while we both, as friendly competitors, wrestled with the mysteries of Tirpitz's life. Dr. Raffael Scheck helped me unravel the twisted strands of Tirpitz's life in the 1920s, and shared friendship and archival comradeship with me in Freiburg. Dr. Keith Bird, a friend of many decades, helped with his unrivaled knowledge of the bibliography of the German Navy. Thanks also to Prof. Eric C. Rust for many valuable suggestions. Robert Sloan of Indiana University Press provided patient and cordial help. Eliz Alahverdian, Art Curator at Adelphi University gave indispensable help with maps and illustrations.

In the fall of 1990, on my second visit to Freiburg, I had the good luck and great pleasure to meet Dr. Rolf Hobson of the Norwegian Defence Studies Institute. We became and remain close personal and family friends. The author of a pioneering work on Tirpitz's naval strategy, he read the entire manuscript with a keen and critical eye, to my immense benefit.

My wife Lorraine Kelly, my son Matthew Kelly, and my longtime friend Edward Case read the manuscript as non-experts, improved my writing and thinking, and somehow tolerated my preoccupation with Tirpitz. I owe them much. All errors in the book are mine.

Patrick J. Kelly
Adelphi University
October 2010

ABBREVIATIONS

BEF   British Expeditionary Force

CIGS   Chief of the Imperial General Staff

DDP   German Democratic Party

DNVP   German National People's Party

DVP   German People's Party

E   Etatsabteilung (Estimates Department of the RMA)

GHQ   General Headquarters

HAPAG   Hamburg-Amerika shipping line

K   Konstruktionsabteilung (Construction Department of the RMA)

KPD   Communist Party of Germany

MK   Marinekabinett (Naval Cabinet)

N   Nachrichtenbüro (Press Bureau of the RMA); Nachrichtenabteilung (Press Agency of the RMA)

OHL   Oberste Heeresleitung (Army High Command)

OK   Oberkommando (Naval High Command)

RMA   Reichsmarineamt (Imperial Naval Office)

v   Verwaltungsabteilung (Administrative
    Department of the RMA)

w   Waffenabteilung (Weapons Department of the RMA)

z   Zentralabteilung (Central Department of the RMA)

MAP 1 The North Sea. *Courtesy of Eliz Alahverdian.*

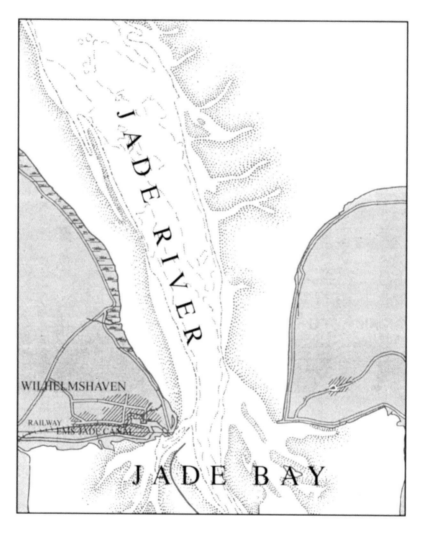

MAP 2 Wilhelmshaven. *Courtesy of Eliz Alahverdian.*

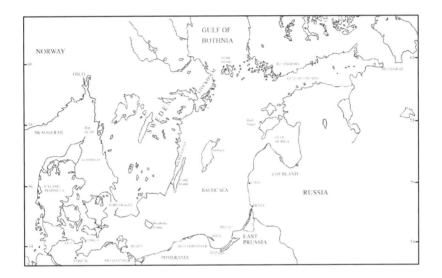

MAP 3 The Baltic Sea. *Courtesy of Eliz Alahverdian.*

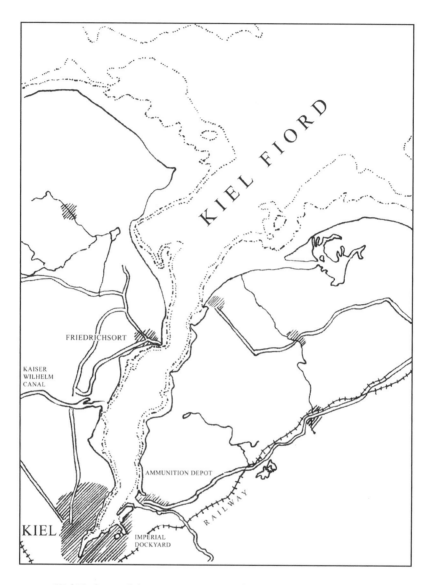

MAP 4 Kiel Harbor and the eastern terminus of the Kaiser Wilhelm Canal. *Courtesy of Eliz Alahverdian.*

1
INTRODUCTION

On 3 August 1914 gray-clad German troopers crossed the Belgian and Luxemburg frontiers to begin, in that theater, the greatest conflagration Europe had ever seen. Nestled in the fenlands of the North Sea coast, the small, drab German city of Wilhelmshaven overnight became a household word. In its harbor and in the nearby Jade, a lagoon-like body of water, sheltered from the stormy North Sea by a great sand bar, there gathered the most powerful fleet ever assembled in continental Europe, the mighty German High Seas Fleet. Fifteen of the most modern (Dreadnought-type) battleships, soon joined by two more in trials, and four speedy battlecruisers lay poised for an expected Armageddon with the even mightier British Grand Fleet, which then had twenty-two Dreadnoughts and ten powerful battlecruisers.

A few dozen leagues to the north, on the small island of Helgoland, lookouts scanned the horizon in wary anticipation of the British Armada. Smaller warships, based in Helgoland, formed a picket line to the north and west, ready to wireless the alarm.

To the south, the presence in an Austrian Adriatic base of the German battlecruiser *Goeben* alarmed the British Mediterranean command. Halfway around the world, in the German colony of Tsingtau on the Chinese Shantung Peninsula,[1] a small squadron of older German cruisers excited the same fears for British forces in the Pacific. This impressive array of German naval might was, in large measure, the life's work of Grand Admiral Alfred von Tirpitz.

As recently as 1897 most ships of the Imperial German Navy were obsolescent museum pieces, many of them foreign-built. Depending on how one measured, Germany, an industrial giant, had a fleet that ranked only fifth or sixth among the world's navies, with just a handful of modern ships. As the French Revolution proved, nations could create, train, and arm huge military forces over a short period of time; navies, however, were another matter. To construct and maintain a formidable navy required vast amounts of coal and steel, large numbers of skilled workers, highly sophisticated machine tools and engineering, and complex organizational entities to manage the process. Failing heroic measures, a large modern ship needed at least three or four years to complete, and usually another year for trials. Some of the essential fleet-building elements were in place in Germany by 1897, but a master organizer was needed to initiate and direct such a complex systematic undertaking.

The naval zeal of William II (r. 1888–1918) was an indispensable pre-requisite for a large fleet, but his mercurial temperament and erratic work habits provided little progress on naval matters during the first nine years of his reign. To finance a first-class navy required vast sums of money. Absent were a plausible program, public enthusiasm, and parliamentary support from a society not previously noted, except in a few coastal cities, for its maritime interests.

Alfred Tirpitz, who brought the German Navy to second in the world by 1914, was the son of a respected Prussian country judge. In 1865, at age sixteen, he joined the navy to escape the rigors of the classroom. How could such an unpromising middle-class youth rise to one of the highest positions in the Second Reich? How could he ultimately challenge the might of the British Royal Navy? How could he become the most effective politician in the entire history of Imperial Germany, save only the incomparable Otto von Bismarck? This biography addresses these questions, along with the failures and doleful consequences that followed from those same unlikely successes.

Tirpitz[2] is best remembered for his work as State Secretary of the Imperial Naval Office (Reichsmarineamt, or RMA) from 1897 to 1916. During those years he persuaded the Imperial Reichstag to pass five naval bills (1898 and 1900, with amendments in 1906, 1908, and 1912) that produced the world's second-largest navy. The laws were mainly directed toward the construction of sixty modern battleships and battlecruisers by 1920. In 1914 the exigencies of war essentially brought the construction plan to a halt; nevertheless, the partially fulfilled program was a remarkable, if tainted, achievement. Tirpitz had to overcome enormous political and diplomatic obstacles, the fecklessness of William II, and even the opposition of powerful elements within the navy itself.

THE NAVY AND THE CONSTITUTION

To understand the character and magnitude of the challenges Tirpitz faced, it is necessary to examine some of the peculiarities of the Constitution of the German Empire that Bismarck put into place shortly after the founding of the Empire in 1871.

By the standards of a world accustomed to the idea of a nation-state, even a federal one such as the United States, the German Empire was an odd creation. The official name of the Empire was "The Federated Governments of the German Empire." Sovereignty was not vested in the Emperor but in the Bundesrat, an unelected body comprised of what amounted to ambassadors from the various German states. Prussia, with over 60 percent of the territory and population of the Empire, was the dominant force within the Bundesrat, and held veto power over anything it enacted. The King of Prussia was President of this union of states and, solely by virtue of this position, was styled the "German Emperor." In many respects he enjoyed far more power as King than as Emperor.

A rough analogy would be as if all of the United States east of the Rocky Mountains were one of the fifty states, and the rest of the country were divided into the other forty-nine. If we call the largest state "Columbia" and give the states hereditary governors, then the Governor of Columbia would, ipso facto, be President of the United States. Even if the smaller states had considerable power over their domestic affairs, one can imagine how significant in national affairs the Governor of Columbia would be.

In peacetime the larger German federal states had their own armies; only in wartime would they be partially subordinated to the King of Prussia. Technically, under the Empire, there was no such thing as a German Army. At first many services, including post, customs, and railroads, were left to individual federal states.[3]

The Prussian Parliament (Landtag) had a three-class suffrage system, which overrepresented rural, aristocratic, and agrarian interests, and underrepresented cities and the fast-growing urban population. The

Imperial Reichstag was elected by universal and equal manhood suffrage, although it was never redistricted between 1871 and 1918 to reflect vast population movements from rural to urban areas. Royal prerogative precluded the Reichstag's direct participation in military and foreign affairs, and it could not initiate legislation, which first had to come from the Bundesrat. The Reichstag's main power was to vote on the national budget. In the background lurked the fear (or hope) of a repetition of what had happened for several years in the 1860s, when Bismarck taxed and spent money in defiance of the Prussian Landtag that, on paper, had a budget right similar to that of the post-1871 Reichstag. In Tirpitz's time, William II sometimes blustered about a government coup, with army backing, against the Reichstag. Under the Empire, this would have been harder to do than in Prussia, because the other federal states would probably have opposed what they would see as a Prussian power grab. Some groups in the Reichstag, such as the Bavarian wing of the Catholic Center Party, were much more concerned with the interests of their own states than those of the whole Reich.

Compared to other parliamentary systems, the position of the Imperial Chancellor was similarly unusual. Unlike, for example, the British Prime Minister, leader of the ruling party, the Chancellor and his cabinet did not rely on a parliamentary majority, but were chosen by and served at the pleasure of the Emperor. This arrangement often created awkwardness for the Chancellor, as well as the danger of serious instability if the Emperor and the Reichstag were irreconcilably at odds on an important issue.

The Imperial Navy, founded in 1871, was truly a national institution, without cumbersome constitutional ties to individual states. Under Bismarck there was a Chief of Admiralty, who simultaneously exercised both military command of the navy, directly subject to the Emperor, and the task of dealing with the Reichstag, under the aegis of the Chancellor. Shortly after William II ascended the throne in 1888 he demanded more direct control of the navy. He therefore split the Admiralty into three parts, modeled, he thought, on the army's organization. A High Command (Oberkommando, or OK), led by a Commanding Admiral, conducted solely military matters and thereby was not "tainted" by contact with the Reichstag. A State Secretary of the RMA, another naval officer, would deal with the Reichstag about the naval budget. Although a member of the Chancellor's cabinet, he was still subject to military discipline. A Naval Cabinet (Marinekabinett, or MK) handled personnel matters within the navy. This apparently logical arrangement led to fierce internecine battles, in which Tirpitz was seriatim engaged for both sides, first as Chief of Staff of the OK and later as State Secretary of the RMA, when he had to refute his prior claims to OK supremacy. Tirpitz was no simple sailor turned minister, but he was at the nexus of a complicated process of institutional creation/reformation that reached into many dimensions of governmental and extra-governmental life.

INTERPRETING TIRPITZ

Tirpitz's achievement has attracted many interpreters, one of whom was Tirpitz himself.[4] As with many memoirs, Tirpitz's were exculpatory. He argued that, in a predatory world, Germany needed a powerful fleet of battleships to protect German coasts, trade, and economic interests, particularly from the British Royal Navy. He proposed a counterintuitive defense of Germany's worldwide interests, the concentration of almost the entire fleet in home waters. The idea came to be called the "risk theory," a form of deterrence, first articulated publicly in the preamble to the 1900 Navy Law. An enlarged German fleet would eventually create a situation whereby a British naval defeat of Germany would incur losses that would leave the Royal Navy exposed to the combined French and Russian navies. He argued that, instead of risking a pyrrhic victory, the British would make political concessions to Germany, particularly in the realm of trade and colonies. If the risk theory were correct, a German fleet concentrated in home waters would make its weight felt all around the world and serve as a lever for German world policy (Weltpolitik). If the British failed to see the logic of the scheme, Germany, with its small but growing fleet, would be an attractive alliance partner for France and, especially, for Russia, who were Britain's two principal opponents in colonial questions around 1900. He did not address how Germany could become an ally of France while still in occupation of Alsace-Lorraine, the principal spoils of the war with France in 1870–1871.

Every ship added after 1900 would, he argued, increase the navy's deterrence value. Early on there would be a "danger zone," during which the young fleet might be vulnerable to British preventive attack. To pass the danger zone safely it would be essential to avoid provocative foreign policy actions until the fleet was "ready." He was vague about when the danger zone would end but was confident that it would be sometime before the full fleet of sixty battleships and large cruisers was complete in 1920.

Tirpitz boasted that, with the 1900 naval law, he had established an "iron budget," which obviated the need to go to the Reichstag for ship construction money every year, as had been the case before 1898. Freed from the vexing annual interference of Parliament, the fleet could grow at the pace of three large ships per year as it finessed the danger zone. In hindsight, Germany was less secure against Britain with a large fleet in 1914 than it had been with a much smaller one in 1900; Tirpitz later attributed this situation mainly to the "bungling" of Chancellors Bernhard von Bülow (1900–1909) and Theobald von Bethmann-Hollweg (1909–1916).

Official histories, most published naval memoirs, and later German conservative historians, particularly Hans Hallmann and Walther Hubatsch,[5] defended Tirpitz. Hubatsch has suggested that the fateful choice made in 1897 to establish a navy based on fixed laws was, in itself, sufficient to involve Germany in a hopeless arms race:

> He [Tirpitz] belongs to that type of *homo faber* that was brought forth in an age of technology. But technology at the turn of the century was in the position of making itself independent. The naval laws, like the Schlieffen Plan and the clockwork of mobilization, withdrew from the necessary political and diplomatic influences. . . .
>
> The mechanically unfolding, long-term Navy Law became an instrument of the political leadership, and was never arranged to the degree necessary to correspond to the total interests of foreign policy.[6]

According to Hubatsch, if Tirpitz did not completely foresee the political effects of his policy, then the fault lay with the Foreign Office.

Another view held that Tirpitz and Germany were not trapped by technology but that Tirpitz was, by nature, a militarist. Gerhard Ritter has written that Tirpitz's solution to Germany's political problems with Britain was "build more, until they come to us," the reply of a "typical militarist." Ritter defined militarism as "the erroneous belief that political problems can be mastered by military exertions alone."[7]

With very few exceptions, such as Carl Galster and Wolfgang Wegener,[8] the navy's official history and published memoirs era reflected Tirpitz's view. Recent scholarship has demonstrated how assiduously the Weimar era navy protected Tirpitz's image and justified his ideas.[9]

Beneath the official silence, some of Tirpitz's former close associates wondered what had gone wrong. In 1926 retired Admiral Eduard von Capelle, Tirpitz's closest aide for eighteen years and the master of dealing with the Reichstag, heard from a former subordinate, Vice Admiral Carl Hollweg, also retired. The latter lamented that the true story would probably never be told:

> There are in Germany only two men who would be, because of their own experience, in a position to write such a book on the theme of fleet building and the causes of the war. These are Your Excellency and Admiral Dähnhardt [Capelle's former deputy], who were both in Berlin during the whole Navy Law period and were knowledgeable about all things. Tirpitz himself is too much of a partisan to write such a book credibly. Thus, it will happen that the "professors" and other people who work only on the basis of "files and documents" will be victorious with their view that building a fleet was a fundamental error, and led to our misfortune.[10]

Despite Hollweg's misgivings, the "official" version held up for a surprisingly long time. The only major exception was Eckart Kehr,[11] who died tragically in 1933 at the age of thirty. Virtually ignored when published, Kehr's work saw Germany's naval and foreign policy driven more strongly by the need for the aristocratic ruling classes to defend their hold on Germany from socialism and democracy than by legitimate defense needs. Kehr's interpretation emphasized what he saw as the primacy of domestic over foreign policy in building the fleet.

Hollweg's prediction about the "professors" only began to materialize in the early 1960s, when the German Naval Archives, which survived the war almost intact, became available to historians. The first book to explore in depth these new holdings was Jonathan Steinberg's *Yesterday's Deterrent: Tirpitz and the Birth of the German Battle Fleet*. Steinberg argued convincingly that Tirpitz, from the moment he took over as State Secretary of the RMA in the summer of 1897, clearly intended to build a "fleet against England." His second contention, which came under attack from later historians such as Volker Berghahn, was that Tirpitz, of bourgeois origins himself, operated with the Reichstag in a much more collegial and parliamentary manner than his more traditional and conservative colleagues. Steinberg thus gave Tirpitz a "liberal" flavor.

The views of Volker Berghahn have, for almost four decades, largely defined the field of naval policy in the Tirpitz era. His impressive scholarly work is based on extensive, multi-archival research, including the massive Tirpitz Nachlass, acquired by the German Naval Archives in the late 1960s.[12] Berghahn examined what he called the "Tirpitz Plan," down to the point in 1908 when it was clear that the plan was in substantial difficulty. Two other historians, Wilhelm Deist and Michael Epkenhans, with much the same viewpoint as Berghahn, published complementary and supplementary studies. Deist exhaustively examined Tirpitz's great propaganda efforts, and Epkenhans, with special emphasis on construction policy, covered the period from 1908 to 1914.[13]

Berghahn agreed with Steinberg that the fleet was anti-British from the outset. He developed Kehr's suggestion of a close link between the agrarian/aristocratic domination of Germany's political system and Tirpitz's fleet construction program. The fleet's purpose, according to Berghahn, was to become a central element in a far-reaching compromise between Germany's aristocratic and industrial elites to stabilize the Wilhelmian system against the rising power of socialism. A broad coalition (*Sammlung*), including industry, that would have the lucrative task of building the fleet, and agrarians, who would get a higher grain tariff, would reach out to the large Catholic Center Party to form a barrier against Social Democrats. Even the workers would be palliated by jobs to build the fleet and by sharing, psychologically if not financially, in the fruits of expanded imperialism. Foreign policy would be tailored to avoid provoking the British until the fleet was far enough through the danger zone to make the risk fleet idea operative.

This short summary does not do full justice to the nuances of Berghahn's ideas on the link between domestic stabilization and fleet building, addressed in more detail below. Berghahn posited that the 1900 Navy Law set up a construction plan, the "iron budget," that obligated the Reichstag, for example, to replace small coastal battleships with powerful seagoing battleships many times their size.

Although lucidly presented, and undeniably true in many particulars, Berghahn's view is, in some respects, open to question. Could Tirpitz have conceived such a comprehensive plan in 1897–98? Could such a ramshackle system as William II's Germany have carried out such a far-reaching plan? Did Tirpitz's later efforts demonstrate such a disciplined approach? Did Tirpitz's *own* motivation, the prime concern of a biography, foster an attempt to stabilize a whole vast system?

In a review of *Der Tirpitz Plan*, Steinberg raises some trenchant questions:

Much evidence exists to show that diplomats had only the vaguest contacts
with the military ministries and certainly Tirpitz had very little contact,
or much sympathy, with the men on the Wilhelmstrasse [Foreign Office].
All too often, nobody knew what anybody else was doing, and that was
sometimes seen as a good thing. A system of government so absurd seems
hardly capable of any decision at all (and frequently was not). Was it up to
the rational, coherent, farsighted, and, above all, coordinated strategy which
Der Tirpitz Plan assumes? I doubt it . . .

   Tirpitz wanted to build battleships. He never wanted to build a
"system-stabilizing fleet," nor would he have understood what it meant.
Dr. Berghahn overlooks the fact that *systemstabilisierend* is a historian's
category. In a very subtle sense, Dr. Berghahn has fallen into a kind of
anachronism by sliding away the barrier between the intentions of the actors at the time and the understanding of those intentions by an analyzing
historian after the events.[14]

One need not agree entirely with Steinberg to recognize that such questions deserve careful consideration.

Another important aspect of Tirpitz's goals is the question of what he
meant by building a fleet "against" Britain. His postwar writings give the
strong impression that he expected war against Britain from the beginning; his prewar actions indicate, however, that he wanted much more to
deter the British than to fight them. Did he intend to build a fleet equal
to or superior to the Royal Navy? Or, perhaps, did he just want to build
the largest fleet that Germany could, given its other financial and political
priorities, a fleet not large enough to provoke the British preventive attack
that he feared? In these and other questions, the problem of hindsight
leaps out. This biography strives to judge the prewar Tirpitz in the prewar
context, what he knew, believed, and did, in so far as that is possible.

Another historian raised the question of intentions in a somewhat
different way:

It was a foolhardy assumption that England would ever tolerate the rise of
German naval power to the point where it would seriously jeopardize the
British command of the seas, on which the independence and prosperity
of the British Isles depended. . . . [Tirpitz] had reached the conclusion
that England might one day choose to destroy German foreign trade and
colonial enterprise. Yet why [he thought] this same England, suspected of
such evil designs, should watch impassively the building up of German
naval strength [through the Navy Law] was one of the mysteries of Tirpitz's
mind.[15]

Such anomalies in Tirpitz's thought and behavior give pause to a an
historian. The vast majority of people who have studied him, with the

partial exceptions of Kehr and Carl-Axel Gemzell, the latter of whom concentrates on operational planning,[16] proceed from the assumption, explicit or implicit, that Tirpitz's policies may be explained by entirely rational means, even when this postulate leads to confusion or contradiction.

To address these dilemmas, a fresh perspective, highly respected in the discipline of political science, if used sparingly and in a nuanced way, can prove helpful as the historian grapples with questions of context. Graham Allison and Philip Zelikow, in a revised edition of Allison's work, *Essence of Decision*, suggest three different but interacting points of view through which to examine the processes and contexts surrounding political decisions.[17] Allison described these as the Rational Actor Model (Model 1), the Organizational Behavior Model (Model 2), and the Governmental, or Bureaucratic, Politics Model (Model 3).

Model 2 does not deal with individual behavior but with that of organizations as whole entities. As such, it is somewhat useful in the study of Tirpitz. On matters in which it does apply, such as the universal feeling of chagrin in the navy for its ineffectiveness in the Franco-Prussian War, the feeling was fully shared by Tirpitz as an individual. Another example would be the desire of virtually all officers for expansion. Their promotion prospects would accelerate far faster than the army's glacial pace. Gemzell's work, in particular, elucidates the Model 2 aspects of the navy.

Model 1, the Rational Actor, assumes the protagonist chose a calculated solution to a strategic problem by an examination of the goals the government was pursuing when it acted, and if that action was a reasonable choice.[18] This approach is the default method most historians use to interpret most situations. An analogy might be the idea of the "economic man," to maximize utility and minimize cost in a rational world. Goals and objectives are articulated, alternatives and possible consequences considered, and the option with the highest potential net payoff for the national interest is chosen.[19]

Tirpitz famously prided himself on rationality and persistence in pursuing his goals. His personal motto was, *"Ziel erkannt, Kraft gespannt"* (recognize the goal, and then energetically pursue it). He frequently functioned as a rational actor. A few of many examples of rationality include his very successful work in the Torpedo Arm (1877–1889); his work on tactics, especially while Chief of Staff of the Oberkommando (1892–1895); organization of the great propaganda campaign to support the Navy Laws;

the seemingly rational structure of the Navy Laws themselves; and his judicious dealings with private contractors, from the torpedo years to the outbreak of war in 1914.

Allison's Model 3, Bureaucratic Politics, or *Ressorteifer*, is an aspect of governmental behavior that is more important in understanding Tirpitz than has previously been recognized. This model sees governmental behavior as often the result of bargaining among groups of officials who occupy positions atop major organizations within a system. Each official represents one point of view, encompassing numerous interests, who compete with other such groups and leaders for roles in the direction of governmental priorities.[20] On most major questions there are legitimate grounds for disagreement. Each group can present a case that its policy can best defend or promote the national interest. Sometimes a particularly resourceful bureaucrat could, under the right conditions, achieve a kind of de facto hegemony over portions of the national agenda. Such was the case with Tirpitz, who had great success in hijacking the priority agenda, not only from other organizations like the army but also within the navy itself.

As Tirpitz narrated the Reichstag's approval of the First Navy Law in his memoirs, he revealed that the law provided protection, not just from the Reichstag meddling and the whims of the Emperor but from skeptical elements within the navy itself:

> I needed a Bill that would protect the continuity of the construction of the fleet on different flanks. The circumstance that was most in the Bill's favour was that it intended to make the Reichstag abandon the temptation to interfere each year afresh in technical details, as they had hitherto done when every ship had become the "exercise for debates"; and the Admiralty had not demanded what was most important in reality, but that which they could get passed in the interplay of changing majorities. But with party coalitions which treated ships as objects of compensation, it was impossible to construct such a naval armament as was demanded by a generation of patient, uniform growth.
>
> I never did discover, however, how to ward off the frequent interference of the *Emperor*, whose imagination, once it had fixed upon shipbuilding, was fed by all manner of impressions. Suggestions and proposals are cheap in the navy, and change like a kaleidoscope; if the Emperor had spoken with some senior lieutenant, or had seen something abroad, he was full of new demands, constructing, reproaching me with backwardness and even thinking to rouse me by means of warnings. Apart from several threats to

resign, I could only secure the continuity of development, which was the fundamental factor of success, by means of legislation. The third side from which chaos threatened and against which I needed a law was *the navy itself.* (My emphasis)[21]

In other words, Tirpitz needed the legal establishment of a naval construction program against not just the Reichstag, as Berghahn argues, but against the Emperor and the navy, too. Tirpitz was clearly trying to stabilize a system, but the system was his own narrow one. In the light of this point, it is hard to argue that the navy was an instrument to stabilize the Prussian/German monarchical system.

Tirpitz acted in the bureaucratic politics manner in many other situations as well. A few of them include the scorched-earth turf wars he waged against the RMA while he was Chief of Staff of the OK (1892–1895); after 1897 his ruthless expansion of the RMA's purview within the navy, especially the dissolution of the OK in 1899; his encouragement of bizarrely inappropriate operations plans against the British in the OK years and after; his refusal to permit the peacetime designation of a wartime fleet commander; and his relentless prioritizing of construction over readiness. The consistent goal of such inconsistencies was to concentrate power in the hands of organizations he led, first the OK and then the RMA.

No historian should blindly follow models developed by theoreticians. Concrete evidence must always take precedence over theory. The Allison categories are not mutually exclusive, and in some cases none may apply; but if their insights lend greater clarity to aspects of Tirpitz's life, their judicious use can add to our understanding of his work. This book attempts to examine the rational, irrational, and bureaucratic sides of Tirpitz's career. Often these were intermingled, not least in Tirpitz's transition from rational strategist to Social Darwinist ideologue of seapower in the late 1890s. Sometimes his *Ressorteifer* was in service to this ideal, and at other times it became an end in itself. The task of a biographer is to try to disentangle and understand the complicated threads of Tirpitz's career.

In their postwar private correspondence, some of Tirpitz's closest subordinates had second thoughts about the fleet-building policy they had helped to create. In November 1925 Capelle wrote to Hollweg about Tirpitz's opinion:

The total number of ships and the three tempo should be retained, and the ratio to England should be 2:3, therefore 60 German to 90 English. . . . We would build three new ships each year; England would build four and one half. The goal was to provide us with good defensive chances.

But Capelle then asked "Was this not a utopia?" to think that Germany could permanently maintain such a pace.[22]

Hollweg replied:

A fleet of 60 German ships was a utopia, considering the increase of displacements and the process of technology. The Grand Admiral's nightmare was always that his Navy Law might be infringed upon. He held to his idea too rigidly and his mistake was that he did not want to believe that the German people were sufficiently accepting of the idea of seapower, so that they could have held fast to the basic idea of the Navy Law without the rigid commitment of Tirpitz's particular law, which the times made obsolete.[23]

To another officer, Capelle wrote regarding Tirpitz's bureaucratic politics methods, "Tirpitz is an outspoken *Kampfenteur* (battler). Tirpitz in a responsible position and Tirpitz in opposition are two very different people." He then cited some examples of Tirpitz's bureaucratic behavior noted above. Capelle said that if Tirpitz had been named Chancellor before the war, which had been at least a remote possibility in 1911, then "I have no doubt at all that Tirpitz before the war would have pursued an English policy [i.e., taken a more accommodating position], even at the cost of the navy. His wild hatred towards England is of more recent [i.e., wartime] origins."[24]

With an interpretive framework outlined, it is possible to examine the life of this remarkable man who rose from middling origins to great prominence and responsibility, and then suffered crushing defeat, only to rise again, in a more modest way, in the Weimar Republic.

2
TIRPITZ'S EARLY LIFE

Alfred Peter Friedrich Tirpitz was born on 19 March 1849 in Küstrin an der Oder in the Mark Brandenburg, Prussia.[1] Oral tradition in his father's family claimed that the family name had been Czern von Terpitz, originally from Silesia and Bohemia. The Thirty Years' War brought impoverishment and forced the family to surrender the ennobling "von."

The earliest Tirpitz who can be documented was Christian Ferdinand (1707–1790), a trumpeter and musician. His son, Jacob Friedrich (1750–1830), Tirpitz's great-grandfather, was an army trumpeter for a Prussian dragoon regiment from the Küstrin area. He became a salt factor and overseer of the salt monopoly in Sonnenburg.

Jacob's middle son, Friedrich Wilhelm (1782–1862), Alfred's grandfather, was a lawyer and notary, first in Sonnenburg and later in Frankfurt an der Oder. His wife, Ulrike Rohleder (1788–1862), was the daughter of a government official in Sonnenburg and a descendant of noble Hugenot refugees. The eldest child of Friedrich and Ulrike was Rudolf Friedrich Tirpitz (1811–1905), Alfred's father. He went to classical gymnasium in Berlin at the Gray Cloister, with a schoolmate named Otto von Bismarck. He studied law at Heidelberg, joined the mostly aristocratic Saxoborussia Corps, and was known as a boxer and duelist. Most unusual is that he drank milk instead of beer. The twenty-one-year-old Rudolf met and fell intensely in love with seventeen-year-old Malwine Hartmann (1815–1880). Once he secured an appropriate position, they were married in 1843. Rudolf had a long and successful career as a jurist. He began as a local magistrate in Küstrin and Frankfurt an der Oder, and capped his career as an appellate judge, sitting in Berlin, for the whole Mark Brandenburg.[2] Rudolf's education and career are clear indications of his status in the upper bourgeoisie.

Malwine's grandfather was Peter Immanuel Hartmann. He was a Baltic German from Dorpat, a Professor of Medicine who had studied with Immanuel Kant in Königsberg. His son, Peter Emmanuel, was a prominent physician in Frankfurt. Malwine's mother was Anna-Luise Anna, the daughter of a wealthy French family who had fled the 1789 Revolution.

Rudolf and Malwine Tirpitz had three children in Küstrin: Olga, Max, and Alfred. In 1850 they moved to Frankfurt and had a fourth child, Paul, in 1854. Olga later married a Frankfurt gymnasium director. Max became an infantry officer in the 48th Line regiment, served honorably in the Franco-Prussian War, and died in a riding accident in 1892. Paul died in 1890.

The home life of the Tirpitz children was typical of the German bourgeoisie. Malwine was an attractive, lively woman who had, as a tutor, a sister of the poet Heinrich von Kleist. In Frankfurt, and later in Berlin, the Tirpitz home was frequented by officials, jurists, officers, and professors. Malwine encouraged the children to put on plays at home, although Alfred was not an enthusiastic participant. Her letters to Alfred were full of family and social matters.[3]

The single greatest influence in Alfred's life was his father.[4] His values and habits were quite remarkable, and his personal ethic thrifty and spartan. Until his ninety-third year he slept on a hard bed with the windows open and began every day with a cold bath. During his military service he feared diving off a board, so every day he forced himself to jump from the highest board. Although he could not rid himself entirely of the fear, every day the dive became easier. He believed that if one did not have the courage to act, one must create the courage. He inscribed "Die Pflicht vor Allem" ("Duty above All") in a copy of Schiller's works that he gave to his grandson. Rudolf revered the ideas of Kant, Fichte, and the heroes of the Prussian Wars of Liberation, such as Scharnhorst and Gneisenau. Like many of the Prussian bourgeoisie, he sympathized with the liberal ideas of the 1848 Revolution; nevertheless, he was unwaveringly true to the Hohenzollern dynasty.

One might expect that such a severe magistrate would be a distant father, but Rudolf's letters to Alfred abound with a degree of openly expressed affection highly unusual for a German father of that era.[5] Well into Alfred's manhood, his father addressed him in letters as "mein lieber Dicke" ("my dear Fatty"). The Tirpitz children grew up in a warm, secure, loving household. Alfred spent lazy summers in Frankfurt wandering the sandy banks of the Oder and exploring the nearby pine forests.[6] He watched military parades in the small garrison city.

The children had a lot of freedom. Alfred was less dutiful than his siblings, and often came home from school with torn pants and ink stains on his shirt. He got into stick-waving fights with other boys. More than once the neighborhood watchman brought him home. Although he could be ingratiating with his teachers, and showed occasional signs of life in the classroom, his overall school performance was mediocre at best. He sometimes played pranks on his teachers, and his work habits were lazy. When one of his teachers told his distraught father that Alfred was dumb, the cheeky boy told his father that he was happy with the remark because now he would not even have to try! All this was in marked contrast to his dutiful older brother, Max.

The classically educated Rudolf sent his two older sons to the Realschule in Frankfurt for their secondary education. Like most educated fathers, Rudolf wanted his sons to attend university upon completing the abitur diploma. Alfred explained his father's school decision as the result of his own inadequacy in the exact sciences.[7] In the Realschule Alfred studied religion, German, French, Latin, mathematics, history, geography, and science. In his last half-year there he began to study English.[8] Alfred later blamed his lack of scholarly achievement on old-fashioned teachers who were unable to communicate with their students. The crisis came halfway through what should have been his penultimate year. At Christmas 1864 the fifteen year old got an overall grade of "moderate" (*mässig*). His father's ambition that Alfred would attend university was in severe jeopardy.[9]

Alfred was at the first great crossroads of his life. Perhaps it dawned on him at last that he had disappointed the hopes of his loving parents. Perhaps, for the first time, he suddenly began thinking about his own future instead of just staying lost in the comfortable embrace of adolescence. He had never expressed an interest in any particular profession.

Around the New Year in 1865 Alfred told his father that his school friend, Curt von Maltzahn, the son of a judicial colleague of Rudolf, had decided to enter the navy. Alfred wished to join him.[10] Many years later he told his first biographer that he simply wanted to escape from the oppression of school ("Raus aus der Schule"). For two weeks his father, stunned at first, mulled the idea over. There was good reason for parental anxiety. In November 1861 the navy's sail corvette, *Amazone*, had sunk without survivors off the Dutch coast. Aboard this training ship were 107 men, including 19 cadets, virtually the entire 1855, 1858, and 1859 classes of officer aspirants.[11] Late in January 1865 Rudolf consented, and inquired at the Admiralty in Berlin to see if Alfred could become a cadet in 1866. Since only three young men had applied as cadets in 1862, and just a few more in 1863 and 1864, the Admiralty was willing to entertain the application of an eager sixteen year old in 1865. The family had to submit a health certificate, a school transcript, evidence that the aspirant had writing skills, and proof that he and his family were of good character (i.e., bourgeois or higher status).[12]

Most daunting for Alfred was the qualifying examination he would have to take. Rudolf hired good tutors, and Alfred, unlike in the past, worked with a will. In April he took the test at the Cadet Institute in Berlin. Alfred later remarked that he was lucky, as the English words he had to identify were among the very few he knew. He remembered the answer to the geography question from a childhood rhyme. To everyone's surprise, including his own, he finished fifth among the twenty-four successful applicants.[13] Maybe he had at last absorbed the spartan work habits of his father.

Although probably unaware of its significance at the time, the exam result determined, for his whole career, his seniority among the "crew" (i.e., class) of 1865. On 24 April he was officially accepted as a cadet and was ordered to report on 15 May to the training ship *Arcona* in Kiel. The carefree boy now had to submit to the discipline of the nascent Prussian Navy.

ORIGINS OF THE PRUSSIAN NAVY

Chance placed sixteen-year-old Alfred Tirpitz into the navy at a time of kaleidoscopic change.[14] He entered shortly after a war against Denmark, the first of Bismarck's three wars of unification, each of which had great impact on the navy. By the 1840s the steam revolution had begun in earnest, although most steamships still had a full panoply of sails. The Crimean War, and especially the Civil War in the United States, made it clear that the future of naval warfare rested with armored ships.[15] By 1865 Prussia had gained territory on the Baltic and North Sea coasts and was at last in a position to create an adequate network of bases.

To understand Prussia/Germany's maritime position when Tirpitz was a young officer, an overview of events prior to 1865 is necessary. German maritime traditions dated back to the middle ages. Particularly notable was the Hanseatic League, a federation of city-states, many of them German (e.g., Hamburg, Bremen, and Lübeck), that stretched from Russia to the North Sea. For centuries Hansa cities dominated trade in northern Europe, especially in the Baltic. However, the rise of powerful states, especially Sweden, England, and Holland, eclipsed the Hansa, and by the mid-seventeenth century about 70 percent of Baltic trade was in the hands of the Dutch. The rise of Brandenburg-Prussia, an acknowledged kingdom only by the early eighteenth century, had little direct impact on maritime matters. The most notable exception, Frederick William, the Great Elector of Brandenburg (d. 1688), built a small navy in 1675. In the mercantile spirit of the day, the Great Elector founded a fort on the African Gold Coast and set up a company on the Dutch model, mainly to carry on the slave trade. He also gained possession of Emden, the first Prussian port on the North Sea. After his death the colony, the company, and the navy were dissolved.

By the mid-eighteenth century English domination of Dutch trade created an opportunity for German cities on the Baltic. Emden traders petitioned Frederick the Great (r. 1740–1786) for protection of their Asiatic Trading Company from the English. Frederick saw no need for numerous warships because of the vulnerable position of Hannover, an English possession, in northern Germany. When England was hostile to Prussia, Frederick could deter English disruption of Prussian trade by threatening Hannover. When Prussia and England were allies, as in the Seven Years War (1756–1763), its merchant ships had little to fear from the English. This episode was one of the first of many cases in German history where land power and seapower interacted. Frederick advanced Prussia's maritime position in 1772 with the acquisition of Danzig and West Prussia during the First Partition of Poland.

After Napoleon's defeat in 1815 the Congress of Vienna created a new territorial dispensation in Europe. The hundreds of German states of the old regime were consolidated into the thirty-nine states of the new German Confederation, which had the approximate borders of the old Holy Roman Empire that Napoleon had abolished. The largest power of the Confederation was the Habsburg Empire, only part of which was within it. The expanded Kingdom of Prussia was second in size, even though East and West Prussia were left out of the Confederation. Two other changes had monumental consequences for Prussia. To contain the danger of a resurgent France, Prussia acquired large territories in Westphalia and along the Rhine. Later discoveries of coal and iron, particularly in the Ruhr Valley, provided a basis for Germany's prodigious industrial growth later in the century. The second change affected Prussia's maritime situation. Although Emden, its sole North Sea port, was lost, Prussia acquired the island of Rügen, plus the last remnants of Swedish Pomerania on the mainland, and consolidated its hold on the mouths of the Vistula (Danzig) and Oder (Stettin). By 1815 Prussia controlled the Baltic coast from Memel to Mecklenburg. The potential for sustained maritime commerce was present, at least in the geographical sense.

Hamburg, favorably located near the mouth of the Elbe, made treaties with England in 1815 to provide a degree of protection for its worldwide trade. Prussian Baltic trade revived more modestly, partly because of the need to pay heavy tolls to Denmark for Atlantic-directed trade. After 1815 sentiment gradually began to grow among Prussian maritime interests to provide protection for seagoing trade. The modest outcome of this effort was the construction of the schooner *Stralsund* in 1816, which was armed with ten light guns.[16]

In the early years of Frederick William IV's reign (r. 1840–1858), naval development faced a set of questions which, unresolved, would resonate for half a century. The first conundrum was the "mission" of the navy. Was it coastal protection, defense of trade, or naval supremacy, at least in the Baltic? The second, related question regarded the kinds of ships to build, especially when ship technology was changing. Because each mission required different kinds of ships, the result was paralysis. Neither the king nor his ministers could decide, so virtually nothing was done.

In the 1840s the rising nationalism of the German bourgeoisie, fueled partly by the defenseless state of German maritime commerce around the world, weighed in for the first time on naval questions. The work of political economist Friedrich List served as a catalyst. In 1841 he published *The National System of Political Economy*, which coincided with tension between Prussia and France. List argued that industrial economies could not develop well under free trade, which he felt most benefited the more advanced economies. Needed was a Confederation-wide tariff union, broader than the Zollverein (tariff union) that Prussia had inaugurated in 1818 and which some of the other German states had joined. Behind tariff walls, protected from foreign competition, struggling domestic industry could develop. He also called for a federal navy to protect German coasts and trade. List's message found a wide audience throughout Germany.

In February 1848 France revolted against the conservative order. A month later so did many other parts of Europe, including most of the states of the German Confederation. Thrones were threatened everywhere. Metternich fled Vienna. Frederick William IV saved his crown only by giving up absolutism. Delegates assembled at the Federal Diet in Frankfurt from all over the German world. The 1815 enabling legislation of the Confederation had proposed a common defense, but Prussian/Austrian rivalry had prevented the formation of a Confederation army, let alone a navy. Just before revolution broke out, Frederick VII of Denmark, in January 1848, moved to incorporate Schleswig and Holstein directly into his kingdom. Although he already ruled both, Holstein was a member of the German Confederation and Schleswig had a substantial German minority. Denmark's action outraged growing German patriotism throughout the Confederation. Danish troops moved in, but the Prussian Army soon intervened. Danish vessels seized defenseless Prussian merchant ships, encouraging pro-navy feeling throughout the Confederation.

Within the Hohenzollern family a navy had one outspoken advocate, Prinz Adalbert of Prussia, cousin of Frederick William IV, who had been trained as a soldier. The Prussian Navy had only the small *Amazone*, a sail corvette, and a few old gunboats. Just a tiny handful of officers held Prussian naval commissions. Their leader was a Dutchman, Jan Schröder. His most promising lieutenant was a young Prussian, Eduard Jachmann. The Federal Parliament also assembled a small fleet and agreed on six million thalers to support the fleet. Most of the money was not forthcoming, as the Parliament could not levy contributions from its member states. A small Confederation fleet under the leadership of Rudolf Brommy had an inconclusive engagement off the coast of English-controlled Helgoland. Adalbert did his best to rally support for the fleet in Frankfurt and Berlin, but by the summer of 1849 reaction against the fleet was returning to Germany and his efforts failed. The Danes maintained an effective blockade, but the Prussian Army reestablished the prewar status quo of Schleswig and Holstein, which remained under the rule of Denmark in an unincorporated way.

The tiny Prussian Navy had cooperated with the Confederation only tepidly and ineffectively; nevertheless, it inherited the meager remnants of the Confederation fleet. For the first time Prussia established an Oberkommando (High Command) for the navy, theoretically at least, independent of the army. In 1861 General Albrecht von Roon, the Prussian War Minister, subsumed some of its duties into a new Ministry of Marine, with Roon as head. Until 1870 Prinz Adalbert continued as military chief of the navy.

The navy's greatest achievement under Adalbert was the acquisition, in 1853, from the Grand Duke of Oldenburg, of a marshy area adjacent to the Jade. A railway connection to Prussian-controlled territory in Minden was slow to materialize, because Hannover would not consent to a right-of-way. After the conquest of Hannover in 1866, the railroad was built and the site was formally dedicated as the naval base of Wilhelmshaven in 1869. Prussia thereby gained a base near the mouths of the Elbe, the great avenue of commerce for Hamburg, the Weser, and the Ems. The small Eider Canal connected the Baltic to the Elbe, but it drew just 3.5 meters. Prussia once again had a North Sea base.

Besides the problems of ships and bases, the Prussian Navy of 1850–1865 had two other major dilemmas: the lack of suitable wharves and shipbuilding facilities for steamers, and the need to create an officer corps. The former problem was not solved until the 1880s, but the latter began to be addressed in the 1850s. A navigation school in Danzig could only accommodate a small number of cadets. More experienced men had to be sought among foreigners from the merchant marine. Tirpitz later noted in his memoirs, "the influx of these uneducated sea-dogs from the merchant service of those days brought many a joke into our mess; we called them *Hilfsbarone* [auxiliary barons]."[17] A "Prussian" naval officer corps conflicted with the need for greater overall numbers. In 1853 a Sea Cadet Institute was founded in Stettin (later moved to Berlin, then Kiel). It was loosely modeled on the ten-year-old U.S. Naval Academy. The

four-year regimen of studies provided for substantial sea duty, usually in
Amazone. Most cadets in that era were sons of nobles, army officers, civil
servants, and the upper bourgeoisie. About forty cadets entered each year,
but attrition was very high. Interest was further depressed with the sinking
of the *Amazone*, in 1861, with most of three classes of cadets aboard. A
small but steady stream of ships was built, including, in 1855, the navy's
first screw steamers, the twenty-four-hundred-ton *Arcona* and *Gazelle*.[18]
Over the next decade four sister ships followed, although by the end of
the 1850s other countries began to build ironclads, a feat then beyond the
capacity of German shipyards. The small navy conducted cruises to the
Mediterranean, the Americas, and East Asia. It showed the flag, trained
cadets, and tried vainly to seek out territorial acquisitions in Asia.[19]

The Danes, at the end of 1863, again raised the issue of incorporating
Schleswig-Holstein into Denmark. Otto von Bismarck, Minister-President
of Prussia since 1862 under William I (r. 1858–1888, first as Regent, then
as King) had forced the Prussian Diet (Landtag) to surrender its constitutional right to approve the military budget. The Danish crisis gave Bismarck a convenient foreign distraction in the midst of Prussia's domestic
troubles. He responded, to the chagrin of German nationalists, by ignoring the Confederation Diet. Instead, he joined the Austrians to present
the Danes with an ultimatum. In February 1864 a joint Prussian/Austrian
force moved into Schleswig-Holstein. The Danes blockaded Prussian
ports. In May a formidable pair of Austrian armored frigates arrived in
the North Sea under the command of Captain Wilhelm von Tegethoff.
After heavy fighting he drove away the Danish blockade squadron from
Hamburg and Bremen. At the end of the war Prussia, over the protests
of many German nationalists, took possession of Holstein and its well-
developed deep-water port of Kiel. Austria, as part of Bismarck's cynical
maneuver, got Schleswig.

In April 1865 Tirpitz reported to *Arcona* at the newly conquered Prussian port of Kiel. The navy he entered was weak but slowly increased its
number of ships and officers. It was still completely overshadowed by the
accomplishments of the army, a comparison that was to become even
more embarrassing in the Austrian conflict of 1866 and in the Franco-
Prussian War of 1870–1871. To build modern ironclads in domestic yards
was beyond the realm of possibility. The great achievement of the navy
was that, by 1866, Prussia/Germany was well on its way to the founda-

tion of the proper geographic basis for a second-class naval power. From Memel, on the Russian border, to Kiel, the entire southern littoral of the Baltic was securely in Prussian possession. Conditions on the North Sea were still primitive but had potential for improvement with the prospect of a railroad connection to Wilhelmshaven, and with the construction of suitable dockyards there. The remaining geographic dilemma, remedied only thirty years later, was the need for a modern Baltic/North Sea canal. Alfred Tirpitz, all things considered, entered the navy at an opportune time.

3
THE ASPIRANT, 1865–1870

On 24 April 1865 seventeen-year-old Alfred Tirpitz arrived at the newly established Prussian Baltic base of Kiel and swore the oath that marked the beginning of his career. On 15 May he boarded a large ship for the first time in his life, the corvette *Arcona*, then serving as a watch ship for Kiel harbor. Senior officers did not pay much attention to cadets, who were left in the care of the petty officers. Tirpitz, like many others, suffered from homesickness. He missed his mother and his indulgent home life in Frankfurt. He also witnessed, with distaste, his first flogging.[1]

On 14 June Tirpitz and his comrades of the crew of 1865 boarded the British-built sailing frigate *Niobe*, their seagoing home for the next year.[2] Its captain was one of the navy's most distinguished officers, Commander Carl Batsch. Among his cadet shipmates were six who later became admirals: Wilhelm Büchsel, Oscar Klausa, and Iwan Oldekop, who were personally close to Tirpitz; Otto von Diedrichs, a few years older than the others because of prior service in the merchant marine; plus Richard Geissler and Oscar Boeters.[3]

Niobe, purchased from England in 1862, was a replacement for the ill-fated *Amazone*. Twelve of its twenty-eight guns were removed to make room for cadets and ships' boys. The ship departed Kiel for a few weeks on the Baltic, which gave the cadets their first taste of seasickness. They were given new uniforms and a short home leave before their first great nautical adventure. They received a small monthly stipend but had to pay many of their own expenses. Families had to subsidize their sons, which limited the naval officer corps to those who could afford it. This practice made the group more socially homogeneous.[4]

Batsch planned a cruise to the Azores, the Canaries, and the Cape Verde Islands. *Niobe* was scheduled to return to Kiel by mid-April 1866.[5] After some short trips around Danzig it passed through the Fehmarn Belt, the nautical border with Denmark, and exchanged stiff salutes with ships and fortifications of its recent enemy.[6] In Kiel it joined the Prussian brig *Rover*. The cadets were given a few days ashore and a chance to mingle with other cadets and officers. Aboard *Rover* were Lieutenant Eduard von Knorr and Sea Cadet Gustav von Senden-Bibran, who would later play important roles in Tirpitz's career.[7] Also in Kiel was the Austrian screw sloop *Erzherzog Friedrich*.

On 30 September *Niobe* and *Rover* set off from Kiel. Held back by contrary winds in the Skagerrak, *Niobe* arrived at Plymouth on 5 October. Years later Tirpitz reflected on his first visit to England:

> As a sea-cadet I soon found from my own experience that Prussians were still esteemed in England. Between 1865 and 1870 our real supply base was Plymouth where Nelson's three-deckers . . . lay in long rows up the river. Here we felt ourselves almost more at home than in the peaceful and idyllic Kiel. . . . In the Navy Hotel at Plymouth we were treated like British midshipmen, even in regard to prices. . . . Our tiny naval officer corps looked up to the British navy with admiration, and our seamen sailed in those days quite as much in English-built ships as on German. . . . We grew up in the British navy like a creeping plant.[8]

Sound chains, faultless rope, and smooth-running engines were English products then. "In those days, we could not imagine that German guns could be equal to English."[9] Jörg Duppler has documented how dependent on Britain the Prussian/German Navy was in its early days. Engines, guns, and ships were better when imported. Dockyard repairs of any complexity were done abroad, mainly in Plymouth. German ships abroad, especially outside Europe, used British bases for supplies and services, including coal.[10] In the age of sail, ships could operate for months without touching land. Steam and the consequent frequent re-coaling made access to bases indispensable. In peacetime this meant that the Prussian Navy depended heavily on the European imperial powers.

Ships of many flags crowded Plymouth Harbor. The cadets saw Nelson's flagship, *HMS Victory*, visited the Royal Dockyards, and attended a performance of Macbeth at a local theater.[11] The cadets could scarcely have had a better introduction to the might, wealth, and reach of the British Empire.

Niobe left Plymouth on 7 October, heading south for the Portuguese island of Madeira. For Tirpitz and most other new cadets, it was their first experience of the rigors of sailing in the open Atlantic. Navigation training, sailing drills, and elementary gunnery exercises with practice ammunition filled each day.[12] Atlantic squalls gave cadets their first hair-raising experience of reefing sails while *Niobe* pitched and yawed in waves of a size not seen in the Baltic. Masts and rigging took damage. Calmer seas and strenuous repair work put the ship back into order. *Niobe* pulled into Funchal Roads, Madeira, on 23 October. Boats selling oranges and clamoring for news from Europe greeted them. Sail and boarding drills, punctuated by a visit ashore and a trip up the island's highest mountain occupied two weeks in port.[13]

On 4 November *Niobe* left Madeira for the Portuguese Cape Verde Islands. Three weeks ashore at Porto Grande included a soccer game with *Rover's* cadets. Gunnery drills became increasingly sophisticated. Tirpitz particularly remembered a very dangerous and strenuous sail exercise, when he suddenly looked down from his high perch and saw an enormous shark in the waters beneath.[14] A Christmas visit to a Russian steam frigate was followed, on 28 December, by Captain Batsch's feared test on seamanship, navigation, and gunnery. The cadets had to direct fire at a target floating at a distance of 300 meters. They were disappointed to miss thirty-four out of thirty-six shots.[15] Batsch had predicted a dismal result. He complained that thirty-seven cadets (the crew of 1864 was also aboard) were too many for the officers of one ship to instruct, particularly in gunnery.[16]

On 23 January 1866 *Niobe* left Porto Grande and arrived at Cadiz, Spain, on 21 February for a six-week stay. Cadiz, like Plymouth, was a crossroads for ships of many nations. Warships and merchantmen mingled in the harbor, a reminder that Spain, unlike landlubber Prussia, was a world power. Cadets went on an excursion to Seville, visited the Royal Dockyards, enjoyed shore leave, and saw their first bullfight.[17]

Niobe left Cadiz on 3 April and arrived in Lisbon six days later for a short visit. In Lisbon, Batsch heard alarming reports that war might break out between Prussia and Austria over Schleswig-Holstein, jointly taken from Denmark in 1864.[18] Batsch heard that the Austrian Navy's steam warship *Erzherzog Friedrich*, which *Niobe* had greeted before leaving Kiel, might be cruising in the English Channel. Batsch departed immediately for Plymouth, since *Niobe* would stand no chance against such a modern ship.[19]

In the Channel *Niobe* spotted a ship lying-to that resembled the Austrian warship. The latter got up steam and seemed to be bearing down on *Niobe*. As Tirpitz put it later:

> I was then No. 3 at the muzzle-loading gun, and it was my duty to put in the cannon balls; by my side lay my pike, ready to hand in case the enemy should grapple and put through the porthole. Other people stood ready with poleaxes, which were to strike in the hull of the enemy vessel, and use as steps.[20]

Fog descended during the night. When it cleared near Plymouth, the mystery ship raised the Norwegian flag. "We youngsters were disappointed in our joyful anticipation of a fight."[21] After a few days at Plymouth, *Niobe*, without incident, arrived at Kiel on 15 May. The last days of the cruise presented terrors of a different sort: oral and written final examinations in navigation, gunnery, and seamanship. Twenty-three cadets passed the exams. Tirpitz, Büchsel, Klausa, Diedrichs, and Oldekop received royal commendations.[22] The exhausted, but now hardened, Alfred Tirpitz returned home for four weeks leave. A month later he received his promotion to Sea Cadet. The pampered mama's boy of 1865 returned to Frankfurt as a young man, and as a full-fledged officer of the King.

APPRENTICESHIP: *GAZELLE*, JUNE–AUGUST 1866

On 14 June 1866 Prussia went to war with Austria and its smaller German allies, including Hannover. Two days later Tirpitz reported to *Gazelle*, a screw corvette of 2,400 tons.[23] It carried a crew of 380, under Commander Aneker Schau. Because the war lasted only seven weeks the squadron never saw action.[24] Tirpitz noted later that the Prussian Navy rejoiced about Austrian Admiral Tegethoff's decisive victory over the Italians at

Lissa. The navy still thought of Tegethoff as the German comrade who had fought at their side against the Danes two years earlier.[25]

Tirpitz's strongest memory of *Gazelle* was an accident that almost cost him his life. On 25 July, just outside Kiel, a crewman fell overboard. Several sailors, led by Tirpitz, noticed the accident and launched a boat that then tipped over in the choppy waters. The crewman, a strong swimmer, saved himself by grabbing a life jacket. Tirpitz, a poor swimmer, was thrown out of the boat. His uniform dragged him down. For ten minutes he struggled, at first unnoticed, then sank and lost consciousness. Another boat was finally launched and sailors pulled him out, half drowned, with a wounded hand.[26] Prudently he did not share this story with his parents.[27]

MUSQUITO: AUGUST 1866–JUNE 1867

The end of the Austro-Prussian War allowed the Prussian Navy, soon to be the Federal Navy of the newly founded North German Confederation, to return to its normal training regimen. Prussia's annexation of Hannover and Schleswig-Holstein gave the Confederation firm control of the German North Sea coast. Bismarck's triumph also resolved the long-standing conflict with the Prussian Diet, which retroactively legalized naval expenditures dating back to 1862.

In August 1866 Tirpitz was posted as a watch officer to the brig *Musquito*[28] for his second overseas cruise. British-built in 1851, Prussia had purchased it in 1862. It was a small sailing ship of 627 tons, with a crew of 150 under Commander Adolph Berger.[29] *Musquito*, in company with *Niobe* and *Rover*, departed Kiel on 6 October for Plymouth. One night on watch, Tirpitz forgot his overcoat. In an unusual gesture to a subordinate, Berger loaned him his own. The next day, because of an error by the incompetent navigation officer, they almost went aground off the Danish coast, to the captain's chagrin.[30]

Upon departure for the Mediterranean, Captain Berger required that two sea cadets take navigational sightings with that officer. When Tirpitz and his friend, Büchsel, took their turn, they announced that the officer's estimate was 80 to 100 nautical miles off. The captain defended the navigator, saying: "That is madness, for if your estimate is correct, we should be near Cape Finisterre." Just as the captain was about to scold the cadets, a ship's boy in the crow's nest shouted "Cape Finisterre in sight."[31]

By the end of the year Tirpitz noted that, in 1866, he had spent 116 days at sea, sailed 8,000 nautical miles, and visited fourteen different places.[32] On 30 December, in Villafranca, Tirpitz wrote to his parents about how the crew had celebrated Christmas with a dance aboard *Musquito*. He had waltzed with a young American woman with an income of $200,000 per year.[33] He did not tell them, however, that he and a comrade took a trip to Monte Carlo. He was enjoying a profitable day gambling when a casino official kicked him out with the remark, "You are too young, sir." Sick at heart he met his comrade, who had gone broke. The kind-hearted Tirpitz loaned him his winnings, and the young officer blew it all. Luckily they still had return tickets to Villafranca.[34] Soon Tirpitz was repaid, just in time for sightseeing trips to Genoa, Livorno, Pisa, and Florence. The glories of the Uffizi and the Pitti Palace inspired him to write eloquently of the paintings and statues of the Renaissance.[35] In April *Musquito* began the trip home. The return to Kiel on 10 May was uneventful, except for rumors of tension with France.[36] The young sea cadet, by then eighteen, had another year of sea duty to his credit. From the tenor and diction of his letters he had become more articulate, and far more worldly-wise.

GEFION, JULY–AUGUST 1867

Tirpitz's next assignment was to the three-masted sailing frigate *Gefion*. Built in Denmark in 1843, Schleswig-Holstein rebels had captured it in 1849. For the summer of 1867 it was fitted out as a training ship. For budgetary reasons, like most of the older ships in the navy, *Gefion* was only mobilized for training and summer maneuvers.[37]

Tirpitz was glad to be living at sea, albeit mainly in Kiel, because he would not have to pay for land quarters. Whenever possible the thrifty Tirpitz discouraged his indulgent father from sending him the usual subsidy of 10 marks per month.[38] The officers and the sea cadets had a *gemütlich* relationship. They often gathered in the evening at a wine bar.[39] Like most officers, Tirpitz was well aware of his standing in the seniority pecking order. He proudly sent his father a copy of the navy's rank list. Although in the navy for just over two years, rapid expansion of the officer corps already made him 127th out of 239.[40] Future promotion opportunities were glittering. His father replied, prophetically, "Rise up, my boy, to

Grand Admiral! The sooner, the better." Older brother Max, mired in the almost static army list, had no such prospects. Although his father mildly reproved Alfred for taking up smoking, the pride of the father in his once wayward son was obvious.[41]

THETIS, AUGUST 1867–AUGUST 1868

The apprenticeship of Sea Cadet Tirpitz continued with a year aboard *Thetis*, a sailing frigate converted into an artillery training ship. Prussia acquired it from Britain in 1855. From August to October 1867, and again in April 1868, its commander was Captain Arthur von Bothwell. In the interim, Lt. Commander Max von der Goltz (October–December 1867) and Lt. Commander Adolph Butterlin (December 1867–April 1868) acted in his place, perhaps because Bothwell was ill.[42] Goltz was later Tirpitz's superior at the Oberkommando der Marine (1892–1895).

Thetis took short sea trips to fire four hundred or so shots at floating targets. The practice was necessary because, at the time, the navy's gunnery standard was abysmal. Tirpitz welcomed the chance to hone his gunnery, as he was slated to attend the Kiel Naval School the following year. He worked diligently to sharpen his French and English.[43]

By January Kiel harbor was frozen over. Tedious stretches of superfluous night watch alternated with strenuous artillery study. For fun there was ice-skating and, for the first time in Tirpitz's life, an active social calendar. His seniors introduced him to the niceties of etiquette for frequent winter balls.[44]

Most of the time the first officer, Butterlin, was "sick" (read: drunk), provoking Captain Bothwell's nasty sense of humor. One morning the ship was awakened by a fire alarm, whether real or just a drill the cadets could not tell. Recruits on board panicked. Bothwell had brought an army officer friend aboard to share in the joke. The base commander's response to the prank was to order *Thetis* to lie in the harbor and break communications with the shore until further notice.[45] Such a bizarre episode did not help cadets cramming for artillery examinations.

Conditions on *Thetis* grew so bad that the tough Lt. Commander Eduard von Knorr came in as first officer for a few weeks to clean up the mess. Knorr's remarkable unpublished autobiography provides a rare look at the seamy side of life in the navy. According to Knorr, *Thetis* was a troubled ship. There were no exercise or duty rosters. Officers could come and go as they pleased. Acting Captain Butterlin was a hopeless drunk. The hapless Bothwell was a tool of his wife, a seductive brunette. She had free access to the boats, craftsmen, and materials of the ship. Knorr visited the wife and found her wearing a negligee at noon. She proposed "friendship" to him if she could continue to plunder the ship. The outraged Knorr refused and spent the next two weeks whipping the ship and the crew into shape. "The mess was no longer a cheap tavern . . . where the commandant and his entourage could drink at the expense of the mess." The ship was cleaned. Exercises and training began. At the end of three weeks Bothwell managed to get rid of Knorr, who was replaced by the more "pliable" Goltz.[46]

Tirpitz's letters from this period only hint at the goings-on. Perhaps he did not want to alarm his parents, or maybe he enjoyed the lax regime. In any case, in August 1868, he passed the artillery exam and left *Thetis* to begin two years at the Kiel Naval School.

NAVAL SCHOOL AND SHORE DUTIES:
AUGUST 1868–APRIL 1870

Tirpitz was a member of the third class of the Naval School, the reorganized successor of the old Sea Cadet Institute. Prinz Adalbert founded the school in 1866. At that time it was the navy's only school for officers. Its Director was Lt. Colonel C. A. Leibe. The school drew faculty from among officers and civilian professors of the University of Kiel. Lieutenant Friedrich Hollmann, who later befriended Tirpitz, taught naval service knowledge and English.[47] The principal emphasis at the school was mathematics, astronomy, and natural science. Other subjects included seamanship, navigation, gunnery, ship architecture, engines, French, English, signaling, gymnastics, and fencing. The class consisted of thirty-six sea cadets and ten sublieutenants. Classroom work was strenuous: twenty-two lectures of ninety minutes each week.[48] Six hours a week of physics and chemistry gave Tirpitz headaches.[49]

In November, to his parents' consternation, a few students came down with typhus, although the epidemic soon passed. On 3 November 1868 Tirpitz witnessed his first torpedo experiment, which, he noted, had a "fearsome effect."[50] He sat on a discipline board for sailors and heard sixteen cases of drunkenness and sleeping on watch.[51] In Tirpitz the student, one can see a foreshadowing of the methodical work habits that characterized his later life: "The lectures are such that one cannot easily follow them; but we are expected to grasp them immediately, and this is to some degree disadvantageous to me, because I must always think things through first, and then I really know it." [52]

On the eve of final examinations, Tirpitz was confident. "I hope I will not lose my cold-bloodedness [i.e., clearheaded rationality]—I have done my duty well."[53] The results justified his confidence. He tied for eighth among the forty-six candidates. Two who surpassed him were already sublieutenants. His overall grades were almost 80 percent, which was considered "very good."[54] Promotion to sublieutenant came on 22 September 1869. He was the fifth promoted from among the crew of 1865, in accordance with his seniority within the crew.

For the next ten months he had shore duty, first as a company officer for a reserve division of sailors in Kiel. He made time to take supplementary courses in astronomy and mathematics at the University of Kiel. His achievements in gunnery earned him a first assignment in Berlin, from December 1869 to the end of April 1870, as a member of the artillery test commission. As he noted in his memoirs, the commission decided that Krupp, not Armstrong, the English company that the navy favored, should become the navy's artillery provider.[55]

Land-based assignments increased Tirpitz's money problems. As a sea cadet he received 35 marks per month. Taxes, laundry, and rent consumed about 29 marks, which left only 6 marks for evening meals and everything else. Rudolf's 10 marks per month was both necessary and welcome, as long as Alfred was not at sea.[56] Promotion would provide a raise but also added expenses for uniforms and social demands.

In letters home between August 1868 and April 1870, Tirpitz mentioned several respectable young ladies. There is no extant evidence about whether Tirpitz had a sex life at the time. If he did it would likely have been among lower-class women in Kiel. Not surprisingly sexual license was apparently common at the Naval School. In 1866 Director Leibe informed Berlin that 25 percent of that year's cadets had been diagnosed with syphilis. The situation was so bad that Leibe called in the Baltic Station Chief, Rear Admiral Jachmann, to brace the young men for immoral behavior.[57] There is no indication that Tirpitz ever had syphilis, but that does not necessarily mean that he was not sowing wild oats along with his fellow sailors.

4

THE YOUNG OFFICER, 1870–1877:
A TASTE OF WAR

Consolidation of the North German Confederation, which by 1867 included all the German states north of the River Main, had important maritime consequences. With the addition of Hamburg and other Hanseatic cities, the Confederation possessed the world's third-largest merchant marine. Greater only were those of Britain and the United States.[1] In Berlin the team of Roon as Naval (and Army) Minister, Prinz Adalbert as Commanding Admiral, and Jachmann as Operational Commander in October 1867 got the new Reichstag to approve a ten-year program for sixteen armored ships, twenty unarmored corvettes, and eight avisos (dispatch boats), all steam-powered. The navy's proposed goals were encouragement and protection of worldwide trade, defense of the North Sea and Baltic coasts, and, most ambitious, the development of a modest capacity to threaten enemy trade, fleets, and harbors.[2] The navy's expansion meant a shift from long-term volunteer sailors to three-year conscripts. Their sheer numbers would greatly increase the navy's training burden.[3]

By 1870 the navy had three powerful armored frigates, the French-built *Friedrich Carl* (6,000 tons), and two British-built ships, *Kronprinz* (5,800 tons) and the huge *König Wilhelm* (9,800 tons), then the world's largest and, on paper at least, most powerful warship.[4]

Franco-German relations in 1870 were strained by Bismarck's failed attempt to put a Hohenzollern on the Spanish throne. Bismarck's publication of the provocative Ems dispatch on Bastille Day (14 July) 1870, goaded Napoleon III into war against the Confederation and its south German allies.

KÖNIG WILHELM, MAY 1870–MAY 1871

Sublieutenant Alfred Tirpitz reported aboard *König Wilhelm* on 1 May 1870 as a watch officer. An armored steam frigate, fully equipped with sails, it had a designed top speed of fourteen knots, a crew of 750, and mounted eighteen 24-cm and five 21-cm guns.[5] On 9 June, with no war in sight, *König Wilhelm* departed Kiel. Mechanical problems dogged the squadron that straggled into Plymouth for repairs. As Tirpitz later put it, they even tried to sail, "but the hulks refused to move." Since *König Wilhelm*'s hull had not been scraped for several years, it was dragging sixty tons of mussels that reduced its top speed to ten knots.[6] Serious engine damage forced a long stay in Plymouth. On 10 July it left Plymouth, only to be stopped by a dispatch boat with rumors of war. News that a superior French squadron was seeking them sent them homeward to defenseless Wilhelmshaven. After a nervous passage, the squadron arrived in Wilhelmshaven on 16 July.[7] Construction of the docks was incomplete, however, and so the squadron had to keep to the outer harbor in the Jade. Since Germany had no dockyards large enough to repair the heavy armored ships, any serious damage would be crippling.[8]

War fever swept over Germany, and Tirpitz was no exception. "It is a holy war, not begun by overweening arrogance as in 1806, but with every seriousness and vigor, which allow us hope for the best." "Every German found in the presence of the French will be shot like a dog." He nevertheless realized that only the three German armored frigates could effectively fight the much larger French fleet, and that to fight them would be futile.[9]

When Prinz Adalbert left to join the army it was a demoralizing statement of the navy's irrelevance, and the navy was shocked and humiliated. Despite two timid and fruitless short forays, the North Sea Squadron accomplished little, and the Baltic Squadron achieved even less. German land victories eventually led to the withdrawal home of the French fleet. The navy's meager glory consisted of the brave November victory of Eduard von Knorr on the gunboat *Meteor* against the larger French *Bouvet* outside Havana,[10] and the brief commerce raid of the corvette *Augusta* in the Bay of Biscay in January 1871.[11]

As fleet flagship *König Wilhelm* had a surfeit of officers, and Tirpitz had to switch his cabin's bed for a hammock.[12] He and other junior officers spent nights on watch fending off German mines that had broken off in heavy seas and came drifting into the roads with the tide. When winter came *Wilhelm's* situation became very dangerous. The harbor entrance had not been sufficiently dredged. To enter, coal and munitions had to be offloaded. On 22 December a storm pushed huge amounts of ice against the hull. Floes came in as high as the gun batteries and cut anchor chains. A smaller ship resembled an "ice palace." The next day, with much difficulty and some essential goods tossed overboard, *König Wilhelm* at last entered the inner harbor. For Tirpitz and his shipmates the war was essentially over.[13]

For the next six months *Wilhelm* sat in the harbor, except for occasional gunnery exercises when the weather improved. Life onboard settled into a dreary routine. Anyone who has been to Wilhelmshaven, even now, would share Tirpitz's bleak opinion of the place. A flat, marshy landscape, a dull, featureless town with few amenities, and drab, stormy weather made Wilhelmshaven an unappealing billet. According to Tirpitz, "compared to [Wilhelmshaven], Kiel is a paradise."[14]

Although his brother Max had been wounded and received an iron cross, Alfred felt no personal envy. Nevertheless, he was disappointed that the fleet did not have another chance to go to sea.[15] To the dismay of all sailors, the navy had been so marginalized that the government at first refused to give sailors the traditional war service medal. Although the decision was later reversed the insult rankled, and had an influence in the 1890s when the navy designed absurdly aggressive war plans that would have been impossible to execute.

BLITZ, MAY 1871–SEPTEMBER 1872

With the war over, Tirpitz's miserable Wilhelmshaven existence came to an end in May, when he became first officer on the steam gunboat *Blitz*. It was only 420 tons, and had a crew of seventy-two. The full-rigged boat had two guns, one 15 cm and the other 12 cm, with a top speed under steam of 9.3 knots. Lt. Commander Glomsda von Buchholz was captain, with only two other officers, Tirpitz, and his old friend and crew comrade, von Ehrenkrook.[16]

Blitz was the designated German police ship in the North Sea. Initially this involved mundane duties such as taking soundings off the coastal islands. "I rejoice in this trip," Tirpitz declared, "since I assume it will be interesting and instructive and will be a relatively comfortable life."[17] In contrast to cadet life, "as an officer, one is indeed a god, especially now as first officer on a gunboat."[18] Congenial duties included visits to resort islands and chauffeur service for Prinz Friedrich Carl, a nephew of Emperor William I who, like his older cousin Adalbert, had a strong interest in the navy. Tirpitz formed a friendship with the Prince, which gave him entrée into high social circles.[19]

In September 1871 Sublieutenant Tirpitz displayed for the first time, albeit in a very private way, the ability to write a provocative memorandum on naval issues. Later this capacity, not shared by his peers, would catapult Tirpitz's ideas to attention in high places. His father sent him an anonymous pamphlet titled "The German Reich Navy," which Tirpitz rightly guessed came from the pen of the prominent Captain Reinhold Werner. It raised three questions: Is a navy necessary for Germany? What kinds of ships should it have? Where should the ships be built?

Germany's huge wartime losses of merchant shipping and the loss of trade by voyages never made was, for Tirpitz, a strong argument for a battlefleet. A fleet could protect one's commerce and disrupt the enemy's. He doubted then and later that international treaties would protect private property at sea, especially if the British were involved in the war. Powerful armored fleets could bombard German coastal towns, which, Kiel apart, had no real defenses. He called it "stupid" that the French had not done it during the war, although he overlooked the deterrent effect of the army's ability to bombard French towns in retaliation. He concluded that an armored battlefleet was the only practical way to protect coastal cities from blockade or worse. In anticipation of his later ideas, he recognized that a battlefleet was not to conquer terrain but to annihilate the foe in battle, if an attacking enemy were to open itself to the possibility. After victory, one could carry the war to the enemy's coasts and trade routes. Logistics would still require Germany, like other countries, to protect extra-European trade with wooden ships. Tirpitz therefore answered Werner's first question with a resounding yes. It is unclear whether Tirpitz learned such Clausewitzian ideas during his time at the Naval School.

The second question, about ship types, he felt should be left to naval experts and not be open to the press or the Reichstag. Later, in 1897, he changed his mind on this point in a particularly cunning way. Regarding where to build the ships, he had some interesting observations. "We have no master of building armored ships, not one company. . . . Our major dockyards make this obvious." It would have been too embarrassing for the pamphlet to admit that, compared to parts on English ships, Germany's were "woeful" (*jammervoll*). English or French chain inspired confidence; German chain did not, although the German iron industry had recently made good strides. He concluded that, for the near future, large armored ships would have to be built abroad, lest they be of inferior quality. He considered a North Sea–Baltic Canal a pressing necessity. He also wanted to acquire Helgoland from England, as it dominated the Elbe estuary.[20]

In the light of Tirpitz's later career the letter appears prophetic, but only to a degree. He advocated a large armored fleet, though of unspecified size; but on that point he was only echoing the opinion of many officers of that era; but even with its logical holes, one can see in the document the beginning stages of his analytical powers.

In the fall of 1871 *Blitz* took up its duty as a watch ship on the Elbe. The assignment was a kind of atavism, because Bismarck had ordered a watch ship there in 1866 to deter any aggressive designs the Kingdom of Hannover (dissolved later in 1866) might have had on Hamburg.[21] Pleasant months passed at balls, teas, and bird hunts with the elite of Altona and Hamburg. Flirtation opportunities abounded with the daughters of wealthy families, capped by a pleasant Christmas leave at home.[22]

At the beginning of 1872 the hardheaded General Albrecht von Stosch effectively took charge at the Admiralty. *Blitz*'s pleasant but useless idyll ended abruptly in April 1872, when an inspection by the truculent Stosch uncovered the sinecure and ordered a more productive mission.[23] Stosch had encouraged the creation of the first German herring cooperative, based in Emden. On 17 June *Blitz*, with newly promoted Lieutenant Tirpitz as first officer, was ordered into the North Sea to protect the handful of Emden herring boats. On the 28th they left for Aberdeen, Scotland, to top off their coal supply. On the way, the mainmast broke in heavy seas.

A two-week repair in Aberdeen had an unexpected fringe benefit. Tirpitz saw the bleak and haunting beauty of the Highlands and visited Balmoral Castle, Queen Victoria's Scottish retreat.

With the repair completed, *Blitz* reached the herring fishery. It searched among hundreds of Dutch and British boats, looking, in vain at first, for a boat flying the German flag. It finally spotted a familiar-looking boat, but it had Dutch colors. To stop it, *Blitz* had to fire a shot across its bow. The fisherman admitted he was German but explained that if he raised a German flag, English boats would harass him and cut his nets. Near the Shetland Islands they actually found a boat with a German flag, which gave *Blitz* a ton of herring as a gift. Next day a Dutch gunboat commander told Tirpitz that the same boat, flying Dutch colors, had approached him recently for medical help. On another occasion Buchholz noticed a number of idle fishing boats on the German island of Amrum. Upon inquiry he discovered that they refused to go out for fear of the English.[24] The experience of German maritime impotence made a deep impression on Tirpitz. Time and again, even at the summit of the navy, he would cite the fishery as an argument to expand German naval power.

With fishery work over, on 14 August 1872, *Blitz* sailed to Kiel to celebrate the birthday of Prinz Heinrich, second son of the Crown Prince. The boy was about to enter the navy at the age of eleven. Unexpectedly, the Prince and his older brother William (the later Emperor) came aboard *Blitz* to examine its guns. Tirpitz made an insightful observation about thirteen-year-old William, whose mighty navy he later built:

> The children made a very good impression . . . [William's] crippled arm is somewhat noticeable, especially because of his various maneuvers to try to make the bodily characteristic not noticeable. Otherwise the prince gives a quite gifted impression, if one can take an impression from such a brief view.[25]

In September 1872, when *Blitz* was taken out of service, Tirpitz was given the challenging assignment of watch officer on the armored frigate *Friedrich Carl*. He wrote his father: "I am very young for such a position. This is a more difficult job than I had expected."[26]

THE STOSCH REGIME

In April 1871 the Constitution of the new German Empire came into effect. A peculiar kind of political creation, it retained within it the monarchies and states that had existed in 1867. Germany had an imperial and federal superstructure by which the larger states retained, in peacetime, their own armies. In war the armies would be subordinated to the King of Prussia, who was simultaneously the German Emperor. An Imperial Reichstag, with limited powers, coexisted with the old state diets and assemblies. The navy, in contrast to the army, was a truly national and imperial institution, with Emperor William I at its head.

Bismarck also reorganized the navy. Beginning on 1 January 1872 he instituted an Imperial Admiralty to head both the administrative and the operational sides of the navy. Roon surrendered his naval brief, and Prinz Adalbert, in poor health, accepted the honorific title "General Inspector of the Navy" until he died in 1873. All in the navy expected Jachmann's appointment as Chief of the Admiralty; instead, Bismarck picked Lieutenant General Albrecht von Stosch, who had served ably under Crown Prince Frederick in the Austrian war. The Prince was aware of Stosch's interest in naval questions, and he had lobbied Bismarck for the appointment. The disappointed Jachmann retired in 1874. Stosch made Rear Admiral Wilhelm von Henk, a mediocrity, his second-in-command. Captain Carl Batsch, Tirpitz's admired commander on *Niobe*, became Admiralty Chief of Staff, in charge of military matters. Batsch became a Stosch protégé and may well have been influential in fostering Tirpitz's career in later years.[27]

Stosch was a vigorous, energetic man with an ambitious agenda. In 1872 he founded a Naval Academy in Kiel that provided an intensive two-year program for the most promising junior officers. The school, the first of its kind in the world, anticipated by twelve years the founding of the U.S. Naval War College in Newport, Rhode Island. Stosch partially modeled the Academy on the army's Prussian War Academy, although, unlike the army, it was not specifically meant to create staff officers. The earlier training of cadets, at the Naval School, remained much the same as Tirpitz had undergone.[28]

Stosch strongly supported stationing ships abroad to foster German economic interests. He advocated acquisition of colonies, although Bismarck's opposition made that impossible until after Stosch left office. As Tirpitz had experienced aboard *Blitz*, Stosch pushed the navy to work extremely hard, which had both positive and negative results. He abolished cushy billets that consumed scarce officer manpower. The downside was the frequent, exhausting, and often pointless army drillings and watch practices. Stosch misunderstood the technical complexities of the navy. It took more time to assemble and train a ship's crew and to make a demobilized ship ready for sea than Stosch would readily tolerate. His unrealistic expectations led to mishaps.[29]

One of Stosch's great achievements was to offer a building plan that, for the first time, had a realistic chance of fulfillment. With Bismarck's support, Stosch got Reichstag approval in 1873 for an upgrade of the Confederation plan of 1867.[30] He proposed a fleet of twenty-three ironclads, fourteen of them high seas ships. Seven monitors and two floating batteries were for coast defense. Twenty unarmored corvettes, six avisos, and eighteen gunboats were included, mostly for service abroad. Stosch also asked for eight torpedo boats, an entirely new type. The program was to be completed over a ten-year period.[31]

FRIEDRICH CARL, OCTOBER 1872–APRIL 1874

On 1 October 1872 Lieutenant Alfred Tirpitz reported aboard the armored frigate *Friedrich Carl* as a watch officer. One of the few French-built ships in the German Navy, it displaced 6,900 tons and had a full set of sails. Captain Reinhold Werner, a capable officer, was in command. Werner also led a squadron that included the corvette *Elisabeth* and the gunboat *Albatross*.[32] Werner planned an eighteen-month cruise to the West Indies, South America, and Japan. Tirpitz was responsible for the third half-battery, with Curt von Maltzahn as a subordinate.[33]

During a stop in Porto Santo Tirpitz led a riding party through the lush tropical hills. On All Saints Day he noted, "The dumb, bigoted people streamed like sheep into church."[34] In Madeira he rode up a mountain with Commander Alfred Stenzel, who later was his instructor at the Naval Academy.[35] The squadron crossed the Atlantic uneventfully—the first time a German armored squadron had done so—and arrived at the British colony of Barbados on 28 November.

On 6 December the squadron went to La Guaira to pay an official visit to Caracas to inquire about a debt problem, a typical event in the age of imperialism. On the 14th they sailed to Porto Cabello, which Tirpitz, in the universal European manner of the time, characterized as a "nigger place" (*Negerort*). German tradesmen from Caracas, such as apothecaries and hat makers, visited the ship.[36] In Curaçao Tirpitz observed that most of the people there were manumitted Negroes, although Dutch orderliness predominated. The white population consisted "unfortunately overwhelmingly of Jews, and much of the uncomfortable side of their characteristics shows."[37] After a visit to Haiti to resolve more debt problems the squadron sailed to Havana, where it provisioned for a trip around South America and on to East Asia.

On 13 March 1873 Werner received sudden orders from Berlin to re-cross the Atlantic. The squadron sailed to Plymouth without knowing the reason. Consistent with the uncertainty of the naval profession, Tirpitz and his colleagues speculated on the possibility of war with England or Russia, or a renewed conflict with France.[38] They arrived at Plymouth on 16 April, none the wiser. *Friedrich Carl* went to Wilhelmshaven to refit. Only then did Tirpitz learn that they were being sent to Spain.

In February 1873 the new Spanish King abdicated amid growing discontent. The moderate republicans of the Spanish Parliament declared Spain a republic. Royalists, Basque separatists, and left-wing republicans rose in revolt, and a bloody, multisided civil war broke out. The lives and property of foreigners were at risk. Germany, along with Britain and others, sent warships to protect their interests.

On 29 June 1873 Werner's squadron of *Friedrich Carl, Elisabeth*, and the gunboat *Delphin* arrived off Malaga. Tirpitz heard the frightened cries of German nationals and businessmen. He noted, "The devil is surely loose in Spain." Tirpitz complained that Spanish ships did little to ameliorate the chaos. Its ships were unprepared and its officers took siestas.[39] A small British squadron, led by the armored frigate *Swiftsure*, joined forces with the Germans and both agreed to protect each other's nationals. Since Werner was senior to the British commander, he took the lead. In the midst of the revolutionary confusion, rebels seized the Spanish ironclad *Victoria* and the frigate *Almansa*. On 3 August, when *Victoria* and *Almansa* returned to Cartagena, Werner and the British seized them. The fleet landed twelve hundred armed sailors to protect the city from imminent rebel attack, enabling Tirpitz to acquire some experience as a leader of sailors in a land operation.[40] Werner operated throughout at the request of local German Consuls, in meticulous cooperation with the British commander, and with the permission of local Spanish officials. The German press at home cheered his decisive intervention, and Spanish citizens feted *Friedrich Carl*.[41]

On 6 August the startled Werner received a telegram from Stosch, sent at Bismarck's direction, which relieved him of command for exceeding Bismarck's orders. Bismarck did not want to help the moderate republican government to consolidate its rule, as he saw political advantage in continued unrest. Werner was ordered to Gibraltar and then home to face a court martial. Hermann Przewisinski, captain of *Elisabeth*, was made commander of the squadron.[42] Tirpitz felt shame at leaving the British in the lurch. Bismarck's indifference disheartened German nationals on the Spanish coast, who turned to the British for help.[43] Werner subsequently was acquitted in the court martial. Also, because he had the support of Stosch, the Emperor, and the German press, his career did not suffer.[44] Tirpitz felt that Bismarck had committed an injustice, but, as he noted in a letter, "errare humanum est."[45]

By January 1874 the situation in Spain calmed down enough for the German squadron to depart. *Friedrich Carl* left Gibraltar on 28 February and returned to Wilhelmshaven in mid-March. The long voyage to the Caribbean, and his experience with revolution in Spain, international cooperation, and diplomatic complications, added to Tirpitz's awareness of a complex world. For unclear reasons, Werner gave him an ambivalent fitness report. Though recognizing his talent, energy, and writing skill, Werner wrote that "he would be a more outstanding officer if he possessed more inner discipline." Tirpitz sometimes took on his seniors. "I only consider him suited for higher positions," Werner continued, "if he can prove that he fully understands how to be a better subordinate."[46] Tirpitz apparently still had not learned to suffer fools, if not gladly then at least tactfully. This curious incident is an early example of Tirpitz's stubbornness and willingness, greater than that of his peers, to challenge higher authority.

On 15 April 1874 Tirpitz became navigation officer on the brig *Musquito* in Kiel. Its main mission was training ships' boys.[47] Tirpitz was delighted to return there. "I have acquired a certain homey feeling for Kiel." He was glad to be away from the "natureless" region of Wilhelmshaven.[48] Training duty was combined with purposeless and mind-numbing watches. "I believe the men in Berlin do not think of night watches as work."

On 1 June the entire complement of *Musquito*, including Commander Johann Pirner, transferred to the small steam corvette *Nymphe*.[49]

It transported Prinz Friedrich Carl on a visit to the Kings of Denmark and Sweden. As was customary for ships in home waters, it participated in the September fleet parade before the Emperor.[50] Tirpitz's billet as navigation officer on *Nymphe* was a good one. He was deputy to the first officer and, as such, was exempt from specific watch duty.[51] The extra time allowed him to prepare artillery and tactical essays for his application to the competitive Naval Academy. On August 23 he learned officially that he and five other young officers would constitute the fall 1874 class of the Naval Academy.[52]

NAVAL ACADEMY, OCTOBER 1874–MAY 1876

In March 1872 Stosch had established the Naval Academy, not an analog to the U.S Naval Academy. The Naval School, which Tirpitz attended in 1868–69, was its parallel. The Naval Academy initially provided two years of postgraduate training for a select group of sea officers. Like the Naval School, it drew faculty from naval officers, land-based civilians, navy officials, and academic lecturers, principally from the University of Kiel. Colonel C. A. Leibe commanded both the Naval Academy and the Naval School. To apply, an officer submitted essays on military and naval history, artillery, navigation, ship construction, engines, and maneuver tactics. Because the fleet was short of officers for summer maneuvers, the term ran from October to the end of June. The curriculum encompassed both scientific and more general academic subjects, including mathematics, astronomy, physics, chemistry, naval organization, fortifications, administration, artillery, shipbuilding, and steam engines; less technical subjects included military and naval history, logic, ethics, culture, literature, military and international law, English, French, and Danish.[53]

Tirpitz wrote required essays on naval aspects of the U.S. Civil War and a critique of the Battle of Lissa. He wrote about ship handling in bad weather, rules of the road at sea, currents and winds of the Atlantic, technical gunnery questions, building armored ships, and engine problems.[54] Tirpitz sweated over this formidable assignment while aboard *Nymphe*.

Lieutenant Tirpitz began class on 23 October 1874. Initially he had to scramble in mathematics. Danish was easy, but he complained about his English instructor.[55] His letters home during that year said little about coursework, so one might conclude either that he was very well prepared

or that the curriculum was not as formidable as it appeared.[56] He was
excited by his expected promotion to Lt. Commander in the fall, when
his salary would at last be high enough to end his father's subsidy, and
make it possible to marry.[57] Max, who had been in the army two years
longer than Alfred's service, had only just been promoted to Lieutenant,
a good example of how much faster the expanding navy could promote
than could the static army.

Tirpitz served for the summer of 1875 as a battery officer aboard the
German-built armored corvette *Hansa*. It participated in the fleet parade
before the Emperor in September.[58] Temporarily blinded in one eye by
an accident, Tirpitz worried about his gunnery demonstration in front
of Stosch, but all went well despite his fears.[59] After exasperating bureaucratic delays, the long-awaited promotion to Lt. Commander became
official on 18 November 1875.

The second year of the Naval Academy was less technical than the
first. In a letter home, Tirpitz joked: "Since I have finished studying the
philosophers and other worldly wise men, I am now struggling, against
my Tirpitz-like nature, to always put my best foot forward."[60]

In the spring term Tirpitz's truculence, which Werner had already
noted, led to open conflict with Commander Alfred Stenzel, his instructor in military and naval history, whose significance in German naval history Rolf Hobson has highlighted. Tirpitz characterized Stenzel, whom
he had met on the *Friedrich Carl*, as a "mistrustful and eccentric man."
Tirpitz made some public statement, perhaps in class, that Stenzel believed would put him in an awkward position with the Admiralty. Stenzel
made a hard accusation, which Tirpitz believed he could not let pass but
instead pursued with "somewhat provocative vigor." The unspecified matter went to Werner, Baltic Station Chief, but apparently was settled before
reaching the Admiralty. Tirpitz reluctantly accepted Werner's judgment
as final.[61] Such amazingly bold action against a superior apparently did
not harm Tirpitz's career. Perhaps his old mentor, Batsch, looked after
him from his powerful post in the Admiralty.

The other matter that engaged Tirpitz's attention in the spring of 1876
was Curt von Maltzahn's long-contemplated decision to leave the navy for
the army. Maltzahn was unhappy about some of his assignments and also
about bureaucratic delays in promotion. Tirpitz was finally able to per-

suade Maltzahn to remain in the navy, partly by noting how much slower promotion was in the army.[62] By May Tirpitz completed his coursework and prepared to rejoin the fleet, half expecting to go to Asia for two years. His academic and technical training at the Academy had enhanced his knowledge and skills, even if it had not dampened his temperament. He was well prepared for the challenges that lay ahead. The great historian of the French Navy, Theodore Ropp, has pointed out that German officer training at that time "was the best given in any European navy."[63]

KRONPRINZ AND KAISER, MAY–SEPTEMBER 1876

On 1 May 1876 Lt. Commander Tirpitz reported to Wilhelmshaven for service aboard the English-built armored frigate *Kronprinz* as a battery officer. It displaced 6,800 tons and had a crew of 543.[64] Captain Otto Livonius was in command as part of the summer armored squadron led by Rear Admiral Batsch aboard *Kaiser,* accompanied by *Friedrich Carl* and the new *Deutschland.*

Upon arrival, Tirpitz recalled his dislike of Wilhelmshaven. "The water is just as dirty, and the region just as desolate as before." As chief of artillery for the *Kronprinz's* sixteen guns, he had nine officers under him, most of them inexperienced.[65] The assassination of two German Consuls in Salonika prompted Bismarck to send the armored squadron on its first foreign intervention. Bismarck feared that the situation might lead to open conflict between Austria and Russia in the Balkans.

On 25 June 1876 the squadron arrived in the Levant via Plymouth, Gibraltar, and Malta, British bases all. The immediate crisis was disarmed when the Turks quickly hanged six purported assassins in full view of the squadron. Tirpitz was skeptical and suspected that the men might not have been personally guilty but had been hanged as a palliative. "Hanging is the order of the day here, and seems to be regarded as a sport."[66]

Tirpitz took advantage of his first visit to the Levant by tracing Xerxes' route on his invasion of Greece. He visited Athens and even saw snow-capped Mount Olympus.[67] *Kronprinz* cruised to Naples and Pompeii and then returned to Salonika and 100-degree heat. A successful gunnery exercise under Batsch's keen eye won Tirpitz the praise of a man he greatly admired. At dinner, Batsch asked Tirpitz if he had ever been to

Japan. Tirpitz's reply that he was likely to be going there in the fall was a measure of how unaware young officers were about their future assignments.[68] Tirpitz did not share his great fear of getting sick in East Asia.

The Admiralty could not afford an extended foreign sojourn of the armored squadron, and Stosch wanted to bring it home for training in the Baltic. The Foreign Office wanted the ships to stay in the Levant. Stosch negotiated a compromise that allowed *Kronprinz* and *Friedrich Carl* to remain, with the others ordered to return home.[69]

With no prior warning, and at the request of the influential Batsch, Tirpitz, Klausa, and some others transferred to *Kaiser*, where Tirpitz took over as gunnery officer. "The sea officer gets a touch of the feeling of the wandering Jew," Tirpitz wrote to his parents: "Never mind how this has happened, I am content." He joked that "it is really unnatural for a man to live on the sea, for why is man given two legs if not to use them?"[70] Perhaps Batsch had discerned a better way to use Tirpitz's talents than to send him to Japan.

Kaiser was a new (1874) English-built armored frigate of 8,900 tons. Its captain was Max von der Goltz, Tirpitz's superior at the Oberkommando in the early 1890s.[71] Upon reaching Germany, Tirpitz had a few weeks of home leave and took the cure for almost two months at Carlsbad, a custom of the day for those who could afford the time and money.[72] Sometime that fall he received word that he was about to undertake the hardest challenge of his young life. On New Year's Day, in 1877, he reported to the Torpedo Experimental Commission in Berlin.

5

THE CREATION OF THE GERMAN
TORPEDO ARM, 1877–1889

THE TORPEDO ARM UNDER STOSCH

When Tirpitz joined the Torpedo Commission, the first halting steps had already been taken in the evolving technology that would culminate in the sleek, deadly underwater missiles of the twentieth century. One idea was to put a mine at the end of a spar and use it as an exploding ram. Another was the Harvey tow torpedo, a floating charge on a tether attached to a boat, with the intention of turning the boat away at the moment of attack and allowing the charge to strike the target. Both these methods required almost suicidal bravery on the part of crews of improvised 10-knot torpedo boats. Nevertheless, by the early 1870s, most naval powers were trying out variations of these weapons. The possibility, even if remote, of sinking expensive battleships with cheap torpedoes was too tempting to resist, especially for smaller navies.

A more dynamic approach was the self-propelled "fish" torpedo. An English engineer, Robert Whitehead, director of the Firma Stabilimento Tecnico in Fiume, pursued this concept, the outcome of which would be the modern torpedo. In 1867 the Austrian government bought Whitehead's patent. As early as 1869 a delegation from the North German Navy visited Fiume. By 1873, with Stosch in charge, the Imperial German Navy purchased torpedoes under license from the Austrian government and Whitehead.[1]

Stosch explored torpedo development in the context of his ambitious ten-year expansion plan.[2] In 1873 Stosch set up a Torpedo Experiment Commission under Commander Alexander Graf von Monts, who or-

dered one hundred torpedoes from Whitehead. At the same time Stosch
commissioned, from an English yard, the construction of *Zieten*, a large
torpedo vessel of 1,170 tons, which was especially designed to test the
Whitehead torpedo.[3] By 1876, when *Zieten* was completed, disappointing experiments with the spar and tow torpedoes confirmed the focus on
the Whitehead torpedo. Commander Eduard von Heusner, director of
the new torpedo depot at Friedrichsort, near Kiel, was put in charge of
technical development of the Whitehead torpedo. His assistant was Lt.
Commander Otto von Diedrichs, Tirpitz's old shipmate from *Niobe*.[4]

On 1 January 1877 Stosch appointed twenty-seven-year-old Lt. Commander Tirpitz to be the officer in charge of detonators and warheads in
the Torpedo Commission.[5] There is no contemporary evidence to suggest
that anyone regarded this as other than a routine assignment.[6] After a
few months of orientation in the Torpedo Commission Office in Berlin,
Tirpitz privately felt anxious. He wrote to his parents in April, saying, "the
whole torpedo story seems to me more and more regrettable." Stosch was
making demands impossible to fulfill.[7]

In May Tirpitz accompanied Heusner to Fiume to learn firsthand
about torpedo construction. He met Whitehead and his family, and noted
that Russian, French, Danish, and Portuguese officers were also studying
torpedo assembly.[8] Upon his return to Kiel in June, Tirpitz noted the large
number of German officers there who had become invalids from service
in the tropics, a prospect he had come to dread. Already present were the
first hints of his lifelong hypochondria.[9]

The work was frustrating. There was no praise from Heusner or
Stosch. The latter kept a keen eye on torpedo development but underestimated its difficulties. "Stosch wants the matter to be developed as easily
as training with a pike."[10] "I hear, I see, nothing but torpedoes. I dream
that I have become one myself."[11] On 18 September 1877 Stosch watched
Tirpitz, as torpedo officer of *Zieten*, score three direct hits with practice
Whitehead torpedoes at a stationary target 730 meters away.[12] Stosch
still had doubts and polled a group of officers, including Tirpitz, about
the torpedo's feasibility. Tirpitz's written response so impressed the gruff
Stosch that he called it "exemplary."[13]

Although Tirpitz had less than a year's experience with torpedoes, his
document anticipated, to a remarkable degree, both the future course of
torpedo development and ideas that were to characterize his work when
he moved to a much larger stage in 1897.

Perhaps influenced by the experience of sitting impotently in Wilhelmshaven aboard *König Wilhelm* during the war with France, he began with words he would use much later:

> It is characteristic of battle on the open sea that its sole goal is the annihilation of the enemy. Land battle offers other tactical possibilities, such as taking terrain, which do not exist in war at sea. Only annihilation can be accounted a success at sea.

In 1877 steam had called into question time-honored tactical principles. In the conflict between guns and armor, the latter was at least temporarily ascendant.[14] If a torpedo could be built that would strike under the waterline, the most powerful armored battleship might sink. "Compared to the gun it is a very cheap means of destruction." Such a task would be almost impossible for spar or tow torpedoes. "The Whitehead torpedo is . . . the first that promises military feasibility."

There followed a sober discussion of the unripe character of the Whitehead torpedo. Torpedoes built for the Adriatic tended to sink in the Baltic because of the specific gravity of that less saline sea. Another was that single-screw torpedoes were hard to keep on a straight course. Range was limited. Firing tests from moving ships had just begun and were fraught with pitfalls. He recommended the establishment of a group of specially trained torpedo mechanics and engineers.[15] He estimated that, with a double-screw torpedo, the probability of hitting a 30-meter-wide stationary target at 750 meters was about 90 percent. Tirpitz's memo identified almost the whole agenda for torpedo experiments over the next few years.

On the question of a delivery system, he believed that *Zieten* already posed a threat to enemy warships, but he shrewdly observed: "If war were to come now there are too many unknown factors and I can only promise success if I assume that the mere existence of the torpedo would have a moral effect on the enemy and influence his maneuvers."

He rejected a general introduction of the torpedo into the warships of the navy, but to try it on a few ships would have an advantage: "the whole Front would come in contact with the new weapon." Another approach would be to equip the steam-powered auxiliary boats of the large ships with torpedo tubes.

Finally, he raised the concern that would dominate his work throughout the 1880s: Should Germany develop special ships with the torpedo as their principal weapon? He dismissed the idea of building more 1,170-ton ships of the *Zieten* type as too large, expensive, and vulnerable to gunfire. Instead, such vessels should be as small, fast, and cheap as possible, and designed to operate in coastal waters.

This memorandum marked Tirpitz's public debut as a thinking man in a navy where rough-and-ready sea dogs were the norm. His ideas were clear, balanced, and logical. He criticized the helter-skelter methods other navies were using to introduce the weapon and advocated the calm, systematic, incremental, and empirical approach that would become the hallmark of his entire career. Despite his junior rank and Stosch's continued, though abating, skepticism about the torpedo, Tirpitz had drawn favorable attention to himself. Now it remained for him to carry out the daunting mission.

Events in the Russo-Turkish War made his remarks seem prophetic. In December 1877 and January 1878 Russian boats fired Whitehead torpedoes at Turkish ships. They sank a Turkish sentinel boat in the harbor of Batumi, the first combat success of a Whitehead torpedo. It sparked a frenzy of torpedo boat building and experiments in virtually all European navies.[16]

In March 1878 Stosch sent Tirpitz to Fiume to arrange the return of unsatisfactory torpedoes ordered the previous year. It was his first opportunity to negotiate independently with a contractor. To Stosch's satisfaction, Tirpitz got Whitehead to take back half of them. He also investigated a new detonator and conducted experiments with various types of tubes.[17] During his work in the Torpedo Arm, Tirpitz would negotiate with a great variety of suppliers, very important experience for his future work. Upon his return in May he became Director of Torpedo Development and assumed command of *Zieten*, while Heusner went to Berlin to take overall command of the torpedo department at the Admiralty. In practice this meant that the young officer had autonomy in his work, though Stosch kept a watchful and supportive eye on him and took his side in bureaucratic conflicts with the Kiel Dockyard. As Tirpitz put it many years later: "Since I was 29, I have had the good fortune to be employed uninterruptedly in positions of independence."[18]

In his end-of-season report, Tirpitz noted that several navies were achieving promising results but that torpedoes were still unreliable. "The great expectation . . . which discovery brings with it is not realizable at the first stage of the process." But the idea will soon "come to life in a practical form." "The torpedo will only be critically significant after a further development period whose duration will have to be measured in years."[19] Despite this cautious statement, Stosch was pleased enough to write:

> I am happy about the report of the commander of *Zieten* on the current status of the torpedo experiments. These experiments finally and for the first time are being carried out in systematic order according to objective principles. I want to express my appreciation to Lt. Commander Tirpitz for this.[20]

The German Navy's first public firing of an armed torpedo took place on 26 June 1879 in the Wiecker Bight, with the old dispatch boat *Preussischer Adler* as the target. Its hull was coated with iron for the occasion. Tirpitz and Torpedo Engineer Voigt loaded two torpedoes, each with 20 kg of explosives, into a steam launch. Tirpitz fired the first, which hit the target from 200 meters and exploded, although it ran on the surface most of the way. The observers, who included Rear Admiral Franz Kinderling, Chief of the Baltic Station, and a number of other senior officers, said the shot was a failure because the torpedo did not run at its designed depth of 3 meters. Tirpitz replied that this was done deliberately to see if the detonator would explode on the surface. He then fired the second torpedo, which ran true at the right depth and blasted the target again. Senior officers sheepishly offered congratulations. Tirpitz was learning how to finesse the opposition of superiors.[21] The success likely helped restore Stosch to the good graces of the Crown Prince, who partly blamed Stosch for the disastrous collision of two armored ships in the English Channel the year before.[22] As a result of these experiments, Stosch decided to equip all large warships with steam launches armed with torpedoes.[23]

The use of steam launches was tested in the squadron maneuvers of 26–27 July 1880. The fleet, five armored ships and a dispatch boat, anchored for the night and secured itself with nets, watch boats, and searchlights against an attack by torpedo-armed launches. The attack came early in the morning of the 27th, and predictably failed because the squadron was on full alert and well protected.[24] The test was biased, but the preparations demonstrated the difficulty of attacking a fleet at anchor near the shore. This again raised the possibility that fleets would have to be attacked at sea, only possible with boats larger than steam launches.

The next day's inspection became one of Tirpitz's greatest triumphs. *Zieten* came steaming at full speed (16 knots) into the harbor. At 400 meters Tirpitz fired a single torpedo from an underwater tube. *Barbarossa*, an old barracks ship, was hit amidships. A cloud of smoke and smashed bits of wood erupted into the air. For a moment the ship did not move. Then it sank slowly with a huge hole in its side.[25]

This test, the first public one to fire from an underwater tube, created great enthusiasm in the Admiralty for torpedo development. It seemed to prove both that large ships could effectively fire torpedoes and that small, swift, relatively cheap boats bigger than the steam launches might be feasible.[26] It was an enormous display of confidence by Tirpitz that he was willing to risk failure before such a prestigious audience. On Stosch's behalf, Tirpitz's nominal superior at the Admiralty, Graf Schack von Wittenau, wrote:

> The Chief gave me the mission to write to you that the news made him very happy. To lead and carry out a military maneuver with such skill and success as you have is excellent. He only regrets that, due to the circumstances of the day, he could not tell you this personally.[27]

In August 1880 the new corvette *Blücher* (3,400 tons) replaced *Zieten* as mothership. *Blücher* served as the torpedo training ship for the majority of German sea officers for a generation.[28] The tender *Ulan* was added to Tirpitz's command to relieve *Blücher* of routine tasks.[29]

At the end of 1880 Lt. Commander Hunold von Ahlefeld and Lieutenant Georg Alexander Müller joined the Torpedo Commission. They were among the first and were later among the most important members of what soon became known as the "Torpedo Gang."[30]

Instinctively uncomfortable with a single supplier, and consistent with Stosch's desire that Germany should become self-sufficient in material, Tirpitz experimented with the first German-made torpedoes, built by the Schwarzkopff firm of Berlin. To inhibit rust, they were made of bronze and were potentially cheaper, faster, and of longer range than the Whitehead model.[31]

Incremental change, painstaking work, and winters spent digesting the lessons of the previous year to prepare for the next brought material improvements to the Torpedo Arm. At the fleet review and inspection on 17 September 1881, with the Emperor present, the Torpedo Commission took center stage. Orchestrated to the minute, *Ulan* and four launches in flotilla formation swept past the imperial yacht and fired accurately at an anchored target.[32] Then *Blücher*, under Tirpitz's command, at full speed, fired one of the new bronze torpedoes at 400-meters range. It sank the old barracks ship *Elbe*. Ten sheep had been placed aboard to test the force of the explosion. Two that were within 10 meters of the blast had broken legs.[33] In recognition of his outstanding service, Tirpitz was promoted to Commander on the spot, an unusual honor, although he was due the promotion soon anyway.

By 1882 no one doubted that torpedoes had a role to play in future wars, Tirpitz and the Admiralty began to focus more directly on how to deliver them against targets. With the consent of the Reichstag, that liked inexpensive torpedo boats, and was susceptible to the "torpedo craze" that was sweeping Europe, Stosch modified the naval building plan of 1873 to provide for ten large and twelve small torpedo boats.[34] The firm Weser of Bremen was commissioned to build seven boats of the *Schütze* class. The crews were limited to thirteen men because of the persistent shortage of officers, which permitted only one per boat.[35] Tirpitz thought too many of these boats were built before experiments determined the right type. They had been ordered as a hasty response to a Russian war scare in 1882.[36]

On the night of 10–11 September 1882 came the first torpedo boat exercise against a fleet outside a harbor. It became known as the "Battle of Fehmarn Sound." Batsch, Chief of the Baltic Station, scripted the general scenario, which gave torpedo boats the main role. The plan assumed that an "Eastern power" declared war on Germany on 10 September. On the same morning an enemy squadron of four armored frigates and a dispatch boat, under Captain Wilhelm von Wickede, left Danzig, perhaps to attack Kiel Harbor.[37] Defending Kiel were *Blücher* and three small ships that served as scouts, plus a group of four *Schütze*-class torpedo boats under Lieutenant Commander Paul Jaeschke.[38] Tirpitz's defending ships were to patrol Fehmarn Sound, a strait about 15 km wide between the German island of Fehmarn (which was about 80 km east of Kiel Harbor) and the Danish island of Lolland (see Figure 5.1). The attacking torpedo boats were to conceal themselves close to shore at the Marian Light on Fehmarn Island. Wickede had discretion about whether to pass the Sound by day or night, what formation to use, and about whether to pass the Sound on the German side, the Danish side, or in the middle.[39] The defending forces also had several options that depended on where and when the enemy tried to force the Sound.

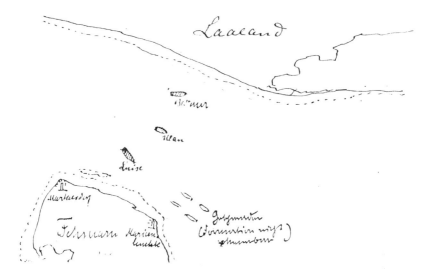

Upon the declaration of "war," Tirpitz spread his small squadron that night across the 15-km width of the Sound. *Blücher*, the fastest, he stationed as near to the Danish shore as possible without losing sight of *Ulan* (commanded by Lieutenant Hugo Pohl), the next ship in the picket line.[40] Pohl spotted the enemy.[41] Wickede's "attackers" were screened in front by a dispatch boat and four torpedo boats. Upon receiving the signal, Jaeschke's four boats steamed out at full speed from Marian Light and took the squadron from the rear.[42]

In the post mortem Stosch credited Tirpitz's screen with spotting the enemy quickly, and criticized Wickede for hugging the German shore, precisely where he would be most vulnerable to torpedo attack. The referees awarded the torpedo boats a hit on the rear of the frigate *Preussen*. The torpedo boats escaped unscathed, although their attempt to attack the squadron the next day near Kiel was unsuccessful. Stosch, who previously had skeptically referred to the torpedo boats as *"Blitzboote,"* concluded that "the best defense of the harbor is to take the offensive, and the whole fleet should throw all its force against the enemy."[43] Even though he still saw the cannon as "the king of weapons," the "battle" was such a tremendous success for the torpedo that he dropped his final hesitancy about sea-going torpedo boats. It still remained to be tested whether the *Schütze*-type boats were the right kind. After fall maneuvers Tirpitz convinced Stosch to support more torpedo boat experiments and to put funds for eighteen more boats in the next year's estimates. The maneuvers enhanced Tirpitz's reputation within the navy and weakened the opposition of some of senior admirals to the torpedo initiative.[44]

The Stosch era ended with his resignation on 20 March 1883. He was worn out by his frequent conflicts with Bismarck.[45] Stosch had laid the groundwork for a plausible system of active coastal defense with torpedo boats and enough armored ships to form a "sortie fleet" to break a blockade by anyone but the British. When he left, Germany had the world's third-largest navy and perhaps (qualitatively, at least) the world's best torpedo force. Though many had resented the appointment of a general rather than an admiral as Chief of Admiralty, most of the naval officer corps, including Tirpitz, regretted his departure.

THE TORPEDO ARM UNDER CAPRIVI

To the shock of the navy, Stosch's successor was not the capable Admiral Batsch but another general, Count Leo von Caprivi, whom the admirals saw as an enemy of the navy. Caprivi was a distant relative of Tirpitz's father. In his letters to his wife from 1884 on, Tirpitz referred frequently to "Uncle Leo" and enjoyed easy access to him.[46] His obsession, that "next fall" a two-front war would break out with France and Russia, dominated Caprivi's time as Chief of the Admiralty (1883–1888). As Tirpitz wrote in 1885, "Uncle Leo infects even unbiased people with his view of war."[47] Since large armored ships took a long time to construct, Caprivi built none, except for the *Siegfried* class of coastal defense ships. By 1888 the German navy had fallen in rank to the sixth-largest navy in the world. Conversely, Caprivi was an ardent torpedo boat enthusiast. These were cheap, could be built quickly, and were popular in the Reichstag.[48] Tirpitz had fought for six years to get Stosch to see the value of torpedo boats; now, with no effort at all, he had a superior more enthusiastic than he. Tirpitz, who had never considered torpedo boats a *substitute* for a battle-fleet, spent the next six years trying to moderate Caprivi's fervor.[49]

In 1883 the Schwarzkopff firm in Berlin began to produce bronze torpedoes under a licensing agreement with Whitehead. Characteristic of his later dealings with contractors, Tirpitz opposed giving Schwartzkopff a monopoly:

> Because a share-holding company which has a monopoly easily pays too
> much attention to its annual dividends, and not enough to the development
> of the product. . . . because of the tendency towards home-production that
> was growing in the larger foreign navies, no foreign money would have
> come to Germany as a compensation for us.[50]

Tirpitz encouraged the development of the navy's Torpedo Depot
at Friedrichsort as a competitor to Schwarzkopff, a practice he was later
to use in building battleships. The company even suggested that he buy
some of its shares, which quickly trebled because of its navy contracts.
"Naturally I did not buy any shares, and would have dismissed any official
who acted otherwise."[51]

Tirpitz secured the winter command of *Blücher* for a long-time member of the Torpedo Gang, Lieutenant Commander Max von Fischel.[52] He
spent the winter, as usual, shuttling between Kiel and Berlin, assessing the
prior year's work and planning for the next. Tirpitz helped Caprivi draft
a memo enthusiastically endorsing torpedo development. The document
went to the Reichstag on 11 March 1884 to explicate Caprivi's ideas on
fleet development.[53]

While in the Torpedo Arm, Tirpitz, when in Berlin, would occasionally attend lectures of the renowned nationalist historian Heinrich von
Treitschke. He even claimed to have dined with Treitschke and to have
asked for his private advice on political matters.[54] It is curious that he never
mentioned this connection in his voluminous correspondence with his
parents at this time.

Caprivi was not alone in his "torpedo intoxication." From the mid-
1870s to the late 1880s and beyond, the French Jeune École, led by Admiral Théophile Aube, struggled to redefine naval strategy with the torpedo
boat as a centerpiece.[55] Aube confronted the awkward question of how
to defeat the British at sea when their economic resources and historical
commitment to traditional forms of seapower were substantially greater
than France's. Aube thought the solution lay in technological change.
The "mastadons," British [and Italian] battleships, could be defeated by
the "microbes" of French torpedo boats. A sustained blockade of the
French coast would be rendered impossible by night attacks on the blockaders with swift, small, and inexpensive torpedo boats. One well-aimed
shot could sink a vastly more expensive battleship. Once the blockade
was broken, swift commerce raiders would strike ruthlessly at Britain's

Achilles' heel, namely, its trade-based national wealth and dependence on foreign sources for food. Even modest success in commerce warfare would cause maritime insurance rates to skyrocket and thereby paralyze trade. France could thus hope to win a *guerre industrielle.* Such ideas were seductive, even compelling, in 1884–85. Younger naval officers in France were attracted to torpedo and cruiser warfare that offered opportunities for initiative and independent command, previously monopolized by a hidebound, aristocratic officer corps.[56]

At that time Aube's rocky term as Minister of Marine (January 1886 to May 1887) lay in the future, and the considerable inadequacies of French torpedo boats were not yet apparent.[57] The French greatly underestimated the amount of political will and stability needed to carry out any coherent naval program. Aube's own views were not as radical as those of his most ardent followers. He did recognize the need for a battlefleet for use against Italy and Germany. In one sense he was prescient. The fear of torpedoes and mines was to virtually paralyze battlefleets in both the North Sea and the Adriatic during World War I.[58]

Caprivi sought to win consensus within the navy for a fleet based solely on coastal defense and torpedo boats. In 1883 he canceled Stosch's armored ship program. In January 1884 he convened a meeting of senior admirals (Blanc, Knorr, Wickede, and Monts) to suggest abandoning the building of armored ships in favor of torpedo vessels. The admirals argued vainly for the replacement of existing armored ships.[59] In March 1884 Caprivi submitted his program to the Reichstag. In the accompanying memorandum he admitted that the fleet ultimately could not do without some armored ships; but because of uncertainty about which type of battleship could survive a torpedo attack, "a navy like ours cannot afford the luxury of failed experiments." The navy would have to await other countries' experiments before committing Germany's resources to a particular type. Meanwhile, since war with France and Russia could come at any time, the navy would have to rely on existing forces and additional torpedo boats, which could be built quickly. To Caprivi's surprise the Reichstag accepted, for patriotic reasons, and almost without discussion, his whole program for 150 torpedo boats over a period of years.[60]

It was Tirpitz's task to decide what kind of torpedo boat to construct.[61] Consistent with his later views, he resisted building large numbers of boats simultaneously, recognizing that if he made an incorrect choice,

Germany could wind up with a fleet of inadequate or obsolescent vessels. Partly as a result of the tests described below, in 1886 the prospective number of boats was cut from 150 to 70.

There was substantial disagreement even about how large the new boats should be. Germany had shallow river mouths and shoaled coasts. Some officers wanted a greater number of boats with a draft small enough to operate in such waters. Others favored fewer vessels of a larger type, to operate alongside the armored squadron at sea. The upper limit in size would be determined by cost and by the chronic officer shortage that provided for only one officer per boat. Tirpitz favored the larger type because he wanted them to sail with the fleet; but he saw the need for extensive experiments before skeptics could be convinced. In the spring of 1884 the Admiralty awarded contracts to the English firms Thorneycroft and Yarrow, and to the German firms Weser, Vulkan, and Schichau to build sample boats of varying designs.[62] By September 1884 the Thorneycroft, Vulkan, Weser, and two Schichau boats had completed their trials and were ready for rigorous high seas testing.

The five boats, and *Blücher*, with Tirpitz in command, sailed from Kiel to Cuxhaven in good weather.[63] The Weser boat had difficulties and had to seek refuge. As the four other boats and *Blücher* arrived at the Elbe, the two S (Schichau) boats collided. One, commanded by Lieutenant August von Heeringen,[64] had its rudder bent. The other sprang a leak. A potential disaster seemed in store for the test. Because it was not possible to repair the boats in Cuxhaven, Tirpitz tried to use materials aboard *Blücher* to fix the damage. As repairs were under way, bad weather was reported. A more faint-hearted (or less ambitious) officer might have been deterred; Tirpitz saw the storm as a welcome opportunity to test the boats in rough weather. On 27 September *Blücher* and the four boats (Heeringen's and the other S-boat; Pohl,[65] aboard the Thorneycroft; and Paschen, aboard the Vulkan) set off for Kiel. A storm came in from the south-southwest. The first day went well, but the storm worsened. At night Heeringen signaled *Blücher* that his rudder was failing. Instead of turning back, Tirpitz boarded Heeringen's boat in the darkness and heavy weather, and tried to jury-rig a manual rudder. Soon after, *Blücher*, now under Ahlefeld's command, lost sight of Tirpitz's boat in the darkness. Since the other S-boat was leaking as a result of collision damage, and Vulkan and Thorneycroft were in trouble in the force 8–9 winds, Ahlefeld was compelled, with a heavy and fearful heart, to seek shelter in Kristiansand Harbor. From there he sent a worried telegram to the Admiralty that Tirpitz's boat had vanished during the storm. The next day Ahlefeld began anxiously to search along the Danish coast. At last, early in the morning of the 29th, a telegram arrived in Kiel from Frederikshavn, a Danish port on the east side of Jutland, reporting that Tirpitz had arrived safely with a damaged rudder. He and Heeringen looked so battered and filthy that at first they were refused hotel accommodations.

In the storm the Vulkan boat had proved only marginally seaworthy, with insufficient range. The Thorneycroft was technically very good, but not seaworthy enough. The S-boat, though far from perfect, had demonstrated sea-keeping qualities necessary to survive a very bad storm. It also had good range and economical engines. One could argue that Tirpitz, who had favored the S-boats from the beginning, had loaded the dice in their favor by his brave and ruthless behavior during the storm. Nevertheless "storm night" became a legend in the navy, and Tirpitz used it successfully to press for larger boats. Tirpitz acquired a dashing reputation in Kiel. A local song about the torpedo boats had, as a refrain, "There go Tirpitz's wild and daring hunters, the sea Cossacks." Tirpitz learned that he had been dubbed "*Kossackenhetmann*" (cossack chief).[66]

On 6 December 1884 Caprivi issued contracts for twenty-two S-boats.[67] Within a few years Schichau gained a monopoly that lasted well into the 1890s.[68] This was a problem for Tirpitz that foreshadowed later conflicts with Krupp, who would have a monopoly of armor and heavy guns once the great fleet buildup began in 1898.[69] Nevertheless, torpedo boat construction was simple and cheap enough for there to be a plausible threat to use other contractors, so Tirpitz could pressure Schichau to keep its prices in line.

In 1884 Caprivi gave Tirpitz the welcome charge to develop torpedo boat tactics and to begin a preliminary study of fleet tactics, seriously neglected in the German Navy, as in most others.[70] Tirpitz formed the navy's first experimental torpedo boat division of six units. Caprivi hectored Monts, the Commander of the Exercise Fleet for 1884.

> The training of crews for battle and the thoughts of the whole squadron should be directed towards war. . . . This is to be the opposite of "parade training." The time for exercises is short and should be used to the utmost for battle training.

Caprivi ordered a reduction in pointless military drills, a relic of the Stosch era, and urged practice of night attacks and even boarding exercises![71] In the summer and fall of 1884 Tirpitz concluded the first systematic development of individual and group torpedo boat tactics.[72] He spent the whole winter digesting these lessons and preparing for the next year's exercises.[73] He also went on his honeymoon.[74]

While Tirpitz was away until the end of January, Count Schack retired. Tirpitz succeeded him as head of the Torpedo Department of the Admiralty.[75] The reshuffling left some significant administrative problems unresolved. The Imperial Dockyards were sometimes uncooperative. The power to have the final word on torpedo boat design was still shared with the Admiralty's Construction Department and with private contractors.[76]

Tirpitz was sensitive about secrecy in many aspects of torpedo work. In the fall of 1884 his old comrade, Commander Iwan F. J. Oldekop, wrote to him for more information about German torpedo development, so he could keep a knowledgeable eye on comparable British work.[77] Tirpitz took almost six months to reply in a way that gives a rare insight into the interaction of his personal and service life:

> You must once give wing to your fantasy and put yourself in the position
> of a young husband on his honeymoon. Then you will forgive me that I
> did not answer your friendly letter of last October. When I returned here, I
> found such a flood of business that I hardly knew what to do. But I will try
> to make up for it now.

He admitted to Oldekop that the Germania and British-built Yarrow boats were failures, but that the Thorneycrofts were better than the S-boats in some respects. He still believed that the efficient engines and bad-weather endurance of the S-boats should tip the scales in favor of the latter.[78]

It was becoming clear that a divisional structure required the leader's boat to be larger than the others to accommodate administrative and command tasks,[79] and to free the commander of ship handling. The first thought was to use "motherships," such as *Blücher* or *Zieten*, to lead the divisions.[80] The drawback of this approach was that the leader would not be present at crucial moments in battle when the division actually attacked.

By 1885 two divisions were organized into a flotilla that undertook an ambitious program of exercises for the summer.[81] Tirpitz led the flotilla on intensive individual and group maneuvers. One division focused on picket duty with the armored squadron, while the other would stalk the big ships by day and try to attack them by night.

In his year-end report[82] Tirpitz argued that the torpedo boats should always operate in divisions, not individually or attached to particular large ships. "Almost without exception, individual deployment miscarried." Boats steaming in divisions were the best way to provide reconnaissance for the fleet and to attack an enemy formation. He was confident that as long as Germany had mobile torpedo boat divisions it would be impossible for an enemy fleet to stay in German waters. He admitted that this could change over time. "Measures beget countermeasures." Command and control as well as endurance problems for boats operating with the fleet required investigation. He admitted frankly that there was a lack of combat experience with torpedo boats. There was no certainty as to what would happen in a real battle; but he asserted that by experimenting with realistic exercises Germany had gained about a one-year lead on other navies. His point was clear. Senior fleet officers had to pay more attention to the risks, opportunities, and potential of the Torpedo Arm.

In 1886 Tirpitz persuaded Caprivi to set up a Torpedo Inspectorate in order to gather all aspects of torpedo development under one office. It included procurement, control of construction, training, weapons, manpower, and maintenance.[83] This clarification freed Tirpitz from most administrative problems and jurisdictional conflicts with other organizations.

By 1885 the question regarding the type of torpedo boats to build was resolved for the duration of Tirpitz's service as Inspector. Between 1885 and 1889 another thirty-five S-boats were built in addition to the six from 1884.[84] The non-Schichau boats were gradually put in reserve or used for training. The S-boats ranged between 98 and 113 tons with a top speed of about 20 knots and with three torpedo tubes, two on deck and one in the bow, all above water, as underwater tubes had not yet proven feasible. S-boats had sufficient range and endurance to cruise with the armored ships, although coal consumption went up enormously at high speed.

In 1887 Schichau delivered the first two larger boats that could lead torpedo boat divisions into battle.[85] These were 300 tons, with seven officers and thirty-nine men and an armament, besides three torpedo tubes, of six 3.7-cm guns. The division leader, relieved of the task of ship command, could devote full attention to leading a division of six to eight boats.

The additional guns were designed to attack or defend against enemy torpedo boats. Without fully realizing it, Tirpitz had built the world's first torpedo boat destroyers. Ironically his great adversary of later years, Sir John Fisher, in 1892 designed superior 27-knot boats for the same purpose. Measures begot measures. Through 1918 Britain retained superiority in this ship type.

By 1886, with homogeneous boats organized into divisions, more sophisticated work began with formation steaming, signaling, and coordinated attacks. In contrast to the Torpedo Arm, the armored squadron lacked any but the simplest tactics.[86] The rules of 1876 were still in effect. The only battle signals permitted were "open fire" and "attack the enemy." There was a vague idea of closing with the enemy to bring about a melee, wherein captains should "act according to circumstance." The sinking of the armored ship *Grosser Kurfürst* in a collision with *König Wilhelm* in 1878 had left squadron commanders paralyzed with fear about risky maneuvers. As the growing skill of torpedo boat commanders permitted ever more daring evolutions, captains of large ships looked on in amazement mingled with horror. Caprivi hoped the example of the torpedo boat flotilla would inspire the others, but he was disappointed. During the 1886 maneuvers Vice Admiral Wilhelm von Wickede, the squadron commander, complained to Caprivi that Tirpitz had too much independence in directing the flotilla. Caprivi replied icily: "My dear excellency, there is only one indispensable man in the navy, and that is Tirpitz."[87] "Uncle Leo's" good opinion was not an unmixed blessing. It created envy and anger in others. Tirpitz feared his position would become precarious if Caprivi departed.[88]

Caprivi's pressure and the success of the torpedo boats began to attract favorable attention among some older navy men. Rear Admiral Carl Paschen, squadron chief in 1887, noted that the torpedo boat maneuvers were the most interesting part of the exercises, and even suggested that senior officers study them for possible application to handling the larger ships.[89]

Caprivi's confidence in torpedo boats was such that in 1887 he assigned them a lead role in an offensive war plan, a *coup de main* by torpedo boats and the armored squadron against the French Northern Fleet in Cherbourg before it could be reinforced from the Mediterranean. The plan had many questionable assumptions, including Britain's benevolent neutrality, since the German fleet would need to refuel in the Channel.[90] Nevertheless, it was the first coherent war plan that took note of the growing capabilities of the torpedo force.

To foster tactics, in January 1888 Caprivi queried a number of senior officers. A hypothetical German fleet of twelve armored ships and three torpedo boat divisions would face an enemy of about equal strength, approaching in line abreast formation. Some officers did not take it seriously. Knorr, abroad at the time, later wrote: "I was happy that this . . . mostly purposeless exercise passed me by."[91] Caprivi asked what formation the German fleet should adopt and how it should attack. Most officers answered in a literal and uninspired fashion.[92] Tirpitz wrote a two-hundred-page response that answered the questions directly but also addressed a variety of contingencies and gave him license to discuss lessons of his torpedo work.[93] His response was by far the most comprehensive.

More important than Tirpitz's response was his cover letter.[94] A "clarifying consensus" about tactical questions in the officer corps was necessary, if the fleet was to work together:

> I personally believe, although it is not a conclusive belief, that such a consensus is achievable in peacetime and that this possibility would substantially improve our chances in case of war because the qualities necessary to do this—system, perseverance and a military vision—can be found in a not insignificant degree in our national character. . . . We should spread out the systematic and programmatic work over several years.[95]

He wanted critical questions addressed one at a time, in an empirical way, in squadron exercises. Each answer would lead to other questions to be answered in turn. Three or four years would be necessary to reach substantial results. The process is exactly what Tirpitz put into practice in 1892, when, as Chief of Staff of the Oberkommando, he worked to improve fleet tactics.

Equally notable in the memorandum was Tirpitz's proposal for an attack formation. He suggested a variation of line ahead called "Staffel."[96] That only a minority of the officers who responded to Caprivi's questions favored any kind of line ahead formation is a testimony to the lack of consensus.[97] Tirpitz himself later changed his mind and favored a partial line abreast formation.

On 15 June 1888 Prince William ascended the throne upon the deaths of his grandfather and father. The eldest grandson of Queen Victoria, he had shown a lively interest in naval matters from an early age. The Torpedo Arm had not escaped his attention. In 1884 he had witnessed a torpedo shooting exercise aboard *Blücher*.[98] In 1886 he visited the first Schichau division boat.[99] Along with his brother, Commander Prinz Heinrich, who led a division of torpedo boats, he sailed to England for his grandmother's jubilee in June 1887 aboard *Blitz*, with Tirpitz in command. To the amazement of British torpedo experts, the flotilla accompanied *Blitz* across the North Sea. The boats made a striking impression with their range and seaworthiness. This occasion marked the true international debut of the German Torpedo Arm. It was also the first chance for Tirpitz to have sustained personal contact with the future Emperor.[100]

William II intended to lead the navy personally. Caprivi understood this and resigned three weeks after the succession, as he did not share William's passion for a large navy. He also knew a dismantling of the Admiralty was coming.[101] Monts was named as his replacement. He and several other senior officers such as Knorr had long resented the independence of Tirpitz and the young officers in the Torpedo Arm. Tirpitz's sarcastic private nicknames for Monts included "the Great Count," and "Alexander the Great."[102] When Monts, at the maneuvers, dismissed the torpedo flotilla as "parade ships," Tirpitz asked to be relieved and given a sea command.[103] He had to stay on until 25 March 1889, when the planned reorganization of the navy would be complete. William II wanted to devolve the Admiralty into three organizations: the Oberkommando (High Command, or OK) to assume the command function; the Reichsmarineamt (Imperial Naval Office, or RMA) to handle administration and deal with the Reichstag; and the Marinekabinett (Naval Cabinet, or MK) for personnel matters.

The Emperor wanted to divide the Admiralty's functions to enhance his direct authority. His younger brother, Prinz Heinrich, already a Captain by 1889, because of the fast promotion track reserved for royals, noted that dividing the navy into five parts (at that time, the OK, the RMA, the MK, and the Baltic and North Sea Stations), each of which would report directly to the Emperor, meant that the latter had *direct* control of each branch of the navy. This arrangement would also ensure that the Commanding Admiral, Head of the OK, would not be "tainted," as he asserted the State Secretary of the RMA would be, by direct dealings with the Reichstag.[104] To put the matter, roughly, into a U.S. Navy context, it would be as if the Secretary of the Navy, the Chief of Naval Operations, and various other major naval commands each reported directly to the President.

Tirpitz quickly realized that such a measure would split the Torpedo Inspectorate into command and administrative parts. Throughout the winter of 1888–89 Tirpitz made desperate but unsuccessful attempts to save the Inspectorate.[105] His promotion to Captain on 24 November 1888 was small consolation for what he saw as the destruction of his twelve years of determined effort. Despite a superb qualification report—"he has served with extraordinary distinction. He inspired his subordinates with enthusiasm for their work and shows a particular zest for the initiative"[106]—Tirpitz feared that all his work had been for naught. He took command of the armored ship *Preussen* that, ironically, his torpedo boats had "sunk" at the "Battle of Fehmarn Sound."

ANALYSIS OF THE TORPEDO YEARS

Were German Torpedo Boats the Best in the World in 1889?

Leading authorities on the German Navy agree that the German Torpedo Arm was the best at that time.[107] Perhaps even more significant is that Theodore Ropp, the historian of the French Navy, agrees.[108] Ropp states that France's 58-ton torpedo boats built by Admiral Aube in the late 1880s were a "complete failure." Arthur J. Marder, the historian of the Royal Navy, does not address the point directly but notes that, on a cruise in the Channel in 1887, within a space of three weeks, nineteen of twenty-three British torpedo boats had serious mechanical problems. In sheer numbers, Britain, France, and Russia had as many or more. Germany, under Stosch and Caprivi, gained a qualitative advantage in usable high seas torpedo boats.[109] In April 1889, after he left the Torpedo Arm, Tirpitz wrote an extensive and quite objective review of his work in the torpedo years. Part of it was a warts-and-all comparison of German torpedo boats with those of Britain and France. While crediting the British with substantial progress, he was already aware of the glaring deficiencies of the French approach.[110] Yet, after 1892, Britain surged into the lead in usable destroyers, a type superior to the German torpedo boat, and never relinquished it. Measures begot countermeasures.[111] After he came to power in 1897 Tirpitz still saw the Torpedo Arm as a personal domain, and often held back its later development. He clung to his old feeling that torpedo boats had to be small, and he ignored the shortcomings of his own creation. The Front fought bitterly to slowly increase its size. The German Imperial Admiralty Staff (Admiralstab) wanted a greater radius of action so that the torpedo boats could fight in northern English waters. Tirpitz answered in 1911 with a reduction in the size of the proposed boat type, with the contention that their "range would suffice for war in the German Bight." He underemphasized necessary escorts in favor of the overriding battleship construction priority, an example of bureaucratic politics.[112]

Who Were the Torpedo Gang?

In 1918 Tirpitz wrote:

> I spent the best eleven years of my life in the torpedo section among "our black comrades, of the wild and daring chase." We were bound to our incomparable crews by ardor and mutual comradeship in storm and danger. We officers of the torpedo section constituted a corps within a corps, the united spirit of which was everywhere recognized, but also envied and opposed.[113]

In 1937 Admiral Adolf von Trotha, a close collaborator of Tirpitz after 1906, but too young to have been in the Torpedo Gang, wrote of Tirpitz's method of managing men:

> From the first day an officer would be appointed, Tirpitz would make great demands. This soon showed if a man was up to the job. If his ideas and work methods were satisfactory, Tirpitz soon opened to him his innermost thoughts. But if there was no meeting of the minds or—the worst case—he proved to be a person who remained stuck on trivialities or administrative questions, Tirpitz would set him aside and find another way.[114]

During his torpedo years Tirpitz developed a cadre of younger officers, many of whom later became important and influential in the navy; but except for a few obvious examples like Heeringen, Müller, Pohl, and Braun, no one up to now has identified who they were. See the list of twenty-four in the appendix to this volume.

The list includes ten men who served under Tirpitz at the OK; all the commanders of the High Seas Fleet from 1913 to 1918 (Ingenohl, Pohl, and Scheer); and five of the six Chiefs of the Admiralstab between 1902 and

1915 (Büchsel, Fischel, Heeringen, Pohl, and Bachmann). During the war Tirpitz had bad relations with Müller, Pohl, and Ingenohl. Büchsel, who generally had good relations with Tirpitz, was only marginally a torpedo man. Fischel, who was very close to Tirpitz in his torpedo days, battled him for institutional reasons when Fischel was Chief of the Admiralstab. Only Heeringen[115] and Bachmann remained close to Tirpitz during their terms as Chiefs of the Admiralstab.

The inclusion of some on the list may be the result of simple coincidence of assignment. Nevertheless, it is justifiable to include in the Torpedo Gang Ahlefeld, Bachmann, Fischel, Ingenohl, Jaeschke, Truppel, Winkler, and Zeye, along with Braun, Heeringen, Müller, and Pohl, as mentioned above.[116] Taken together, during the prewar years, they constituted a talented and formidable "mafia" within the navy.

Conclusions

A detailed study of the torpedo years affirms Berghahn's judgment:

> Tirpitz was from the beginning an unusual sea officer. In the breadth of his interest for technical, political, and "philosophical" problems, and in his piercing and cool intellect he seems to have far surpassed his comrades. . . . Not the least of his many noteworthy characteristics was his unsurpassed sense for the systematic, and the tenacity with which he pursued his goal, once he recognized it.[117]

The development of the Whitehead torpedo, a robust type of torpedo boat, and the strategy and tactics that went with them, demonstrated the combination of vision, painstaking empiricism, and ruthless energy characteristic of his later work.

As he was to do with William II, Tirpitz courted, manipulated, and, when necessary, discreetly stood up to Stosch and Caprivi, his principal superiors. He persuaded an often reluctant Stosch of the value of the torpedo, and pushed him toward the beginnings of a "blue water" strategy. He retained a genuine, though not uncritical, respect and affection for Stosch even after the latter's death.[118]

Tirpitz's *Ressorteifer* tendency was not predominant during the torpedo years. In his Tirpitz biography, Michael Salewski argues that, "as Torpedo Inspector at least, Tirpitz was no *Ressortegoist*."[119] He correctly points out that, for all Tirpitz's enthusiasm for the Torpedo Arm, he never lost sight of the ultimate goal of a battlefleet. Tirpitz had little respect for less critical torpedo enthusiasts like the French Admiral Aube. He recognized during the torpedo years, though perhaps not later, that torpedoes and torpedo boats, like cut flowers, had a short usable lifespan and needed to be improved continuously in the light of rapid technological advances. It is clear from his 1889 memo on torpedo development that he saw torpedoes as a useful addition to a battlefleet, not a replacement for it.

Nevertheless, even in the torpedo years, *Ressorteifer*, Allison's Model 3 of bureaucratic politics, was present, at least *in ovo*, though in nothing like the magnitude of the post-1897 period. The creation of the Torpedo Inspectorate in 1886 gave Tirpitz a virtually self-contained sphere that embraced all peacetime aspects of the Torpedo Arm and freed him from vexatious interference. The Inspectorate was a kind of small-scale model of the later all-embracing Navy Laws, when Tirpitz fended off meddling from other elements of the navy, and balanced the Emperor and the Reichstag off against each other. The resignation in 1888 of his patron, Caprivi, left his carefully constructed organization in disarray. Despite his brilliant successes and growing reputation, the Torpedo Arm was too small a base, and his lack of seniority in a tradition-riddled navy did not provide him the power to preserve his work. Things would be different after the 1898 Navy Law made him indispensable to an Emperor hungry for the prestige of a world-class navy. Only then would he have the institutional base and seniority to carry his battlefleet idea close to completion.

6

INTERIM, 1889–1891

Late in 1883 or early in 1884, while Tirpitz struggled with the complexities of torpedoes and torpedo boats, the thirty-four-year-old officer fell in love. The young lady, Marie Lipke, was a fetching twenty-three year old from a wealthy bourgeois family. By early 1884 they were engaged. Their correspondence at the time shows Tirpitz as the eager suitor. "How much I love you and desire you . . . do you feel this desire at least a little bit?" Marie fretted that Alfred might find her boring.[1] They married on 18 November 1884 at the Garrison Church in Berlin.[2] After a happy and protracted honeymoon they lived in Kiel in a house subsidized by Gustav Lipke, Marie's father.[3]

Marriage for a naval officer was a complicated business. The groom needed imperial marriage consent (*Allerhöchsten Konsens*), for reasons both financial and social. Officers needed enough money to support a family, lest they be overwhelmed with debt. Brides, too, had to have financial means, and a wife with low social status was considered unsuitable. The practical effect of such rules was to prevent officers ranked below lieutenant from marrying. Young officers searched for wealthy, socially acceptable young women so actively that, in 1894, the Marine Kabinett censured officers for advertising in the newspapers for a suitable match. Although there were no written rules, young officers were discouraged from seeking Jewish wives, even if the latter were financially and socially suitable.[4]

Commander Tirpitz's family was wealthy and prominent enough to clear these hurdles. Marie Lipke was a baptized Protestant, born in

West Prussia in 1860. Her mother was Karoline Rothpletz, daughter of a rich Swiss/Baden family. Gustav Lipke was born in 1820 in Berlin to a wealthy, assimilated Jewish banking and business family. At eighteen he converted to Protestantism. He attended Gymnasium and the University of Berlin. He was a lawyer who had served in the Prussian Diet (1873–1879) and in the Imperial Reichstag (1878–1881). He was a liberal ally of Carl Twesten and an opponent of Bismarck. He was a very successful man, both through inheritance and his own enterprise.

Marie Lipke was quite a catch for a rising and ambitious officer. Only by later Nazi standards, unimaginable in 1884, would she be considered half-Jewish; nevertheless, Gustav's Jewish origins seem to have been a closely held family secret. It is not even certain that Tirpitz himself knew about it, although given his relatively tolerant religious views it might not have made any difference.[5] Early in the marriage, Marie had political opinions of her own. Unlike her husband, Marie was no great admirer of Bismarck, to the point that Tirpitz gently chided her with the appella- tion "my darling democrat" (mein geliebter Demokrat).[6] After her father's death, and particularly once Tirpitz himself became engaged in politics, their friendly differences vanished.

If one can judge by their correspondence, the marriage seems to have been happy. Children followed quickly. Ilse, Tirpitz's favorite, was born in 1885, eleven months after the wedding. Wolfgang (1887), Margot (1888), and Max (1893) followed. In 1892 the family moved to Berlin. In 1897, when Tirpitz became State Secretary of the RMA, the family moved into the spacious official residence on Leipzigerplatz. Until his dismissal in 1916 Tirpitz lived adjacent to his office.

Time and mischance took a toll on the family. Mother Malwine died in 1890 at the age of seventy-five. Rudolf lived on until 1905. He died, hale and hearty almost to the end, at ninety-four. Brother Max died after a riding accident in 1892. In 1889 Gustav Lipke died of injuries after he was hit by a beer wagon in Berlin.[7] Upon his death, Marie inherited a very large sum.[8]

Tirpitz, perhaps through Marie's maternal relatives, became friendly with the Grand Duke and Duchess of Baden who, in the late 1890s, gave him a plot of land on the side of a hill overlooking the small and lovely Black Forest spa of St. Blasien. Tirpitz built a comfortable home there, which still stands. Its most striking feature is a broad, wraparound porch, from which one can view the town and its scenic valley. Once Tirpitz became State Secretary, St. Blasien served as the family's vacation home. Forest walks with the children were interspersed with intensive work. Much planning for naval legislation took place there. RMA officers were frequent visitors. While there, Tirpitz stayed in constant contact with Berlin, first by telegraph and, after 1910, by telephone.[9]

Part of Marie's inheritance from her father was a property in Alghero, Sardinia. The estate was on the wild, bandit-ridden, northwestern coast of the island. A steward administered its grazing land, vineyards, and ten thousand olive trees. The family visited there rarely, but Alghero was a great favorite of Ilse, the adventurous eldest daughter.[10]

Alfred and Marie were affectionate and attentive parents. They traveled frequently, often with the children. Italy, especially its Riviera, was a favorite place. Visits to Marie's relatives in Zürich were common. Tirpitz sent Ilse and Margot to study at Cheltenham Ladies' College in England, which Marie had attended as a girl. Ilse, who quickly perfected her English, was amazed by the school's freedom from rote German-style learning.[11]

Tirpitz was not very interested in Berlin society. Marie liked to shop and, given her privileged upbringing, enjoyed parties and balls. As State Secretary, Tirpitz had to represent the officer corps socially, which meant giving and attending more social events than he would have liked. Balls and parties were held at the RMA for officers and selected political notables, including the Imperial Chancellor. William II was a frequent, if somewhat disconcerting, visitor. He was so enchanted with Ilse's beauty, poise, and English skill, that he called her "my little cruiser." Every year in June the Emperor held Kiel Week, during which there was a gala international regatta with yacht races, balls, and other festivities. He liked to think of it as the German answer to the Cowes Regatta, hosted by his grandmother, Queen Victoria. In Kiel Tirpitz mingled with foreign royalty and dignitaries such as Winston Churchill and Admiral John Jellicoe.[12] Tirpitz disliked the lavish displays of Kiel Week, and especially William II's bombastic pride in his growing fleet which Tirpitz wanted to keep as inconspicuous as possible.[13]

In 1909, at a ball in her home, the vivacious Ilse met a young Foreign Office lawyer from a distinguished but not particularly rich Prussian/Hanoverian family, Ulrich von Hassell. Even though Ilse was besieged with suitors, it was love at first sight. Ilse, then twenty-four, later wrote of their fairy-tale courtship that was not without elements of farce. In the time-honored way that daughters manipulate doting fathers, Ilse used cunning and patience to convince her skeptical father that the intelligent and responsible Ulrich was worthy of his first-born daughter. In the end, love conquered all. They married in 1911, and Tirpitz embraced his new son-in-law with enthusiasm.[14]

When time permitted, Tirpitz read about history, politics, and war, and an occasional novel. He gave his son Wolfgang a copy of Clausewitz.[15] An admirer of Kant and Schiller, he also read the nationalist historian Heinrich von Treitschke. Although Protestant, he did not share the anti-Catholic prejudices of some of his peers.[16] As State Secretary, he courted the pivotal Catholic Center Party, to the dismay of some of his colleagues. Only very few times in his vast correspondence did he make comments that stereotyped Jews.[17] Clearly, however, he was no anti-Semite. His father wrote to him and Marie in 1898, deploring the "nonsense" (*Unsinn*) of anti-Semitism.[18] During the war he noted his opposition to anti-Semitism and welcomed the patriotic support of German Jews.[19]

Tirpitz's correspondence, as early as cadet days, was rife with complaints of all manner of physical ailments. Rheumatism, lung disease, and back trouble seemed to assail him frequently. His own family believed he was a hypochondriac. He often came to the family table late and disinclined to eat, but once there he ate a lot, very fast. His partiality for oysters and red wine perhaps accounted for some of his stomach troubles. He took more medicine than some thought was necessary and suffered from insomnia, but at sea he slept through the worst weather.[20]

When World War I started, hard news was not long in coming. Wolfgang von Tirpitz was a young officer aboard the light cruiser *Mainz*. On 28 August 1914, in a confused action in the fog off Helgoland, a superior British force sank *Mainz* and two other light cruisers. Despair gripped the family until a message arrived from Churchill via the U.S. Embassy in Berlin. "Tell Admiral von Tirpitz that his son is safe and unwounded." Wolfgang was one of the 348 survivors of *Mainz* whom the British had pulled out of the North Sea.[21] He spent the remainder of the war as a prisoner.

The family had only just begun to come to terms with that event when a further, horrible bulletin arrived. On 8 September 1914, on the Marne, Reserve Lieutenant Ulrich von Hassell of the 2nd Regiment of Prussian

Guards Infantry was gravely and, it was feared, mortally wounded by a bullet lodged in his heart. Six months of hospitalization ensued. The bullet could not be extracted for fear that the operation would kill him.[22] Ulrich completed his recuperation with Ilse in the Tirpitz home. He carried the bullet for the rest of his life, although he was never again fit for military service. Considering the annihilating toll that the war took on junior infantry officers, the terrible wound may have been a perverse stroke of luck.

SHIP COMMAND, 1889–1890

Captain Alfred Tirpitz left his post as Inspector of the Torpedo Arm on 25 March 1889. For a month he was "available to" the Chief of the Baltic Station, Vice Admiral Eduard von Knorr. Such a designation was common for officers between assignments. While in Kiel, Tirpitz took the opportunity to write an extensive history of the development of the Torpedo Arm. It was not addressed to anyone in particular, but he sent copies to influential people like Stosch, Caprivi, and Senden, perhaps hoping it would come to the Emperor's attention.[23]

On 29 April 1889 Tirpitz assumed his first command of a large ship. The armored frigate *Preussen*, laid down in 1873, displaced 7,700 tons, with a crew of about five hundred, and was armed with four 26-cm and two 17-cm guns in turrets. Under steam it had a top speed of 14 knots, although it was originally equipped with three masts for sails. In 1885 it was refitted with underwater torpedo tubes and torpedo nets, eloquent evidence of the influence of Tirpitz's torpedo work in the fleet. On 1 July 1889 *Preussen* joined the II Division of the maneuver fleet. The division's commander was Rear Admiral Friedrich Hollmann, who later became Tirpitz's great adversary.[24]

In the fall and winter of 1889–90 *Preussen* and the three other armored ships of the II Division went to the Mediterranean for training. The episode was significant because it was the first example in the German Navy of keeping a group of large ships in commission for a full year. They escorted *Hohenzollern* on visits to Athens and Constantinople, and returned home in the spring of 1890.[25]

On 2 May 1890 Tirpitz became commander of the armored corvette *Württemberg*. Laid down in 1878, it was one of the first large German ships built without sails. It displaced 7,800 tons, had a top speed of 14 knots and was armed with six 26-cm and eight 8.7-cm guns. *Württemberg* joined the maneuver squadron in the summer of 1890. That summer, for the first time, four full divisions of torpedo boats joined the maneuvers. William II, to the annoyance of some officers, preempted precious exercise time by having the fleet escort *Hohenzollern* on visits to Copenhagen and Christiania (later Oslo), and other Norwegian harbors.[26]

Ship command did not give Tirpitz much opportunity to influence fleet development. As he later related, he tried to make the most of his time in the fleet. He rigorously trained officers and crews:

> This secured a high certainty of movement, which attracted much notice when I was able to proceed with apparent daring as commander of *Preussen* and *Württemberg* in first operations with heavy ships in squadron forma- tion; in reality my ability to do so was due to practice, but it was often want- ing in the older ships, owing to the weakness of their individual training.[27]

Another officer had a somewhat different opinion:

> In the fleet [Tirpitz] had the reputation of being a "bad driver" (*schlechter Fahrer*). On the other hand, his trainees (sublieutenants and sea cadets) liked him because he spoke to them in detail about strategy and tactics, something which officers on other ships never did.[28]

After Caprivi stepped down from the Admiralty, he and Tirpitz con- tinued to correspond on naval and political matters,[29] even when Caprivi became Chancellor after Bismarck's fall in March 1890. Upon leaving *Württemberg* in September 1890, Tirpitz was originally slated to become Dockyard Director at Kiel. Caprivi felt that such a position would be a waste of Tirpitz's talents. In the summer of 1890 Caprivi took advantage of a hunt with William II to propose Tirpitz for the more central post of Chief of Staff of the Baltic Station under Vice Admiral Knorr. On 27 September 1890 Tirpitz assumed this job, and could observe the growing friction between Vice Admiral Max von der Goltz at the OK and Hol- lmann, newly appointed State Secretary of the RMA.[30]

When Tirpitz became Baltic Chief of Staff his purview expanded from the narrow world of torpedoes and ship command to broad con- siderations of national interest. Bismarck's worldview had focused on the continental balance of power and the isolation of France. The 1879 defensive alliance with Austria-Hungary gave the latter security against an attack from Russia, but because Bismarck held the whip hand, the treaty also restrained Austria-Hungary from aggressive moves against Russia. A further defensive alliance in 1882 gave Italy a degree of security but, in Bismarck's time, assured that Italy would refrain from joining Austria-Hungary's potential enemy, Russia. Bismarck avoided an alliance with Russia, partly because he could not dominate gigantic Russia as he could his lesser allies; nevertheless, he tried to keep a loose diplomatic connection with Russia through a "Reinsurance" Treaty that would deter warlike coalitions against either party. Bismarck also maintained wary, but correct, relations with Great Britain that culminated, in 1890, with the exchange of the German colony of Zanzibar for the tiny, but strategic, island of Helgoland that shielded vulnerable German harbors and river mouths in the North Sea.[31] As Knorr pointed out, in a war with France a German Helgoland would be easy prey for the superior French Navy. In a war with Britain, it would be invaluable, though vulnerable, but, in 1890, such a war was inconceivable.

By 1890 Bismarck had seemingly achieved his long-term goal of isolating France. His role as referee between Russia and Austria-Hungary limited the risk of great power wars in the Balkans. His great nightmare, a two-front war against France and Russia, had apparently become almost impossible.[32] When William II dismissed Bismarck in March 1890 and replaced him with Caprivi, it was unclear what effect the Emperor's widely proclaimed but ill-defined policy of a "New Course" would have on Bismarck's subtle and intricate network of alliances and alignments.

CHIEF OF STAFF OF THE BALTIC STATION, 1890–1891

In the fall of 1890 Tirpitz became Chief of Staff of the Baltic Station under the command of Eduard von Knorr. Knorr was one of the few naval heroes of the French war. His little *Meteor* had battered a larger French ship in single combat outside Havana Harbor. A contemporary subordinate described Knorr as a tall and erect man, with an outspoken personality. He had a blond full beard and deep blue eyes, which exuded fire and "the spirit of a dozen lieutenants." A man of choleric nature, who blushed easily, his nickname was "Red Eduard." Given his fiery nature, work under him was not simple, especially because, in some ways, he still thought in terms of the age of sail.[33]

Knorr respected Tirpitz's knowledge and diligence and supported some of his initiatives, though he was sometimes uncomfortable with him as a subordinate. Knorr wrote later:

> It was his [Tirpitz's] way not to devote his whole ability and knowledge to the work of that position. He used the strength and means available to him as Chief of Staff (Baltic) to gather things he could then use for later opportunities.[34]

During his time at Kiel Tirpitz wrote three important memoranda. The first, dated 1 February 1891, was "Reasons for the Retention of an Oberkommando with a Powerful Competence."[35] It was Tirpitz's opening shot in the turf wars endemic in the navy since the Emperor terminated the Admiralty in 1889. On paper, the division into the Oberkommando, the Reichsmarineamt, and the Marine Kabinett seemed an apt parallel to the Prussian Army, with its General Staff, Prussian War Ministry, and Military Cabinet. The parallel was deceptive. The army was a Prussian institution, whereas the navy was an imperial one. By far the most important difference was that the navy's mission was the development of an effective fighting force, whereas the army had long been a mature, successful, and self-confident institution.

For the navy, the question was which branch, the RMA or the OK, should have principal responsibility for fleet development. Chancellor Caprivi would have preferred that the Admiralty had been kept; but he had no choice except to accommodate the new dispensation. Caprivi tried to ameliorate the quarrels by persuading the Emperor to issue a Cabinet Order on 21 October 1890 that gave the lead role to Hollmann's RMA in the creation, maintenance, and development of the navy. The Commanding Admiral, through the OK, was assigned the "military" tasks analogous to those of the Chief of the General Staff. A subsequent Cabinet Order of 17 March 1891 did not clarify matters much.[36]

Tirpitz's 1 February memo argued that only the OK could efficiently carry out the "military" aspect of the navy, and then only if it had sufficient power and purview to do the job properly. Since the 1870s the navy had expended enormous effort on military questions but had little to show for it because of a lack of persistence and continuity, "a work, which like that of Sisyphus, is always begun anew, and never bears fruit." In an expression he would rue in 1899, when he persuaded the Emperor to abolish the OK, Tirpitz argued that the military task should fall principally to the OK, because civilians in the Reichstag had influence over the work of the RMA.

The memo directly invoked the name of Clausewitz and the idea of decisive battle to delineate what he saw as the major purpose of the navy. Tirpitz advocated, as he had in his response to Caprivi's twelve tactical questions, the kind of painstaking bottom-up development that had worked in the Torpedo Arm. The only organization that could provide such continuity and focus was the OK.[37]

The second, April 1891 paper was "Our Further Maritime and Military Development."[38] It was widely circulated among senior officers, and the Emperor may have read it. The paper summarized the existing, rather muddled, condition of military development in the navy. Tirpitz gave a comprehensive consideration of strategic, tactical, and organizational aspects, none of which had assimilated fully the technological changes of the last decade.

Tirpitz tried to clarify where there was and was not a consensus in the officer corps. He argued that most officers agreed that coastal defense with small vessels and fortifications should be supplementary to the role of a battlefleet.[39] But how should a fleet be organized to operate in a large-scale European war? He cited Clausewitz's axiom that war is the continuation of politics and required concentration of one's entire force for battle. Mobilization exercises and theoretical calculations were not enough. Tirpitz urged work to determine how to bring about a decisive battle. He proposed systematic exercises of the type employed in the Torpedo Arm. The "consensus" in favor of decisive battle had to be robustly bolstered with a far deeper practical understanding of specific means—training, preparation of reserves, and deployment of ships and manpower—as well as specific proposals for fleet exercises for the fall of 1892.

The third memorandum was titled, "Manuscript about the New Organization of our Armored Fleet."[40] This paper was a response to Hollmann's proposal for the following year's estimates to set up a "doubling" system. Comparable ships would be paired. One ship would be permanently manned with a full crew, and the other laid up over the winter. If war came in winter, half the crew of the first ship would go to the second. The other half of the crew of both ships would be made up of reservists and recruits. Tirpitz was horrified that no ship would have a fully trained crew as it set off for war. Tirpitz considered how a conscript navy could maintain maximum crew readiness for winter mobilization, when much of the fleet was laid up. He proposed a more efficient manning system during the year, and the year-round manning of a portion of the fleet. Readiness, continuity and esprit de corps would carry tactical experience over from one year to the next. This would provide a good first step toward organizing the fleet for war. Organization, tactics, and training had to be centered on quick and effective concentration, together with the ability to keep the whole fleet at sea for more than just a few days at a time.

As Hobson argues, in Tirpitz's three 1891 memos there was no sign he was yet aware of the ideas in Alfred Thayer Mahan's influential and persuasive book, *The Influence of Sea Power upon History*, published the previous year. More curiously, there was also no indication of any attempt to define how strong a German fleet would have to be to engage in battle with its potential enemies of the time, France or Russia or both.[41] Real-world comparisons were surprisingly absent.

Tirpitz understood that Senden, as the Chief of the newly established MK, with daily access to the Emperor, would be an important factor, both in policy debates and in intra-service jockeying. Tirpitz took pains to keep in touch with him,[42] and made sure Senden received copies of his important memoranda.

Gustav von Senden-Bibran was the son of an old Lower Saxon noble family. He joined the navy in 1862 at the age of fourteen. He served briefly with Tirpitz on *Thetis* in 1869, and both worked in different posts at the Admiralty for part of the time Tirpitz was in the Torpedo Arm.[43] As Chief of the MK, he was noted for his diligence, and had the unenviable task of traveling, and dining daily, with the endlessly peripatetic William II. In the 1890s he often found himself as a de facto mediator in the stormy turf wars between the OK and the RMA.[44] Senden was a lifelong bachelor and an anglophobe with a tactless streak.[45] The later Chancellor Hohenlohe explained:

> Senden's significance for the Emperor lies in the fact that His Majesty has only a superficial knowledge of the navy, but since he wants to govern it by himself, he cannot ask questions or appear to be taught. If he has ideas for the navy, or any desires or thoughts, Senden has to put it in the correct form. With [Senden] the Emperor is not embarrassed to ask questions or allow himself to be taught.[46]

Hopmann characterized Senden as an honorable man who was captive of no party, who strove to work objectively,[47] especially early in his career at the MK. Tirpitz, even then, carried on a regular correspondence with Senden.[48]

Tirpitz learned to be wary around the volatile Emperor. He wrote to Marie in July 1889 about an after-dinner gathering with the Emperor and some senior admirals. Although Tirpitz was glad to hear that the Emperor had read his memo on torpedo development, with the liquor flowing, "I intentionally did not allow myself to catch his eye." On that evening he enjoyed William II's favor, but he was afraid that "the day will come when the backlash [*Rückschlag*] will occur."[49]

The ambitious proposals in the three 1891 memoranda made it clear that the next appropriate post for Tirpitz after the Baltic Station would be Chief of Staff of the OK. Some of Tirpitz's opponents wanted William and Senden to place him as Dockyard Director at Kiel, a position appropriate for his seniority; but this was not a strategic post and might have shunted him aside for years. His major ally was Imperial Chancellor Caprivi, who wrote to Tirpitz on 28 March 1891 about a conversation he had recently had with the Emperor. When Caprivi objected that Tirpitz was needed elsewhere than in the Dockyard, William agreed, and even said he regarded Tirpitz as the torch bearer (*Träger*) for the tactical and strategic training of the navy. This, of course, pleased Caprivi. The bad news was that William thought that Tirpitz should first get some experience running the Dockyard but that the Emperor would keep in touch with him. It is clear that Caprivi's intervention alone did not suffice to get Tirpitz the OK Chief of Staff job.[50]

Tirpitz may have made his own luck. On 6 April 1891, a few days after Caprivi's letter, William II presided over an evening in the Kieler Schloss with a group that included senior admirals and the ninety-year-old retired Field Marshall Helmuth von Moltke. Tirpitz was there, too, though very junior in such exalted company. While Tirpitz remained silent, the Emperor encouraged a discussion of naval development. The talk went around for hours, with no fresh ideas. Finally, in utter frustration, William II blurted out: "This filthy mess [*Schweinerei*] must stop." At that point Senden, who had probably read Tirpitz's memo of a few days before on that very subject, nudged him to speak. Tirpitz articulated some of his organized and coherent ideas on fleet development and appeared to make a favorable impression on the Emperor. The reactions of the other cowed officers is not recorded but may well be imagined.[51]

Even this remarkable coup was not enough to win Tirpitz the OK position. It probably took Hollmann's distasteful "doubling" proposal for manning the fleet that provoked Tirpitz to write his fall 1891 memo on manning to change William II's mind in December.[52] The upshot was that, on 21 January 1892, Tirpitz stepped into the lion's den as Chief of Staff of the OK.

7
OBERKOMMANDO DER MARINE, 1892–1895

When Tirpitz became Chief of Staff to Admiral Max von der Goltz, Commanding Admiral in the Oberkommando der Marine (OK), it was a time of critical uncertainty within all the world's navies. A generation had passed since the last great naval battle, and a "fog of peace" had descended, analogous to Clausewitz's famous expression, the "fog of war."[1]

By the end of the 1880s confusion reigned in most of the world's navies about virtually all major strategic, tactical, and technological questions. The last great naval battle had been the Austrian victory over the Italians at Lissa in 1866. It was fought by a potpourri of wooden ships and ironclads, under both sail and steam, using not just artillery but also ramming, a tactic that dated from classical times. Austrian Admiral Wilhelm von Tegetthoff had used a triple line abreast V formation to slam perpendicularly into a larger and more modern Italian fleet that was in line ahead. Execrable Italian leadership complicated any rational analysis of the battle, and it provided only a muddled guide for future development.[2]

During the long maritime peace after Lissa, technology changed in kaleidoscopic fashion. Experimentation took place to a degree unprecedented in naval history. Some ships, such as the small German coastal defense battleships of the *Siegfried* class, were obsolete before they were completed.[3] By 1890, to the regret of many older officers who saw reefing sails in a gale as the ultimate test of manhood, a consensus had at last emerged that warships should shed their sails.

During the 1880s, except for the Italians, who built ever larger battleships, European navies, under the influence of the French Jeune École, slowed down construction of armored battleships, whose dominance appeared threatened by gnat-like swarms of cheap and swift torpedo boats. Manufacturers experimented with ever thicker armor competing with ever more powerful artillery. Would future wars be fought in the traditional way by large battleships, albeit now armored and steam-powered, or by cruisers and torpedo boats engaging in commerce raiding on the enemy, as the French Jeune École insisted? With no war to test the various hypotheses, the experts differed in their opinions.[4]

The "fog of peace" also affected the Imperial German Navy. Humiliated by its passivity and ineffectiveness in the Franco-Prussian War, the navy longed to emerge from the army's dominant shadow.[5]

The accession of twenty-nine-year old William II in 1888 seemed to promise better times for the navy. Son of the eldest daughter of Queen Victoria, he had repeatedly asserted his intention to do for the navy what his grandfather William I had done for the army;[6] nevertheless, from the very beginning, the Emperor's interest was a mixed blessing for the navy.[7] His enthusiasm was welcome, but his belief in his own expertise in naval matters created no end of problems. For the first nine years of his reign, he wavered between a battleship and a cruiser navy. He could change his mind from one to the other virtually overnight.[8]

In 1889 he divided the navy into three parts to safeguard his power of command (*Kommandogewalt*) in the navy, exercised through the OK, against the possible meddling of parliamentarians, with whom Hollmann and the RMA had to deal. In this way William II could entertain the illusion, which he took all too seriously to suit his admirals, that he, personally, commanded the navy.[9]

There were strategic questions as well. If naval war ever came, who would be the enemy? France? Russia? Denmark? Or would it be some combination of the three? In the wake of Bismarck's dismissal in 1890 the looming Franco-Russian alliance made the question urgent. In those innocent days, not the slightest thought was given to the absurd proposition of a naval war with Britain.

Should the navy emphasize immediate preparedness, always expecting a war "next spring," which was Caprivi's strategy (1883–1888)? This policy would favor torpedo boats, which could be constructed quickly. Or should larger ships, which required years to build, be ordered for future fleets? Should the fleet be scattered among Germany's ports and designed strictly for coastal defense; or should it be concentrated in one place for battle on the high seas? Should the navy build cruisers and gunboats to defend Germany's foreign trade and attack the commerce of a wartime enemy? Would war come before or after the prospective 1895 completion of a canal connecting the North Sea and the Baltic? Such uncertainties had concrete implications.

A navy manned by conscripts created the incessant need for an over-burdened sea officer corps to train every year the one-third of the men who were raw recruits. If war broke out in the late fall or winter, new recruits would sail into battle. Because of its low salinity, much of the Baltic was frozen during the winter. Through the 1880s most of the fleet not on foreign station was taken out of service for half the year.

Particularly vexing was the problem of which tactics to adopt should battle ever come. The navy of the late 1880s was comprised largely of museum pieces, some principally sail-powered. Only a few were homoge-neous enough to operate together effectively. Captains were wary of sail-ing too close together for fear of collision. Admirals resisted disciplined, prearranged formations and evolutions because it might crimp their abil-ity to act according to circumstances. The continual need to train new men, plus the climate, limited to a few precious summer weeks the time the fleet could exercise together. After 1888 weeks of practice time would often be squandered to escort the Emperor on trips to the Cowes regatta or on visits to fellow sovereigns.

Theoretical debates raged over whether hypothetical battles should be fought at long range, short range, or in melée. Should the ram, the torpedo, or artillery be the principal weapon, and which formation, or combination of formations, could most advantageously emphasize each weapon? In practice, German tactical exercises in the 1880s mostly con-sisted of formal and sterile evolutions, far more suited to naval parades than to prospective battles.[10]

In his torpedo years Tirpitz mustered large numbers of relatively homogeneous small boats for exercises. He could experiment with tacti-cal formations and methods of attack much more readily than could commanders of larger ships. In the Torpedo Arm began the first tenta-tive efforts to dispel the "fog of peace," by learning how steam-powered warships should be deployed in large numbers in battle. It was also in the Torpedo Arm that enthusiastic subordinates gave Tirpitz the nickname

"Master" (*Meister*), which was later also used sarcastically by some of his opponents.[11] Because of his extensive experience in maneuvering groups of torpedo boats, it was natural for Tirpitz to apply the lessons learned there to tactics for large armored ships.

TACTICS

In all countries, the state of naval battle tactics for armored steamships in the 1880s was rudimentary.[12] The typical scenario would have a battle begin with a "long range" artillery duel at 400 to 500 meters. The guns could fire at much longer range, but accuracy for the largest guns was so abysmal that they could not hit anything moving beyond that distance. The respective fleets would continue to fire as they approached. Battle would culminate in a ramming melée, similar to Lissa. Few noticed that artillery and ram tactics were intrinsically incompatible. Faith in the ram as the decisive weapon lasted into the 1880s and well beyond,[13] a kind of parallel to the army's faith in the bayonet. A German fleet commander had available only two overall battle commands to his captains: "ran an den Feind" (approach the enemy) and "Gefecht" (battle).[14] Any commands more complex, it was felt, would hamper initiative in particular situations. Most tactical exercises, therefore, were formal tactics suitable for fleet inspections and demonstrations but hardly for battle.

On 20 January 1892 Tirpitz arrived at the OK as Chief of Staff. With the support of Commanding Admiral Goltz and the connivance of Senden at the MK, who controlled personnel assignments, Tirpitz brought with him bright, eager subordinates who had served with him in the Torpedo Arm, many of whom later became admirals.[15] The Chief of Staff position gave Tirpitz, for the first time, a conspicuous platform for his restless ambition, energy, convictions, powers of persuasion, and systematic thinking.[16] Although Goltz himself was a forceful man, he was willing to give Tirpitz wide latitude to develop his ideas

The Goltz/Tirpitz combination immediately began a major shakeup. William II gave control of the tactical development of the navy, previously somewhat ambiguous, exclusively to the OK in the spring of 1892.[17] For the first time, in the fall maneuvers of 1892, every ship in home waters, including training ships, obsolete sailing ships, and tenders were all pressed into service, in a close approximation of the memoranda Tirpitz had written in 1891.[18] Although the I and II divisions, of four ships each, of the maneuver fleet were all armored ships, they were of several different types and ages. In five weeks of exercises Tirpitz imposed more exacting standards on captains than ever before. To concentrate artillery fire, intervals between ships were reduced from 400 to 300 meters, and the large ships had to dim their running lights at night. Some of the older officers grumbled, remembering past collisions and near misses. As Albert Hopmann, who was there, put it, "hairs stood on end and men cursed."[19]

A problem intrinsic to realistic simulations in peacetime quickly became apparent. In war, neither side knows the exact intentions of the other. In peace, when the "enemy" is one's own ships, to avoid catastrophe special measures had to be taken, such as reduced speed. Battle scenarios had to be at least partially pre-scripted and both sides had to know at least the main idea of the exercise. Realism had to be compromised for safety's sake, and the analysts had to extrapolate what *might* have happened in an actual battle. Even in the freest scenarios, the two sides had to collude to some degree.[20]

Tirpitz complained bitterly, though privately, that in September 1892 the Emperor's meddling cost eight days of practice time.[21] The heterogeneity of the fleet also interfered with realistic practice. It required a great stretch of the imagination to see little coastal defense "battleships" of the *Siegfried* class fighting real enemy battleships on the high seas. Only the four ships of the *Brandenburg* class, still under construction, offered hope of providing at least one homogeneous division of modern, seaworthy battleships. Goltz and Tirpitz were unhappy with timid and feeble efforts of captains unused even to semi-realistic war training. In 1894 Goltz criticized the officer corps after the 1893 maneuvers for their deficiencies in strategy and tactics. He encouraged them to study naval history and, especially, "the works of Captain Mahan."[22]

In 1892 and 1893 serious tactical work began on the important question of whether to force a melée or to stand off in an artillery duel at ranges too long for torpedoes to play much of a part.[23] Another key point was whether it was better to attack in line abreast or line ahead. Line abreast allowed some of the fleet's guns to bear sooner on an enemy line of either type. It lent itself readily to close-range battle with the possibility of ramming. Torpedo boats could shelter behind the line abreast, then dash ahead at the critical moment to attack when the enemy was within torpedo range, at that time about 500 meters for accurate fire. One of the key disadvantages of line abreast, recognized at the time, was that it was very hard for a leader to turn and maneuver the whole fleet, especially in the presence of the enemy.

In contrast, line ahead, whether "deep" (single straight line) or "Staffel" (see diagrams) had a big advantage in maneuver because it could be based simply on "follow the leader," with complicated signals unnecessary. Line ahead was also better for broadside artillery duels, though the art of gunnery then could not guarantee many hits at ranges greater than 800 meters. Line ahead also made more difficult close-range fire by torpedo boats, a point of great importance to Tirpitz at the time. In 1892 it was assumed that one side could *force* a melée by attacking line abreast, even if the other side did not wish a close-range battle. Also, formation in single line ahead formation was thought to be weaker the longer it was. Closer intervals between ships helped, but this factor de-layed broader acceptance of line ahead. Since neither formation could keep together unless it steamed at the speed of its slowest ship, the need for homogeneous divisions (four ships) and squadrons (eight ships) soon became apparent as these maneuvers were tried.

Another development was the work of Admiral August Thomsen in the Artillery Inspectorate from 1890 to 1895.[24] Thomsen gradually im-proved gunnery sufficiently so that longer-range accurate firing was at least conceivable.

Dienstschrift VI,[25] an analysis of the 1893 maneuvers signed by Goltz, drew two important conclusions:

> Last year's and this year's experience make it seem that ship types exercise a greater influence on tactics than previously assumed, and we therefore must pay more attention to type homogeneity. It is still an open question whether assault tactics are better in line ahead or line abreast. The type of ship is decisive: line abreast for ships with strong bow armament and relatively weak broadsides, or line ahead for ships with strong broadside armament like the *Brandenburgs* and our old cruisers.

The document shows how determined the OK was in 1894 to force a close battle. The memo proposed that battle formation should be in the form of a T (see diagram). One squadron (eight ships) would lead in line abreast, with the flagship behind its center leading another squad-ron in line ahead. This approach, it was thought, would maximize the

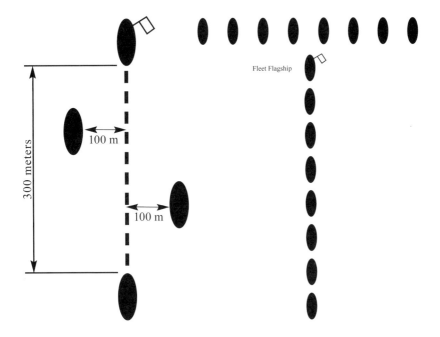

Fleet Flagship

300 meters

100 m

100 m

advantages of both formations for battle.[26] The T remained the standard battle formation for the fleet into the late 1890s. It was also the standard formation in the famous Dienstschrift IX (Directive IX) of 16 June 1894, although historians have almost completely ignored the tactical part of that document.[27]

In August 1894 the "fog of peace" dramatically, but misleadingly, lifted with the Battle of the Yalu. A Japanese fleet comprised mostly of cruisers defeated, by a storm of middle artillery fire, a Chinese fleet armed with heavier guns. The *Brandenburg* class, just coming into service in 1895, suddenly appeared inadequate. This class had a predominantly big-gun armament of six 28-cm guns in double turrets but with weak middle artillery (a foreshadowing of *HMS Dreadnought*). Some admirals, notably Hans Koester, who had recently assumed leadership of the maneuver fleet, insisted that the *Kaiser Friedrich III* class of battleships, then in the planning stage, have a main armament of only four 24-cm guns, with no fewer than eight 15-cm guns. This heavy secondary armament could put up a storm of shellfire, as the Japanese had done at the Yalu. To the dismay of Goltz, Koester had the Emperor's ear, and five ships of this type were ultimately built.[28] The *Kaiser Friedrich III* class is a perverse example of the interaction of ship type and tactics, since secondary armament on that scale was almost abandoned later on.

In the spring of 1895 Eduard von Knorr replaced Goltz as Commanding Admiral. Goltz was in poor health and disgusted by the ship type decision. Knorr was not as deferential to Tirpitz as was his predecessor. Antagonism with Knorr fairly quickly led to Tirpitz's departure from the OK. As Tirpitz wrote to his wife's aunt, "personally, I would be happy to depart in the fall from Berlin and my present burdensome post. . . . It is hard to see a way out."[29] Under Koester's seagoing leadership, but organized by Tirpitz, the 1895 maneuvers were of particularly great tactical significance.[30] They tried a melée simulation for the first and last time, with ambiguous results. Koester in *Brandenburg* with a sister ship "attacked" a German fleet that was defending Wilhelmshaven. Since long-range gunnery had improved substantially, some admirals, though not Tirpitz, who was still wedded to the T formation, questioned the efficacy of close-range battle. Further, it was becoming clear that other countries were beginning to adopt line ahead. In September 1895, at the end of fall maneuvers, Tirpitz stepped down as OK Chief of Staff.

Most historians, and Tirpitz himself, have regarded his tactical work in the OK as an unadulterated triumph. It is quite true that, between 1892 and 1895, skill, competence, and aggressiveness had improved enormously in the fleet. Koester won a deserved reputation as a stern and highly gifted taskmaster and tactician. He trained the officers who, in 1916, led the fleet at Jutland. For his important part in this process, Tirpitz deserves great credit. In his tactical work, Tirpitz operated very much as a rational actor.

There was, nevertheless, a hidden contradiction in German tactical doctrine, hitherto unexplored. It parallels the strategic contradictions discussed below. Only Curt von Maltzahn seemed to get a hint of it.[31] If one accepts the premise that the only worthwhile goal for a battlefleet was attack and annihilation of the enemy, peculiar conclusions can arise.

In the long history of naval warfare decisive battles of annihilation, like the Nile and Trafalgar, were rare. They occurred either because one side made a big mistake (Lissa) or was caught by surprise in an unfavorable position (the Nile) or was confronted with a new tactic (Trafalgar). Most battles in the age of sail were artillery duels fought in line ahead. In most cases, unless *both* sides were willing to fight a battle to the death, either an indecisive engagement ensued or, at most, one side had a marginal tactical victory.

The only way to have a chance to "annihilate" the enemy would be through close combat or melée. The only way to assure close combat against an enemy in line ahead, increasingly popular in the 1890s, would be to charge line abreast, whether in a T formation or with the whole fleet abreast. With long-range gunnery improving, such a maneuver would have amounted to a kamikaze charge into full broadsides, while attacking ships could only bring bow guns to bear.

In the late 1890s, perhaps under Mahan's influence, it began to dawn on some admirals that a line-ahead defense trumped a line-abreast attack. The obvious conclusion was that the best battle formation was mutual line ahead with long-range artillery duels. But such battles were almost never decisive! Although the Germans were slow to realize it, without superior forces one could not force a battle of annihilation without first facing one's own annihilation, assuming competent enemy leadership. This fact alone, even without the contradictions in German strategy discussed below, would doom a campaign against an enemy who was not equally determined to fight to the death. Consequently, it appears that Tirpitz's (theoretically) unfailingly aggressive tactics would have been self-defeating. This is a conclusion he never overtly acknowledged, although his experience in tactical exercises should have demonstrated it. The tactical passivity of the High Seas Fleet during the war illustrated the tactical contradiction outlined above, although it was then also tempered by the perceived need for political restraint.

STRATEGY

A biography of Tirpitz cannot present a comprehensive treatment of all aspects of German strategy in the 1890s.[32] Nevertheless, the impact of his strategic thought in the 1890s was anomalous and long-lasting. The traditional mission of the German Navy in the 1870s and 1880s was to secure Germany's coastal cities against attack, to keep shipping lanes open by breaking any blockade, and to prevent hostile landings. Important, but secondary, were the defense of German overseas trade and attacks on the enemy's trade. At that time the only conceivable major enemies were France, Russia, or both. There was also the possibility that Denmark might join in some hypothetical war. Both Stosch and Caprivi had entertained the idea of a "sortie fleet." Germany's armored fleet would be concentrated in Wilhelmshaven, then sortie (a term significantly derived from army usage) to break a French blockade and open German ports to necessary imports.[33] Even then, when the basic mission was defensive, the sortie fleet, later combined with flotillas of torpedo boats, had a strongly offensive flavor. Under Caprivi (1883–1888), partly because of his belief that war was always going to come "next spring," no large armored units were added to the fleet except some that Stosch had already ordered. Nevertheless, as Lambi points out, while "Caprivi's strategic thinking, as related to operations, gradually became more offensive. . . . it . . . became more defensive as it related to construction."[34]

In the evolution of his strategic thought, Tirpitz was relentlessly offensive-minded from the start. In September 1871 the twenty-two-year-old sublieutenant, smarting from the navy's humiliating war experience, wrote his father a prophetic letter in which he argued in fiery terms for a battlefleet with which to prevent the French blockade. He wanted enough armored ships to attack and annihilate the French fleet.[35] The theme of offensive war by battlefleet was unaltered throughout Tirpitz's career, including his time in the Torpedo Arm, when he envisioned torpedo boat flotillas operating in concert with a battlefleet.[36]

In the three memoranda he wrote while Baltic Chief of Staff, his aggressiveness was no less than it had been in 1871.[37] In the 1 February 1891 paper he argued that the navy's organization should have a strong OK as its most important arm because "the planned working out of our strategy, tactics, training, and organization must be controlled by the vision of what will probably be the most important hour of decision for our fleet."

In the April 1891 memo he asserted that there was a consensus in the officer corps about "the necessity to strike the enemy's seapower in open battle." It is unlikely such a consensus actually existed in 1891, but the statement represented the view that Tirpitz wanted to imbue into the officer corps.[38] Both Knorr, then his superior, and Wilhelm Büchsel, Tirpitz's crew comrade and head of the military section of the RMA, concurred in his emphasis upon seeking out open battle.[39] The third 1891 memo sang the same song. Preparation for decisive battle should be the focus of all the navy's effort.

As Hobson has put it, there is no discussion in any of these memoranda about how strong the fleet should be, compared to the enemy's strength, in order for the fleet to seek out battle.

Nor did they discuss whether a significantly weaker German fleet should try to avoid what would be inevitable defeat in battle and instead try to exert some influence as a fleet-in-being, or to carry out a more effective coastal defence against the intruder than it could after having been mauled on the high seas.[40]

These points raise an interesting question that hitherto has rarely been asked: why the almost mindless concentration on the offensive in the 1890s, and why the almost total blindness to the virtues and strengths of the strategic defensive? Perhaps, as the insightful Maltzahn, reflecting on Dienstschrift IX, suggested,

> It comes from the thought, that for the officer corps a certain exaggeration of the offensive side must create a counterweight against the recent tone of resignation to the inevitable. . . . [Aggressive rhetoric] was only designed to spring us loose from our coasts and . . . we would only create a fleet *capable* [my emphasis] of the offensive.

The most convincing explanation for this aggressive ethos, which seems so far removed from reality, comes from Hobson's recent works.[41] He sees two complementary explanations. One was the development of a distinctive "Prussian School" of naval thought. The other was the navy's institutional motivation.

On the first point Hobson presents a persuasive, nuanced argument that in the German Naval Academy a particular version of Clausewitz's thought was dominant, that decisive battle was the *only* means in war, whatever the war's political or military objectives. In 1894, in Dienstschrift IX, Tirpitz tried to infuse some strategic purpose into offensive battle by a rudimentary definition of the idea of command of the sea. The strong offensive bias remained, as witnessed by the OK's 1895 operations plan against France, discussed below.

The institutional motivation was partly to expunge the humiliation of sitting impotently, iced-up in port, in Wilhelmshaven during the French war and, indeed, from having found no combat role since 1848.[42] Similar was the desire, universally held in the navy, to escape the domination of the army's reputation. The army's swift victories may have pressured the navy to act quickly if it were to have any part at all in a future war. Another reason might well have been to accommodate the Emperor's overheated offensive fantasies.[43] Both views are good examples of Allison's Model 2 behavior, which he calls organizational in that the views were pervasive throughout the whole navy.

Central to a consideration of Tirpitz as a naval thinker is the famous ninth in a series of tactical and strategic memoranda of the OK titled "General Experiences from the Maneuvers of the Fall [1893] Practice Fleet," issued on 16 June 1894.[44] This document was perhaps the most influential one in the history of the Imperial German Navy. Its nominal author was Commanding Admiral Goltz, but all knew that the voice behind it was Tirpitz's. It is very likely that Lt. Commander Otto Braun, Head of Department A III of the OK, in charge of operational plans for the western theater, also played a substantial role in drafting it.[45] He had earned Tirpitz's trust for his stellar work in the Torpedo Arm.[46]

Dienstschrift IX noted the fruits of years of tactical and strategic experiments, while it realistically recognized the limitations of peacetime exercises. The second part of the document, "The Natural Purpose [Bestimmung] of a Fleet Is the Strategic Offensive," was less cautious in its assertions:

> In recent times, when the sea became the best highway for commerce between individual nations, ships and fleets themselves became instruments of war, and the sea itself became a theater of war. Thereby the acquisition of sea supremacy [Seeherrschaft] became the first mission of a fleet; for only when sea supremacy is achieved can the enemy be forced to conclude peace.[47]

The specific missions would include, besides cooperating with the army, blockading the enemy's coasts, hindering commerce through neutral intermediaries, damaging the transatlantic interests of enemy states, and bombarding and destroying enemy coastal cities. Such a purely offensive plan, which downplayed coastal defense and protection from a blockade, seems more a hortatory manifesto than a concrete statement of Germany's maritime defense needs. Although Tirpitz agreed that in a land war the strategic and even tactical defensive had certain advantages, he asserted that in war at sea "there is no tactical defense in this sense."[48]

In castigating the use of a fleet as a defensive tool, Tirpitz unwittingly prophesized the dilemma the navy that would face the in 1914–18:

> Advocates of a defensive fleet proceed from the assumption that the enemy fleet will come to them and that the decision must take place where they

wish it. But this is the case only very infrequently. Enemy ships need not
stay close to our coasts . . . but they can stand out to sea far from one's own
works. Then our own fleet would have only the choice between inactivity,
i.e., moral self-annihilation, and fighting a battle on the open sea.[49]

Up to this point Dienstschrift IX was a fairly straightforward document in the Clausewitzian adaptation to sea war, which, as noted earlier,
Hobson has called the "Prussian School" of naval thought. By a careful
study of Tirpitz's correspondence in the early 1890s, especially with Curt
von Maltzahn, his friend from boyhood, Hobson concludes that Tirpitz
first read Mahan in about February 1894, that is, *before* the publication
of Dienstschrift IX.[50]

Hobson's analysis of Mahan provides a useful means to understand
the evolution of Tirpitz's ideas. Hobson draws on important strategic
thinkers such as Julian Corbett, Herbert Rosinski, and Azar Gat to craft
a new synthesis of some of Mahan's ideas.[51] Hobson makes an important
distinction between Mahan, the clear-sighted thinker on operational matters in wartime, and the muddled navalist, imperialist, and Social Darwinist Mahanian view of a necessary and direct link between seapower
and national, political, and economic development in peacetime. Such a
link was an ideological leap of faith not based on evidence or experience.
As Hobson pungently puts it: "Quite how the RMA and its warships could
conquer and retain markets more effectively than businessmen producing
quality goods at competitive prices, neither Tirpitz nor Maltzahn even
bothered to explain."[52] One might add that Mahan did not adequately
explain the connection either.

If part of Dienstschrift IX was clearly still in the Prussian School's
Clausewitzian tradition,[53] another part exhibited the first signs of Tirpitz's
reading of Mahan's peacetime seapower ideology, which was to blossom
further in Tirpitz's thought in late 1895, after he left the OK.

> A state that has maritime interests, which amounts to the same thing as
> world interests, must represent them and make its power tangible beyond its
> territorial waters. The worldwide projection of national trade and industry,
> and, to a certain degree, of high seas fisheries, world commerce, and colo-
> nies, are impossible without a fleet capable of the offensive. The conflict
> of national interests, and a lack of confidence of capital and the business
> world would, over time, wither away the economic life of the state if there
> is no national power upon the seas. . . . Therein lies the most important
> (*vornehmlichste*) purpose of the fleet.

> Germany lost its status as a nautical and world state when the seapower of
> the Hanseatic League disappeared. The world trade of Holland went from
> first to seventh place after de Ruyter's fleet was defeated. On the other hand,
> we can see how the business-oriented United States is creating an offensive
> fleet for itself in order to acquire maritime trade and interests.[54]

Such a reductionist view of the world economy that ignored, for instance, the huge burden of land defense the Dutch had to assume against
Louis XIV, illustrates that in this part of Dienstschrift IX Tirpitz was viewing the world through the spectacles of Mahan's seapower ideology. Even
the more Clausewitzian parts of Dienstschrift IX ignored one of Mahan's
keenest operational insights: the influence of geography upon seapower. It
is hard to see how Germany, geographically stoppered in the North Sea
and the Baltic by the British Isles, could wage a transatlantic war with
France, its only conceivable maritime opponent in the 1890s, apart from
Russia. In fact, the document pays no serious attention at all to strategic
aspects of geography. Although Tirpitz mentioned the strategic defensive,
he dismissed it out of hand and failed to regard it, as Mahan had, as the
only viable option for a fleet disadvantaged by numbers and geography,
that is, as a "fleet in being"[55]

Tirpitz acknowledged that offensive war in the age of steam differed from that in the age of sail, but he vastly underestimated the differences, especially in the crucial realm of logistics. Under sail, the only
logistical limitation on a ship's endurance was water and provisions. The
voracious appetite of steam-driven warships for coal imposed a wartime
limit of one or two weeks before fuel got dangerously short. Re-coaling
at sea was clumsy and difficult. Cranky engines and boilers often broke
down at inconvenient times.[56] Tirpitz's voyages as a young officer should
have taught him just how short seagoing endurance was. In wartime,
logistics outside home waters would depend on the tenuous cooperation
of neutrals. Tirpitz argued that offensive war would require a certain
ruthlessness (Rücksichtlosigkeit) against neutrals. Such a draconian policy
might have worked against small countries like Denmark, Holland, and
Belgium, but even they had no helpful bases outside European waters.
The few German bases abroad were far away from the North Atlantic.
The same logistical factors that would limit a wartime battlefleet's mo-
bility would have a similar effect on waging cruiser warfare. The huge
real-world drawbacks of offensive war make its advocacy in Dienstschrift

IX seem more an exercise in religious faith than in hard-headed military planning.

Another aspect of Dienstschrift IX, which, in 1900, Tirpitz would develop in quite a different form, was the idea that only a fleet designed for offensive action would enhance Germany's alliance value to other powers and thereby improve its diplomatic position. Tirpitz asserted, without further argument or elaboration, that a defensive fleet would be without alliance value.[57]

The parts of Dienstschrift IX discussed above can therefore be seen as a powerful, in-service broadside for an offensive fleet rather than just for coastal defense or cruiser warfare. At best, they might be seen as aspirational tracts for the distant future. Perhaps they were driven more by the institutional motives of the navy, or rather of one segment of the navy, or by Tirpitz's personal ambition than by a serious attempt to define a fleet policy.

Eminently sensible, in a rational way, was the effort to define ship types as battleships (or ships of the line), two types of cruisers (large and small), and torpedo boats.[58] Tirpitz wanted to end the proliferation of ship types, some of which had become obsolescent museum pieces. Battleships would be heavily armed and armored ships that could deal out, and withstand, heavy caliber shellfire. They would vary between 8,000 and 15,000 tons, and need not be particularly fast (16 knots), with a range of about 3,400 nautical miles at 10 knots. At that time Tirpitz advocated a mixed armament of heavy and medium guns.

Large (first class) cruisers would be faster than battleships (19–20 knots), with a range of 5,000 nautical miles. They would have less armor than battleships but enough to stand in the line of battle in a pinch. They should have large numbers of medium-caliber guns. Tirpitz was undecided whether large cruisers should have heavy artillery. They should scout for the battleships, and be able to hunt and defend against torpedo boats. Small (third-class) cruisers should be fast enough (18–19 knots) to escape from battleships. They should displace 2,500 to 3,000 tons, be armed with 12- to 15-cm guns, and have a range of 5,000 nautical miles at 10 knots.

Torpedo boats should be small and considerably faster than battleships to attack the enemy's battle line at the crucial moment. Although they possessed a low coal capacity, Tirpitz was unrealistically sanguine about their seaworthiness and the possibility of frequent re-coaling at sea.

The type delineation was a great advance, although Hollmann and the RMA paid no attention. In particular, reduction of cruisers to only two types was a good idea. The plan was to have a cruiser fast enough to run away from any ship it was not strong enough to fight. Dienstschrift IX did not entirely dismiss the *Siegfried* class of small coastal defense battleships, but it implied that their day was waning. Omitted were some of the old types such as corvettes, frigates, and dispatch boats. Of course, in 1894, the type reduction was purely hypothetical because Hollmann still controlled the budget.[59]

The second great advance of Dienstschrift IX was to designate the *size* of the fleet Tirpitz believed was needed for offensive deployment. His yardstick was a ⅓ superiority over whichever was larger, the French North Sea Fleet or the Russian Baltic Fleet:

17   Battleships (two squadrons of eight each, plus a flagship)
 6   First-Class Cruisers
12   Third-Class Cruisers
 6   Torpedo Boat Flotillas

Tirpitz also implicitly acknowledged, by specifying fleet size, that a measure of superiority, and not just a mindless attack, was necessary to undertake the strategic offensive against an (unnamed) Franco-Russian Alliance. If the enemy fought on the open sea, he would be defeated. If he skulked in port, his coasts would be bombarded, his harbors blockaded, and his overseas trade destroyed. Despite such grandiose generalities there is not a hint in Dienstschrift IX of the fundamental tactical problem of how to force a decisive battle, apart from a ritual presentation of the T formation.

The full extent of strategic unreality in the OK during Tirpitz's tenure is exemplified in the 1895 operations plan against France and Russia.[60] The plan, which closely resembled one drafted in 1892, took advantage of the marginal superiority of the German fleet over the French Northern [Channel] Fleet for the first ten or so days of mobilization. Analogous to the Schlieffen Plan, to attack the Russian Baltic Fleet first would fail because the Russians, if a superior German fleet showed up, would surely retreat to the safety of the Gulf of Finland.

Without going into operational details, the plan called for departure for the Channel by the fifth day of mobilization. A blockade of the French Channel ports would be declared, and the fleet would move against Le Havre. If the French admiral there would not come out, shelling Le Havre would surely force the French warships in Cherbourg to rally immediately to the aid of Le Havre. It was assumed that public pressure and panic would force Paris to order the fleet out, so the German fleet could conveniently annihilate it before French reinforcements arrived from the Mediterranean. The plan also assumed that repair and resupply could occur in English ports. Clearly the benevolent neutrality of England was assumed.

Only a navy completely blinded by offensive fantasies could put forth such an absurd plan. In real life, the French Northern Fleet would simply sit in port to await reinforcement from the Mediterranean. Even if Germany's allies tied them down in the Mediterranean, the French Northern Fleet would simply wait for the blockading Germans to run out of coal. To some degree, the illusory nature of such plans was acknowledged. On 12 December 1893 William II annotated a table that showed the great superiority of the combined Russian Baltic and French Northern Fleets with the comment, "The larger the enemy, the greater the honor."[61]

How ironic that there was a perfectly viable way to defend Germany's naval interests. Even against a numerically superior Franco-Russian force, geography had blessed Germany with splendid interior lines, especially after the Kaiser Wilhelm Canal connected the Baltic and the North Seas after June 1895. If the French tried to blockade Wilhelmshaven, the German fleet could either attack or wait for the French to run out of supplies. If the French tried to pass into the Baltic, the Germans could either use the canal to beat them to Kiel or harass French communications in the North Sea. It is hard to attribute the lack of such a sensible strategic defense to anything other than an irrational intoxication with the offensive and the influence of seapower ideology.

Tirpitz left the OK in September 1895. He left behind many of the Torpedo Gang, including Otto Braun, his closest collaborator in strategic planning. They continued to influence Knorr to put together a proposal for the Emperor late in November 1895.[62] The memo pointed out Germany's woeful position by 1901 relative to the French and the Russians, who were embarking on serious shipbuilding programs. By then, German superiority in old armored ships from the Stosch era would be irrelevant because they would be obsolete, and the Franco-Russian superiority in new ships would be overwhelming. To keep a 30 percent margin of superiority over either the French Northern Fleet or the Russian Baltic Fleet, Knorr proposed a fleet of seventeen large battleships (most of them replacements for the old ships), the same number proposed in Dienstschrift IX. The number did not include the eight *Siegfrieds*. The 30 percent margin, which, theoretically, based German construction upon the building done by other powers, provided the first plausible rationale for a coherent construction program since the time of Stosch. Although Tirpitz had left the OK, his ideas remained, at least in the OK.

Brutal obstacles remained. The Emperor, Hollmann, and, ultimately, the Reichstag still had to be persuaded. From 1890 on, Hollmann had impeded the OK at almost every turn. The intra-service rivalry between the OK and the RMA was a major factor.

TURF

In 1889 William II, keenly ambitious to expand the navy and exercise his command power over it in greater than just a formal sense, had split the Admiralty into three parts. The OK, answerable to him alone, would be the executive command of all military aspects of the fleet. The RMA, responsible both to the Emperor and to the Chancellor in its dealings with the Reichstag for the annual appropriations, would handle the administrative and technical side. The MK, under Senden, was concerned with personnel, and served as the Emperor's personal secretariat for naval matters[63]

On paper the division of authority among the three offices looked clear-cut. In practice, conflict between the OK and the RMA began four weeks after the division.[64] Senden and, ultimately, the Emperor functioned as referees in endless disputes, some petty, some major. The split created a dilemma not only for the navy but also for the Emperor. Did he side with Goltz and the OK and respond to its continuous flood of flattering memoranda that emphasized his role as Supreme War Lord? Or did he side with the unpretentious, genial, pragmatic Hollmann, a personal friend, who was his agent to get money out of the Reichstag?[65] In practice, as usual, the Emperor wavered.

Tirpitz, during his torpedo years, had a cordial relationship with Hollmann and regarded him as one of the few senior officers who had supported him then. After three and a half years of conflict with him while he was at the OK, Tirpitz characterized him as "devoid of principle and adapted only to the needs of the moment."[66] Especially difficult for the OK was when Caprivi was Chancellor (1890–1894). Despite his warm personal relationship with Tirpitz, and his past experience with the navy, Caprivi tended to favor the RMA. Caprivi had left the Admiralty because he disliked the incipient threefold division. As Chancellor he had to retain it, but he thought he could minimize its disadvantages by shoring up the RMA and trying to limit the OK to military functions in their narrowest sense.[67]

The barrage of flying brickbats is evident in a personal letter Tirpitz wrote to Senden on the question of who should draft exercise regulations for the fleet:

> I feel it is again my duty to write to you that it is organizationally incorrect and is, in the long run, untenable if the *purely* military regulations and writings, which to a certain degree stem directly from the command powers of the Emperor, are made a part of the *Ressort* (Competence) of the State Secretary, which, as time goes on, inevitably will become more and more dependent on the Chancellor, and which, above all, will depend on a Reichstag elected by general suffrage.[68]

Typical objects of conflict included the following: which office would design exercise rules for the fleet (the OK); who would have the final say over tactics (the OK); and who would control the "development" of the navy, including the determination of ship types (the RMA). Each side hoarded information, and would give it to the other office late or not at all. Other matters included to whom the Artillery Inspectorate should report (both the OK and the RMA); and which office had the right to issue service memoranda (the OK). Many other issues, including petty points of protocol, were also contested.[69]

With Tirpitz's drafts pouring kerosene on the fire, the OK won many of the battles, but victories on the most important matters went to the RMA. Of particular interest, in the light of later events, were the first relatively timid attempts to develop a propaganda campaign in favor of the navy. In January 1894 the Emperor asked the OK and the RMA to devise a means to reach out to the public.[70] Hollmann was not very interested in doing so and left it to the RMA department heads, where it dissipated. In 1895 Hollmann even gave control of the periodical *Marine Rundschau* to the OK. Goltz gave supervision of propaganda to Tirpitz, who put it in the hands of aides Ingenohl and Heeringen, leading members of the Torpedo Gang. Ingenohl cultivated contacts with the press. For the first time, in 1894, the fall maneuvers were publicized. By the end of the year public opinion about the navy began to improve.

The Emperor became personally involved in the campaign. On 8 January 1895 he gave a naval lecture to a group of Reichstag deputies. Hollmann had primed him to speak in favor of a cruiser proposal. The day before, Tirpitz had briefed him on the need for a battlefleet. To the frustration and bemusement of Tirpitz,[71] and to the confusion of the deputies, the Emperor advocated both views simultaneously.

Tirpitz's fledgling propaganda campaign had two important results. The mild agitation may have helped to pass Hollmann's subsequent 1895 program (addressed below). According to Deist, the leading expert on Tirpitz as propagandist, the campaign's modest success emboldened the OK to submit their November 1895 battleship scheme to the Emperor.[72] Far more important in the long term, it gave Tirpitz and Heeringen a trial run for the brilliantly successful propaganda campaign of 1897–98, instrumental in the passage of the Navy Law of 1898.

Among the many RMA victories over the OK between 1892 and 1895 was Hollmann's doubling scheme, which he saw as a way to save money. Tirpitz pressed unsuccessfully to oppose the practice of laying up most ships for the winter. In reaction, Hollmann declared: "Heavens, you want me to keep the ships in commission in the winter! It is hard enough just to get them ready for fall maneuvers and then to get them in order again for the spring."[73] Despite Tirpitz's plan for year-round manning, the doubling system, disastrous for readiness if war should break out in the winter, remained in effect until 1898, when Tirpitz controlled the RMA.[74]

Hollmann won on the cruiser type question. The OK recognized the need for some cruisers but wanted to limit them to two types, heavy and light. Hollmann and the Emperor wanted a further, middle type. Cruisers were popular with both the Emperor and the public in the age of imperialism. Almost every year Goltz would ask Hollmann for battleships. The advice would be ignored and cruisers provided instead.[75]

From 1892 until he left the OK in September 1895, Tirpitz staunchly defended the idea that fleet development should be the product of the military authority of the OK.[76] He was frustrated that Hollmann simply ignored all OK's proposals for fleet development and ship types. Nevertheless, as early as 1892, his old mentor Stosch had warned him:

> I would like to repeat to you that the battle against the State Secretary
> [Hollmann] is a mistake. . . . Even the Emperor cannot coerce the State
> Secretary when the latter presents his opinion. His financial responsibilities
> make him a force. . . . In your place, I would strive to become a powerful
> State Secretary myself.[77]

Tirpitz ignored this advice at the time, but hard experience later changed his mind, and late in 1895 he had a sudden and complete conversion. In the historiographic debate over Tirpitz, this important suggestion from Stosch has hitherto gone unmentioned and deserves serious emphasis.

Tirpitz's notes to Goltz between 1892 and 1895 bristle with complaints about Hollmann's refusal to provide the OK with money. It was sometimes difficult, for example, to obtain all the money necessary to put many ships into commission for tactical maneuvers.[78] Tirpitz and Goltz together had waged ferocious competence battles over many issues, but they failed to make inroads on the all-important question of the material development of the fleet. The best-wrought military plans would come to nothing, if the person who controlled the money refused to act. As Tirpitz wrote to Senden at the end of 1892:

> In the moment when we are faced with a fateful question which means
> everything in the matter of organization, the RMA, with one stroke, brings
> it to nothing. At this moment, the OK can provide not a penny to any
> officer or office.[79]

CONCLUSIONS

An examination of Tirpitz's years at the Oberkommando reveals great accomplishments and equally great contradictions. Ruthless and methodical tactical practice discarded some obsolete formations and gave both individual ships and groups of ships experience in coordinated formation maneuvering and battle practice. Such rigorous and disciplined work laid the groundwork for two further decades of increasingly sophisticated tactical work under Koester and others. Ultimately the navy reaped great dividends from these efforts at Jutland. In this respect, Tirpitz behaved as a rational actor.

The fundamental tactical contradictions were not resolved, or even addressed, between 1892 and 1895. With improvements in gunnery, and assuming competent leadership on the enemy's side, to close in line abreast with an enemy in line ahead became increasingly dangerous for the attacker; but without close range or a melée, decisive battle became very difficult to achieve. Conversely, to attack in line ahead against an enemy in the same formation was a formula for a stalemate or at best marginal victory, even if the other side was willing to slug it out. Hyper-aggressive rhetoric, and its embodiment in reliance on the T formation, remained after Tirpitz left the OK. The chance that a capable commander would adopt it in a real war soon receded, and with it any hope of a successful battle of annihilation. Clearly this flaw was partly a product of organizational behavior, thinking pervasive in the navy. The memory of the navy's ineffectiveness in prior wars and jealousy of the army's success led to unrealistic offensive tactical schemes.

The OK under Tirpitz perpetuated strategic illusions. Aggressive operations plans were hallucinatory. Sensible defensive schemes, such as using Germany's great geographical advantage in a war with France and Russia, were not even considered. More important in the long term, Tirpitz, without acknowledgment, succumbed to Mahan's ideology of seapower. Tirpitz as strategist, in this era at least, deserves low marks.

On the question of ship type, Goltz and Tirpitz, by their rational approach, made great advances, even though the Emperor and Hollmann frustrated them by ignoring their advice. In its proposal to drop such types as gunboats and dispatch boats, in downplaying the role of the *Siegfried* coastal defense ships, and by trying, unsuccessfully at first, to limit Germany to two clearly defined cruiser types, the OK served the navy well between 1892 and 1895, even though the RMA paid no attention. Tirpitz learned the importance of propaganda and earned his first spurs as a turf warrior in the OK. When he left in September 1895, he was frustrated that many of his plans were thwarted. In turf matters, Tirpitz showed strong signs of the kind of bureaucratic politics (*Ressorteifer*) that was to characterize much of his work after 1897. On 13 May 1895, the very day Goltz stepped down from the OK, Tirpitz was promoted to Rear Admiral, in strict accordance with his seniority as always.

8

ON THE VERGE OF POWER, 1895–1897

When William II became Emperor in 1888, Germany was in the midst of explosive population and economic growth.[1] Between 1871 and 1910 the population of the Empire grew from 41 million to 65 million. Urban dwellers more than doubled and the annual population growth was 1 percent, after emigration slowed down in the early 1880s. Coal production grew sevenfold, and iron and steel production even faster, so that by 1900 German industrial power had caught up to that of Great Britain. Globally Germany was second only to the even faster-growing United States. Foreign trade grew alongside industry. Exports of industrial goods and imports, principally foodstuffs and raw materials, became increasingly important to the economy. Burgeoning growth continued in the German merchant marine, although the vast bulk of foreign trade was with other European countries.[2]

There was a concomitant growth of an industrial working class. The discriminatory three-class voting system within Prussia muted the number of seats of Social Democrats, but in the Imperial Reichstag the Socialist vote rose from 1.4 million in 1890 to 2.1 million in 1898, 27 percent of the total. The geographic distribution of seats, unchanged since 1871, limited Socialist seats to 56 (of 397) in 1898; but the trend of growing legislative representation seemed clear to contemporaries, as frightening to parties of the right as it was heartening to those of the left. The largest single party, the Center, represented Catholic interests and consistently won about 100 seats. Conservatives worried about how these two parties, anathematized by Bismarck as "enemies of the Reich," would function in the post-Bismarck era.

In 1884 Germany joined other European powers with the sudden acquisition of a substantial colonial empire. For complicated diplomatic and domestic political reasons, at the Congress of Berlin Bismarck acquired Togoland, the Cameroons, German Southwest Africa, German East Africa, and eventually the Marshall Islands, part of New Guinea, and a number of the Solomon Islands.[3] Bismarck saw colonies as a means to occupy his European rivals abroad, and showed little interest in them for their own sake. The accession of William II and his dismissal of Bismarck in 1890 seemed to signal a great shift of attitude, but the exchange of Zanzibar and its environs for Helgoland in July 1890 greatly disappointed colonial enthusiasts.[4] Despite fashionable talk of "world policy" (Weltpolitik) and "world empire" (Weltreich), Germany seemed to be treading water rather than gaining new colonies.

CAPRIVI AS CHANCELLOR, 1890–1894

On 17 March 1890, to general surprise, William II appointed Count Leo von Caprivi, formerly Chief of the Admiralty, to be Imperial Chancellor. The expectation had been that the Emperor, once he shed Bismarck, would appoint a compliant puppet. Instead, Caprivi had a reputation as a moderate and as a man of personal integrity, who had resigned from the Admiralty in protest against the Emperor's meddling.[5] Perhaps the erratic William II picked a relatively strong Chancellor in fear of a backlash from the supporters of Bismarck, who was sulking in retirement.[6]

Caprivi reluctantly undertook the Chancellorship in the spirit of a soldier sacrificing for his king. Innocent of intrigue, he was surrounded by schemers like Friedrich von Holstein, the gray eminence at the Foreign Office, and Johannes von Miquel. Despite the mercurial Emperor and conniving politicians, recent research has suggested that Caprivi had at least a rudimentary idea of a grand strategy for Germany.[7]

Caprivi saw that the Bismarckian alliance system was untenable in the long term because of its inherent contradictions. He therefore supported William II's decision to drop the Reinsurance Treaty with Russia, although he recognized that the consequence of this was a rapprochement and, by 1894, a defensive alliance between France and Russia. He also understood that German policy had to take into account domestic

changes owing to massive industrialization. In the long run he feared a
two-front war with France and Russia[8] but, since his aims were purely
defensive, he did not favor, as some did, preventive war. One obvious step
was to strengthen the army, which he accomplished in the Army Bill of
1893. His naval experience enabled him, unlike his predecessor, to look
beyond purely land war. Industrialization had made Germany far more
dependent on imports, especially food and raw materials. An effective
enemy blockade would, in a long war, threaten Germany's ability not just
to feed the army but even to survive. He therefore negotiated tariff reduction treaties with some of Germany's neighbors and even reduced the
grain tariff on Russia, which brought him the wrath of agrarian interests.
They wanted to keep Bismarck's grain tariffs and were partly successful
in rolling back Caprivi's economic reforms.

In the Admiralty Caprivi had been no advocate of a large navy; nevertheless, he had no confidence that in wartime the Declaration of Paris of
1856 would protect food imports. Germany, to endure a long war, needed
a fleet strong enough to prevent both bombardment of coasts and ports,
and a close blockade. If successful, this policy would keep open enough
oceangoing trade to prevent the starvation of the population and the
strangulation of German industry.[9] The limited aim, to prevent an airtight
blockade, was consistent with Stosch's ideas. Caprivi differed substantially
from the goals Tirpitz would later propose for a battlefleet. The Emperor
wanted an enlarged fleet but had no clear idea of its purpose. Caprivi
was the only one of William II's post-Bismarck chancellors who had both
a coherent and potentially effective economic policy, combined with a
military policy that focused on the defensive. Opposition by agrarian
interests brought Caprivi down in 1894.

In October 1894 the Emperor appointed seventy-five-year-old Prince
Chlodwig Hohenlohe-Schillingsfürst as Caprivi's successor. Hohenlohe
was a Catholic, with no particular ties to any party, and was seen by all
as a transitional figure; but he was sufficiently cunning to last until 1900
as Chancellor.[10]

THE NAVY AND THE REICHSTAG, 1890–1895

Friedrich Hollmann took office in April 1890, a month after Caprivi
became Chancellor. Under construction were the four ships of the *Brandenburg* class that the Reichstag had approved during the "honeymoon"

period shortly after William II's accession in 1888. The *Brandenburg* class was a new departure for Germany. The ratio of heavy guns, six 28-cm, to intermediate artillery was much higher than customary.[11]

After 1890 getting money out of the Reichstag for ship construction was hard. The Center, Social Democratic, and Progressive parties were consistently negative. By 1891, the Emperor's honeymoon over, other parliamentarians dragged their feet even in the replacement of the imperial yacht *Hohenzollern*. Only the funding for the remaining small coastal defense battleships of the *Siegfried* class had a relatively easy time, as most parties could agree on the need for coastal defense.

A further complication every year was that the Reichstag had to approve construction installments (four for large ships). Some members, not just the Social Democrats, considered new ships to be toys for the Emperor's amusement, which was sometimes not far from the truth. Others quibbled over whether to build battleships or cruisers and complained that the Emperor either had no plan or, worse, limitless (*uferlose*) plans to expand the navy. Tirpitz was later able to take good advantage of this rhetorical flourish.[12]

In the spring of 1893, when Caprivi was pushing to expand the army, he also argued on behalf of the navy. He made the case that war could threaten vital seaborne imports. By May 1893, when the Army Bill failed, Caprivi dissolved the Reichstag and campaigned for a Reichstag "patriotic" enough to pass it. The Progressive Party split over the issue. Conservatives and their allies gained enough seats to pass the bill. The Center Party lost a few seats but remained the largest single party with ninety-six members. Ludwig Windthorst, Bismarck's great opponent, had died in 1891. Ernst Lieber, an influential Center Deputy and later its leader, began, timidly at first, to see an opportunity for the Party. He could use its sometimes pivotal position to trade occasional support for the navy measures, such as repeal of the remnants of Bismarck's anti-Catholic Kulturkampf (struggle for civilization).

Center collaboration bore its first fruit in the March 1894 vote on the navy budget, which approved a first installment for the battleship *Kaiser Friedrich III*.[13] Its armament differed radically from the *Brandenburg* class, with less heavy artillery, only four 24-cm, but with eighteen 15-cm guns. The Emperor and Admiral Koester pressed for this change based on their reading of the "lessons" of the Sino-Japanese War (see chapter 7).

Despite approval of the *Brandenburg* and *Kaiser Friedrich* III classes, the Emperor, through most of the 1890s, remained a cruiser supporter. Even though the Emperor had read Mahan with enthusiasm, the book's pro-battleship orientation eluded him. The cruiser preference reasserted itself in the 1895 estimates, which proposed no new battleship but a large armored cruiser, plus three second-class cruisers of the *Hertha* class, a type that Tirpitz had specifically derided in Dienstschrift IX.

Hollmann's successes and failures in the Reichstag through 1895 betrayed no specific pattern, only what he thought he could get in any given year. The patternless mass of cruisers and contradictory battleship types deliberately ignored the sensible advice in Dienstschrift IX, while Tirpitz uneasily spent his final months as Chief of Staff of the OK under Knorr.[14]

TIRPITZ AT LARGE, SEPTEMBER 1895–MAY 1896

On 30 September 1895 Rear Admiral Alfred Tirpitz stepped down as Chief of Staff of the OK. He reported to Kiel as "available" to the Chief of the Baltic Station. It was understood that early in 1896 he would depart for China to command the cruiser squadron. He seemed happy to be leaving behind the blizzard of paper wars with the RMA to take up a seagoing post.[15] He tried successfully to ensure command of the gunboat *Iltis* for his favorite officer, Lt. Commander Otto Braun. He told Diedrichs that taking the China post would be seen in Berlin as a step up in his career, and any other available post would be seen as a setback.[16] It is clear that in early December 1895 he had no idea that he would become State Secretary of the RMA upon his return in April 1897.[17]

The fall maneuvers of 1895, the last under Tirpitz's direction, continued his campaign to train the "hoplites" into a "phalanx." Baltic maneuvers matched two full squadrons (albeit including many small or obsolete ships) against each other, and included practice in line ahead and T formation tactics.[18] Although Tirpitz left the OK, many of the Torpedo Gang stayed behind. Hollmann had refused until the last minute to share with the OK what his building plan was for the 1896–97 estimates. Alarmed by the implications of ambitious French and Russian fleet plans, Knorr ordered Heeringen and Braun to develop a memorandum that stated objectively the deterioration of Germany's relative naval position. Knorr wanted to trump Hollmann's position with the Emperor.[19]

Tirpitz's name was not on the consequent OK document, "Draft Plan for the Renewal and Expansion of Fleet Material," dated 28 November 1895, but his fingerprints were all over it, even though he apparently played no direct role in its crafting.[20] Since the early 1890s, the OK pointed out, Germany's potential enemies, France and Russia, had expanded their battlefleets, whereas Germany's strength had decreased since the 1880s. A comparison of the modern battleships of the French Northern Fleet and the Russian Baltic Fleet with the German Fleet showed an enemy superiority of thirteen to four in 1896, and twenty to five in 1901. After then it would get worse, given the French and Russian building plans. By 1901 each would have, in northern waters, twice Germany's numbers, and Germany would be unable to defeat either, even if each attacked separately. The situation with overseas cruisers would be equally dismal.

Knorr argued that to have a probability of success on the strategic defensive the German Fleet would have to be at least 30 percent stronger than the largest northern fleet. He proposed a long-term plan and be-lieved that the Reichstag's negative attitude had to be linked in the public mind-set with the financial and economic power of the Empire. The as-serted linkage between peacetime economic development and fleet size reflected Dienstschrift IX. Knorr adopted Tirpitz's limitation of ship types to battleships of 10,000–11,000 tons, armored cruisers of 7,000–7,500 tons, and third-class cruisers. Second-class cruisers were omitted, in accord with Dienstschrift IX.

To achieve 30 percent superiority over either northern fleet, Knorr wanted twelve additional battleships and three more armored cruisers by 1908. By then there would be two squadrons of battleships, plus a fleet flagship. Knorr wanted 420 million marks for construction between 1896 and 1908, which, on an annual basis, would only be slightly more than Hollmann was already spending. This plan was a clear usurpation of the RMA's fleet development role.

Knorr argued that a well-defined, coherent, long-term plan would appeal to the Reichstag. By implication, he was criticizing the short-term opportunism of Hollmann's legislative style, a practice that gave credence to the complaints of the anti-navy deputies that the goals of the navy (and the Emperor) were limitless.

The OK proposal was a clear forerunner of the plan Tirpitz presented to the Reichstag in 1897. It was also the first systematic building initiative since Stosch's in 1873. The modest proposal, suitable for a defensive war, was more a product of sober calculation than of seapower ideology.

For once, Knorr's prodding got William II to push the RMA to respond to the OK's design instead of ignoring it. On 16 December the Emperor ordered Hollmann to cooperate. Hollmann set up within the RMA a Z (Ziel, or Goal) Commission to study the problem.[21] William II endorsed the OK idea of seventeen battleships, and eight *Siegfrieds*, but forcefully contested the exclusion of second-class cruisers. The very next day Senden, at the Emperor's order, sent Tirpitz a copy of the OK's 28 November memorandum and asked him:

1. To what degree does the OK program correspond to your experience, and what changes do you think are necessary?
2. How should we craft a program for the expansion of the navy in order to form a basis for the future?

Tirpitz was ordered to keep this task strictly secret, and not even to let Knorr or Hollmann know he had seen it.[22]

The charge gave Tirpitz the chance of a lifetime. At this point one can begin to address a central question. In his career Tirpitz adduced many arguments for building a world-class battlefleet, and appealed to many different diplomatic, political, military, and economic interests. It is difficult to wade through the many, often contradictory, rationales he gave to try to find, without reductionism, the central core of his motivation. The period of feverish activity during December 1895 and January 1896 provides telling clues.

Tirpitz violated the secrecy injunction by confiding in his mentor Stosch. Tirpitz had been a ferocious advocate for the institutional interest of the OK against those of the RMA. In issues great and petty he had represented the State Secretary of the RMA as tainted in military decisions by his relationship to the Reichstag. Around the turn of the year 1896 it seems to have dawned on Tirpitz that the power of the purse would, in the end, prevail over the OK's blustering on fleet development. In the OK he had complained that military initiatives, even if well designed and intended, could be frustrated by the OK's inability to provide even a penny.[23] Perhaps it was at this point that Tirpitz recalled the letter Stosch had sent him in 1892 advising him to seek the post of State Secretary.

Stosch had argued that the OK could do little without the RMA's
cooperation:

> I would like to repeat to you that the battle against the State Secretary is
> a mistake. . . . Even the Emperor cannot coerce the State Secretary when
> the latter presents his opinion. His financial responsibilities make him
> a force; his representations in the Reichstag give him authority, and the
> steady contact with the Emperor, who harbors so many secret little wishes,
> gives him the power, where the OK only possesses a field of attack. The
> State Secretary must be a man of brains and character, and have power,
> otherwise the navy will not go forward. You can attack the person of the
> State Secretary, but may never attack the power of the office. Your battle
> against the power of the Cabinet I must also consider tactically wrong. You
> do not have the power to go against the State Secretary and the Cabinet
> simultaneously. In your place, I would strive to become a powerful State
> Secretary myself.[24]

In the memo that he wrote for the Emperor, Tirpitz implicitly, but
clearly, had himself in mind as State Secretary. It was a complete betrayal
of his previous strident OK advocacy. One can only imagine Knorr's
(and Goltz's) rage had they read the memo, dated 3 January 1896. This
epiphany of perspective was a major turning point in Tirpitz's life.

While Tirpitz scribbled away during Christmas week, momentous
events intervened. On 31 December 1895 news reached Europe that
Dr. Leander Starr Jameson had led eight hundred men from the Cape
Colony for a filibustering raid into the Boer Republic. His men were
quickly rounded up, but William II reacted hysterically. In a meeting
with Senden, Hollmann, and Knorr on 3 January 1896, he fulminated
about sending troops to support Boer President Paul Kruger and spoke of
seeking a protectorate over the Transvaal. The explosive Kruger Telegram
followed, pledging German support for the Boers. The reaction in both
Germany and Britain set off the first of many vituperative Anglo-German
press wars. The rage of the British press caught the Germans by surprise,
although clearly the British had always considered South Africa a vital
imperial interest. German nationalist intellectuals took the opportunity
to call loudly for Weltpolitik, in concert with the British if possible, but
against them if necessary.[25]

Even before the Jameson Raid, Tirpitz tried out on Stosch various
arguments to present to the Emperor in response to the OK's 28 November draft. Tirpitz offered broader ideas than ever, some clearly inspired by

Mahan's imperialistic side. He cited the example of Colbert, Louis XIV's Minister, who built up French seapower and mercantile interests. Tirpitz suggested an unprecedented concentration of maritime interests in the RMA. Perhaps he also recalled his personal experiences in the herring fishery and Germany's reliance on foreign ports, coal, and repair facilities for the navy, and the merchant marine. This dependency had meant that Germany lived what Tirpitz called a "parasitic existence" abroad. Such peacetime economic activities could only develop in a healthy way through the growth of a powerful navy. "Parasitism must be replaced by the principle *civis germanus sum.*" In an echo of Mahan's Social Darwinism, Tirpitz wrote that Germany would decline in the next century unless it vigorously asserted its maritime interests. He also noted, in a line that would later receive great emphasis from Kehr and Berghahn, that the great new national mission, and the profits it would accrue, would be "a strong palliative against educated and uneducated Social Democrats."[26] Whether this point was a central core of Tirpitz's "plan," as Berghahn argues, or was simply another in his eclectic array of arguments, is addressed below.

Stosch's reply detailed his failed efforts as Chief of Admiralty to gather under his control general maritime interests that foundered on the parochial interests of some of the German maritime states, but mostly because of Reichstag opposition. He had also urged seizure of the Netherlands to strengthen Germany's North Sea position, but "the highest authorities" (*entscheidene Stelle*), presumably Bismarck, had said no. On a more optimistic note, which Tirpitz underlined in the document, Stosch hoped that the Reichstag would support fleet expansion if a zealous and skillful State Secretary could restrain the Emperor and guide the Reichstag. It would be very helpful to the navy if the Emperor agreed to limit the growth of the army estimates. Although Tirpitz had not brought it up in the original letter, Stosch offered advice on how to humble (*ducken*) England. He believed Tirpitz would have the Emperor's help to make the international position of the British as uncomfortable as possible, but what Stosch had in mind was not a war with Britain. He wanted Germany to stand on the sidelines with the other continental powers while Britain fought France and Russia.[27] It is possible that in this remark Stosch inspired the anti-English feeling in Tirpitz's 3 January 1896 memo to the Emperor.

The memorandum, unlike the 21 December letter to Stosch, addressed the military rationale of the original OK proposal. Tirpitz agreed with the OK that two full squadrons of battleships, plus a fleet flagship, were necessary. He suggested two additional battleships as material reserve, a total of nineteen, plus the eight old *Siegfrieds*. Tirpitz wanted three more armored cruisers than the OK's plan for service both at home and abroad, and two fewer light cruisers. He agreed that such a fleet should be completed by 1908, at a cost just 64 million marks higher than the OK's request. A fleet this size, he argued, would protect Germany's interests in a war with the French Northern and the Russian Baltic Fleets, as the OK had intended.

Most of the document was an examination of the peacetime implications of seapower, with Mahan's ideological influence quite apparent. Most striking was the comment that "even the most powerful sea-state of Europe would be more accommodating towards us if we had two or three well-trained squadrons to throw into the political balance, and, if necessary, into a conflict." Tirpitz did not explain how such a magical situation could actually materialize. In this statement Tirpitz, for the first time, named even mighty Britain as a country that would have to take into account an enhanced German fleet in the European political balance. This notion suggests an unrefined form of the "risk theory."

He repeated the idea of a "palliative," and advocated an appeal to the educated classes on the necessity of a fleet to protect German economic interests. He even detailed how to conduct a propaganda campaign on an unprecedented scale. More tentatively, he argued that the RMA could become a super ministry that would amalgamate most maritime interests such as fisheries, pilot services, the Kaiser Wilhelm Canal, and aspects of the merchant fleet and the colonies, then controlled by other Reich ministries or by individual states. He recognized that such a great reform would be politically difficult, but he argued that the growth of individual maritime interest groups had spawned a vast amount of red tape.[28]

The document, seen at the time only by the Emperor and, probably, Senden, amounted to Tirpitz's job application for the position of State Secretary of the RMA. Who better than he, who had influenced the OK memo, could best carry out its recommendations? Left unmentioned, of course, was that Tirpitz had spent more than three years arguing that the OK, and not the RMA, should have the lead role in fleet development.

As Tirpitz nervously awaited his interview with the Emperor at the end of the month, the latter, still enraged by events in South Africa, importuned Chancellor Hohenlohe for more cruisers at once, even before the ships proposed in the OK's long-term plan.[29] Tirpitz anxiously approached Senden on 12 January with his fears that the Emperor's cruiser obsession would scupper the whole OK program.[30] The cruiser idea received only tepid support from National Liberal leaders, with both the Conservative and Center Parties opposed.[31] Senden, enraged, proposed what amounted to a government coup with one-party rule. He suggested that "an energetic man with powers as State Secretary must bring about a change, perhaps Tirpitz."[32]

The meeting with William II on 28 January 1896 did not discuss the military side of the OK proposal, which seems to have been considered a given. Instead the conversation dealt almost entirely with what Tirpitz believed was necessary to pass an effective Navy Law in the Reichstag. At first Tirpitz said that his nerves were too weak for such a duty. The Emperor told him that he could have leave until the spring, after Hollmann had dealt with the 1896–97 estimates. Tirpitz suggested, disingenuously, that he had no talent for parliamentary battles. The Emperor dismissed this statement; but then Tirpitz presented to the Emperor what looks almost like an ultimatum. Tirpitz said that the proposal would have no chance unless the Chancellor and Prussian Finance Minister Miquel would publicly state that the fleet was necessary for Germany's economic future. If he were State Secretary, he would need the whole government behind him and would be able to tell what he called the unvarnished truth. If the Emperor could not agree to such conditions, he should name someone else as State Secretary! He would need not only the Emperor's full confidence but the latter's agreement that he would be discreet in public while the proposal was under consideration. These were practically the very same terms that Tirpitz demanded and was granted in 1897, when he actually assumed the position. William II agreed to the terms. Hollmann would deal with the 1896–97 estimates, and then Tirpitz would be appointed to carry out the OK program in the spring.

The program could only succeed if the annually approved ship installments were replaced by Reichstag agreement to a longer-term commitment. Tirpitz also insisted that during the parliamentary battle no new army increases would be requested. The Emperor also agreed to consider, but did not consent to, the vast expansion of the RMA's powers over Germany's maritime interests.[33] The interview appeared to be a triumph for Tirpitz, but it was a short-lived expression of confidence. Getting the Emperor's attention was one thing; keeping it was quite another. Perhaps the Emperor was also nervous about having such a powerful minister. By late January word leaked out in naval circles that Tirpitz was to be the new State Secretary. Old friends and comrades guardedly sent congratulations, and some petitioned Tirpitz for a position in the RMA.[34]

On 12 February Stosch, anxious about the Transvaal furor and fearful of British hostility because of trade competition, asked Tirpitz how Germany could wage a naval war against the British.[35] Tirpitz replied the very next day. Bound to secrecy, he did not tell Stosch of his prospective appointment as State Secretary. He acknowledged that his assignment to Asia was questionable, and he seemed dismayed about it, since the strain of Berlin politics was beginning to tell.[36]

> It was my burning wish to go there. Also, it would have been good for my nervous system to leave demanding intellectual activity for a year and a day and to linger a long distance from Madrid. I must now wait and see what fate has decided for me.

Contrary to public opinion and his own initial view, Tirpitz was convinced that Germany had acted stupidly about Transvaal. For such a situation, Germany's alliance value depended not on the army but also on a fleet. No fleet meant that England could disregard Germany. "Our policy now lacks any concept of the political significance of seapower." The good side of the Transvaal fiasco, he wrote, was that,

> I would even consider it useful to open the eyes of our wrong-headed politicians to have an even greater humiliation than this. First, that it would definitely dampen Anglophilia. Second, it would dispose the nation to create a fleet as suggested in Dienstschrift IX.

Tirpitz rejoiced at the possibility of using anti-English feeling as a powerful means of agitation for the expansion of the fleet, that is, to create a convenient scapegoat as a political rallying point.

> I therefore believe we should withhold our talons versus England, and in the next twelve years create a suitable fleet of a strength not much different than that of your memorandum of 1872.

Regarding an actual war then with the British, Tirpitz was deeply pessimistic. Ruthless blockade in the North Sea and the Baltic, loss of colonies and overseas trade, and havoc on Germany's coasts would be the result. Even if Germany could successfully assault the Thames estuary in the first few days of a war, and cause temporary panic in London, he doubted whether such short-term success could bring about a favorable compromise peace. Germany could not hope to withstand a British counterattack. If Germany, instead, stood on the strategic defensive, the only hope would be an alliance with France and Russia, and even then the British would win, if at considerable cost. Despite flashes of bravado, Tirpitz still thought in terms of the strategic defensive against the Royal Navy.

This letter is a kind of first draft of the risk theory, with its mention of a battle near the Thames and a crude assessment of alliance value. Also present was the dual dilemma that would bedevil Tirpitz during his years in power. How, on the one hand, could Germany use the English naval "threat" to arouse popular support for an expanded navy and, on the other, withhold Germany's talons for twelve years, as if the British would not take note of the agitation and threaten to act accordingly?

During February Tirpitz, through Senden, continued to push his agenda of getting the Emperor to expand the competence of the RMA. Senden met with Hermann von Lucanus, Chief of the Civil Cabinet. The latter objected to a naval takeover of commercial activities because the Bundesrat would object.[37] Tirpitz acknowledged that the Emperor could not simply conjure up a navy by an act of his will, but needed to reckon with the Reichstag and public opinion.[38] Senden did his best. In a memo to himself, written early in March, probably for a conversation with the Emperor, Senden complained of Hollmann's lack of initiative and failure to obtain Reichstag support for the Emperor's cruiser project. Senden still wanted to get rid of Hollmann, once the 1896–97 estimates were passed. Tirpitz, he wrote, was a very energetic and ambitious man with whom the Emperor would have to be more conciliatory than with Hollmann.[39]

A clear picture of Tirpitz's thinking at that juncture emerged in a speech draft that, with typical thoroughness and perhaps some overconfidence, he had prepared in March 1896 to make in the Reichstag upon his prospective appointment.[40] In defense of the OK proposal for seventeen armored ships, Tirpitz pointed out that it was only three more than Stosch had asked for in 1873. He examined, in purely military terms, Germany's prospects in possible wars with France or Russia or both. He ignored the possibility that the two great neutrals, Britain and the United States, would uphold neutral rights and keep German trade open via Holland and Belgium. If the Reichstag failed to accept the government proposal to complete a fleet by 1908, Germany would have meager prospects, even against Russia alone. If the program was accepted and Germany achieved a 30 percent advantage over the stronger northern fleet (France), it would be possible to defeat each northern fleet separately. If the French waited for their Mediterranean fleet to come north, even a united French fleet would have a hard time blockading German ports for an extended period. Although he did not use the Mahanian term, what he was really suggesting, in that eventuality, was a respectable German "fleet in being." The idea was alien to the tactical and strategic ideas he had labored over in the OK. There was at least a hint of Caprivi's strategic idea that, if the army did not win a quick victory, the navy could keep some ports open, relieve the army of coastal defense duty and, perhaps, retain some continued maritime commerce, which would ameliorate the food shortage.

Tirpitz also raised the possibility of a naval war with the British. Barring an increase in the German fleet, the situation would be hopeless. As he had written to Stosch, all German ports would be blockaded and bombarded, maritime trade halted, and colonies seized. The only hope Tirpitz saw in such a situation was political, and only then if the proposed 1908 fleet was already built. Tirpitz assumed that, in a war with Britain, Germany would have no maritime allies. At least Britain would have to pay a political price by transferring some ships from the Mediterranean. He optimistically asserted that if the British had to attack Germany, annihilation of the German fleet might cost them serious losses. In a best-case scenario, he asserted that the prospect of such losses might make the British accommodating rather than fight to the finish, and perhaps later have to face a coalition of the other maritime powers. This wildly optimistic view was a further stage in the development of the "risk theory" as a rationale for fleet building against even a vastly superior navy. It also smacks of an attempt to paper over an insoluble problem, an approach that Tirpitz would later develop in a more artful fashion.

Just as the trap door seemed about to open under Hollmann's feet, he slipped the noose. To the dismay of both Tirpitz and Senden, Hollmann persuaded the Reichstag that the navy was not planning a large expansion. The deputies accepted Lieber's suggestion that, to end limitless fleet plans, it was necessary to accept a carefully planned and gradual expansion of the navy, mainly through the replacement of obsolete ships.

Hollmann's proposal for one battleship and three cruisers met with Reich-stag approval.[41]

Tirpitz threw in the towel. He complained sarcastically to Senden that the government had "blown a cruiser fanfare" and rued Hollmann's assurance that as long as he was in office there would be no limitless fleet plans. Tirpitz felt that he had been cast in the role of the "wicked uncle" and that the threat of replacing Hollmann had rallied the Reichstag in favor of the proposal. He realized that, had he been appointed in April 1896 he would have been in an impossible situation.[42] Even William II saw the handwriting on the wall and departed for his usual round of spring travel. Senden wrote Tirpitz on 31 March with the questionable solace that the Emperor had charged him to say that "things delayed are not things denied," with assurances that he still wanted to move in Tirpitz's direction.[43] Words from such an erratic source must have been cold comfort.

Tirpitz prepared to depart for Asia on good terms with Knorr, who in April 1896 still saw him as an advocate of the OK program. He was still unaware of Tirpitz's plans to expand the RMA to the detriment of the OK.[44] Tirpitz's astonishing *volte face* was the clearest manifestation yet that he was willing, even eager, to throw overboard his previous position in order to enhance his own power and to get what he wanted within the navy. Although the effort miscarried at the time, his behavior was a classic example of bureaucratic politics, since by April 1896 Tirpitz identified the future development of the navy with his own leadership of it.

TIRPITZ IN EAST ASIA, 1896–1897

China's declining empire was a magnet for the economic and imperial interests of the industrially more advanced powers. The British acquisition of Hong Kong in 1847 inspired the cupidity of others. China also faced challenges in the south from France, in the north from Russia, and in the east from Japan. All sought a foothold in China with an eye toward territorial concessions. The United States, although it did not seek territory, coveted its share of the lucrative China trade. In the Treaty of Peking, of September 1861, China conceded to Prussian (and later German) warships the right to protect German trade and missionaries.[45]

By 1895 the volume of German business in China was a distant second to that of Great Britain. In that year British tonnage clearing Chinese ports was 20.5 million, compared to Germany's 2.4 million. At that time

361 British and 92 German firms operated in China. Japan was third with 34 firms. Germany was China's second-largest foreign banker, and Krupp had a virtual monopoly as an arms supplier. German missions, both Protestant and Catholic, proliferated in China. Patriotic German Catholic missionaries were particularly concentrated in the Shantung peninsula.[46]

In August 1894 war broke out between China and Japan. The latter won a quick victory, including the virtual annihilation of the Chinese fleet. The resulting Treaty of Shimonoseki in April 1895 awarded Korea to Japan, although it was later amended to provide Port Arthur as compensation to Russia at China's expense.

The outbreak of the war caught the attention of William II who, in September 1894, created a Cruiser Division for East Asia.[47] After the Treaty of Shimonoseki, Germany wanted a base in China to free its warships from dependence on Britain and Japan for coal and repairs. Hollmann, Knorr, and the Chancellor enthusiastically supported the idea, although Marschall, Holstein, and the Foreign Office, fearing diplomatic complications, were still reluctant. Eight sites could plausibly be considered. These consisted of Kiaochou Bay and Wei-hai-wei on the Shantung peninsula; Amoy, an island on Samsah Bight, which had served as a makeshift base for the German Navy since the 1860s; Swatow, between Hong Kong and Amoy; Mirs Bay, north of Hong Kong; Chusan Island, south of Shanghai; Montebello Island, off the Korean coast; and the Pescadores Islands, off Japanese-held Formosa.[48]

Rear Admiral Otto Diedrichs, Tirpitz's successor at the OK, helped Knorr prepare a document about potential bases for a meeting with the Emperor on 8 November 1895. The base had to have a deep harbor, protected from heavy seas and the typhoons that were common in the region. It had to be defensible against attack from sea or land, and also be close enough to major shipping lanes for commercial purposes. Knorr's geographic preference was to obtain a place between Shanghai and Hong Kong. An island would be better than a mainland port for defense against civil unrest. He also thought an island would be easier to acquire. In short, Knorr wanted something like a Hong Kong. Although Diedrichs, who had much experience in Asia, preferred Kiaochou, Knorr selected four possibilities: Amoy, Chusan, Kiaochou, and Samsah.[49]

Knorr's fourth choice was Kiaochou Bay, on the southern side of the Shantung peninsula. Reports had praised its harbor, potential nearby coal reserves, and the possibility of improving its wretched inland communications by railroad construction. Not a treaty port, there would be relatively fewer diplomatic complications. It was a long way north of Shanghai and Hong Kong, reputedly subject to icing over in the winter, and promised to be expensive to develop.

With this formidable mission in mind, Tirpitz left his family in Kiel and sailed from Hamburg for New York on 2 May 1895.[50] He arrived on 11 May, and noted the expanse and magnificence of Central Park. After a few days he left for Chicago via the "Overland Express." He visited Niagara Falls and rolled over "endless prairies" to Chicago. Tirpitz marveled that such a large city could arise out of wilderness within a few decades. He observed that Chicago was already the third-largest German city in the world. Germans lived side-by-side with Slavs and Scandinavians. As the father of two daughters, he approved of the education and diligence of American women. He found them "highly amusing, clever, and beautiful," and liked their modesty in dress, even when he saw them, to his amazement, riding bicycles. In Wyoming they were even allowed to vote!

He passed through the American desert and found it "much worse than the worst of Sardinia." In Salt Lake City he saw his first American Indian and found the former lords of America "a sad sight." He saw giant redwoods, thriving farms, and the bustling commerce of San Francisco. He regretted that he could only spend a few days in California.

On 21 May he sailed from San Francisco aboard the U.S. steamer *China*. Tirpitz's sailor's eye noted the improvements that the U.S. Navy had recently made to Pearl Harbor. On 9 June he awakened to the magnificent sight of Tokyo Bay. He noted the remarkable fact that, only thirty years before, Japan had been more backward than medieval Europe. He found the fervor of Japanese patriotism impressive. He sailed to Shanghai, and on 13 June he took over the Cruiser Division.

His command consisted of the old large cruiser *Kaiser* as flagship (Captain Hugo Zeye, an old comrade of Tirpitz's from torpedo days), 8,900 tons, with eight 26-cm and seven 15-cm guns, and a top speed of 14 knots; the sister ships, second-class cruisers *Irene* (Commander DuBois), and *Prinzess Wilhelm* (Commander Adolf Thiele), each of 5,000 tons, with four 15-cm and eight 10.5-cm guns, with a top speed of 18.5 knots; the third-class cruiser *Arcona* (Commander Gottlieb Becker), 2,600 tons, with ten 15-cm and four 10.5-cm guns and a top speed of 14 knots; *Cormoran*

(Commander Alfred Brinkmann), a fourth-class cruiser of 1,800 tons, eight 10.5-cm guns, and a speed of 15.5 knots; and the gunboat *Iltis* (Lt. Commander Otto Braun), 570 tons, with both engines and full sailing tackle, two 12.5-cm and two 8.7-cm guns, with a speed of 8.5 knots.[51] Tirpitz had taken pains to obtain a command for the able Otto Braun, who had served him superbly in the Torpedo Arm and in the OK.[52]

Tirpitz's orders were to show the flag, protect German citizens (including missionaries) and trade, and to seek out possible sites for a base in China. More mundane duties, including training and ship maintenance, occupied more of his time than he would have liked. On the question of bases, orders arrived from Knorr on 4 July to investigate Amoy, Quemoy, and Samsah Bight, as well as the Chusan Islands. Knorr had dropped Kiaochou Bight off the list.[53] Tirpitz, very likely because he had read a favorable assessment of it, had a strong initial preference for Kiaochou. Its location, climate, and potential for economic development were appealing, as was the lack of diplomatic strings attached to Chusan and Amoy. In his memoirs Tirpitz argued that he had continued to support Kiaochou from beginning to end.[54] The real story is more muddled.

Tirpitz's first initiative as Chief of the Cruiser Division was to take aside Braun, commander of *Iltis*, and confide his preference for Kiaochou. He gave Braun secret orders to go to Kiaochou to inspect the harbor and environs. Initially Tirpitz did not relay the order to the OK, probably because he was supposed to investigate the other sites first.[55]

Early in the morning of 23 July 1896, Braun set off for Kiaochou Bay. By 6:00 PM strong winds blew in from the east, and by 8:00 PM, just as *Iltis* was rounding the eastern tip of Shantung, it became a fierce typhoon. Braun took in all sails and proceeded under engine power. Inexorably, amid mountainous seas under a blackened sky, *Iltis* was driven toward shore. At 10:30 it struck a rock, and soon the tiny boat split in two. The stern sank, along with Braun, all the officers, and all but ten of the men. Survivors clung to the bow, which was wedged onto a rock.[56] A few days later *Cormoran* and *Arcona* returned the survivors to Chifu, along with the remains of twenty-five of the seventy-five casualties. Braun's body washed ashore and was found a few days later, stripped of his belongings.[57] Braun had been widely recognized as the most promising young officer in the navy. As Ahlefeld wrote in condolence, "the navy has lost a beautiful hope . . . even more, a man of unusual strength. . . . You have lost not only a friend, but a tireless helper and an insightful co-worker."[58]

The disaster was not just a personal one. Tirpitz spent most of August dealing with details of burials and the regrouping of his shaken command. At home, the opposition press leaped on the tragedy and demanded a public inquiry.[59] Tirpitz had to awkwardly explain to Knorr why Braun had received such orders, and why a larger ship had not been sent on the mission.[60] At the same time Tirpitz was carrying on discussions with German Ambassador Eduard von Heyking about possible base sites. While Tirpitz tentatively proposed Kiaochou and Heyking Amoy, they agreed that many places required further investigation and harbor surveys.[61] On 13–14 August Tirpitz, aboard *Kaiser*, made his first visit to Kiaochou Bight.[62] On 22 August Heyking wrote to the Foreign Office (received in Berlin on 11 October) about Tirpitz's interest in Kiaochou. Because he had heard that Port Arthur was not ice-free year-round, Heyking wrote that Russia saw Kiaochou as part of its sphere of influence and that Russian ships had sheltered there the previous winter.[63] Heyking's assertions, and wariness of offending the Russians, confused the issue for over a year.

Tirpitz sent his own report on the base question on 13 September (received in Berlin late October). He eliminated Chusan because of English opposition. Samsah would have to await a visit later in the fall. Amoy remained a possibility because Tirpitz had learned from British contacts that, despite its treaty status, Britain would make only small difficulties if Germany were interested. He reserved his most favorable comments for Kiaochou Bay. Its customs revenues were up in recent years. A good climate, the possibility of exploitable coal reserves, and a hinterland with terrain favorable for building a railroad line also made it attractive. It was the only relatively good harbor north of Shanghai.[64]

From 13 to 21 September Tirpitz visited Vladivostok. The trip was intended to show the flag, to get to know Russian officers and the efficiency of their fleet, and, if possible, to get a sense of Russian ambitions in Chinese waters.[65] He met with the governor and the naval commander, Admiral Alexiev, who told him, unofficially, that Russia had no designs on Kiaochou.

From Vladivostok Tirpitz sailed to Japan for an extended visit, mostly because *Kaiser* needed repairs. In Yokohama he visited the German Naval Hospital, a modern facility for German sailors and civilians. On 6 October he had an audience with the Emperor of Japan in Tokyo.[66] The Mikado was dressed in a French-style uniform and seemed to Tirpitz somewhat uneasy. Tirpitz presented his captains and was most impressed by a tour of the palace led by a German-speaking guide. The palace was enormous and made almost entirely of wood. A display of bronzes, jewels, and pottery embellished the walls. Tirpitz admitted to Marie that the ambience was far more beautiful than the rococo and baroque style of William II's palace in Berlin. He toured a museum with richly decorated swords, armor, and idols on display. In Nagasaki he toured the first city the Japanese had permitted Europeans to live in. Everywhere he went in Japan he found inspiring landscapes and exquisite gardens.

Upon his return to Chusan on 26 October Tirpitz found problems waiting. Heyking, in response to an abrupt telegraphic inquiry from Berlin about whether Tirpitz and he had agreed on a basing site, impulsively replied: yes—Amoy, since he was loath to disappoint the Emperor with an ambiguous answer.[67] The next day in Berlin Tirpitz's September letter arrived, which favored Kiaochou, and the situation was again confused. While Tirpitz was in Japan, *Cormoran* and *Arcona* were at the site of the *Iltis* tragedy, doing salvage work. Several ships in the division were in need of repair. Since the Nagasaki dockyards were booked for months to come, Tirpitz had to make reservations in Hong Kong for *Irene*.[68] During November and December Tirpitz visited Samsah, Amoy, and Chusan.[69]

On 6 November Tirpitz received a telegram from the OK to send a ship to Manila, in response to appeals from the Consul and businessmen there, who feared a Filipino uprising. He replied on 21 November, bewailing the condition of his ships. Dock reservations were precious and required nine months advance notice. *Kaiser* was due in the dockyard on 1 December. Engine problems limited *Prinzess Wilhelm* to half-speed. *Irene* would not be out of the dock for four weeks. *Cormoran* and *Arcona* were investigating base sites.[70]

In Berlin the Emperor directed Knorr to clarify the OK's base position. The OK consulted former Chinese Tariff Director Hans Detring, a staunch advocate of Kiaochou.[71] Knorr was persuaded but hedged his bet by support for the seizure of Amoy at a later date.[72] The Emperor ordered Knorr to devise a plan to seize and occupy Kiaochou Bay and Tsingtau, the Chinese village at its entrance. Knorr arranged in December to send a naval engineer, Georg Franzius, to investigate Kiaochou and some other sites.[73] Senden wrote Tirpitz on 22 November that the Emperor and the navy were very interested in Kiaochou and that Tirpitz's view was now ascendant.[74]

Tirpitz, of course, did not know until weeks later that his view of Kiaochou was popular in Berlin. On 2 December he complained that the OK was still enthusiastic about Amoy, and he doubted they would listen to him in Berlin.[75] A few days later Tirpitz performed the most amazing turnabout of the whole question. On 7 December, from Hong Kong, Tirpitz, in a letter to Knorr, completely changed his position.[76] Tirpitz now concluded, probably on the basis of an article in the *North China Daily* (Shanghai), that China had agreed to lease Kiaochou to the Russians. Oddly he expressed skepticism about the truth of the article. He advocated, instead, an investigation of Fukien in the Yangtze delta and the nearby island of Amoy! Why the sudden change of opinion from a man usually so stubborn? In his memoirs Tirpitz did not even mention this surprising development. The same reluctance and passivity popped up again in November 1897, when Germany actually seized Kiaochou. Available contemporary documents do not provide an answer for this puzzle. Perhaps Gottschall got it right by suggesting that Tirpitz, as in 1897, suddenly feared that a future Asian conflict might jeopardize his cherished fleet proposals;[77] at that time, however, it was not at all clear that he would replace Hollmann. Perhaps the stress of the recent month had afflicted Tirpitz with a bout of depression. The upshot was that the Emperor decided to delay any action until Franzius, due in China in February, concluded his study.

Tirpitz was frustrated by what he considered the OK's excessive demands, especially when many of his ships needed serious repairs. Unaware of the decision in Berlin, he feared he would get orders for an immediate seizure of Amoy or somewhere else. It was hard to get confidential information to or from the OK by telegram, as the only telegraphic connection was through Heyking in Peking.[78] He complained bitterly about the duplicity of Heyking, whose dispatches the Emperor found entertaining but who had lied earlier by telegraphing that Tirpitz had agreed with him in favor of Amoy. He also complained about confusion over whether China had promised Kiaochou to Russia.[79]

Tirpitz had already sent *Arcona* to Manila, but he got orders to go there himself. On 21 December Tirpitz sailed to Manila on *Irene*. Nervously he wrote to Marie that "I am always presented as an opposition figure, and therefore I have striven mightily to accommodate the OK, but the odds against me are too great. If I come out of this affair with honor and reputation intact, I will be very happy, and my ambitions would be satisfied."[80]

When he arrived in Manila he discovered, as expected, that the situation was not nearly as bad as German businessmen had claimed. Although the uprising was a serious one for the Spaniards, German interests were in no danger. He grumbled to Marie that the "crisis" had been a waste for the Cruiser Division.[81] On 3 January 1897 Tirpitz left Manila for Hong Kong.

While in Hong Kong he met the American Admiral George Dewey aboard his flagship *Olympia*. He wrote to Marie, "living out of a suitcase is uncomfortable, especially when one is not a private gentleman, but an official person and a big man [*sic*]." He also gave a candid insight into British commercial practices in Hong Kong: "I am astonished by the tolerance which the English display. Germans come here en masse, pay no taxes, and make themselves wealthy. I doubt we would be so generous."[82]

Early in January Tirpitz's pessimistic December report on Kiaochou arrived in Berlin and reinforced the Emperor's decision to await Franzius's inspection.[83] Tirpitz also wrote privately to Senden and denied the clear intent of his September report, which had strongly recommended Kiaochou. He claimed that he had only said Germany should not cross Kiaochou off the list! He complained that he was in complete ignorance of events in Berlin on the base question, even though he had caused part of the confusion. His fear of conflict with Britain over any aggressive German move in China loomed very large. "If it finally comes to a real conflict between England and us, observers would laugh up their sleeves at our ruin."[84]

These letters were Tirpitz's last contribution to the base question during his time in Asia. Despite his claim of unwavering support for Kiaochou in his memoirs, Tirpitz's efforts to identify an appropriate base in China were, in the short term at least, a failure. The *Iltis* tragedy, with its concomitant loss of the redoubtable Braun, the chicanery of Heyking, unclear directions from Berlin, and a coerced and fruitless trip to Manila, all added to his troubles. As Gottschall clearly demonstrates, Diedrichs was the only person in authority, officer or politician, from 1895 to its seizure in November 1897, to advocate steadfastly for Kiaochou.[85]

While Tirpitz was in Asia, political information from home was rare and incomplete. In Hong Kong or Japan he had sporadic access to news snippets from Reuters and other telegraphic services, plus the occasional letter from Ahlefeld, Müller, or Senden. With the full realization that Tirpitz then had little detail on most matters, it is necessary to look briefly at the events in Berlin that led to his recall.[86]

After Hollmann's triumph in the Reichstag in March 1896, the OK-RMA war resumed on many fronts, including gun calibers and cruiser types. The biggest battle was whether the OK's fleet proposal, or something like it, would go before the Reichstag. The Emperor fluctuated wildly in his sentiments. Trapped in the middle was Chancellor Hohenlohe, who was also hampered by the fact that the two main issues in 1896, fleet expansion and a proposed reform in the code of military justice, were both centrally related to the Emperor's cherished powers of military command.

Senden won the first round when, on 28 May 1896, the Emperor, without consulting the Chancellor, approved a Naval Cabinet Order to prepare a large-scale campaign designed to spread propaganda about Germany's existing and potential maritime interests.[87] The Emperor, however, was still not clear on the substance of the proposal. On 29 June Hollmann, traveling with the Emperor on an inspection of the Kaiser Wilhelm Canal got him away from Senden. Hollmann argued that fleet expansion could be achieved only a little at a time because of the Reichstag's heated objections to "limitless" fleet plans. Rapid technological change made it unwise to focus mainly on battleships. William II agreed to abandon the OK's battleship program. The OK did not learn of this decision until mid-September! Hollmann had won another apparent triumph. What if Hollmann had been consistently able to pass estimates that were large enough to satisfy the Emperor but small enough to mollify the Reichstag? As Hallmann has pointed out, in 1896 Hollmann was only fifty-four years old and might have remained State Secretary for another ten years. Tirpitz, perhaps, would have headed the OK but not the RMA. The grand plans of Dienstschrift IX and the OK program of November 1895 had only Tirpitz and his followers as advocates. Most other senior officers were skeptical or cautious.

Hollmann decided to err on the side of pleasing the Emperor. On 12 November 1896 he gave the Reichstag his draft for the 1897–98 estimates. It provided for only one battleship, a replacement for the elderly *König Wilhelm*. He asked for two new second-class and one new fourth-class cruiser, along with a number of smaller vessels, including a replacement for *Iltis*. The construction budget was 70 million marks, an eye-popping

39.5 million over the previous year. On 20 November Lieber apologetically told Hollmann it was impossible. Even fleet-friendly parties warned Hollmann he was going too fast.[88]

Tirpitz's direct involvement with events in Berlin was small. His name came up prominently in the press early in September 1896. Rumors arose about "limitless" fleet plans. Articles asserted that William II had called upon Tirpitz to examine such a plan. Although not precisely identified as such in the press, these articles referred to his meeting with William II in January 1896, when Tirpitz not only accepted the OK fleet plan but proposed a greatly expanded RMA to carry them out.[89] This development put Tirpitz in an embarrassing position with Knorr, who was still unaware of the meeting.

Tirpitz did not hear about newspaper speculation until mid-November. He suspected that Hollmann had planted articles to quench rumors of a large fleet proposal. He wrote to Knorr that, clearly, the OK's fleet plan had leaked to the press, and added, somewhat sheepishly, "I would like to note that if something in which I was involved really was proposed, and Your Excellency was not informed about it, that would obviously only be done by direct order of His Majesty."[90] Knorr jotted a big question mark on his copy. Upon receipt of the letter in early January, Knorr wrote to Hollmann to ask if he had planted some of the articles. Hollmann replied that William II had been the source of the original leak to the press about his meeting with Tirpitz.[91]

Knorr wisely replied to Tirpitz's letter that it would be futile to pursue the matter any further and that he considered the matter closed, unless he heard again from Tirpitz. Somewhat disingenuously, the latter replied that, if he had met with the Emperor, it was to discuss the OK's plans, not his own. Nowhere did he mention his idea of a vast expansion of the RMA.[92]

In January 1897 Tirpitz was quite pessimistic. In a letter to Senden, he wrote:

> The RMA proposal filled me with pain. The great chance we had [the previous year, as a result of the Jameson Raid], despite all the uproar, if we had moved forward without any falsehoods, with purpose, goals, and clear limits for the navy, is now past and without prospects for a long time, unless a sudden political disaster comes to our aid. And so neither you nor I will experience a similar favorable moment for the final health of our navy.[93]

Tirpitz had overestimated the Emperor's patience and underestimated Hollmann's incompetence. Already, on 9 February, Müller wrote Tirpitz that Hollmann was "finished" and that it was inconceivable that Hollmann could survive budget negotiations. Tirpitz would replace him, at the latest in the fall.[94]

By the beginning of March 1897 Hollmann was in trouble on two fronts with the aroused Emperor. The OK-RMA conflict over competence had become so embroiled that William II tried to create an Imperial Committee to resolve the conflict once and for all. Hohenlohe, prodded by Hollmann, Marschall, and Holstein in the Foreign Office, asserted that such a committee was unconstitutional. The Emperor's rage increased when, on 8 March, the Reichstag's Budget Commission savaged Hollmann's 70 million construction budget. Hollmann compounded the problem when he, out of nowhere, trotted out Stosch's 1873 memorandum that had advocated fourteen battleships. When the deputies calculated the horrifying sums this would cost in subsequent years, they were appalled.[95]

Tirpitz, back in Hong Kong, knew little of these events. Early in February he came down with a serious lung infection that made it impossible for him to go to sea for six weeks. He called it bronchitis, but it may have been a severe flu or even pneumonia. He received Müller's letter about Hollmann's prospective dismissal with skepticism. He wrote to Marie that he hardly thought it possible that he would take over the RMA because his health was so debilitated.[96] A week later he wrote to her again, telling her that he would prefer Hollmann stayed, because, for lack of health and energy, he did not feel capable of replacing him.[97]

On 12 March the Budget Commission passed the estimates, but cut 12 million from the 70 million in construction funds that Hollmann had promised the Emperor. Hollmann submitted his resignation, even though he had actually achieved an increase of 27.5 million over the previous year. The success was not enough to appease the Emperor. The resignation created another problem that William II had not anticipated. As Chancellor Hohenlohe pointed out, a minister's resignation over a budget defeat would make it look alarmingly like Germany was functioning as a parliamentary system! Despite the Emperor's grumbling about a government coup against the Reichstag, he saved face by putting Hollmann on extended leave of absence.[98] On 31 March 1897 Tirpitz was ordered to

return to Berlin to become State Secretary. He accepted on the condition that he would be granted two months convalescent leave when he
arrived home. On 13 April 1897 he left Nagasaki for a rather leisurely trip
home, since he did not arrive until 3 June. Upon leaving, he wrote in a
melancholy mood to Marie: "My flag went down for the last time in my
life, the end of a sailor's career. It was difficult for me."[99] Rear Admiral
Otto Diedrichs succeeded him.

    While Tirpitz traveled, Senden and the Emperor sprang into ac-
tion. Knorr and Büchsel, the Acting State Secretary, received orders to
prepare proposals similar to the OK's 28 November 1895 program; the
Emperor, however, insisted that instead of 30 percent stronger than either
the French or Russian Northern Fleets, it should be half as strong as the
combined French and Russian Northern Fleets.[100] As usual, William II
preferred to insult rather than court the Reichstag. He was particularly
harsh on the critical Center Party. On 2 May Knorr gave the Emperor
a plan with a strategy to concentrate the fleet in home waters. It should
seek battle on the open seas. On 10 May Knorr proposed a bloated fleet of
twenty-eight new and twelve old battleships, seven new armored cruisers,
and twenty-one protected cruisers. The RMA cut the total to twenty-eight
battleships in all, and estimated that the cost would be a staggering 675
million marks. On 19 May, at a meeting with the Emperor in Wiesbaden,
the RMA returned to three instead of two classes of cruisers and suggested
that the program be completed by 1910. The total thirteen-year construction cost was to be 833 million marks, an average of 54 million marks per
year. Max von Fischel, head of the Military Department of the RMA, put
it into the form of a law draft by 24 May.[101]

    All was prepared for Tirpitz's arrival. The RMA and the OK had at
last developed a unified plan for fleet strategy, tactics, and finances for an
alliance-worthy fleet. It seemed that all Tirpitz had to do was to sign on
and carry out a plan that others had developed.

9
TIRPITZ ASCENDANT,
1897–1898

PREPARATIONS

There is no available written record of Tirpitz's thoughts as he sailed home from New York. The voyage did little to help his severe bronchitis, but his fevered brain must never have rested. When he debarked at Bremerhaven early in June 1897, he entered the most complex, difficult, and delicate situation he had ever encountered. The array of problems he faced, aspects of which he had to deal with almost simultaneously, was truly staggering.

Only thirteenth in seniority, he had to seize the initiative from his old boss, Eduard von Knorr at the OK, and from other senior admirals in powerful places, many of whom still favored a cruiser strategy. As Hopmann later wrote, "even in the RMA there was opposition to the Navy Law, and it was prophesized that the introduction of such a law would lead, within a few months, to Tirpitz losing his job."[1] His crew comrade Büchsel was Acting State Secretary of the RMA, from Hollmann's dismissal at the end of March to Tirpitz's official installation on 18 June. Knorr and Büchsel, at Senden's strong urging and at the Emperor's orders, did not wait for Tirpitz's return but devised a unified OK-RMA scheme. Nevertheless, Tirpitz had his own ideas and Knorr, especially, would need persuading.

William II was, in the summer of 1897, preoccupied with a massive government reshuffle, of which Tirpitz's appointment was a part. The changes inaugurated what some historians have called an era of "personal rule." The sclerotic, but cunning, Chancellor Hohenlohe remained in office. New men came in, including, most notably, Bernhard von Bülow as

Foreign Secretary, who replaced the more cautious Baron Marschall von Bieberstein. None of them except Bülow were fleet enthusiasts.

Tirpitz had to develop his own building program, with a rationale convincing enough to make plausible a huge and long-term financial commitment from the government, the Parliament, and the country, with further demands on the cumbersome imperial tax system. A first step in this direction would be a reorganization of the RMA Departments that dealt with parliamentary and financial matters.

Tirpitz had felt, at least since his letter to Stosch of 21 December 1895,[2] that opinion in the country was gradually moving toward fleet expansion. He believed that a massive propaganda campaign, under his direct control, was essential to fire up a broad range of constituencies in favor of a battleship-based navy. This effort, unprecedented in scale and sophistication, was to demonstrate how much better than his ministerial colleagues Tirpitz understood the demagogic side of politics.

He needed the Emperor's wholehearted support. He had to get his new ministerial colleagues in line. He had to appeal to the Federal Princes and their representatives in the Bundesrat. Then he had to undertake what most observers felt was the hardest task of all: to entice a skeptical Reichstag, more hostile than friendly, to agree to a long-term proposal that could jeopardize, or at least abridge, its zealously guarded budget right.

If any one of these imperatives failed Tirpitz would be disgraced and either dismissed or reduced to impotence, as had occurred with Hollmann. Any chance for rational, long-term development of the navy would probably disappear for years, or perhaps forever. Physically ill, undoubtedly nervous, but ferociously determined, Tirpitz knew he was playing for the highest stakes. Many aspects of the situation looked unpromising.

Although Tirpitz's competence within the navy was well known, many in the Reichstag and elsewhere saw him as an advocate of limitless fleet plans, and feared that the Emperor had simply designated a man abler than Hollmann to gratify his desire for more "toys" (i.e., ships). The decisive Center Party, under Ernst Lieber's leadership, cautiously took no early public position. It favored a plan that would bind the government to avoid a "zigzag" course but that would not bind the Reichstag. Tirpitz was nervous about the parliamentary situation.[3] In July he wrote to one of his wife's relatives "One enters our parliamentary witch's cauldron as a decent man, and a few years later one comes out beaten to a pulp."[4]

His friend Felix Bendemann was supportive, but, typical of Front officers, Bendemann worried about the navy's shortage of officers and men for a greatly expanded navy.[5] Admiral Hans Koester, the Station Commander in Kiel, warned that it would create a shortage of officers and absorb resources needed for preparedness, as did Tirpitz's old friend, Rear Admiral Iwan Oldekop. Diedrichs, Tirpitz's successor with the cruiser squadron in Asia, prophetically feared that fleet expansion might be a power play for Tirpitz to become, in effect, head of the navy. Expansion might also risk a collision course with Britain. Vice Admiral Guido Karcher wrote privately that Tirpitz would not be happy until "he alone possesses everything."[6] Some of his colleagues scented unseemly ambition in him even before he got started.

One potential problem was conspicuous by its absence. A rational observer might expect that the far more prestigious army would contest the navy's fiscal demands. Chapter 1 describes the peculiar constitutional circumstances by which the "German Army" was, in some jurisdictional respects, a collection of state armies ultimately under the wartime control of the Emperor as King of Prussia, even though the Imperial Reichstag funded it. Although the navy received annual appropriations, Bismarck had wrested from the Reichstag a system whereby the army was funded at first for seven and, after 1893, for five years at a time. This practice somewhat abridged the Reichstag's budget right and prevented it from "meddling" annually in the army's appropriations. One of Tirpitz's prime goals was to craft an analogous arrangement with the Reichstag to permit long-term planning for the navy.

Between 1897 and 1911 the army was relatively quiescent in budget matters. Its initially dominant share of national defense expenditures shrank substantially relative to that of the navy. There were two principal reasons for this counterintuitive behavior. The first was that William II, from the time of his accession in 1888, loudly and frequently proclaimed that he wanted to play a role in the navy similar to that which his grandfather, William I, had done in creating Europe's mightiest army. The second reason was subtler but equally trenchant. All great powers needed an army for national defense. The Prussian Army had an additional task: to defend domestic order and the existing social and political situation against potentially revolutionary threats. Echoes of revolutions in France, and living memories of the revolutions of 1848 in Germany, tweaked the fears of the ruling classes, particularly when burgeoning industrialization expanded a bourgeoisie that was potentially unsympathetic to the semi-authoritarian Bismarckian Constitution. Even more frightening to some was the fast-growing urban and industrial working class, whose patriotism was suspect in an age of increasing social democratic sentiments. Many members of the elite believed that only a politically reliable army could provide a secure bulwark against revolution.

Conscription provided the army that had won the wars of national unification between 1864 and 1871, and was essential to a Germany trapped by geography between France and Russia. The politically safest army would be the traditional one, with mostly nobles as officers and mostly peasants as soldiers. The inexorable facts of demography meant that the faster the army expanded, the more that bourgeois non-nobles would be needed as officers, and the more urban workers would be its soldiers. Thoughtful officers recognized the danger. The result was that, between Caprivi's Army Bill of 1893 and the rising fear of war in 1910–11, the army was not eager to expand at a higher rate than the overall increase of the population. This phenomenon might be an example of the type of organizational interest in Allison's Model 2. For these reasons, and others too complex to address here, Tirpitz could, for more than a decade after 1897, and without significant army opposition, substantially increase the navy's relative share of the defense budget.[7]

Tirpitz, with satchels full of documents, soon left for Bad Ems to begin his sick leave. Months would pass before he and his family settled in at his spacious home at the RMA office at Leipzigerplatz 13 in Berlin. This "leave" was his first opportunity to study in detail the combined OK-RMA proposal that the Emperor had approved on 19 May. Knorr agreed, in the interest of battleship building, to set aside jurisdictional disputes with the RMA for the duration. Tirpitz had his first meeting as State Secretary designee with William II on 15 June.[8] Based on notes in his own hand, Tirpitz found the Emperor surprisingly accommodating.[9] He asked that William II help him obtain full cooperation from the Chancellor and the government, including the Foreign Office (by 18 June its head was Bülow); the Imperial Treasury (Max von Thielmann); and Prussian Finance Minister and Vice President of the Prussian State Ministry, the influential Johannes von Miquel. Tirpitz needed the active cooperation of them all to convince the press and the Bundesrat that an expanded fleet was an economic necessity.

Tirpitz also asked that his office, with some help from Bülow, be allowed to take the lead in the Reichstag, and that he be permitted to speak fairly openly about the strategic and tactical aspects of the proposal. He felt it imperative that no other naval officer should be permitted to oppose it publicly. He demanded a free hand to select the officers who would assist him, and also the sole responsibility to advocate publicly for the plan. He wanted complete control of both the tone and content of propaganda materials, with a special bureau in the RMA to manage the publicity campaign. He warned the Emperor that he did not believe the Navy Bill would be a good issue over which to dissolve the Reichstag early (regular elections were scheduled for the summer of 1898) and that there should be as little conflict as possible with the Reichstag. Tirpitz clearly wanted to follow a policy of persuasion rather than threat.

Once again, as he had done with the Emperor in January 1896, he raised the question of expanding the purview of the RMA, especially to the harbor and canal portfolios of the Interior Ministry. Nevertheless, he agreed to proceed slowly in such matters, except those regarding the press and parliamentary bureaus of the RMA.

The building plan, which, in its July form, included nineteen battleships, the existing eight small coastal battleships, and sixteen large and thirty small cruisers, differed substantially from the OK-RMA plan, mainly because it eliminated the Emperor's cherished *Hertha* class of medium cruisers. William II's immediate consent on this point amazed Tirpitz. At first he thought his imperial master had misunderstood, but this uncertainty was dispelled when the latter inquired about what, then, to do with existing medium cruisers. The Emperor also consented to the rationale for the fleet plan, which stated explicitly the need to strengthen German political power. He dismissed the possibility of cruiser war against Britain because of Germany's geographic position and lack of foreign bases. Cruiser war against France or Russia, or both, would fail as well because neither had much foreign seaborne trade and their colonies were well defended. The confrontation, then, could only take place, in a phrase later to become famous, "between Helgoland and the Thames." How a two-squadron battlefleet, not to be completed for about ten years, could be a serious threat to Britain was not immediately clear. Neither Tirpitz's handwritten notes nor the printed version included the concept of "alliance value" that Tirpitz had noted on prior occasions, although in his memoirs he names it as a prime reason for the proposal.[10]

Tirpitz omitted from the printed form of the proposal[11] a tantalizing criticism of the OK's operations plan against France. Because it is crossed out in Tirpitz's handwritten notes of 15 June, it is unclear whether or not he presented it to the Emperor that day:

> It is based on assuming the strategic defensive in the Baltic and the North Sea. We are supposed to await the arrival of the enemy and then to strike. The purpose is supposed to be to keep open our sea trade. I believe that the enemy will not come and that we would wait with our fleet while France cuts us off from ⅔ to ¾ of our imports by blockade in the Channel and off northern England. But that is not my business.[12]

This comment is Tirpitz's first recorded mention of the possibility of a distant blockade. Although it dealt here with France, it presaged the later British decision to adopt just such a plan. Curiously Tirpitz does not seem to have reckoned with the possibility that the British might adopt a distant blockade on the eve of war. Later he did not pressure the Admiralty Staff to study this contingency that would have undermined a central tenet of the risk theory. Particularly the odd last sentence—"but this is not my business"—smacks of a bureaucratic politics mentality, even when Tirpitz was otherwise clearly in rational mode.

To put flesh on the bones of the Emperor's decisions, Tirpitz had to recast financial estimates previously prepared for the OK-RMA draft. At the beginning of June 1897 Tirpitz met Commander Eduard von Capelle, who had prepared those estimates. As Capelle later told the story, Tirpitz's first reaction to him was, "Ach, how can I work with someone who is a calculator?"[13] Within days, Tirpitz learned just how valuable Capelle was. Capelle became his chief adviser on parliamentary and fiscal matters in a collaboration that lasted until Capelle retired in 1915. Lt. Commander Harald Dähnhardt was Capelle's able assistant on the 1898 Navy Law.

As Tirpitz puts it in his memoirs:

> My predecessor Hollmann used to read all the documents relating to his office personally. I restricted myself to the preparation of the [1898] Navy Bill, and left the current business to my deputy [Büchsel]. In Ems and St. Blasien, where the bronchitis, which I brought with me from the tropics, was to be cured, I gathered round me the men whom I had chosen to work out the Navy Bill with me. The older parliamentary experience of von Capelle, his critical mind, his logical style, were a happy balance to my disposition, which was more given to working by intuition. He was less a fighter than a master of finance; together with Dähnhardt, who carried

on urbane intercourse with the Reichstag deputies, he controlled the
financial side of affairs, which, in view of the poor state of the revenue,
was a tricky art in itself. While I generally went straight for the goal, von
Capelle espied the difficulties and objections as well as the different ways of
overcoming them; he was always the first to find the weak points to which
our opponents could hitch on, but he was not perhaps so good with the
imponderabilia. He was . . . indispensable to me for the parliamentary side
of the work.[14]

Adolf von Trotha, who later worked with Capelle, described the Tir-
pitz/Capelle partnership:

[Capelle] was at that time, because of his personality, a good moderating
counterweight to the more free-wheeling Tirpitz. He would listen quietly
to Tirpitz's hard-driving plans without much response. Then, a few days
later, he presented in a thoughtful and tactful way the difficulties, financial,
and, above all, parliamentary, which the plans would meet. In the ensuing
conversations, Tirpitz would then formulate the right policy.[15]

Tirpitz later claimed that "my method of work always had Nelson's
'we are a band of brothers' for its motto. . . . If one is faced with a big piece
of work, one must try to avoid doing everything oneself."[16] He applied
this leadership style, developed in the Torpedo Arm, to the Navy Laws
of 1898 and 1900.

On 19 June Tirpitz ordered a special committee of the RMA to assemble the facts and figures for convincing financial arguments supporting a first draft of the Navy Bill.[17] It consisted of Capelle, Dähnhardt,
and two longtime RMA civil servants. Capelle became the lead official
on estimates matters.[18] Capelle and Dähnhardt shuttled between Berlin
and Ems, and later St. Blasien, Tirpitz's summer retreat in the Black Forest, where they could avoid the bureaucracy and social engagements of
Berlin. Tirpitz continued his sick leave which the Emperor had extended
to mid-September.

Throughout July and early August drafts and estimates flew back
and forth via letter or courier between St. Blasien and Berlin.[19] Tirpitz
decided that the law should run to 1905 instead of the original 1910 in the
memorandum that followed his meeting with the Emperor on 15 June.
Since eight of the older battleships would still be usable in 1905, eleven
new ones would have to be laid down between 1898 and 1905, a total of
nineteen (two squadrons of eight ships each, plus a flagship and two other
ships as material reserve). The annual "tempo" of battleship building for

those seven years would thus be 2:2:1:2:1:1:2. This "acceleration" in building," as Steinberg points out, "was the first of many in Tirpitz's career."[20] Each successive Navy Law accelerated the building in one way or another. Along with an average of one large cruiser a year, three large ships would be built annually up to 1901. Tirpitz understood that an even, predictable number of annual ship contracts could provide economies. Contractors and the Imperial Dockyards could expand their facilities, confident that they would not lose money to the overcapacity that would come with irregular demand. This factor also provided a wealthy constituency for shipbuilding, and reinforced the attraction of continuing the three tempo beyond 1900.

Tirpitz, on 17 June, appointed his young comrade from the Torpedo Gang and OK days, Commander August von Heeringen, to head a new department in the RMA, M II, a "Section for News and General Parliamentary Affairs" (later to be styled Nachrichtenabteilung, or N), which reported to Hugo von Pohl, another Torpedo Gang member. In appearance a modest press office, it was possibly the first modern propaganda ministry. The main task of the organization was to discreetly launch a propaganda blitzkrieg. Tirpitz, as Chief of Staff of the OK, had wrested control of the navy's very modest publicity operation from the RMA. Tirpitz had persuaded the Emperor on 15 June that the RMA should control publicity for the Navy Bill, to the exclusion of the OK and other parts of the navy.

During the campaigns for the 1898 and 1900 Navy Bills, Heeringen, a man of great energy and personal charm, was the officer in the RMA closest to Tirpitz.[21] Heeringen set off like a whirlwind.[22] He had Mahan's second and third volumes translated. He recruited trustworthy retired officers to give speeches and write articles. He solicited information from all naval sources, especially from attachés and foreign stations. He invited journalists to observe fall maneuvers and trials. He visited and corresponded with scores of editors of important newspapers. The German Colonial Society and the Pan-German League provided platforms, speakers, and money. Tirpitz later claimed that the public aspects of the propaganda campaign were paid for by private contributions.[23] The propaganda campaign got a huge and unexpected boost with the appearance, in London on 11 September, of a vehemently anti-German article in the *Saturday Review* that ended with the words "*Germania esse delendam*

[Germany must be destroyed]," an echo of Cato's call for the destruction of Carthage.[24] Little noted in England, it was a tremendous sensation in Germany and made the Navy Bill seem like a timely riposte.

Heeringen went on a grand tour of German universities and recruited some of the most distinguished names in German academic life to write and speak about German maritime interests.[25] They constituted a powerful reinforcement, given the enviable prestige of professors in German life, even though they numbered only a few dozen. Upon Professor Gustav Schmoller's recommendation, Heeringen hired Ernst von Halle, an economist and political scientist. From a prominent Hamburg Jewish family, for professional advancement he had changed his name to his mother's. Halle was put in charge of scholarly propaganda. Until his death in 1908 he directed scholarly activities in the RMA. He skillfully assembled statistics on all aspects of maritime activity, and was a principal editor for the RMA's *Nauticus*, which published its first issues early in 1898.[26]

Despite M II's public functions, the RMA blandly said that it was merely a press office for the navy. In a lame attempt to maintain official deniability, Tirpitz hoped to deflect accusations that the navy was conjuring up agitation.[27] Heeringen was so ubiquitous that Tirpitz's great parliamentary opponent, Eugen Richter, punned that the demands of the Navy Law "were very salty, and tasted like herring"[28] (*Hering* in German).

With the propaganda campaign roaring, Tirpitz and Capelle put the final touches on the cost tables, which was difficult because Tirpitz had moved the completion date up to 1905, five years sooner than the OK-RMA plan. In this version the navy would have its own septannat (1898–1905). To save money, Tirpitz reduced the annual sailor intake from 1,722 to 1,139. This point raised howls in the Front, whose officers worried where sufficient crew would come from. He also decided not to keep both squadrons permanently in commission, a contradiction of his position in the past. He chose to limit battleship size to about 11,000 tons and large cruisers to about 9,000 tons. This decision kept costs down but later opened Tirpitz to the accusation that he was building ships not competitive to those of other nations.[29] The money saved would be applied to construction. This was an early example of the conflict between short-term readiness and long-term building. Tirpitz moved the construction of new torpedo boats into the regular estimates and out of the legally determined ship establishment. This saved, on paper, 44 million marks from the construction budget. The seven-year construction total was 410 million marks, a yearly average of 58.6 million, only about 10 million more per year than Hollmann had gotten from the prior Reichstag. The proposal, made public late in the fall, would seem surprisingly moderate to the deputies, the opposite of the limitless plan that Tirpitz's enemies had anticipated.[30]

Throughout August Tirpitz negotiated with Prussian Finance Minister Miquel and Treasury Secretary Thielmann. Chancellor Hohenlohe, though not enthusiastic, loyally supported the bill. Miquel, who was trying to cobble together a coalition (Sammlung) between the industrial and the agrarian interests, dragged his feet grudgingly.[31] In a letter to Thielmann, Tirpitz explicitly, though disingenuously, denied that his fleet proposal was intended to compete with France, let alone with Britain. The 1905 fleet would be of modest size, which many in the navy thought was too small.[32] He assured Miquel that competition with England was an "*Unding*" (absurdity), although by then Germany would have a fleet that England would have to respect.[33]

Capelle reassured Miquel that the bill was not limitless and should win a sympathetic hearing from the Reichstag. Capelle warned against heavy-handed tactics, such as threats of dissolution. Persuasion, not force, was necessary. He felt that the plan could stand on its own merits. Threats might make otherwise friendly parties vote no, lest they be repudiated in the ensuing forced election. Capelle was confident that a moderate program and moderate tactics would have the best chance. He assured Miquel that the navy's presentation would be along objective, technical, and military lines. Miquel agreed that the Reichstag would have to be handled gently, "if only someone could convince the Emperor to give a few good speeches in favor of constitutionalism, and to give more public recognition to the Reichstag."[34] When William II reaffirmed his whole-hearted support for the bill,[35] on 23 August, Miquel assented.

Tirpitz set off to win support in the Bundesrat. He met with a warm reception from his old patron, the Grand Duke of Baden. Among others, he met with the Senate of the City of Hamburg, and with Prince Regent Luitpold of Bavaria. The most contentious issue in the Bundesrat at the time was between the Emperor and Bavaria over the question of military justice reform.[36] Tirpitz tried quietly, but in vain, to do what he could to help the Bavarians on the justice issue.[37]

On 23 August Tirpitz had a very important meeting with the elderly and infirm Bismarck at his estate in Friedrichsruhe. At the 15 June meeting Tirpitz had persuaded the Emperor to name a new cruiser, *Fürst Bismarck*, as an olive branch to the old Chancellor who still had many friends in the press and the Reichstag.[38] Tirpitz was very nervous about the meeting, which he had carefully arranged with the help of Senden and Bülow.[39] The ostensible reason for Tirpitz's visit was to persuade Bismarck, who had already declined an invitation to attend the christening for health reasons, to permit a daughter-in-law to do the honors. The real reason was to seek Bismarck's blessing for the bill, or at least to head off his opposition to it. Bismarck had previously criticized "fantastic" fleet plans and the building of "parade ships." He graciously put the nervous Tirpitz at ease by recalling his school days at the Gray Cloister in Berlin with Tirpitz's father, Rudolf. Tirpitz advocated his fleet plan on the same grounds put forth by Bismarck's War Minister Roon in 1867. He prompted Bismarck to write that:

> I find that the whole request corresponds to our needs, even if I would have proposed more reliance on cruisers. But this viewpoint would not prevent me, if I were in the Reichstag, from voting for the proposal, since our experts consider it correct.

Tirpitz succeeded in preventing the opposition from claiming Bismarck's support. To give opponents no chance to use the cruiser remark against the bill, Tirpitz let it be known that he had a letter from Bismarck in favor of the proposal, but he delayed release of its contents until after the law was safely passed.[40] Bismarck's imprimatur proved very helpful with nationalists and agrarians in the Reichstag.

In Tirpitz's meetings with Princes and Bundesrat representatives, the most frequent question was how to pay for it. Tirpitz, Thielmann, and Miquel were confident that rising tax revenues from a growing economy would cover anticipated costs.[41] Some representatives feared, however, that continued progress in warship technology would soon make the RMA's cost estimates obsolete. Tirpitz gave bland assurances that, after a long period of technological change, ship types had settled down into battleships, large and small cruisers, and torpedo boats. He was confident that they would not change substantially in the near future. They could be established by a long-term law, and there was little likelihood of an ugly surprise.[42] Unclear from the evidence is whether this contention was a deception or whether Tirpitz believed it at the time. Hollmann's practice had been to lowball the first installment of a ship in the hope that the Reichstag would make up the difference in following years. Tirpitz clearly hoped to get and keep credibility with the deputies. Nevertheless, as events were to show, within a year of the passage of the law in April 1898, per ship cost estimates proved far too low. In fact, escalating costs, even before the Dreadnought-class ships, led to huge increases in tonnage and complexity. These costs dogged the RMA in future years, and were a prime, though underplayed, factor in all later amendments of the Navy Law.

Despite these objections, Tirpitz's intelligent and persuasive arguments, with massive tables and charts to back them up, carried the day. The draft went to the Bundesrat on 29 October.[43] It seemed clearly presented, politically benign, moderate in its demands, and, above all, required no new taxes. Approval by the Bundesrat was by then automatic. Tirpitz had united the Emperor, the Chancellor, the Cabinet, and the Bundesrat behind his idea. Though a great triumph, it was meaningless until it also passed the Reichstag.

THE NAVY LAW IN THE REICHSTAG

Tirpitz now had to persuade the same Reichstag that had forced Hollmann's resignation to pass not simply a one-year appropriation but to bind itself to a fixed program of increasing naval expenditures for the next seven years.[44] During the summer of 1897 many observers, including the powerful and canny Miquel, had opposed Tirpitz's naval program because the Reichstag would never accept it in such a binding form. With the Emperor's help, such government roadblocks had yielded, but the political parties remained to be convinced.

National Liberals and Conservatives (except the agrarian faction, which was lukewarm at best) were Tirpitz's enthusiastic allies, "patriotic" parties he could count on. On the other side were the "enemies of the Reich," the ardently anti-imperialist Social Democrats, disaffected Poles and Alsatians, and the small, but vocal, Eugen Richter faction (Freisinnige Volkspartei). The decisive party was the Catholic Center. With 96 deputies out of 397, the Center could tip the balance for or against the bill. Center opposition had cost Hollmann his position less than a year before.

To win Center votes, Tirpitz first had to convince the Emperor to avoid making inflammatory public statements in favor of the bill, lest complaints escalate that the fleet was the Emperor's plaything. With William II relatively quiet, Tirpitz at least had a chance to have the deputies hear his arguments.[45]

Early in August Miquel had approached Ernst Lieber, leader of the Center Party, and had asked him to accept a long-term naval plan. However, Lieber responded that the pace of technological change made a long-term commitment impossible. Nevertheless, he indicated his willingness to meet Capelle.[46] Heeringen even advised that not only Capelle but Tirpitz himself should meet with Lieber.[47]

On 13 October Capelle wrote to Lieber at his home in Camberg to request a meeting.[48] Lieber's reply showed the difficulties that faced the leader of a party with strong factionalism and centripetal tendencies. Lieber asked that Capelle not come to Camberg:

> I am more sharply watched by all sides [of the Center Party] than the secret police watch the worst anarchist. A naval captain from the RMA, even in civilian clothes, could not travel here unnoticed.

Lieber worried that he had too many pressures both from within and outside the party to allow any indiscretion. Only in Berlin could such a meeting have complete privacy. A poor man with twelve children, Lieber agreed to come to Berlin if the RMA secretly reimbursed him for travel expenses.[49]

This letter reflected Lieber's difficult position within his own party. The Center was really of three factions of about equal size. The leadership group generally went along with Lieber's decisions. The Bavarians looked mainly to their sectional interests and dissented with the Reich over reform of the military penal code. The Bavarian Center deputies were also under extreme pressure at home from the Bauernbund (Peasant League), which threatened the Center's position there and was vehemently anti-imperialist. No amount of persuasion could have won the Bavarians for the Navy Bill. The Rhineland faction, led by Richard Müller from Fulda, was the third group. The Rheinlanders, like Lieber, were often willing to cooperate with the government, but only if they got something in return. They wanted the repeal of the remnants of Bismarck's Kulturkampf, which had refused civil rights to Catholic religious orders, especially the

Jesuits. Lieber was also under great pressure from Georg Cardinal Kopp, Archbishop of Breslau. Lieber already feared Kopp was denouncing him in Rome as a friend of the government and was trying to rouse the bishops of Germany to depose him as Center leader.[50]

The extreme discretion of Tirpitz and Capelle helped Lieber in his predicament. On 16 October Capelle sent him particulars of the bill and said Tirpitz and he would be glad to pay his way for a trip to Berlin. Capelle added that Tirpitz recognized Lieber's awkward situation, and would do his best to address Lieber's and his party's objections.[51]

Lieber met secretly with Capelle at Tirpitz's office on 22 and 23 October, and met with both Capelle and Tirpitz on Sunday, the 24th. They gave Lieber an advance copy of the law draft. Notes in Lieber's hand on the draft provide an outline of their discussions. The draft invoked a memorandum by War Minister Roon in 1867, and claimed the law was just a fulfillment of it. According to Roon, besides the defense of Germany's trade and colonies, the goal should be the "development of our own offensive potential, not only to destroy enemy sea trade, but also to attack enemy coasts and harbors. To carry out the defensive part of our mission we need to be able, under certain circumstances, to seize the offensive."

Lieber cringed at the document's offensive tenor to such an extent that Tirpitz replaced these phrases with words drawn instead from Stosch's 1873 memorandum that had referred only to "development of our own offensive capacity" without elaboration. Tirpitz and Capelle also convinced Lieber that the technological change had slowed, so that ship types could be fixed. This was the same objection Miquel had raised originally. Lieber was partially convinced of the need for a fixed program, but he worried about its cost.

He suggested three ways he might be able to support the bill. The first was if shipbuilding costs were limited to 50 million marks per year; the second was that the septannat had to be made more flexible (six to eight or five to nine years); the third was to fix the battlefleet and allow flexibility in the number of ships for service abroad.[52]

Tirpitz did not say so directly, but the latter two suggestions would have fatally undermined his concept of a fixed Navy Law. The building program would have again been at the mercy of the Reichstag, something he wished to avoid at all costs. Lieber left Leipzigerplatz 13 with 400 marks in his pocket "for your expenses in the interests of the navy now and in the future."[53] This was hardly enough to be a bribe, but it was certainly intended to court Lieber's goodwill.

On 27 October Lieber took his problems to Hohenlohe. He complained of pressure from Cardinal Kopp and the bishops to oppose the government. Lieber was still willing to help the navy, but he also said that the Reichstag would approve nothing without settling the military penal reforms or repealing some of the prohibitions against the Jesuits.[54] In return, Hohenlohe unburdened himself to Lieber:

> If the old Kaiser still lived or Frederick ruled, said Hohenlohe, no one would be thinking of the "naval question." Naturally, if the navy takes up the mission, they carry it to excess and find reasons everywhere to support their convictions in science and experience. . . . The taxpayers would have to spit out [spucken] many hundreds of millions and leave their purses permanently open.[55]

Clearly Hohenlohe's heart was not in the Navy Bill, even as he prepared to send it to the Bundesrat. With these prophetic words, he seemed to recognize at work a process resembling that of organizational politics. Actually, it was more a case of bureaucratic politics, since it was Tirpitz's policy and interests at stake, and many within the navy were wary of him.

On 6 November news reached Berlin of the murder of German Catholic missionaries in Shantung. On 12 November Admiral Diedrichs, Tirpitz's successor in China, seized Kioachou for Germany.[56] Tirpitz's part in this affair is somewhat surprising. In his memoirs he claims that he favored the annexation straightforwardly; on 10 November, however, he wrote to Hohenlohe that he "considers the action against China unfavorable for the Navy Bill, and in its present form objectionable, since . . . we must reckon with the possibility of war [with Russia]."[57] He tried the same line of argument with Bülow.[58]

William II later wrote, "Hohenlohe was precisely the one who with vigor and dash aided and warmly supported me in the Kiaochou affair while the Foreign Office had shat in its pants and Tirpitz stood aside and grumbled."[59] On 14 November Tirpitz nervously wrote to the Grand Duke of Baden that potential differences with Russia over Kiaochou "would probably create some alarms in the press and would come at a time undesirable for the Reichstag negotiations, since it would arouse further excitement. . . . Any unfavorable excitement could sink our enterprise."[60]

In spite of his professed rationale that Germany needed a fleet to protect and expand Germany's interests overseas, Tirpitz was prepared to sacrifice them at the slightest hint that they might endanger the precious Navy Bill. Later, during the Russo-Japanese War, it appeared that Kiaochou might come under pressure from whoever won the war. Tirpitz, in a conversation with Albert Hopmann, who was an observer in Asia in the first months of the war, asked the latter what should be done with it (Kiaochou)? Hopmann answered, "maybe exchange it." Tirpitz replied: "For what? It would have been better if we had not seized it."[61]

Petter goes so far as to say that Tirpitz saw actual, as opposed to theoretical, imperialism as a threat to his building program because it would have strengthened cruiser sentiment. After the annexation of Kiaochou in 1898, Tirpitz accepted the new situation, but he fought *against* making it a defensible war harbor, or "mouse hole," for the cruiser squadron. He wanted a commercial harbor and, supported by enormous investment from the RMA on infrastructure (ca. 100 million marks to 1907), it became economically significant. According to Petter, Tirpitz found Kiaochou useful mostly in domestic politics. He earned the goodwill of Catholics, who had missionaries there. Even anti-imperialist politicians such as Eugen Richter regarded Kiaochou as a positive model.[62]

To help his cause in the Bundesrat, Tirpitz made several vain attempts to persuade William II to back off his hard-line position on the part of the military penal reforms unwelcome to the Bavarians.[63] The military justice reform bill, after great Bundesrat turmoil, went to the Reichstag on 16 December. Against all expectations, it ultimately passed comfortably in May 1898. Tirpitz's anxiety on this score turned out to be unjustified, but this was not obvious in December 1897.[64]

Krafft von Crailsheim, a Bavarian Bundesrat representative, wrote to Tirpitz to try to persuade him simply to propose a set of estimates, and to delay a legally established fleet until after the scheduled 1898 Reichstag election. Tirpitz replied: "After the events in recent years in which the navy estimates went back and forth, I fear very much that such a stone set in motion by your proposal could not be stopped." On the crucial point of legal establishment of ship types and numbers, he declared:

> I believe the Reichstag will assent. . . . In evidence, I adduce my conviction that it would be a serious political mistake for the Center to reject the naval proposal. The smart politicians of the Center would not make such an error. They will also not let pass an opportunity to demonstrate their

capability to govern and to jump on the bandwagon of a national issue, whose popularity will grow from year to year.

He also rejected the idea of a government coup because the goal could be accomplished without the uncertainties that a coup would engender.[65]

Admiral Prinz Heinrich, the Emperor's brother, offered his support. After reading the proposal, he wrote: "I must, after diligent study, confess that the request is somewhat modest [*etwas bescheiden*], but empirically and objectively based." In a phrase that harkened back to Luther, he wrote: "Little monk, little monk, you are on a difficult road" [*Mönchlein, Mönchlein, du gehst einem schweren Gang*].[66]

The Bundesrat approved the draft on 27 November. Three days later the Emperor opened the Reichstag with a speech that emphasized the importance of the Navy Bill.[67] The draft law contained seemingly clear and simple demands. The fleet establishment would be nineteen battleships: eight coastal armored ships, and twelve large and thirty small cruisers; torpedo boats and smaller ships were excluded. The established ships had to be completed by fiscal year 1904–1905. The law set the lifespan of individual types at twenty-five years for battleships, twenty years for large cruisers, and fifteen years for small cruisers, and, absolutely central to Tirpitz's idea, committed the Reichstag to provide money automatically for replacements once the ships reached their statutory maximum ages. To leave torpedo boats out of the establishment would put another 44 million marks into the annual estimates over seven years, but this was no problem because torpedo boats had always been politically popular.

The rationale (*Begründung*) asserted that technical change had reached a point that made fixed and distinctive ship types possible. It reviewed the technical, tactical, and strategic arguments for the legal establishment of two full squadrons of battleships. The rationale offered vague and bland assurances that the Reichstag's budget right was not threatened. It outlined the missions of the battlefleet in the modified way that Lieber had proposed, reminiscent of Stosch's 1873 memorandum:

> The mission of the battlefleet is the defense of the coasts of the nation.
> . . . Against larger seapowers the fleet has only the significance of a "sortie
> fleet" (*Ausfallsflotte*). Any other objective is ruled out by the limited naval
> strength that the law provides.

For the next seven years a total of eleven battleships, new and replacement, would have to be built. The average annual construction budget was set at 58.6 million marks, only slightly more than Hollmann had received the previous spring.[68]

The apparent clarity, transparency, and purposefulness of the plan made a favorable impression compared to Hollmann's. Tirpitz had turned the tables on those who had fought "limitless" fleet plans. Here was a plan *with* a limit, in ship numbers at least. Any further expansion would have to be approved by a future Reichstag. Its political purpose seemed entirely defensive, with strategy, tactics, technology, and cost tied neatly together.

Along with the law draft, the RMA published "Die Seeinteressen des deutschen Reiches." Halle and M II compiled this document, which demonstrated, with facts and figures, the enormous and spectacular growth in population, trade, industry commerce, merchant marine, fisheries, and colonies that Germany had experienced since 1871. Imports had more than doubled, exports had almost tripled, and merchant tonnage under the German ensign had grown more than tenfold. Germany had become, within a quarter of a century, the world's second-largest trading power.[69]

Despite such growth, Germany had slipped badly from its 1883 position as the world's fourth naval power, and had dropped not just in relative but also in absolute terms. The clear assumption of such a statement, promoted by Mahan's writings and the imperialist values of the time, was that maritime interests and naval power should increase proportionately, lest neglect of the navy lead to economic ruin. No one seemed to notice that maritime states such as Norway and the Netherlands had large maritime interests without large navies. As the great historian of the French Navy, Theodore Ropp, once acidly put it:

> The idea that a navy should be proportionate to the maritime interests
> of a country was a relic of the days when it was necessary to police the
> seas against the Barbary Pirates, or force civilization on the Chinese. As a
> doctrine of national defense against another first-rate European power, it
> was as irrational as the notion that an air force should be proportional to the
> "air interests" created by a Lufthansa or a Pan American.[70]

Such heretical thoughts were, at the time, largely confined to Socialists and other anti-imperialists.

Tirpitz, in a fit of nervousness as the Reichstag opened, worried that the government and the deputies might strike a deal and vote only for the first year's installments rather than a long-term and binding law. When he heard whispers to this effect, he confronted Hohenlohe and said that if the Reichstag could not accept the proposal as it was, it would have to be dissolved.[71] Tirpitz was gambling, but he believed he held a winning hand, confident that his propaganda machinery could carry the day in an election over the naval issue. The government's attitude against such amendments stiffened.

The Navy Bill went before the Reichstag for its first reading from 6 through 9 December.[72] Hohenlohe, Tirpitz, Bülow, and Thielmann spoke. In his maiden Reichstag speech, Tirpitz argued as if the law were a self-evident necessity. It would banish time-worn accusations of limitless fleet plans. He asserted that, because technology had slowed, the ships would cost no more than outlined in the government's tables. Within a year this statement turned out to be nonsense, but coming from the government's leading naval expert it carried a certain authority. Tirpitz argued that the fleet was purely defensive, to prevent a blockade. He conceded that cruisers were more popular than battleships, but asserted that, with the latter, by 1904 "you can create enough ships so that even a seapower of the first rank would hesitate three times before attacking our coasts." This was the only occasion Tirpitz even indirectly mentioned the British.

The Social Democrats, as expected, made bitter and sarcastic attacks against Tirpitz and the naval program. The Conservatives agreed to support the bill but made it clear that their agrarian faction expected compensation for yielding to industry's desire for a fleet.

On 7 December Eugen Richter delivered a vehement personal attack on Tirpitz, but his following was small and his influence limited. Tirpitz rebutted Richter's characterization of the law as an eternal one (Äternat). The replacement clause meant only that what the Reichstag legally established now would also be necessary in the future. With some glee, he turned Richter's decade of criticism of limitless fleet plans against him. How could a limitless fleet plan be prevented, except by a limited law? Lieber said that the Center knew that its position would ultimately determine the outcome, but it had not yet reached a decision. He recognized the need to expand the navy, but criticized the government for its hard line on the military penal code and the anti-Jesuit laws. He then suggested that an upper limit be placed on naval expenditure. This idea was akin to the compromise Lieber had proposed to Tirpitz at their secret meeting on 24 October, Tirpitz feigned surprise at the suggestion, and, to everyone's amazement, most deputies agreed to consider it.[73] He disingen-uously said, "The idea is new to me." The Center did not explicitly balk at the notion of a fixed ship establishment and automatic replacement.

Delayed by the Christmas recess and other business, the Navy Bill came up in the Budget Commission on 24 February 1898. During the interim the propaganda campaign peaked. The Center's crucial position made Bavaria and the Rhineland special targets for agitation.[74] Lieber worked to organize firmer support within the Center.[75]

To parry anticipated attacks from the Reichstag that the law would infringe on the budget right, Tirpitz had Prussian Finance Minister Miquel prepare a long memorandum to address such objections.[76] Miquel claimed that it was a misunderstanding to assert that the Navy Law would impair the budget powers of the Reichstag. He argued that most gov-ernment expenditures came from continuing appropriations, which the Reichstag could not revoke unilaterally. This meant, he went on, that the Reichstag could not assert an annual power of review. He used the example of annual estimates for completing construction of the Reich-stag's own building, which was based on a long-term building plan. Each annual installment had to be provided because in a building plan one stage leads to the next.

As leader of the nine Center deputies on the twenty-nine-member Commission, Lieber held the balance of power there, as long as he kept his own party's support. Together the "patriotic" parties, the National Liberals and the Conservatives, could only muster eleven votes. With the help of two splinter parties, the pro-navy members had altogether just thirteen votes, not a majority. Pro-navy petitions, the fruit of Heeringen's campaign, flowed in by the hundreds. Tirpitz and Capelle, flanked by a bevy of aides, sat in on the Commission hearings, which began on 24 February.[77]

Lieber accepted the squadron principle, which meant that the estab-lishment of a whole double squadron, and not individual ships, would be voted up or down. The consequences of this decision, apparently harm-less and even beneficent as it seemed to signal the end of "limitless" fleet plans, would not become clear until the next Navy Law was proposed, with a second double squadron.

At the second session Lieber proposed a fixed upper limit for expen-ditures on the septannat. Tirpitz evaded a direct answer, but it was clear that he would accept a limit. He was cagy enough not to name a specific figure lest he later be accused of breaking a promise. His willingness to compromise on this point, already suggested in his secret meetings with Lieber the year before, mollified some reluctant Centrists.[78] Lieber contested Richter's accusations that an *ternat* was unconstitutional. He cited Miquel's argument, and said that if multiyear appropriations were suitable for the army, they were also suitable for the navy. If the Reichstag was bound, so, too, was the government. If the government accepted the proposed financial limit, it would be bound for seven years.

At the third meeting Lieber even quoted Mahan and proposed that, if new sources of revenue were necessary to pay for the law, the money should be raised not by imperial taxes (which the particularists among the Center could not have accepted) but by proportionate matricular contributions from individual states. The additional money from the states should come from a direct tax on incomes over 10,000 marks in most states. The Center wanted to have the "strong shoulders," those who would reap the profits for shipbuilding, to bear the cost, not the "weak shoulders" of ordinary people who would have to pay higher prices on consumer goods. The "patriotic" parties, who represented propertied and moneyed interests, balked. Richter, presciently, asked what would happen after the septannat expired. Tirpitz evaded the point by saying, "to estimate the consequences of a law over a generation seems to me not a good idea."

On 5 March the National Liberal von Bennigsen tried to break the deadlock. He offered a compromise that any money needed for the navy over and above that provided by ordinary income should not come from new or increased indirect taxes and, according to Bennigsen, thereby spare the "weak shoulders." He fudged the message, however, when he exempted tariffs, a principal source of Reich revenue, from his definition of indirect taxes. As flaccid as it was, Bennigsen's amendment provided a face-saving device for Lieber to claim that the "weak shoulders" would not be affected.

In that session a curious incident occurred that illustrated how little the deputies comprehended what they were doing. Richard Müller, from Fulda, a leader of the Rhineland faction of the Center and an opponent of the Navy Bill (he voted against it in the final reading), proposed to shorten the term of the law from seven to six years, without reducing the number of ships. No doubt Müller felt that he was limiting the period of the Reichstag's commitment by one year. In effect, his amendment ac-

celerated the building program. Tirpitz was delighted and accepted the
"compromise."[79]

The volatile Center had still another surprise. At a party caucus on 8
March, in response to a stiff warning from Lieber that political necessity
dictated acceptance of the naval bill, a number of Center deputies, led
by Dr. Alois Fritzen, revolted against the leadership.[80] Fritzen wanted to
make it possible for the Reichstag alone to change the critical automatic
replacement clause. The law draft provided that the consent of both
the Bundesrat and the Reichstag were necessary to change the replacement tempo for ships that exceeded their age limit. The Bundesrat had
the right to veto a Reichstag attempt to reduce the replacement tempo.
Fritzen's amendment would have endangered the automatic apparently
inexorable substitution of new ships for old which was a major reason
why Tirpitz wanted the law.[81] Tirpitz was both furious and apprehensive:
if the Rhineland Centrists could be won to Fritzen's view, passage of the
law would be at grave risk. He immediately threatened Lieber that "the
omission [of the Bundesrat] was unacceptable to me and that in case the
government accepts it, I would be compelled to submit my resignation. I
hope that the Center will reconsider."[82]

Tirpitz well understood how eager the Center was to enhance its
position as the decisive party. If Tirpitz resigned and the Navy Bill failed,
the Center would have lost its chance to swing the balance of power and,
perhaps in return, get government support for some of its programs, such
as repeal of the Jesuit Laws. The party would then return to unavailing
opposition. As Steinberg rightly points out, Tirpitz, merely an administra-
tor under the Chancellor, had no constitutional right to resign as a result
of a parliamentary defeat, let alone over a disagreement within a single
parliamentary party. Although not a Cabinet member in the British parliamentary sense, he acted like one on this occasion, and this behavior
won him support in the Parliament. He took the Reichstag seriously,
cultivated its leaders, and occasionally made known his dependence upon
them. Lieber, head of a party that Bismarck had characterized as an "enemy of the Reich," trusted him enough to pass the Navy Bill. By an odd
paradox, his self-created vulnerability to defeat in the Reichstag was, in
this instance, one of his greatest strengths.[83] Clearly, however, Tirpitz was
not a "liberal" as Steinberg claims.

The bill passed the Budget Commission on 17 March, with Müller's
amendment and Bennigsen's slightly modified one. The final debate in

the Plenum featured more sharp attacks from Richter and August Bebel, leader of the Social Democrats. Ironically Bebel was laughed down by all parties except his own, when he warned that the expanded fleet would lead to conflict with England.[84] This reaction demonstrates the absurdity with which conflict with Britain was viewed at the time. The Bavarian Center deputies, except for Hertling, opposed it, but the leadership group and the Rhineland faction supported it. Two-thirds of the Center Party was sufficient for a respectable majority (212 to 139) on 26 March.

The National Liberals and moderate Conservatives supported it for nationalist reasons, and it suited their economic interests because it meant contracts for industry. Many of the agrarians backed the navy in spite of their anti-imperial, anti-industrial orientation, because they were confident that they would be compensated by tariffs on foodstuffs, as they were to be in the tariff bill of 1902. In this sense the Navy Bill was, in part, a product of Miquel's *Sammlungpolitik*.[85]

Although it still functioned as a Catholic confessional Party on religious matters, the Center was the only party with support from all economic classes. In that sense, paradoxically, the Center was the only truly national party. Historians like Hallmann and Bachem agree that Lieber wanted the Center to operate as a "government" party on some issues in order to help its own agenda, and to demonstrate that it, too, was patriotic.

Perhaps the clearest analysis of the Center Party's role in the Navy Law comes from John Zeender, who had access to the broadest array of materials. Zeender argued that Lieber was under great pressure, both from Cardinal Kopp and the ultramontanes (the pro-papal party) to get rid of the vexing remnants of Bismarck's Kulturkampf. Lieber feared that if something were not achieved soon, the Center would collapse from within. On most non-confessional questions the Bavarian Centrists, under great pressure from the Bauernbund, already went their own way. The Rhinelanders would support Lieber in non-confessional questions only if they were compensated. Lieber felt that he could only deliver the goods if the Center was the decisive force in forming government majorities on national questions. Other center leaders felt the same way. On 25 November 1897 the maverick Bavarian Center leader Georg Hertling wrote to Lieber: "Regarding the naval proposal I also consider it not permanently desirable that the Center always stand in the opposition in so-called national questions."[86] Lieber, therefore, if he was to keep the party together and achieve its major goals, was forced to assert a kind of hegemony for

his party. Lieber's needs and ambitions were integral to the passage of the
Navy Law. It is hard to see how such a law could have been passed had the
Center been opposed or severely splintered. Hollmann had tried to exploit
Lieber's position but without the energy, drive, or coherence that Tirpitz
brought to the task. Tirpitz and Capelle read Lieber well and pressed
the relationship to the limit. After passage, Tirpitz wrote gratefully to
Lieber:

> Permit me to give you a purely private expression of feeling. The prejudice
> existed in wide circles in Germany, especially in the northern and central
> parts, that your party was against the forward initiatives of the German
> Reich. . . . As unjustified and unjustifiable as this prejudice was, it existed,
> and was held like a dogma of faith. After this winter, this evil weed, which
> crippled Germany's growth, has been pulled up by the roots. Thereby a
> new future is opened for our country. Thank you. You can be proud.[87]

Tirpitz and, to some degree, Bülow were quickest to understand that
the Center Party, especially Lieber, Hertling, and others in the leadership
faction were trying to move the party in a new direction on "national"
questions, like naval policy. They were prepared to support the government in ways they had not done previously in order to preserve their
position as the swing party. Röhl argues persuasively that such accommodation rendered unnecessary, except in the eyes of some extreme army
officers, the idea of a government coup against the Reichstag.[88] Even after
Lieber's incapacity in 1900 Tirpitz and Capelle, in all subsequent Navy
Bills, covertly tested the waters with the Center leadership, even during
the 1907 election campaign when the government actively campaigned
against the Center.

Another significant question raised during the preliminaries to the
1898 Navy Law is what connection, if any, it had to Miquel's idea of Sammlungspolitik. According to Kehr and, in a more sophisticated version,
to Berghahn, Tirpitz and others such as Miquel and Bülow intended
the 1898 Navy Law as the first step in a system-stabilizing initiative to
reunite conservative industrial and agricultural interests. The coalition
(Sammlung) was intended to thwart Social Democracy and to reinstate a
version of Bismarck's earlier cartel of iron and rye. A detailed discussion of
this question is beyond the scope of this work but, as this chapter and the
writings of Geoff Eley point out,[89] in 1897–98 Tirpitz's industrial and, in
theory at least, imperialist and navalist goals were more of a threat to the
delicate industrial/agrarian balance than a reinforcement of it.

There is very little evidence that Tirpitz, in 1897–98, cared for anything beyond a narrowly focused "Tirpitz plan" to expand the fleet, rather than the broadly based "Tirpitz Plan" (Berghahn) to stabilize the whole imperial system. In the RMA's negotiations with Miquel in the summer and fall of 1897 there is no evidence that Tirpitz was striving for any goals beyond naval expansion, and he explicitly opposed using the navy as a battering ram for an election called before the Reichstag's statutory expiration in the summer of 1898. Tirpitz's eager wooing of the Center Party, many of whose members' interests did not coincide with those of a Sammlung-style coalition, and the economic sugar plums conjured up by the RMA's propaganda machine included no emphasis on agrarian interests but instead focused only on industry and trade. In 1897, as later, Tirpitz's conspiratorial efforts were confined to the interests of the navy as he saw them. He was rarely hesitant to propose, in confidential intra-government conversations at least, measures such as an inheritance tax that would be anathema to Sammlung interests.

For the first time Tirpitz showed himself to the Reichstag and to the country as a master politician. He overcame his inner nervousness with a remarkable outward display of charm, confidence, moderation, and apparent flexibility. Hindsight gives an unwarranted sense of inevitability to the First Navy Law. In less than a year from debarking in Bremerhaven, he brought home a very long shot. He turned chaos into order within the navy and defeat into victory in the Reichstag. He harnessed the erratic Emperor to his agenda and rode him to get the support of a government apparatus mostly indifferent to naval expansion. With Heeringen's very capable help, he galvanized a mostly apathetic nation into one that was aware of and keen on its maritime and naval interests, and he sowed the seeds of future large-scale agitation that might be difficult to control.

The Emperor showed Tirpitz his gratitude by an extraordinary step. Despite opposition from many of its members, he appointed Tirpitz to the Prussian Ministry of State. He wrote to Hohenlohe:

> Upon his return from China, with a weakened constitution, cheerfully and alone he undertook the huge task of informing an entire nation, fifty million combative, short-sighted, and ill-tempered Germans, and he persuaded them of an opposite opinion. He accomplished this apparently impossible mission in eight months. Truly a powerful man![90]

One obvious question is what Tirpitz anticipated for the future in April 1898? In his memoirs, written in 1918, he notes:

In the winter of 1898/9 I was still firmly resolved to keep to the six years'
limit. It was, however, always quite clear to me, and I also expressed myself
to this effect in the Reichstag, that the first Navy Bill would not create the
fleet in its ultimate form. It was frankly stated that we would have to bring
forward supplementary demands after the conclusion of the six years' limit.
. . . I had in mind the idea of proceeding "in spurts," nursing the Reichstag
as much as possible meanwhile.[91]

Tirpitz may well have had this idea in mind in 1897 through April
1898; but there is very little evidence in the documents that he had informed the Reichstag of what would come after 1904. He had not denied
that there might be an attempt at further expansion. This is different,
however, from making an affirmative declaration of intent, as Tirpitz
claimed in his memoirs. There is one solid, if vague, piece of evidence
about his future intentions during this period. On 11 August 1897 he wrote
to Senden:

If we succeed in passing the law, in 1905 there would be a very good basis
for a further rounding off [*Abrundung*] of the navy. But we need not now
present the sums, which would only be required in the future.[92]

Clearly Tirpitz had an idea, albeit an indistinct one, of proceeding in
something like a "stepwise" fashion (Berghahn) after 1905 (actually 1904,
in the law's final form), but there were no specifics, even in the secret
deliberations of the RMA, at least up to April 1898. Nor, at that time,
is there concrete evidence of the "system stabilizing" grand design that
Berghahn and others have called the "Tirpitz Plan." By 1898 Tirpitz was
certainly, as Hobson has pointed out, a believer in the navalist ideology
of Mahan, and recognized that some industrial and economic interests
favored fleet expansion. At this time it seems far-fetched to see Tirpitz
as the fabricator of a broad-ranging way to stabilize the shaky imperial
political system. He then had his hands full with the consolidation of his
new-found power within the navy. There is little evidence that he was
thinking then in government-wide systemic terms. Lambi shares this
view: "It is questionable if it was coherently planned."[93]

Steinberg and Berghahn are certainly convincing that, as early as
his memo to the Emperor of July 1897, the fleet was to be built "against
England." The real question is what the phrase "against England" meant
in the context of 1897–98? In his maiden Reichstag speech of 6 December
1897 Tirpitz referred to a fleet that, by 1905, even a first-rank naval power

would have to think twice before attacking. In the context of showing the Reichstag that the intentions of the bill were purely defensive, this was almost an incidental public remark. That Tirpitz was not trying to convince the Reichstag that the 1898 fleet was "against England" in any literal sense is well illustrated by the derisive laughter that Social Democratic leader August Bebel drew when he made that very accusation. The British themselves barely noticed the 1898 law.[94]

In 1897–98, the OK had no remotely credible plan for a war against England. The nineteen battleships, even when completed, would have posed no threat to England, even if they had, by some bizarre circumstance, been able to attract France or Russia, or both as an ally.[95] Only the Second Navy Law would create a plausible threat. The most credible reason in 1897 to plan a fleet "against England," albeit secretly at that point, was that the British were the only potential rival worthy of the name. Here Tirpitz may have begun to shift from rational actor to bureaucratic politics, as perhaps he also did in his opposition to the annexation of Kiaochou, even though the scale of the 1898 law was defensible on rational actor grounds. How could one plausibly build a really substantial fleet without a first-class "enemy"? Tirpitz may have believed, consciously or unconsciously, that the only way he could persuade a nation of landlubbers to expand a fleet for the general purposes of enhancing and defending its world position would be to use the Royal Navy as a target. As the Kruger Telegram and the *Saturday Review* article had aptly demonstrated, dislike and envy of the British had provided *Agitationsmittel* (good slogan material) throughout the country, which could be translated into money and support in the Reichstag. Although in 1897–98 Tirpitz, in public, deliberately muted (without ignoring completely) the British "threat," a politician as clever as Tirpitz could not help but notice its potency, particularly if he was thinking of a further expansion after 1904. Tirpitz's vehemently anti-British memoirs, written in 1918, should therefore not be trusted about what his intentions were in 1897.

BUREAUCRATIC POLITICS UNLEASHED: THE DISSOLUTION OF THE OBERKOMMANDO

Since the dissolution of the Admiralty in 1889 there had been continuous turf wars between the OK and the RMA. Senden in the MK and the

Emperor periodically served as mediators. The OK argued that the RMA, in dealing with the Chancellor and the Reichstag, tainted the command power of the Emperor, to whom the OK was directly and solely subordinated. Tirpitz, as OK Chief of Staff (1892–95) had furiously attacked Hollmann and the RMA to get exclusive control, in the critical question of fleet development, for the OK. His mentor, Stosch, had warned Tirpitz of the great financial power of the State Secretary, and had urged Tirpitz to seek the position himself.[96]

By June 1897 the shoe was on the other foot. The Emperor had charged Tirpitz, as head of the RMA, with the duty of fleet development, a task Tirpitz had stridently sought when he was in the OK. Although Knorr supported the law draft, and in the summer of 1897 agreed to a cease-fire in the turf wars, he rued Tirpitz's aggressive and ultimately successful attempt to put Kiaochou under the RMA's aegis.[97] As early as December 1897 the intramural dispute began to heat up again. Tirpitz complained to Knorr about the OK's authority over ships on foreign station without the knowledge or consent of the RMA.[98] Tirpitz had rigorously upheld this prerogative of the OK as its Chief of Staff. Officers within the OK, such as Rear Admiral Carl Barandon and Captain Henning von Holtzendorff, urged Knorr to fight back.[99] OK press leaks about minor jurisdictional conflicts with the RMA irked Tirpitz. In his response to Tirpitz, Knorr reprised how he had set aside his misgivings about the law draft, and that he and his staff had put their shoulders to the wheel in comradely fashion and continued to do so. He accused Tirpitz of meddling in the OK's authority over ships abroad. Knorr argued that this was a threat to the Emperor's command power that had to be exercised by a body wholly independent of the Reichstag.[100] Tirpitz again turned to William II, who, as so often before, deferred a decision.[101]

Tirpitz even went so far as to seek an opinion from a leading constitutional law professor, who agreed that the Emperor could exercise his command power through either the OK or the RMA. The professor advised that the legal character of the command power allowed the State Secretary to act directly as an officer on such matters, regardless of his relationship with the Reichstag on other concerns.[102] This was not an opinion Tirpitz would have welcomed in 1892; but by 1898 he was wearing a different hat.

Once the Navy Law passed, Tirpitz shifted into full-scale attack mode on the OK, to the dismay of old friends like Felix von Bendemann, then a squadron commander in the fleet. On 24 April 1898, in a memo to the Emperor, Tirpitz laid his cards on the table.[103] He apologized, with dubious sincerity, for raising the organization question. He then made a proposal tantamount to a partial recreation of the old Admiralty that William II had abolished in 1889. Although the OK would retain command of the fleet in home waters, the RMA, because of its mission of fleet development, should take control of the navy's operational planning. Just as brazenly, he asked that the RMA take over command direction of ships on foreign station, fisheries, and other maritime matters. It should also have the sole responsibility to deal with the highest Reich and state offices on behalf of the navy. Such a measure would, for example, effectively terminate the OK's ability to deal with the Foreign Office. He demanded a status equivalent to that of the Prussian War Minister.

The proposal, if implemented, would also have had disruptive effects on the seniority system. In any organizations made subject to Tirpitz, admirals senior to him would have had to retire or be reassigned to other posts not subject to him. Tirpitz tried to ameliorate the problem by conceding to the Emperor, in his 24 April letter, that if ships on foreign station had a commander senior to Tirpitz, that commander would be directly subordinated to the Emperor. The havoc that this proposal would have created for senior admirals was probably an important, though little noted, reason for the peculiar form the reorganization eventually took in 1899.

The scope of such a bureaucratic power play was breathtaking. It resembled the plan for a super-RMA that Tirpitz had pushed on the Emperor in January 1896. In a letter to Senden on 28 April, he wrote:

> I place . . . my powers in the service of His Majesty, but it is impossible for me to assume responsibility for an organization which, in my judgment, cannot function and which would make my position unbearable. If an organization were to be introduced which is against my convictions, I would not be able to take the responsibility for it.[104]

What emboldened Tirpitz to attempt such a coup is unclear.[105] Very likely the intoxicating experience of passing the Navy Law had also led to a sense of hubris and a belief in his own indispensability. He also sought the support of Foreign Secretary Bülow.[106] Such arguments were the hall-mark of his expanded bureaucratic politics (*Ressorteifer*). Tirpitz was try-ing to vastly increase his power over the navy. He was prepared to gamble for the highest stakes, once the Navy Law was an accomplished fact.

A hint of the denouement came a few days later with a pained and sorrowful letter from Senden.[107] Tirpitz's clearly implied threat to resign upon a first difference of opinion carried the risk of "breaking your con-nection" with the Emperor. Obedience, wrote Senden, is the central duty of an officer. Without directly saying so, Senden was appalled that Tirpitz was acting like a civilian minister in a parliamentary government, free to resign over a policy disagreement rather than to behave as a loyal military officer. He accused Tirpitz of an injustice against an Emperor who had spent ten years developing the navy, and who had no firm opinion about an alternative naval organization in the face of frequent organizational conflict. To ease the sting of the letter, he concluded by professing his loyal and comradely feelings for Tirpitz. Senden may have ruefully re-called his words to the Emperor on March 1896, when he characterized Tirpitz as an ambitious man, not easy to control.[108]

Polite but unrepentant, Tirpitz replied that the organization ques-tion was not his first difference of opinion with the Emperor since June 1897. The Emperor, he wrote, had done many things against his recom-mendation, but that was "certainly proper if the Emperor wills it so."[109] The organizational question was so important that the Emperor could no longer use a man who differed from him on a matter of such conse-quence. Regarding an officer's duty of obedience, Tirpitz concluded that "to expect an officer in a highly responsible position, in all circumstances to carry on, even against his deepest beliefs would, in my opinion, lead to pernicious [*verderbliche*] circumstances." William II at first wavered, and showed indications of giving Tirpitz most of what he wanted.[110]

Knorr counterpunched with a long letter to William II in which he asked, rhetorically, whether the State Secretary, alone within the navy, should control all maritime interests.[111] Should the leader who is mainly responsible for the navy in wartime have little accountability in peace-time? Was Trafalgar of less importance to the development of English sea interests than the work of the Admiralty? "Tirpitz does not answer this question, but it is the key to the riddle," Knorr stated in his letter. Knorr saw that if Tirpitz's proposal were accepted, naval policy would be directed by "bureaucratic interests [*ressortmässige Marinepolitik*]." I see in this a direct danger for the real interests of the navy." Control of ships abroad would put many functions of the Foreign Office in the RMA's hands. Knorr replayed an old refrain when he referred to "the placing of the imperial command power under an office responsible to parliament, i.e., under the parliament itself." Tirpitz's proposal would split the fleet in two, with one command for the home fleet and another for ships abroad, provoking even greater friction between the OK and the RMA. He also cautioned against conferring status on the RMA analogous to that of the Prussian War Ministry, which reported directly and solely to the sovereign, and not partially to the Parliament like the RMA.

In an appendix, Knorr noted:

> I humbly remember Kiaochou. If then the State Secretary had in his hands the political deployment of foreign ships, he would have thrown his whole weight into the scales to hinder action.[112]

The OK's order draft tried to accommodate the RMA in small ways. Knorr accepted the shift of the journal *Marine Rundschau* from the OK to the RMA. He agreed to expand the RMA's competence into some areas under the control of the Ministry of the Interior, such as harbors and canals. He rejected any attempt to undermine the OK's command functions.

Many Front officers rallied to Knorr.[113] The Emperor found Knorr's memo "objective" and clearly stated. He agreed that Tirpitz had gone too far, too fast. At the same time William II definitively rejected Tirpitz's resignation attempt.[114] He wrote: "You have obviously been inclined to consider objective matters too readily from a personal standpoint." The Emperor, perhaps sincerely, perhaps to save face for Tirpitz, attributed his "misjudgment" to overwork, both in his parliamentary activity and in the pressing duties of his office. The Emperor expressed full confidence in his service and repeated his advice that Tirpitz should take a rest. Organizational questions must take second place at the moment. He agreed to consider Tirpitz's ideas for organizational reform in a few months, when he returned from his travels.

Tirpitz, with typical stubbornness, made another attempt to resign, this time because of "my weakened health" and the stress the OK had caused by "undermining" his personal authority. Again the Emperor refused to accept it.[115] In a letter to Hohenlohe, Tirpitz complained bitterly that the OK fought dishonorably by using personal attacks, namely, that he was power-hungry.[116] Tirpitz, after his great triumph in April, was angry and frustrated. The Emperor, aboard his yacht, offered Tirpitz some hope that he really was considering a future reorganization. In passing the Navy Law, "you have succeeded surprisingly fast." As long as the law is not complete, "I cannot do without your valuable service."[117] In his repeated efforts to resign, Tirpitz showed the nerve of a tightrope walker. Could he have been certain that the erratic Emperor would refuse it, and that he could leverage resignation threats to get what he wanted? What if he offended the sovereign enough to accept the resignation? Would there have been a Second Navy Law, with all its negative results for Germany? In hindsight, great historical consequences depended on this delicate personal relationship.

Tirpitz had no choice but to obey and stay in service. While the sovereign went about his annual cruises, Tirpitz sulked and plotted while taking the cure at Bad Nauheim. His deputy, Büchsel, kept him posted from Berlin.[118] Senden was caught in the middle, between Tirpitz, Knorr, and his imperial master. On Tirpitz's central issue, subordination of ships abroad to the RMA, Senden seemed to lean in Tirpitz's direction; but he emphasized that the Emperor needed more time to decide about reorganization. He also hinted to Büchsel that he was preparing to expedite Knorr's departure. Through the retired Admiral Hollmann, once again on congenial terms with the Emperor, Tirpitz heard, via Pohl, of the Emperor's bitter annoyance at him for his audacious resignation attempts, coupled with his recognition of Tirpitz's indispensability. On a less optimistic note, Pohl also reported there were many complaints from naval officers about the RMA's move for dominance within the navy. There was even speculation that Bendemann might replace Tirpitz.[119]

The Emperor consulted his brother, Prinz Heinrich, a division commander in Diedrichs's Asian Cruiser Squadron. The Prince unburdened himself at length in support of a strong OK.[120] Although he had previously supported Tirpitz, on this matter he felt that Tirpitz was "absolutely wrong."

> I find it incomprehensible that Tirpitz is so shortsighted. . . . His continuing threat of resignation is not entirely loyal. A monarch with the courage to let Prince Bismarck go would not hesitate to let a Tirpitz go upon his own wish, though it would make me sad to see one of our finest men go. No man on this earth is indispensable.

In July 1898 the Emperor decided to delay the reorganization question until winter. Senden's own view seemed to lean against Knorr. He perversely cited Knorr's submission of anti-RMA documents that demonstrated Tirpitz's arguments as OK Chief of Staff. Senden criticized Knorr as "personal and not objective" for pointing out Tirpitz's *volte face*. He concluded that the personal difference between Tirpitz and Knorr was irreconcilable. His informal poll of naval officers revealed a consensus that Tirpitz should be kept at a distance from the Front and from command responsibilities in general.[121]

Tirpitz himself was characteristically pessimistic. He thought Knorr might go in the spring but that he might be let go even sooner, before any organizational changes. He thanked Büchsel for defending him and complained that Senden was attacking him, but he stubbornly stuck to his proposal while claiming it would not destroy the OK. His cure at Bad Nauheim was going well, although he had been told by doctors that he had a stress-induced heart problem.[122] The Emperor had another characterization of Tirpitz's malady, and perhaps a more apt one. William II told the Chancellor that Tirpitz found it hard to obey because he was neurasthenic, that is, ill from stress and emotional conflicts, with a wide array of symptoms including fatigue, depression, and worry, with pains of indistinct origins.[123]

In September Prinz Heinrich wrote to Tirpitz in a more conciliatory tone than he had written his brother the month before. Nevertheless, he stated his disagreement clearly:

> One cannot tailor an organization to present personnel, but one must think of the future and therefore not make a Tirpitz into Chief of Admiralty, someone who could not later be replaced. . . . My heart hurts to be in opposition to "my dear old master," but I have a friendly duty to express my sincere beliefs.[124]

Tirpitz replied with a convoluted, even lame argument that his present position on the direction of ships abroad had not changed since 1892! He claimed that he had gone to Hollmann then and had asked for elbowroom to develop the fleet's organization and tactics, while recognizing the RMA's decisive role with ships abroad. Hollmann had rejected that offer, but Tirpitz argued to Prinz Heinrich that this incident proved his own consistency. He disingenuously asserted: "Personally I have no par-

ticularistic attachment [*Localpatriotismus*] for an office [*Behörde*], neither
before nor now." He apologized for his disagreement with the Prince, but
said it was absolutely necessary to expand the reach of the RMA to ships
abroad.[125] The letter is a clear example of a bureaucratic politician deceiving himself so that he appears to be a rational actor, even in his own eyes.
In 1904 Tirpitz even told Michaelis, then a junior officer in the RMA, that
the Emperor had forced him, against his beliefs, to countersign the order
to dissolve the OK, and that he considered it better to combine development and administration in the hands of one officer, as had been true of
the Admiralty from 1873 to 1888.[126]

In December the Emperor solicited ideas from the whole navy about
reorganization. This seemed a victory for Tirpitz, but the Emperor also
made it clear that there were two conditions. The Commanding Admiral, or whoever succeeded him, would continue to oversee the battlefleet
and ships on foreign deployment. The North Sea and Baltic Commands
would retain authority for officer assignment to ships and exercises.[127]
Tirpitz and the RMA immediately began to draft a plan that would be
to their advantage.

A revealing meeting took place at Leipzigerplatz 13 on 14 February
1899 with Tirpitz, Fischel, Capelle, and Heeringen attending.[128] The
agenda was either to emasculate or dissolve the OK. Heeringen suggested that the real power of command devolve from the Commanding
Admiral to station chiefs and the fleet commander. The Commanding
Admiral would retain only vaguely supervisory powers equivalent to an
Army Inspector General. Fischel went further, suggesting that the station
and fleet chiefs be directly subordinated to the Emperor. Capelle inter-
jected that the Admiralstab's planning functions be expanded to include
command of ships abroad, with the Commanding Admiral limited to
inspection. He also warned, though in practice this was impossible, that
Tirpitz should keep a low profile personally because many officers would
find the scheme offensive. Fischel audaciously proposed that the very title
"OK" be abolished. Such an approach would doubtless strengthen the
Emperor's direct command power.

Capelle suggested that reserve division battleships be placed under
the station chiefs rather than the fleet chief. Purely for bureaucratic power
reasons, he argued that if this was not done, the fleet chief would have
a strong power base against that of the RMA. Tirpitz had reservations

about going this far, but he decided to leave the question to the Emperor. Centralized fleet command also contended with the Emperor's known desire to have four or five men to choose from for wartime command, lest the decision be made solely by seniority, in which case an unsuitable choice might be inevitable.

On 14 March 1899 William II issued his final decision, to dissolve the OK and redistribute its functions.[129] This was a remarkable document, which remained in force, with few changes, until the outbreak of war in 1914. It created quite a bizarre command structure. The Admiralstab Section of the old OK became the Admiralstab, responsible for operational planning, intelligence, and direction of ships abroad. The Admiralstab, along with the Chiefs of the North Sea and Baltic Stations, the Inspectorate of Training, the Chief of the I Squadron, and the Chief of the Overseas Cruiser Squadron would all report directly to the Emperor.

Equally astounding was the fact that no fleet chief was named. He would be appointed annually solely to lead the summer exercises of the maneuver fleet. This meant that no one knew in advance who would lead the fleet if war suddenly broke out. William II took his personal leadership of the navy so seriously that, to preserve his free choice of wartime fleet commander, he crippled the fleet's ability to coherently prepare for war under a known commander. A better example of the Emperor's negative effect on the navy would be hard to find.

In an act of supreme flattery and remarkable folly, Tirpitz wrote:

> Only Your Majesty can make the great, responsible decisions about an offensive and coordinate the operations of the fleet with those of the army. Only Your Majesty can—e.g.,in a coalition war—adjust the military situation to the political one.[130]

The combination of the Emperor's vanity and the RMA's bureaucratic triumph over the OK was lethal. The army was never coordinated with the navy. Endless confusion and continued turf wars remained. On paper, the dissolution of the OK in that particular manner looked like only a partial victory for Tirpitz. The Admiralstab, though not nearly as powerful as the OK, won the direction of foreign deployment that Tirpitz had originally coveted. Bureaucratic battles would continue after 1899, especially between the RMA and the Admiralstab, but also, as the fleet grew, with an ever greater number of Front officers. Tirpitz appeared to be only one among equals of those officers who reported directly to the

Emperor. As Prinz Heinrich put it, "previously we had battles between two places. In the future we will fight among seven."[131] In reality, Tirpitz was, by a wide margin, first among these "equals." Parallel reporting lines to the Emperor meant that Tirpitz could avoid problems with more senior admirals because he had top seniority within the RMA. He also had what then counted most, the lead task of the navy to build the fleet. Even though he was not beyond being challenged by others, the role was powerful armor indeed. Many senior officers feared that Tirpitz's power grab would adversely affect the navy in important areas like training and preparedness. Vice Admiral Guido Karcher wrote Diedrichs that Tirpitz would not be satisfied "until he alone possesses everything."[132]

As soon as Tirpitz, the rational actor, won passage of the 1898 Navy Law, Tirpitz, the bureaucratic politician, stepped to the fore. The latter destroyed centralized military control in the navy, except by the distracted and erratic Emperor, who was utterly incapable of exercising it save in a ceremonial way. The reorganization had long and deleterious consequences both for the navy and for the nation.

Knorr retired immediately, and Tirpitz wasted little time using his newfound power against political opposition within the navy. The retired Vice Admiral Victor Valois published a book early in 1899 in favor of cruisers if war came with Britain. Tirpitz's boyhood friend, Curt von Maltzahn, an instructor at the Naval Academy, wanted to publish a manuscript titled *Seekriegslehre* (Lessons of Naval War), in which he questioned the exclusive use of a battleship strategy in a war against a superior seapower, and pointed out the advantages of commerce warfare. Tirpitz got the Emperor to criticize Valois' book, to enjoin publication of Maltzahn's, and to silence unauthorized statements from active and retired officers.[133] Vice Admiral Iwan Oldekop, his old comrade from cadet days, was Inspector of Training. He had both sheltered his subordinate Maltzahn and written letters critical of the Navy Law and the reorganization. He rightly feared that Tirpitz's power would have a chilling effect on intelligent young officers. Tirpitz forced Oldekop into retirement without even the courtesy of a hearing.[134] The ugly side of bureaucratic politics, which could turn lifelong friends into enemies, was fully in play in the immediate aftermath of the 1898 Navy Law.

The new dispensation had the Emperor and Senden meet weekly, on Tuesday and Saturday, with, respectively, Tirpitz and the Chief of the Admiralstab. The meetings with the Admiralstab dealt mainly with operational planning. Meetings with Tirpitz addressed naval policy in general, construction, and domestic political questions pertinent to the navy. With the MK, the Emperor personally decided on promotions of sea officers and many relatively minor matters such as permission for officers to marry. The Emperor also frequently visited naval bases, particularly Kiel and Wilhelmshaven, and meddled in annual maneuvers.[135] He operated hands-on in many matters, including the most trivial. He paid virtually no attention to what should have been his overriding duty, the coordination of national defense between the army and the navy. The Emperor's management style was to have negative consequences for the security of the nation.

10

THE SECOND NAVY LAW, 1899-1900

The ink was scarcely dry on the Emperor's signature to the Navy Law when a new pressure group rose to promote the German Navy.[1] On 30 April 1898 Viktor Schweinburg, editor of Krupp's paper, the *Berliner Neueste Nachrichten*, founded the Deutscher Flottenverein (German Fleet Association) in Berlin. Its professed purpose was

> the arousing, cherishing, and strengthening in the German people of understanding for and interest in the meaning and purpose of a navy. . . . The Navy League considers a strong German navy a necessity, especially for securing the coasts of Germany against the danger of war, for maintaining Germany's position among the world powers, for protecting the general interests and commercial relations of Germany, as well as the honor and security of her citizens engaged in business abroad.[2]

The Flottenverein was an attempt by the big industrialists like Krupp to start a massive lobbying effort for the navy. Trade was much less represented in the founding group than industry was. In 1897 the industrialists were more reticent than later in openly touting the Navy Law for fear of an adverse effect on agrarians in the Reichstag.[3] In March 1898 Krupp's hand was forced by the attempt of a Berlin cod liver oil factory owner, J. E. Stroschein, to found a Deutscher Reichsmarine Verein (German Navy Association). He formed a committee and began an educational effort to promote knowledge of the navy in the name of simple patriotism.[4]

Krupp feared that the new group was too idealistic to represent the interests of heavy industry. Krupp chose Schweinburg as an intermediary between industry and naval agitators. The industrialists hoped to channel patriotic emotion for a larger navy into lucrative contracts for themselves.

The idea of a navy league was not new. Other countries, like Great Britain, had them. There was an attempt as early as 1895 to start one, but it failed because of a lack of interest by Hollmann's RMA. The earlier group wanted to raise money to pay for a ship, but ships were so expensive by then that such an initiative could not succeed.[5]

Tirpitz hesitated at first about a Flottenverein. It could take over the long-term propaganda role that Heeringen and N had orchestrated for the 1898 law; but he feared that N's propaganda role, if too obviously involved with heavy industry, might jeopardize the RMA's political relationship with the Center, and might also alienate the agrarians. In the euphoria of the 1898 Navy Law, Tirpitz, with William II's explicit permission, joined the Flottenverein and encouraged RMA officials, retired officers, and even active sea officers to follow suit. By the end of 1898 Tirpitz evidently had second thoughts. Conflict within the Flottenverein and its blatant association with heavy industry was embarrassing and hard to control. Academics such as Schmoller tried to persuade Schweinburg to broaden its base and give it a less party-political character. By December 1898 Tirpitz realized that he could not control the Flottenverein as he might have wished. Heeringen continued to supply it with materials, but Tirpitz's enthusiasm waned when he felt that it pushed its agenda to the detriment of his own more nuanced approach. Instead of the Flottenverein's drumbeat for ever more ships, Tirpitz and Heeringen understood the role of timing and feared a premature propaganda campaign.[6]

This problem became apparent in the genesis of the 1900 Navy Law, and was even more telling between 1901 and 1908. Tirpitz's credibility in the Reichstag was predicated on his reputation for objectivity, moderation, and trustworthiness. He took great pains to husband this impression. A Flottenverein publicly belligerent toward the RMA might squander one of Tirpitz's greatest assets.

During 1898 the Flottenverein's numbers were relatively small—only a few thousand. Since it was theoretically apolitical, large numbers of government officials, and army and navy officers, could and did join after 1898. Heavy industry and shipping interests pitched in. A patriotic facade, supposedly not interested in political and economic advantage, suited their interests. With the Spanish-American War in 1898, and Germany's colonial troubles in Samoa in 1899, popular enthusiasm for naval expansion again began to grow. By mid-1899 the Flottenverein had 130,000 members. Six months later it had almost 250,000. By 1906 it was just short of 1 million.[7]

In individual states princes assumed protectorates for the organizations. Its national protector was Prinz Heinrich of Prussia. There were more than fifty regional organizations, and almost fifteen hundred local ones, many of which had aristocrats as sponsors. For the 1900 Navy Law, the Flottenverein sponsored three thousand lectures and published more than six million copies of books and pamphlets on naval matters. Membership dues in 1900 brought in 348,000 marks, but 411,000 additional marks were spent. The supplementary funds came from industrial moguls like Krupp, who tried to stay in the background as much as possible.[8]

One reason the Flottenverein grew so fast was that other patriotic societies, such as the Pan-German League, the Colonial Society, and so on, joined en masse. People from these groups were called "corporate" members. Others could join as individuals. Membership dues were scaled according to the individual's ability to pay. Many less navalist young people joined because local branches had regular dances, teas, and the like.[9]

Early in 1899, to Tirpitz's consternation, the Flottenverein, the Pan-German League, and others began to agitate for a new Navy Law. They were checked temporarily by the Social Democrats, who published an indiscreet letter from Schweinburg to the local chapters that urged naval expansion to assist industry. In November 1899 the letter induced some of the "Flottenprofessoren" to form their own group, the "Freie Vereinigung für Flottenvorträge," to propound their pro-navy arguments untainted by money from industry. Secretly it was close to Heeringen, and N funded it. This episode caused a reorganization of the Flottenverein that included Schweinburg's departure. General August Keim assumed leadership of propaganda activities. Most professors soon returned to the fold, and the Flottenverein absorbed most of the people and the functions of the "Freie Vereinigung."[10]

There was great potential for differences of opinion between the RMA and the Flottenverein. In November 1899 Tirpitz told the Bundesrat that "the agitation has begun to move in a direction which does not correspond to the government's." In the previous summer he had acknowledged that the Flottenverein "put business interests above objective considerations."[11] Tirpitz's real troubles with that group began after 1900.

THE IMPERIAL TAX SYSTEM

Fleet development, as it became more expensive after the 1898 Navy Law, was influenced by the peculiarities of the German tax system under Bismarck's Constitution of 1871.[12] The government had estimated the annual budget of the Bundestag and the Reichstag. Before the 1898 Navy Law the only major longer-term appropriation was the army budget, which by then went to the Reichstag only every five years. Even then the Reichstag could vet only additional expenditures. Tirpitz roughly modeled the financial limitations of the 1898 Navy Law on this pattern; however, to expand the fleet further during the six-year period of the law or modify the financial limits, or both, he would have to return to the Reichstag.

Bismarck had feared that the Reichstag would threaten the power and wealth of the conservative elites were it allowed to levy direct taxes, such as those on income and inheritances. Article 70 of the Constitution restricted the right of direct taxation to the federal states that were less democratic. The Reich's taxing powers were limited to tariffs, postal and telegraph services, and indirect taxes on consumption, such as tobacco and alcohol. The Reich government could only borrow for "extraordinary expenditures." Over 80 percent of the Reich's expenditures were for the army and the navy. If Reich income from indirect taxes fell short of military needs, the budget would have to be balanced by "matricular contributions" from the federal states. In this way the wealthy would not be exposed to democratically inspired progressive taxes on wealth and income.

Bismarck's tariffs on grain and industrial products in 1879 not only provided protection for domestic producers but also increased Reich income. Some feared that this good fortune would make the Reich too flush with cash, and therefore too spendthrift. To address this "problem" the Reichstag passed a measure, the Franckenstein Clause, whereby any annual income over 130 million marks had to be sent back to the states, which would, in turn, return some of it to the Reich as so-called matricular contributions. Caprivi's tariff reductions in the early 1890s decreased

Reich income and strained the system. Reich expenditures increased. Franckenstein Clause payments to the states dwindled and were exceeded by increases in state matricular contributions. The process created pressure on the Reich from the states to raise tariffs and to use loans to support the ordinary budget. In the early 1900s, as the power of the left slowly grew in the Reichstag, opposition to the grain tariffs increased, which hit the poor hardest via a higher price for bread. The Social Democrats and part of the Center Party were particularly sensitive on this point.

As naval construction put increasing pressure on the budget, Tirpitz found himself drawn further into parliamentary battles over loans, higher matricular contributions, and the need for finance reform that would allow the Reich government, for the first time, to levy direct taxes. This pressure substantially inhibited Tirpitz's ability to build ships large and powerful enough to compete qualitatively with other navies, especially Britain's. The pressure essentially began in 1906, when Tirpitz found himself in a dilemma. He had to choose between retaining the financial confidence of the Reichstag, and build inferior ships, or construct progressively more expensive Dreadnought-class battleships and battlecruisers.[13] His bland assurances to Lieber in 1897 that technology had stabilized quickly proved to be wrong, This conundrum made Tirpitz appear more parliament-friendly than conservative interest groups and even some naval officers would have liked.

PREPARATIONS FOR AN UNEXPECTED NOVELLE

After the glittering success of the 1898 Navy Law, with construction established through 1904, that summer Tirpitz repaired to St. Blasien for a well-deserved respite. Appearances were deceiving, for he was preparing for his campaign against the OK.

In the quiet of his study, he also planned ahead for fleet development. Tempting gaps remained to be filled. The three tempo would last only through 1900. It was already foreseeable that the price of shipbuilding and armor was creeping upward and threatened the Reichstag's financial limitations. Sometime that summer Tirpitz noted:

> After the expiration of the sexannat [the 1898 Navy Law] or, if technically and organizationally feasible, even earlier, a naval-political and parliamentary situation [should] be created from which the expansion of the navy can

be effected without difficulty, while still preserving the freedom that the Navy Law gives His Majesty.[14]

International events began to heat up in ways that seemed to highlight the utility of naval power in foreign policy. In April 1898 the Spanish American War broke out. In October the Fashoda Affair entered its acute stage. A large British expedition under General Kitchener came south along the Nile and encountered Captain Marchand's much smaller French force that had marched east from French West Africa. French opinion rapidly escalated to calls for war. Cooler diplomatic heads prevailed, and the crisis abated. A key factor in its resolution was that British naval superiority made it obvious even to the most ardent French colonialists that Marchand could not be succored. The impotence of Spain and France because of their naval inferiority did not escape notice in Germany.

Tirpitz later wrote: "In the winter of 1898–1899 I was still firmly resolved to keep to the six year limit." But, he noted, the time was coming when Germany

> [would have] to decide whether the political step towards real seapower was to be ventured upon or whether the whole enterprise was to remain a systematic demonstration. Personally, I was determined to proceed from the first step to the second, paying attention meanwhile to the political situation at home and abroad.[15]

Tirpitz's fidelity to the timing of the sexannat was less than his memoirs suggested. At an RMA meeting of 28 October 1898 he ordered the strictest secrecy, even from other branches of the navy, regarding new fleet initiatives.[16] He had Capelle compose a speculative memo about the navy's further development.[17] Capelle examined how capital expenditures under the existing sexannat could be spent to expand the navy's construction infrastructure for a hypothetical second sexannat that would build a third squadron of battleships. He also speculated about how further expansion of imperial docks and harbors in a second sexannat could address the needs of a third sexannat for a fourth squadron! Capelle spread the proposals over time to make it more palatable to the Reichstag. As early as the fall of 1898 Tirpitz was speculating far beyond the 1898 Navy Law.

On 28 November 1898 Tirpitz, for the first time, raised the question with the Emperor of a Novelle (amendment) to the Navy Law.[18] Tirpitz offered him a series of options. Regarding personnel and material needs, and the anticipated financial pinch owing to rising costs, Tirpitz noted that there were two choices, depending on whether the navy observed the six-year limit or acted before it expired. The Emperor would have to decide, by 1902 at the latest, whether a *Novelle* should be added in 1904 (the expiration of the sexannat), 1903, or 1902. The latter date was desirable because it was a year before the expiration of the sexannat, when the navy's estimates would not have begun to fall because of a lowered building tempo. Tirpitz did not want the deputies to become accustomed to falling estimates. The year 1902 was also when some of Caprivi's trade treaties would have to be renegotiated, and it was a year before a new Army Bill.[19] The 1898 Navy Law, Tirpitz said, had left many needs unfulfilled, including cruisers for service abroad and a re-designation of the *Siegfried* class as battleships for purposes of replacement. These ships were not legally due for replacement until 1910, and replacement of the *Siegfrieds* could hardly justify a Novelle that would only begin to build ships in seven or eight years. To address the need to maintain the three tempo after 1900, he proposed a third battle squadron, plus large and small cruisers and a flying squadron of battleships for service abroad. In total, he suggested a fleet with forty-five battleships, a stunning increase of 130 percent over the nineteen battleships of the 1898 law.

In order to mollify the Reichstag in the event that there was an early Novelle, the 1898 law would have to be executed as planned without exceeding the cost limits. Other needs would have to be subordinated for the duration. If the Emperor decided on no premature Novelle, the navy could marginally exceed the spending limits to meet some pressing needs of the Front.

The Emperor agreed that the RMA should begin to plan for a third battle squadron and put money into dockyards rather than coastal forts. He postponed a decision on the third squadron, but it was clear from the context that it would be in place before 1904. Tirpitz's subsequent adherence to the financial limits was only a cloak to keep the naval question from exploding before he could act at a time of his own choosing. The major question was when to introduce the proposals.[20]

Tirpitz's wish to keep the expansion an RMA in-house secret was soon frustrated. By December 1898 rumors were flying about a new naval proposal. The speculation caused a minor sensation at the first reading of the 1899–1900 estimates. In the Reichstag on 15 December Lieber asked Tirpitz to quash the rumors, but Tirpitz kept silent. He repeated the request on 30 January 1899 before the Budget Commission. Tirpitz misleadingly replied that the government and the Reichstag had agreed on a six-year program the previous spring. He claimed not to have taken seriously the speculation in the December plenary about a new proposal. As a result he had not answered, and noted the RMA's strenuous efforts to stay within the statutory financial limits. To accommodate the Budget Commission, he said:

> I declare expressly that there is no intention to present a new fleet plan. On the contrary, there exists the greatest determination in all parts of the naval administration to carry out the navy law and to stay within its given limits.[21]

Lieber's question created a problem for Tirpitz. He knew that support from Lieber and the Center was absolutely crucial to pass any future proposal. In 1897 he had consulted Lieber before he went to the Reichstag. He had not informed Lieber of the speculative conclusions of the 28 November 1898 meeting, and was in no position to admit publicly that a shortening of the sexannat was under consideration. Paradoxically he had to mislead in order to keep Lieber's confidence and hope that future events would allow him plausible reasons to renege on his pledge to adhere to the original law. He understood the importance of maintaining a good-faith relationship with the Reichstag. This behavior did not make him a "liberal," but it does show that he understood it was in his self-interest to treat the Reichstag with respect rather than contempt.

Consistent with the decisions of the previous November, Capelle juggled the estimates so that a Novelle in 1904 would not cause a startling increase in the estimates for that year. He wanted to hold down the 1900–1902 estimates as much as possible, and make the 1903 estimates as high as possible within the existing financial limits.[22] He saved millions in short-term economic measures, such as the abridgement of coastal defense projects. Much of the hoarded money went to expand the imperial dockyards in Wilhelmshaven. Tirpitz decided to tender early contracts for the two battleships of the 1900 estimates, because lower bids were available then than would be later, although no money could actually be dispersed early.[23]

With his usual solicitude for the limits of the possible in the Reichstag, Capelle, in February 1899, pondered scenarios for an early Novelle. Based on the ideas of the previous fall, he considered a 1902 or 1903 Novelle that would have a third battle squadron for home waters, large and small cruisers for fleet reconnaissance, plus two large cruisers and three battleships for foreign service, to be completed by 1908 and followed by yet another Novelle to replace *Siegfrieds* with battleships. The twenty-five-year replacement clause of the 1898 Navy Law would perpetuate this large fleet into the distant future.[24] Such a flight of long-term fantasy was unusual for the normally pragmatic Capelle, and so it is likely that Tirpitz pushed him to make the proposal.

Meetings with the Emperor in this period also dealt with the need to postpone the interests of the Front in matters such as manpower and training questions in favor of construction. They discussed the naval situation in France and one of Tirpitz's favorite subjects in which to "educate" the Emperor: the futility of a commerce war in the steam era. Tirpitz also suggested that the situation in Asia demanded stationing additional modern ships there. This contradicted his memo of July 1897, which insisted that modern ships should be concentrated in home waters. Particularly notable was his observation that in a war with Japan the fleet should not be bottled up in Kiaochou,[25] a riff on his often proclaimed exhortations about the need for foreign bases. At a meeting on 2 May 1899 William II told Tirpitz that he would decide in the spring of 1900 about the timing of the Novelle.[26]

Tirpitz's statement to the Reichstag had temporarily squelched rumors of an early Novelle, but events were conspiring to raise the issue again. In early spring in 1899 domestic attention was riveted on the government's attempt to pass a canal proposal for the Mittelland/Ruhr area. The canal question was closely linked to the naval one, since the agrarians saw both as symbols of the emerging domination of industry over agriculture. Miquel tried to bridge the gap between industry and agriculture by combining the two in his *Sammlungspolitik*. Naval and canal projects threatened to make the alliance stillborn. In March 1899 the government put the canal bill before the Prussian Diet. It was rejected in August after a long and bitter fight. If the government hoped for another Navy Bill, it would have to drop the canal, lest the agrarians oppose the navy and make a pro-navy majority impossible.[27] This episode is another example, as Eley has pointed out, of the lack of any overarching, system-stabilizing "Plan" to use the navy to enhance a coalition to strengthen the monarchy. Clearly agrarian and naval/industrial interests were much more in conflict than in concert. "There is little indication," according to Eley, "that Tirpitz saw beyond the naval issue in any coherent way at all."[28]

While the Prussian Diet debated the canal, the Samoan controversy involving Germany, Britain, and the United States became acute. Relations with Britain grew strained.[29] The crisis lasted until November 1899 and once again showed Germany's relative impotence in the face of superior British naval power. In October 1898 Chancellor Hohenlohe had asked Tirpitz if Hamburg could be held against a British attack.[30] He replied that holding Hamburg mattered little, since war with Britain meant the extinction of colonies and trade, and a blockade "from Wilhelmshaven to Memel." "We could do nothing," Tirpitz declared, "except make peace as swiftly as possible. War with England would be madness." He concluded that all anti-English policies must cease until Germany had a fleet strong enough to pass the danger zone. "An alliance with Russia and France would be of no use to us."[31] In effect, he advanced a policy of passivity toward Britain at the present time in order to challenge Britain in fifteen or twenty years. This view calls into question the short-term utility of the risk theory, the deterrence value of which would grow only slowly over time. For the same period he wanted to limit readiness to foster construction. This example of *Ressorteifer*, in which his departmental interest often trumped common sense, is an example of bureaucratic politics, the subordination of other important naval functions to the master goal of construction.

Despite or perhaps because of his pessimism, Tirpitz told Hohenlohe in May 1899 that, to avoid losing its world-power position, Germany would have to expand the fleet by around 1901. By then, he said, Germany would be well placed to use resentment over Samoa against Britain to pass a new Navy Law, another example of his contradictory attitude toward the British naval threat. To placate the Center, Tirpitz also thought it desirable to repeal the anti-Jesuit law.[32]

The summer of 1899 was uncomfortable for Tirpitz. To ease his frazzled nerves, in July he took the cure in Bad Nauheim. His old friend, Ahlefeld, Shipyard Director at Kiel, wrote to him: "I'm glad I'm not in your hot kitchen."[33] Tirpitz fretted over agitation for action right away. He was apprehensive about the British reaction to a Novelle at that time and hoped for one in 1901. That date, he believed, was the soonest he could credibly return to the Reichstag.

While still taking his cure, he received a report from the Nachrichtenbüro about the political situation.[34] Halle assumed that the Novelle would be no later than 1901 and perhaps as early as 1900. Capelle annotated the memo. His cautious approach was everywhere evident. Halle's memo emphasized that, if possible, the initiative must appear to come from the Reichstag rather than the RMA, and that it should have the broadest possible base of support. He was confident that help would be forthcoming from the Pan-German League, the Colonial Society, the Flottenverein, and the League of Heavy Industry. Capelle asked, sarcastically, "How many votes [did these groups have] in the Reichstag?" Capelle feared that the industrialists' obvious domination in the Flottenverein might discredit the campaign and anger the agrarians.

Halle assumed unrelenting opposition from the Social Democrats and Eugen Richter. Once again the navy's fate would be in the hands of the Center. He saw the need for concessions to them but still hoped not to "hit the so-called national parties over the head." Capelle suggested, "[Repeal the] Jesuit Law?" Halle proposed offering a Cabinet or Prussian Ministry post to a Center notable and to try to make the Center, in certain questions, "a government party in all but name." Halle wanted to pay for a Novelle in a way that was acceptable to the Center such as through a national inheritance tax. Capelle noted, however, that a national inheritance tax "would knock our best friends in the country over the head," namely, the Conservatives and the National Liberals. Drawing on Capelle's ideas from the spring, Halle suggested a third battle squadron, replacement of the *Siegfrieds*, a "flying squadron" of four battleships for service abroad, plus an appropriate increase in cruisers.

By early May, as noted in his letter to the Chancellor, Tirpitz was leaning toward a Novelle for 1901. Halle's memo reinforced this judgment. In his memoirs Tirpitz frankly admitted that the primary considerations were financial and political.[35] By the summer of 1899 it became even clearer that the financial limits of the 1898 law were too low. The price and size of battleships were increasing.[36] But to ask the Reichstag to lift the financial limits in 1899 or 1900 was awkward. The deputies might ask embarrassing questions about intentions for 1904 and after. The navy would be in the position of enduring the trials of a general debate without the reward of a Novelle. Therefore, a budget increase had to go to the Reichstag accompanied by a Novelle. This maneuver became characteristic of Tirpitz's relations with the Reichstag. It recurred in both 1906 and 1908, when Novelles were deliberately timed to coincide with ship type and cost increases much greater than the navy had previously anticipated. The Novelles were used partly as a "cover" for awkward increases in construction costs.

A second reason for a fall 1900 Novelle was that the building tempo for battleships and large cruisers would drop from three to one after that year. Under the 1898 law the tempo from 1898 was 3:3:3:1:2:2:1. Tirpitz considered the three tempo to be the "normal" rate German industry could most efficiently sustain. The simplest resolution would have been a Navy Bill with a permanent three tempo. Nevertheless, he knew that the Reichstag would never have accepted such a severe abridgement of its budget right. In time, he hoped that the automatic replacement clause would create a permanent three tempo. Once the Reichstag accepted the principle of a fleet organized into squadrons, it had to accept or reject whole squadrons and could not accept or reject individual ships, as had been the practice in Hollmann's time.

Another reason for a 1901 Novelle was that both Tirpitz and Foreign Secretary Bülow believed that the international situation had changed substantially since 1898. Tirpitz cited, as reasons for a fleet increase, Samoa, Diedrichs's awkward encounter with Dewey in Manila Bay, the Fashoda confrontation between Britain and France, and the looming Anglo-Boer clash in South Africa.

Tirpitz may also have had wanted to settle the navy's needs before some of Caprivi's trade treaties expired in 1902, which was certain to lead to a furious battle between industry and agriculture over tariff increases. Another consideration, although it did not materialize, may have been to avoid conflict if the army sought a large increase in its estimates, due for reconsideration in 1903.

Tirpitz's nervousness about the annual September meeting with the Emperor at Rominten was apparent in a letter he wrote to Büchsel in August.[37] He saw himself as "a man who is caught between millstones." He was frustrated by the problem of the timing of the Novelle, but he felt that the situation was not yet ripe: "It is clear from preliminary work that the Novelle request must be much larger than I had sketched out last winter."

He evidently recovered his nerve, because on 28 September at Rominten he presented a program that included elements of the plan of November 1898, plus Capelle's and Halle's ideas from the spring and summer.[38] He envisioned a fleet of forty-five battleships, all but five permanently in home waters, along with twelve large cruisers and thirty small cruisers. Such a fleet would require two additional steps. The first would add the third battle squadron, plus five battleships and four large cruisers for service abroad. The second step would be to add a fourth battle squadron, after the *Siegfrieds* were replaced beginning in 1910.

When the goal was reached, in around 1917, Germany would be so powerful that

> only England would be superior. But even against England, when other factors such as geographical situation, weapons systems, mobilization, torpedo boats, tactical training, planned organizational expansion, and unified leadership by the monarch [Tirpitz apparently felt obliged to slip in this bit of flattery], we would no doubt have good chances. . . . England will have lost any inclination to attack us for general political reasons and because of the sober calculations of their businesses. Such a mass of seapower . . . will enable Your Majesty to pursue overseas policy on a grand scale.

These remarks showed Tirpitz at his most mercurial, out of touch with reality. To consider Germany's geographical position superior to Britain's was a cardinal mistake. (The deterrence question is discussed later in this chapter.) The prior year he had warned Chancellor Hohenlohe of the fiasco that a war with Britain could bring. In the meeting with William II, he did not emphasize that it would take twenty years of uninterrupted building to result in a fleet the size he was dangling before his sovereign's eyes.[39]

Tirpitz asked for a 1901 or a 1902 Novelle, with the timing decision to be made in the spring of 1900. Senden spoke against it, fearing that Tirpitz underestimated parliamentary difficulties. Nevertheless, William II authorized him to go ahead with the planning. Given Tirpitz's strong predilection for the three tempo, it was likely, as the year went on, that Tirpitz would push for 1901, unless political circumstances made it impossible to amend the 1898 law sooner.

Tirpitz went to great pains to keep his plan a secret, which hampered his ability to create a consensus for it, even within the sea officer corps. He asked Bülow, who had the Emperor's ear, to prevent premature leaks.[40] He even enjoined publication of a book (*Seekriegslehre*) by his boyhood friend, Curt von Maltzahn. The book publicly designated England as Germany's main naval opponent.[41] Clearly Tirpitz had no intention of taking the risk theory public before he had to.

The Emperor shattered Tirpitz's cautious timetable. At the launching of the battleship *Karl der Grosse* in Hamburg on 18 October, he made his famous inflammatory statement: "We bitterly need a strong German fleet" (*Bitter Not ist uns eine starke deutsche Flotte*). Whether prompted by the outbreak of the Boer War, or simply by a childish inability to keep a secret, the statement took the initiative out of Tirpitz's hands. Thus the Emperor had put the RMA into the difficult and embarrassing situation which Tirpitz had taken such pains to avoid. If the naval administration applied the brakes, or simply kept quiet and did nothing, the public would take it as an open disagreement between the Emperor and the RMA. Tirpitz saw no choice but to accelerate the detail work on the Novelle, still in its rough planning stage. He wanted a delay, at least until the bill could be put into proper form with the same massive documentation as there had been for the 1898 law. The Emperor wanted it introduced immediately.

Tirpitz set out to create consensus for the initiative among the officer corps. This was particularly difficult in the fall of 1899, because many officers had raw feelings over the dissolution of the OK the previous spring. In a confidential meeting with officers at the Wilhelmshaven Casino,[42] he reviewed the progress since 1897 and proudly underlined how he had won the nation's enthusiasm for the navy. In a general way he revealed his intention, over time, to double the size of the fleet. He warned of parliamentary difficulties and appealed for the support of the officer corps. He foresaw conflicts among powerful domestic interest groups about the forthcoming tariff question, for which the canal battle of the summer was only a prelude. The army question could arise again in 1903 and might compete with the navy for resources. At the same time, the situations in Samoa[43] and South Africa had inflamed public opinion. Rhetorically he asked the officers whether the naval administration should leave unused what he called the present "window of opportunity." William II's speech forced Tirpitz to abandon his customary secretive ways. He anticipated that soon the naval question would be loudly debated in the national press. He acknowledged that the battle would be harder than in 1897–98.[44]

As Tirpitz predicted, the newspapers created a storm in late October. Only the papers under the control of heavy industry were unconditionally in favor of a Novelle. The Emperor's speech was a painful shock for the agrarian papers, which demanded that the Ruhr/Mittelland Canal be permanently dropped in exchange. The Center press vainly hoped that the Emperor's speech was just his personal opinion and not an announcement of a Novelle. It argued that the 1898 sexannat should remain in force.[45]

On 23 October Tirpitz temporarily pushed the imperial genie back into the bottle with flattery.[46] Not without irony, he offered the Emperor "the thanks of the navy for the epoch-making speech in Hamburg," a mighty impulse that "unchained a great movement." Because a Reichstag interpellation was now certain, the government would have to concede that a Novelle was coming, and he suggested the year 1901, with the announcement held off until the fall of 1900. In the short range, Tirpitz asserted, we must simply say that no Novelle was intended for 1900. It would take time to prepare and to steer opinion in the right direction. The Emperor concurred with Tirpitz's time line.

The next day an article in the official *Norddeutsche Allgemeine Zeitung* stated that no Novelle was contemplated for the following spring, because the 1898 law corresponded to Germany's present maritime interests. If circumstances required, the article hinted that a change in the sexannat would have to be considered.[47]

On 26 October Tirpitz saw Chancellor Hohenlohe. Tirpitz claimed to have been so impressed by the favorable public response to pro-navy agitation, and by England's growing difficulties in South Africa, that he changed his mind again. He wanted a Novelle proposal earlier, either immediately in response to an interpellation or by government initiative in the fall of 1900. Why he changed his mind within days is unclear. His only hesitation seemed to come from the difficulty of preparing a fully formulated bill and supporting tables by mid-November. Bülow and Lucanus, Chief of the Civil Cabinet, were also eager to act in the next Reichstag session. The more cautious Chancellor was reluctant, because it would require putting off a revived Canal Bill and a Navy Bill might require concessions to the Center on the Jesuit Law. Tirpitz wanted to pass the bill while the British were heavily engaged in South Africa. The Chancellor warned that trouble in the Reichstag would outweigh other advantages, and he felt that Tirpitz had overstated public enthusiasm for a Novelle.[48]

Hohenlohe's weakness was such that Tirpitz, without the Chancellor's permission, wrote an unsigned article on 29 October in the *Norddeutsche Allgemeine Zeitung*. It highlighted the drop in tempo in 1901 and publicly, for the first time, argued the need for third and fourth squadrons and for dropping the 1898 cost limitations. Because Tirpitz was a member of Hohenlohe's Cabinet, this was an act of gross insubordination. Within the next few days, the old and tired Chancellor withdrew his opposition. On 2 November the Emperor announced to the federal princes that a Novelle would be introduced that winter.[49] The same day Tirpitz explained to the Bundesrat that, despite his best efforts to stay within the limits of the 1898 Navy Law, the Spanish-American War had shown the necessity of thicker armor, despite its increasing price. If there were no Novelle, new ships would be weaker than those of other nations. He conceded that he had had a role in driving the process, and argued that the Emperor's speech and the reaction to it had forced him to act. No new taxes were contemplated. The cost could be covered by loans, with a minimal increase in the continuing budget.[50]

Four days later Hohenlohe sent a letter, obviously written by Capelle or Tirpitz, to the princes that justified the need for another double squadron.[51] Replies were not universally favorable and contained complaints, particularly from Bavaria, that cited needs for the army and for social purposes.[52]

Ever since the Emperor's speech, the Etatsabteilung, the Nachrichtenbüro, and other departments in the RMA worked feverishly to prepare a draft, as well as massive sets of tables and statistics for the Reichstag and for negotiations with the Reich Treasury.[53] The first draft provided for an increase of one squadron of eight battleships, plus two large and six small cruisers. Replacement of the eight *Siegfrieds* with battleships would create a fourth battle squadron. Three additional large cruisers would be for service overseas. The material reserve would increase by two battleships and one large and one small cruiser. The financial limits were dropped altogether. In an appended note, Capelle wrote that the *Siegfrieds* would begin to be replaced in 1910.[54] As late as 8 November Tirpitz still wanted to include battleships for service abroad, since he ordered that tables be prepared to include this. The plan, including five battleships for service abroad, would have assured continuation of the three tempo until 1916.[55]

At an RMA meeting on 8 November Dähnhardt presented the first draft of the Begründung. First and foremost, if the financial limitations were dropped, the Novelle would be an even more one-sided Reichstag commitment than the 1898 law. His justification was that fixed sums of money did not allow sufficiently for increasing costs. Other countries were also expanding trade and navies, particularly Japan and the United States. He presented the ritual argument of a large fleet to protect Germany's ever growing economic interests. For the efficiency and financial health of the private and imperial dockyards three large and three small ships per year were the optimum number, an implicit acknowledgment of the existence of a "military-industrial complex." Germany needed another double squadron, with reserves, of thirty-eight battleships in a home fleet. Four additional battleships for service abroad would be requested in a Novelle in 1911. The most politically significant part of the draft Begründung was the statement that "our strength must be such that our fleet has a chance of successfully withstanding an attack from the greatest seapower." This idea formed the kernel of the risk theory.[56]

Even though the "risk" idea became the main public rationale of Tirpitz's naval policy, he feared to express it too openly. On the one hand, the British Navy was a handy whipping boy for mass agitation; on the other, Tirpitz, for many years, feared a preventive attack on the fleet while it was weak. He worried about British action, even though Britain at the time was heavily preoccupied with the Boer War. On 16 November he wrote to the German Naval Attaché in London:

> We must know if the English government plans to introduce into Parliament any naval proposals as a result of the German Novelle, and if they consider us an opponent at sea, or whether it has made references to the German fleet.[57]

No doubt Tirpitz would have preferred more discretion about the anti-British dimension of the Novelle. The high-handed actions of the British against the Boers made it impossible to justify any large Navy Bill without some public reference to England.[58]

Reich Treasury Secretary Thielmann was not as sanguine as Tirpitz on finances. He was not prepared to offer a long-term and binding financial plan. He agreed that Reich revenues would likely increase, but he pointed out that social programs and the army would consume a portion of the revenue growth.[59] The Emperor chimed in with a threat to dissolve the Reichstag if the deputies rejected the Novelle, a prospect the Chancellor feared would create chaos.[60]

On 29 November the government informed the Bundesrat that a Navy Bill was under preparation for two double squadrons of battleships.[61] At the first reading of the 1900 naval estimates on 11 December, the government made a similar declaration in the Reichstag.[62]

Tirpitz sprang into action to pave the way. At the end of December the Schweinburg Affair in the Navy League was at its height. Tirpitz was forced to act after the Social Democrats published Schweinburg's letter to local chapters of the Navy League urging a Novelle to help industry. Tirpitz was afraid that this letter would discredit the Novelle in the eyes of both the agrarians and the Center. On 2 December he asked Krupp to use "all your influence" to quickly remove Schweinburg from the Secretaryship of the Navy League.[63]

Even more central was his relationship with Lieber and the Center. Lieber, a year before, had feared a Novelle and had warned Hohenlohe against it.[64] As Capelle told the story later,[65] Tirpitz had struggled with his conscience over whether to keep to his prior assurances to the Reichstag to stick to the six-year commitment, but he decided to "sacrifice" himself (i.e. renege on his prior promise) in view of military considerations and ordered Capelle to begin secret negotiations with the Reichstag. Capelle immediately approached Dr. Wilhelm Barth, a Progressive deputy with whom he was friendly, to ask his advice. Barth confidentially told Capelle that if Tirpitz were pressured by unconditional necessity, and was willing to "sacrifice" himself, it would make sense to go for the whole double squadron and not to make the mistake of asking for too little. If properly presented, Barth believed, it would pass. Tirpitz agreed. Capelle wrote that Lieber was upset about the idea. The latter had complained and scolded, and made accusations about Tirpitz and Capelle.

Tirpitz tried to pacify Lieber. In a letter of 6 December Tirpitz acknowledged that he had heard that Lieber was upset but that he had not spoken to him personally. Tirpitz claimed that he had only done this out of consideration for Lieber's difficulties lest he be seen as too close to Tirpitz. He expressed his confidence that Lieber would again support the navy. This expectation came from Tirpitz's understanding of Lieber's eagerness to keep his party's decisive position, and he also understood Lieber's mortal fear of a Reichstag dissolution.[66]

Lieber was again caught in the crossfire between factions of his party, although he had more control over the party than he had had in 1897–98. Tirpitz tried to enlist Civil Cabinet Chief Lucanus to support the repeal of paragraph 2 of the Jesuit Law. "The longer we delay this kind of accommodation, the more difficult it will get,"[67] he wrote. Tirpitz, who cared nothing for the retention of the Jesuit Law, did his best to help; nevertheless, Conservative and National Liberal opposition made the repeal impossible.

The debate on the estimates began on 11 December. A Novelle was announced but without details.[68] The National Liberals offered strong support; Richter and the Social Democrats chided the newly promoted Vice Admiral Tirpitz for breaking his earlier promise that he would stick to the sexannat. Lieber and the Center at first took no position. It was clear that the Center would be decisive, and that the Rhineland faction again held the balance of power within the party. Although Tirpitz was optimistic that he could win over the Center, the issue was by no means clear when the Reichstag adjourned for Christmas.

Fate intervened in the last days of 1899. Events in South Africa made passage of the Novelle almost a certainty. Tirpitz could hardly have planned it better himself. The British had blockaded Delagoa Bay in South Africa to keep the Boers from receiving supplies from European sympathizers. British cruisers seized three German packet boats on their way to South Africa. After a search, all were released except *Bundesrath*, whose captain was falsely accused of carrying contraband. The German government protested vehemently, until Lord Salisbury, in mid-January, ordered *Bundesrath*'s release, apologized, offered compensation, and assured that German ships would no longer be stopped.[69] Tirpitz was delighted at the seizure. "Now we have the wind we need to blow our ship into port; the Navy Law will pass."[70]

The *Bundesrath* Affair produced an uproar in the press. The Center papers dropped their opposition. A wave of Anglophobia swept through the "national" parties, including the agrarians. Even the Anglophile Hamburg merchants were angered.[71]

The Emperor was impatient that Tirpitz had not yet officially introduced the Novelle. On 10 January he wrote to Hohenlohe to demand that Tirpitz present it within eight days. He claimed that "the Admiral is rather conceited" and wants to "cut a good figure." Tirpitz has been "tinkering with it since 18 October." "It is well known that under Bismarck law proposals were drafted and introduced within a single day."[72] Tirpitz was miffed at this childish imperial harassment.

The draft law and supporting tables were ready for the Emperor by 15 January. Between the plans outlined in rough form at the meeting of 8 November and the final version, there were three handwritten and four printed law drafts.[73] The final draft called for an increase of one fleet flagship, two squadrons of eight battleships each, two large and eight small cruisers as reconnaissance forces for the home fleet, with two battleships and one large and two small cruisers as material reserve. For service abroad, the proposal called for five large cruisers or battleships.

The fleet would be reduced by the eight *Siegfrieds* which would be replaced after their twenty-five-year lifespan by eight of the battleships noted above. By 15 January Tirpitz asked for large cruisers instead of battleships for service abroad, and so he dropped the "or battleships." The battlefleet, after the law was completed in 1920, would number four squadrons, including reserves of thirty-eight battleships and their reconnaissance forces.

The Begründung presented the danger of blockade by a superior opponent. Germany would face economic stagnation and, eventually, strangulation. Misleadingly, in view of the anti-English orientation of the 1898 law, it said that the prior law did not consider the possibility of war "against a great seapower [i.e. the British]."

Germany could not defend its overseas interests with 42 cruisers while the strongest seapower had 206. The defense of overseas interests had to be in home waters. To explain how this could be done, the Begründung gave the first public declaration of the risk theory:

> In order to protect under the existing circumstances Germany's world trade and colonies, there is only one means: Germany must possess a fleet so strong that a war, even for the strongest seapower, would contain so much danger that through such a war its own existence would be put into question. For this purpose it is not unconditionally necessary that the

German battlefleet be as strong as that of the greatest seapower. Such a
great seapower will in general not be in a position to concentrate its whole
striking power against us. But even if it should succeed in meeting us with
great superiority, the defeat of a strong German fleet would still so greatly
weaken the opponent that in spite of the victory it achieved, then its own
power position would no longer be succored by a sufficient fleet.

To achieve this goal, Germany would need four battle squadrons with
their accompanying auxiliaries.[74] The 1898 Navy Law had provided only
two. With four squadrons, special coastal defense ships would no longer
be necessary. Cruisers abroad could defend Germany's interests in a war
against a lesser seapower.

If a fleet of this size was necessary it had to be built as soon as possible.
Because of rising costs in ships, guns, armor, and so on, the Begründung
deemed it impossible to stay within the sexannat and its financial limitation. The best assurance of steady and economical growth was to keep the
three tempo for large ships and to arrange new and replacement building
accordingly, while keeping to the age limits of twenty-five years for battleships, twenty for large cruisers, and fifteen for small cruisers.

Such a program would cost 1,306 million marks for shipbuilding and
arming, an average of 81.6 million marks per year. The entire sum for na
val purposes over the next sixteen years, including a capital budget for improvements in docks, harbors, and so forth, and continuing expenditures
for wages, ship maintenance, and the like totaled 3,722 million marks.[75]

Under the Emperor's command authority, battleships had to be built
in squadrons. The law would acknowledge that the Reichstag had the
will to create a fleet. Without this commitment, it would be extremely
difficult to acquire personnel and material, and to get private building
yards to invest the vast sums of necessary capital.[76]

The Begründung anticipated possible objections to the legal establishment of the fleet and gave pointed refutations. What if the political,
financial, and technical assumptions behind the plan were to change over
such a long period?[77] The government anticipated no radical changes, but
if such change occurred the two houses would always be in a position
to modify the law. Did not the very introduction of the Novelle prove
that the method of legal establishment was incorrect? The Begründung
pointed out that the sexannat part of the law applied only to new construction. The rest of the law—maintenance of the fleet, personnel, and

replacement of ships over the age limit—was truly an *Äternat* (eternal law).

The Bundesrat rubber-stamped the Novelle on 16 January.[78] Debate in the Reichstag began on 8 February.[79] The propaganda campaign was by now in full swing. In a spectacular show for Rhinelanders, Heeringen sent a division of torpedo boats all the way up the river to Karlsruhe.[80] He also persuaded cigarette and chocolate companies to put pictures of German warships on their packets. Toy companies sold model warships.[81] Naval propaganda was even directed at the army. For example, articles in the *Militär-Wochenblatt* argued that a stronger battlefleet would take the burden of coastal defense off the army and prevent a blockade so that the army could be fed in wartime.[82]

Once again, all would depend on the Center and, to a lesser extent, the agrarians. To Tirpitz's dismay, Lieber fell seriously ill at the end of January. Dr. Franz Schädler and Adolf Grober replaced him as floor leader, and Aloys Fritzen became the reporter for the naval estimates in the Budget Commission. On the first day of debate, Schädler spoke guardedly in favor of the fleet, tacitly in the hope of compensation, especially wine tariffs, popular in the Catholic wine-growing areas.[83] On 27 April the Center openly stated: "No tariff, no fleet."[84] Social Democrats attacked the law saying that it would ignite an arms race. As before, no one in power listened seriously. Richter proposed that the cruisers intended for service abroad not be included in the law, especially since none would be built until 1906 anyway.

A sterling example of Capelle's work methods with opponents is how he handled Richter on this point. Capelle approached him privately after Richter stormed out of the debate. In response to Richter's complaint about taking up the cruiser question six years before it was necessary, Capelle slyly replied that the navy was only trying to be clear and straightforward with the Reichstag. When Richter asked why not take them up later, Capelle shrewdly saw in this comment the possibility of a compromise. Even though Richter would vote against any bill, perhaps others would find the idea appealing.[85]

On 12 February the bill went to the Budget Commission. Most of the debate concerned how the law would be paid for. The Commission finally settled on a tariff on wine, brandy, and champagne, which both the Center and the agrarians wanted. Ultimate acceptance of the law was never

seriously in doubt after the *Bundesrath* Affair. When Treasury Secretary
Thielmann finally accepted a tariff on foreign champagne and certain
other wines, the delays cleared up. On 22 May the Budget Commission
reported favorably to the plenum.[86] By then the agrarians were given assurances that their needs would be addressed when the Caprivi tariffs
expired in 1902 and after. Tirpitz had previously hoped to keep the navy
law separate from tariff policy; but once he saw that the Center would
accept it, he indicated his willingness to go along with the agrarians on
future tariff reform.[87] This decision was opportunistic on Tirpitz's part
and not an aspect of any wide-ranging "plan."

The Navy Law did not emerge unscathed from the Commission.
Because of the complicated financial provisions in the 1898 law and the
navy's desire to drop them, the Commission recommended that the old
law be repealed instead of amended. The remainder would be incorporated into the Novelle to form an entirely new law. Since this changed
nothing except to get rid of the vexing limitations, Tirpitz was happy to
comply.

Tirpitz made another "concession" that he secretly favored. Center deputy Müller (Fulda), the "opponent" of the navy who had served
Tirpitz so well in 1898, moved that ships for foreign service, not due to
be started until 1906 anyway, be deleted from the law, the same idea
Richter had inadvertently given to Capelle. The fleet would then consist
of thirty-eight battleships, fourteen instead of twenty large cruisers, and
thirty-eight instead of forty-five small cruisers. In exchange for this "concession," Müller made another motion, also accepted, that would drop
the financial limitations altogether. Tirpitz accepted this package with
alacrity, with the explicit provision that he would ask for cruisers again
when he needed them.

Why he was so willing to do this is illustrative of his method of
operation:

> As we could not put down more than three big ships in a year, owing to
> the limitations of our technical arrangements . . . the six [large] cruisers
> which were cancelled were not ordered until 1906. Thus the cancelling of
> them did not really amount to anything. On the occasion of their rejection,
> however, in 1900 I remarked that we would introduce a supplementary
> demand for them within the specified period [i.e., 1906 or before]. Hence
> the demand for these cruisers in 1906. I preferred the *whole* of the foreign
> service fleet to be cancelled in 1900; this left a sufficiently big item for the
> supplementary demand.[88]

Implicit in Tirpitz's acceptance of the deletion was his belief that he could retain the Reichstag's confidence over the next six years. He clearly did not realize in 1900 how fast costs would escalate. In the years before 1906, Tirpitz was therefore forced to put his relationship with the Center ahead of other demands, such as those from the Front.

There is a curious document from this period in the files of the Etats Department, dated early February 1900, giving a cost estimate for a third double squadron—another nineteen battleships plus accompanying cruisers and torpedo boats. If completed, it would have meant fifty-seven battleships and twelve large cruisers in European waters. Although initialed by Dähnhardt, there is no evidence that anything was done with it but to deposit it in the files. This was a harbinger of similar thought pieces beginning in 1903, but, without further evidence, the historian cannot attribute any contemporary significance to it.[89]

On 12 June 1900 the Reichstag, by a two to one margin, accepted the bill unchanged. Tirpitz's second double squadron and its reconnaissance forces became part of the legal establishment. The Reichstag did not pass the new law solely for reasons of "hurrah patriotism" and economic self-interest. These factors were important to the National Liberals and the Conservatives, even including the Agrarians to a degree.[90] The case of the Center was more complicated. Although the Center press remained cool toward the Navy Bill, even its historian, Karl Bachem,[91] admits that the gratuitous seizure of the *Bundesrath* and consequent agitation made serious inroads on Center voters and deputies. Bachem also emphasizes the effects of the statistical evidence, which showed a startling increase in maritime trade, defenseless in the face of an envious England. That the French introduced a large Navy Bill on 30 January lent credibility to Tirpitz's argument that other powers were building.[92] The lawyers and small businessmen of the Center delegation could not be expected to see strategic flaws in anything as sophisticated as the risk theory. Deputies of all parties, except the Social Democrats and the Richter faction, were used to following the government's lead in defense matters, especially when they appeared so organized and documented.

Bachem also claims that the government had dropped hints that when the Navy Law passed, the Jesuit Law would be repealed. He even asserts that the government tried to make it appear as if the Pope supported the Navy Law.[93] Tirpitz had tried to persuade the Emperor in favor of repeal, but he failed owing to the opposition of Bülow and Lucanus.[94]

Tirpitz never promised Lieber anything on the subject, except that he would try. In 1900, like in 1898, the Center had a choice between attaining at least nominal "hegemony" in the hope of getting something or returning to opposition and getting nothing.[95]

The European reaction to the law was surprisingly mild. The French and the Russians were favorably disposed toward German naval expansion.[96] The British reaction was lukewarm. On 13 June 1900, the *Times* wrote:

> We not unnaturally regard the growing naval ambition of Germany with a certain feeling of genuine sympathy, which is, nevertheless, not unalloyed with concern. . . . Paper programs are not always performances.

Still, the article admitted that the Navy Law might have an effect on the growth of the British navy.[97] British attention was then focused on the Boer War, and the 1900 law passed with little notice in the British press.[98]

The 1900 Navy Law marked the culminating moment in Tirpitz's naval career. Despite his repudiation of a public commitment to the sex-annat, he persuaded the Reichstag to approve a bill that, over time, would double the size of the navy and catapult Germany well beyond the modest establishment of the 1898 law. He even devised a clever scheme—the risk theory—which would protect Germany's bustling overseas commerce in the absence of either overseas bases or a force of cruisers comparable in size to other imperial powers. He had won a bruising bureaucratic battle within the navy with the dissolution of the OK, which completely fragmented naval command. All important positions in the navy now reported directly to William II, and Tirpitz was the most influential among them. His *Ressorteifer* ascended within the navy as well as against outside agencies. He was not totally dominant, however. He was subject to the whims and pouts of his imperial master to whom he was indispensable because he could tame the lions in the Reichstag. Challenges would occasionally arise from the new Admiralstab and the Front; nevertheless he was in an unparalleled position to enforce his will upon the navy.

In his congratulations, William II wrote of "the difficulties with which you have had to contend," and that he had seen "with what energy and true diligence you have waged the battle," and that Tirpitz had achieved "the highest goals I have set."[99] On 12 June 1900, the same day the law passed, Tirpitz was raised to the hereditary nobility. He and his descendants would be entitled to add the coveted "von" to their names.[100] Tirpitz graciously credited Capelle. "The great goal would not have been achieved without you. I assure you of my present and lifelong gratitude."[101]

As Kehr has pointed out, 1900 was the last year advocates could claim that construction was necessary because of fast growing economic development. Since the economy began to falter late in 1900, any further such assertions would have met with public derision. The Emperor's impetuous speech of 18 October 1899 got Tirpitz to take up the gauntlet, and helped the bill to victory at the last moment when economic arguments seemed to support it.[102]

BUDGET RIGHT

The 1898 Navy Law contained financial limits that pinched the RMA almost immediately. To escape this dilemma was one of Tirpitz's principal reasons to amend the sexannat before it expired in 1903. The 1900 law not only doubled the fleet, but also lifted the financial limits. Tirpitz quietly boasted to the Emperor that he had secured, for shipbuilding at least, an "iron budget." In his memoirs he wrote that the 1900 law

> allowed a free hand as regards finances. The Reichstag surrendered the possibility of refusing money for the new types of vessels [e.g., later on for Dreadnoughts] that were increasing in size and cost, unless it was prepared to bring upon itself the reproach of building inferior ships.[103]

Central to Berghahn's view of Tirpitz is the idea that the fleet was built both against England and against the Parliament. The iron budget, in this view, signified a profound and long-lasting victory over the Reichstag. Because the latter had legally established the size of the fleet by squadron, it seemed morally obligated to provide the money, and actually did so each year, according to the nonbinding cost estimates appended to the Navy Law. It would seem as though the Reichstag's compliance is absolute proof that the 1900 law had, indeed, established an "iron budget." In fact, compliance concealed a deeper and more problematic reality, and the assertion of an iron budget is an exaggeration.

After 1900 the navy labored under a financial limitation, albeit self-imposed. Even before Dreadnoughts came in 1905–6 to skyrocket shipbuilding costs, the fact is that Tirpitz did all he could to live within the nonbinding limits of the cost projections the RMA made in 1900. He still had to ask the Reichstag each year for the naval estimates. As long as he stayed within or very close to the figures projected in the 1900 addenda, the passage of the annual estimates was a pro forma matter. He knew that if he exceeded them significantly he might be in trouble. He also knew that he would have to return to the Reichstag in 1906 if he hoped to get the overseas cruisers that were dropped in the 1900 law, and this prospect seems to have made him cautious in his estimates requests from 1901 to 1905, even when he was under great pressure from the Emperor and interest groups to do otherwise. Juggle funds though he might, and raid the capital budget to meet increasing shipbuilding costs, he never in that period asked for significantly more than he had projected in 1900. This practice, he felt, was absolutely essential to preserve the good will of the Reichstag.

Tirpitz's caution, which continued through the 1906 Novelle, was justified. As Fairbairn has pointed out, in the 1898 and 1903 election campaigns the fleet's opponents attacked the Novelle with great effectiveness based both on cost and the regressive nature of the Reich's tax system. The Richter left liberals and the Social Democrats attacked both fleet and tariffs with great gusto and, especially with the latter issue, achieved significant electoral gains. The Center deputies who supported the fleet did so to highlight their swing status in the Reichstag; however, they explained their central role to their voters as the party that *limited* (Fairbairn's italics) the government's naval demand, and they claimed credit for scaling down excesses. The Center pitched its election appeal as the party of prudent thrift. It boasted, somewhat misleadingly, that it had avoided new taxes on mass consumption items and had kept the burden from falling on the poor. Conservatives avoided, as far as possible, any mention of the fleet in their campaigns, or, when they did, they linked it with the army in a generally patriotic context. Among the larger parties, only the National Liberals had genuine enthusiasm for the fleet, and this advocacy apparently did not advance their electoral success in those two elections.[104] The point of the 1906 amendment was not just to add cruisers; it also continued the three tempo beyond 1905, and got the Reichstag to accept a new and much higher table of shipbuilding costs to build ships competitive with the British Dreadnoughts.

Another interesting piece of evidence that the navy, within its deepest counsels, did not really regard the budget as "iron" is contained in a
lecture Tirpitz delivered on 10 April 1910 in Kiel before a group of high
officers.[105] The lecture was titled, "The Development and Significance
of the Navy Law." After a historical overview of Prussian/German naval
policy and construction since 1853, Tirpitz explained how he had fundamentally changed and rationalized the process. He noted that the law
had acquired "somewhat of the permanent character of an *Äternat*,"[106]
but he partially contradicted the point with regard to new (as opposed to
replacement) construction:

> The Reichstag has a completely free hand to delay the new construction, as
> the [1900] plan foresees for the years 1901–1905, or in any other time. This
> is naturally a risk, and in this period Richter proposed to delay one of the
> battleships. But the government makes the assumption about the law that
> the Reichstag, which legally established the size of the fleet, also would be
> willing to provide the money in a tempo suited to the financial efficiency of
> the country, i.e., to reach the tempo that the government plan foresaw. *The
> government has not yet been disappointed. Up to now, all new building has
> been approved according to plan.* (My emphasis)[107]

This comment indicates that the Navy Law, to a degree, was a bluff.
Tirpitz had a mighty incentive to keep the Reichstag's goodwill by behav-
ing *as if* he were a parliamentary minister responsible to the Reichstag.
This does not mean he was a "liberal," just that he used a pragmatic approach to get what he wanted. In dealing with deputies and the parties,
Tirpitz functioned as a rational actor, because he wisely recognized that
the bullying tactics that might work with the Emperor and the branches
of the navy would not work in the Parliament.

Crossed out from the lecture draft, possibly because it was decided
that this point could not be shared even with admirals, was the following
noteworthy comment:

> About replacement building the situation is different. The law binds the
> Reichstag to approve the replacement ships in the years envisioned. But the
> Reichstag is *not* bound to approve in full the size of the [financial] install-
> ment the government requests in a given estimate. . . . The government
> wants to pay for a battleship or a large cruiser in four [annual] installments,
> and for a small cruiser in three. But the Reichstag is in no way prevented
> by the law from making the installments so small that a ship could only be
> completed in six, or eight, or ten years. Indeed, to posit the extreme case,

the Reichstag would be observing the *letter* of the law if they approved only ten pfennigs for the building of a given replacement ship.[108]

Granted, this would have been a nightmare scenario, but it shows that the Navy Law was not an *Äternat* in any literal sense. No wonder the navy kept this notion secret.

Eckart Kehr, in the late 1920s, had an inkling of what Tirpitz was up to. When Tirpitz presented the 1900 law,

> he voluntarily gave up the fetters of the septennial budget and instituted an open relationship between the Reichstag and the government. Thereupon the Reichstag felt less shackled, and out of this freedom that Tirpitz had granted it and which the army did not dare to emulate, grew the Reichstag's great sympathy for the fleet and its inclination to approve naval demands more readily than those of the army. From the point of view of the state and the military, the Prussian method of keeping the military at arm's length from the Reichstag, the nation, and the civilian sector, allowing as little parliamentary influence over the armed forces as possible, proved to be less effective than Tirpitz's approach. He enhanced it further in the course of inspection visits by Reichstag deputies by creating the impression that the Reichstag was a control organ for the accomplishments of the navy, an impression that was, characteristically, sufficient to evoke angry protests on the part of the Prussian State Ministry.[109]

Manfred Rauh has argued that Berghahn's view of Tirpitz's claims about the abridgement of the budget right was overdrawn,[110] if he means that Tirpitz successively had to lowball his plans to a clueless Reichstag. Despite his propaganda and occasional trickery, the navy had strong and genuine support, and to the degree that the Reichstag bound itself, it did so willingly for patriotic reasons as well as on political and economic grounds. Tirpitz played most of his cards openly with the Parliament. Rauh goes too far, however, when he sees Tirpitz's peaceful parliamentary involvement, especially with the Center, as somehow a prelude to a parliamentary system. For Tirpitz, a lifelong conservative in most respects, cooperation was a matter of expediency to persuade the Reichstag to build a powerful navy. The Reichstag's support was in response to the political popularity of national defense in that period.

Perhaps Thomas Nipperdey got it right. "Coast defense and then the battlefleet were built [and expanded] not against, but with public opinion." "Alongside traditional Prussian militarism, modern national imperial 'navalism' came about, not only 'from above' but also 'from below.'"[111] Nipperdey agrees that the fleet was built against England, but not, to the same degree, against the Reichstag. Tirpitz may have tried to convince the Emperor that Parliament was helpless, but he himself knew better. He gave the Reichstag the order, rationality, and predictability they craved, and their commitment to the navy was voluntary. The randomness and "cow trading" of the Hollmann era were over.[112] The need to keep building capacity efficient via the three tempo pushed the Reichstag forward. The outcome, foreseen by few in the Reichstag until it actually happened, was a naval arms race, and a merry-go-round that was hard to jump off. As Nipperdey argues:

> The amazing thing was that Tirpitz, who had wanted to bind the Reichstag in constitutional chains, adjusted himself in a thoroughly modern way to the realities of parliament. He was a great and successful tactician, partly through taking care in contacts with the decisive Center Party and via the organization of fleet visits for deputies [including Social Democrats] etc. He used new and modern concepts, mobilized the public, and this influenced the parties.[113]

William Michaelis, a naval officer and keen observer of Tirpitz, later wrote that the admiral had convinced the Reichstag that the government as well as the Parliament would be bound; but that Tirpitz's *Ressorteifer* was such that

> over time, he felt himself so strongly bound by the navy law that he felt he had to reject almost all proposals to improve it between Novelles, with the comment that it would 'endanger the navy law.' He especially used this formula to reject proposals that came from other places, e.g., the Emperor, the Fleet Chief, or the Admiralstab. He did not want to concede that improvement of his infallibly correct work could come from someone other than himself or his closest confidants.[114]

Michaelis recognized in Tirpitz the classic bureaucratic politician.

THE RISK THEORY

At the heart of Tirpitz's justification for a large navy was the "risk theory." First stated publicly in the Begründung to the 1900 Navy Law, the theory's central issue was the relationship between Germany and England. Tirpitz argued that, without a battlefleet, Germany's extensive overseas interests would be at the mercy of British goodwill. During his own experience abroad, from cadet to admiral, German dependence on British bases for coal, repairs, and so on, was enormous. If an Anglo-German war should break out over Britain's jealousy of Germany's growing sea trade, like the earlier wars Britain had waged against other European countries, or even if Britain simply abandoned its free-trade policy, Germany would suffer grievously. Without a fleet, Germany would have no leverage over British policy. The only way to obtain such leverage, Tirpitz argued, would be the construction of as powerful a fleet of battleships as possible to be concentrated in the North Sea. If Germany had such a powerful fleet, Britain could attack it and probably defeat it; but, in the process, Britain's naval position against the other continental naval powers, France and Russia, would be gravely endangered and its supremacy lost. This potential threat would, Tirpitz believed, enhance Germany's attractiveness as an ally to France and Russia, both of them on bad terms with Britain at the turn of the century. Alternatively, to counter the possibility of a continental alliance, Britain might come to terms with Germany, and the German fleet would thereby have alliance value (*Bündnisfähigkeit*). In 1900 the possibility that Britain would come to terms with France and Russia was considered very remote.

To defend worldwide trade the fleet would, paradoxically, be concentrated in the North Sea or, as Tirpitz had put it in 1897, "between Helgoland and the Thames." This approach was Tirpitz's seemingly elegant deterrence strategy to deal with the insoluble geographic dilemma of how to defend German interests abroad. The scheme further assumed that Britain would, from the outset of a war, attempt a close blockade of Wilhelmshaven and other German ports. Tirpitz argued that Germany's fleet would not have to be as large as the Royal Navy in order to pressure Britain, since he felt that world political conditions would not allow the Royal Navy to concentrate most of its battleships in home waters. During the indeterminate period while the German fleet was growing, Germany would have to pass through a "danger zone," when the fleet would be too weak to defend itself against a sudden preventive attack. Once Germany passed through the "danger zone," Britain would have to pay too high a price for going to war with Germany.

Although he was, at first, vague about the numbers necessary to deter a British attack, Tirpitz was confident that when the 1900 Navy Law approached completion, sometime around 1915, the fleet could, via damage threatened under the risk theory, successfully discourage the Royal Navy from attacking.

Scores of historians have spilled barrels of ink to try to discern the purposes and feasibility of the risk theory. To understand the problem in its original context, it is necessary to focus initially on the period from 1900 to 1905, that is, before the "Dreadnought Revolution" substantially changed the situation. A comprehensive review of the risk theory is beyond the scope of this biography, but the most trenchant critiques of it are those by Kennedy and Hobson.[115]

In 1898 Great Britain had thirty-eight first-class battleships, and Germany had seven; thirty-four first-class cruisers, and Germany two.[116] Clearly Germany started far behind in modern ships. One contradiction of Tirpitz's approach was that he hoped to expand the fleet as quietly as possible so as not to provoke the British, but, as the 1900 law showed, through propaganda campaigns he rode the tide of already existing anti-British feeling in Germany, as the *Bundesrath* seizure had demonstrated. Even with Bülow's cooperation, he could not turn German Anglophobia on or off to suit his convenience. Nor could he keep in harness the volatile Emperor's occasional public outbursts.

Another assumption of the risk theory was that the British, if faced with an Anglo-German crisis against Tirpitz's mature fleet, would be unable to reinforce the always formidable fleet in home waters with powerful units based in Gibraltar or Malta. Even a remotely rational Whitehall would not allow a conflict in Asia or the Eastern Mediterranean to jeopardize its central mission to defend the sea lanes at home. Tirpitz could concentrate his whole battleship force in the North Sea, but as Britain's "risk" grew, ships would be returned home in proportion. Paradoxically construction of the risk fleet created a predictable feedback effect that began in 1902, when the Admiralty began to rethink its existing fleet distribution.

A related paradox was that Tirpitz, who ostensibly wanted a fleet to enhance German world policy, almost invariably opposed ventures abroad that might upset the risk theory applecart, such as heavy German naval deployment to China during the Boxer Rebellion in 1900 and the Venezuelan debt crisis of 1902. He even opposed alliance proposals to Russia in 1904–1905, when the risk theory should have made him sympathetic to it. An early harbinger of this attitude had been his nervous

opposition to the seizure of Kiaochou in 1897, lest it complicate negotiations with the Reichstag. It was almost as if he believed that Germany
could hide for more than a decade while the fleet was being built and then
pop out as a full-blown contender for world power when the fleet neared
completion. For such a policy to succeed would require an astonishing
degree of blindness on the part of Germany's potential adversaries. For
decades, the British Admiralty had supported a "two power" standard: for
Britain to have a fleet as large or larger than those of the next two powers,
France and Russia, combined. Tirpitz seems to have implicitly assumed
that when Germany passed first one and then the other, somehow the
two power standard would go into abeyance.

A further remarkable assumption of Tirpitz's system was that, if war
came, the portion of the Royal Navy in home waters would immediately
charge across the North Sea to impose a close blockade. The British
would willingly subject themselves to attrition via German mines and
torpedoes until they conveniently were whittled down to a size Germany
could contend with. The assumption is all the more surprising in the
light of what Tirpitz, in 1897, had written in a critique of an OK operations plan for war with France. The enemy would not engage in open
battle in the North Sea or the Baltic but instead would simply blockade
the English Channel and the northern exits of the North Sea. German
exports and imports would be cut by about 70 percent, with minimal risk
for the French.[117] In the first years after the 1900 law, Tirpitz never gave
serious consideration to the possibility that the British could frustrate the
risk fleet and ruin the German economy by doing the same, or perhaps he
did think about it, but rejected the idea, lest it upset his all-important plan.

Tirpitz also made sure that his battleships were unusable in any
context other than what the risk idea envisioned. Since their range was
limited, they could not operate outside home waters any further than
Cherbourg. Crew quarters on the battleships were cramped and uncomfortable, badly suited for extended cruises. Also, Helgoland was actually
a long way (more than 300 nautical miles) from the Thames estuary
and northeast of it. Any attack that far south on the English coast would
expose the German fleet to being cut off from its base, even by a fleet
based well to the north.[118] This fact alone brings into question the idea
that Germany would take offensive action "between Helgoland and the
Thames."

A further oddity of the risk theory was that, in theory, German sea-
men had to be prepared to sally forth on what amounted to a suicide
mission to weaken the Royal Navy on behalf of other powers. Officers
might be ready for such self-sacrifice, but it is hard to see how conscript
sailors might feel the same. As Heeringen put it in 1911:

> It is in the long run completely impossible that our fleet can live with the
> idea that our purpose is only to be a risk for England, that is, that our defeat
> could nevertheless affect England's maritime position vs. the neutrals. To
> maintain our morale our fleet needs a militarily feasible chance of victory
> against England.[119]

These contradictions and mistakes in judgment were increasingly
apparent in 1904 or before. The situation became worse with the coming
of the Anglo-French Entente and the British shift to Dreadnoughts.

These blunders by the same cool, rational, and goal-oriented Tirpitz,
who had demolished the OK and persuaded a half-willing Reichstag to
accept his long-term design for fleet building, seem to defy explanation.
Kennedy, baffled by these conundrums, speculated that Tirpitz, after all,
wanted a German fleet as large as the Royal Navy,[120] despite the fact that
the few documents pointing in that direction are overwhelmed by evidence that Tirpitz clung stubbornly to the expensive, but limited, scope
of the Navy Law, and resisted the pressure and temptation to expand the
fleet still further.[121]

Hobson has a more convincing approach to Tirpitz's strategic blindness to the consequences of the risk theory. In a detailed analysis, he
shows how Tirpitz evolved from a clear-sighted thinker who accepted
some of the more sensible ideas of Mahan, to a man swept away by Mahan's irrational notion of the magical political and imperial dimensions
of seapower, heavily infused with Social Darwinism.[122] Tirpitz, in a Mahanian act of faith, argued from the beginning that there was a direct and
proportional relationship between Germany's sea trade and the size of its
battlefleet. Increases in the fleet would lead to increases in trade, and vice
versa, and that "the military situation against England requires ships of
the line in as great a number as possible."[123] A complementary explanation
for Tirpitz's obstinacy in the face of such contradictions would be that his
persistent belief in the risk theory was, in part, a product of bureaucratic
politics. Tirpitz strove for order, stability, and personal control against
all other parties, the Reichstag, the Emperor, his colleagues within the

navy, and even against any diplomatic initiative that, in his view, might increase the chance of a British attack before his fleet was "ready" at some indeterminate time in the future.

Another question to consider is whether the risk theory's main purpose was offensive or defensive.[124] The core of his famous Dienstschrift IX (1894) is the argument that the German battlefleet should always assume the strategic offensive. In the early 1890s, chagrined over the passivity of the fleet in the Franco-Prussian War, the OK devised several versions of wildly optimistic offensive operations plans against possible enemies.[125] By November–December 1899, the Admiralstab dropped the operation plan for a suicidal rush on the Thames estuary at the outbreak of war.

The consensus among historians who have studied the risk theory most closely is that Tirpitz's fleet was built primarily against Britain, to be predominantly a defensive one against the Royal Navy.[126] It was a deterrent against an attack in the waters near Helgoland. Of course, as analyzed later, it could only work tactically if the British actually attacked and attempted to establish a close blockade, another assumption central to the risk theory. Later this was to evolve into the idea of a 2:3 ratio Tirpitz estimated would give Germany "sufficient defensive chances." If Germany could build sixty large ships, Britain would have to build ninety. As Hobson points out, this ratio was a substantial modification of Tirpitz's earlier ideas on the strategic offensive.[127] For an attacker to have a good chance, conventional wisdom saw the knife edge of success to be a 4:3 ratio of superiority. Conversely, the defender needed to have a ratio of at least 3:4 to stay on the knife's edge. It is not completely clear, except perhaps for Tirpitz's belief in the political (as opposed to the strategic) aspect of seapower, that a 2:3 ratio would be sufficient for deterrence. Of course, in the years between 1897 and 1905, before Dreadnoughts, such calculations were only theoretical and very long term, given the crushing British superiority at that time. The principal way that the risk fleet was anti-British was political, in the sense that it provided a rationale and a whipping boy to justify Tirpitz's demands on the resources of the country to sustain the Navy Law and his bureaucratic empire.

Also implicit in the risk theory was that the fleet would make Germany more attractive to potential alliance partners who also had naval power. Alsace-Lorraine effectively excluded France as a potential ally, so

THE SECOND NAVY LAW, 1899–1900

Russia would be the likeliest candidate to supplement deterrence while Germany passed through the "danger zone." Surprisingly, if one is to take the risk theory seriously, there is no contemporary evidence that Tirpitz attempted to influence foreign policy in that direction, and there is evidence that in 1904–1905 Tirpitz actively opposed a potential Russian alliance, lest it provoke the British. Also curious is that nowhere in the records is there evidence that Tirpitz sought help from the United States to restrain British ambitions.[128]

Something he could reasonably count on early in this period was continued Franco-Russian tension with Britain over colonial matters, which continued unabated until negotiations led to the Anglo-French Entente in 1904. The notion of "alliance worthiness" seems for Tirpitz more like a "talking point" for domestic politics than a matter of substance. He seems to have ignored or overlooked what would have been the central question for any potential ally: the mighty German Army, the mainspring of Germany's semi-hegemonic position on the continent.

A central point of Berghahn's interpretation of Tirpitz's naval policy is the idea, famously expressed in Tirpitz's letter to Stosch of 21 December 1895, that the fleet would be a "palliative against educated and uneducated Social Democrats."[129] Construction surely provided some jobs, but, as Salewski has pointed out,[130] much of the cost of the fleet was borne by the regressive 1902 tariffs. The single phrase in that Stosch letter and his consequent notes for a meeting with the Emperor are apparently the only times Tirpitz claimed that the fleet was a "palliative" against the Social Democrats. This single phrase has received huge emphasis from Berghahn and others, who see it as a link to manipulative social imperialism. Many historians do not find it convincing as a central tenet of Tirpitz's policy.[131]

Even some of Tirpitz's closest comrades were cynical about the risk theory. Michaelis, who was in the RMA for part of the Tirpitz era, wrote:

> The risk idea was only meant as a shield against the adamant opponents
> of the fleet's slogan against limitless fleet plans. Capelle told me: "The
> Reichstag does not want the truth from us, but a suitable formula with
> which the sensible ones can guide those who are stupid." In my opinion the
> risk idea has no serious military place.[132]

Michaelis added, perhaps in hindsight:

In war the risk idea would bring us the further disadvantage that an English commander, in order to avoid the risk we had announced, would hold back his battlefleet in a way which would make it difficult for us to take the offensive because of the strength relationship.[133]

Tirpitz himself said in 1911, when the ratio was a relatively favorable 14:9, "our chances in a war with England are thoroughly unsatisfactory. Naturally, I cannot concede this in public."[134] Clearly the risk theory, if it is to be taken at all seriously, was, at best, just a throw of the dice.

Father, Rudolf Tirpitz, 1811–1905. *Courtesy of Agostino von Hassell.*

Newlyweds Alfred and Marie, 1884.
Courtesy of Agostino von Hassell.

Tirpitz and Marie in Sardinia, ca. 1888. *Courtesy of Agostino von Hassell.*

SCHMIDT & WEGENER   KIEL.

Tirpitz and Ilse, early 1890s.
Courtesy of Agostino von Hassell.

Left to right: Ahlefeld, Prinz Heinrich, Tirpitz, early 1890s.
Courtesy of Agostino von Hassell.

Tirpitz ca. 1905, at the height of his power. *Courtesy of Agostino von Hassell.*

Tirpitz in March 1896, on the eve of departing for Asia.
Courtesy of Agostino von Hassell.

Admiral Eduard von Capelle, Tirpitz's Chief Aide for the Navy Laws.
Courtesy of Wikimedia Commons.

Admiral August von Heeringen, Tirpitz's agitator for the first two Navy Laws, later Chief of the Admiralstab. *Hildebrand, 6:68.*

The Emperor in all his glory, ca. 1910. *Hildebrand, 1:62.*

Left to right: von Diedrichs, Fischel, Fritze, Zeye, Meuss, von Prittwitz, Büchsel, Koester, Funke, Oldekop, Kirchhoff, von Holtzendorff, Vüllers. *Mantey.*

Left center: Tirpitz (Chief of Staff), von der Goltz (Commanding Admiral); right front: von Senden (Chief of the Naval Cabinet). *Mantey.*

SMS *Zieten*, ca. 1879, Tirpitz's first command, an early torpedo vessel. Note torpedo tubes in the bow. *Courtesy of Agostino von Hassell.*

William II, Tirpitz, and Holtzendorff, ca. 1912.
Courtesy of Agostino von Hassell.

D-1, the Imperial Navy's first destroyer, ca. 1886.
Courtesy of the U.S. Naval History and Heritage Command.

SMS *Siegfried*, early 1890s, coastal battleship later replaced by the powerful Dreadnought SMS *Helgoland.* *Courtesy of the U.S. Naval History and Heritage Command.*

HMS *Dreadnought*, the first of its type, 1906. *Courtesy of the U.S. Naval History and Heritage Command.*

SMS *Nassau*, the first German Dreadnought. *Courtesy of the U.S. Naval History and Heritage Command.*

SMS *Goeben*, ca. 1914, the battlecruiser that helped bring the Ottoman Empire into the war. *Courtesy of the U.S. Naval History and Heritage Command.*

Spee's squadron departs Valparaiso, Chile, on 18 November 1914 for its rendezvous with destiny in the Falklands. *Courtesy of the U.S. Naval History and Heritage Command.*

U-boats in harbor, ca. 1912. *Courtesy of the U.S. Naval History and Heritage Command.*

SMS *Blücher*, armored cruiser sunk at the Dogger Bank, 24 January 1915.
Courtesy of the U.S. Naval History and Heritage Command.

Tirpitz as Reichstag Deputy, ca. 1925.
Courtesy of Agostino von Hassell.

11

THE "QUIET" YEARS, 1900–1906

PROSPECTS

When raised to the hereditary nobility in June 1900 Tirpitz, at age fifty-one, was in his mature prime. His public image, in newspaper photos and editorial cartoons, was dominated by his famous forked beard. His once trim body, hardened by years of strenuous outdoor work in the Torpedo Arm, was gradually softening. Eight years of desk work had taken its toll. Unchanged were his piercing eyes, which still glittered with intelligence and ambition. He was at the peak of his powers.

He could be ruthless, as in 1899, when he persuaded his imperial master to dismantle his chief rival within the navy, the Oberkommando. He became the biggest fish in the naval pond, though, as a junior Vice Admiral, he was not on top of the navy's seniority list. He succeeded in manipulating the erratic Emperor, not by flattery or subservience, but by a shrewd combination of defiance and resignation threats, mingled with tact and occasional tactical accommodation. His indispensability for the Emperor's lifetime dream of a formidable fleet allowed Tirpitz to get away with such behavior. Until 1914, when the navy's mission suddenly changed from construction to combat, Tirpitz preserved his ascendancy.

With a superb staff that included a leavening from his old Torpedo Gang like Harald Dähnhardt, and with Eduard von Capelle as his right-hand man, Tirpitz ran the administrative part of the navy with skill and tight-fisted efficiency. He cleverly manipulated, cultivated, and concili-ated Reichstag parties and even some individual deputies with success not seen since Bismarck's day. Tirpitz, more out of expediency than principle, placed great store in preserving the political capital he had accumulated by staying within the financial limits of the 1898 Navy Law. The Reichstag repaid him by accepting a doubling of the prospective fleet and the provision of a more generous, but still predefined, financial table as the costs of new and larger ships rose.

Despite his success, Tirpitz faced many challenges after 1900. Could he stay within budgetary limits if shipbuilding costs increased more than anticipated? What should be the next step in the development of the fleet? Would the hard-pressed Front officers, who were as interested in fleet readiness as in fleet expansion, accept Tirpitz's view that shipbuilding took priority? Would the international situation stay quiet enough to permit an undisturbed and gradual expansion of the fleet over a number of years? Would the British catch on to the possibility that they might be the target rather than just the benchmark for German fleet development? Could Tirpitz keep the support of the impressionable Emperor for his priorities? Could he retain the indispensable support of the Center Party for fleet development?[1]

On the surface the years between 1900 and the modest appearing 1906 Novelle seemed the most tranquil of his nineteen years as State Secretary of the RMA. In reality, and mostly out of the public eye, foreign, domestic, and intra-service complications were afoot that would threaten the apparently invincible edifice of the Navy Law.

The first six years of the new century provide a signal opportunity to consider whether Tirpitz was operating an overarching, system-stabilizing "Plan" to undercut threats to the imperial constitutional system; or if Tirpitz was actually engaged in a more narrowly defined "plan" to manipulate the Emperor and his government, the Reichstag, and the rest of the navy, and also to impose his own vision of a navy created to enhance his personal power and that of the RMA.

One key to understanding why Tirpitz took the latter course rather than the former is to apply, in a nuanced way, the bureaucratic politics model to events after 1900. Historians have recognized, especially for the pre-1897 period, the role of goals specific to the entire officer corps in its universal desire to expand the fleet.[2] These motives included the never forgotten humiliation of inactivity during the war with France; the desire to have prestige comparable with the army's in the eyes of the nation; and the seldom publicly articulated desire for promotion that a rapidly expanding navy could offer to ambitious officers. These motives are consistent with Allison's organizational behavior model.

Tirpitz certainly shared these feelings, but he went further, into the bureaucratic politics model. A long-term commitment from the Reichstag and, above all, the positing of England as the only enemy that would justify the creation of a fleet on a grand scale changed things. After 1898–99 Tirpitz himself switched substantially from the organizational behavior model to the bureaucratic politics approach, the only way to center power in the RMA and himself. He channeled into his own design not only the Emperor and the Reichstag but also other powerful and senior naval officers. The anti-English orientation, which he would mute for opportunistic reasons from 1900 to 1906, had to be strong enough to gather patriotic support when needed for naval appropriations and yet not so stentorian as to provoke active English enmity. Hobson has articulated that Tirpitz, especially after about 1896, evolved into a sink-or-swim Mahanian Social Darwinist, but he was quiet about it publicly. He was able to subdue or magnify his anti-English feeling as it suited his purpose to advance his "plan," narrowly defined. Tirpitz had neither the power nor the influence to implement a broader, system-stabilizing "Plan" that the Emperor, given his erratic nature, could not have implemented even if such a broad design had really existed and he had actually understood it.

CONSTRUCTION 1898–1905

The RMA's most tangible works were the warships built during the period from 1898 to 1905. The first group of battleships Tirpitz laid down was the *Wittelsbach* class and its four sister ships. These well-armored ships displaced 12,800 tons, had as a main armament four 24-cm guns, the same as the previous *Kaiser Friedrich III* class. They had secondary armament consisting of eighteen 15-cm guns and a speed of 17 knots. They cost about 22.7 million marks each. Except for better armor and a little more speed, these were only a slight improvement over previous ships.[3] In general, the Imperial Dockyards in Kiel and Wilhelmshaven built ships cheaper than private yards, but their capacity was strained once the avalanche of orders for battleships began after the 1898 Navy Law.[4]

Comparable British battleships show that Tirpitz was competing quantitatively, not qualitatively. The ships of the *London* and the *Duncan* classes were larger at 14,000–15,000 tons, faster at 18–19 knots, had superior heavy guns, four 28-cm, and were similarly armored.[5]

The first group of German battleships built under the 1900 Navy Law, at a cost of about 24 million each, was *Braunschweig* and its four sisters. They were laid down in 1902–1903, displaced 14,400 tons, had a designed speed of 18 knots, and were slightly better armored, and a knot faster, than the *Wittelsbachs*. The biggest improvement in the *Braunschweigs* was an increase in the caliber of its main armament to four 28-cm guns. This marked a return to the gun size of the *Brandenburgs* of the 1890s that had six 28-cm guns. The new 28-cm guns could be fired much more quickly. Their secondary armament was fourteen 17-cm guns, four of which were in turrets instead of casements.[6]

Their British contemporaries were the *Queen* class (two ships) and the *King Edward* class (eight ships), the former 15,000 tons and the latter 16,350 tons. Both classes had four 30.5-cm main armaments, but the *King Edwards* had a powerful secondary armament of four 23-cm and ten 15-cm guns, and armor slightly thicker than on the German ships.[7] Clearly British battleships laid down between 1902 and 1905 were qualitatively superior to Tirpitz's.

The last German pre-Dreadnoughts were the *Deutschland* class (5 ships), built between 1903 and 1906. They displaced 14,200 tons and had the same armament and speed as the *Braunschweigs*, with some minor improvements.[8] They were controversial within the navy because they were substantially smaller and less heavily armed than the *King Edwards*, and the last two British pre-Dreadnoughts of the *Lord Nelson* class, which displaced almost 17,000 tons and had four 30.5-cm and ten 23.4-cm guns.[9]

The first large cruiser laid down (March 1900) under Tirpitz's stewardship was *Prinz Heinrich*. Because Tirpitz hoarded every possible mark for battleships, it was built on the cheap. Armed with only two 24-cm guns (instead of the four in its immediate predecessor *Fürst Bismarck*) and ten 15-cm as a secondary armament, it displaced 9,800 tons and had a designed speed of 20 knots.

There followed in 1901 and 1902 the sister ships *Prinz Adalbert* and *Friedrich Carl*. They had a lighter but quicker firing main armament of four 21-cm guns, displaced 9,875 tons, had a speed of 20.5 knots and were designed to provide reconnaissance for the battlefleet.

The 1903 and 1904 large cruisers *Roon* and *Yorck* were identical in armament to the *Prinz Adalberts*, but slightly larger (10,300 tons) and a little faster (21 knots). The 1905 and 1906 large cruisers *Scharnhorst* and *Gneisnau* later became famous during their daring and fateful odyssey across the Pacific under the command of Vice Admiral Maximilian von Spee in 1914. These ships, a substantial improvement over prior ones, were competitive internationally in size and speed for armored cruisers. The most striking difference was that their main armament was doubled to eight 21-cm guns, with a reduced secondary armament of only six 15-cm. They were bigger (13,000 tons) and faster (22.5 knots) than Tirpitz's prior cruisers.[10]

German large armored cruisers of the 1899–1906 era were comparable in quality to the French- and Russian-built cruisers, but they were generally inferior to their British counterparts. The same was true of German light cruisers of that era, about three per year. Tirpitz clearly followed a policy of gradual and incremental improvements.

Despite complaints from the Emperor and the Front, Tirpitz built smaller battleships than the British for financial reasons and for the crucial consideration that bigger ships could not pass through the Kaiser Wilhelm Canal without a very expensive widening of the canal. The continual increase in the size of British battleships, and rumors of still bigger ones, put Tirpitz into a very uncomfortable position by 1905. Similar size and speed differences existed between the large and small cruisers of each side. The type differentials led to an enduring (and partially unfounded) sense of inferiority among German sailors.

WORKADAY LIFE AT TIRPITZ'S RMA

It is revealing to take a candid look at Tirpitz's work life as State Secretary of the RMA. The papers of William Michaelis provide a rare glimpse into this milieu. Michaelis was the son of a construction engineer, and a good example, though he married a rich woman, of the bourgeois class that constituted a majority of the sea officer corps. Born in 1871, he entered the navy in 1889. He was the head of his "crew" and consequently highest in seniority among his peers. He shuttled between sea service and land postings at the RMA and the Admiralstab. His career ended as a Rear Admiral, with a brief stint as Chief of Admiralty in 1920.[11]

At the Naval Academy, Michaelis learned strategy, tactics, and naval history, laced with illustrations from Clausewitz and Mahan, from Rear Admiral Curt von Maltzahn, who was also Director of the Naval Academy from 1900 to 1903. Tirpitz and Maltzahn had fallen out in the 1890s, because Maltzahn differed subtly from Tirpitz's idea of all-or-nothing battleship offensives.[12]

In October 1903 Lieutenant Commander Michaelis came to work in the Military Department of the RMA under Vice Admiral Otto Diedrichsen. During his first days at the RMA he met his old friend, Commander Harald Dähnhardt, to whom he lamented not knowing how to address the many civilian officials in the RMA. Dähnhardt replied:

> That is very simple—you just call everyone Herr Geheimrat [the second-highest rank]. If he is an Excellency [the highest rank], he is delighted for being taken for someone younger. If he is just an office worker, he is flattered, and with the rest you are correct.

At first Michaelis seldom saw the State Secretary. One of his first commissions was to visit the Station Chiefs to persuade them that Artillery and Torpedo Inspectors should report to the RMA as well as to them. Michaelis thought this was unnecessary, as "it was just based on the idea that the RMA wanted a voice in all parts of the navy." This was a first example for Michaelis of the extent of Tirpitz's *Ressorteifer* within the navy. He sought the advice of a more experienced colleague, who replied, "What then? The State Secretary wants to do this? It is madness. Write on the memo: to be taken up again after six months. Now let it rest until the old man is reasonable."

As Michaelis gradually proved his competence, he would occasionally meet directly with Tirpitz. On several occasions Tirpitz complained about the navy's organization that allowed so many officers direct access to the Emperor. He claimed that the Emperor had forced this arrangement upon him shortly after he took over the RMA! Sometime later a baffled Michaelis discovered in the files some of the documents from 1898–99, when Tirpitz had demanded the abolition of the OK. He could not determine whether Tirpitz was lying or deceiving himself. In the Front at the time, Michaelis noted, "everyone believed that Tirpitz introduced this system in order to be unhindered in playing each group off against the others."[13]

In one ongoing disagreement between the two, Michaelis had demonstrated how removed Tirpitz was from the realities of life in the Front. Tirpitz had the idea that keeping a whole crew intact on a given ship for three years was the most efficient way to man the fleet. No doubt this was true for any individual ship, at least in the third year; but given the massive annual turnover of one-third of the conscripts, Michaelis saw the need to balance each crew among first-, second-, and third-year recruits to avoid the nightmare of having one-third of the fleet manned entirely by raw recruits. "He [Tirpitz] did not understand the difficulties of training a crew comprised solely of recruits." Michaelis got his way, at least in the short run, which shows that Tirpitz could be flexible in matters that did not impinge directly on the Navy Law. Tirpitz seemed to have forgotten his recruit-training days as a young officer.

Michaelis was involved in preparations for the 1906 Novelle. "Whenever the State Secretary had a question, he wanted an immediate answer." The relevant expert would prepare a memo for the Etatsabteilung to examine and perhaps add to the material sent to the Reichstag. After Michaelis prepared one such memo, Capelle told him:

> Your writing is very interesting, and I learned much from it; but it contains an error in that it is obviously *true*, but the Reichstag does not want to know the truth. We should give them slogans with which the navy's friends can club the navy's opponents. *Mundus vult decipi.* [The world wants to be deceived.]

This episode shows how the RMA played on the credulity and patriotism of the deputies. Michaelis, a hard-liner toward the Reichstag, was inwardly disgusted

> with the way Tirpitz sought to win over the loudest shriekers in the Reichstag. He let [Matthias] Erzberger [of the Center Party] have access to the most secret files of the RMA—and even let him use RMA official cars. . . . The young men of the RMA had to go arm in arm with Social Democratic deputies. This may have been for the greater good, but I did not find this witch's policy very nice.

Michaelis worked in increasing proximity to Tirpitz between 1903 and 1906, and provided a classic picture of Tirpitz as the bureaucratic politician:

The *Ressort* feelings [*Ressortempfindlichkeit*] of the State Secretary made for much superfluous work. At every moment he feared that an interloper wanted to amass competencies that belonged only to him and the RMA. Thereby he interfered in matters that did not concern him as Chief of Naval Administration. He drew the circle of his interests very widely. The result was, naturally, continuous uncomfortable conflicts. He was always contending with the Foreign Office, but also with the Admiralstab and the Fleet Chief, whom he expected to behave as subordinates. He saw them as pens that should write as he ordered.

In July 1905 Heeringen took over the General Navy Department. He made Michaelis his confidential secretary, and he took part in many conversations with Tirpitz. He also attended Reichstag sessions along with Heeringen and Capelle. The latter revealed to him one of the RMA's great secrets:

> Capelle told me about the inside context of the Navy Law. Now I knew that the most important part was the annual appropriation [so much for the idea of the Navy Law made of iron]. The rest, the age of the ships, the formations, and the official rationale [*Begründung*] were only embellishments [*Ausschmückungen*]. Even the risk idea, which I doubted, Capelle declared to me was only a shield against the Reichstag slogan of limitless [*uferlosen*] fleet plans.

This misdirection, overlooked by most contemporaries and historians, is considered in detail in the examination of later Novelles.

Michaelis admired Tirpitz's energy, vision, and "dazzling persuasiveness when he came to a decision after much to and fro, and the forcefulness with which he carried out his decisions." He nevertheless was disappointed that Tirpitz built battleships with size and gun caliber inferior to the British. He was unsympathetic to Tirpitz's commonsense view that any battleship was a compromise between factors like speed, protection, gun power, and range. He clearly did not understand the huge financial pressure Tirpitz was under as the size and expense of ships accelerated. The pressure increased exponentially when Britain began to build Dreadnoughts.[14]

In the early phases of Dreadnought building, Tirpitz sometimes had to be devious even within the RMA. When Vice Admiral Rudolf von Eickstedt, head of the Construction Department (Konstructionsabteilung, or K), more a sailor than an engineer, dragged his feet, Tirpitz often discreetly went outside the chain of command to consult Eickstedt's subordinate, Dr. Hans von Bürkner, a highly skilled professional engineer.[15] Adolf von Trotha, to avoid the embarrassment of carrying out Tirpitz's orders, often sneaked past Eickstedt's office in the Leipzigerstrasse to visit Bürkner in the RMA's Voßstrasse building.[16]

GERMANY AND THE WORLD, 1900–1903

Tirpitz and Bülow came to office in 1897 in the Cabinet of Chancellor Hohenlohe (Bülow replaced him in 1900), when popular feeling in many circles responded enthusiastically to the idea of Weltpolitik, or "world policy." The term "Weltpolitik" was linked in propaganda with fleet expansion and connoted, to many, economic and colonial expansion on the British model. This call resonated with many, except for agrarians, a few old-fashioned liberals, and Social Democrats, all of whom dismissed Weltpolitik as imperialistic saber rattling.

A minority of keen-eyed observers saw through the facade. An anonymous journalist wrote in the *Hamburger Correspondent* in 1901:

> What an irony of history: [Chancellor] Caprivi, the "Troupier" who did not want to know much about colonies, navies, and overseas policies, through the redeeming act of his trade policies led Germany into the ranks of the great world powers. Count Bülow, who achieved a place in the sun via the purchase of the Caroline and Marianas Islands, who strengthened our navy and foresees our future blooming on the ocean, lends a hand to the shrinking of our world trade and surrounds Germany with tariff walls.[17]

Among some involved in international trade, the prospect of rising tariffs, applied reciprocally by Germany's trading partners, seemed to them to weaken, not strengthen, Germany's world position.

Tirpitz and Bülow realized the danger that the British would some day see the growing German fleet as a threat. The navy would have to pass through a "danger zone" of unspecified length before it could defend itself against British attack. As one historian put it, the optimum policy during that time would be *"Zeitgewinn und Flottenbau,"* that is, play for time and build a fleet, but be quiet about it lest the British be provoked.[18] Because Tirpitz sometimes needed to emphasize the British "threat," most notably in the preface to the Navy Law of 1900, it was important to keep as quiet as possible afterward, when paper ships were turning into real ones at the rate of three per year. If followed consistently, which it was not, especially after 1904, this policy led to the paradoxical conclusion that Germany must avoid major conflicts at all costs until the fleet was built. In effect, to practice Weltpolitik in the future, one must foreswear Weltpolitik for a decade or more.

Tirpitz, despite his extremely bellicose anti-English statements after 1914, was far more consistent in advocating passivity than Bülow was. In November 1897, only a few months after taking office, he opposed the acquisition of Tsingtau lest potential conflict with Russia jeopardize the passage of the 1898 Navy Law. It is an intriguing mystery how either Tirpitz or Bülow could have seriously thought it possible to keep a gag over the mouth of the mercurial Emperor, even for a short time, let alone for a decade or more.

In May 1900, just before the Navy Law passed, the Boxer Rebellion created an acute situation for the European legations in Peking.[19] In early June Vice Admiral Felix von Bendemann, Chief of the Asiatic Cruiser Squadron, sailed to Taku to join British, French, Russian, Japanese, and American contingents. On 10 June Admiral Edward Seymour, the British commander, led an allied force of about two thousand men, including six hundred German sailors and marines, toward Peking. A week of bloody fighting followed, and Seymour had to retreat. After this reversal the allies decided to consolidate their position at Taku. Under Captain Hugo von Pohl, a member of Tirpitz's Torpedo Gang, an allied landing force successfully stormed the Taku forts. During the battle Krupp-made Chinese guns sunk the German gunboat *Iltis* (the luckless replacement for Otto Braun's ship). Along with the assassination of the German Minister in Peking on 22 June, this misfortune enraged William II when the news arrived in Berlin on 3 July.

That very same day, without consulting either Tirpitz or Bülow,[20] the Emperor ordered the dispatch to China, under Field Marshall General Count von Waldersee, of an expeditionary force of twenty thousand, together with a division of the newest German battleships and several cruisers. This constituted the largest fleet by far that Germany had ever sent outside European waters. Even though Peking had already been taken by the time the force arrived, to many the expedition seemed to exemplify

Weltpolitik in action. Waldersee famously remarked as he was about to embark for China, "We should pursue world policy, if only I knew what that should be. For the moment it is only a slogan."[21]

Tirpitz was typically nervous about sending such a large portion of his newest battleships so far away. He saw the German strategic center suddenly moved to Asia without a compelling political or strategic reason. He also did not want to pay for it. Thinking like a typical bureaucratic politician, he saw that sending a large army contingent to China might be a way for the army to overtake the navy in public opinion and in the Reichstag.[22] On 14 July he wrote to Prinz Heinrich: "The military complications in China are very unfavorable for the fast development of our fleet." Significantly Tirpitz had not been present at the meeting in which the Emperor decided to send the force, though he reluctantly acquiesced.[23]

Always concerned about the reaction of the Reichstag, Tirpitz worried about the debate over estimates the next winter, "which will be very much over budget as a direct result of the war situation in China. Thereby Weltpolitik unfolds in a way in which the navy steps into the background even before it has grown sufficiently."[24]

With no new fleet bill pending, Tirpitz tried to keep the growing German fleet as inconspicuous as possible. In 1901, when retired Vice Admiral Otto Livonius wrote an article in the *Deutsche Revue* favoring a fleet equal to Britain's, London Naval Attaché Captain Carl Coerper reported on the reaction of the British press. The Nachrichtenbüro wrote a refutation.[25] When Prinz Heinrich visited England in October 1903, he warned Tirpitz that "the cat was out of the bag" about German naval expansion, and concluded, "we could have been further along than we are now, had we understood how to keep quiet."[26]

Another example of Tirpitz's effort in this direction could have miscarried. In October 1902 he asked N to prepare a brochure about a hypothetical Anglo-German war.[27] The draft posited a Battle of Helgoland in 1906, in which German trade was stopped in its tracks, colonies seized, a blockade imposed, industry hard-pressed, and the German fleet crushed; the British, however, suffered more casualties than expected. The German economy would collapse, but the battle would also leave England vulnerable to attack around the world, with the Americans left in control of Canada and most transatlantic trade. Cooler heads prevailed, and the brochure never appeared. Tirpitz had hoped that such a horrendous scenario would throw cold water on the radical press of both sides; however, Bülow wisely argued that it might be seen as the harbinger of a new naval proposal.

The navy soon had another opportunity to project its power abroad, in a manner typical of the age of gunboat diplomacy. During a civil war in Venezuela, European traders, including Germans and Englishmen, had suffered severe losses. The Venezuelan government repeatedly refused to pay for damages. In the fall of 1902 the Germans joined the British and the Italians to blockade the Venezuelan coast.[28] Tirpitz opposed the blockade, consistent with his desire to avoid conflict while in the danger zone. Holstein of the Foreign Office had a blunter view: "Tirpitz has no stomach for a fight." Tirpitz may also have worried about the need to go to the Reichstag to pay for the intervention.[29] A German squadron of three small cruisers and the gunboat *Panther*, together with British and Italian forces, began a blockade. Impetuous German bombardments of shore installations provoked the ire of President Theodore Roosevelt. He mobilized the fleet under Admiral Dewey to "protect" South America from violations of the Monroe Doctrine. Bülow retreated before the "big stick." The blockade was lifted in February 1903 after negotiations with Venezuela were completed.

In spring 1903 an incident occurred that provided a revealing picture of Tirpitz's relations with the Emperor and the Chancellor. Upon the death of the Russian Naval Minister, William II ordered Tirpitz to make a condolence visit to St. Petersburg. To Tirpitz's discomfort, he also was charged with showing Nicholas II plans for the newest German battleship. Tirpitz found the order both surprising and distasteful. Before he left for Russia, he told Bülow about the mission. Bülow replied that he had to carry out the Emperor's order, a reply that disappointed Tirpitz. He wrestled with his conscience about what to do. Finally he decided not to inform the Czar. When he returned and ruefully reported this to Bülow, he was surprised when Bülow said: "I am very grateful you took this upon yourself." Such evasion of responsibility earned Bülow the epithet "the eel." The Emperor apparently forgot the order and never asked Tirpitz about it again.[30] It is hard to imagine how two such feckless masters could be participants in an overarching system-stabilizing Tirpitz "Plan."

INTERLUDE IN THE UNITED STATES

Tirpitz's third and last visit to the United States occurred between 22 February and 11 March 1902, with the entourage of Prinz Heinrich, on a ceremonial visit to christen his imperial brother's new racing yacht. *Meteor*, built in an American yard, was a result of William II's wish to have a boat superior to those of his British cousins. Recall that Tirpitz had previously crossed the United States in 1896 and 1897 on his way to and from Asia.[31]

Two other officers on the trip had a substantial impact on Tirpitz's later life: Captain Georg Alexander von Müller, a Torpedo Gang member, then close to Tirpitz, and a department head in the MK; and Lt. Commander Adolf von Trotha, from the RMA's Central Department (Zentralabteilung, or Z), later personally close to Tirpitz.[32]

They met President Roosevelt, and watched as Alice Roosevelt, his vivacious eighteen-year-old daughter, christened *Meteor*.[33] They left for a whirlwind train journey through the eastern and central states. They visited Philadelphia, Baltimore, Annapolis, Buffalo, Detroit, Chicago, Milwaukee, St. Louis, and Chattanooga, where they rode a funicular up Lookout Mountain, the site of a famous Civil War battle, and Boston, where the Prince received an honorary doctorate from Harvard. The most complete written record of the trip is Müller's, in which he noted the ubiquity of American industry, the sagaciousness of American politicians, despite their often humble origins, the striking physical condition of officer cadets, and their spartan training. He was surprised to see so few fat officers, implicitly a slight to the beer-drinking and sausage-eating habits of their German counterparts. Harvard also impressed him, especially the easy exchanges between distinguished scientists and industrial leaders, a phenomenon that he felt would be good for Germany. He was perhaps most struck by the New York elite, whom he met at a luncheon on 26 February. Present were such luminaries as J. P. Morgan, John D. Rockefeller, Mark Twain, and Alfred Thayer Mahan, many of them self-made men.

Tirpitz briefly reported his impressions to the Emperor and the Prince.[34] On 28 February he spent a rainy hour and a half at the Naval Academy. He was amazed that the U.S. Navy spared no expense in training its midshipmen, 40 million marks for new buildings alone. He admitted that he was envious, but "this would not work for us as a model," because Germany must concentrate on building the fleet "and use all available means on it." He admitted that American midshipmen were physically more robust than German cadets but noted that midshipmen stayed at the Naval Academy for four years, not two. He dismissed their substantial engineering training by noting that it would be socially "impossible" for Germany to combine the sea officer and engineering officer corps. He observed that "the two navies have fundamentally different ideas about organization, training, and administration" but "came to similar conclusions about strategy and tactics." "We came to our conclusions by practical experience, while the Americans only did it in a theoretical way."

Most tantalizing of Tirpitz's remarks was a private conversation he had with Mahan, who Tirpitz recorded as saying, "the German Army is unsurpassed in training, organization, and buildup and I am convinced they will do the same in the creation of a navy." One can only wonder what transpired in the rest of this conversation, the only one on record between these two maritime giants.

ORGANIZATIONAL MATTERS 1901–1903

With the dissolution of the OK on 10 March 1899, the RMA assumed some of its functions. The peacetime duties of the Admiralstab were essentially confined to the preparation of operational plans. The Nachrichtenbüro (N) was given independent status. It separated from the Zentralabteilung (Z) and was made solely responsible for the publication of *Nauticus* and *Marine Rundschau*, and for press relations, the assembly of naval information from other countries, and the distribution of news within the navy.[35]

With his victory over the OK, Tirpitz seemed dominant within the navy. The Chief of the First Squadron, and, after 1903, the Fleet Chief, had operational control of the fleet, and was not obligated to apply operational plans that the Admiralstab designed. The Admiralstab was empowered to transmit the Emperor's orders to the Cruiser Squadron abroad, and to coordinate with the Foreign Office.[36]

The first head of the Admiralstab was Felix von Bendemann, who served until December 1899 when he took command of the Asian Cruiser Squadron. His successor, Vice Admiral Otto von Diedrichs, was more ambitious and therefore more threatening to Tirpitz. For example, Tirpitz interfered with the Admiralstab's ability to direct overseas ship opera-

tions with the excuse that his office had priority over all financial alloca-
tions. Despite Diedrichs's complaints to the Emperor, Tirpitz, because
he controlled the finances, usually had considerable influence over naval
operations abroad.[37]

Tirpitz, with the support of the Front, throttled Diedrichs's plan for a
separate corps of Admiralstab officers to work in the Front. He prevented
Diedrichs from increasing the small (only eight officers initially) Admiralstab, because of the officer shortage. He blocked Diedrichs's plan to move
the Naval Academy to Berlin. Tirpitz's universal excuse to turn down such
requests was that they had to wait until the fleet was complete. He even
accused Diedrichs of bureaucratic empire building![38] One of Diedrichs's
few successes was a collaboration with the General Staff, and he even
went so far as to arrange for an exchange of liaison officers.[39] Tirpitz also
bested Diedrichs in having the Naval Attachés in London, Washington,
Paris, Rome, and St. Petersburg report directly to the RMA. The Admiralstab learned only what the RMA chose to share from attaché dispatches.[40]

Diedrichs, an honorable sailor but no keen bureaucratic warrior,
finally became weary of Tirpitz's bullying.[41] He received the Emperor's
permission to retire. His replacement, whom Tirpitz hand-picked, was
Vice Admiral William Büchsel, who officially took over the Admiralstab
in October 1903. Büchsel, Tirpitz's old friend and recently his chief subordinate at the RMA, was more compliant with Tirpitz's wishes. Senden
had supported Diedrichs on some issues, which is one of the reasons why
Tirpitz's relations with Senden began to sour after 1900.[42]

In dealing with the Admiralstab during the Diedrichs era, Tirpitz
acted as a ruthless empire builder. He was without mercy in the defense
of the RMA's role in fleet development and in the expansion, wherever
possible, of the meaning of "development" even when it contradicted the
objective interests of the navy.

The Admiralstab had greater latitude in its function of operational
planning. The 1899 plan against the Dual Alliance (France and Russia)
was similar to the hallucinatory 1892 plan against France, an immediate
offensive against the Channel ports before the French Mediterranean
Fleet could arrive. This plan, as in 1892, tacitly assumed the use of British
ports for coaling, repairs, and so on, and further assumed that the French
Fleet would come out and fight as a result of the shelling of their ports
rather than take the obvious and sensible course of awaiting reinforce-

ments. This scenario became even more remote when Russian attention turned to Asia in 1903–1904.[43] Despite many discussions of the plan inside the Admiralstab and with the Emperor, because of its obvious flaws it remained a dead letter.

Operations plans against Britain in the seven years after the 1898 Navy Law were a counsel of despair. There was no thought of a suicidal offensive. German trade would be driven from the seas. A ruthless blockade of Wilhelmshaven and the Elbe estuary was expected. Unless the army seized the Danish islands, which Schlieffen steadfastly refused to do, Kiel would suffer the same dismal fate. Economic ruin and food shortages would quickly follow. In his 1904 plan Büchsel acknowledged that Britain might prefer to strangle German trade at a distance. In that case Germany would have to inflict economic pain on Britain by raiding its commerce. Tirpitz did not like the purely defensive character of this plan, but he could do little about it until he had more ships.[44] This wretched prospect sheds light on Tirpitz's fear that the British would subject the German fleet to a sudden surprise attack. Tirpitz went to great lengths to avoid tension with the British. The Japanese surprise attack on Port Arthur gave credence to this fear. Publicly Tirpitz uttered nothing like the bold words of the preface to the 1900 Navy Law that contemplated conflict with the "strongest naval power."

Another conflict was between Tirpitz and Admiral Hans von Koester, who, from 1899 to 1903, was Chief of the Summer Exercise Fleet and simultaneously Chief of the Kiel Naval Station. Hopmann characterized him as the "Exercise Master" of the German navy, clever and thoughtful about how he handled his commanders, ships, and weapons. Hopmann praised his firm, energetic, benevolent personality and leadership qualities, although he conceded that Koester, unlike Tirpitz, did not have a creative dimension.[45]

After the fall 1902 maneuvers Koester asserted that he was the real leader of the naval striking force, and he demanded direct access to the Emperor. Koester saw himself as the guardian of the fleet's war readiness, which should have the highest priority. He fought to extend his competence at Tirpitz's expense. Like Tirpitz, he did not take the Admiralstab seriously, viewing it as comprised of paper pushers as opposed to active Front officers. Tirpitz fought stubbornly against the fleet command, opposing even its objectively justifiable requests.[46]

By 1903 the fleet had a sufficient number of modern ships to form a first division (four ships) and by 1906 a second division, which together constituted a squadron. Koester wanted not just squadron command but also a permanent fleet command. Tirpitz favored the existing method, whereby, for two months in the summer, ships in home waters would exercise under a temporary fleet chief, the part-time position Koester had held since 1899; at all other times the Emperor held the virtual command. It seems obvious that a modern navy had to have a designated commander were war suddenly to erupt. Unbelievably to modern eyes, Tirpitz opposed the idea. It is instructive to consider Tirpitz's reasoning and how he used the Emperor's vanity to frustrate a peacetime fleet command all the way up to 1914.

Tirpitz admitted that a permanent fleet command would have some training advantages, but he claimed (unfairly, in view of Koester's track record) that it would leave too little scope for the autonomy and initiative of future squadron chiefs. Such a change would lead to formal evolutions suitable for parades but not for battle. Tirpitz argued that the selection of a peacetime Fleet Chief would be based on seniority, whereas in war the Emperor would need the freedom to choose the most suitable of all senior admirals. A Fleet Chief, Tirpitz believed, would consider all ships in home waters as his domain and would oppose even temporary detachment of individual ships or groups of ships. Once a Fleet Chief's three-year term expired, he would have to retire for seniority reasons and could not serve in that or any other capacity.[47] At Rominten, at the end of September 1903, Tirpitz had an angry confrontation with Senden and Koester over preparedness and fleet organization.[48] After a bitter exchange with Senden, his old ally, Tirpitz's view prevailed, again by a threat to resign. The idea prevailed that Koester, as Fleet Chief, would interfere with the Emperor's direct relationship with the fleet. Koester failed to become Fleet Chief, but he was appointed full-time head of the active battlefleet, without control of the reserve fleet and without the certainty that he would be fleet commander in the event of war.

Once again Tirpitz defeated a sensible measure for a known fleet command in advance of war, which would have benefited both training and readiness. Tirpitz acted out of fear that a powerful fleet chief would become a formidable bureaucratic rival within the navy.

Koester's battles with Tirpitz over penny-pinching on ship types and readiness resonated in the fleet. In 1905 Hopmann, who had observed the Russo-Japanese War firsthand, confided to his wife:

> We have ships that we designated as battleships, but that are, in reality, metal tubs, accompanied by small cruisers. We have gunnery and battle exercises that are precisely thought out, but which are very problematic for real war. Our officers and commanders spend half their service time sitting at a typewriter. I still doubt that this is a good brew for a war, despite all the good characteristics and advantages that we possess.[49]

EARLY NOVELLE PREPARATIONS, 1901–1905

The most secret and important work of the RMA in the years immediately after the 1900 Navy Law was in the Etatsabteilung (E). By 1902 Senior Commander (Fregattenkapitän) Harald Dähnhardt took over the drafting work under the watchful eye of Capelle, who until January 1904 was director of E. He was then promoted to head the Administrative Department (Verwaltungsabteilung, or V) but remained in overall charge of relations with the Reichstag. E's major task was to prepare the annual estimates and to develop ideas for further Navy Law amendments. To outward appearances, this was a straightforward task. During parliamentary negotiations over the 1900 law, Tirpitz had agreed to strike six overseas cruisers. Reichstag members had pointed out that these ships would begin construction only in 1906. Tirpitz, to the surprise of some, readily agreed, but he reserved the right to reintroduce the cruisers in the future. Tirpitz privately welcomed the legitimation of a future amendment. The actual Novelle of 1906 resembled the 1900 proposal with respect to cruisers. A public observer would assume that nothing much had changed in E's calculations during the six-year interim. In reality, and in secret, even sometimes from the Emperor and other officers in the navy, E examined a great variety of possibilities, some of which vastly exceeded the six-cruiser Novelle.

Several factors influenced Tirpitz's calculations. One was the foreign situation, particularly Anglo-German relations that periodically worsened during the period. Berghahn argues that Tirpitz's feelings toward Britain were a form of "brinksmanship,"[50] but from 1901 to 1905 Tirpitz implemented a policy of silent appeasement. Because of Germany's maritime weakness, the fear of a negative British reaction was an important factor in his assessment of various Novelle ideas.

A second consideration for the RMA was money. Tirpitz feared getting involved in any conflict whatsoever, even as part of a coalition, as was the case in China and Venezuela, but the finances mattered seriously as well. When recession came in 1900–1902 Tirpitz felt pressure from industry and the Flottenverein to build more ships.[51]

A central factor in understanding Tirpitz's situation from 1900 to 1905, underestimated by historians, with the exception of Berghahn,[52] was the financial bind the navy was in soon after the passage of the 1900 law. The law was accompanied by cost estimate tables for the years to follow. As long as Tirpitz needed money over and above that projected in 1900, he felt that he had to retain the Reichstag's confidence by keeping to that total. This fact, which both the Front and the Emperor overlooked or underestimated, governed his actions in a wide variety of ways. Tirpitz had, to some degree, entrapped the Reichstag into his vision of building a great fleet; but the Reichstag had, de facto, trapped him into sticking to his own original projections. Adept at switching money among budget categories, he often had to rob Peter to pay Paul to meet construction costs that substantially exceeded original projections. Matters dear to the Front—from fleet readiness to coastal fortifications to food subsidies for officers' casinos (mess halls)—had to suffer to cover rising costs for shipbuilding and guns and armor.

Revenue projections that underlay the 1900 law soon proved overly optimistic, even after new grain tariffs began in 1902. Treasury Secretary Thielmann and his successor, Hermann von Stengel, vainly pleaded for government economies. Since the dominant parties opposed direct federal taxes and resisted increased state contributions, the Treasury became ever more dependent on loans. Though the financial crisis would not peak until several years later, the shoe began to pinch painfully.[53] Since the navy was the fastest-growing part of the federal budget, Tirpitz's law contributed substantially to a looming financial crisis that ratcheted up social and political pressures.

The first hint of planning for a Novelle came in late 1901. Under the 1900 law the three tempo would drop to two in 1906. On 6 November 1901 Capelle proposed, and Tirpitz tentatively accepted, a Novelle of five battleships and four small cruisers for service abroad. The rejected 1900 request had been for six large and four small cruisers. Capelle explained that the need to use battleships instead of large cruisers abroad was based on the China intervention, where all the seapowers had sent their stron-

gest ships. The proposal would secure the three tempo until 1911. The
tentative plan was to put the Novelle forward in the winter of 1904–1905.
Tirpitz ordered the preparation of tables outlining personnel, costs, and
so on.[54] To propose it for 1904–1905 was not a very big change, since it
applied to construction beginning in 1906. The tentative shift from large
cruisers to battleships was significant, however. Theoretically intended for
service abroad, they could easily be added to the home fleet.

The order leaked to the Social Democrats. *Vorwärts* published it on
29 January 1902, and called it "naval absolutism" that Tirpitz would repeat
a request that had been turned down in 1900. Tirpitz's old opponents,
Bebel and Richter, complained of "great political plans" in Asia and of
"Chinese adventures." Tirpitz calmly admitted that the document was au-
thentic, but he reminded the Budget Commission that he had told them
in 1900 to expect a later request for foreign ships. He blandly expressed
surprise at the accusation of deception. His rejoinder calmed the waters
somewhat but made the country aware that Tirpitz had plans, though
perhaps in a slightly different form (battleships instead of cruisers) than
originally presented in 1900.[55] The disclosure of expansion plans received
wide notice in the British press.[56]

Early in 1902 Tirpitz gave general guidance for E's work that included
a possible winter 1905 Novelle.[57] Throughout 1902 work continued in
an unhurried fashion. In the winter of 1901–1902, the Admiralstab had
conducted naval war games predicated on a war between the Triple and
the Dual Alliances. The exercise suggested that, to prevent a junction
of the French and Russian fleets, a group of large armored cruisers was
necessary.[58] On 12 December 1902 E proposed a Novelle for 1904 with only
two battleships but with the intention of adding four large and five small
cruisers with a three tempo through 1911. Battleships would replace the
eight *Siegfried* coastal defense ships before their twenty-five-year lifespan
expired. In theory, two battleships could maintain German prestige in
Asia, and the four cruisers could become a "flying squadron" for use
where needed, including in the North Sea.[59]

In another variant E suggested two battleships and five large and no
small cruisers with the three tempo through 1912. Savings from unbuilt
small cruisers would cover the increasing expense of the larger ships.
Capelle believed that neither plan would create diplomatic difficulties
and was optimistic about their reception in a future Reichstag.[60]

In May 1903 Dähnhardt prepared a plan with a further twist:[61] to request two battleships and five large cruisers but to add the battleships to the home fleet as "material reserve" rather than designate them for Foreign Service. Each division of four battleships would have one further ship as material reserve, assuming that the flagship for each double squadron was also made a material reserve ship.[62] With a "flying squadron" of four large cruisers, plus one in reserve, the navy could meet foreign emergencies without drawing strength from home waters. The inclusion of the "foreign" battleships, and the malleability of the idea of "material reserve," demonstrated how Tirpitz did not take seriously the separate classifications of ships in the legal ship establishment. As Capelle had told Michaelis, such terms were artifices, simply excuses to amass more battleships in home waters.

While Tirpitz and his family summered in their Victorian home in St. Blasien, Capelle and Dähnhardt worked out three additional possibilities.[63] Proposal I provided five large foreign cruisers and two battleships for the material reserve, the same as in the May draft. Proposal II would add a third double squadron, nineteen more battleships (making a total of fifty-seven), plus six large and fourteen small cruisers. This *Seewehr Schlachtflotte* would be analogous to a militia for the army. Proposal III, even more ambitious in a way, was simply to establish a permanent three tempo of two battleships and one large cruiser per year. The battleship lifespan would be *increased* from twenty-five to thirty years. The plan would add twenty-two battleships and six large and twenty-two small cruisers. About timing Capelle noted, optimistically, that it should be implemented after the Reich's financial situation had improved by favorable trade treaties or by new taxes. In any event, if the three tempo were to continue, it had to be no later than 1906.

Capelle explained the pros and cons of each variation. The most modest, Proposal I (two battleships and five large cruisers), would meet few objections in the Reichstag because it resembled the original 1900 proposal; it would rouse little opposition abroad; it would strengthen the Foreign Service fleet; and each division would have its own reserve battleship. It would only uphold the three tempo through 1912 and would require a further Novelle no later than 1913. The request would not fuel a massive propaganda campaign nor provide a plausible excuse for dissolving the Reichstag.

Proposal II would have the advantage of "reaching our final goal in a single step," that is, the provision of enough ships to deal with "the strongest opponent." The three tempo would last until 1925. The size of the fleet proposed was large enough to threaten the Reichstag with dissolution if it balked; its size, however, would also provoke substantial opposition, especially within the Center Party, and whether the consequences of dissolving the Reichstag would be favorable to the navy was unclear. It would possibly poison Anglo-German relations, with incalculable consequences, and weaken the Foreign Service fleet. One crippling disadvantage that Capelle apparently did not consider was that the Seewehr and the thirty-year lifespan for battleships would keep many very old and obsolete ships that would be no better than "floating coffins" against even small numbers of more modern ships. Berghahn disagrees: "For the British Navy a confrontation with a completed Seewehr Schlachtflotte could have had catastrophic results."[64] Surely he is mistaken on this point. Fisher, whose opinion about old ships differed, campaigned to scrap them to economize on money and manpower. Large numbers of superannuated 1890s battleships would be expensive and more of a liability than an asset to the German fleet. They would have been impressive on paper only, as Fisher well understood.

Proposal III, a permanent three tempo, would be clear and simple. No further Novelle would be needed, and the Foreign Service fleet would increase at the rate of one large cruiser annually. The disadvantages would be large, however. The 1900 law would have to be repealed and superseded. The Reichstag would resist an obvious Äternat, and correctly feel its budget right substantially abridged. Its threat to veto further programs would diminish or disappear. Worst of all for Tirpitz, the Reichstag might agree to the three tempo but limit it to a stated period, perhaps ten years. Government acceptance of a time limit would mean the end of the automatic replacement of obsolete ships. If the government rejected such a "compromise" and dissolved the Reichstag, opponents in the subsequent election could claim that they would guarantee the government's needs for ten years. What more could the government want? If this scenario transpired, any future development of the navy would be left "in the air," and the RMA would have to begin anew from where, legislatively, it had been in 1897. Such an outcome would also be disastrous from the point of view of bureaucratic politics and would saddle the navy with obsolete ships.

Capelle concluded that the choice between the three alternatives would not be primarily financial in the short term. All retained the three tempo from 1906 through 1912, and the shipbuilding cost would be about the same for each. The choice would be based on the foreign and domestic situations at the time the proposal was made public. If circumstances permitted, Capelle favored Proposal II, the third double squadron. If this were impossible, he favored a "modest" program akin to that of Proposal I (two battleships and five large cruisers), with a further Novelle in 1913, to keep the three tempo. He rejected, as the worst proposal, the permanent three tempo because of the navy's dilemma if the Reichstag offered a compromise. Capelle's assessment of the situation illustrated once more the degree of the RMA's dependence on the Reichstag.

Tirpitz himself was less committal, sent the memo back, and asked Capelle to continue work. Tirpitz's refusal to make a decision shows how flexible he had to be. As the 1906 deadline drew nearer, he had to consider the financial situation, relations with the Reichstag, and the foreign, especially British, reaction.

Tirpitz's thinking at the time was reflected in a memo Dähnhardt wrote in July 1903, in which he sought to profile the British mentality.[65] He believed that anti-German opinion in Britain was mainly based on trade envy. Some thought Germany was systematically planning an attack, perhaps after an occupation of Holland, and British agitators hoped to provoke a crisis to ensure continued trade superiority. The Admiralty was getting "nervous." The British were trying to enhance their enormous superiority to make them even more able to strike an annihilating blow against Germany. Dähnhardt raised a crucial question:

> Is it possible for Germany to achieve its goal to make its fleet strong enough so that if England were to attack Germany it would put its own world position in jeopardy? . . . Will we not always be outnumbered by England as we are now?

Dähnhardt operated on the optimistic assumption that England was incapable, in the long term, of keeping to as high a tempo as in the past year (three new and four replacement ships). If Germany implemented Proposal II, he estimated that by 1926 (!)England would be unable either to conduct an annihilating attack or to keep an effective blockade. He implicitly assumed what Tirpitz had in 1898 and 1900: that England could not possibly man a fleet of that size, since it would require the unthinkable—conscription. This view was clearly overblown and ignored Fisher's efforts to economize on men and money by scrapping old ships. He further assumed that if England truly felt threatened, the richest country in Europe, and one that did not have a large army, could not man a fleet on a life-and-death matter of national security. Conspicuous by its absence was any hint that trade or other sources of conflict could be settled by negotiation.

Such thinking, which reflected Tirpitz's own, is another example of bureaucratic politics. If one is determined to use a hammer as one's only tool, even if other means are available, one will employ any and all means of willful blindness to see any problem as a nail and nothing else.

Upon further reflection, Dähnhardt reached the sobering conclusion that, instead of the expansive Proposal II, a more modest measure was called for. He had the nightmarish vision that if the RMA introduced it, there would be a huge uproar in the Reichstag that the navy's ambition greatly exceeded the six dropped cruisers of 1900. He concluded that it was enough to keep the three tempo going for a few more years, and only later try to get a third double squadron.[66]

While E was speculating about Novelle plans, Tirpitz, based on bitter experience, kept the Emperor in the dark. During his Hubertusstock meeting with the Emperor in September 1903, he was deliberately vague and argued that Novelle content would depend on the attitudes of Reichstag parties. Further, he would "need time to prepare my parliamentary friends."[67]

Tirpitz had good reason to be cautious. In the 1903 Reichstag elections, mostly fought over tariffs and other tax issues, the Social Democrats, hostile to the navy, gained more than twenty seats. The National Liberals made only minimal gains. During the campaign the Center was nervously defensive about its support of the navy and held its normal proportion of seats. To assert, as some historians have, that the fleet was successful in propping up the regime is therefore questionable.[68]

Despite Tirpitz's discretion, the Emperor heard that E was preparing specific Novelle plans. He bombarded Tirpitz with a flurry of questions about type and number of ships. He also pushed for larger, faster, and stronger ships, an issue that would dog Tirpitz for years. The old temptation to meddle in construction plans bloomed anew.[69] On 14 November Tirpitz admitted that technical change in battleships was escalating, but he made the excuse that the RMA could do little more until a Novelle passed. The cost tables of the 1900 law allowed 18 million marks per battleship. Tirpitz hoped to increase this to 28 million marks in a Novelle. This was another example of how bound Tirpitz was by his own law. He argued that it would be hard to increase the home fleet based on a Foreign Service Novelle, and did not mention Dähnhardt's Proposal II for a third double squadron. He did say, however, that it might be possible to obtain a fifth squadron. Finally, Tirpitz warned William II against leaks that might imperil Novelle plans. The Emperor agreed and tentatively decided that the Novelle should ask for battleships instead of cruisers.[70]

On another front, ship design, the Emperor's restlessness could not be stayed. According to Trotha, between the fall of 1903 and the summer of 1905 the Emperor sent Tirpitz eleven separate construction projects, mostly about his schemes for a "fast battleship." The diversion complicated the workload of both the RMA and Tirpitz himself. He had to repeatedly tell the Emperor that if the legally established type distinctions were obscured, the law might be threatened. Tirpitz, to the dismay of the Konstructionsabteilung, yielded to enormous pressure to allow William II to publish anonymously in the first 1904 issue of *Marine Rundschau* an article that designated the Argentinean cruiser *Moreno*, with its four 25.4-cm and fourteen 19-cm guns, a model for German large cruisers. The article drew a refutation from the hapless Hopmann, who was ignorant of the real author. Tirpitz, to avoid a comical war in the press, and to spare the Emperor embarrassment before Senden, persuaded the Emperor, in a rare one-on-one interview, to drop the matter. William II took the private rebuff personally, and it contributed to William II's later bad feelings toward Tirpitz.[71]

YEARS OF TURMOIL, 1904–1905

Late in 1903, a large tribal rebellion broke out in German Southwest Africa (now Namibia) brought on by the abusive behavior of German officials and traders. By January 1904 it was clear that a large expeditionary force was necessary to suppress it. Years of bloody fighting followed, marked by brutal German atrocities. The war gradually embittered relations between the government and the Center, which objected to the outrages.[72]

Dähnhardt drafted yet another Novelle proposal. This one provided eight battleships, another in reserve, and two large and six small cruisers.[73] For the first time Tirpitz confidentially revealed his "plan" to some of his "friends" in the Reichstag during negotiations for the 1904 estimates. They responded negatively to a full squadron but showed surprising interest in shortening the lifespan of the old *Sachsen* and *Siegfried* classes from twenty-five to twenty years. Clearly the deputies did not understand the implications of this suggestion, because it would require a four tempo for a number of years. On 15 February 1904 Tirpitz ordered E to examine this possibility and to suggest when it might be introduced.[74]

E drafted a proposal to shorten battleship life to twenty years, to be introduced in the fall of 1904 with a building tempo of 4:4:4:4:1:1:1:1:1:1:2:2:2 from 1905 to 1917. Another law would be needed in 1909 to reintroduce the three tempo. The RMA would also ask for 27 million marks per battleship.[75]

William II resumed pestering Tirpitz with plans for large cruisers and a fast battleship. Although the next year's cruiser would have 21-cm guns, he wanted 24-cm guns.[76] Tirpitz patiently explained that every ship was a compromise, and such a cruiser would lose too much in speed and range to be of use to the fleet.[77] William II's next salvo was a sketch in his own hand for a heavily armored 19.5-knot, 14,000-ton battleship, with four 28-cm and either eight 24-cm or ten 21-cm guns. He also suggested that the ship have turbine engines, and sent a *direct* order to the Konstructionsabteilung in the RMA to design such a ship, much to the annoyance of both Tirpitz and K.[78]

At a staff meeting on 25 April 1904 Tirpitz pondered how to deal with the amateur ship designer. The latter, from his annual Mediterranean cruise, struck again with a 15,000-ton battleship project with four 28-cm and sixteen 21-cm guns.[79] At the meeting Tirpitz noted that "the money question will always be the decisive factor." The Emperor's project would cost at least 30 million marks. He then made another remark which he would later contradict. He acknowledged that the Italians and the British were building bigger ships than Germany, and asserted that numbers would count more than the superiority of individual ships.[80] On other occasions he argued that German ships were qualitatively superior. He complained to Prinz Heinrich that he could not convince the imperial brother that the type questions in his proposal would fudge the legally established type distinction and jeopardize the Reichstag's confidence.[81]

In June 1904 Capelle began work on plans that did not involve a four tempo, one that would shorten the lifespan of *Siegfrieds* and older battleships ships, and add five large cruisers. Unstated was the assumption that an additional Novelle would follow in 1911 or 1912 to continue the three tempo. When Capelle wanted to meet with the Treasury in anticipation of revenue needs, Tirpitz denied permission, probably for fear of a leak.[82]

In the fall of 1904, when William II returned from his travels, he wanted a Novelle that would ensure early completion of the second double squadron, which under the 1900 Navy Law would occur in 1920. Capelle's three tempo plan of June 1904 would have completed it a few years earlier. The Emperor wanted it completed by 1914, with a four-battleship tempo from 1906 through 1909. On 1 November Tirpitz ordered E to prepare financial tables for that plan. He liked the idea of a four-battleship tempo, but only building battleships would interrupt cruiser development for four years. On 15 December he ordered a plan for a four tempo that would include one cruiser a year.[83] Later in December the Emperor, disturbed by an abrupt rise in Anglo-German tension, tried to revive the idea of a third double squadron. Tirpitz said no, afraid that the Reichstag would reject both its cost and its offensive character. Such was the semi-panic in the navy at the time that Tirpitz feared Britain might use it as an excuse for preventive war. Also shaken, Capelle suggested a deferral of the Novelle to 1907.[84] The causes of this internal turmoil require examination.

DIPLOMATIC BOMBSHELLS, 1901–1905

Between 1897 and 1901 Anglo-German relations had two contradictory trends. One was German Weltpolitik and Tirpitz's Navy Laws that required time-limited doses of Anglophobia. German foreign policy, in theory, was based on the avoidance of conflict with Britain while the "danger zone" continued and the fleet was still incomplete. This approach was rendered difficult by William II's sporadic excitability (e.g., China, Samoa, the Boer War), inflammatory rhetoric, and jealousy of British royalty. The other trend was the inclination of some British politicians and a few German officials to explore the possibility of an Anglo-German alliance. This move foundered partly because of Bülow's belief that an alliance with Britain would mean Russian hostility. Germany preferred to play off one against the other while trying to stay on reasonably friendly grounds with both,[85] the German idea of the "free hand."

Tirpitz wanted public Anglophobia to be limited to the eve of the Navy Laws, but he was upstaged by the enraged reaction of the press to the Boer War (1899–1903). The British press, no stranger to Germanopho-

bia, began to awaken to the possible consequences of a future powerful
German Navy instead of seeing it as a welcome balance to the French
Navy.[86]

Prinz Heinrich's British visit in May 1902, as commander of a powerful squadron of eight battleships, had made an impression. A *National
Revue* correspondent wrote:[87]

> For the first time in our history, a foreign force, superior to any squadron
> we have in commission in home waters, has been at work on our coasts.
> . . . The force comes today as a friend, but in the future it may come as an
> enemy—for Germans have openly avowed the purpose of building a fleet to
> destroy the British naval predominance.

In October 1902 the Admiralty first became convinced that the German
Navy was built with England in mind. The Earl of Selborne, First Lord
of the Admiralty notified the Cabinet:[88]

> The Admiralty had proof that the German Navy was being constructed
> with a view to being able to fight the British Navy; restricted cruising
> radius; cramped crew quarters etc., meant that the German battleships were
> designed for a North Sea fleet and practically nothing else.

As the Admiralty awakened and the German fleet grew, Tirpitz's
fears of the danger zone became a persistent narrative embodied in the
term "Copenhagen." During a crucial moment in the Napoleonic Wars
in 1807, while Denmark was neutral, a British force suddenly appeared in
the Danish Straits and, in an act of surpassing ruthlessness, bombarded
Copenhagen and seized the Danish fleet.[89] A British preventive attack on
German ports had been in Tirpitz's thoughts since 1897. The risk fleet
idea to deter British attack contained a paradox. Might not a gradual
buildup of the German fleet invite the very "Copenhagen" it was supposed to prevent? His fear helps to explain his seemingly peculiar passivity
in foreign affairs. Although he had little direct influence in that sphere,
the mere existence of the fleet had great impact abroad. How ironic that
the creator of what was supposed to be the principal instrument of Weltpolitik favored a peaceful and restrained foreign policy for the decades it
would take to construct the fleet. In his memoirs Tirpitz lamented "sensa-
tional interventions" such as the Kruger telegram, the China expedition,
and the landing in Tangiers in 1905.[90]

The Anglo-French Entente of 8 April 1904 was an unpleasant shock,
although it was, at first, just a colonial agreement between two long-term

rivals. Another reason for the Entente was the 1902 British defensive alliance with Japan. The looming Russo-Japanese War threatened conflict between England and France, Russia's ally for a decade. Anglo-French complications in Europe on behalf of their warring allies in Asia would have been a serious problem for both. Initially the agreement was not anti-German on the British side, although its architect, the cunning and far-seeing French Foreign Minister Theophile Delcassé, may have wished it so. A long-term German naval threat was, at the time, not yet a major issue with the British.

In June 1904 King Edward VII visited Germany for Kiel Week. To Tirpitz's chagrin, Edward VII's vainglorious nephew assembled virtually the whole German Navy in home waters. The display clearly impressed the King and his naval advisers. Tirpitz would have preferred more discretion.[91]

That summer the Admiralty began a gradual concentration of the Royal Navy in home waters, which Tirpitz had believed to be impossible in 1900. Fisher became First Sea Lord in October 1904. The Home Fleet grew to twelve battleships, equal to the number Germany had in commission in 1904. The Atlantic Fleet, in Gibraltar with eight battleships, could provide quick support in home waters. The Mediterranean Fleet was cut from twelve to eight battleships. As an Admiralty committee reported in February 1905: "The deployment of the German Navy, and the uncertain attitude of that power, has rendered a redistribution necessary as regards our force in European waters."[92]

On 8 February 1904 the long-anticipated Russo-Japanese War broke out. To reinforce its Far Eastern Fleet, the Russians decided to send the Baltic Fleet halfway around the world.[93] The Hamburg-Amerika shipping line (HAPAG), supplied coal for the fleet. It created a great outcry in Japan and Britain that Germany was not observing the traditional obligations of neutrals.[94]

On the night of 21 October 1904 the Russian fleet passed through the North Sea's Dogger Bank near Hull. In an almost farcical fiasco, inexperienced Russians fired on English trawlers that they mistook for lurking Japanese torpedo boats. The British reacted with fury, not only against the Russians but even more so against the Germans for supplying them.[95]

Taken aback by the furor, William II, Bülow, and Holstein believed that the time was ripe for a defensive alliance with Russia. The idea of the "free hand" was temporarily forgotten. Foreign Secretary Richthofen and Tirpitz opposed it. The "Copenhagen" complex had an effect that far outweighed the "alliance value" corollary of the risk theory.

Tirpitz was so nervous that a Russian alliance would provoke Britain that he wrote directly to Richthofen on 1 November to argue that an alliance with Russia would avail Germany little and might cost much. Contrary to the risk theory, "the military value for us of an alliance with Russia is essentially nothing in a naval war." He asserted that France would join England and Russia as an ally [in fact, a very unlikely event in such a war] and would "disrupt the functioning of our military apparatus." At war with Japan, Russia would be so crippled that it could not attack in the west even if it stuck with its French ally. He was convinced that "our eastern border can be considered, in fact, unthreatened."[96] At first the Czar was interested, but, as the Dogger Bank incident died down, his advisers talked him out of it. The Russians then allowed negotiations to end.[97]

The uproar over the Dogger Bank incident began the already planned redistribution of the Royal Navy. Fisher called home four battleships from the Mediterranean Fleet and carried out sooner than anticipated concentration in home waters. William II commented that it was "a result of the sly policy of Delcassé, who has defended himself against us with England."[98]

As if to confirm the Copenhagen narrative, on 3 February 1905 Arthur Lee, First Lord of the Admiralty, told his constituents that if war were declared on Germany, the Royal Navy would "get its blow in first, before the other side had time even to read in the papers that war had been declared."[99] This was more inflammatory even than the 1897 *Saturday Review* article titled "*Germaniam delendam esse* [Germany must be destroyed]." Such irresponsible statements by a Cabinet member were almost ignored in England but created consternation in Germany. A threat perception gap, where each side felt threatened by the other but neither believed it was threatening anyone, began to grow. This became a characteristic of later arms races, where both sides felt they were acting only defensively.[100]

Throughout December and January the Admiralstab worked frantically to update its operations plan against England. The plan assumed that France was likely to join Britain. The navy's plan had an odd twist, revelatory of the incoherence of German war planning;[101] to avoid choking off imports, it would guarantee the neutrality of Belgium and the Netherlands while the army passed through Belgium on the way to

France! Fisher's redistribution seemed to portend preventive attack, with predictably disastrous consequences. If the British entered the Baltic, the Great and Little Belts would have to be seized and occupied. If the Danes resisted, the army would crush them.

The army would have none of it. Schlieffen bluntly told the navy that every available man was needed elsewhere.[102] The army wanted to invade Belgium and keep Denmark neutral, and the navy wanted to do the opposite. The army got its way, leaving the navy with nothing resembling a feasible plan.

FIRST NEWS OF HMS *DREADNOUGHT*

In London Coerper began to hear rumors that the Admiralty was considering enormously larger battleships. He also noted rumors that Japan was contemplating a battleship of 19,200 tons with twelve to fourteen 30.5-cm guns. Most alarming of all, on 20 February 1905, he confirmed that the Admiralty had decided to build an 18,000-ton battleship with twelve 30.5-cm guns. Such an all-big-gun armament was a radical departure. HMS *Dreadnought* was on the way.[103]

Tirpitz was shaken by the news. His first thought was that English belligerence, to which he attributed the larger ship type, made it imperative for Germany to return to the idea of the cruiser Novelle.[104] Subsequent research by British naval historians has demonstrated that Fisher was simply anticipating developments in Japan and the United States, and did not have Germany primarily in mind.[105] What matters here is not Fisher's actual intention but rather what Tirpitz *thought* it was. Clearly Tirpitz and William II believed that the Dreadnought and later the Invincible battlecruiser type was directed mainly at Germany. They claimed that Britain, and not Germany, was responsible for the ensuing arms race.[106]

On 11 February Tirpitz met with the Emperor, still enraged by Lee's speech the week before.[107] Tirpitz tried to dampen William II's wrath and insisted that a third double squadron or a four tempo Novelle were out of the question. He conceded that larger battleships (though not necessarily Dreadnoughts) were essential; the cost, however, would be a great burden for the Reichstag and the Reich's meager purse. There were two choices for a three tempo: either shorten the lifespan of the older battleships, meaning three battleships a year (offensive, not defensive, in the eyes of the Reichstag) or return to the 1900 cruiser proposal. Tirpitz agreed that the choice could temporarily be left open, but he indicated a strong preference for a cruiser Novelle, with two battleships and one large cruiser per year through 1911. The Emperor reluctantly agreed, and it seemed that by mid-February 1905 the content of the Novelle was agreed upon.[108]

Tirpitz feared that going beyond the cruiser Novelle would increase the possibility of conflict with England. Money was a thorny problem. Matching the size of British ships would mean having to widen the Kaiser Wilhelm Canal, which would be ruinously expensive. With the self-obsessed view of the bureaucratic warrior, Tirpitz was convinced that Fisher had built *Dreadnought* primarily because the canal and German dockyards could not accommodate ships that large. Tirpitz had to choose: either build inferior ships or widen the canal. Based on his extensive studies of Fisher, Marder concludes that not "a scrap of evidence" indicates that the canal was a factor in Fisher's ship-type increase.[109]

Despite growing pressure from the Flottenverein, Tirpitz concluded that he should proceed with the six cruiser Novelle.[110] The twists and turns in the Novelle proposals over the preceding years had varied in size relative to Germany's diplomatic freedom of action, the attitudes of key parties in the Reichstag, and the Reich's general financial situation. As these factors became more unfavorable, the Novelle regressed to its original size. The time was not ripe to jeopardize his life's work with a rash initiative. On 20 February 1905 he informed the Budget Commission that he would propose a cruiser Novelle in the fall.[111] Reichstag reaction was mild and generally favorable. At that point there was little notion of the enormous prospective cost increase, and most deputies were not sympathetic with the Flottenverein's aggressive battleship ideas.[112]

The RMA feverishly worked on the design of larger battleships. The first two projects were a ship with four 28-cm and twelve 21-cm guns (similar to William II's idea of the previous year) and a ship with eight 28 cm guns. The latter, if approved, would have been the first German Dreadnought, albeit a small one. Both types could still have passed through the Kaiser Wilhelm Canal. As yet, Tirpitz was not thinking of 18,000-ton behemoths.[113]

While on his annual Mediterranean cruise, William II reluctantly landed at Tangiers to support the Moroccan Sultan against French inroads. This initiative, of which Tirpitz had no foreknowledge, touched off the First Moroccan Crisis.[114] In Messina he saw Italian plans for a new

battleship with eight 30.5-cm guns, while Germany was only contemplating 28-cm guns. Tirpitz responded that such a ship could not manage
the rough waters of the North Sea. Indeed, such a leap in size might
jeopardize the Novelle for both political and parliamentary reasons. He
reminded the Emperor that the Reichstag would not support a German-
led arms race. Germany had to wait and see, and build larger ships only
if it appeared forced to do so by others.[115]

Eickstedt, Chief of K, had technical objections that reinforced Tirpitz's reluctance to build Dreadnoughts. He stated flatly that K then only
had the capacity to design a ship with six 28-cm guns, not eight, and the
ship could make only 20 knots, not 22, as the Emperor wanted.[116] Tirpitz
reminded William II that a fast battleship would obscure the law's distinction between battleships and large cruisers. Nonetheless, with an eye to
the future, Tirpitz ordered K to study the eventual feasibility of a 22.5-knot
battleship, with six or eight 28-cm guns, plus an even faster cruiser with
eight 21-cm guns.[117]

By May 1905 the first Novelle draft was ready. Tirpitz told E to ignore rapidly rising costs and to try to limit discussion of costs in the 1906
estimates to a battleship price of 31 million marks.[118] Upon reflection,
Capelle decided that this was the wrong way to go. He explained why in
a detailed analysis of the possible effects of concealing the scope of the
cost increase.[119]

Capelle conceded the superficial advantage of separating the price
increase from the Novelle, but he believed that sharper minds in the
Reichstag would feel deceived. If the Reichstag cried foul and was dissolved, then the navy might be hurt in the subsequent election. To keep
the Reichstag's confidence, it would be better if the Novelle and the
estimates were discussed together, with the increase in ship size frankly
discussed, including real approximations of ship costs between 1906 and
1917. Capelle's wisdom, good sense, and pragmatism proved compelling
to Tirpitz. On 2 June Tirpitz agreed to send the Novelle and the estimates
to the Reichstag together.[120]

By the end of July the Novelle and estimates drafts went to the Treasury for comment.[121] The Novelle, only one paragraph long, simply provided for an increase of five cruisers for service abroad, plus one for the
material reserve. The estimates added eight more torpedo boat divisions
to make a total of twenty-four by 1917.

For the first time the estimates provided a small sum for research and for the development of U-boats, a type that France, England, and the United States had been testing since 1900. Tirpitz's conservatism about U-boats became a huge issue during the war. He waited until 1906, he said, because the primitive vessels available before then would be of no use for the fleet or for a commerce war, a strategy he did not want to encourage anyway. Tirpitz argued that resources deployed any sooner would be wasted in *"altes Eisen"* (junk). Only a few visionaries foresaw the U-boat's immense potential for raiding commerce in 1906, or even in 1914.[122]

In the spring and summer of 1905 Coerper forwarded information on *HMS Dreadnought*, and some of the news was scary. At the end of April First Lord Lee said that it would be "the strongest the world has ever seen and will be built in the shortest conceivable time." Coerper learned that the ship would have turbine engines, a first for battleships. It would steam at 21 knots and have ten 30.5-cm guns.[123]

In response, the Emperor demanded a 22-knot, 19,000-ton fast battleship. Tirpitz countered that over 16,000 tons would reopen the expensive canal question and alienate the Reichstag.[124] This time the Emperor did not buy the argument. He asked Bülow about widening the canal. Bülow typically, was more optimistic than Tirpitz. He believed that he could overcome both expected agrarian opposition and cost questions in the name of the canal's commercial importance, a rationale that would lift the blame from the navy. The Emperor assured Tirpitz that the cost of widening the canal, 60 million marks, need not deter construction of larger ships, because the burden could be placed on the Interior Ministry.[125]

Tirpitz spent the summer pondering whether to build Dreadnoughts. Dähnhardt, Capelle, and Senior Commander Reinhard Scheer,[126] Head of the Central Department (Zentralabteilung, or Z), helped him weigh the options. Tirpitz, under enormous pressure but free from the cost of the canal, saw the logic of a type increase. For once he backed down to the Emperor. New tables increased the battleship cost from 31 million to 36.5 million marks and for cruisers from 24 million to 27.5 million marks.[127] The 1906 battleships (*Nassau* and *Westfalen*) were to be 18,000 tons with twelve 28-cm guns and twelve 15-cm guns, and with a speed of 18.75 knots, though he made no attempt to shift from reciprocating to turbine engines. The 1906 large cruiser (*Blücher*) was to be about 15,000 tons with twelve 21-cm guns.[128]

The decision marked the beginning of German Dreadnoughts, but their design created difficult problems for K. The keel of *Nassau*, the first, was not laid until the spring of 1907. It is fair to say that Tirpitz opposed building Dreadnoughts until the combined pressure of the Emperor and Fisher forced him to. If he did not follow the British, he could be accused of sending German sailors into battle in "floating coffins." Later he was accused of this anyway when comparable German Dreadnoughts were smaller than British ones.

Tirpitz's conservatism, combined with the Reich's financial difficulties, and his need to keep faith with the Reichstag, made Fisher's initiative awkward. Only afterward did he console himself with the thought that Fisher had wiped the slate clean. The huge British superiority in pre-Dreadnoughts would become increasingly irrelevant as both sides built more Dreadnoughts. Although Fisher had guaranteed himself a short head start, the realization that both sides were starting from scratch made it clear that an arms race was likely. When Fisher later built the battlecruiser *Invincible*, the competition spread to another ruinously expensive type.

THE 1906 NOVELLE BEFORE THE REICHSTAG

By the end of September 1905 the draft law and the estimates were complete. The Emperor approved them unchanged on 4 October.[129] The canal bill was successfully fobbed off on the Interior Ministry.[130] Tirpitz ordered strict secrecy to keep the British from knowing that Germany was about to build Dreadnoughts.[131]

The "modest" six-cruiser scope of the 1906 Novelle, with the three tempo continued through 1911, had been public since Tirpitz announced it in the Budget Commission on 20 February 1905. The Flottenverein was clearly disappointed. In April 1904 it had proposed four[!] double squadrons that would cost more than 3,000 million marks. Center deputies were delighted when Tirpitz repudiated their grandiose designs.[132]

After the Novelle announcement, pressure began to rise once more. On 6 October Tirpitz heard that the Flottenverein was pressing for a larger Novelle. On 22 October Count Ernst von Reventlow, a well-known, right-wing polemicist, wrote to Tirpitz that the public "expected" that older battleships would be replaced before their twenty-five-year lifespan; Tirpitz replied coolly.[133] The naval enthusiasts pressed the more

pliable Bülow as well. It was a measure of how little Bülow understood
Tirpitz's design that Bülow asked if Tirpitz could assure that the danger
zone would be passed after the next four years. The Chancellor, who
was supposedly Tirpitz's closest partner in a "system-stabilizing Tirpitz
Plan," had no real comprehension of what Tirpitz was doing. Bülow even
tried to persuade Tirpitz to expand the Novelle shortly before it went to
the Bundesrat, and expressed his willingness to take on the consequent
political risk. Tirpitz warned that such a course might bring on war. He
privately felt that Bülow was trying to place the blame for the small Novelle wholly on his shoulders. In that way Bülow could escape the wrath
of the Emperor and the patriotic Right.[134]

Otto Prince Salm and retired Admiral Thomsen visited Tirpitz just
before the bill went to the Bundesrat. They wanted early replacement of
the older battleships and a four-battleship tempo. It was a heated meeting.
Trotha stood outside the closed door and heard Thomsen accuse Tirpitz
of offering the nation "stones for bread."[135] Tirpitz rebuffed them, pointed
to the "Copenhagen" danger, and argued that the Reichstag would not
support offensive measures. He also argued that high new loans and taxes
would undercut the desperately needed financial reform that Bülow was
trying to get under way. Salm and Thomsen went away empty-handed,
but the agitation continued.[136]

The Novelle and the naval estimates passed the Bundesrat on 15
November, and on the 27th Bülow sent it to the Reichstag.[137] The RMA
updated the economic statistical survey that had accompanied the 1898
Navy Law. It demonstrated the growth of German maritime interests
and, implicitly, the need for more cruisers to protect those interests.[138]
This Mahanist line of thought is no more persuasive than to say that Luf-
thansa could not thrive without a powerful German Air Force or that the
huge Norwegian merchant marine could not exist without a formidable
Norwegian Navy.

From 1906 to 1917 the plan, including ships already projected in the
existing law, envisioned eighteen battleships, thirteen large cruisers, and
twenty small cruisers. The three tempo would continue through 1911
and then would drop to two. According to the new and all-important
table of estimates, annual expenditures would grow from 252 million
marks in 1906 to 330 million marks in 1917. The Novelle and the new

estimates table added more than 900 million marks to the 1900 projections.[139] Even so, this table, much sooner than expected, proved miserably
inadequate because of still further acceleration in the cost of large ships.
Large cruisers cost 27.5 million marks (*Blücher's* cost in 1906). *Von der
Tann*, Germany's first (1907) Invincible-type battlecruiser, later cost 36.6
million marks. This quantum leap, and not the desire for a four tempo,
would make another Novelle necessary within two years. In 1906 Tirpitz
was "low-balling" the Reichstag without realizing it.

Both the canal and the navy had to be paid for, along with the Reich's
other revenue needs. The government asked for an increase in beer and
tobacco tariffs, and some automobile, travel ticket, and bill of lading taxes.
By far the most controversial for the right-wing government parties was a
Reich inheritance tax. Though modest, this levy would be a move toward
a direct tax by the Reich.[140]

As in the past, the deputies were more interested in the tax proposals
than in the navy itself. Neither deputies nor the press seemed to grasp
the real issue; they saw only the number of ships and their cost. Flottenverein agitation made Tirpitz seem like a moderate. By January 1906 their
propaganda machine turned personal against Tirpitz with the accusation
that he was sending sailors to their death in "floating coffins."[141] They
missed the real significance of the Novelle. Retention of the three tempo
at a time of escalating ship growth meant participation in an arms race.
Few saw the implications of ships of a new and revolutionary type. Tirpitz
tried to keep these aspects as obscure as possible, lest the deputies fully
understand the situation.

Once again the Center clearly would be pivotal. Conservatives and
National Liberals wanted a larger bill.[142] The Center liked its apparently
moderate scale. Over the next month the Center even made overtures to
shorten the lifespan of the older battleships.[143]

The major attacks came, predictably, from the Social Democrats.
Bebel, their leader, argued that an arms race was hopeless for Germany;
Bebel, however, like almost everyone else, overlooked the significance of
the transition to Dreadnoughts.[144] Tirpitz spoke in a calm, measured tone.
He emphasized the moderate number of ships. He argued that displacements would have to increase for technical and strategic reasons, without
referring to specific countries. Both he and the official press soft-pedaled

the decision to build Dreadnoughts. Without objective outside experts, who existed in Britain but not in Germany, the press also missed the significance of the Dreadnought transition.[145]

On 15 December the bills went to the Budget Commission. Agitation for a shortened lifespan or a third double squadron, or both, reached its peak. The Moroccan Crisis roused patriotic feeling even among non-chauvinists. As a contingency, Tirpitz prepared for an attempt in the Budget Commission to shorten battleship lifespan to twenty years. He even calculated a building plan on the twenty-year assumption that would, however, be configured to retain the three tempo.[146]

At a meeting on 3 February 1906 the Emperor wavered in his support of Tirpitz's Novelle and criticized him for not using the enormous agitation to obtain more ships.[147] William II pushed Bülow to advocate shortening the lifespan of the older battleships even to eighteen or nineteen years. Bülow, with his usual facile optimism, claimed he could get it through the Reichstag in light of Delcassé's false allegation that he had been offered 100,000 British troops.[148]

Tirpitz reminded the Emperor why he had accepted the modest Novelle in the first place. A three tempo of two battleships and one large cruiser was technically and developmentally the best for the navy. Even more important was fear of a "Copenhagen" if Germany overreached. He saw the danger in 1906 to be as great as it had been in 1905. Preventive war would destroy the results achieved over a decade.[149]

Capelle prepared a memo demonstrating that there would be almost no chance to pass a large proposal, even if the danger of preventive war were ignored. The Center would not go along.[150] On 8 February Bülow admitted to Tirpitz that such a Novelle was impossible. The Emperor was, nevertheless, furious at Tirpitz for his obstinacy. Tirpitz had to again resort to threatening resignation to get the Emperor to accept the modest Novelle. Once again Tirpitz acted like a quasi-parliamentary Cabinet member. Only because Tirpitz was indispensable did the Emperor finally back down on 15 February.[151]

The next time that Tirpitz saw William II, on 3 March, the latter should have been exultant, since it was then that he gave final approval to the plan for *Nassau*, Germany's first Dreadnought. This impressively powerful ship was designed to be 18,700 tons, 19 knots, with twelve 28-cm and twelve 15-cm guns, as well as formidable armor. Instead the Emperor was extremely cool.[152]

The Budget Commission accepted the Novelle and the estimates unchanged, with opposition only from the Social Democrats and the left-wing progressives. By late March 1906 the Moroccan Crisis made it clear that the British were prepared to back the French. Germany's weakness and isolation were obvious to all. The final acceptance, without debate, of the Novelle on 19 May, and of the estimates on 25 May by large majorities, was almost anticlimactic.[153]

The ease of passage made the Emperor even more furious at Tirpitz. As marginalia to an article in the *Neue Politische Korrespondenz* of 16 March, William II wrote: "*Flaussen! Man hat nicht genug seinerseits gefordert und fühlt nun, dass die Leute, die darauf hinweisen, recht haben* [Humbug. We did not demand enough. Now we feel that the people who advised asking more were correct]."[154]

Tirpitz heard of this remark on 30 March; a few days later he submitted his resignation. William II promptly apologized and returned the letter. Tirpitz asked, and received permission, for leave. He sulked all summer at St. Blasien and even left there slightly uncertain as to whether he would indeed resign. He finally relented when he heard, through Müller, that the Emperor was remorseful.[155]

The 1906 Navy Law and estimates provide a nuanced example of Tirpitz as the classic bureaucratic politician. At first glance the moderate size of the Novelle seems surprising. Older historians such as Willy Becker, who interpret Tirpitz's motivation as simply "*Baueifer*" (avidity for building), are at a loss to explain it.[156] Similarly historians like Fernis partially miss the point when they see the 1906 Novelle as simply a fulfillment of the cruiser part of the draft 1900 law.[157] The moderate size of the 1906 Novelle was owing to Tirpitz's fear of preventive attack, combined with his dependence on the Reichstag for any new initiatives, as well as the Reich's difficult financial situation. In the heat of patriotic feeling linked to the First Moroccan Crisis, he might have asked for and gotten more, but he knew his empire would be swept into uncertainty if interrupted by a disastrous war. He knew he would have been blamed if Germany lost badly in such a mismatch. He certainly considered larger alternatives to a cruiser Novelle, but he rejected them all in 1905, mostly out of fear of a "Copenhagen" crisis and what that would have done to his well-functioning bureaucratic empire. By 1905 he was in a position of strength to achieve his goals, and such bureaucratic politicians are notably risk-averse. If he were fully convinced that he could have gotten more without war or parliamentary complications, he might well have done so. *Ressorteifer* had convinced him to double the fleet in 1900, using the "strongest seapower" as a convenient measuring stick to provide a plausible reason to expand. That was a risk but a necessary and, he thought, manageable one. Once the law was in hand, he used the limited personal influence he had in foreign affairs to try to get the Emperor and Bülow to lie low in colonial and diplomatic matters. From 1904 to 1906, though he misjudged and vastly overestimated Britain's inclination for preventive war, he became extremely cautious about further expansion because of his genuine though misplaced fears.

It is true that the existence and prospective future growth of the German Navy played a secondary though real role in forming the Anglo-French Entente. However, the timid beginnings of Anglo-French military conversation resulted principally from the ill-considered German diplomatic offensive in Morocco and the fear of a German land attack on France. No evidence indicates that Tirpitz played much more than a spectator's role in the First Moroccan Crisis. Tirpitz could have used the consequent Anglo-German hostility to push for a larger Novelle, as he had in 1900; instead, for the complex reasons outlined above, he chose a more moderate approach.

The Dreadnought transition, rather than the 1906 Novelle per se, started the great naval arms race. For that both Tirpitz and Fisher share the blame. Whatever the reasons that prompted Fisher to build Dreadnoughts, it greatly magnified what was already a low-intensity arms race, since both powers were starting virtually from zero. Tirpitz began to build Dreadnoughts only very reluctantly, but once he did so the temptation was great, and he succumbed to it in 1908. Thus began the huge arms race, the first in the twentieth century. The risk theory, which apparently had received its death blow with Fisher's reforms and the Anglo-French Entente, gained new credibility as a narrative after the *Dreadnought*, even though it actually remained a chimera reflecting propaganda more than reality. Devaluation of the tremendous British advantage in pre-Dreadnoughts made it appear possible for Germany to deter the "greatest seapower" all by itself.

12

SOW THE WIND, 1906–1908

THE RMA IN 1906

The RMA's diverse workload and Tirpitz's success as a bureaucratic warrior employed sixty mostly senior sea officers, by far the largest levy in the navy except for the fleet itself.[1] Many of them were long-term RMA officers, whereas the Admiralstab had thirty-six officers, most of them quite junior, who rotated frequently in and out of the fleet. The RMA employed fifty-seven senior civil servants (none in the Admiralstab), plus clerks, scribes, and so on. The Admiralstab had only one admiral (Büchsel), whereas the RMA had six rear admirals or officers of even higher rank.

The RMA still had a leavening of Tirpitz's Torpedo Gang, who, by 1906, were of high rank. These included Tirpitz's close personal friends: Vice Admiral Hunold von Ahlefeld, Rear Admiral August von Heeringen, and Captain Raimond Winkler. Other torpedo men included Captain Reinhard Scheer and Captain Harald Dähnhardt. The latter two reported to Rear Admiral Eduard Capelle, Director of the Administrative Department (V).

Just departed for the fleet were Commanders Adolf von Trotha, who had served under Scheer in the Central Department, and William Michaelis. The latter had served as confidential secretary to Heeringen. Trotha had served in a similar capacity for Tirpitz for the prior five years. Although Trotha, after 1906, never again served under Tirpitz, their correspondence of hundreds of letters testifies to the closeness of their relationship.[2]

Trotha had a gift for ingratiating himself with powerful men. First he served Tirpitz, while officially a subordinate of Scheer, and then Müller in the MK from 1909 to 1913, where he had close access to the Emperor. He became Scheer's Chief of Staff when the latter took over the High Seas Fleet in 1916. After the war he was briefly Chief of Admiralty under the Republic, but discredited himself by his "neutrality" toward the Kapp Putsch. After Tirpitz's death, he became an ardent Nazi.[3] Trotha was one of few officers with substantial Front credentials who understood the magnitude of Tirpitz's achievement in winning the Reichstag for the navy. He saw what Tirpitz had to do, to the disappointment of many Front officers, to operate in the world of parliamentary politics.

Trotha's duties from 1901 to 1906 included preparing matters subject to the Emperor's decision. He defended Tirpitz from Front complaints, including his reluctance to create a Fleet Command before it was "absolutely necessary." This had deleterious effects on training and readiness, as seen in Tirpitz's conflict with Koester in 1902 and after.[4] Trotha saw this practice as the "normal conflicts of a healthy organization."[5] One advantage of Tirpitz's view was that sooner or later Prinz Heinrich would take his turn as Chief of the Active Battlefleet. Though he was a man of considerable personal charm, and much more stable than his imperial brother, no one wanted to see him as wartime Fleet Chief. Trotha defended Tirpitz against the charge that he did not provide enough money for readiness and other pressing needs of the fleet. He agreed with Tirpitz that the tight-fistedness of the Reichstag for anything but construction made such needs wait until the development phase was over.[6]

ACROSS THE NORTH SEA

Early in 1906 events eased Tirpitz's fears of a preventive attack. In December 1905, with the Moroccan Crisis at its height, Tirpitz shepherding the Novelle through the Reichstag, and *Dreadnought* on the stocks at Portsmouth, British elections in January 1906 returned a gigantic Liberal majority. The new Foreign Secretary, Sir Edward Grey, renewed his predecessor's vague "commitment" to support France against Germany at the Algeciras Conference and continued military conversations with France that the Conservatives had initiated;[7] there were indications, however, that the Liberals intended to modify British naval policy.

In their last days in office the Conservatives defined their shipbuilding policy in the "Cawdor Memorandum," after Lord Cawdor, then First

Lord of the Admiralty.[8] It proposed construction of four large armored ships per year. The new Liberal Prime Minister, Sir Henry Campbell-Bannerman, at first accepted this program.

Many Liberal candidates had run on a platform of arms reduction in favor of social welfare programs. The party was divided over armaments. The Liberal Imperialist faction, led by Herbert Asquith (at the Exchequer until 1908), Grey, and Lord Richard Haldane, were more aware of the potential threat of Tirpitz's navy than the Liberal "Little Navy" wing. This group, led by Campbell-Bannerman and, after his death in 1908, by David Lloyd George and Winston Churchill, were far less willing than the Liberal Imperialists to sacrifice social welfare for Dreadnoughts.

In the spring of 1906 a popular clamor arose for a reduced naval program. Dreadnoughts and, still in deep secrecy, three Invincible-class battlecruisers were under construction. In May 1906 Fisher and the Board of Admiralty agreed to drop one ship of the 1906–1907 program. With the Russian proposal for another peace conference at The Hague in 1907, the government persuaded the Admiralty to ask for only two Dreadnoughts in the 1907–1908 estimates, with a third to be laid down if the conference was unsuccessful in arms reduction.

This change in the Cawdor Program produced howls of protest from Conservatives and the navalist press. Fisher, in particular, was pilloried and accused of selling out to the "cheese paring economists" of the government; but Fisher was satisfied with the reduction, since Britain had such a commanding lead, both in pre-Dreadnoughts and Dreadnoughts under construction. Even if the Admiralty ceased building for two years, Britain would still be superior to Germany.[9] In the spring of 1909 the Royal Navy would have four Dreadnoughts and three battlecruisers at sea, while neither France nor Germany would have any. Russia's naval defeat in the war with Japan left its navy virtually out of consideration. The subsequent direction of the British naval program would depend on the results of the upcoming Hague Conference on Armaments.

EARLY NOVELLE PLANS

With the British Liberals in office and their relatively modest building plans, Tirpitz saw a possibility for expanding the fleet further. The Algeciras Conference, in practice a German defeat, ended the Moroccan

Crisis. British solidarity with France had strengthened the Anglo-French Entente, whereas Bülow and Holstein's original purpose had been to weaken it. Bülow, exhausted, suffered a heart attack on 5 April and was out of action for several months.[10] Ironically the German diplomatic defeat also increased Tirpitz's freedom of action, because fear of preventive war diminished. In a further irony, a novel titled *The Invasion of 1910* by William LeQueux portrayed a sudden German attack in home waters, with catastrophic British losses to gunfire and torpedoes. This book followed Erskine Childers's *The Riddle of the Sands* (1903), which similarly depicted a German sneak attack. Early in April 1906 the curious Emperor held a naval meeting about it. The Admiralstab dismissed the novel, but the episode showed that fear of a "Copenhagen"-like assault was not limited to the eastern side of the North Sea.[11]

Heartening to Tirpitz was the Center's favorable attitude toward the 1906 Novelle and its estimates. The party had also suggested shortening the lifespan of the older battleships. Tirpitz had already floated the idea of a shorter lifespan to Bülow on 13 November 1905.[12] Shortly after his departure for St. Blasien on leave, and several weeks before the Novelle passed its third reading, on 6 April Tirpitz asked Capelle, Dähnhardt, and N to consider how to direct a campaign for yet another Novelle. The Flottenverein was already complaining loudly that the 1906 Novelle was completely insufficient.[13]

Dähnhardt, in less than a week, gave Capelle a number of possibilities. His initial plan envisioned a twenty-year lifespan for battleships, four additional material reserve ships, and four more large cruisers plus one material reserve for use with the battlefleet. The increase in material reserve illustrates a kind of dodge. Since, by law, the battleships were organized in two double squadrons, it would violate the law if battleships were added that were *not* "material reserve." With thirty-eight battleships (two double squadrons of sixteen each, two flagships, and four material reserve ships), the addition of four ships, even if officially designated "material reserve," would make possible, de facto, a fifth squadron if all eight material reserve ships were to comprise another squadron.

Dähnhardt proposed an increase in the battleship price to 40 million marks and to 35 million or 40 million for large cruisers. He estimated the cost at an extra 673 million marks. Equally significant, the plan featured a four tempo for a series of years.[14] Dähnhardt's second plan was similar, except that it could be introduced, if circumstances warranted, as early as the fall of 1907. It provided only two additional material reserve ships, which would make a total of forty battleships, and a possible five squadrons. He estimated that it would cost an additional 530 million marks, including the price increases.[15] A further alternative would be to introduce Plan 2 in 1912 (the first year of the two tempo) and would require a four tempo between 1913 and 1917.[16]

Dähnhardt suggested several other similar choices for bills in either the fall of 1908 or of 1909, with a three tempo or a four tempo, depending on the number of material reserve battleships and large cruisers in the original plan. In his marginalia on Dähnhardt's work, Capelle showed his preference for a three tempo in the fall of 1909. Dähnhardt preferred a four tempo.[17]

Dähnhardt had an unwitting ally in the Emperor. Müller, on 3 May, informed Tirpitz, that William II wanted a large Novelle within a year in order to shorten the lifespan of the older battleships and contain a four tempo. Tirpitz replied cautiously, perhaps because he wanted to keep the work already in progress from the Emperor. A radical departure from previous methods might endanger the Navy Law.[18]

Tirpitz at first was on Capelle's side. He ordered plans based on a twenty-year battleship lifespan, keeping the three tempo. Capelle agreed that the addition of two more material reserve battleships (totaling sixty large ships) and a twenty-year lifespan, would amount to a permanent establishment of the three-battleship tempo. Even just two additional new ships would make a five-squadron battlefleet possible. The rapid rise in ship prices, faster than anticipated, convinced Capelle that another Novelle, with a new table of ship prices, would soon be necessary, certainly before 1910. Four days *before* the Reichstag gave final approval to the 1906 Novelle, Capelle was thinking of even higher ship prices. On the timing, he rejected the fall of 1907, because that would be just before the five-year term of the Reichstag expired and so a feasible threat of dissolution would not be possible. Because 1910 would be too late to cope with rising costs, Capelle favored the fall of 1909.[19]

Capelle allowed Dähnhardt to present his dissenting view to Tirpitz, an unusual event. He abandoned the idea of a 1907 Novelle and instead suggested a two-step process. The first, as Capelle wanted, would stabilize the three tempo with a twenty-year battleship lifespan and two material reserve battleships. The second would be a temporary four tempo via either five large cruisers for home waters or eight new battleships to form another whole material reserve double squadron.

Dähnhardt wanted, in 1910, either just the first step, with the second to follow later, or both steps simultaneously, if foreign and domestic considerations permitted. To wait that long would protect the navy from accusations of "having no plan" or of taking a "zigzag course." He counseled against informing the Emperor, but he thought that Müller should have a hint of the information so that he could convince William II that a Novelle the following year was impossible.[20]

On 18 May 1906 Tirpitz ordered E to work along the lines of Dähnhardt's ideas. One plan would stabilize the three tempo by adding two more material reserve ships. The second, if political conditions allowed, would be for another "flying squadron" of five large cruisers. Tirpitz rejected Dähnhardt's idea of another double squadron of battleships. If both proposals passed, it would mean a four tempo from 1911 to 1915. Tirpitz also investigated shortening the construction time of battleships and large cruisers from four years to three. This innovation was not feasible for financial and technical reasons; the *potential* was there, however, and therein lies part of the genesis of the naval scare of 1909.

Tirpitz agreed with E on timing. The winter of 1906–1907 would be too soon after the latest Novelle. The winter of 1907–1908 would be unfavorable, since, as noted, it was expected to be the end of the Reichstag term and so he could not credibly threaten dissolution. The winter of 1908–1909 would probably also be objectionable, because in the first term of the new Reichstag the parties, particularly the Center, that had never emphasized support of the navy in its campaigning would be bound by their election promises.

Tirpitz was inclined to favor the winter of 1909–1910. Between 1906 and 1909 Germany would have laid down eight Dreadnoughts, a full homogeneous squadron, although most of the ships would still be under construction. Thereafter there would probably be a further increase in ship size, with the need for a new and higher table of ship costs. After 1911 the battleship tempo would drop to one, an opportune time to increase it.[21]

Tirpitz's calculations were based upon political and financial considerations that had nothing to do with the risk theory. Once again Tirpitz acted as a quasi-parliamentary politician and wanted to obtain as much as he could without endangering the Navy Law. He was no navalist fanatic, but he operated as a bureaucratic politician to preserve his personal and institutional power by keeping the Navy Law intact.

The British disarmament resolution and seemingly pacifist attitude eased his anxiety and gave Tirpitz the nerve to consider a four tempo.[22] After the Algeciras Conference, fears related to the British fleet redistribution receded, encouraging, rather than retarding, another Novelle. At this early planning stage, Tirpitz seems not to have considered that a four tempo would provoke a British reaction. He was even skeptical that Britain could or would maintain its own four tempo if Germany adhered to the three tempo.[23] Tirpitz's illusion continued even after 1908, when it became glaringly apparent that the British had both the means and the will to far exceed a four tempo.

INVINCIBLE

Coerper, in London, heard that the Admiralty was considering another type increase. On 23 May he learned that Armstrong had contracted to build 13.5-inch (34.3-cm) naval guns, and that 16-inch guns were under consideration. Coerper concluded that Germany must soon reckon with post-Dreadnought battleships of 20,000 tons with 34.3-cm guns.[24]

Coerper soon received the alarming news that *Invincible* and its two sisters would be armed with eight 30.5-cm guns. *Invincible* would be a weaker armed and armored, but faster, Dreadnought, a quantum leap in cruiser type that would, at a stroke, render obsolete all the world's armored cruisers. "*Also Linienschiff*" [therefore battleship], wrote the Emperor on the margin of the report, implicitly chiding Tirpitz for opposing his long-cherished plans for a "fast battleship."[25] Tirpitz's first response was denial. He had believed that *Invincible* would merely be a slightly improved *Black Prince* armored cruiser. He replied to Coerper that the information on *Invincible's* guns was incompatible with its anticipated displacement and speed.[26] *Blücher*, with twelve 21-cm guns, was a pygmy by comparison.

The menacing news got RMA departments busy. They soon concluded that Germany could not wait until 1910 for its own battleship-type increase. The four *Nassaus* were secretly laid down during the summer of 1907. Bürkner's design had sixteen watertight compartments. Their reciprocating engines needed a large amount of space amidships, and this precluded superfiring turrets for lack of space for ammunition hoists. The only practical way to include six two-gun turrets was a hexagonal arrangement, with one turret fore, one aft, and two on each side. Therefore a broadside was only eight of the twelve guns.[27]After only a division (four ships) of *Nassaus*, Germany's 1908 battleship projects would have to have twelve 30.5-cm guns instead of 28-cm, like *Nassau*, and the change would require a 20 percent displacement increase. The cost would be ruinous, more than 44 million marks, 10 million more than provided in the cost tables.[28] The RMA could make up this sum from other branches of the navy only with the greatest difficulty.

Capelle asked rhetorically, "Why could we not introduce a Novelle in the next year or two?" He answered: because if one wanted a Novelle in circa 1908, it would be such an "unusual step," because it would have to demand significantly *more* than the present one "in order to make the initiative generally comprehensible" [to the deputies]. Second, it would need a purely objective rationale (organizational reasons within the navy, structure of the navy law, and so on) or else "people would see it as an exercise in *foreign policy*." We have no purely objective motive. At home it would be perceived as defensive, abroad as offensive. What should *we have to ask for?* We would have to take up the old cry of the Flottenverein: build more, build faster. Capelle's observation that the Flottenverein would see a four tempo as "too little," proved partly prophetic and partly mistaken. Capelle concluded that an early Novelle would take the fleet into an obvious power struggle with the Reichstag, something he did not want to provoke. He also expressed horror about what a quick Novelle would do to the nightmarishly divisive tax question.[29]

Dähnhardt lamely suggested that a new estimates table be introduced in the winter of 1907–1908 and that a Novelle be delayed until 1909–1910, but he could not ignore the complications of such an approach.[30] In this atmosphere the Navy Law was a greater bind on the government than on the Reichstag.

At a meeting on 14 July 1906 Tirpitz decided on a different approach. He ordered the preparation of two new tables of estimates for 1909–1917. The first envisioned a three tempo for the entire period, with a battleship price of 44 million marks and a large cruiser cost of 36 million. The second was a four tempo (two battleships and two cruisers per year) with the same prices. He ordered a plan for a battleship with twelve 30.5-cm and twelve 15-cm guns, and for a large cruiser with eight 30.5 cm guns. He tentatively decided to broach the ideas with the Emperor in late September. Tirpitz contemplated a Novelle, or at least a new estimates table, no later than the winter of 1908–1909. He warned his guests at St. Blasien to tell no one who was not directly involved, even within the RMA.[31]

Tirpitz was extremely reluctant to raise prices on both ship types simultaneously. A cruiser with eight 30.5-cm guns would cost 44 million marks, as much as a battleship.[32] There was no enthusiasm in the Reichstag for such an increase. Tirpitz heard that "even old Kardorff [a National Liberal navalist] complains of the monstrous cost of the ships." Since the Admiralty had not announced *Invincible*, he still cherished the notion that Coerper's information was incorrect.[33] Capelle even suggested that, next winter in the Reichstag, Tirpitz declare his regrets for the great type increases and publicly blame future cost increases on the British.[34] Tirpitz decided to delay a definitive decision until the Reichstag session in the fall clarified the parliamentary situation. British delays in officially announcing the type increases caused a problem, because by November at the latest he would have to submit his estimates to the Bundesrat, and he could not appear to be escalating type increases.[35]

Throughout August and September 1906 there was a minor navy scare in Britain. German secrecy about construction details set off speculation in the navalist press that Germany was building battleships of 19,000 tons or more. A semi-official article in the *Naval and Military Record* on 20 September calmed the rumors with the observation that German docks and slips were not large enough to accommodate warships of that size.[36]

Reports from Captain Philip Dumas, British Naval Attaché to Germany, in the summer and fall of 1906, show little insight and much misperception. Dumas got a remarkable degree of free access to German dockyards. Although he carefully followed the debates over the 1906 Novelle, he completely missed the significance of large increases in construction appropriations. In contradiction to the article cited above, he grossly overestimated German dockyard capability for building Dreadnoughts. He also had no comprehension of the strict accounting constraints that Tirpitz was under. British ignorance on this point had serious consequences during 1909.[37]

Tirpitz's position within the naval bureaucracy improved in late July, when Müller took over the MK from the retired Senden, who in recent years had usually supported the Front against the RMA. Müller was optimistic that he could bridge the personality conflict between Tirpitz and William II.[38]

Reports from the British press gradually became more explicit about type increases, and navalists like Reventlow began to ratchet up the pressure.[39] Capelle worried about the impact of the news that the first German Dreadnoughts would have only 28-cm guns and the cruiser project only 21-cm guns. The navy had promised during the Novelle debate to build ships of equal value to those of other nations. Such disappointing news would put the RMA in a bad light. Despite his earlier advice to wait, it seemed that Capelle was beginning to rethink his timing advice and even toyed with but rejected the idea that Tirpitz should go to the Reichstag with a new table of costs in 1907, because it would raise the tax question shortly before an election.[40] Tirpitz told Capelle that he had briefly thought of a trial balloon to that effect about a large cruiser, "but I dropped it because of its effect on His Majesty that would make the situation more dubious," and he deferred discussion with the Emperor until September. "It is certain that England will have a type and caliber increase. Then we cannot retain the 28-cm gun, and the sooner the better for the next Novelle."[41]

An ominous note sounded from another direction.[42] The Admiralstab learned of French fleet redistribution that dispatched some strong units to the Mediterranean from Brest. The obvious implication to Büchsel was a tacit agreement between Britain and France to cede defense of the Channel to the former. Nevertheless Büchsel still clung to the old plan, in the event of war with France alone, to attack French Atlantic ports. By 1906 such a war was more unlikely than it had ever been. The German Naval Attaché in Paris had some good news. Fisher's Dreadnought program had brought French battleship building into disarray.[43] The French did not lay down their first Dreadnought, *Courbet*, until 1910. All the other powers were similarly affected. The first Dreadnoughts of Japan, the United States, Italy, and Russia were not laid down until 1909. Austria had to wait until 1911.[44]

In August and early September RMA departments worked feverishly to prepare for the meeting with the Emperor.[45] On 19 September[46] Tirpitz had to decide, despite the lack of complete information on the Invincibles, whether to make a quantum leap in size for the cruiser of 1907. The conservative Eickstedt wanted to stay with the 21-cm guns of *Blücher*. At most he was willing to go to a 24-cm gun. Tirpitz argued that political considerations favored an immediate displacement increase, since the Reichstag, scheduled to end its term in 1908, was in its penultimate session. Its last year would be less favorable for the navy. Ahlefeld, Capelle, and Heeringen agreed. The latter suggested that, for one year at least, 28-cm guns like *Nassau's* would be adequate. Tirpitz agreed, but when Eickstedt favored only six 28-cm guns, he insisted on eight, as much for political as military reasons, since the Reichstag might balk at an inferior ship.

By the 28 September meeting, Müller had calmed William II from his anger against Tirpitz. The latter told William II that the Invincibles were originally assumed to be 15,000 tons, but Tirpitz relayed Attaché Coerper's reports of eight 30.5-cm guns. Although Tirpitz was not entirely convinced, prudence and politics made him assume it was so. He wanted to proceed with an increased cruiser estimate in the spring of 1907, and advocated the eight 28-cm guns that were an RMA consensus. He alerted the Emperor to the great cost and technical difficulties of moving directly to cruisers with 30.5-cm guns. The British initiative would allow the Germans to blame them.

Because of type increases both in battleships and cruisers, a Novelle would be necessary within two or three years. When and how that would come about depended on political and financial circumstances. Tirpitz made it clear that Germany must avoid provocative engagements abroad in the next few years that might revive Anglo-German tension. Such tension could gravely jeopardize Novelle prospects. The real reason may have been that Tirpitz was still afraid of a "Copenhagen"-style attack. William II agreed to do his best to keep things quiet for a time.[47] Once again Weltpolitik at the present time had to be sacrificed for Weltpolitik in the future, further evidence that, for Tirpitz, preservation of the Navy Law and his own power took precedence over all other considerations.

On 28 November the Emperor accepted Tirpitz's recommendation that the 1907 battleships, *Posen* and *Rheinland*, would have twelve 28-cm guns. This measure assured that the first division (four ships) of German Dreadnoughts would be homogeneous. The move to 30.5-cm guns would have to wait for the 1908 project.[48]

By the fall of 1906 Tirpitz believed that he had largely charted the course he would follow for the next few years. Money for cruiser *Von der Tann* would be slipped into the 1907 estimates. The ship was a significant innovation, since it was the first large German warship with turbine engines.[49] Novelle plans would continue, based on either a stabilized three tempo or a four tempo. Studies would continue on shortening building time from four years to three. Such plans, which at every stage strongly considered the politics in the Reichstag, are hardly those of someone who dominated the Reichstag but of a leader who, like it or not, had to work *with* politicians to achieve his goals. There were problems ahead, particularly the knotty one of how to pay for it. A federal income tax or inheritance tax, or both, would be very difficult to achieve. Bülow warned Tirpitz that there would be a deficit of 145 million marks in the 1907 budget, and he called for strict economy.[50] Tirpitz's calculations had to be rethought when, at the end of 1906, circumstances allowed Tirpitz, after all, to accelerate his timetable.

A STROKE OF LUCK

Late in 1906 the Herero insurrection in Southwest Africa lingered painfully. The Center Party, never enthusiastic about the expedition, paid more attention than the "patriotic" parties to dreadful German atrocities.[51] The crisis between the Center and Bülow reached its height in December 1906. Led by Matthias Erzberger, the Center rejected a proposal to reorganize the Colonial Office and to provide more money to suppress the rebellion. They would compromise only if troop numbers in the colony were reduced immediately. The Right, the government, and William II himself saw the Center opposition as a challenge to the Emperor's power to wage war. When the money bill met defeat with a vote of 177 to 168 by a combination of the Center Party members and Social Democrats, Bülow dissolved the Reichstag and called for new elections a year before its five-year term expired.[52]

Bülow saw the election as an opportunity to end the government's dependence on the Center for a majority. He appealed for a "patriotic" vote against the Center. He did not really expect to make dramatic inroads into the notoriously stable Center electorate, but the vehemence of Bülow's campaign alienated many Center deputies who had been friendly in the past. This jeopardized Bülow's expectation that the Center would still support the government on some issues in the new Reichstag.

He appealed to Conservatives, National Liberals, and Progressives, including followers of the recently deceased Eugen Richter, to form a coalition against the Center and the Social Democrats on the "national" issue. The campaign was a success, albeit a temporary one. The parties of the Bloc won a slender majority, but it was a partial failure in that the Center even made some gains and, with 105 seats, were still the single largest party. The Social Democrats were the big losers. For the first election since their founding their numbers diminished; nor did the Bloc, riddled by internal contradictions, retain much coherence after voting the government credits to carry on the war in Southwest Africa. Bülow's tactics in the short run had succeeded beyond his expectations.[53]

Tirpitz had previously opposed Reichstag dissolutions, but he was, rather quietly, in favor of this one.[54] His dilemma was how he could support the government while not making enemies of his "friends" in the Center. During the campaign he was careful never, personally, to criticize the Center; but he also had to be careful not to alienate Progressives, who were strongly anti-Center.

He walked the tightrope impeccably. The outcome, a Bloc majority, worked to his advantage. He no longer had to worry about introducing a Novelle in the last session of a Reichstag. The election was fought on an issue that did not concern the navy, namely, the Herero Uprising. He avoided the anger of Center leaders like Peter Spahn who were favorably disposed toward the navy. The radical navalists played a very active and anti-Center role in the election.[55] The election turned out to be a stroke of luck. It resolved the Reichstag situation without damage to the navy's chance for a Novelle. The possibility existed for a Novelle before the winter of 1908–1909 although, on many issues, the Bloc parties had little in common. As one Progressive deputy put it, the Bloc was like the "pairing of a carp pond with a rabbit hutch."[56]

CRISIS IN THE FLOTTENVEREIN

A striking consequence of the campaign was that it caused a crisis within the Flottenverein.[57] It had savaged Tirpitz in the spring of 1906 because of the "moderate" nature of the 1906 Novelle. The organization missed the huge importance of the battleship cost increase that allowed Germany to build Dreadnoughts. The Flottenverein's sole criterion for Navy Bills was more ships, ignoring costs, diplomatic complications, and political realities.

In the summer of 1906 Tirpitz began to think about how to prepare public opinion for a future Novelle.[58] During the election campaign the national leadership of the Flottenverein went out of control. Against Tir-

pitz's wishes, General Keim carried the campaign into Bavaria, with blatant "political" activity, in violation of its officially "non-political" charter.
The unending anti-Catholic statements in the heart of Catholic Germany
created an enormous uproar.[59] Prince Rupprecht of Bavaria threatened to
resign his protectorate over the Bavarian Flottenverein. Tirpitz supported
Rupprecht against Keim and Bülow, who was unmoved even when the
Bavarian army threatened to force its officers to resign from the Flottenverein. Bülow wavered but ultimately consented to accept Keim's resignation, but, typically, he did nothing to bring it about.

Late in 1907 Prince Rupprecht and other Catholic princes resigned,
and it began to seem that the Flottenverein was coming apart. Only the
personal intervention of the Emperor led to Keim's deposition in January
1908, after he had criticized Tirpitz's four tempo Novelle as too small.[60]
Under Keim's direction, the Flottenverein was no longer Tirpitz's puppet. Only under Keim's successor, the retired Admiral Hans Koester, who
assumed leadership in June 1908, did the Flottenverein work in concert
with the government, although Koester, to retain credibility within the
organization, had to appear independent of the government.

The selection of Koester did not allay Tirpitz's anxiety. He wrote to
Müller:

> Although the Flottenverein can be occasionally vexing for us, we have good
> reason to keep it. We never know when we will again have an urgent need
> for it. Pro-fleet opinion could turn around very suddenly, as soon as the idea
> breaks through that, in a general European war, we would have to seek our
> salvation in the army, and not in the fleet. There are already some straws in
> the wind in that direction.[61]

This comment turned out to be prophetic during the rise of army-based
radical nationalism in 1912–13.

THE HAGUE CONFERENCE AND THE
ANGLO-RUSSIAN ENTENTE

In September 1905 Russia proposed to reconvene the Hague Peace Conference and, in April 1906, announced that its program did not include
arms limitation, only questions of international law. The British, on the
other hand, saw this as a way to carry out its election pledges to reduce
arms expenditures. They secured Italian and American support to discuss

arms limitation. France and Russia were only lukewarm about arms limitation, but neither wanted to oppose the British directly.[62]

These powers were relieved when Germany and Austria refused to discuss arms limitation. The British position was not entirely humanitarian, although the Liberals tried to make it appear so. While the Prime Minister preached international disarmament, the Admiralty and government spokesmen were at pains to tell Parliament that reductions in their building program in no way jeopardized Britain's naval supremacy.[63]

As expected, Tirpitz's attitude paralleled the Emperor's. He had fought too hard—within the navy, within the government, and in the Reichstag—for his plan to let an international agreement rob him of his Navy Law. Tirpitz had unwitting allies in the Admiralty who were no less "realistic" than he. An Admiralty Memorandum to Grey admitted:

> From the standpoint of pure opportunism . . . our present naval position is so good that we might express our adhesion to the principle on the condition that other countries were willing to do likewise.

The memo criticized disarmament on the familiar grounds of inadequate controls. Many nations, especially Germany, would object to having other nations fetter their freedom of action. In this way, attempts at disarmament might start, rather than prevent, a war.[64]

A peculiar but revealing aspect of the Hague Conference was Tirpitz's support of the *expansion* of belligerents' rights under international law.[65] In the practical context of a war between Germany and Britain, neutrals like the Netherlands and Denmark would find their imports greatly constrained by a British blockade, lest they re-export goods by land to Germany. The German Foreign Office, logically enough, argued for a limitation of belligerents' rights to keep open such a "windpipe" for Germany. Mahan, in a *volte face* of America's traditional protection of neutral rights, joined Fisher in wanting to expand belligerents' rights, since the United States had joined the ranks of the world's great navies.

By 1904 Tirpitz strongly opposed the abolition of the right to capture.[66] In March 1906 the RMA reported on Germany's vulnerability to blockade. As Lothar Burchardt has shown, the RMA presented a gruesome and exaggerated picture. The report ignored the possibility of protests by neutrals. Tirpitz saw no remedy other than to construct more warships.[67]

Tirpitz agreed with Mahan and Fisher. He argued against the Foreign Office and the ministries of trade and the interior to preserve the right to capture. He maintained that the primary cause of Anglo-German tension was trade rivalry. The "City of London" wanted to eradicate German trade, and feared its own trade losses. To keep the right of capture would therefore be a deterrent to British attack. As Jost Dülffer has noted, Tirpitz's emphasis on trade envy diverted attention from the real cause of the tension, the rapid growth of the German fleet.[68] Tirpitz successfully persuaded William II to support the retention of the right to capture. At the Conference, this decision made the Germans look like quasi-pirates, especially when the British actually voted to abolish the right to capture.

Captain Rudolf Siegel, German naval delegate to the conference, supported Tirpitz's view. As elegantly described by Barbara Tuchman, Siegel's reasoning suggested

> the mind of a chess player trained by a Jesuit. The purpose of a navy, he pointed out to his government, was to protect the seagoing commerce of its country. If the immunity of private property were accepted, the navy's occupation would be gone. The public would demand reduction in warships and refuse to support naval appropriations in the Reichstag. In short, Captain Siegel made it clear that if the German navy was to have a *raison d'être*, property must be left open to seizure, even in the interest of the enemy.[69]

This bizarre argument, rarely openly expressed, made perfect sense in the context of bureaucratic politics and a Mahanist view of seapower. It was a rationale to justify the need for the Navy Law and a reinforcement of Tirpitz's position of power.

Talk of arms limitation quickly died out. The British advertised their willingness to at least exchange confidential naval information.[70] Marschall von Bieberstein, the German delegate, argued that even so mild a measure as an information exchange might be the first step in allowing Britain to retain, by diplomacy, what she was in danger of "losing," specifically overwhelming naval supremacy. With arms limitation the two-power standard could be maintained with little effort.[71] The failure of the Hague Conference had important consequences. The Liberals had to honor their promise to lay down the third Dreadnought of the 1907 program. Publication in November 1907 of the 1908 Novelle signaled the onset of a new arms race.

The Anglo-Russian Entente, signed on 31 August 1907, constituted an attempt to settle outstanding differences in Persia, Afghanistan, and Tibet. It was published immediately, had no secret clauses, and only concerned matters outside Europe.[72] Nonetheless, it provided relief for British anxiety about the attitude of Russia in an Anglo-German conflict. The agreement made a further mockery of the "alliance value," of the risk theory.

PREPARATIONS FOR THE 1908 NOVELLE

Tirpitz thought the election result of January 1907 was as favorable as the government could get, but he did not want to press too far. The existing three tempo, he felt, had to be made, de facto, permanent. This "moderation" would carry weight in the Reichstag and presumably would facilitate yet another cost increase. He rejoiced in the heavy defeat of the Social Democrats but still advocated a cautious approach.[73]

During and after the election campaign, Capelle and Dähnhardt assessed the effects of the election and the still modest British building program. They tried to estimate the chances of wringing a new cost table and Novelle from the Reichstag.[74] As more details poured in from Coerper about the size of the Invincibles and the transition to 34.3-cm guns for the battleships, it was increasingly obvious that it was impossible to stay for long within the 1906 cost tables, even if a little more was added in 1907 for Von der Tann. They agreed that the timing for a general increase should coincide with Bülow's expected tax reform proposals. If a new cost table were presented before the tax reform, the navy might be blamed for the tax increase.

Another timing problem was that if the RMA went to the Reichstag in the fall of 1907 with a new table and then a year or two later introduced a fresh Novelle with yet another cost table, the Reichstag's confidence in the RMA might be shaken. Once again cries might arise of "having no plan" and "taking a zigzag course." They feared arousing sentiment to return the cost estimates to an annual basis, which would undermine the Navy Law.

The RMA needed to persuade the Treasury to push a general tax increase to cloak the navy's increased appetite. Although a tax increase was also needed for the colonies, the army, pension funds, and so on, the navy wanted to evade most of the blame. If there were no tax increase, the navy could only limp along until the inevitable budget crisis in 1908 or 1909. How, then, were the 30.5-cm guns, already planned for the 1908 battleships, to be paid for?

On balance, both Capelle and Dähnhardt felt that it was better to bite the bullet and propose a cost increase together with a Novelle. Contrary to their advice regarding the timing of this in the summer of 1906, they felt now that the cost increases alone compelled them once again to increase both together in 1908, even though it would be so soon after the 1906 Novelle. To wait any longer would mean financial disaster for the RMA. Capelle had originally favored a delay for the Novelle until 1912, with a new cost increase in 1907. Either Tirpitz or Dähnhardt persuaded him that the two should again go together.

The previous year E had contemplated both a three and a four tempo. They decided against the latter because they were unsure, given the gigantic cost increases, whether the Reichstag would allow it. Furthermore:

> E believes that even if the Reichstag situation were good, the actions of
> the Liberal government, with an annual tempo of three or even two ships
> would make it seem impossible for us to temporarily go over to the four
> tempo. . . . If we go to the four tempo, we would be tarred with the stigma
> of starting an arms race and, even worse, the Liberals in England would be
> replaced by the Conservatives. Thus, even if there is a majority in the Bloc,
> we must not have a four tempo, and therefore it would be better for us to
> stabilize [i.e., perpetuate] the three tempo and make us independent for all
> time from political accidents.[75]

Tirpitz refused this prophetic advice in the summer of 1907, to his peril; but his closest aides were aware that a naval arms race might result.

On 17 February 1907 Capelle summed up E's advice.[76] The most urgent need was a new cost table. So soon after 1906, the only plausible excuse for a three tempo Novelle, already guaranteed through 1911, would be to shorten the battleship lifespan to twenty years. Capelle wanted the Novelle to serve as camouflage for an increased cost table. He also suggested a reduction in the number of annual installments from four to three, with delivery of ships a year sooner, which would increase the annual estimates even more. He also wanted 10 million marks per year for U-boats. Altogether the total cost would be 700 million to 800 million more marks than the 1906 law. A larger Novelle would play havoc with other construction needs, such as the increase in ship size, and so a moderate Novelle was a necessity to bring the total large ship establishment up to sixty. The two material reserve ships could be requested for 1916 and 1917, since the shortened lifespan would assure the three tempo until then. Tirpitz seemed content.[77]

A later draft increased the (1908) 30.5-cm battleship cost to 48 million marks and the eight 30.5-cm to 45 million. The enormous increase was 11.5 million more per battleship and 16.5 million more per cruiser.[78] Even the Emperor saw the good sense of a "modest" three tempo Novelle and agreed to drop his insistence on a four tempo.[79] The upshot was that Tirpitz, by April 1907, committed himself to a three tempo Novelle and ordered RMA departments to begin the detail work and the preparation of cost tables,[80] with a shortened building time of three years. In May the Construction Department (K) said it would be feasible. The bottleneck was heavy artillery, but Krupp assured K that he could deliver 30.5-cm guns as fast as he could deliver 28-cm guns.[81] This exchange demonstrates that Tirpitz was actually planning the "acceleration" which Asquith had accused him of in 1909, although he could not have done it without the Reichstag's consent.[82] Clearly Tirpitz had the capability of building ships in three years but to the detriment of other priorities and at a higher cost.

By the spring of 1907 the government knew that the huge deficit would require a new tax bill that would have to rely, at least partially, on direct federal taxes. The savvy Heeringen argued that the fall of 1907 was a good time for the Novelle, because the navy could stake its claim for a piece of the future tax increase. It could not miss the opportunity because large tax increases were rare, and the shakiness of the Bloc parties meant that the navy had to move fast. If the Novelle did not increase the overall establishment of ships, passage would be less difficult. The shortened building time would, he thought, assuage the disappointment of the navalists' demands for even more ships. Since the Novelle would increase neither the tempo nor the establishment of ships, he anticipated no foreign outcry.[83] As Heeringen put it, "In fact we are the driven and not the drivers" in displacement increases. He also implored Tirpitz to keep specific ship plans secret, even to the point of disguising the amount of the supplementary ship costs in the estimates.[84]

At the critical RMA meeting of 17 May, there was still some uncertainty about what the British were up to, but the consensus was that the newest Dreadnoughts would be at least 19,500 tons. Japan was projecting 21,000 tons and the United States 22,000 tons. Tirpitz stated:

> We are therefore required to keep our expansion within certain limits if our initiative is to be considered reasonable and not extreme. The RMA has won the confidence of the Reichstag and of the larger and better-informed part of the German people that our initiatives in fleet development are suited to the needs and circumstances of the Reich, and we have been consistent. This confidence has brought us to the position that naval proposals meet hardly any resistance. It is all the more important to retain this reputation and their willingness to cooperate, because development is still not completed, and one cannot foresee what configuration it will assume in the following years.

A clearer statement of Tirpitz's relationship with the Reichstag would be hard to find.

Tirpitz feared that if Germany exceeded the 22,000-ton figure, it would appear provocative. The conservative Eickstedt objected to a large increase, but he was ignored in favor of Bürkner who thought it was feasible. All agreed on 30.5-cm guns, but Tirpitz decided against turbine engines for the 1908 battleships because of cost, though he insisted on them for cruisers beginning with *Von der Tann*. The 1908 cruiser, *Moltke*, would also be 22,000 tons with ten, as opposed to eight 28-cm guns on *Von der Tann*. Each type could be built for about 46 million marks.[85]

By the end of May the draft and the estimates table were ready. Both Bülow and the Emperor approved.[86] Through June and most of July work continued on small refinements. As late as 28 July 1907 Tirpitz was still planning a three tempo Novelle.[87]

TRANSITION TO THE FOUR TEMPO

To get acquainted with the new Reichstag, Tirpitz, from 3 to 8 June 1907, instituted, for the first time, a "parliamentary trip" to Kiel, Flensburg, and Sonderburg. He personally lectured Bundesrat and Budget Commission members. He allowed them to witness a fleet maneuver. This clever and gracious move showed Tirpitz at his quasi-parliamentary best with the new Reichstag, while he simultaneously kept lines open to Center Party members and reminded them that they were not his enemies.[88]

The subsequent good feeling made it easier for E to reach out to deputies. In the past Tirpitz's aides had always begun with the Center

Party. However, given the new political Bloc of National Liberals, Conservatives, and Progressives, Tirpitz started with the latter, but not before Dähnhardt, in the spring, had made some informal approaches to Spahn of the Center Party. Given the Center's position as the scapegoat in the prior election campaign, the contact apparently made Capelle uneasy.[89]

In July Dähnhardt visited Dr. Ernst Müller-Meiningen, a leader of the Progressives, proportionally the biggest winner in the elections. The party had become much more government-friendly since the death, in 1906, of Tirpitz's old enemy, Eugen Richter.[90] Although Müller-Meiningen was an "angry, almost fanatical Center hater," Dähnhardt found him "somewhat surprised" to learn that "we would be forced in the next year to ask for more money than in the previous cost table," although he was not surprised that the RMA had to keep pace with other countries. When Dähnhardt gave him cost numbers, he asked what plan the Treasury had to raise taxes. Dähnhardt did not know. It was clear to the latter that both the Center and the Progressives were expecting a move to raise taxes. The deputy seemed to have no insuperable objections to shortening ship replacement times.

This was all welcome news, but then the deputy touched the sorest of sore spots for Tirpitz. He asked why the government, in view of the frequent increases in ship types, did not simply rely on annual appropriations without an overriding law. Dähnhardt countered that such a view might put the navy completely at the mercy of fluctuating Reichstag majorities. He reminded Müller-Meiningen that last year the law had helped Tirpitz thwart the thunderous demands of the Flottenverein. The meeting ended cordially, with the deputy agreeing to speak favorably about the navy within the party. The deputy's disturbing remark, however, had alarmed Tirpitz.

During the Czar's August 1907 visit, William II committed an indiscretion for which Tirpitz was partly responsible. He told his cousin Nicky that, during a practice torpedo boat attack, Tirpitz had said, "I wish *Dreadnought* were over there [i.e., the target] and that Fisher was in the middle of it." The Czar gave a forced smile, and the story found its way to Edward VII.[91]

Center leader Spahn, in a speech on 14 August, noted that Germany had to follow the lead of the United States, which had ordered 23,000-ton Dreadnoughts at more than 40 million marks each. He spoke in favor of shortening battleship lifespan to twenty years and for an increase in the ship estimates to at least 40 million marks. It is unclear whether the RMA instigated this speech, but the Center probably wanted to resume its position of hegemony on naval matters. Spahn may have expected that the Progressives would split over the issue and once again leave an opportunity for the Center to provide the decisive votes.[92]

In a letter to Bülow on 14 August, Tirpitz was still focused on the three tempo. He wanted, "in view of the foreign and domestic situation, to appear as small and harmless as possible."[93] While Tirpitz spent the late summer at St. Blasien, Capelle and Dähnhardt were trying to line up Reichstag support for the three tempo Novelle. The cautious Capelle was mystified by Spahn's benevolence toward the navy. "I am breaking my head over his motive." The advantage of Center support was obvious, but Capelle was afraid that it would drive away the Center-hating Progressives and lead to renewed accusations that Tirpitz was a "Center man." On the other hand, it might stimulate a situation in which parties competed to support the navy. He worried about what would happen when the public discovered the *"dicke Ende"* (price to be paid) of higher taxes. Capelle advocated a policy of watchful waiting.[94] On 1 September Capelle spoke to August Stein, editor of the *Frankfurter Zeitung,* and was gratified that Stein saw the three tempo Novelle as a bulwark against exaggerated Flottenverein demands.[95]

Tirpitz worried that the Progressives and the National Liberals would be upset by Spahn's speech and see it as an attempt by the Center to regain hegemony by stealing their thunder. Tirpitz wrote to Capelle on 13 September: "It would be quite a joke if the Progressives rejected [the Novelle] and the Center accepted it." Press coverage was more favorable than he had expected. These were the first hints that he was beginning to think bigger.[96]

The exact point when Tirpitz decided for a four tempo is unclear. It was after his 13 September letter to Capelle but before he saw Bülow on 21 September. Relations with Britain were relatively quiet and offered no excuse to demand more ships. But that cut both ways, because there was now little perceived danger of war. As the advocate of disarmament at the Hague Conference, Britain could hardly suddenly come on as Mars.

In his postwar writings, Tirpitz explained the four tempo in both domestic and technical terms:

> There had been a regular race between the Center and the [Progressives] for the adoption of a Supplementary Naval Bill in the summer of 1907, before we had actually decided upon the Bill at the Admiralty.[97]

The leaders of the Center and the National Liberals told him that a majority of the Reichstag expected a Novelle in 1908. Given the need to shorten battleship lifespan, "it would have been irresponsible if the naval administration did not seize upon these favorable circumstances and offer to introduce a proposal which, without departing from our old goals, would realize them faster."[98]

These valid points still do not explain fully the untypically sudden four tempo decision. One main reason was to go along with the National Liberals and the Progressives to keep the Bloc's hegemony. Spahn had not spoken in favor of the four tempo. To push the Center that high, while retaining the existing ship establishment, would show that the Center were followers, not leaders, which would satisfy the Bloc parties. Since the law did not increase the ship establishment, the Center could hardly oppose increasing the tempo, especially when there was no danger of a British attack, as Tirpitz had thought there was in 1905–1906.

Why was the three tempo idea, with a shortened lifespan, suddenly abandoned when the Emperor, the Chancellor, and the necessary parties were completely onboard, and when only two additional ships in 1916 and 1917 would reach the promised land of sixty ships with a twenty-year replacement period? Tirpitz had doggedly fought for the idea since 1897 and had deflected Flottenverein attempts to increase it. There is no documented definitive reason for the change, but there are hints in Tirpitz's reaction to E's preliminary discussions with the parliamentarians. A three tempo Novelle, along with an even more important new cost table, would make Tirpitz vulnerable to assertions, like Müller-Meiningen's, that there need not be a Navy Law at all if costs had to be recalculated every year or two. Why not simply use annual estimates? A twenty-year lifespan would mean that in the four years from 1908 to 1911 eleven battleships would have to be replaced and the building tempo would have to increase. Under a three tempo Novelle only eight battleships would be replaced in that period (the other ships would be cruisers). In practice, the 1908 Novelle's three tempo would only become effective in 1911. Why not wait until 1911, deputies might ask; but if building costs were not raised before 1911, Germany could only build obsolete ships based on an

outdated cost table. Flottenverein accusations that the navy was too modest would gain the ring of credibility, if not truth. Tirpitz felt compelled
to propose something substantially more, principally to camouflage the
inexorable increase of the cost tables, and hence the march of "progress."
Otherwise, the Navy Law might be at risk.[99] The ultimate irony was that,
if indeed Tirpitz had set out to emasculate the Reichstag with an "iron
budget," growing costs wound up placing the yoke of dependency on his
own shoulders. In the end it was Tirpitz's dependence on Parliament that
pushed him to a four tempo to have a plausible excuse to raise per-ship
appropriations.

For reasons of bureaucratic politics, to protect the Navy Law at all
costs, and for related reasons of domestic politics, Tirpitz courted an
intensified arms race in the mistaken belief that the British could not
counter even a temporary four tempo. The temptation of starting over
from scratch, with the British advantage in pre-Dreadnoughts swiftly
deteriorating over time, proved too much for Tirpitz, as long as it was
compatible with the domestic political situation.[100] All the old shibbo-
leths, like "risk theory" and "alliance value," were gone by 1908, replaced
by what was, at best, a crude theory of deterrence.

Only the canny Holstein, an observer in retirement, saw through the
charade even before the four tempo, and wrote to Bülow:

> The naval policy is of benefit to the naval trust (armor plating, etc.) and the
> promotion of naval officers. For the rest of Germany it is detrimental and
> an indubitable danger, both in foreign and domestic affairs. The Kaiser's
> speeches about the fleet, the Navy League, and the convulsive naval arma-
> ments—these are the things which have consolidated an overwhelming
> naval superiority against us. . . . For that reason this naval policy is sterile.
> If it is nevertheless continued . . . then it would fall into the category of
> dangerous playthings.[101]

Tirpitz absented himself from September maneuvers while he
mulled over the fateful decision.[102] On 21 September he visited Bülow at
his estate in Norderney to argue for the four tempo.[103] As usual, Tirpitz
sugar-coated the proposal for the Chancellor. He noted that the clamor for
a fleet increase was louder than expected and "acceleration" was gaining
currency as a slogan.

The Reichstag's June junket through naval installations had gotten a
warm response. The quiet international situation made a four tempo acceleration seem safe from preventive war. The Novelle could be made to

appear modest, and new estimates tables could easily be inserted. Tirpitz gave Bülow no hint of his secret fears that the new estimates tables could metastasize into a threat to the Navy Law by a return to annual estimates. Next to the Flottenverein's push for a six tempo, four would appear moderate. Domestically it would help keep the Bloc intact. To persevere with the three tempo would appear to be a concession to the Center.

Tirpitz acknowledged the possibility of foreign complications. Britain was tranquil at the moment, but the Anglo-Russian Entente foreboded encirclement, which would demand more ships in the future. He told Bülow that he had already spoken with sympathetic deputies about a three tempo Novelle, and asked Bülow's consent to speak to them about the four tempo. Bülow found Tirpitz's case convincing and already knew that the Emperor would be enthusiastic. The next day, without even a mention of the four tempo, Bülow wrote to Holstein:

> Tirpitz impressed me as being quite sensible during his recent visit. He is convinced we will never be able to match the English, and, in opposition to many currents and despite many technical supplements, he is holding firm to his Naval Bill that is designed gradually to build up a fleet that is only intended for defensive purposes.[104]

Surprisingly Bülow did not seem even dimly aware of the diplomatic consequences of the four tempo, or even of the hole it would blow in a budget that would place a bigger tax reform/increase squarely on his shoulders. The tax question would predictably and severely exacerbate class conflict and the domestic situation. Perhaps Bülow realized, as Capelle had pointed out to Tirpitz,[105] that the initial cost in the 1908 estimates would be relatively modest, and a really big deficit would not appear until 1909. Bülow's insouciance is further proof that there was no "Tirpitz Plan" to stabilize the monarchical system, even while Tirpitz *had* a plan to maximize his own power and that of the RMA.

At Rominten, on 29 September, Tirpitz presented the same case to William II.[106] Tirpitz's intention at that time, as the British were to accuse him of in 1909, was clearly to accelerate the building time as well as the tempo. As Tirpitz anticipated, the Emperor accepted the package with enthusiasm. Tirpitz recorded his thoughts shortly thereafter:

> His Majesty regarded the proposal as self-evident and a bagatelle. . . . When I told him that the previous negotiations with the deputies only concerned the [three tempo] Novelle . . . and not the present one, H.M. said that was a matter of indifference to him! He rejected the significance of money

troubles. England cannot complain about the sudden building of a mass of Dreadnoughts. He noted that it was good that I had now come to agree that the lifespan of battleships would have to be shortened. *Its significance for the stabilization of the three tempo he seemed not to recognize or to value. On the whole, the audience was depressing for me, since for ten years I have incessantly struggled for this goal.*[107] (My emphasis)

William II, like Bülow, understood neither what Berghahn later called the "Tirpitz Plan" nor the more modest version of Tirpitz's "plan" argued in this biography. One can almost sympathize with Tirpitz's frustration that something he had struggled so hard to achieve was not understood by his principal client after all that time.

After William II's decision, events moved rapidly. On 3 October Tirpitz finally informed the Treasury about the four tempo and its increased money demands. Capelle detailed for Treasury Secretary Stengel the foreign, domestic, and parliamentary reasons for the four tempo and the increase in per-ship appropriations. The total cost of the 1908 Novelle, mostly for ships, guns, and armor, was about 945 million marks higher than the 1906 estimate (to 1917). The Treasury made no complaints about the cost, probably because, in August, it had announced an unexpected surplus of 27 million in the 1906–1907 budget because of increased tariff revenue.[108]

The Novelle simply provided that battleship lifespan be reduced to twenty years. The four tempo of three battleships and one large cruiser per year would last from 1908 through 1911. In 1912 the tempo would fall to two per year until 1917, when it rose to three. The tables allowed 47 million marks per battleship and 42 million per large cruiser. Capital and continuing expenses increased, and the U-boat service doubled to 10 million per year. On 30 October the program went to the Bundesrat,[109] where it was approved unchanged.

There was some initial nervousness in the British press. The Admiralty seemed to take the announcement calmly, and the *Times* simply recommended a return to the program of four large armored ships per year.[110] Press protests only began in earnest in December and early January. Even then the Liberals went ahead with their 1908–1909 plan of only two ships, on the basis of their great head start in Dreadnoughts. Not until the Tweedmouth Letter became known, early in March, did the Liberals take further action.[111]

German press reaction was highly favorable. The Conservative and National Liberal papers favored the four tempo but would have liked more. The Flottenverein wanted more and only grudgingly accepted the four tempo. Center papers were reserved but not opposed. Progressives proclaimed their support. Only Social Democrats and a few others were adamantly against the four tempo.[112]

The only opposition that might have been formidable came from retired Vice Admiral Carl Galster. In the fall of 1907 he published a small book/pamphlet that advocated cruisers and U-boats instead of more battleships. He saw the need for a battlefleet but felt that Germany could only mount Kleinkrieg against an opponent as strong as the Royal Navy.[113] No one but the Socialists paid attention.

THE 1908 NOVELLE IN THE REICHSTAG

The first reading of the Novelle and the estimates took place in plenary sessions between 28 November and 5 December 1907.[114] Tirpitz stressed technical aspects of the law: the price increase, the need for a full double squadron of Dreadnoughts, and so on. Bassermann even suggested that another Novelle be introduced in 1911 so that the tempo would not sink precipitately from four to two. Bebel, who had seen through Tirpitz's designs from the beginning, stated that no one could believe that there would not be another Novelle before 1917, likely in 1912. The Social Democrats were so marginalized that no one else heeded the warning.

More troubling to Tirpitz was a speech by the Progressive Wiemer on 30 November. He raised the same sensitive issue that he had during the previous summer that had been a carefully concealed problem for Tirpitz since Lieber had raised it privately in October 1897. "The present proposal proves how regrettable it is to bind fleet development to a long-term law when naval and technical developments move so fast."

Spahn (Center), known to favor the law in principle, deferred taking a definite position before it went to the Budget Commission. This gave Tirpitz some nervous moments, as did the Moltke-Harden trial that was going on at the same time. It absorbed much press attention and at one time threatened to dissolve the Bloc. Simultaneously the crisis within the Flottenverein was at its height. It prompted the resignation, in December, of Prince Rupprecht from the Bavarian branch of the Flottenverein.[115]

For these reasons the Center was reluctant to commit itself publicly too soon. Although fierce navalist propaganda had helped prepare a receptive atmosphere for the Novelle, the crisis had little other effect on the Novelle's progress.

Despite public calm, Tirpitz expressed his inner anxiety in a letter of 5/6 December to Müller.[116] Bassermann's idea, to reinstitute the three tempo for a period of years after 1911, was premature, but he thought he could manage it privately with Bassermann. He lamented that, despite their support, the Conservatives had no love for the *"grässliche Flotte"* (hideous fleet). He thought the Center would foreswear any feelings of revenge for their scapegoating in the prior election. Their support in the naval question was essential if they were to regain any vestige of their previous hegemonic position. As long as his rationale appeared logical and plausible, the Center would not abandon the navy. Wiemer's comment against a legal establishment he dismissed as obviously unacceptable, although he was nervous about a rumor Dähnhardt had heard that the Center might support Wiemer's idea in the Budget Commission, despite sworn enmity between the Progressives and the Center. In the end he was confident that the Bloc would stand fast in support of the navy. If, against all expectations, there were no majority, the only alternative would be to dissolve the Reichstag and use the navy as the main campaign issue.

The Novelle and the estimates went before the Budget Commission from 3 to 13 December 1907, and on 9 and 10 January 1908. In these sessions Tirpitz softened Center reluctance with the dubious argument that no new taxes would be necessary for the next few years. He had persuaded the Treasury to rely more heavily on loans and to give the navy a larger share of existing tax income. He blandly avoided the question of a future Novelle by pointing out that no one could predict what the situation would be in the next four or five years.

Only Social Democrats clearly saw that the Novelle would intensify the arms race. As long as huge new taxes were not required, the Commission, including the Center, accepted Tirpitz's technical arguments without embarrassing challenges.[117] Once again, as Capelle had once told Michaelis, "the Reichstag does not want the truth from us, but a suitable formula with which the sensible ones can guide those who are stupid."[118]

The debate showed how weak the opposition was. The Bloc and the Center favored it overwhelmingly, and the parties even allowed passage of the Novelle and the estimates without a formal resolution of the money question, an unprecedented change. Only the Social Democrats protested the absence of this control. The third reading of the Novelle and the estimates was an anticlimax. Both passed with large majorities, with only the Social Democrats and the Poles in dissent. It was a remarkable triumph for Tirpitz, and showed both how great his skill and credibility were, and how inattentive most of the Reichstag was.[119]

The Bloc and the Center proclaimed rejection of any naval competition with Britain. It did not dawn on them until much later that this was precisely the effect of the 1908 Novelle.[120] Once again, the "threat perception gap" was about to come into play, although it was not at its peak until the following year.

Initially the British government reacted calmly. William II put them on guard with another colossal indiscretion.[121] On 16 February 1908 he wrote a letter to Lord Tweedmouth, First Lord of the Admiralty, to assure him that the fleet was not built as a "challenge to British naval supremacy" and that "the German fleet is built against nobody at all." The Emperor consulted with neither the Chancellor nor Tirpitz. Only Müller had seen it and did not realize its significance.[122]

Tweedmouth compounded the indiscretion when he sent the Emperor, a few days later, a copy of the British naval estimates for 1908–1909, a week before they went to Parliament. When Grey heard of the letter and its reply, he was dumbfounded. Grey had King Edward VII write to his errant nephew on 22 February and tactfully chastise him for the "new departure" of direct communication with a member of the British Cabinet. Shortly thereafter, Tweedmouth lost office. Reginald McKenna, more anti-German, replaced him. Colonel Repington, the *Times* military correspondent, heard of William II's letter and published an exposé of it on 6 March. The Emperor's disavowal of competition rang hollow. Repington used the article to highlight the German "threat." Partly as a result of this imbroglio, McKenna acceded to Fisher's request for four and, if necessary, six large armored ships for the 1909 program. The Novelle, together with the renewed awareness of the German "threat" in Britain, began the train of events that led to the naval scare of 1909.[123]

The 1908 Novelle marked the high point of Tirpitz's influence within the navy, the government, and the country. Müller, Chief of the Naval Cabinet, was friendly. By 1908 Tirpitz had succeeded in his campaign to eliminate the Admiralstab as a rival and to persuade the Emperor to agree to limit its size to only twenty-eight officers.[124] He had convinced himself, as well as Bülow and William II, that no serious consequences would follow the introduction of the four tempo. This argument was self-justifying, because if trouble later came with the British it would "prove" that the four tempo had been necessary to defend Germany. Tirpitz got himself and his country into this ensnaring paradox, from which neither was able to emerge safely.

13

THE WHIRLWIND RISES,
1908–1911

The 1908 Novelle, and the less celebrated but equally important ratcheting up of the ship cost table, was a great victory. Shipbuilding increased at an energetic pace. Money poured in to expand imperial and private shipyards, as well as Krupp's great armor and artillery forges.

In June 1908 Tirpitz arranged a junket for Reichstag and Bundesrat members. From Danzig to Kiel to Wilhelmshaven, the parliamentarians inspected fortifications and fleet exercises. Tirpitz explained the need for quiet, steady work over the next few years, and radiated confidence that the navy was spending the public's money efficiently and wisely.[1]

The 1908 Novelle was a potentially provocative act. Tirpitz tried to soft-pedal it, but he feared that British Conservatives would raise a hue and cry and demand a corresponding expansion of the Royal Navy or, even worse, replay the "Copenhagen" cries heard in 1904–1905.[2] Just as threatening for Tirpitz were British diplomatic attempts to limit the arms race.

The British Liberals had social reform markers to redeem with their constituency. In the spring of 1908 there was a cabinet reshuffle. Herbert Asquith replaced the mortally ill Campbell-Bannerman as Prime Minister. David Lloyd George took Asquith's position as Chancellor of the Exchequer. Winston Churchill became President of the Board of Trade. Reginald McKenna replaced the hapless Tweedmouth at the Admiralty.

The four tempo Novelle gave Liberals two choices to avoid being savaged by Conservative navalists. They could increase the 1909 building program or reach an arms control understanding with Germany. Accustomed to annual parliamentary appropriations, they had little grasp of the long-term nature of the Navy Law or of Tirpitz's extraordinary tenacity in upholding it. Perhaps they thought that the Germans were like the French, who often announced ambitious building programs that were never fulfilled.

In May 1908 Fisher convinced the Admiralty that at least four large ships were necessary for the 1909 program, with an additional two contingent upon German actions. Grey threatened to resign if the Cabinet did not accept the 4/6 program. Lloyd George and Churchill were reluctant to support as many as four. Both factions looked to negotiations with Germany to ease the situation and to spare them the embarrassment of calling for economies on armaments while then increasing naval estimates.[3]

In Foreign Office circles suspicion of Germany was growing. In 1907 Sir Eyre Crowe reminded Grey that Britain traditionally had opposed any continental power (e.g., Louis XIV or Napoleon) that threatened continental hegemony. Crowe argued that Germany, intentionally or not, was moving in a hegemonic direction and should draw Britain's opposition.[4] Despite Crowe, Grey was determined to try negotiations.

By the summer of 1908 Bülow, too, was interested in diplomacy. He felt pressured by Germany's growing diplomatic isolation and the pressing need to implement tax reform to pay for the navy. Grey approached German Ambassador Count Paul Wolff-Metternich to discuss the naval question. They spoke informally between March and August 1908. Although the conversations led to nothing specific, the exchange revealed each side's priorities.[5] A complicating factor, then and later, was Coerper's successor as Naval Attaché in London, Captain Wilhelm Widenmann, a partisan of Tirpitz who consistently undermined Metternich.[6]

Grey argued that Britain, with its tiny army, could never threaten Germany regardless of how superior its navy; but if Germany's navy became superior, its army could conquer England. The size of the British battleship-building program depended on Germany's. Grey, whose threat perception acumen was as obtuse as Tirpitz's, failed to acknowledge the havoc that a British blockade could wreak on the German economy. He was also ignorant of how the German Navy Law worked. With annual appropriations, Britain could easily vary its program from year to year. He seemed unaware of the German fear that arms control might destroy the Navy Law and bring back the chaos of the 1890s.

Metternich, and to a certain extent Bülow, stood in the middle. Metternich dutifully passed British views on to the Emperor, who often riddled his dispatches with sarcastic marginalia. In July Metternich met twice with Grey and Lloyd George. They were ignorant of the German domestic complications brought on by the suggestion of an immediate reduction in the building tempo and a permanent 2:3 ratio in future construction. The Emperor was indignant that Germany would have to slow its program first to hope for a friendship with Britain. Tirpitz entirely concurred.[7] Bülow was a bit more flexible and naively inquired about the possibility of British neutrality in a Franco-German war in exchange for a tempo reduction.[8] Metternich replied that an unconditional neutrality agreement was unavailable because of the Anglo-French Entente that had widespread support in Britain.[9]

Tirpitz contested Metternich's belief that the naval rivalry and not trade was the principal source of Anglo-German antagonism. He would not acknowledge that using the fleet as a "lever" against Britain was working contrary to his professed expectations. A construction slowdown would mean a retreat from the world stage. Who could guarantee that a neutrality agreement would hold if Conservatives returned to power? He denied that the four tempo intensified the rivalry, but then he used the increased tension to justify the four tempo in the first place.[10] Since Tirpitz had the Emperor's ear, the talks petered out.[11] Without consulting Tirpitz, William II told Metternich to inform Grey that Germany did not intend to create another Novelle.[12] This unnerved Tirpitz. Faced with Galster's renewed criticism of battleship policy, as well as the growing public awareness of the cost of the four tempo, he suggested to William II at Rominten, in September 1908, that Germany not completely halt talks. He feared that the odium of failure would fall on Germany, but he did not want to abandon the possibility of another Novelle.[13]

A few weeks later William II blundered again. He gave an interview to an English journalist and intimated that while *he* was a friend of Britain, most of his subjects were not. He claimed that some British critics were "mad as hatters" for their suspicion that the German fleet was directed against them. After all, during the Boer War he had drawn up a campaign plan and sent it to Queen Victoria, despite German sympathy for the Boers! Because he sent a copy of the interview to Bülow before publication, he had acted constitutionally. Bülow erred stunningly when

he returned it to the author unredacted. On 28 October the interview
was published in the *Daily Telegraph*. The press exploded on both sides
of the Channel. Even the most "kaisertreu" conservative papers attacked
William II for the indiscretion. Other papers railed against his "personal
regime." The error was just as much Bülow's fault, but the public blamed
the Emperor. Bülow's lame defense of the Emperor in the Reichstag
further bruised his fragile ego. He had to promise that he would take no
future political step without the Chancellor's advice. In the short run the
affair improved Bülow's political position enough that he tried to leverage it into a naval agreement. Ultimately, however, it poisoned his good
personal relationship with the Emperor and became a major factor in
his downfall.[14] The British reacted on 12 November. Asquith redefined
the two-power standard and asserted the government's determination
to uphold it, but he did not publicly announce the 1909 estimates, as
the government was still divided on some specifics. The informational
vacuum led to loose talk in the British press about a German invasion.[15]

The Bosnian Crisis, which began in October 1908 with the Austrian
annexation of Bosnia-Herzegovina, heightened international tensions
still further. Bülow, to avoid complete isolation, openly backed Austria-
Hungary with an ultimatum against a humiliated Russia that had been
caught selling out the interests of its ally, Serbia. This successful bullying
of Russia helped to form the mind-set that led to disaster in 1914.

While the Emperor lay abashed by the *Daily Telegraph* Affair, Bülow
made a last attempt to get naval conversations restarted.[16] Before he could
deal with the British, he had to reach an understanding with Tirpitz.
On 30 November he asked Tirpitz whether and when Germany could
confidently meet a British attack.[17] Tirpitz replied that the growing fleet
had made a British preventive attack less rather than more likely, but he
had to concede that the danger zone still lay ahead.[18] Tirpitz had clearly
evaded the question.

Since Germany could not out-build Britain in battleships, why not,
Bülow asked, instead of expensive Dreadnoughts, improve coastal fortifications and build U-boats to make a blockade more difficult? Why not
then go back to the three tempo and alleviate British fears? Easing the
tempo would make passage of the danger zone possible without inviting
preventive attack.[19] It galled Tirpitz that Graf Friedrich von Baudissin,
Büchsel's successor as Chief of the Admiralstab, supported Bülow.[20]

Tirpitz's reply demonstrated that he and Bülow had exchanged the positions they had held about the size of the 1906 Novelle. Now it was Bülow who feared preventive attack, while Tirpitz argued that the danger was no greater than before. He believed that the naval scare, then just beginning, had been "arranged by the British Conservatives and ship-building interests to pressure the Liberals to increase their program." Any tempo reduction would require a new Novelle and would be interpreted as a retreat before British blackmail. He threatened to resign if Bülow tendered a three tempo plan to William II.[21]

Tirpitz argued that Germany could not accept any naval agreement without a reduction in the British advantage large enough to rule out a preventive attack. He criticized the Emperor's assurance that there would be no Novelle in 1912. His "concession" was that he would back a ten-year agreement with Britain that would bind Germany to a three tempo if the British agreed to build no more than four ships per year.[22] Because the four tempo was due to sink to two in 1912, this clearly was no concession. Such an agreement would gain Tirpitz four ships above the existing establishment of fifty-eight. He would accept only military concessions, because he believed a vague political agreement would be useless. In March 1909 the naval scare erupted full force during the estimates debates in the Commons.

Early in 1909 Grey resurrected his proposal of an informal agreement to exchange information, so that the naval scare, by then raging, would be less likely to recur. Grey wanted to allow the mutual inspection of shipyards. The Emperor and Tirpitz, always secrecy-minded, opposed the idea. They complained that the British government did not trust the German government's official statements, as if they would ever trust British official statements. Although Germany announced its building program long in advance, specific details, apart from cost, were more closely held in Germany than in Britain. Germany would therefore gain less from such an exchange.[23]

In March–April 1909 Bülow tried again for a deal with "concessions" to Britain, in return for a colonial settlement and a political agreement. The Emperor would only consider "concessions" that kept the existing program intact. Germany would promise no further Novelles only if Britain agreed to a defensive alliance, a neutrality pact in which each would refuse to join an alliance against the other, or an entente that would guarantee the territorial integrity of both (i.e., German retention of Alsace-Lorraine), an absurd proposition.[24] Tirpitz, like William II, felt that Germany had to retain the possibility of a 1912 Novelle, even though the RMA had not yet decided whether to pursue one. Though it might be renounced later in return for political compensation, Tirpitz stubbornly clung to a 3:4 ratio as the only possible basis for arms reduction.[25] The British dismissed the idea out of hand.[26]

Bülow's swan song on the naval question came at a meeting on 3 June 1909. Also present were Tirpitz, Bethmann-Hollweg, Moltke, Schoen, and Metternich.[27] Bülow reiterated his fears of a preventive war. Metternich feared that the offer of a 3:4 ratio might precipitate a war. Tirpitz opposed slowing the tempo without a 3:4 ratio and pointed out that the tempo, failing another Novelle, would fall to two in 1912 anyway. He even suggested that Germany not take the initiative to offer a 3:4 ratio but instead wait for the British to do so! In that event it would be possible *without a change in the Navy Law*, to reduce the tempo from four to three in the normal estimates, presumably by adding one ship to one of the two tempo years after 1912. Obviously both Metternich and Tirpitz were indulging in rhetorical excess.

This statement was a reversal of his position the previous December, when he had said that any reduction in the battleship schedule would require another Novelle. Bülow wanted a slower tempo to pass the danger zone more easily; Tirpitz admitted that the danger zone would exist until the canal was finished in about 1915. How he made that calculation was not apparent, as he could not have known how many ships the British would have by 1915. It was clear to all that no diplomatic initiative was possible.

Between 1906 and 1909 Tirpitz had shifted his ground substantially. In 1906 he had opposed a four tempo for fear of preventive war; in 1909 he supported the four tempo amid a war scare in Britain much worse than in 1905. Tirpitz was correct that the temporary four tempo would not spark a war, although there was virtually no chance of a unilateral British war under any circumstances. The fateful leap to the four tempo made "face" a greater issue than in the past. To reduce the tempo before 1912, the year the reduction was scheduled, might implicitly suggest that his prior judgment had been faulty or dangerous. Tirpitz would not be the last institutional leader to resist vigorously any public hint that he had made a mistake. The confidence of the Reichstag and his control over the navy were Tirpitz's coin of the realm. How unlike Tirpitz it would have been to let Bülow, or later Bethmann, chisel away at his life's work without a fight. Since Tirpitz still had the Emperor's support in 1909, he could dish the politicians and diplomats who wanted to exchange his future battle-ships for what he considered to be shadowy promises without substance.

THE NAVAL SCARE OF 1909

Germany's adamant position on arms limitation talks crystallized a con-sensus between Liberals and Conservatives in Britain that Britain's naval supremacy had to be upheld, by a massive effort if necessary.[28] The Lib-eral Imperialists and the Conservatives both had an interest in navalist sentiment: the Conservatives to accuse the Liberals of insufficient vigor in national defense, and the Liberals to steal their thunder. Even Churchill, then a "little navy" man, saw clearly that the time was not yet ripe for pushing social reform ahead of preparedness.[29] The Liberals tried to do both. Lloyd George's "people's budget" caused a constitutional crisis, and ultimately reinforced the willingness of the British elite to tax them-selves instead of placing the greatest burden on "weaker shoulders." The German elite did the opposite by its reliance on indirect taxes to pay for defense.

A major reason for the naval scare was the British system of annual estimates. A certain amount of scare-mongering was a time-honored us-age. Particularly in need of a scare was the Liberal "little navy" faction to press them domestically, as Fisher admitted to Widenmann.[30] The Brit-ish naval budget process began within the Cabinet. Early in January the political press would speculate about how it would affect national security and various vested interests. The press fed on leaks from Cabinet factions, and pro-navy lobbies contended publicly with Radical and pacifist groups.

The estimates were published around 1 March and stimulated press comparisons with potential rival navies. The public debate often affected international relations between January and April. Instead of a long-term building program like Germany's, the British system every year projected needs for the next several years (the time it took to build a battleship in

British yards). Technology, budget practices, and political culture led to an annual debate not only on the Royal Navy but also on the German Navy—the recognized scapegoat for increasing naval budgets.[31]

In Germany the Navy Law and the estimates tables were known years in advance, and freed Tirpitz from the need of an annual propaganda campaign, unless it was a Novelle year or required an unforeseen estimates increase, as in 1906 and 1908. To avoid such annual conflicts was a major reason why Tirpitz had devised the Navy Law and took pains to keep his expenditures close to previous predictions. By controlling the timing of Novelles, Tirpitz could also, within certain limits, control the timing of great public debates on naval policy. Meanwhile, the RMA could gradually indoctrinate the population. The Reichstag's increasingly favorable attitude demonstrated the success of this policy. The process led to the slow development of a public narrative favorable to the navy.

In the British naval debates of March 1908 the question of Germany shortening ship-building time, "acceleration," had arisen, but it was not taken seriously except by extreme navalists. In the fall and early winter of 1908–1909 rumors proliferated that Germany was accelerating its production of guns, armor, and turrets in order to make warship production faster.

McKenna recommended to the Cabinet, on 8 December 1908, a program of six large ships for the 1909 estimates, a compromise between the economists, Lloyd George, and Churchill, who wanted four or even fewer, and Fisher and the navalists, who wanted eight.[32] Grey informed Metternich on 18 December of a significant increase in the naval estimates the following spring, unless Germany reduced its program.[33]

The Admiralty had reached potentially startling conclusions about Germany's building potential over the next few years. The two Dreadnoughts of the 1906 program (*Blücher* was correctly excluded) and the three of the 1907 program had all been laid down in 1907. Together with the eight of the 1908 and 1909 programs, these ships would bring the total to thirteen capital ships, if they were completed by 1912.[34] Early in 1909 Britain had ten Dreadnoughts built or under construction, plus the two in the 1908 estimates and the six in McKenna's 1909 program. If all were completed by 1912, the ratio would be 18:13, hardly consistent with the two-power standard; but if the Germans shortened construction time, they might have seventeen or even twenty-one by 1912.[35]

To reach these conclusions, the Admiralty had pieced together information that had trickled in during 1908. In the summer of 1908 several
German yards, notably Germania in Kiel, had expanded considerably.
The four tempo had made such expansion both necessary and inevitable,
but the Admiralty saw it as sinister. The Second Sea Lord, Admiral John
Jellicoe, had heard from private sources that the Krupp works in Essen,
the main supplier of guns, turrets, and armor, had recently expanded
its capacity by 30 percent (consistent with a jump from a three to a four
tempo). Krupp had also secretly bought up large quantities of nickel,
indispensable for armor. In December 1908 the Admiralty saw the 1909
naval estimates and noted that the first two (of four) annual installments
for the 1908 ships were only slightly less than the total of the first three
installments for the earlier ships. Again, the Admiralty put an ominous
spin on information fully explainable by the four tempo and the increased
per-ship allowance. The Admiralty interpreted these figures as meaning
either that the Germans were building larger ships, as indeed was the
case, or, as the Admiralty concluded, that Germany had accelerated by
shortening shipbuilding time.

In October 1908 the Admiralty learned from public sources that shipbuilders had assembled materials for capital ships under construction
in advance of their laying down. This news was harmless and hardly
surprising, since the type question had delayed laying down *Nassau* and
its sisters for more than a year. More alarming were rumors that material for ships of the 1909 program were purchased in October 1908, well
in advance of Reichstag authorization, which was not due until 1 April
1909.[36] On 15 December Widenmann denied the latter to McKenna.[37] By
18 March Metternich was forced to admit it. He conceded that the RMA
had promised contracts for two of the four 1909 ships to two separate firms
in October 1908. The other two contracts would not be awarded until July
1909. The RMA had promised them for financial reasons. Because of the
demands of the four tempo, several firms conspired to form a trust and
raise the price. To break the trust, the RMA had promised two contracts
early at a favorable price. Any materials purchased by contractors in advance of 1 April 1909 would be at their expense and risk. They would have
to await Reichstag approval before money was disbursed.[38] In the hysteria
of the moment, the belated admission did little to stem the hue and cry.

In January Fisher noted to McKenna that it was a "practical certainty"
that Germany would have seventeen Dreadnoughts and Invincibles by

the spring of 1912, not thirteen as the German schedule indicated. Furthermore, there was a "possibility" that if Germany used all its shipbuilding resources without restriction, it would have twenty-one capital ships
by 1912, whereas Britain would only have eighteen. They argued that
authorizing eight ships, and not six, in the 1909 estimates was imperative.[39]

Whether naive or malicious, these assertions were wrong. Ironclad
German budgetary rules, under tight scrutiny by the Treasury and the
Reichstag, would prevent any large sum from disbursement without authorization. Tirpitz would have had to (and did not) go to the Reichstag
to reduce the annual building installments from four to three, or at least
get a large increase in the amounts of the early installments.[40] The Admiralty's allegations were an example of cherry-picking bits of data to "prove"
a predetermined conclusion.

The Admiralty's suggestion created a serious crisis within the Cabinet. The economists lined up against the Admiralty and the Liberal Imperialists. After a stormy meeting, Asquith finally offered a proposal that
everyone could accept. The government would seek authorization for four
ships, with another four contingent to be laid down depending on the situation in Germany. In Churchill's words: "The Admiralty had [originally]
demanded six; the economists offered four; and we finally compromised
on eight."[41] Repeated German protests and denials were ignored, and
Asquith's "compromise" was accepted. In May Lloyd George published
the budget that was to lead to two general elections and a constitutional
weakening of the House of Lords. His proposed inheritance tax made
Conservatives more apoplectic than did the German Navy.

In an odd outcome, the four contingent Dreadnoughts were authorized without reference to Germany. In April 1909 the Admiralty learned
that Austria was considering the construction of three or four Dreadnoughts. In July 1909 the government received parliamentary consent
for the additional four ships because of Austrian, and consequent Italian,
building. Germany scarcely received mention in the debates.[42]

German archives prove conclusively that Tirpitz had no intention of
acceleration in 1908, but he had considered it. In December 1905, while
the Novelle and the estimates were under consideration, Budget Commission members had inquired about shortening the building time. In
January 1906 the RMA investigated the possibility. The time needed for

building *Nassau-* and *Blücher*-type ships could be shortened to twenty-eight to thirty-two months under two conditions. The first, deemed "possible," was the swift delivery of guns, turrets, and armor from Krupp to the dockyards. The second, considered "uncertain," prohibited design changes during construction. Such acceleration would cost an additional 20 to 25 million marks per year, a large sum from a tight budget. The Reichstag would have to approve the reduction of annual installments from four to three. At a lower cost, allowing for technological change, large ships could be build in thirty-two to thirty-four months, but about six months of sea trials would still be needed.[43]

Some 1906 Novelle plans included a reduction of installments from four to three, which, by 1916, would mean that three additional large ships would be completed than was possible with four installments. To save money and deal with technical problems, the building times would be reduced gradually over a period of years.[44] Krupp promised that within two years he could deliver large guns within thirty months after they were ordered, but he would first have to expand facilities.[45]

By the spring of 1907 Krupp told the Construction Department (K) that it could supply 30.5-cm guns as fast as it had 28-cm guns.[46] The tables of the three tempo Novelle of the summer of 1907 provided for a decrease in installments for large ships to three.[47] The Technical Department (Technische Abteilung, or B) objected. Although ships could be built in the Imperial Dockyards in thirty-six months, B believed that doing so in forty-two months was preferable to avoid delaying ship repairs, having to hire more workers, and so on.[48]

When Tirpitz decided, in August–September 1907, to go to the four tempo, any mention of acceleration was dropped. This was done for financial reasons, since the four tempo and increased ship prices had already led to a great increase in the estimates.[49] This policy was still in force in the summer of 1908, despite the Krupp expansion that the Admiralty considered so sinister. In June 1908 Carl Ziese, director of the Schichau Yard in Danzig, received a Reichstag delegation, which asked him why so much more time was needed to build a battleship than a transatlantic liner. Ziese complained bitterly that the discrepancy was the result of the slow delivery of guns and armor, and that the nine-hour day in German yards cut production by 15 percent compared to British yards. He accused

Geheimrat Theodor Harms, head of the RMA's Technical Department, of fraternizing with the Social Democrats and making things too easy for Schichau's workers.[50]

By the end of 1908 the expansion at Krupp was sufficiently advanced to enable the completion of capital ships in twenty-seven to thirty-two months, excluding the sea trials; nevertheless, the RMA held fast to the timeframe specified in the contracts, thirty-two to thirty-six months.[51] Although the Admiralty was technically correct that acceleration was *possible*, Tirpitz still had no intention of doing so.

The question remains regarding the early promise of ship contracts in October 1908 to the firms of Schichau and Blohm & Voss. Tirpitz had told the Reichstag on 29 March 1909 that the two ships had been promised early, subject to the later consent of the Reichstag. He explained the danger of a trust to bid up the price of the four ships in the 1909 estimates. He had scuttled the trust by promising (though not signing) contracts for a battleship and a battlecruiser at a relatively cheap price to the two firms in October 1908, under the usual terms, thirty-six months after the contract was actually signed. Not a pfennig would be paid until that moment.

In this way the two Imperial Yards that were due to become vacant in the summer of 1909 could be played off against the other private yards to get a cheaper price. The contracts for the last two battleships would not be signed until late summer, and these ships would not be due for completion until three years afterward. He absolutely denied the acceleration allegations of Asquith and Balfour.[52] Heath, the British Naval Attaché, admitted to a friend of Müller: "You know, it's just a political move. He [Asquith] made those statements for party reasons."[53]

Tirpitz's statement was inaccurate in only one respect. On 1 March Schichau began work on one of the ships. When William II heard of this, he was angry, as it gave formal justification to British assertions of acceleration. Tirpitz noted that the contracts were only signed on 8 April, and he had not discovered until late in April that Schichau had started a month early with its own money and at its own risk in order to avoid a temporary layoff of some of its workers. In any event, the early start would not affect the delivery date.[54]

Tirpitz was bitter that the British had trusted neither his statements nor those of his government about acceleration. He was right to feel offended for his involuntary role as scapegoat. German anger at what seemed to be deliberate British misperception led to the gradual isolation of the British Naval Attaché.[55]

The results of the naval scare were greater in Britain than in Germany. Churchill later admitted:

> There can be no doubt whatever that, as far as the facts and figures were concerned, we [Lloyd George and Churchill] were strictly right. The gloomy Admiralty anticipations were in no respect fulfilled in the year 1912. . . . There were no secret German Dreadnoughts, nor had Admiral Tirpitz made any untrue statement in respect of major construction. . . . [While we] were right in the narrow sense, we were absolutely wrong in relation to the deep tides of destiny.[56]

In the latter sentence Churchill referred to the situation in January 1915. Without the four contingent ships, the Grand Fleet would only have had twenty-one ships (allowing for one that sank and five under refit) to counter Germany's twenty.

The naval scare in Britain had several other important results. One outcome was the beginning of the Imperial Fleet. During the summer of 1909 Australia and New Zealand each offered to pay for a battlecruiser. The naval scare also led to a growing sense of the inevitability of a war with Germany, and a loss of faith by all except the Radical wing of the Liberal Party in the possibility of a naval agreement. After the naval scare, the two-power standard was virtually scrapped. Germany was the recognized opponent upon whose actions the government predicated naval plans.[57]

Bülow's failure to deliver a naval agreement, in an impossible situation, was one element that led to his demise. Another was the slow crumbling of the Conservative, National Liberal, and Progressive Bloc. Although all three parties supported the war in Southwest Africa and, more warily, the 1908 Novelle, the crucial problem was how to pay for it. In the winter of 1909 Bülow proposed direct (inheritance) taxes and additional indirect taxes. National Liberals and Progressives favored an inheritance tax that would mostly affect large landowners. Conservatives opposed this tax at any price. After a long and arduous struggle, the Conservatives voted no and broke up the Bloc. They found an eager collaborator in the Center Party, which had not forgotten Bülow's hostility during the last election campaign.[58] The Bloc dissolved, and a "black-blue" coalition of the Center and the Conservatives replaced it. On 26

June 1909 Bülow resigned. His glittering but fuzzy idea of Weltpolitik was in shambles. An arms race raged out of control, and his diplomatic efforts had failed to curb it. The aftermath of the *Daily Telegraph* Affair fatally eroded his influence with William II, and Tirpitz won the competition for the Emperor's ear. Bülow left to his successor the attempt to draw nearer to Britain.

DIPLOMACY UNDER BETHMANN, 1909–1911

Theobald von Bethmann-Hollweg, Reich Minister of the Interior, succeeded Bülow as Chancellor on 14 July 1909. The new Chancellor had a reputation as a moderate. He knew little of foreign affairs and was not an advocate of Weltpolitik. He would have to devote much of his attention to domestic politics and finances. He saw the need to improve Germany's shaky diplomatic position by again trying to approach the British on the naval question.

The first step toward any such initiative was with Tirpitz who, given his influence with the Emperor, could stymie negotiations.[59] The British eight tempo of 1909 was a very impressive statement of their determination to preserve supremacy; Tirpitz still believed, however, that Britain could not, in the long term, sustain a two-power standard. Tirpitz grasped at straws to maintain the illusion that Germany could compete with Britain. He seized upon a remark made in the 1909 estimates debate in the House of Commons. A Member of Parliament (MP) had noted that by 1914 Britain should strive for a 20 percent superiority in capital ships. Such a ratio, 6:5, would exceed Tirpitz's wildest dreams. In an act of exceptional self-deception, Tirpitz read great significance into the fact that neither the Admiralty nor the government contradicted the statement. In a draft letter to Müller, apparently not sent, he wrote: "Perhaps this offers a chance to improve our military strength ratio with England in a way such as we could never have previously hoped."[60] He believed that Britain had revealed its exhaustion by calling upon the Dominions (Canada, Australia, and New Zealand) to help with the cost of building Dreadnoughts. This thought may have influenced Tirpitz's sudden eagerness for negotiations, and his hope that he had found a willing collaborator in the new Chancellor.

Bethmann met Tirpitz on 11 August 1909 and was surprised to find him apparently willing to compromise.[61] Tirpitz offered a five-year agreement, by which he would, in 1910, reduce the tempo to three and then, from 1911 to 1914, reduce it again to two ships per year. In exchange, the British would limit themselves to four ships in 1910 and three per year thereafter. He would promise no Novelle in 1912. In 1914 the relative strengths of Dreadnoughts built and in construction would be 24:32, a ratio of 3:4. On the surface this appeared to be a great concession, but Tirpitz left much unsaid. German tempo would have to revert to three after 1914 in order to follow the replacement paragraph of the navy, and the British total would have to include ships built for the Dominions. In reality, this proposal amounted to no more than a repackaged version of the 3:4 ratio that he had offered to Bülow.

The Emperor embraced the idea with enthusiasm, deceiving himself into thinking that the British would regard a 3:4 ratio as a concession. On 1 September Tirpitz sent Bethmann a proposal he considered even more conciliatory. He would reduce the German tempo to two through 1910, if the British would reduce theirs to three (including Dominion ships) during the same period. In effect, however, this was the same offer. Tirpitz felt that the British Liberals would favor such a plan but he anticipated Fisher's resistance. If they accepted the plan, well and good; if not, the odium for rejection would fall upon them.[62]

On 14 October Bethmann spoke with British Ambassador Goschen about a political understanding that he hoped would guarantee the European territorial status quo in exchange for relaxing the building tempo. He did not raise Tirpitz's idea for mutual arms limitation, as he felt it would put his cards on the table too soon. In any event, political discussions would have to precede a naval agreement.[63] Grey refused this arrangement and countered with the idea that an exchange of naval information would be the best way to approach an agreement. Bethmann replied, on 4 November, with an offer to discuss political and naval questions simultaneously, with an eye toward a neutrality agreement. The latter was as unpalatable to Grey as Bülow's previous efforts, partly because it would bring Alsace-Lorraine into the discussion and affect relations with France. Grey used the approaching general elections to defer negotiations.[64] For the next eighteen months Britain would be convulsed with the struggle between the Liberals and the House of Lords. Although the Liberals won the election in January 1910, their small majority now made them dependent on their Labour and Irish partners, which crimped their freedom of action.

The failure of the negotiations and Britain's preoccupation with domestic affairs led to an almost two-year hiatus from serious discussions of a naval agreement. Tirpitz's brief honeymoon with Bethmann ended. He began to see the latter as another, more powerful Metternich on naval questions. The new Treasury Secretary Adolf Wermuth displayed an aggressive attitude toward naval spending.

The proposals Tirpitz had made in the fall of 1909 were never presented, but even if the 3:4 ratio had been offered, it would certainly have met a flat rejection. The Admiralty would never accept a plan that reduced only the building tempo and not the number of ships in the Navy Law. Conversely, the Germans would not consider a naval agreement unless it clearly stated that Britain would not align itself with Germany's enemies in the event of war. The British did not understand the threat the Germans saw in the Anglo-French Entente, nor did the Germans realize the extent to which the British were threatened by the German fleet. This gap in perceptions continued and grew as the Dreadnoughts piled up on both sides.

In March 1910 the Admiralty estimates included four battleships and one battlecruiser. This was sufficient even though Germany was building three battleships and one battlecruiser, since German acceleration had not materialized and the economists had to be appeased because of the narrow Liberal majority.[65] Bethmann doggedly tried again to revive a reduced tempo in exchange for an undefined political agreement.[66] On 14 August 1910 Grey dropped the idea that the Navy Law itself, and not just the tempo, had to be reduced. He proposed instead an information exchange, but in return for a tempo reduction he was only willing to say that Britain was not a member of a group of powers directed against Germany.[67] On 12 October Bethmann accepted, in principle, an information exchange as a confidence-building measure, but he wanted to know what Britain would exchange for a pledge not to introduce another Novelle.[68]

Negotiations lapsed in December 1910 owing to yet another British general election, this time over the constitutional position of the House of Lords on Irish Home Rule. On 16 December 1910 the two sides agreed to separate the information exchange from other issues. Resolving the details was left to the RMA and the Admiralty. Tirpitz had mixed feelings about the information exchange. On the one hand, "twenty years ago this kind of exchange with England . . . would have been considered absurd. England has never done this with anyone else, and it would be a blow to their prestige." Psychologically it would be advantageous for Germany, but because England could build ships faster, England, he argued, would have the real advantage of being able to observe and incorporate German improvements. Any exchange proposal would have to be simultaneous and binding for the next fiscal year so that the British could not steal a march. Tirpitz insisted that, for the subsequent year, both sides should have a free hand.[69] After haggling over minutiae, an agreement seemed imminent by July 1911. The Agadir Crisis intervened, however, and the effort came to naught.[70]

Grey tried to revive the subject of a general naval and political understanding on 8 March 1911. He agreed to discuss both simultaneously but wanted to limit the political side to particular points of friction, such as the Baghdad railway.[71] To understand Tirpitz's view in this question, it is necessary to review his train of thought at the time. On 24 October 1910 he met with William II and comprehensively restated his position. Although he tried to resurrect the risk theory, his real agenda became clear with this admission:

> If the English fleet can be permanently made strong enough so that an attack on Germany is no risk, German naval development, from the historical standpoint, would have been a failure and the naval policy of Your Majesty an historical fiasco.[72]

This argument was a classic example of the "sunk costs" fallacy, which is a frequent defense of failed policies. A war must be continued so that those who have fallen must not have died in vain. Vain leaders such as William II and committed bureaucratic institutionalists such as Tirpitz were, and are, virtually incapable of admitting a mistake or miscalculation.

Tirpitz suggested that the growing sentiment in Britain was that an attack on Germany involved no risk at all. With Conservatives strongly clamoring to impose a standard of "two keels to every German one," Tirpitz saw three alternatives: a 1:2 ratio that directly contradicted the risk theory; a 3:4 ration that was momentarily unfeasible; and a 2:3 ratio, the only remaining possibility. He was willing to negotiate on this basis but only if the fifty-eight ships stipulated in the Navy Law were retained. Such an understanding would require the British to build almost ninety capital ships.

In conversations with Capelle that preceded the meeting with the Emperor, Tirpitz worried about the problems that might arise from Bethmann's opposition to a 1912 Novelle.[73] Without the Novelle, Germany would slip to a two tempo from 1912 to 1917. The British would have the "easy" solution of building only four ships a year, putting the onus to compete on Germany. Capelle had argued for a 2:3 ratio; if the British rejected it, the onus would then be on them. They agreed that Germany should be willing, for the next five years, to keep a two tempo only if the British would agree to no more than a three tempo during that time. This consideration was likely the genesis of Tirpitz's willingness to accept a 2:3 ratio.

The 2:3 proposal, like the 3:4 of the year before, contained more poison than appeared on the surface. In 1909 Lloyd George had suggested a 2:3 ratio, but Tirpitz wanted to retain the entire ship establishment delineated in the Navy Law. The British might have considered this, but they would have excluded the Dominion ships from the tally and would not have given a neutrality agreement for it. Even if both sides accepted a 2:3 tempo until 1913 or 1914 (as Tirpitz had suggested the previous year), Germany, in order to preserve the Navy Law, would return permanently to the three tempo after 1913 or 1914. The proposal was also deceptive, because the overall relationship would have been about 3:4 in 1914 and very close to that ratio for years after.

That Tirpitz was willing to accept a 2:3 ratio in the long term demonstrates that his intentions were then defensive and that the maximum-sized navy he could aspire to was one of fifty-eight to sixty-two capital ships. At optimistic moments he had hoped that the British could not build ninety or so ships; however, the eight tempo of 1909 and the British capacity to continue to build four or more per year made it clear that Germany could not do better than about a 2:3 ratio, which Tirpitz defined as a sufficient defensive opportunity. Given his prior belief that a one-third superiority, that is, a 4:3 ratio, was the minimum necessary to take the offensive, the fact that Tirpitz would concede a 3:2 superiority, substantially larger than the 4:3 ratio, indicates that, by 1911, he was willing to accept *less* than what he had previously defined as a sufficient defensive opportunity.[74]

Tirpitz complained bitterly that Bethmann, Foreign Secretary Kiderlen-Wächter, and Metternich refused to present the 2:3 offer to the British.[75] He believed that his plan was a "concession," whereas Bethmann knew better. Tirpitz's and Widenmann's thorough misunderstanding of the diplomatic situation was evident in Tirpitz's optimistic interpretation of Widenmann's dispatch of 14 March 1911. In reporting on the parliamentary debate over the naval estimates, Widenmann quoted McKenna: "We have taken as a reasonable margin of security 30 of these ships as against 21. The 21 German ships will be delivered to the shipyards in the spring of 1914." Tirpitz and Widenmann interpreted the statement to be a "capitulation," giving up on the two-power standard. They castigated Bethmann for not seizing this diplomatic "opportunity." William II was "jubilant" and saw it as justification for not acquiescing to Bülow's more conciliatory approach.[76]

Actually the German "triumph" was a blip in British domestic politics. The recent election had left the government with only a small majority and therefore more vulnerable to interest groups within the party such as Radicals, Labour, and advocates of Irish Home Rule. Grey had to appease his domestic critics and ease diplomatic tensions with Germany. Had the Germans been more conciliatory, it is interesting to speculate whether Grey would have felt pressured to respond in kind. In practice, the two-power standard had already fallen with the four tempo, but most important to Tirpitz was the ratio between Germany and Britain. He ignored the fact that, in a war, France and Russia were likely to be aligned with Britain. The Liberals were determined to maintain British superiority over Germany come what may.

The real danger for Tirpitz and his bureaucratic empire would have been a permanent two tempo after 1911, because it could not rise again to a three tempo for replacement purposes after 1917.[77] When he pondered a 2:3 *ratio*, he risked that it would translate into a permanent German two *tempo* that would ultimately cut the German fleet by one-third. Tirpitz's works published after the war give the impression that, in 1911, he was willing to agree to a 2:3 *ratio* but in fact that was not the case. May 1911 was too late to discuss a reduction in tempo because from 1912 to 1917, without a Novelle, the German tempo would only be two in any case. To cut the tempo further, or not return to the three tempo after 1917, would permanently scuttle the Navy Law. Tirpitz pointed out that it might be necessary to add a few ships during the two-tempo interval to "remind" the Reichstag that the three tempo was the "normal" rate. This would require yet another Novelle. Bethmann could only conclude that "a naval agreement is in fact not possible." Tirpitz implicitly acknowledged that even talking further could be dangerous to Germany because, "if they come to us with a proposal for a naval agreement, it could only be the kind that we would have to reject, and in this way the odium of rejection would be placed upon us."[78]

Bethmann told the British that it was too late for an agreement based upon tempo reduction. He tried once more, in vain, for a general political understanding.[79] If there had ever been a chance for a 2:3 agreement, either in Tirpitz's bogus way or in a more honest one, it ended in 1911. The chances for such an agreement had always been small. Even Müller did not believe that the British would have accepted a 2:3 ratio.[80]

One historian has noted that Grey never revealed to Parliament that the Germans had offered a slowing of the arms race for a political agreement. The British public never had the chance to choose between the Cabinet's Entente policy and a naval and political agreement with Germany. It is curious that Bethmann never publicly revealed an offer that might have given British radicals a chance to pressure their own Cabinet. Perhaps Bethmann realized that Tirpitz's conciliatory appearance would be unmasked in the glare of publicity. Perhaps he refrained out of simple courtesy, or maybe he feared the wrath of the Emperor and the navalists.[81] In any case, as British Naval Attaché reports show, they continued to misunderstand the German naval system and had no idea of the large role played in naval affairs by questions of cost and taxation.[82]

TIRPITZ, THE REICHSTAG, AND THE TREASURY, 1908–1911

Passage in the Reichstag of the 1908 Navy Law with the four tempo raised Tirpitz's reputation to new heights; but even before Bülow's departure in the summer of 1909 potential trouble spots surfaced. Germany's international isolation and the cost question, with its tax consequences, stirred up the conservative press. By 1909, with the four tempo in place, navy spending approached 50 percent of the army's.[83] The growing need for finance reform, as well as pressure on the states to increase matricular contributions, gave Conservatives serious pause. Such unrest demonstrated the likelihood of huge naval expenditures destabilizing, rather than stabilizing, conservative monarchical control.

In the winter of 1908–1909, disturbed by the naval scare, Matthias Erzberger, the "coming man" in the Center Party and a sometime Tirpitz collaborator, complained that "it was a great mistake" that the government had not pursued the British offer for naval arms reduction. Progressives and the Center worried about the need to bring naval expenditures more in line with the taxing power of the state. Even some Conservatives felt that the fleet was simply too expensive.[84] Trotha, by 1908 a staff officer in the fleet, noted the increasing anti-navy sentiment in the press. Trotha conceded that the 1908 Novelle would not have passed in the spring of 1909, had it been delayed until then:

> We are certainly not, in the foreseeable future, to increase naval building. . . . The near future will require us to stay within the present limits of the Navy Law, which cannot be changed without an emergency, otherwise we would risk defeat.[85]

Budget Commission debates about the 1909 naval estimates were troublesome. Tirpitz had to defend against British accusations of acceleration and address the issue of whether the Navy Law could be maintained. Progressive Deputy Schrader questioned whether Germany could afford to continue building at the existing rate. Despite Tirpitz's assurances that the money was available, Schrader's inquiry threatened the Navy Law. In response to comments in the press regarding Admiral Galster's push for cheaper cruisers, torpedo boats, and submarines, Tirpitz argued, disingenuously, that, within the navy, opinion was unanimously against Galster, who concluded that a naval war against Britain would have to employ Kleinkrieg methods. Tirpitz argued that the 1906 cruiser Novelle showed that he had not ignored cruisers. The ability to conduct a worldwide Kleinkrieg varied among states. France, for example, with two coastlines and many foreign bases with coaling stations, could pursue such a war with prospects of success; Germany, however, "to a certain degree is in a geographical corner, and has only one [major] foreign base [Tsingtau]."

In a statement remarkable in the light of later events, Tirpitz told the Budget Commission:

> Today a close blockade in the old sense is no longer possible. Light ships would be close in, with large cruisers behind them, and the battlefleet would stand a few hundred miles away.

In an even more surprising comment, Tirpitz remarked:

> A deployment of the Royal Navy, as Deputy Erzberger suggests, of a blockade in the north of England or at Dover would contravene international treaties. That would be no [legal] blockade, and the mighty United States, e.g., would not refrain from trying to trade in the blockaded region. The Sea War Law Conference recently established that no neutral countries could be blockaded.[86]

These two statements, taken together, reveal a conundrum. Tirpitz acknowledged the likelihood of a distant blockade, but German naval planning in 1909 and after assumed a close blockade. The statement is juxtaposed with another, that international law, and the threat of American intervention, would prevent a distant blockade in the North Sea. Tirpitz's view on this point was correct in theory but woefully lacking in practice. This point has received attention neither from contemporary naval strategists nor from later historians.[87]

Despite Reichstag hesitations, the estimates passed in their original form. Resentment of Britain and the naval scare brought even skeptical deputies into line. Once again navalist agitation in Britain reinforced the dynamism of the arms race, and trumped growing misgivings over the cost of the navy and its implications for tax policy. After the 1907 election the Center, with Erzberger at the fore, took a purely opportunistic position on military matters; by December 1909, however, with the Bloc in tatters, the Center joined the Conservatives and, on arms matters at least, again became a pro-government party and even adopted a favorable attitude toward the army.[88]

As Reichstag support for further Novelles wavered, trouble loomed for Tirpitz with Bethmann's new Treasury Secretary, Adolf Wermuth. For the three years that he served, from 1909 to 1912, Wermuth was the most formidable adversary that Tirpitz had ever faced. Wermuth called for draconian economies in all departments. He candidly parsed the Reich's income, expenditures, and growing debt, and warned of a "complete catastrophe" in the near future.[89] The canny Capelle saw that, unlike previous Treasury Secretaries who had called for thrift, Wermuth really meant it. In September 1909 Capelle wrote to Tirpitz: "The *strength* of the Treasury is that, in fact, it does not have enough money, that the introduction of new taxes for the 1910 estimates is hardly feasible [*angängig*], and that the Chancellor would hardly give his consent [to new taxes]."[90]

Capelle judged that Wermuth was exaggerating the woes of the financial situation and saw a ray of hope for the navy. Capelle offered Tirpitz three possibilities: push for the introduction of new taxes; pass off the necessary economies onto other branches of the government, which, in fact, could only mean the army; or make some concessions at the navy's expense. Tirpitz could pursue a mixed version of all three strategies. Both the army and navy would eventually have to pressure Wermuth to introduce new taxes. Capelle counseled prudence and restraint against attacking the Treasury; to act otherwise might bring blame upon the navy for the financial situation.

Tirpitz was beset by complaints from within the navy that he was too accommodating with the Reichstag. In response, in April 1910 in Kiel, he took the unusual step of addressing a group of higher officers and some cadets at the Naval Academy.[91] Fearful that the Navy Law was taken for granted, he reminded his audience of the history of the navy's relations with the Reichstag before 1898. Only with a long-term Navy Law could fleet development proceed without "cow trading" over annual appropriations. It would be dangerous for the navy if he did not maintain reasonably good relations with the Reichstag. He acknowledged that the Reichstag's commitment to new construction was as much moral as political. He evidently omitted the part of the draft that discussed frankly how troublesome the Reichstag could become over replacement ships. Even Tirpitz's most influential opponent within the navy, the newly appointed Fleet Chief Admiral Henning von Holtzendorff, felt obliged to assure Tirpitz that the officer corps stood behind him in the need to preserve the Navy Law.[92]

During 1910 and early 1911 Tirpitz's relations with the Emperor deteriorated somewhat. Fairly typical were disagreements in December 1910 over technical details in the construction of the *Nassaus*. Tirpitz complained that the Emperor continually sought advice on technical matters from non-experts. Frustrated, Tirpitz turned to the retired Admiral Friedrich Hollmann, a crony of the Emperor, to seek advice on who should replace him as State Secretary, knowing full well that Hollmann would bring the question to the Emperor.

Throughout 1910 and 1911 the navy and other Reich offices waged a guerrilla war against Wermuth's stringent economies. There was extensive correspondence over Wermuth's attempts to limit mess allowances for everyone from common sailors to admirals.[93] Another issue was Tirpitz's attempt to secure an additional building in downtown Berlin for the RMA and other navy departments that were scattered around the city. On this point Capelle advised "judicious concessions."[94] A more significant conflict concerned what was to be done with the proceeds of the sale of two obsolete battleships to the Turks in July 1910. Wermuth wanted the 17 million marks to go to the Treasury, whereas Tirpitz wanted to use the money to cover the navy's burgeoning needs, a result of the underestimated costs in the 1908 Novelle tables.[95] This was a sign of how the navy's

parliamentary situation had so deteriorated since then that, as noted, Capelle strongly advised against bucking the Treasury on the matter so that
it did not appear that the navy had made an error in the cost tables two
years earlier, which would shake the Reichstag's confidence in the RMA's
calculations. Capelle was pessimistic about a three tempo Novelle in 1912.

Capelle was also worried about the 1912 Reichstag elections. The
bourgeois parties were tearing one another to pieces (*zerfleischen*). The
Social Democrats could rebound from their 1907 defeat with their many
popular issues such as finance reform, suffrage in Prussia, and the anticipated 1911 Army Bill. Were the navy to ask unexpectedly for additional
funding in 1911, it could easily become the scapegoat for the financial
situation. Were an Army Bill to be postponed until after 1911, and even
a small Navy Bill submitted that year, "one may well imagine the storm
it would cause in the army." Capelle feared that such a proposal would
"not only cost the RMA its political credit" but might also cost the navy
its State Secretary.[96]

During the debate on the naval estimates in February 1911, even
pro-navy deputies were enthusiastic about the prospective reduced costs
in 1912 because of the drop in tempo to two ships per year. The only way
Tirpitz could stave off further difficulties was to prevent Bethmann from
trading a long-term drop to a two tempo for a naval understanding with
Britain. If the Chancellor achieved such an agreement, Tirpitz's plan for
a fleet of sixty large ships would be severely jeopardized.[97]

Paucity of naval enthusiasm from the Center and other swing parties,
and pressure from Bethmann and Wermuth, made Tirpitz, in the spring
of 1911, pessimistic about the continuation of the three tempo. He even
suggested that a future Novelle might better be proposed by another State
Secretary.[98] In his fourteen years in office Tirpitz had had his ups and
downs, but the spring of 1911 may well have been his lowest point. There
seemed no obvious way to restore his political fortunes.

RELATIONS WITH THE ADMIRALSTAB AND
THE FRONT COMMAND, 1903–1911

While Tirpitz engaged in the 1906 and 1908 Novelles,[99] and coped with
the diplomatic efforts of Bülow and Bethmann to come to a political/

naval agreement with Britain, he also battled over strategic and bureaucratic matters with the Admiralstab and the newly founded Office of Fleet
Commander in 1903.

Admiral Otto von Diedrichs had retired in frustration in 1902 upon
losing bureaucratic battles with Tirpitz and the RMA. His successor as
Chief of the Admiralstab was Vice Admiral Wilhelm Büchsel (1902–1908),
Tirpitz's crew comrade and former shipmate. Walter von Keyserlingk
served for three years under Büchsel in the Admiralstab and described
him as tall and handsome, a quick study, and an optimist by nature. Despite his personal friendship with Tirpitz, which continued through his
Admiralstab years, Büchsel tried to revive Diedrichs's effort to create an
Admiralstab officer corps. The corps would work out of a central office
but should also have Admiralstab officers in the Front advising higher
officers.[100] To give the Admiralstab the feel of an elite corps, Büchsel
proposed uniforms that would set them apart, as General Staff uniforms
did in the army. According to Keyserlingk, "such an initiative made the
new idea into a laughing stock even faster than would otherwise have
been the case."[101]

Tirpitz worried that expanding the size and function of the Admiralstab might re-create an office akin to that of the Oberkommando, the dangerous rival for power that he had destroyed in 1899. Therefore, in 1904,
he managed to remove the authority of the Admiralstab in Berlin from
Admiralstab officers in the fleet. Because the Front always complained
of officer shortages, Tirpitz enlisted its support against the Admiralstab's
expansion efforts. As Pohl told Michaelis when the former became First
Squadron Commander in 1909, "Do not believe that I will allow myself to
be ruled by an Admiralstab officer; I have been in the fleet long enough
to know what I have to do."[102] When Büchsel tried to bring the Cadet
School and the Naval Academy under the Admiralstab, Tirpitz, in 1907,
persuaded the Emperor to place the Naval Academy under the RMA.[103]
Tirpitz's ability to defeat the Admiralstab is a classic example of his skill
at bureaucratic politics. Although the "threat" from the Admiralstab was
minor, Tirpitz gelded it but also used it as a counterweight to another
threat, the Fleet Command. The Admiralstab's primary peacetime function was to prepare war plans. Even in that capacity its scope was limited,
as Tirpitz had complete control over the types and numbers of naval

ships. Only when war began in 1914 did the Admiralstab rise at Tirpitz's expense. Büchsel, an easygoing man, seemed not to take the bureaucratic battles personally.[104]

Beginning in 1901–1902 the inexorable three tempo started to pour out of the shipyards and into the fleet. One of the curiosities of German fleet organization, little noted by historians, is that, until 1903, there was no fleet commander. For a few weeks each summer the fleet would assemble for joint exercises, after 1899 under the general command of Admiral Hans von Koester, who the rest of the year was Commander of the First (and only, at the time) Battle Squadron. During the rest of the year the fleet was under the Emperor's direct command.

The keen-eyed Hopmann was privy to Tirpitz's reasoning on the question. Tirpitz saw that a permanent Battlefleet Command would have training advantages. His excuse to oppose it was that, since the fleet was built by squadrons (eight ships), a fleet commander might crimp the initiative of squadron leaders and result in formal tactics more suitable for the sand table than for battle. Tirpitz saw that the selection of a fleet commander in peacetime would be based on the ironclad process of seniority. If a war suddenly came, the fleet commander should be the most capable among the senior admirals, no matter what his peacetime position. Another "problem" would be that a fleet commander might consider within his domain all ships in home waters, not just the battle squadrons. He might oppose temporary detachment of ships on other important missions.[105] The last of these two rationales reveal Tirpitz's real reason for opposing a fleet commander position. He would be an increasingly formidable bureaucratic rival to Tirpitz as the battlefleet grew. Tirpitz was willing, with the Emperor's collusion, to leave the fleet in a position of not knowing who its wartime commander would be. This odd arrangement did not threaten Tirpitz's power base.

In 1903, when a Second Squadron was being formed, William II succumbed to the obvious and made Koester Commander of the Active Battlefleet (renamed the High Seas Fleet in 1907), though there was no guarantee that Koester would command it in wartime. Koester was one of only a few admirals senior to Tirpitz. Although he had occasional personal and bureaucratic conflicts with Tirpitz, the navy recognized him as a skilled trainer and tactician who encouraged initiative on the part of subordinate commanders.[106]

His successor, in 1906, was Prinz Heinrich, the Emperor's brother, a marginally competent, if hardly brilliant, officer. He had spent his whole life in the navy and, as a royal, was promoted faster than seniority warranted. He was a longtime friend and supporter of Tirpitz, dating back to the torpedo years.[107] His "minder" and Chief of Staff was Captain Wilhelm von Lans, no friend of Tirpitz.[108] As Fleet Chief he had low-level bureaucratic conflicts with both the Admiralstab and the RMA, but he continued Koester's work on tactics and gunnery. He was horrified by the thought of war with Britain and was skeptical of the possibility that his English relatives would allow an attack on Germany.[109]

Prinz Heinrich's successor as Fleet Chief from 1909 to 1913 was a horse of a different color. Admiral Henning von Holtzendorff, a man of tremendous personal charisma, was a distant relative of Naval Cabinet Chief Müller. Michaelis served on his staff when he was Commander of the First Squadron and described him fulsomely. He was from an old aristocratic family with large holdings in Pomerania. He had many noble Prussian relatives and was an intimate of the imperial family. Tirpitz disliked the fact that Holtzendorff wanted to change some of Tirpitz's tactical ideas from the 1890s. According to Michaelis, Holtzendorff thought day and night about how to defeat the Royal Navy, rather than just lead a risk fleet.[110]

STRATEGIC PLANNING

Completion of the Kaiser Wilhelm Canal in 1895 gave Germany a huge geographic advantage in a war with France and Russia. With a secure connection between the base at Kiel and the Elbe estuary, the German fleet could rapidly concentrate either in the Baltic or the North Sea as conditions demanded, a classic example of interior lines. If a French fleet tried to pass the narrow Danish waters to enter the Baltic, the threat to Danish neutrality would arouse British ire, and it would expose French communications in the North Sea to German interdiction from Wilhelmshaven.

Two developments altered this favorable situation. The first and most obvious was that, beginning in 1904 with the Dogger Bank incident, Germany had to plan seriously for a possible naval war against the Royal Navy. The second complicating factor was that when the Dreadnoughts *Nassau* and *Westfalen* began sea trials in October 1909[111] and finally joined the

High Seas Fleet in May 1910, Germany lost its interior lines. Ships of that size could not pass through the canal. If they were based in Kiel and events required a move to Wilhelmshaven, they faced a voyage around Jutland and would present a tempting target for British attack. Until the widening of the canal was completed in 1914–15, this geographic reality presented a conundrum for German planners, along with the bigger problem of how to defend against a potential enemy far more formidable than France or Russia. The loss of interior lines was a major reason why Tirpitz had initially been reluctant to build Dreadnoughts. The "fleet against England" came at a ruinous geostrategic cost.

Büchsel struggled from 1902 to 1908 to come up with plausible answers to these insoluble dilemmas. There is no need here to go into the tortuous history of operations plans against Britain during the Büchsel era.[112] Büchsel tried to persuade Schlieffen to invade Denmark, to ease the navy's strategic position. Schlieffen, and later Moltke, refused, since their eyes were focused on Belgium, with scarcely a man to spare for operations against Denmark. Büchsel even had the perspicacity, unremarked at the time, to observe in a 1902 memo a possibility that could undercut all planning against Britain. "We must keep in mind that the enemy's most dangerous tactic is to blockade us from a distance and to avoid any offensive actions." As Lambi notes, this was probably the first anticipation on the German side of the wide blockade strategy that the British actually adopted in the war.[113] Büchsel's problem was compounded by Fisher's fleet redistribution back into home waters. Tirpitz had assumed in 1897 and 1900 that overseas commitments would keep most of the Royal Navy away from the Channel; instead, every time the German Sisyphus rolled the stone up the hill, British Home Fleet reinforcements rolled it back down. Büchsel settled on a North Sea defensive plan based on Wilhelmshaven and the Elbe estuary. If, as expected, the British mounted a close blockade, submarines and torpedo boat attacks might whittle down the blockading forces enough for a fleet attack.[114]

In 1908 Admiral Graf Friedrich von Baudissin replaced the retired Büchsel. Not personally close to Tirpitz, he was well known to the Emperor. He had a reputation as a clever seaman and saw himself as a representative of the Front, as opposed to the Berlin-based paper pushers.[115] During 1908 Baudissin campaigned for a more aggressive plan for a war with Britain.[116] If the High Seas Fleet were passive, German Atlantic

commerce would be cut off. He therefore favored attacks on the blockaders with the whole fleet as far north as Scotland, ideally on the night
before war broke out, a prospect realizable only if Germany were planning its own "Copenhagen."[117] He excited the temporary enthusiasm of
the Emperor, and managed to get Moltke and the General Staff not to
object were the fleet to be used offensively. Baudissin came in conflict
with Tirpitz when the former demanded that ships in reserve be crewed
in advance of a possible war. Tirpitz did not like either the money this
would cost or that it would impinge on the RMA's responsibility for organizing reserve mobilization. Baudissin lasted only about thirteen months
as Chief, departing in early May 1909. Michaelis, who joined the Admiralstab with Baudissin's successor, noted the remark of a former crew
comrade in the office: "Here we change chiefs as fast as an express train
passes by telephone poles."[118]

The new Chief was Vice Admiral Max von Fischel, one of Tirpitz's
oldest torpedo comrades.[119] Fischel tried to keep an offensive spirit, despite the long odds. Such plans were crippled by, among other factors, the
addition of *Nassau* and *Westfalen* to the fleet, bringing on the problem
of where to base them. Their clumsy deployment from the Baltic would
ruin all surprise in taking the offensive.[120] Tirpitz worried that, in times
of tension, visibly offensive measures could sharpen the situation, and he
wanted to preclude the possibility of a sudden German strike.[121]

Michaelis clearly saw the practical disadvantages of the Admiralstab.
The RMA gave the Admiralstab little money for intelligence, while the
RMA's Nachrichtenbüro commanded lavish sums for the same functions.
Tirpitz withheld from the Admiralstab information on vital matters, such
as technology. The Fleet Chief listened to the Admiralstab only as long
as it agreed with what he wanted to hear. The last straw for Fischel came
when, while making a presentation, he saw that William II was paging
through a horse journal. Fischel retired in March 1911.[122] One could
scarcely imagine a clearer example of the peacetime irrelevance of an
Admiralstab under Tirpitz's thumb. Admiral August von Heeringen, another member of the Torpedo Gang and Tirpitz's closest collaborator in
the campaigns for the early Navy Laws, succeeded Fischel.

On 1 October 1909 Henning von Holtzendorff, Commander of the
First Battle Squadron, followed Prinz Heinrich as Fleet Chief. According to Trotha, but not Michaelis, the Holzendorff appointment surprised

the officer corps and gave the impression that Müller, his distant relative, had engineered the appointment.[123] Tirpitz had an old grudge against Holtzendorff, who had served as Knorr's "pen" at the Oberkommando during Tirpitz's successful campaign to get rid of the office.[124]

Holtzendorff questioned the Baudissin/Fischel offensive strategy. He recognized the strategic problem of where to base the *Nassaus*. He doubted, in view of British superiority, the wisdom of taking the offensive at all. He wanted to concentrate in the Baltic in anticipation of a British attack there.[125] Tirpitz favored Fischel's more offensive North Sea deployment. In a war game early in 1911, Holtzendorff tested Fischel's strategy. Its negative outcome cleared the deck for a Baltic exercise the following year. Most upsetting to Tirpitz about Holtzendorff's exercise was the latter's advocacy for naming a wartime Fleet Chief in peacetime, presumably Holtzendorff himself. Tirpitz argued once again that the Emperor should wait to appoint a Fleet Chief until the outbreak of war in order to name the most capable admiral, independent of seniority.[126] Before events could develop further, the gunboat *Panther* landed in Morocco and brought with it great consequences for the naval situation.

CONSTRUCTION, 1909 TO 1911

The four tempo (three battleships and one large cruiser per year) began in 1908. *Oldenburg*, the last of the four *Helgolands* (completed August 1912), displaced 22,800 tons and had twelve 30.5-cm guns. The other two 1909 battleships (completed October 1912) and the three 1910 ships constituted the *Kaiser* class. Although each had only ten 30.5-cm guns, they displaced 24,700 tons, had heavier armor, and were the first German battleships with turbine engines. Saved space allowed an arrangement of turrets so that all guns could fire in a broadside of ten, instead of eight as with previous classes.

All German battlecruisers had turbine engines. *Moltke*, *Goeben*, and *Seydlitz*, were laid down between 1909 and 1911 and were completed 2½ years later. Each had ten 28-cm guns and could cruise at 23–25 knots.[127] Both battleships and battlecruisers, in the Tirpitz pattern, were somewhat slower and less heavily armed than their British counterparts, but they were better protected.

14
DENOUEMENT, 1911–1914

THE SECOND MOROCCAN CRISIS

The explosive events of the summer and early fall of 1911 were triggered by an innocent and routine ship redeployment. The gunboat *Panther*, Southwest African station ship, was due to return to Wilhelmshaven for major repairs. Chief of the Admiralstab, Fischel, on 8 March 1911, asked the Foreign Office if there were any objections if *Panther* stopped in a Moroccan port on its way home in July. The French, in violation of the Algeciras Act of 1906, occupied the Moroccan capital of Fez on 21 May. Foreign Secretary Kiderlen-Wächter agreed to allow *Panther* to visit the port of Mogador.[1]

Late in June Bethmann and Kiderlen decided to challenge the French occupation of Morocco. A handy excuse was to protect hypothetically endangered German nationals in Agadir. The Emperor reluctantly consented, though nervous that it might spoil his upcoming visit to London. Since all the principals were at Kiel Week, Kiderlen called in Heeringen, the new Chief of the Admiralstab, to prepare the necessary orders without clarifying the political context. Heeringen told Michaelis that the Emperor had ordered the immediate dispatch of *Panther* to Agadir. Michaelis asked why the initiative, to which Heeringen replied: "To hoist the flag." Michaelis responded: "The little ship is too weak to make a difference, and, by raising their flag at Fez, the French have declared that Morocco is in their sphere." Heeringen answered: "It is not supposed to conquer Morocco but only to show that we are there, too. As Kiderlen says, it should be a trumpet blast with which we will get compensation from the French elsewhere."[2] Neither Tirpitz nor the Fleet Chief was officially informed.

Hopmann wrote that Tirpitz, had he been consulted, would have strongly advised against the incursion. "During his entire time in office, he was no friend of fanfare, especially any directed against England that threatened to disrupt his life's work."[3] Hopmann was only partly right; for when a Novelle was pending Tirpitz did not hesitate to play the anti-British propaganda card. At other times he tried to lay low. But in the spring and early summer of 1911 Tirpitz was pessimistic about the prospective Novelle to raise the impending two tempo. and so, as the Moroccan Crisis played itself out, he began to see it as a heaven-sent opportunity for expansion, akin to the *Bundesrath* affair of 1900.

The Second Moroccan Crisis originated in the Franco-German rivalry there, but it ended, as in 1906, with a major confrontation between Britain and Germany.[4] Since 1909 the French had substantially exceeded the special rights granted them in the 1906 Act of Algeciras. The resulting insurrection prompted the French, in 1911, to send a force to Fez. German protests to Paris went unheeded. Kiderlen and Bethmann felt that quick action was necessary to address the "affront." The most realistic possibility, in their view, was to concede the French position there in exchange for compensation elsewhere. The Emperor consented, and on 20 June 1911 Kiderlen informed the French of this decision. In this context *Panther* arrived in Agadir on 1 July, creating consternation in Paris and London. Although German interests there were almost nil and in no jeopardy, Kiderlen, to rationalize the incursion, invoked hackneyed phrases about the defense of German lives and property; his real reason, however, was to rattle a saber at the French to improve Germany's bargaining position. This recklessness provoked a furor in Britain and counterpoint nationalist agitation in Germany.

Kiderlen did not inform the navy of the political reasons for dispatching *Panther*.[5] When Tirpitz heard of it later he recognized it as a grave political and tactical blunder, especially since the British had not been informed ahead of time. The unnecessary secrecy is a good example of the chaotic manner in which Germany conducted policy. Tirpitz received unofficial word of the *Panther* decision just as he was departing for summer leave, and, in his memoirs, he remarked: "A flag is easily hoisted, but it is often a difficult matter to lower even a small one with honor."[6]

Foreign Secretary Grey warned, on 3 July, of British interest in the matter. Kiderlen compounded the error by a three-week delay in clarifying his position.[7] The British Conservative press loudly denounced Kiderlen's policy as an attempt to bully France and secure a naval base in Morocco for Germany. The Liberal press was misleadingly moderate and left the false impression in Berlin that, despite Grey's statement, the British might not back France.[8]

The British Cabinet, baffled by Kiderlen's silence, sounded the alarm in the form of Lloyd George's famous Mansion House speech of 21 July. Because Lloyd George was considered a pacifist and an advocate of good Anglo-German relations, the speech carried more weight than had a Liberal Imperialist delivered it:

> If a situation were to be forced upon us in which peace could only be preserved by the surrender of the great and beneficent position Britain has won by centuries of heroism and achievement, by allowing Britain to be treated, where her interests were vitally affected, as if she were of no account in the Cabinet of Nations, then I say emphatically that peace at that price would be a humiliation intolerable for a great country like ours to endure. National honour is no party question.[9]

Lloyd George's uncharacteristically threatening speech caused a sensation in Germany. Tirpitz saw it as a "slap in the face" and a "check."[10] He soon seized the opportunity to begin Novelle preparations, a political impossibility a few months before. The speech sparked fears of war in the German press. During the excitement Lloyds would only sell maritime insurance of fifteen days' duration. Even more ominous were rumors that the Admiralty had canceled a fleet visit to Norway and Sweden in the interest of concentrating the fleet in home waters. The Emperor, too, was frightened. He told Müller: "One does not like to think about [the possibility of war] if all one's sons are at the front."[11] The speech and its subsequent war fears also surprised the Admiralty. Press rumors that the whole German High Seas Fleet had vanished into the North Sea led to a panic in the Cabinet and, in October, resulted in Winston Churchill replacing Reginald McKenna as First Lord of the Admiralty.[12]

Mutual war fears continued through August and into September, even though France and Germany began to bargain for a settlement in August. The crisis eased only in October. In an agreement signed on 4 November 1911 Germany recognized a French protectorate over Morocco in exchange for territorial compensation from the French Congo adjacent to the German Cameroons.[13]

The results of the Agadir Crisis were far-reaching in both Germany and Britain. On 23 August 1911 the Committee of Imperial Defence held a historic meeting to decide on British policy in the event of war with Germany. At this meeting the views of the War Office prevailed. The British Expeditionary Force (BEF) would fight in France if Britain, allied with France, went to war with Germany. The Admiralty had wanted to retain the BEF for operations elsewhere, perhaps on Germany's Baltic coast. Once Churchill became First Lord, the Admiralty made no difficulties in the coordination of plans with the War Office and the French for the quick transport of the BEF to France.[14] The Agadir Crisis, therefore, tightened the bonds that had developed during the previous Anglo-French military conversations. In Germany the crisis raised popular clamor for a Novelle. Tirpitz was only too willing to accommodate.[15]

EARLY NOVELLE PREPARATIONS

As early as 1908 Tirpitz had in mind a Novelle for 1912. When National Liberal Ernst Bassermann mentioned the possibility in the Budget Commission in 1908, Tirpitz remarked in private that the statement had been useful as a trial balloon, as it provoked no unfavorable reaction in the Reichstag. Tirpitz did not respond publicly because he wanted to retain a free hand.[16]

Tirpitz kept his Novelle option open during the 1909–11 naval negotiations. In 1909–10 he would have been willing to give up the possibility of a 1912 Novelle but only if the British made reciprocal concessions.[17] On 4 May 1911 Bethmann once more tried to persuade Tirpitz to agree that there would be no Novelle that fall. Though prospects of a Novelle at the time were bleak, Tirpitz would only forsake it if the British committed to a three tempo over the next six years; otherwise, he wanted to keep the Novelle possibility open sometime during the period of the two tempo (1912 to 1917). The three tempo would return on a permanent basis after 1917. When Bethmann suggested a tempo reduction after 1917, Tirpitz demurred, fearing that it would undermine the Navy Law. A six-year two tempo would also be a threat, because the Reichstag might forget that the "normal" tempo was three. It would be essential, he said, once or twice during that time, to have a three-tempo year to make it less likely that the

Reichstag might balk after 1917 to pay for the third ship. To interrupt the two tempo, a small Novelle would be necessary.[18]

Tirpitz's pessimism for a 1911 Novelle seemed justified. Retired Grand Admiral Hans von Koester had led the Flottenverein since 1909 in a moderate fashion, which was congenial to Tirpitz. Koester worried that the organization was slowly atrophying and that its influence might be hard to reconstitute in a crisis. At a meeting on 28 May the Flottenverein passed a resolution in favor of a three tempo Novelle for 1912. The public response was, distressingly, only minimally favorable. Many in the press and some Reichstag deputies voiced suspicions that the resolution was a stalking horse for Tirpitz, although he had taken no public position on it. As a consequence, Tirpitz, Capelle, and Dähnhardt agreed that the political winds were unfavorable for a fall 1911 Novelle.[19]

There is no evidence to suggest that before the Agadir Crisis and Lloyd George's Mansion House speech Tirpitz was planning a 1912 Novelle. He had not ordered the usual preparation of statistical tables or feelers to his "friends" in the Reichstag. Before August 1911 the usual juggernaut of Novelle preparation was absent. It took the Agadir Crisis, the Mansion House speech, popular clamor in both Britain and Germany, and the test mobilization of the Royal Navy in July to galvanize him into action.

From St. Blasien, on 3 August 1911, Tirpitz wrote to Capelle that a reaction to the threats of the Mansion House speech was imperative, and suddenly prospects for the early Novelle looked promising. "The storm of public opinion can become very strong, and we would be in danger of letting the right moment slip away if we wait until 1913. We must create the possibility of a Novelle in 1912." His initial idea was three or four large cruisers, larger guns, and more personnel for new ships. Tirpitz opined that a Novelle could be justified without reference to the British by citing the inadequacies of Germany's pre-Dreadnought cruisers. Caught up in the excitement of the moment, he even suggested that, if necessary, the Reichstag might provide cruisers by special appropriations outside the Navy Law.[20] Such an idea, if made public, would have courted a return to the accusations of the 1890s that the Reichstag was on a "zigzag course" and undermined the successful formula of the Navy Law.

The normally calm Capelle also seemed overwrought by the crisis. Three more cruisers outside the Navy Law "would not stand in the correct relationship to the *Fashoda* [humiliation] that Germany had suffered."

"For 1912 . . . [what is needed is] either a continuation of the four tempo against England or nothing!"[21] Although Tirpitz did not want a war over Morocco, he felt that the naval situation was gradually improving with progress being made both on the canal widening and the fortification of Helgoland; if Britain tried to veto the Novelle, however, war would inevitably follow, and, in that case, "we would have to let fate take its course."[22]

Tirpitz rejected Capelle's idea of a four tempo Novelle, stating that it would be provocative. He also believed that insufficient trained manpower was available for the new ships of a continued four tempo. A three tempo Novelle, with an expansion in ship size, increased personnel, and additional U-boat money would suffice without succumbing to the demands of radical navalists.[23] Tirpitz even ordered Captain Carl Hollweg, Head of the Nachrichtenbüro (N), to look into the consequences of a public German offer to Britain of a 2:3 fleet (not tempo) ratio. Hollweg concluded that were the British to accept, it would seem at first that Germany had scored a great success; however, it would in fact hamper, and even, de facto, replace the Navy Law, limiting future German possibilities for trade and empire.[24] Such twisted logic again demonstrates the strong hold of Mahanist Social Darwinism in the navy. Battleships, apparently, for economic purposes, were a tool superior to shrewd German businessmen who sold quality products at competitive prices.

Wary of approaching the Emperor for fear of public disclosure, as occurred in 1899, Tirpitz first broached the subject with Bethmann. Tirpitz attributed the diplomatic "defeat" over Morocco to insufficient seapower, for which a three tempo Novelle was the only remedy. Novelle battleships could be combined with material reserve ships to form a third active battle squadron. New battlecruisers would replace the notoriously sinkable *Hertha* class. Loans could cover most of the cost, and "only" 50 million marks would have to come from new taxes. In reality, the money could come only by increasing the inheritance tax. Tirpitz seemed not to understand what a bombshell this proposal would be to government relations with Conservatives. Since the sitting Reichstag was due to expire at the end of the year, he recommended that an agreement with Conservatives and the Center be made before the election in order to form a cartel between them and the National Liberals.[25]

Bethmann felt that a Novelle would endanger peaceful relations with Britain and could amount to a public admission that Germany's Morocco policy was a failure. Even an increased inheritance tax would not provide sufficient funds. Instead of an outright rejection, Tirpitz persuaded Bethmann to delay his decision until after the diplomatic crisis blew over.[26] This was the first minor victory for Bethmann's Novelle-stalling tactics.

William II spoke publicly in Hamburg early in September about the need for a stronger fleet, since by then Tirpitz had told him about the Novelle possibility. Fleet Chief Holtzendorff thought that organization, training, and personnel should take priority over additional ships.[27] Tirpitz was indignant about Holtzendorff's "meddling" and tried to limit his access to the Emperor on fleet development.[28] Hopmann privately agreed with Holtzendorff and favored more gradual and balanced fleet development. He noted: "Tirpitz fears for his life's work, but it is still not really under threat. We have only wanted to go too fast and, like parvenus, filled our mouths too full."[29]

On 6 September the Emperor told Bethmann that any Novelle should wait until conversations with France regarding compensation were concluded, that is, perhaps in a year or more. Then, only a week later, William II wanted a cruiser Novelle that could be justified on the basis of the recent expansion of the French and Japanese fleets! Müller hoped to clarify the confusion at the annual naval audience in Rominten at the end of September.[30] Revealingly, because it was omitted from Tirpitz's postwar writings, in mid-September Capelle, in a conversation with Müller, frankly noted that the fleet "can only have a rationale against England."[31]

As the RMA staff prepared for the Rominten meeting,[32] Tirpitz nervously softened his position when he told the Chancellor in September that the Novelle had to be passed in 1912 at the latest to secure "good defensive chances," unless Bethmann could get the British to accept a 2:3 ratio. Tirpitz would then prepare legislation to maintain German strength at that level.[33]

At Rominten, on 26 September, Tirpitz proposed a *public* offer to Britain of a 2:3 ratio. If accepted, a fall 1912 Novelle could provide a fleet built to that level; if rejected, the odium would fall on the British and the Novelle could be introduced anyway. The Novelle would add three battleships and three large cruisers to the two tempo from 1912 to 1917. With the five existing material reserve ships, a third active battle squadron could be constituted. William II accepted this ingenious idea but still hoped to persuade Bethmann to accept a fall 1911 Novelle.[34] After informing Bethmann of his decision,[35] he asked Koester to kill a Navy League resolution for a cruiser Novelle.[36]

Tirpitz, in early October, changed his mind about the timing of the Novelle and wanted to announce it in the fall of 1911, because at that time it seemed likely that the impending Reichstag debate on the Morocco question would force the government to declare openly if a Novelle was in the offing. Further, the Emperor had leaked hints of it, and this assured public discussion and perhaps awkward questions. Tirpitz wanted Bethmann to make a 2:3 offer public during the Morocco debates. More confident now of public support, he insisted that both the offer and the Novelle proposal be announced *before* the looming Reichstag elections so that it could influence the poll.[37] Capelle, normally cautious on financial matters, wrote in a memo in late October that Britain did not have the will or the finances to continue the shipbuilding competition and therefore would have to approach Germany diplomatically.[38] Whether Tirpitz shared this optimism is unclear.

Bethmann, fearful of the political, financial, and diplomatic consequences of a Novelle, fought back. With Kiderlen, he marshaled the press resources of the Foreign Office against naval expansion. He enlisted the indefatigable Adolf Wermuth, Reich Treasury Secretary, who objected to using loans rather than new taxes to pay for the Novelle ships. Wermuth wanted to avoid raising the Novelle and the tax question before the elections.[39]

The 14 October audience at Hubertusstock was a classic example of the Emperor's governing style, this time to Tirpitz's disadvantage. At a morning meeting he told Tirpitz that Bethmann would either have to introduce the Novelle or be dismissed. In the afternoon Bethmann talked him into not announcing the 2:3 offer and, instead, only hinting at the possibility of a Novelle. If necessary, it could be announced the following spring. This defeat put Tirpitz and Capelle into a very pessimistic mood.[40]

Despite the discouraging news, the Etatsabteilung (E) by 16 October had a first draft for a three tempo Novelle. Dähnhardt secretly showed the draft to Matthias Erzberger of the Center Party.[41] He shared it with deputies Hertling and Gröber, who were favorable toward the Novelle but with some important caveats: it should not be announced before the elections, and it should not be financed with an expanded inheritance tax.[42] As a result of these conversations, Dähnhardt and Hollweg were more optimistic than Tirpitz.[43] Surprisingly, amid the Reichstag polemics during the Morocco debate, a Novelle was not mentioned.[44]

Holtzendorff voiced reservations about the Novelle. He was worried about war in 1911 and felt that more important than a Novelle was the completion of the canal. Germany should avoid war until the High Seas Fleet was entirely made up of modern ships and the canal was passable by Dreadnoughts. Until then, war preparations should have priority over a Novelle.[45] Even within the RMA there was privately held dissension about a Novelle. Scheer, for example, quietly shared his misgivings with Hopmann.[46]

Early in November the second draft of the Novelle and the estimates were ready. Once again, the estimates contained a price increase for large ships, 58 million marks each for battleships and battlecruisers, even though E estimated the real cost at about 60 million marks for battleships and 48.4 million for battlecruisers. Such sleight of hand provided a cushion against the possibility of later size and cost increases.[47]

The draft Novelle would increase the fleet to a total of forty-one battleships (one flagship and five squadrons, of which three would be permanently fully manned), with twenty large and forty small cruisers as reconnaissance and foreign-service ships. The increase of three battleships would make the German fleet two-thirds as strong as that of any possible opponent, large enough to offer "good defensive chances," although it assumed that the British would accept such a ratio. It would also stabilize the three tempo, increase war readiness with a third active squadron, and add more money for U-boats and Zeppelins. The incremental cost over the 1908 table was estimated at 360 million marks.[48]

Bethmann and Wermuth continued their efforts to delay the Novelle and the 1912 estimates. Bethmann persuaded the Emperor to defer debate on the naval question until Tirpitz, Wermuth, and he could agree on a form for the proposal.[49] Bethmann objected to the part that mentioned a 2:3 ratio with Britain. Tirpitz obligingly dropped the reference to the ratio and based the rationale for the Novelle solely on technical reasons—increasing readiness and replacing old cruisers—but he did not alter the three tempo.[50] Tirpitz, on 28 November, received a strong letter from Wermuth with bitter complaints about the Novelle's financial increase instead of the expected economies of a two tempo in 1912. Wermuth wrote that the army needed extra money far more than the navy did. The need for additional taxes threatened to ruin his plans for financial reform. He refuted Tirpitz's contention that British finances could not withstand further naval competition.[51] Hopmann privately thought that Wermuth's mastery of the numbers was far better than Capelle's and Dähnhardt's.[52] In all his years in office Tirpitz had never encountered such fierce resistance from the Treasury. Wermuth had a point. While British construction costs for Dreadnoughts stayed steady or declined slightly (until the *Queen Elizabeth* class), German costs rose from 38.4 million marks for *Nassau* to 46.2 million for *Helgoland* to 45 million for the *Kaiser* class, an increase of more than 17 percent in three years. By 1909 Germany spent almost 20 percent more per battleship than the British did. Battlecruiser unit costs increased from 36.5 million marks to 56 million between 1908 and 1912, a rise of 53 percent, and 30 percent more than comparable British ships. British efficiency, combined with type increases, put Tirpitz at a disadvantage and burdened German taxpayers.[53] Tirpitz's old argument that the British could not afford to compete was proven wrong.

As the 1912 estimates went to the Bundesrat on 28 November, Bethmann told the Emperor that the Novelle would not be included, pending final negotiations about its form and how to pay for it. Tirpitz feared that if the Novelle were left out of the regular Bundesrat debate, Bethmann might find a way to drop it. There would be no mention of it in the upcoming election campaign, which might jeopardize the chances of getting it passed later via a supplementary estimate. Together with Heeringen and Müller, he complained to the Emperor on 9 December.[54]

Bethmann introduced a new tactic that bedeviled Tirpitz and had important short- and long-term consequences. He took advantage of the continuing public outrage over the setback of Agadir to try to awaken a sleeping giant. For more than a decade the army, for reasons of its own, had lain supine while the navy received an increasing share of the overall defense budget. By 1912 the navy commanded fully one-third of the defense budget.[55] Bethmann began to play off the army against the navy. He wrote to Prussian War Minister General Josias von Heeringen, brother of August, Chief of the Admiralstab. Before the Novelle could be settled, Bethmann argued, the Treasury had to know the army's future needs. In effect, he invited the War Minister to ask for a large increase in the army budget.[56]

Tirpitz immediately sent August von Heeringen to his brother, only to discover that Wermuth had been there six weeks earlier and had bluntly asked the War Minister to seek a large army increase to stop the Novelle. The War Minister at first refused. A few weeks later Bethmann asked him whether changed political circumstances (e.g., Italy's expected defection from the Triple Alliance) would demand an army budget increase. Heeringen said yes, although he had to consult the General Staff. Thanks to good relations between the army and the navy, the War Minister agreed to make the army's request small enough so as not to jeopardize the navy's request. He refused, however, to directly join Tirpitz in his battle with Bethmann, Wermuth, and Kiderlen.[57]

Stymied in his gambit, Bethmann tried another tactic. He announced to the Bundesrat that a combined army/navy proposal was in preparation that would have to be included in a supplementary appropriation; however, he gave no hint about the size of either.[58] He enlisted the help of Civil Cabinet Chief Rudolf von Valentini. On 12 December, in Tirpitz's presence, Valentini suggested to the Emperor that he announce a Novelle that consisted only of personnel increases. Müller objected that a two tempo Novelle would preclude a third active squadron. Even though the Emperor rejected the proposal, the next day Tirpitz again considered resigning.[59] In an audience on 16 December, William II assured Tirpitz that Bethmann had given him his word that he would bring up a proposal. This assurance provided no comfort to Tirpitz, whom Hopmann found to be anxious and on edge.[60]

The combined efforts of Bethmann, Kiderlen, Wermuth and Valentini had an effect. The Emperor was aware that if he submitted the Novelle in its unchanged form, some of his ministers might resign and create grave parliamentary problems.[61] These difficulties, plus the nettlesome tax question, prompted William II, on 23 December, to reduce the Novelle by two battlecruisers, leaving three battleships and one battlecruiser. According to this plan, between 1912 and 1917, a three tempo would be in place for four years. The Emperor hoped that this "compromise" would speed the development of a joint army/navy plan, and he wanted it published as soon as possible.[62]

Despite these concessions, Bethmann's resistance continued. He told Müller that he was "considering" a joint army/navy proposal for the spring; but he insisted that he control the timing of the announcement according to the foreign and domestic situation.[63] On 12 January 1912 he even went to the Emperor, without consulting Tirpitz, to see if he would drop the Novelle and include the three new ships in the yearly estimates.[64]

The Emperor turned him down. Bethmann argued strongly for the deletion of at least one of the four new ships. Once again William II wavered
and agreed to consider it after he heard Tirpitz's opinion. At this meeting
Tirpitz reluctantly agreed to drop one ship and to alternate a two and
three tempo for the following six years, but only on the condition that
Wermuth agreed.[65] From Hopmann's diary it is clear that huge monetary
demands on the Treasury from many parts of the government, combined
with the unwelcome Reichstag election results, led Tirpitz to make this
concession,[66] although he did at least keep the three tempo partially alive.

During these tortuous negotiations the Reichstag elections were held.
Despite leaks and rumors in both the German and British press, the prospect of a Novelle was not a major issue in the campaign. The election was
an enormous triumph for the Social Democrats. They won 110 seats, a
strong rebound from their disastrous showing of 1907, when they had won
only 43. The Progressives, the National Liberals, and the Conservatives
suffered serious losses. Even the Center lost seats, although not as many
proportionately as the other parties.[67]

The Emperor accepted Tirpitz's conditions on 26 January, hoping to
announce the Novelle and get it before the Reichstag. If Wermuth did not
accept the compromise, he would be replaced.[68] The stalwart Wermuth
would not budge. When it became apparent that Bethmann would, reluctantly, introduce the Novelle anyway, Wermuth resigned on 12 March.[69]

On the eve of the Haldane Mission, Bethmann had agreed to an
alternating tempo Novelle, but he insisted that he keep control of the
timing of the announcement. The impatient Emperor anticipated making the announcement in his speech at the opening of the Reichstag on
7 February 1912, when he revealed that the government was preparing a
bill to strengthen German arms "on land and sea." Though the speech
had no details, its timing, on the eve of Haldane's arrival, did not augur
well for reopened negotiations with Britain.[70]

THE HALDANE MISSION

In the aftermath of the Franco-German colonial settlement of November
1911, there was sentiment on both British and German sides to investigate
a political or a naval agreement, or both.[71] The two intermediaries were
personal friends of the Emperor—Albert Ballin, Managing Director of the

Hamburg-Amerika steamship line; and Sir Ernest Cassel, born a German Jew but a naturalized Englishman and a noted London banker. Without consulting the Emperor Ballin suggested to Cassel, early in January 1912, that Churchill be invited to Germany to discuss the naval question. Churchill, having been newly appointed First Lord of the Admiralty, declined, but he mentioned the invitation in the Cabinet and kindled an interest in investigating this "German initiative."[72]

Cassel arrived in Berlin on 29 January with a memo authorized by Grey, Lloyd George, and Churchill, stating that Germany must recognize British naval supremacy and the German Navy Law must not be increased but rather reduced or delayed if possible. In return, Britain would not impede German colonial expansion. A third clause proposed an exchange of promises that neither Germany nor Britain would join "aggressive designs or combinations directed against the other."

The Emperor and Bethmann responded favorably but insisted that the British would have to accept the alternating three tempo Novelle as part of the existing Navy Law.[73] This reservation would mean that Germany would still be able to form a third battle squadron. Metternich, the German Ambassador in London and a sharp opponent of Tirpitz, saw that a British offer to avoid any "aggressive" anti-German combination would be virtually useless and that Germany would get no worthwhile concessions without cancellation of the Novelle.[74]

Bethmann hinted to Grey that an arms pact might be possible in exchange for what would amount to a neutrality agreement.[75] The British reply was not encouraging and warned that a Novelle would mean more British spending. If the tempo could be adjusted so as not to require a British increase, Richard Haldane, the Germanophone Minister of War, could be sent to Germany on an unofficial visit.[76] Mutual confusion about the origins of the initiative created an unjustified atmosphere of relative optimism. Even skeptics on the British side could not dismiss, without further exploration, a chance to improve relations with Germany and temper the naval arms race, although Grey, who correctly saw the Emperor as the critical party, noted at one point: "The German Emperor is ageing me; he is like a battleship with steam up and screws going, but with no rudder, and he will run into something some day and cause a catastrophe."[77]

Bethmann wanted to lessen the tension, abate the consequences of "encirclement," and ease the vexing financial and tax situation. Tirpitz heard about the visit only on 5 February. He was angry that amateurs had been used as intermediaries, and he had not changed his view on the need for a 2:3 ratio. Müller agreed that a Novelle should be retained and felt, as Tirpitz later did, that Germany should have presented Haldane with the original six-ship three tempo Novelle and "compromise" by offering the alternating three-ship level."[78]

Haldane arrived on 8 February. Churchill had briefed him, although by all appearances badly, on the nature of the German Navy Law.[79] The next day Churchill, in a speech in Glasgow, coined a phrase that still resonates. Whereas the Royal Navy was a vital necessity to Britain, he said, "from some points of view, the German navy is to . . . [Germany] more in the nature of a luxury." The term "luxury fleet" struck a nerve in both Tirpitz and the Emperor, and the expression was not soon forgotten.[80] The navy and the diplomats were not the only ones watching. Watson, the British Naval Attaché, heard from an unnamed officer in the Prussian War Academy, who expressed "warm approval" of Churchill's statement."[81] Clearly the army was beginning to stir, and this sentiment had major consequences in 1913.

On 8 February Haldane and Bethmann discussed political, naval, and colonial agreements, but the gap between the sides was wide. Bethmann wanted the equivalent of an unconditional promise of neutrality, something Haldane could not consider. When Bethmann said that Germany needed a third active battle squadron, Haldane noted that it would require five or six British squadrons in home waters, and that the Liberals would have to meet every additional Novelle ship with two; if agreement could be reached on that question, however, Britain could consider a colonial settlement favorable to Germany.[82] At one point Haldane noted, in English: "I see that if it were left to us two, we would soon arrange the whole matter satisfactorily; but I have my people at home at the Admiralty, my naval men, they are so difficult to please." Bethmann replied: "And I have mine, too."[83]

The most crucial discussion took place the next day, when Haldane met with the Emperor and Tirpitz. The Emperor gave Haldane a copy of the Novelle which Haldane then put in his pocket without looking at it, stating that he considered it a matter for the naval experts.[84] He politely rejected Tirpitz's proposal for a 2:3 ratio. A long discussion about the Novelle ensued. The Emperor and Tirpitz explained that originally it had called for six more ships over the next six years but that number had been cut to three. They did not explain that the three dropped cruisers had only been deferred, since they were replacements for the old *Hertha* class. Haldane defended the "traditional two-power standard" in naval strength, even though it had long since, de facto, gone by the board. What he apparently meant was a standard of two keels to one to match future additional German ships. Haldane suggested stretching Novelle increases over twelve rather than six years, apparently without understanding how inconvenient that would be for the Navy Law. According to Tirpitz, Haldane said that the British government was indifferent to the Novelle's personnel increases and "recognized" the need for a third active battle squadron. According to Haldane, the former point was mentioned only in passing. This misunderstanding led to serious complications later. To Tirpitz's barely concealed dismay, and without prior consultation, the Emperor, on the spur of the moment, offered to take one more ship off the Novelle so that there would be a three tempo only in 1913 and 1916, with the other ship to be added back sometime after 1917. In exchange, there would have to be a satisfactory British neutrality agreement. Haldane considered this "concession" depressingly small. He offered a not very binding mutual agreement against unprovoked aggression.

As Tirpitz, in a despairing mood, described to Capelle, Dähnhardt, and Hopmann later that day, the notion of a neutrality agreement, thin gruel that it was, meant a gravely threatening first step in the destruction of the Navy Law. He feared that turning down the proposal would put the onus for rejection "squarely on his shoulders." If the British published such a proposal, it would take "the wind out of our sails" in the Reichstag. The whole of the "odium" would fall on him. He thought it unlikely that the British would honor a neutrality agreement, even if they committed to one. Hopmann regretted, in private, that Tirpitz had pursued too hastily "an aggressive policy against England that went beyond our actual power." The Novelle proposal "was, in my opinion, a mistake, and it would have been better to limit it to personnel increases and reorganization within the fleet."[85] Later that day and the next Haldane, Bethmann, and Kiderlen had long discussions about a neutrality agreement and the meaning of the term "aggression." Conversations about colonial questions were more cordial but led to further misunderstandings, since the Germans believed that Haldane had "promised" colonial concessions but Haldane believed that he had not. When Haldane left on 11 February, Kiderlen and Bethmann still mistakenly believed that a meaningful neutrality pact was possible if the Novelle could be reduced further.[86]

In a discussion within the RMA on 10 February, Capelle and Dähnhardt astonished Tirpitz. Capelle expected that the British would accept a neutrality agreement, but he saw that deal as "such a great success for us and such a historic moment for our world position that it should cause the Novelle to disappear completely." It would be a "triumph of our naval policy that Tirpitz could be prouder of than of the passage of a Novelle that had its origins in another situation, and that was now a torso."[87] Capelle's exuberance showed how little he understood British policy and how much he underestimated the Anglo-French bond. For a few days even Tirpitz seems to have wavered in his commitment to the Novelle. One can imagine his consternation when confronted by Capelle's statement. Within the RMA there was a consensus that if Britain made substantial concessions the Novelle could not pass the Reichstag.[88]

Tirpitz later claimed that he would have been ready to drop the Novelle altogether, if the British had made the real concession of an effective neutrality agreement or a mutual arms ratio (presumably 2:3). From Hopmann's diary it is clear that Tirpitz was bargaining not to get an agreement but to save the Novelle, even though he was skeptical that the British would make an acceptable offer.[89]

Tirpitz soon regained his composure. On 22 February Kiderlen, like Valentini had done in December, tried to persuade Tirpitz to introduce the Novelle as it was but without the extra ships. Tirpitz did not see how a third of a ship per year (as in the building plan showed to Haldane) could have much effect on the negotiations. The drop to two new ships offered to Haldane he saw as just another unreciprocated concession. He absolutely refused to reduce the Novelle.[90] The next day Müller tried his hand at compromise. He suggested the same as Kiderlen but wanted to include one ship in the Novelle and wait until 1916 to ask for the other two. Again Tirpitz refused on the grounds that it would appear that Germany was backing down to Britain.[91] He wrote to Müller on 26 February: "The sooner we publish the Novelle, the more we reduce the chance that the English will make even greater demands upon us."[92] Besides his normal anxiety whenever the Navy Law was even remotely threatened, Tirpitz, supported by Widenmann, still refused to believe that the British, beset by labor unrest and demands for expensive social reforms,[93] would be willing to support a two keels to one policy for each additional Novelle ship.[94]

When Haldane returned home, he enjoyed a brief period of euphoria. Soon after, however, the Admiralty's analysts got to work. They were less troubled by the three new ships of the Novelle, or even by the formation of a third battle squadron, than by the increased readiness of the High Seas Fleet that the personnel increase portended. After fall exercises the German fleet usually remained in port for most of the winter in order to train the conscripts who joined the fleet in the late fall. The Novelle personnel increases, they thought, would make the fleet ready for action year-round, which would take great sums to counter. The Admiralty, with an all-volunteer navy, substantially underestimated the gigantic annual training task facing the Germans. Even without the Novelle, the Admiralty found the steady growth of the High Seas Fleet menacing, particularly since the sixteen ships of the 1908–11 four tempo were gradually joining the fleet. Also alarming was the growth in U-boats. Germanophobes in the Foreign Office and elsewhere reasserted their influence. On 24 February Grey gave Metternich a memorandum that incorporated the Admiralty's objection. It was enough to jeopardize whatever small chance there might have been for a naval agreement.[95]

Bethmann pressed Tirpitz to make more concessions, but he would go no further than what the Emperor had offered to Haldane: a three tempo in 1913 and 1916 with the third ship added at some point after the annual three tempo resumed in 1917. He bitterly resented the Admiralty's innuendo that the personnel increases would lead to major changes in the organization of the German fleet.[96]At the audience on 2 March Tirpitz threatened to resign if the Emperor believed that the Novelle, in its present form, constituted a danger of war.[97]

On 1 March Tirpitz requested that the Novelle be published immediately,[98] but Bethmann persuaded the Emperor to let him try one more time for a neutrality agreement. When, on 18 March, Grey finally told Metternich that Britain could accept no such neutrality agreement without disturbing relations with France, the negotiations effectively ended. Hopmann recorded Tirpitz's grim satisfaction that his prediction of British perfidy had come true.[99] The final blow came that same day, when Churchill announced the 1912–13 estimates to Parliament. He bluntly stated that Britain was building only against Germany. If there were no

Novelle, Britain's building program would be designed to maintain 60 percent superiority over Germany. If there were a Novelle, Britain would lay down two ships for every additional German keel. Dominion ships would not count as part of the Royal Navy in the calculation of the ratio. At the same time Churchill offered a "naval holiday," that is, if Germany refrained from building any large ships for a year, Britain would follow suit.[100] Such an offhand proposal clearly shows Britain's ignorance of the way German naval procurement worked and how closely it was linked to German domestic politics, about which they had little understanding.

The Haldane Mission, if it had any chance of success, foundered on mutual misperceptions. Perhaps, as Steinberg has suggested, some misunderstandings in the conversations between the Emperor, Tirpitz, and Haldane occurred because they were conducted in English and German indiscriminately, since all three men were fluent in both; such a conversation could clearly cause confusion in subtle shades of meaning.[101] In hindsight, given the overall diplomatic situation and the increasing closeness of the Anglo-French Entente, little could have been accomplished even assuming goodwill on both sides. Tirpitz's limpet-like attachment to the Navy Law, together with his continuing ability to retain the Emperor's loyalty, made any diplomatic rapprochement impossible. Even Bethmann's, Kiderlen's, and Wermuth's opposition, the most determined Tirpitz had ever faced, could not prevail against him.

THE NOVELLE BEFORE THE REICHSTAG

Consequent to the disappointing news from London, Bethmann had to publish the Novelle. The conflict over timing had elicited resignation threats from both Bethmann and Tirpitz. Bethmann, until the very end, had tried to get Tirpitz to drop the three battleships but to no avail.[102]

The National Liberals, Conservatives, and the Center favored a Novelle, although the latter two parties did not want an inheritance tax to pay for it. Once again the reinforced Social Democrats opposed it strenuously. The Pan-Germans and the Flottenverein engaged in agitation. With the moderate Koester at the head of the Flottenverein, its agitation did not reach the customary level. Tirpitz and Bethmann colluded in an effort to keep the propaganda campaigns from provoking the British.[103]

On 22 March the Novelle, the Army Bill, and the tax proposals to pay for them were published. The Army Bill was small, an increase of only twenty-nine thousand men. Partly out of consideration for the navy, and partly because the army was only ponderously rethinking its future needs, War Minister Josias von Heeringen postponed a great Army Bill to 1913.[104] The Novelle was the same one that Tirpitz had sent to Bethmann on 27 February. There would be a three tempo in 1913 and 1916, and a third ship would be added sometime after 1917. It would call for three fully manned active battle squadrons. For reasons of cost only one-fourth of the reserve ships, as opposed to half of them under the 1900 law, would be kept in full-time service. Crews allotted to the reserve ships would be cut in half, and the manpower saved would be added to the active squadrons. The preamble justified on "technical"(really readiness) grounds the need to have a larger proportion of the fleet ready for battle on short notice. The three additional ships were needed to fill out the third active squadron. The Novelle provided a U-boat establishment of seventy-two, six per year. Tirpitz hesitated to commit more resources to U-boats; it was still unclear to him whether or how U-boats could be effective in a war. For the first time the navy asked for money for Zeppelins. The 1912 Novelle's emphasis on readiness amounted to a partial victory for the Front.

The Novelle did not include a total-cost table as had previous laws but only indicated that the total cost of the Novelle was 210 million marks above the cost of the 1908 law. The Army and Navy Bills together would cost 650 million extra to 1918. Costs would be covered by increased Reich income, assuming that the nation's economic health remained good, plus a small wine tax. With Wermuth's departure the facile optimism of the past had clearly returned under his successor, Hermann Kühn. Wermuth had insisted on an increased and expanded inheritance tax that would have roused huge opposition, especially among the Conservatives.[105]

The bill went to the Reichstag on 15 April 1912. Bethmann and Tirpitz submerged their private differences and commended the bill to the Deputies. Conservatives and the Center were particularly pleased that it contained no inheritance tax increase. A few right-wing deputies criticized its size as insufficient. During Budget Commission discussions, Tirpitz averred that, because of the increased size and cost of modern ships, the Reichstag should not expect another Novelle. The needs of the navy were complete. For once Tirpitz kept his word, as the 1912 Novelle was the final one. A majority, with only the Social Democrats in strong opposition, was never in doubt.[106]

The vote capped Tirpitz's unbroken string of Reichstag victories with a final success. The two and ultimately three extra ships of the 1912 Novelle was the only numerical increase in ship establishment over Tirpitz's original request in the 1900 law. At an Immediatvortrag on 22 May 1912 Tirpitz surveyed his life's work with justifiable pride.[107] When construction of the new ships was complete, sometime after 1918, the navy would possess sixty-one large ships. After 1917 the three tempo seemed secure, as only replacement ships remained to be built.

Tirpitz did not know at the time that the 1912 Novelle would be his last great parliamentary success. The Reichstag's consent was the culmination of fifteen years of general planning. He and his aides glad-handed even parliamentary enemies of the navy to a degree and with a skill unprecedented in the Wilhelmian Reich. Tirpitz and his Etatsabteilung worked very hard to obtain and keep the confidence of parliamentary leaders, especially, but not limited to, those of the Center Party. He took members of many parties on shipyard inspection trips and even to social events. He also paid close attention to a Bundesrat that could not be considered a rubber stamp, especially in questions of taxation and regional interests. He gave extensive statistical and not just rhetorical support to his initiatives. In short, he was a master at "manufacturing consent." Despite claims by historians that Tirpitz had fashioned an "iron budget," even after the hard-fought 1912 Novelle "completed' the Navy Law, Tirpitz himself noted that "the Navy Law was indeed a *lex imperfecta* [incomplete law] and would remain a piece of paper if the Reichstag did not approve the necessary money."[108] Tirpitz was certainly no bourgeois liberal, but Steinberg is correct to point out that Tirpitz used parliamentary methods in ways unusual for a military man in Imperial Germany.

Berghahn is right to assert that Tirpitz manipulated the Reichstag to fulfill the Emperor's aims; however, the evidence also strongly suggests that Tirpitz used the Reichstag at least as much to get the Emperor to do what he wanted and to accept what would be palatable to the Reichstag. An uncountable number of resignation attempts, a score at least, were needed to keep the volatile William II, if not under control, at least manageable. Although Tirpitz was far from the first of William II's ministers to threaten resignation, he developed it into a fine art that was quasi-parliamentary in manner and scope. Such behavior, most especially from a serving officer, was quite unorthodox under the Bismarckian Constitution. To reinforce his bureaucratic power within the navy he used the Navy Law itself to ward off threats to the law from other officers and schools of thought. To keep his grand design intact, he upended men as formidable as Knorr, Galster, Holtzendorff, and even his boyhood friend Maltzahn.

Central to his consolidation of power was the idea of a "fleet against England." This notion, besides its obvious deterrence factor, was a necessary tool to play publicly when a Novelle was pending. The frank Hopmann, in private, expressed it well: "The life elixir of our fleet is the rivalry with England. Without this [our fleet] loses its reason for existence."[109] Most other times Tirpitz worked hard to limit and contain navalist agitation, lest it push too hard and let loose the ruthlessness he ascribed to the British when it was convenient for him to make the accusation. Tirpitz performed a balancing act on a grand scale. No wonder he suffered periodic bouts of nervousness and depression. In August 1914 Tirpitz was to pay a painful price for his seventeen years of impudence with the Emperor and the resentment he had aroused among his fellow naval officers.

NAVAL DIPLOMACY, MAY 1912–JUNE 1914

The 1912 Novelle and the buildup preceding it had serious international consequences. Three important changes took place in British naval policy during 1912: further redistribution of the fleet that concentrated it ever more in home waters; naval conversations with France that culminated in the Grey-Cambon letters of 22/23 November 1912; and the Admiralty's evolving policy to abandon the close blockade that began in 1912. The latter question is examined below in the context of German strategy. The British continued the escalation of ship types with the decision to build the oil-fired battleships of the *Queen Elizabeth* class, armed with 15-inch (38.1-cm) guns.

The redistribution began in February 1912. With a complete third battle squadron, the German fleet would, in a few years, consist of twenty-five battleships and eight battlecruisers. To counter this, Britain would have to have at least forty capital ships at instant readiness in or near home

waters. The Admiralty had to contemplate summoning home six battleships in the Mediterranean as well as seeking French support for British
interests there. On 18 March 1912, in the same speech that proposed a 16:10
ratio and a naval holiday, Churchill announced the reorganization.[110]

At the time of the Novelle, both Austria and Italy were beginning
Dreadnought programs. Although the Admiralty recognized that they
were building primarily against each other, the weak forces the Admiralty had left in the Mediterranean were numerically no match for them.
The Admiralty knew that, in the event of war with the Triple Alliance,
Empire communications through the Mediterranean would be at risk
unless French help were available. The British government, therefore,
had three choices: a binding alliance or naval agreement with France; a
naval increase sufficient to secure both the North Sea and the Mediterranean; or simply following the Admiralty's plan to concentrate forces in
the decisive theater.[111] Public and Cabinet debate on these alternatives
continued through the summer and fall of 1912. The final decision was
a slippery and ambiguous combination of the first and third alternatives.

At a meeting with the Chief of the Imperial General Staff (CIGS),
on 4 July 1912, Churchill put the final nail in the coffin of the risk theory.
The Admiralty had to preserve superiority in the North Sea and "all
other objects, however precious, must, if necessary, be sacrificed to secure
the end."[112] The naval conversations with France, which had lain fallow
since Agadir, resumed. In September the French Brest Squadron moved
to Toulon and concentrated almost all modern units of the French navy
in the Mediterranean. From a purely strategic point of view, this was the
best the French could do, since they were far too weak to face Germany
alone in the North Sea. The need for unassailable supremacy in home
waters justified British naval concentration there.

Such "independent" redistributions naturally raised speculation as
to whether a binding Anglo-French agreement was behind them. Press
in both countries noted the French action that denuded its Atlantic coast
of naval defense. That there was no binding agreement was clearly stated
in the Grey-Cambon exchange of letters of 22/23 November 1912; the exchange, however, did state that the two powers would consult on whether
to act in unison if the "general peace" were threatened. This bit of offhand
diplomacy, combined with the mutual fleet redistributions, constituted a
moral, if not legal, obligation for Britain to defend the French North Sea

coast in the event of a German attack.[113] Despite the original assumptions of the risk theory, Britain was, after all, able to concentrate the great bulk of its fleet at home by the outbreak of the war.

The failure of the Haldane Mission marked the effective end of Anglo-German naval negotiations. On three different occasions, in March 1912 and 1913, and in October 1913, Churchill publicly proposed a 16:10 ratio between the fleets and a naval construction holiday. No diplomatic negotiations took place on either of these ideas, since neither side wanted to rehash the old arguments. Neither Tirpitz nor the German government took Churchill's idea of a naval holiday seriously, believing it had been offered for domestic consumption.[114]

The 16:10 idea met with a more favorable reaction. In fact, Tirpitz "accepted" it in a speech in the Budget Commission on 7 February 1913. In his postwar public writings, Tirpitz leaves the impression that this ratio proposal finally settled the naval rivalry, and that his acceptance of the ratio was a major reason for good Anglo-German relations during 1912–13. What actually happened is more complicated. Churchill proposed the 16:10 ratio counting only British strength in or near home waters, and not counting the several Dominion ships—quite a different prospect from Tirpitz's idea of eight squadrons to five in the total fleets.[115] A major factor in Tirpitz's public accommodation to this ratio was that the Center Party favored it. He privately noted that it only applied to battleship building and would not have the same constraints in the building of cruisers. It also removed from him the public odium for sustaining an arms competition. Tirpitz was therefore content to keep silent publicly, apart from "accepting" the ratio.[116]

After the passage of the "last" Novelle in May 1912, Tirpitz's troubles seemed to multiply. The newly founded Wehrverein, led by General August Keim, ousted in 1908 as head of the Flottenverein, began to beat the propaganda drums in favor of army expansion. Though the Flottenverein worked cooperatively with it, increasing public interest in a new Army Bill gradually pushed the Flottenverein to the sidelines.[117]

Another problem was the continual fast growth of ship size, especially in Britain. The four original Nassau-class battleships had 28-cm guns, as did all German battlecruisers laid down up to 1912. The subsequent ships of the four tempo (1908–11) had 30.5-cm guns. The first five British battlecruisers had 12-inch (30.5-cm) guns. Beginning with the

Lion class (1910), they had 13.5-inch (34.3-cm) guns. The first ten British Dreadnought battleships had 12-inch main armament, the next twelve had 13.5-inch, and caliber accelerated to 15-inch (38.1-cm) with the *Queen Elizabeth* class, the first of which were laid down in October 1912.[118] The *Queen Elizabeths* particularly concerned the RMA because their high speed and very heavy guns combined the characteristics of a battleship and a battlecruiser.[119] Both Italy and France planned to exceed 30.5-cm. In the fall of 1911 Heeringen raised the matter, and Tirpitz, in principle, agreed that gun caliber had to be increased, eventually to 38-cm.[120]

In the summer of 1912 William II,[121] in response to news about the larger guns on the *Queen Elizabeth*, complained that Germany was falling behind in the qualitative arms race. Other countries were considering ruinously expensive triple turrets that Tirpitz did not want. Instead, he preferred the heaviest possible guns, perhaps fewer in number.[122] The Emperor wrote, "since we have excellent engineers, technicians, and officers, why are we always behind? The reason could well be that the administrative staff has a narrow, departmental point of view, and is out of touch with [the viewpoint] of the Front." Feeling threatened, Tirpitz indignantly pointed out that the Emperor was too responsive to the loud complaints of the Front. He made an uncharacteristically stupid, and partly prophetic, remark: "Our principle should be—here is the weapon—make use of it. We did this in 1870 with the needle gun [an infantry rifle] that was dangerously inferior to the [French] chassepot."[123] The comment enraged William II. It took all the diplomatic skills of Müller and Prinz Heinrich to contain his anger lest there be "a very uncomfortable personnel decision."[124] Budget constraints, and the need to keep credibility in the Reichstag, crimped the navy's ability to compete in gun caliber.

Tirpitz's position in the late summer and early fall of 1912 was, as Epkenhans has characterized it, that of "isolation."[125] At odds with the Emperor, the Chancellor, and the Front, especially with Holtzendorff, who at that point was fighting Tirpitz's idea to man a few reserve ships mainly with recruits in order to man more fully the active fleet,[126] Tirpitz feared that a putsch would remove him. He was convinced that "many people are working for my overthrow."[127] Capelle conceded that the Chancellor saw Tirpitz as a "dangerous man" [stated in English] but felt that Bethmann was "too clever" to take the blame for Tirpitz's dismissal, unless he could use Müller and Holtzendorff as a "battering ram." Capelle thought it improbable that Holtzendorff would play such a role.[128]

Capelle apologetically advised Tirpitz to back down in his conflict with the fleet over the recruit question.[129] Tirpitz even had Capelle draft a resignation attempt, ostensibly based on age and illness, which would then leave the timing up to the Emperor, whose twenty-five-year jubilee was coming up in 1913.[130] Though not sent, this letter is evidence of Tirpitz's low spirits in the early fall of 1912.

THE AWAKENING OF THE ARMY AND
NOVELLE FALSE STARTS, 1913–1914

In October 1912, while Tirpitz struggled with opposition on all sides, events intervened over which he had no control. Early that month war broke out in the Balkans. A coalition of Serbia, Greece, Rumania, and Bulgaria quickly defeated the Ottoman Army. With the possibility of Russian intervention and Austria's teetering position, the Reich government accelerated its focus on continental matters. The process had begun the prior year in the wake of the Agadir Crisis, when Bethmann tried to play off the army against Tirpitz. The army had responded in a dilatory fashion, increasing its force by a mere twenty-nine thousand men in 1912. Until late 1912 the army leadership was still thinking as it had since the 1890s, giving priority to its domestic mission—the preservation of order. For that task the loyalty to the monarchy of conscripts from the cities and bourgeois officers was suspect. The growing Wehrverein considered the small 1912 expansion inadequate and pushed with increasing vehemence to reprioritize the army.

The Emperor, in October 1912, alarmed by the international situation, tried to persuade General Staff Chief Moltke and War Minister Heeringen to ask for a stronger army. At first they were not interested, but the Emperor's initiative galvanized some younger officers, notably Colonel Erich Ludendorff, Chief of the Mobilization Section of the General Staff. By the end of November, Moltke proposed full implementation of conscription under the Army Law, an expensive request.[131]

Bethmann, also worried about events abroad, supported Moltke's conversion to a substantial Army Bill for the spring of 1913.[132] In a manner Tirpitz characterized as "childish," the Emperor also proposed a three battlecruiser Novelle. Tirpitz, to the surprise of many, was not immediately enthusiastic. He told Hopmann that the navy's primary need at the time was "to make what we have complete and war ready" and not to worry about four years down the road.[133] Perhaps Tirpitz, ever mindful of the need to keep the Reichstag's confidence, had remembered his pledge of six months before that the 1912 Novelle would be the last.

In early December Haldane met with Prinz Karl Lichnowsky, Metternich's successor as German Ambassador. Haldane warned that if conflict between Austria and Serbia threatened a French defeat in a wider war, Britain could not stand aside.[134] William II exploded with anger and sarcasm about Haldane's remarks. On that very Sunday morning, 8 December 1912, he convened an audience with Moltke, Tirpitz, Chief of the Admiralstab August von Heeringen, and Müller. This meeting, called on the spur of the moment, was the later controversial German Imperial War Council.[135] Müller's handwritten version of the meeting (in N 159/4) gives William II's pessimistic view of Germany's diplomatic position. The Emperor complained that if Germany were to attack France, Britain would join the French. If Austria were to move on Serbia, Russia would attack Austria and bring Germany in. He said that the navy had to prepare for war with Britain, including submarine warfare in the narrow parts of the English Channel. He urged Tirpitz to speed the buildup of the U-boat force.

Moltke's response to this jeremiad became famous: "I believe war is inevitable, and the sooner the better; but we ought to do more through the press to prepare the popularity of a war against England, as suggested in the Emperor's comments." As Müller recorded it:

> Tirpitz observed that the navy would prefer to postpone a great fight for a year and a half [when the canal and the U-boat base in Helgoland would be completed]. Moltke said the navy would not be ready even then and the army's position would get increasingly more unfavorable, for our enemies are arming more strongly than we, since we are very short of money. This was the end of the conference. The result amounted to almost zero. The Chief of the Great General Staff said: war the sooner the better, but he does not draw the logical conclusion from this, that is, to present Russia or France or both with an ultimatum that would unleash the war with right on our side.

As Berghahn correctly puts it: "It is safe to assume that Tirpitz, by advocating a postponement until 1914, pursued a delaying tactic in the hope of avoiding war altogether."[136]

William II ordered War Minister Heeringen to prepare a new Army Bill. On 11 December he told Tirpitz to ask for more ships in the spring.[137]

Tirpitz gave no immediate reply. Capelle's idea was that, in case of a large Army Bill, the navy should ask for a smaller amount to fill the gaps, such as accelerated replacement of the *Hertha*-class cruisers, but should not ask for more. He estimated that chances for a 300-million-mark Novelle would be slim in the Reichstag. The Chancellor and Foreign Office would fear it would provoke the British, as in 1912.[138]

Bethmann, on 16 December, met with Tirpitz and War Minister Heeringen.[139] Heeringen asked for sixty thousand men and 300–500 million marks. Tirpitz said that the large sum for the army required the navy to ask for something as well, even if he conceded the lead to the army. He asked to fill the tempo gap in the Novelle, replace the *Hertha*s in a timely fashion, and provide money for increasing ship costs. Bethmann reminded Tirpitz of his pledge that the 1912 Novelle was the final one. Tirpitz evasively replied that it would not require a Novelle and that the total costs were not clear, even though Capelle had given him a 300 million estimate a few days before. Bethmann grumbled that the combined high costs would exacerbate the difficult financial situation.

Tirpitz had the RMA work out several Novelle projects.[140] These included a three tempo from 1913 through 1920, with two new cruisers added in 1913 and 1915, with net extra costs at 136 million marks over 1912. Tirpitz was pessimistic about the parliamentary prospects less than a year after the "last" Novelle, and prices for ships, oil, coal, and so on, were again rising steeply. Capelle calculated that between 1914 and 1918 the navy would be short-funded by about 111 million marks.[141] Dähnhardt's dreary conclusion was that public opinion would not support another navy increase and obtaining the money would be very difficult.[142] There was already speculation in the press concerning a Novelle. Dähnhardt stringently cautioned Tirpitz against encouraging the press. Tirpitz denied that the RMA was active in the campaign.[143] He told Hopmann that he was quite pessimistic about the navy's political prospects in the shadow of a big Army Bill that would relegate the navy to the background for a long while. He lamented that he had not successfully resigned the previous fall.[144]

Despite the Chancellor's opposition, on 4 January 1913 William II ordered Tirpitz to prepare a Novelle that would include an extra large cruiser for 1914. In his notes Tirpitz wrote: "A Novelle with one ship makes the Navy Law a farce!" If it were to be one ship, it should be the third battleship, dropped from the 1912 Novelle. "If one wants a Novelle it would have to contain three cruisers [stricken from the original version of the 1912 Novelle]."[145] Tirpitz lamented to Hopmann that the Emperor's proposal meant that every year would bring another Novelle. Tirpitz echoed his late Reichstag opponent, Eugen Richter (d. 1906), when he told Hopmann: "For the Emperor, the fleet is mainly still a toy."[146]

The very next day the Emperor changed his mind. On 5 January Bethmann persuaded him that because of the forthcoming large Army Bill, and the risk of jeopardizing relations with Britain, no new Navy Bill should be forthcoming. Instead, a Novelle should be proposed the following year.[147] Hopmann privately noted:

> Therefore, first one thing and then another. Pure William II I.R. It is in and of itself deeply sad, but for us, for the moment, the best solution. We must now pull back, with the danger that we will take second place to the army . . . only to receive a pittance that we must beg for. In general, the decision is of great significance . . . and we adopt again a purely continental policy. We cower before England, but in recent years we have held our heads too high and have had our mouths too wide open. Hopefully it is only a temporary setback.[148]

With the shift to a continental policy, Tirpitz's central position in Reich policy was substantially degraded; to say that it was the end of the Tirpitz "Plan," however, is to overstate what that "Plan" was in the first place. He still held the confidence of many in the Reichstag, but he knew his political limits and what the traffic would bear. Though the Tirpitz "plan" was still intact on paper, future prospects for maintaining even a two tempo Navy Law was dubious, given the need for ever increasing sums. The "power of the purse," though circumscribed by the Bismarckian Constitution, really mattered. Even in 1913 Tirpitz was still the central person in the navy. He had as many political friends as ever in the Reichstag, within the limits of the public's waning interest in the navy. What he had lost was the presence of pliant politicians such as Hohenlohe and Bülow, replaced by men less manageable for his purposes like Bethmann and especially Wermuth. His biggest loss was not so much the Emperor's confidence but rather the latter's weakening ability to dominate and deliver for Tirpitz's aspirations. William II's political "capital," strong in the early days of Tirpitz's time at the RMA, had waned substantially through his countless acts of personal folly, political embarrassment, and diplomatic gaffes. Gone, too, was the superficial plausibility of the idea, which many believed was true at the beginning of the century, that a powerful navy would magically bring with it economic prosperity and political gain. The hard-nosed and effective British response to German shipbuilding showed that no amount of competition would break either their will or their purse.

By the spring of 1913, with a large Army Bill pending, the navy laid low. Negotiations about a "naval holiday" and a 16:10 ratio had petered out, to the satisfaction of both sides. Assuming no new naval initiatives, neither side wanted to awaken a sleeping dog. The Liberal government had serious domestic problems. The narrow majority gained in the 1910 elections required more appeasement than had been necessary after their landslide in the 1906 election. Tirpitz was well aware that his parliamentary allies, especially Erzberger and the Center Party, would support existing programs but were unwilling to expand them.

The Army Bill grew substantially in the course of its preparation because of increasing popular pressure. By 1913 an army-centered popular and radical nationalism was on the march, and the Reichstag was ready to respond.[149] On 28 February Bethmann approved a permanent army increase of 117,000 men, plus commissioned and noncommissioned officers, with a one-time capital cost of 884 million marks in addition to an annual increase of 200 million. This was the largest peacetime military increase in the history of the Empire.[150] Paying for this enormous bill was Bethmann's greatest peacetime achievement. He took advantage of the wave of patriotic sentiment evoked by the tense international situation and the agitation of the Wehrverein and the patriotic parties. The great resistance of the upper classes, particularly the agrarians, to direct Reich taxes, had bedeviled governments for decades. Bethmann's clever idea was to portray the capital levy of 884 million marks as a one-time patriotic sacrifice. The remaining annual 200 million for recurring costs was from increased matricular contributions from the federal states. That Bethmann was able to sell such an idea to the Reichstag is a striking illustration of how national priorities had shifted since Bethmann first broached the subject with War Minister Heeringen in the fall of 1911.[151] The initiative gave Germany a short-term advantage; shortly thereafter, however, the French introduced three-year service for conscripts, and the Russians began to reorganize their army with an increase of half a million men.

In a meeting in October 1913 Tirpitz worried that the great Army Bill of 1913 had left the navy without enough money to expand the fleet and remain competitive in ship size. "If the money is no longer there, the

Reichstag would not have the means, and the whole law would be just a piece of paper." If the three tempo is not sustainable in the long run, "the whole fleet policy would be in vain." This sober realism was followed by a fatalistic expression that Germany might have to roll the dice in a war.[152]

Tirpitz was also concerned that the German fleet, for many years, had not been much of a presence overseas. In June 1913, in a departure from his past attitude, he recommended a flag-showing cruise. In December 1913 a small squadron consisting of two of the most modern battleships, *König Albert* and *Kaiser*, the latter commanded by Trotha, and the light cruiser *Strassburg*, departed Wilhelmshaven. The cruise lasted until mid-June 1914. The vessels visited many ports in Western Africa and South America.[153] In addition to its diplomatic purpose, the cruise was to serve as propaganda so that Tirpitz, at some later point, could justify construction of more overseas cruisers, which would not transgress the tacit 16:10 ratio in battleships. The trip was clear proof that Tirpitz did not expect a war to erupt in the summer of 1914 but was simply delaying when he said, at the "war council" of December 1912, that the fleet would be "ready" by 1914. Had he anticipated a war, he would not have sent abroad two powerful battleships that, in the event of war, would have been at the mercy of the Royal Navy.

Hopmann ended 1913 with a gloomy assessment. Tirpitz and Capelle were also pessimistic. The Zabern affair was an act of exceptional stupidity by the military in Alsace-Lorraine. Other scandals had dismal effects on the political atmosphere. The focus on the army, he thought, would leave the navy short: "Our government is without purpose or strength. Every department [*Ressort*] works in its own interest. His Majesty is removed from all of them and understands nothing."[154]

Despite Tirpitz's pessimism about a fleet increase, he appeared to be in a good position in the Reichstag. True, there was no sentiment in favor of expansion, but there was also no ill feeling for the navy, except from Social Democrats. Relations with Britain, if not warm, were at least stable. Growing concern with recent building in the Russian Baltic Fleet dampened any idea of naval arms reduction.[155] The estimates passed the Budget Commission smoothly in 1914. Tirpitz, in his public statements, referred more and more to the 16:10 ratio as 8:5 squadrons. Britain was increasingly distracted from still further naval expenditures by public pressure for social programs and the increasingly tense question of Home Rule for Ireland.

Beneath his outward serenity, Tirpitz was concerned about his weakening political position and the long-term finances of the navy. As he noted in mid-May 1914, to carry out the *existing* Navy Law would require a great deal of money above the scheduled budgets, "more than we all estimated." England automatically made such expenditures. He blamed Wermuth for starving the navy of funds, negating entirely his earlier belief that the British had neither the money nor the will to keep up. He even called the situation "catastrophic." Public support, including that of the Flottenverein, was much diminished from a few years before. Money was short for shipbuilding and guns, for torpedoes, dockyards, and other items. This large need would create a problem for the Chancellor and the Treasury. He feared to ask for too much, lest it give fuel to his opponents, but a substantial increase, he believed, could not be avoided.[156] Tirpitz was facing up to reality better than Capelle, who noted that, if the British adopted a wide blockade, it would "force us in even higher measure than before to throw all upon the offensive."[157]

Tirpitz told the Chancellor on 22 May that the 1915 estimates required 38 million marks more, plus another 12 million previously obtained from loans. This meant that 50 million marks in new revenue had to be gotten from taxes. In response to the Emperor's demands, Tirpitz wanted money to organize a flying squadron of one large and three small cruisers to replace the battlecruiser *Goeben* in the Mediterranean.[158] Bethmann noted the Reich's "extraordinarily difficult" financial condition.[159] Treasury Secretary Kühn said that the sum was impossible because of the steep cost of the Army Bill, and complained that the navy's prior estimates should have been more accurate. The iron discipline that had kept the navy close to budget for many years was clearly no longer present. Kühn also denied a 1914 supplementary estimate, and offered cold comfort by suggesting the need to economize.[160]

Before examining the events of the summer of 1914, it is necessary to look at the progress the navy had made in U-boats and to consider the relations between the different naval organizations as well as their relation to their tasks.

TIRPITZ AND U-BOAT CONSTRUCTION

In 1900 the submarine was in its beginning stages. John Holland created some promising designs and the U.S. Navy, soon after, ordered six boats based on Holland's design. Buoyed by their Jeune École tradition, the French became the greatest submarine enthusiasts. By 1904 they had twenty-six submarines, with thirteen more under construction.[161] In 1906 the French Navy proposed a plan that would include eighty-two offensive and forty-nine defensive submarines, and they had already begun to integrate submarines into the French fleet.[162]

Vickers built the Royal Navy's first five Holland boats in 1903. As documented by Nicholas Lambert, Fisher, at the same time he introduced *Dreadnought* in 1904, was secretly planning a future fleet based mainly on battlecruisers and submarines.[163]

Tirpitz's reaction to early U-boat development was not enthusiastic. The early U-boats had gasoline-fueled engines, a safety and handling nightmare on a small boat. Only the later diesel boats partly solved this problem.[164] The early boats had limited range and insufficient crew accommodations to remain at sea for even one night. Their low freeboard made surface sailing difficult in the choppy North Sea. Another factor inhibiting Tirpitz's embrace of U-boats was the "lesson" he had learned from his years in the Torpedo Arm. As with his protracted decision to build Dreadnoughts, Tirpitz was always reluctant, for reasons of cost, to be first in the field with unproven technologies. He felt that Germany could learn from the experiments and mistakes of others before making an expensive commitment to a new ship type. Perhaps the decisive reason was that U-boats did not fit in with his original design as outlined in the Navy Law. A fleet of battleships and large cruisers, meant for decisive battle, could use torpedo boats and U-boats only as auxiliaries in a North Sea Armageddon. A large-scale commitment to U-boats, especially if they were designed for Kleinkrieg that focused on commerce war, as advocated by opponents such as Galster, could undermine the painfully constructed edifice of the Navy Law.

To understand Tirpitz's views on U-boats, it is enlightening to track his public statements in the Reichstag in the years prior to 1914. As early as 1900 Richter asked why Germany was not keeping pace with France. Tirpitz replied that the U-boat was of no great value.[165] On 11 May 1904 even Tirpitz's Reichstag ally, von Kardorff, pointed out that Germany, alone among the great seapowers, had not yet constructed a U-boat. Tirpitz replied that the navy was closely observing the field and considering small experiments but that the U-boat's potential for underwater offensive action was still severely limited.[166]

By 1905 Tirpitz felt obliged to ask the Reichstag for money to build a few experimental U-boats.[167] The 1906 estimates contained an appropriation of 1.5 million marks for U-boat development, a figure that rose to 5 million in 1909 and 15 million in 1911. By 1912 the navy was spending 18 million per year for six boats each year with a lifespan of twelve years. This amounted to a projected establishment of seventy-two boats.[168] In the Budget Commission, on 18 December 1907, Tirpitz had to defend himself against Galster-inspired press accusations that Germany was proceeding too slowly in U-boat development.[169] He argued that since France had proven in 1905 that U-boats could be seaworthy, the RMA had investigated a newly developed diesel engine. He invoked his history of having taken a methodical approach to the new technologies of torpedoes and torpedo boats in the 1870s and 1880s, and noted that it was not until about 1884 that the Torpedo Arm began to mature as a feasible weapons system.

In January 1908, when a Progressive deputy noted Galster's remark that, for the price of one Dreadnought, Germany could build ten U-boats, Tirpitz responded sharply and evasively that Germany was ahead of other nations in the number of U-boats suitable for service in the North Sea. He denied that the RMA was neglectful of Kleinkrieg, which, in his definition, could not be pursued without a powerful battlefleet.[170] The following year, in the Budget Commission, he pointed out that had the RMA moved as fast as the French in U-boat development, Germany would then have forty boats that would already be obsolete ("old iron").[171] He noted that a close blockade, as in the Napoleonic wars, was passé. The fleet would have to break through an enemy cordon further out to sea, and only when the blockade was broken through would Kleinkrieg, in Galster's sense, be possible. "Naturally we would have little chance against a stronger opponent without Kleinkrieg; but without a battlefleet we would have no chance at all." In this context Tirpitz's definition of Kleinkrieg embraced only the harassment of the enemy's fleet, not attacks on commerce, the core idea of the Jeune École's understanding of Kleinkrieg.

Before the war most Reichstag parties were content with the RMA's handling of the U-boat question.[172] In February 1914 Tirpitz contentedly announced to the Budget Commission that, as of 1 January, Germany had 24 boats completed with 20 under construction. By October 1914, 36 would be ready. France had 96 at the time, and Britain 101, but some of these had been built as long ago as 1901, and the older ones would be useless except for harbor defense.[173]

The reality was not as rosy as Tirpitz painted it in the Reichstag. The first boats, U-1 through U-4, were finished by 1909. These boats could not operate without a mother ship and were so cramped for space that the crews could not live aboard.[174] They were, contrary to Tirpitz's assurances to the Reichstag, incapable of operating in the rough waters of the North Sea. U-5 through U-8 were ready by the fall of 1910. These improved boats could function for brief periods in the North Sea without a mother ship.

Revealing of Tirpitz's intention for deployment was that the U-boats were initially placed under the Torpedo Inspectorate. The boats were organized into half-flotillas and flotillas, in a manner parallel to the torpedo boats, with mother ships. They were meant to operate mainly with the battlefleet; however, their range was less than that of the torpedo boats, and their surface speed was slower than that of the most lumbering battleship. These characteristics make it appear that Tirpitz added U-boats to the fleet more to deflect criticism in the Reichstag and within the navy than for some strategic purpose. U-boats took money away from both fleet construction and the preparedness of the battlefleet. If they were to become as prominent as critics like Galster would have preferred, the whole premise of a battlefleet and a Navy Law to develop and sustain it would be threatened, along with Tirpitz's preeminent position within the navy. Perhaps Michaelis got it right:

> I thought it was regrettable parsimony applied to the U-boats. Tirpitz only hesitantly began to build them. At the beginning he thought them toys. For a series of years he built only six annually, and the RMA made a big secret out of them. Only at the private initiative of the Fleet Commander [Holtzendorff] and individual U-boat commanders were there occasional exercises of the U-boats against the fleet. . . . In 1912, at the Kaiser maneuvers, the Fleet Commander placed special importance on U-boat participation, because he thought the moment was ripe . . . but Tirpitz expressly forbade their participation. When Tirpitz went on leave, I was sent to his deputy, Capelle, to argue the case. Capelle listened to me quietly and decided "then I must take it upon my own head," and the U-boats participated.[175]

Before the war, despite his later claims to the contrary, Tirpitz subordinated U-boat development to the Navy Law and his retention of bureaucratic power within the navy.

CONFLICT BETWEEN THE NAVAL STAFFS, 1911–1914

For the years immediately preceding the war, in the RMA and the Admiralstab, there exists, besides the normal documentary sources, enlightening personal accounts from two officers who had a bird's-eye view of events. From September 1910 to September 1913 William Michaelis was a Department Head in the Admiralstab and worked particularly closely with Heeringen during his time as Chief from 1911 to 1913.[176] From October 1911 to April 1915, Hopmann was Chief of the RMA's Central Department (Z) and was Tirpitz's right-hand man. Hopmann not only published some fairly revealing memoirs, but many of his private letters and diary entries are published in a volume superbly edited by Michael Epkenhans.[177] From these little exploited sources one can learn not only about policy matters but also about personal relationships between the principal actors, which, if read judiciously, tell much about matters often only hinted at in official documents.

Once in the Admiralstab, Michaelis quickly recognized that its influence in the navy was miniscule. Even if the Chief of the Admiralstab obtained the Emperor's personal consent, there was always the danger that Tirpitz could persuade William II to take the reverse position, especially if Tirpitz worked in concert with Müller at the MK. The implicit conflict was that the RMA governed naval development, defined as broadly as Tirpitz could make it, while the principal responsibility of the Admiralstab was to prepare war plans that few paid serious attention to. For example, the Fleet Command only followed Admiralstab recommendations when these agreed with what the Fleet Commander wanted to do, especially when Holtzendorff held that position (1909–13). Tirpitz meddled in all aspects of Admiralstab work. Not only did operations plans need his prior consent, but he could amend exercise plans that went to the Emperor for approval. Tirpitz starved the Admiralstab intelligence department of funds at the same time that he lavished money on the RMA's Nachrichtenbüro (N), which gathered not only political and parliamentary intelligence but also intelligence on purely military matters.[178] Even given the close friendship between Tirpitz and Heeringen, the latter had to go to great lengths to avoid or correct misunderstandings, and he was often reduced to using Capelle as an intermediary.[179]

One of Michaelis's duties was to provide codes for the fleet. Michaelis hired a typewriter company to design a machine into which clear text could be typed and cipher text produced, and the reverse. Such a machine would have been a forerunner of the later Enigma machine. The Admiralstab requested its introduction, but the cheeseparers of the RMA rejected it for reasons of cost.[180] One can only speculate whether machine ciphers would have reduced or prevented Britain's pervasive reading of German naval ciphers during the war.

A painful task for Michaelis concerned his former Naval Academy teacher, the retired Rear Admiral Curt von Maltzahn, Tirpitz's boyhood friend. Because Maltzahn did not completely follow Tirpitz's line on battleship warfare, Tirpitz had him removed from his position as head of the Naval Academy. The Admiralstab had commissioned the retired Maltzahn to write a history of German naval tactics and, in 1911, Maltzahn tried to persuade Heeringen to allow its publication. Heeringen knew that Tirpitz would not like the publication because Maltzahn had given Commanding Admiral Knorr partial credit for line tactics when Tirpitz had been his Chief of Staff at the Oberkommando. Without revealing the real reason, Michaelis had to tell Maltzahn that the book could not be published.[181]

When Michaelis saw a report of a British torpedo experiment, he sent it to the RMA with a note that the British had switched to compressed air torpedoes to increase range. Instead of being grateful, Tirpitz, according to Michaelis, raged against the Admiralstab, arguing that Germany had the world's best torpedoes, and even told a friend that Michaelis was a "traitor" and a "bird that fouls its own nest." Tirpitz had Hopmann show Michaelis some old torpedoes as "proof" that Germany's were as good as any other. Michaelis was not impressed, nor was he pleased with Hopmann's comment that "I should sing the song of whomever's bread I eat." Only thereafter did German factories change over to compressed air torpedoes.[182] Incidents such as these demonstrate Tirpitz's extreme jealousy about anything that could be construed as criticism, another measure of his bureaucratic arrogance within the navy.

On 2 October 1911 Captain Albert Hopmann took over as Chief of the Central Department (Z) of the RMA. His daily duties included screening materials to determine which should go directly to the State Secretary, and editing all official documents that were released under Tirpitz's signature. He also sat in on all important conversations and meetings that Tirpitz held.[183]

Although he found much to admire in Tirpitz, Hopmann was not without criticism. In November 1911, during preparations for the 1912 Novelle, he spoke with Rear Admiral Reinhard Scheer, the newly appointed Director of the General Naval Department (Allgemeine Marine Departement, or A) in the RMA and fresh from a stint as Chief of Staff of the High Seas Fleet. Scheer, like Hopmann, did not have his heart in the Novelle. They agreed it would overstretch the navy's financial and military resources, and could create political and diplomatic difficulties without a clear goal. Hopmann felt that the Novelle "was only a quirk [*Marotte*] of the Emperor who lacked a clear political rationale for his 'mechanical toy'" (stated in English). Later Tirpitz himself, for the first time, conceded to Hopmann that "the fleet, for the Emperor, was mainly still only a toy."[184]

> I believe that Tirpitz would be happy if he had imposed more reserve on his [Novelle] proposal. He is also less of an oblivious person [*Karnickel*] than Capelle and Dähnhardt, who have also lost sight of the military and practical element and believe that everything has to do with [ship] numbers. They bring us a fleet that is a greenhouse plant that in all its branches lacks a healthy dynamism. . . . What would we do later with 60 capital ships? . . . the ratio, England to Germany, would remain the same, about 2:1. In my view, England could not allow this. Their fleet has missions throughout the world, ours has a mission only in the North Sea; at least that is what we have told the world.[185]

This revealing diary entry demonstrates Hopmann's private skepticism of Tirpitz's rationale for the 1912 Novelle, while, in an act of cognitive dissonance, he tried to let his chief off the hook. Who, after all, gave orders to and had the final say over the work of Capelle and Dähnhardt?

During the winter of 1911–12 a critical question in the navy was the arming of the following years' capital ships at a time when the British were escalating the size of their heavy artillery. After much back and forth, the RMA decided that future battleships, instead of ten 30.5-cm guns, should have eight 38-cm guns in line-ahead double turrets. Future battlecruisers would have eight 35-cm guns. Armament of light cruisers would still be limited to 10.5-cm guns. The Fleet Command wanted guns of this size, because they were the largest that could be manually operated. The Torpedo Inspectorate opposed a large increase in torpedo boat tonnage on the grounds that their increased length would force an inconvenient change in tactics.[186] These decisions would be bitterly questioned when the war came and German light cruisers and torpedo boats were outclassed by their British counterparts.

Despite his occasional private disagreements with Tirpitz, Hopmann unswervingly supported him in contentious matters within the navy, especially against Holtzendorff. During Kiel Week, in 1912, he noted in his diary:

> Tirpitz is the only one who, amidst all resistance, unerringly pursues a high goal. Most others only muddle along [wurschteln] and work just for show and for the effects of the moment. In my view, the spirit of Holtzendorff is very tangible in the fleet-only mutual hostility . . . instead of work in common.[187]

Of course, Hopmann did not note the years of hostility that Tirpitz had aroused within the navy.

In the light of Tirpitz's conflicts with Holtzendorff over fleet deployment and operations plans, rumors circulated, especially in 1912, when the Fleet Chief's term in office was waning, that he might replace Tirpitz at the RMA. Cabinet Chief Müller's close relationship with Holtzendorff was well known.[188] Even Capelle thought it possible that the Emperor, under pressure from the Chancellor, might push Tirpitz out and replace him with Holtzendorff.[189] Tirpitz himself, during his more pessimistic moments, thought that Holtzendorff wanted his job. He told Hopmann that he would do anything to prevent this and feared that the trio, comprised of the Emperor, Müller, and Holtzendorff, would bring down the navy.[190]

In 1911–12, as opposition to Chancellor Bethmann slowly grew, rumors spread that Tirpitz might be the next Chancellor, although Tirpitz dismissed the idea.[191] He was a bit startled, though, when, during Kiel Week in 1913, he was ordered to report immediately to the imperial yacht at a time when Bethmann was in political difficulties. An obvious possibility for such a summons could have been to persuade Tirpitz to become Chancellor. He sought Hopmann's opinion. Only Tirpitz, Hopmann replied, had the nation's confidence to replace Bethmann, and the Emperor would gradually have to come to that conclusion. Tirpitz answered that he was too old (sixty-four at the time) and would have to decline if asked. However, William II was not thinking about matters of high policy and had only wanted to discuss the erection of iron works in Tsingtau.[192]

That Tirpitz had no interest in becoming Chancellor is not surprising. Despite his unbroken string of successes on naval matters in the Reichstag, his ability to control events and dominate the navy would have counted for little if faced with the omnibus duties, responsibilities, and burdens of a Chancellor. The kind of control he had as State Secretary of the RMA would not carry over if he had the fate of the entire Reich in his hands.

NAVAL OPERATIONS PLANS, 1911–1914, AND THE CLOSE BLOCKADE

The Agadir Crisis reawakened a real possibility of war with Britain at a time when fleet deployments and war plans were unsettled questions.[193] Holtzendorff, since 1909, had favored a main fleet deployment in the Baltic, whereas all the contemporaneous Admiralstab Chiefs—Baudissin, Fischel, and Heeringen, with Tirpitz's support—favored a North Sea deployment. Prior to May 1910 the Kaiser Wilhelm Canal had provided great operational flexibility, since every ship in the navy could readily move between Kiel and Wilhelmshaven. The situation changed drastically in May 1910 when the first German Dreadnoughts, *Nassau* and *Westfalen*, joined the fleet. The conundrum of where to base them could no longer be avoided. If based in Kiel, they would face a long and potentially hazardous wartime passage around Denmark, at risk of a British attack while low on coal and far from bases. On 24 October 1911 the Emperor, at the prodding of Tirpitz and Heeringen, tentatively decided to base the newest battleships and large cruisers in Wilhelmshaven.[194] Holtzendorff protested and, Tirpitz-like, threatened to resign if all the ships too big for the canal were removed from Kiel.[195] In his reposte, Tirpitz told the Emperor that to base the fleet in Kiel would concede, not only to the British but also to the German people, that the fleet was not strong enough to prevent a blockade of Germany's North Sea ports. In such a case the nation could rightly question what the enormous tax levies for the fleet had accomplished. The navy's consistent development policy would be seen as "bankrupt." This was a typical bureaucratic "sunk costs" argument. Tirpitz reinforced the point by asserting that a Helgoland Bight deployment would trump one in the Kattegat, whether as an offensive sallying point or as a place of refuge if the fleet was on the defensive.[196] The next day William II made a definitive decision to base the High Seas Fleet, including the Dreadnoughts, in the North Sea.[197] The following month Tirpitz reported that, by April 1914, the widening of the canal would be completed for the Dreadnoughts.[198] The navy's interior lines would be restored. In practical terms, William II's decision settled the question of ship bases up to the outbreak of the war. Holtzendorff grumbled about the decision for another year. His fall 1912 maneuvers were something of a fiasco.[199] In April 1913 Vice Admiral Friedrich von Ingenohl replaced him as Fleet Chief.

Some intelligent junior officers such as Ernst von Weizsäcker, an admirer of Holtzendorff, worried about the scarcity of talented top-level officers in the navy. When Heeringen took ill in 1910, he wrote in his diary:

We are so short of usable senior admirals that we can scarcely spare him. This bad situation is partly because old Tirpitz has retained men as department heads who are factotums, only fit to fill their posts, but who are not usable otherwise. We have very few admirals who are suited to lead at sea.[200]

Still open was the question of whether to use the fleet offensively or defensively. In 1912 the prevailing assumption was that, upon the outbreak of war, the Royal Navy would rush to the Helgoland Bight and quickly set up a close blockade of the North Sea ports. The operations plan of November 1912 incorporated this assumption. Rapid British mobilization was expected to send large numbers of light units to positions off the North Sea coast, with more powerful ships lurking further out at sea. Such a course of action would preclude the Baudissin/Fischel fantasies of a German attack on the British coast immediately upon the outbreak of war. A further complicating factor was that, by 1912, the fleet was so large that it took two high tides to pass the shoals of the Jade. Heeringen's obvious counter to such an aggressive British strategy would be Kleinkrieg-style mine, torpedo, and U-boat attacks to whittle down the blockading forces—in other words, a policy of a strategic defense combined with a tactical offense. German planners gave no consideration to a distant blockade.[201] Although Heeringen had broached the possibility of a distant blockade, Pohl, his successor, failed to pursue it.[202] The November 1912 plan, which had Tirpitz's implicit approval, was also significant in that it ignored the kamikaze-like offensive naval plans dating back to 1892. A more sober reality was beginning to intrude in German planning that had previously been driven by the vanity and fantasies of the Emperor, along with the navy's own deep-seated traditional embarrassment for its minimal participation in the war with France two generations before. Still noteworthy, however, was that this latest plan, just like those that came before, was developed with minimal army participation.[203]

Heeringen told Michaelis about a meeting he had with Tirpitz to discuss an Admiralstab draft war plan. Tirpitz did not believe in a German attack at the outbreak because of numerical inferiority. Instead, he wanted to await the anticipated British descent on the Helgoland Bight. He told Heeringen that a real war plan, as opposed to one on paper, would have to await the actual circumstances that would follow the outbreak of war. Peacetime planning had only educational and morale value, and for those purposes it was always better to emphasize the offensive. Tirpitz's private candor was an admission that ambitious offensive plans were a Potemkin village to appease the Emperor and to maintain morale within the officer corps.[204] Tirpitz's wartime and postwar writings contain no acknowledgment of this uncomfortable truth. When speaking with the Emperor, however, Tirpitz sang a different tune. For example, at a meeting in February 1913, Tirpitz condemned Holtzendorff's maneuvers the previous fall for their defensive strategy, which were partly based on the allegation that German weapons were inferior. The consequent sense of inferiority would, he said, kill the will for victory and reduce the morale and efficiency of the navy in both war and peace. He wanted the Emperor to proclaim that he would not tolerate such pessimism in the naval officer corps.[205] Here is a clear example of Tirpitz's disingenuousness in the service of his bureaucratic empire. With Heeringen he could be candid, but he could not openly endorse a war plan that would seem contradictory to his professed aims.

While the Germans floundered about for ideas on how to use their powerful fleet, geographic and technological circumstances stimulated some strategic rethinking on the western side of the North Sea.[206] A close blockade had been necessary against France and Spain during the age of sail, because they both had direct and ready access to the open sea. Although a close blockade was not without risk, especially from the elements, sailing ships never had a fuel problem. Steam power greatly complicated a close blockade because ravenous coal consumption, impossible to conveniently supply at sea, meant that some ships would always be on the way to or from refueling. Mines and torpedoes from surface ships and submarines made it very hazardous for blockaders to keep station.

By 1904 Fisher and the Admiralty began to reconsider the drawbacks of a close blockade, although its tradition of success and the public expectation of it had kept the practice alive longer than pure, cold calculation would have allowed. As late as 1911 the Admiralty's war plan called for a blockade of Helgoland Bight with light forces, with larger units in support and ready to pounce upon a sortie by the High Seas Fleet.

By 1912 Fisher's successor as First Sea Lord, Arthur Wilson, recognized the dangers and logistical problems of a close blockade and, to the dismay of the truculent First Lord Churchill, replaced it with an "observational" blockade that provided a picket line to the north and west, well outside Helgoland Bight, with the main fleet further to the west. Deeper study revealed that the observational blockade, with a line almost three hundred miles long, would have attritional problems similar to those of a close blockade, only more gradual.

A month before war broke out, the Admiralty made a fortunate decision. A new plan abandoned the observational blockade and took full advantage of the geographic conundrum that the North Sea posed for Germany. With a southern line across the Channel at Dover, and a northern one between the Shetland Islands and Norwegian coastal waters, and with the Grand Fleet based at Scapa Flow in the Orkneys, the North Sea would become a cul de sac for the High Seas Fleet. With this stratagem Tirpitz's last hope of deterrence, or, if that failed, a battle against part of the British fleet within fifty miles of Helgoland, fell. When Heeringen left the Admiralstab in 1913, he told Michaelis confidentially, "I fear that our fleet is too small to win but too large to die gloriously."[207] As Kennedy has put it, "the more [Tirpitz] believed in the risk theory and the deterrence of a British attack, the less convincing was his assumption that the Royal Navy would rush into dangerous German waters."[208]

These secret calculations within the Admiralty to foreswear, in July 1914, the close blockade were unknown on the German side. Büchsel's offhand remark of 1902 about the possibility of a distant blockade, and Tirpitz's comments in a similar vein before the Budget Commission in 1909, stimulated no serious consideration within the Admiralstab.[209] According to Michaelis, in 1912 Heeringen, in a casual but prophetic remark about a war game, said: "If the English really adopt a distant blockade, with a consequent holding back of their battleships, the wartime role of our beautiful High Seas Fleet would be a very unhappy one. The U-boats would then have to [carry on the war]."[210]

In April 1913 the prickly Admiral Hugo Pohl (ennobled a few months later) succeeded Heeringen as Chief of the Admiralstab.[211] In the fall of 1913 Admiralstab intelligence analysis of the 1913 maneuvers of the French and British navies indicated that the British were considering a pullback from a close blockade. Pohl's conclusion based on this information was therefore not about the distant blockade, only adopted in July 1914, but concerned Wilson's observational blockade.[212] Pohl realized that to attack such a distant line would take the High Seas Fleet far beyond the fifty nautical miles from Helgoland assumed in previous operations plans; nevertheless he hoped that, with good reconnaissance, perhaps including airships, an engagement on favorable terms might still be possible. War games in March 1914 were based on these unrealistically favorable assumptions. Pohl concluded that only minelayers and submarines should operate far to the north, whereas the main fleet should energetically combat any British light forces in the vicinity of Helgoland. He did not realize that virtually none would be there. Despite all evidence to the contrary, he followed the decades-long tradition of wooly-headed optimism and still believed that a battle on favorable terms against part of the British Fleet might still be possible, another example of the limitless human capacity for self-deception in a situation where political and bureaucratic forces combine to institutionalize a fallacy. To change strategies would call into question Tirpitz's Navy Law, and his personal power within the navy. The institutional interest of the navy as a whole in this case reinforced Tirpitz's bureaucratic political mind-set. Germany therefore stumbled into a naval war with Britain and the Entente with no coherent plan for naval operations. Captain Carl Hollweg, longtime director of N in the RMA and commander of the pre-Dreadnought battleship *Schlesien*, noted a remark by Tirpitz in May 1914. Tirpitz at the time was visiting Fleet Commander Ingenohl to view a tactical exercise of the High Seas Fleet.

Ingenohl was surprised that Tirpitz showed so little interest. Tirpitz said suddenly: "Yes, and what would you do if, in the event of war, the English did not come to our coasts." The seriousness of the situation was therefore clear to him; but consequential action was lacking.[213]

It seems apparent that Tirpitz, despite his cognitive dissonance, was aware of the distant blockade as at least a possibility, and he himself had no answer for it.

A FATEFUL SUMMER

As the summer of 1914 approached, there were no particular signs that it would differ very much from summers past. Kiel Week preparations were in progress; officers and high officials made plans for leave. Heeringen, Tirpitz's brilliant collaborator of many years, retired in June 1914; he suffered from debilitating angina and hardening of the arteries. Except for a few clashes when he was at the Admiralstab, Heeringen had been a loyal and effective member of Tirpitz's leadership cadre.[214]

The Emperor, in a benevolent mood, invited the whole Board of Admiralty to Kiel Week, though only Jellicoe chose to attend. Müller told Hopmann of his concern about rumored Anglo-Russian naval conversations that might solidify the Entente. Tirpitz, in a dark mood, confided to Hopmann that Britain wanted Germany and Russia to tear each other apart.[215] Sometime in May 1914 Tirpitz lamented to Capelle that "the navy's situation is a disaster," and, because of cost and political circumstances, "we can no longer build the ships that the [Navy Law] envisions."[216] On 15 June the Treasury refused the navy's request for an additional 50 million marks for 1915, and even a supplemental 3 million for 1914, for lack of money. The pivotal Center deputy Erzberger published an article that precluded further new taxes the following year.[217] Tirpitz's low spirits were understandable, but he failed to mention the more important reasons for his dilemma, Britain's unexpectedly vigorous response to his own conceptually flawed designs. Even the Novelle in its original form would have improved the situation only marginally and, if passed, would simply have prompted even more energetic countermeasures from the British. Only in the most superficial way did the 1912 Novelle improve relations with the British, and then only because of the drop in 1912 from a four to a two tempo.

Tirpitz left Berlin for Kiel Week on 21 June. That year it had special significance, because it marked the opening of the widened Kaiser Wilhelm Canal. At last the navy could again operate on interior lines that had been absent for the newest ships since *Nassau* went into service in 1910. Kiel Week, during which the Emperor flaunted German seapower before the whole world, had always discomforted Tirpitz, as he preferred to expand the navy as quietly as possible.[218] On Sunday, 28 June, Tirpitz was entertaining a group of twenty-five British officers and diplomats for lunch, along with some German political notables. As the group was departing at about 5:00 PM, word came suddenly that Archduke Franz Ferdinand, heir to the Hapsburg throne, whom Tirpitz had visited a few weeks before, had died. By 11:00 PM details arrived of the assassination. Hopmann noted that it was "a dreadful deed that could have unforeseeable political consequences."[219] The news was tragic and disturbing, but Tirpitz left the next day to take his scheduled cure at Tarasp in the Swiss Alps, intending to visit St. Blasien at the end of July.[220]

Rivers of ink have been spilled by generations of historians about what happened during the following weeks.[221] Here the main emphasis is on what Tirpitz knew and did during that critical period.[222]

The famous "blank check" meeting, at which William II assured the Austrians that he would support them unconditionally in their quarrel with the Serbs, took place on 5 July. The next day he called in Capelle, Tirpitz's deputy as Under State Secretary. The Emperor assured Capelle that, even if Serbia refused an ultimatum, he believed it improbable that Russia would intervene militarily, since the Czar would not support regicides. He did not mention Britain at all, an indication of an implicit assumption that the British would not become involved in any way other than diplomatic. Capelle was ordered to avoid any measures that might draw political attention or conspicuous expenditures that might be considered a preparation for war. On 5 July Bethmann persuaded the Emperor and Moltke that Austria had to be pushed to act quickly and decisively about Serbia. Such a course would create a fait accompli to present to the Entente. Meanwhile, it was vital to keep outward appearances calm to prevent the semblance of a crisis atmosphere. With these orders, the Emperor left for Kiel and his annual cruise in Scandinavian waters.[223] In his diary Hopmann noted that Capelle advised a discreet completion of the newest ships and measures to make torpedo boats and U-boats ready for war as soon as possible.[224]

Tirpitz's reply betrayed no sense of an immediate crisis. His cure was going very well, and he suggested that Dähnhardt and other officers not come to St. Blasien before 26 July. Were it up to him, he would seek a friendly understanding with Russia and hope to pit the whale against the bear.[225]

Hopmann sent Tirpitz an early draft of the ultimatum for Serbia, and also the first signs of German frustration about the glacial pace of Austrian diplomacy and mobilization preparations; nevertheless, both Capelle and Hopmann were confident that none of the great powers had the appetite for a continental war over Serbia.[226]

On 16 July Hopmann learned that the Austrian ultimatum to Serbia would only be sent on 22 July, after French President Raymond Poincaré started home from his visit to Russia.[227] The departure of the High Seas Fleet for its normal cruise to Norway had a calming effect on the stock markets, so the deception plan was still working, at least with the public.[228]

Widely reported in the press was a long-planned test mobilization of the Royal Navy that included a grand review at Spithead of most of the Home Fleet and subsequent tactical exercises in the Channel.[229] On 20 July Rear Admiral Paul Behncke, Pohl's deputy at the Admiralstab, met with Foreign Secretary Gottlieb von Jagow. The latter asked nervously if he should propose an early return of the fleet and the Emperor. The Foreign Office was considering the possibility, previously discounted, of British intervention. Jagow suggested to Behncke the bizarre idea of a threat to occupy the Netherlands to deter Britain from entering a war. Both Capelle and Hopmann immediately recognized the stupidity of the idea, since it would do Britain the favor of allowing it "the right to pose as protector of all small states," and it would close Belgian and Dutch harbors to Germany. Capelle knew that the General Staff had said in 1905 that it did not have a man to spare to occupy the Netherlands. A sign that Bethmann's plan was in trouble was Jagow's admission that "a great European war is not out of the question."[230] Jagow made a nervous, uncertain, and fearful impression upon Behncke. Clearly the Chancellor's original plan of fast action against Serbia and a localized war as a fait accompli, combined then with a friendship offensive toward the Entente, was beginning to unravel. Bethmann pressed to keep the Emperor and the fleet from returning home early. The navy was increasingly anxious that the fleet might be caught at a severe disadvantage away from its bases if the British entered the war. A "Copenhagen" could result. Capelle wanted the Chancellor to guarantee that no war would begin in the next five or six days (noted as eight days in Hopmann's diary on 22 July).[231]

The forty-eight-hour ultimatum was, at last, given to the Serbs on 23 July, a full twenty-five days after the assassination. That same day William II sent the Admiralstab a telegram imploring it and the Foreign Office to bring the fleet home from Norway very soon. He was clearly chafing under the need to maintain peacetime appearances. Behncke, after consulting with the Foreign Office, replied that the diplomats saw no immediate danger, since French President Poincaré was still on his way home through the Baltic after a visit to Russia. The situation looked safe, at least for the five or six days in question, but Behncke recommended that the fleet be ready to depart sooner if the situation warranted. It is curious that in the three weeks between 6 and 27 July, only one letter (of 10 or 11 July) has been found that came from Tirpitz to the RMA. Of course, he could have been in contact by the relatively primitive telephones then extant, but there is only one mention even of that (in Hopmann's diary on 26 July). Despite getting admittedly incomplete information via Hopmann and the newspapers in his Swiss Kurort, to all appearances he was unusually detached.

The international situation grew worse. Russia declared publicly on 25 July that it could not be indifferent to the fate of Serbia. Austria began serious mobilization preparations against Serbia. Pohl returned a few days early from his leave. War Minister Falkenhayn and Chief of the General Staff Moltke returned on schedule on the 24th and 26th, respectively. Moltke, in particular, began to ratchet up the pressure on Bethmann to seize the moment for war, before Russia completed its scheduled military reforms in 1916.[232]

By 27 July the situation had begun to spin out of Bethmann's control. Serbia had replied to the ultimatum in conciliatory fashion but did not accept all of it. As planned, the result was that Austria broke relations with Serbia. The next day Grey called for an ambassadors' conference in London, in a last-ditch effort to calm the alarming momentum for general war.

Hopmann met Tirpitz, Capelle, and Dähnhardt at the Anhalter Station in Berlin on 27 July. Tirpitz was worried, not about the preservation of peace, as he claimed in his memoirs,[233] but about his fears that British meddling would persuade Austria to partially back down from its ultimatum, a situation that could "easily degenerate into a setback for the Triple Alliance." That afternoon he met with Bethmann and came away with the impression, erroneous as it turned out, that the Chancellor favored such a course. Hopmann relayed to Tirpitz the "wonderful" news that the Emperor was directly issuing his own improvised mobilization plan to the Baltic Station! Tirpitz sarcastically noted: "Now he is playing soldier."[234] Remarkably Tirpitz did not seem disturbed by the possibility of a continental war.[235]

The next day Müller, based on assurances from the Foreign Office, told Tirpitz that the situation was not serious, though Tirpitz warned against trusting Britain and repeated his fear that Austria would slacken its tough line. On that same day Austria declared war on Serbia and shelled Belgrade. The RMA also heard that the Royal Navy was calling up reservists.[236]

The next day the RMA learned of a partial Russian mobilization. According to Epkenhans, as late as 29 July neither Tirpitz nor Pohl expected that Britain would go to war. There is even evidence that Tirpitz planned to return to St. Blasien that same evening, hardly a sign of urgency.[237] That evening Tirpitz and Müller went to Potsdam, where the Emperor told them of Prinz Heinrich's meeting with King George V, who hinted that Britain would stay neutral in the event of war. At this time very few people, and no one in Britain, knew that the Schlieffen Plan called for an invasion of Belgium, even in a "defensive" war. At the same meeting word came from Prince Lichnowsky that Grey had privately told him that Britain would not be able to stand aside in the event of a Franco-German war. Tirpitz remarked that this statement certainly called into question the idea of British neutrality. By this time Tirpitz realized that the situation was indeed serious and that Britain would be involved in a continental war.[238]

By the next day, 30 July, Bethmann and the Emperor were under extreme pressure from Moltke and Falkenhayn to mobilize, as it was clear that a general Russian mobilization was imminent. In this context Bethmann called a meeting of the Prussian State Ministry where Tirpitz was present. The Chancellor said that the situation had become so grave that he no longer believed that a peaceful solution was possible. Once again Tirpitz passively went along with the army's idea of preventive war. Afterward Bethmann agreed that the navy could undertake some preliminary security measures. That afternoon Pohl, Behncke, Prinz Heinrich, and Tirpitz met concerning possible operations plans. Tirpitz made the case that, if the British fleet approached Helgoland, the High Seas Fleet should attack it as soon as possible. At this meeting he did not raise the possibility, as he had with Ingenohl in May 1914, of what to do if the British did not come. Behncke advocated patience until the newest ships were ready and the reserve fleet fully manned.[239] Even so, the RMA was not completely convinced that the British were not bluffing. In this sense the RMA's calculations were no more realistic than those of the Chancellor or the Foreign Office.

With the looming prospect of war with Britain, the question suddenly arose: Who would lead the navy if Germany went to war? Under the Constitution, the Emperor was Supreme War Lord; however, ever since the time of the elder Moltke, there was no doubt that in wartime the Chief of the General Staff was, de facto, in command of the army, a situation the Emperor never dared to challenge. All his life William II had fancied himself a great admiral and effective head of the navy. Every year, to the dismay of his admirals, he meddled in maneuvers and interfered with scarce training time. In 1888 he had abolished the Imperial Admiralty. In 1899, with Tirpitz's connivance, he had fragmented the Oberkommando der Marine, the military arm of the navy. This reorganization, and the bureaucratic warfare that followed, left Tirpitz first among the theoretical equals of the many other parts of the navy that reported directly to the Emperor. These included the Fleet Command and the Admiralstab. As the only officer to maintain his position for seventeen years (as of 1914), and as the successful avatar of the navy's principal mission during that era, Tirpitz had been able to maintain, and even expand, his bureaucratic empire within the navy.

The outbreak of a war would instantly shift the navy's main mission from construction to operations. This change posed a precipitous dilemma for Tirpitz. He had long believed that in case of war all branches of the navy should be under one officer, in effect a reconstitution of the Admiralty. That officer alone would then report to the Emperor. The

Chief of the Admiralstab, Pohl, would be an obvious candidate for the job, but Tirpitz had little confidence in Pohl's capacity to undertake the task, although he conceded that Pohl was a good sailor and squadron leader. "Accordingly, I told the Chief of the [Naval] Cabinet [Müller] that, in the then positions of the parties concerned, the proposed office would have to be entrusted to myself."[240] Tirpitz claimed that, had Pohl been suitable, he would have suggested him for the post. He asserted that later: "When I despaired of any other solution," he offered, in complete defiance of the almost immutable seniority system, to serve under Pohl, if only Pohl would discuss operational decisions with him before they went to the Emperor.

Not surprisingly, given his self-delusion about running the naval war himself, the Emperor, through Müller, rejected Tirpitz's idea of an Admiralty. Müller, on 30 July, crafted a weak compromise: Pohl would "consult" Tirpitz, and if Tirpitz dissented, the Emperor would be notified.[241] In effect, this decision restricted Tirpitz's right of direct access to matters concerning the administrative work of the RMA. In retrospect, Müller noted:

> I had overestimated both the unselfishness of Tirpitz as such, and the goodwill of Pohl genuinely to use Tirpitz's advice in the Emperor's interest. Pohl soon began to complain to me of Tirpitz's pessimism, "which nearly drives one mad." In short, it was a very grave mistake.[242]

At mid-day on 31 July confirmation came in of Russian general mobilization. An hour later William II issued a public declaration of a "state of imminent war," the immediate preliminary to a German general mobilization.[243] In the brief period between the ultimatum and its expiration the next day, Tirpitz vainly tried to find some way to derail war with Russia but, by then, events had long since spun out of control.[244]

Although Bethmann succeeded in uniting the Reichstag for a "defensive" war against Russia, his other mission, to keep Britain neutral, failed. In a critical meeting during the night of 1 and 2 August, Tirpitz met with Bethmann, Falkenhayn, Moltke, and Stumm from the Foreign Office. When Moltke and Falkenhayn explained to the Chancellor the urgent necessity of an invasion of Belgium, Tirpitz saw immediately that war with Britain was about to begin. It is a chilling testimony to the dysfunctional nature of the German system of government that Tirpitz realized that the march through Belgium was, before that moment, unclear to the Chancellor and the Foreign Office.[245] The juggernaut exigencies of the Schlieffen Plan, which required an invasion of Luxemburg on 2 August and of Belgium shortly thereafter, doomed any prospect of peace with Britain.[246] The chance that the British Cabinet might stay out of war, a real possibility under other circumstances, was brushed aside by popular sympathy for Belgium, and by recourse to the time-honored balance-of-power principle.

One of the most remarkable anomalies of the 1914 situation was the singular lack of coordinated planning between the army and the navy, for which Tirpitz bore a share of the responsibility. War planning was the duty of the Admiralstab, not the RMA, but Tirpitz had huge influence over such plans. The greatest responsibility for this failure rests with the monarch, who insisted on the exercise of his constitutional war-making powers but never put in the effort or thought to coordinate the army and navy. There is no evidence that Tirpitz, before 1914, ever used his influence to push William II in this direction. The unchallenged ability of each military organ to develop its own war plan without reference to the other's exacted a high price in 1914.

With the coming of the war Tirpitz's flawed strategic plans were in ruins. With them collapsed the bureaucratic empire he had built to sustain them, or, perhaps, it was the other way around and his bureaucratic empire required such plans to rationalize its existence. The deterrence value of the "risk fleet," and even the later idea of "sufficient defensive chances," had clearly failed in their purpose, although Tirpitz could never admit to this, even to himself. His cherished role as one of the principal men of the Wilhelmian Reich would, in fact, diminish to a minor one, partially because of the peculiar organizational arrangements he had championed for the navy. Tirpitz never acknowledged the important role the fleet had played in the creation of Germany's diplomatic encirclement. The man who had enlisted the Emperor to prevent either a naval or a political understanding with Britain found himself, during the July crisis and even before, eclipsed by a resurgent army. No one consulted him seriously on monumental questions of peace and war. Despite his awareness that the fleet was not "ready" for war with Britain in 1914, he followed in the path of almost all decision makers in all the relevant countries who believed that the risks of war were less than the risks of a concerted effort to preserve peace. By August 1914, in the mind of the German public and, indeed, in the highest councils of the British government and the Admiralty, Tirpitz was the larger-than-life symbol of German naval might. Despite this compelling image, as he himself would only gradually discover, when it really counted in the German government and in the naval high command, the war would make him a much diminished man, and it would wreak uncontrollable havoc on the bureaucratic empire he had worked so long to create and maintain.

15

TIRPITZ AT WAR,
AUGUST 1914–MARCH 1916

GEOGRAPHIC AND MATERIAL PRELUDE

The central theater of the naval war was the North Sea. The north–south orientation of the island of Great Britain was a barrier that made the North Sea a virtual cul de sac. Germany only had access to the open ocean either to the south, through the narrow English Channel, or to the north. At its southern end, where the English Channel begins, less than 30 nautical miles separate Dover from Calais. The North Sea extends north about 700 miles, along the coast of England and Scotland, to the Shetland Islands. About 200 miles east of the Shetlands is the great Norwegian coastal archipelago, inside of which is the old Hanseatic port of Bergen. From Bergen, 400 miles south and slightly east, was the fortified island of Helgoland, 50 miles north of the Jade Bay, and Wilhelmshaven, the home of the High Seas Fleet. From there, initially skirting the Dutch coast, another 300 miles southwest, is Dover and the English Channel. At the northwest corner of the North Sea, in the Orkney Islands, is Scapa Flow, the principal base of the British Grand Fleet. From there, 600 miles away, almost exactly southeast of Scapa, is Wilhelmshaven. The route between the two forms a diagonal that neatly bisects the North Sea.

Besides the geography of the North Sea, an important factor limiting choices, particularly for Britain, was the port situation. The best British naval facilities, ideal for past wars with France, were at Plymouth and Portsmouth on the south coast. Looking north from the Thames estuary, Harwich was suited only to light forces. Rosyth and Cromarty were, at the beginning of the war, insufficiently developed and open to submarine attack; nor were they large enough to accommodate the Grand Fleet. That left only Scapa Flow in the Orkneys, relatively exposed to the rigors of the North Atlantic. Just an anchorage at first, it had no direct access to rail communications. Only the decision, made in July 1914, to undertake a distant blockade made it a feasible choice.

Although Germany had a North Sea coastline of only about 100 miles, it had a highly developed array of commercial ports. The greatest was Hamburg, well inland on the Elbe. Cuxhaven and Bremen, and Bremerhaven on the Weser, were important trade entrepots. The western terminus of the Kaiser Wilhelm Canal entered the Elbe downstream from Hamburg. The naval base of Wilhelmshaven, a fenland in the 1860s, was, by 1914, well connected to the efficient German rail network. The problem with Wilhelmshaven was that shoals and sandbars in the Jade required two high tides for the whole fleet to get to sea. This fact limited quick deployment. Geography also limited the fleet's ability to mount a major attack on the vital cross-channel movement of troops and supplies to France. If the High Seas Fleet sailed the 350 miles to the Channel, it would run the huge risk that the numerically superior Grand Fleet, steaming quickly from the north, might cut it off from its base. Such a raid would probably be futile anyway, because the Channel was narrow enough so that threatened merchantmen could scurry back into port before any attack. The greatest hazard to both fleets in the North Sea was the danger, in such shallow and narrow seas, of minefields and submarine attacks. This risk would increase continuously as the war went on.

At the outset of the war Britain possessed twenty-two Dreadnought battleships plus two more Turkish-owned ships requisitioned from British yards in August 1914. Germany had thirteen, with four more (the *König* class) completed by November 1914, although they would still have to undergo trials. Britain had nine battlecruisers, with *Tiger* completed in October 1914. Germany had four battlecruisers, with *Derfflinger* completed in September 1914. *Goeben* had other business in the Mediterranean. By British standards, German ships were undergunned (11- and 12-inch guns vs. 12-, 13.5-, and 15-inch guns) and were a knot or two slower. German ships excelled in the thickness and quality of their armor and in their unmatched watertight integrity, but these advantages were obvious neither to friend nor foe until battle was actually joined. German Dreadnoughts, built specifically for North Sea battles, had shorter range. Britain had a substantial supremacy in pre-Dreadnought battleships.[1] Before the war and pre-Jutland, Tirpitz was severely criticized for ships that appeared statistically and cosmetically inferior.

The Baltic, too, posed geographical challenges. Its only entrances were through the Danish Islands, via the Little Belt, the Great Belt, and the Sound at Copenhagen along the Swedish coast. Except for a narrow passage on the mainland side of the Little Belt, Denmark mined the passages at the beginning of the war to protect its neutrality. The Germans consented, because the mines also protected them from a major British incursion into the Baltic. As Tirpitz remembered from his torpedo days, the river-fed Baltic was less brackish than the North Sea, and large parts of the Baltic froze during the winter.[2] For several months of the year the weather shut the Russian Baltic Fleet in its base at Kronstadt in the Gulf of Finland. Just before the war Russia began an ambitious Dreadnought program. None of them had been completed at the beginning of the war, although Russia had five relatively modern pre-Dreadnoughts and some large, fast destroyers. In the Baltic both sides assumed the defensive—the Russians because of weakness and the Germans because their attention was directed almost exclusively towards the North Sea. They considered the Baltic command so unimportant that Grand Admiral Prinz Heinrich, the Emperor's brother, left his mostly honorary post of General Inspector of the Navy to assume it. This nepotism was balanced by the decision, supported by the Prince himself, to give him no real authority if the navy undertook major operations there.[3] The Baltic Fleet, with rare exceptions, consisted of an ensemble of older and obsolescent ships that would have been of no use in the North Sea.

TIRPITZ AT WAR: INITIAL PHASE

For all his bellicose postwar writing, Tirpitz clearly did not want a war in 1914. When asked about it before the war, such as at the "war council" of December 1912, Tirpitz, to Moltke's disgust, had advised delay. When war with Britain came it was obvious that deterrence had failed and, along with it, the bureaucratic power Tirpitz had built so painfully and successfully since 1897. If the Admiralty had been re-created under his command, with the RMA, the Admiralstab, and the Fleet Command under one roof, Tirpitz might have been able to hold onto power. He had suggested this arrangement just before the war; but his success in fragmenting the navy left the Supreme Warlord as its sole coordinator. In wartime the Emperor was unwilling to step back and cede real authority to a naval officer, although Tirpitz had expected that he would be the wartime Supreme Commander.[4] The Emperor's vanity had been wounded by Tirpitz's constant manipulations and resignation threats. Müller later noted that, "for ten years the Emperor had held him in deep mistrust."[5] Tirpitz was probably right to do what was necessary to make the flighty William II stick to a coherent program, but it created a festering resentment in William II. Given Tirpitz's status as the creator and public face of the navy, the Emperor needed him to build the fleet but not, he thought, to run a war.

Another cause of Tirpitz's decline in the navy was the rancor he had aroused among officers of the Front and the Admiralstab by his bullying of both, sometimes at the expense of readiness. Officers also resented his assiduous cultivation of Reichstag deputies, including even some leftists. They did not understand that it was the only way Tirpitz could acquire the sums necessary to build increasingly expensive Dreadnoughts. Some also thought him too old, and too bureaucratic in the traditional sense. He was, after all, seventeen years removed from his last sea command. Tirpitz was trapped in his own creation, the peacetime bureaucratic balkanization of the navy, which continued unchanged into the war. Ingenohl, the Fleet Commander, Pohl, Chief of the Admiralstab, and Müller, Head of the Marine Kabinett, had all been members of the Torpedo Gang.[6] Over time, the latter two had developed their own agendas that differed from Tirpitz's. In the unprecedented situation of war, Tirpitz had to figure out what he could achieve in his new position as "adviser." Müller, "to balance Bethmann," engineered an order for Tirpitz to join the Emperor's headquarters entourage.[7]

The first great question facing the naval leadership was how to use the High Seas Fleet in the North Sea. On 30 July 1914 Pohl sent Ingenohl the following operations order:

1. The goal of the operation is to damage the English fleet
    by attacks on the reconnaissance or blockading forces
    in the German Bight, by ruthless mining, and also, if
    possible, a U-boat offensive near the British coast.

2. After warfare has achieved an equality of strength, attempts should be prepared to concentrate all forces to send the fleet into battle in favorable circumstances. If, beforehand, a favorable opportunity to strike should present itself, it must be taken.[8]

Tirpitz, although he did not favor an immediate offensive, was uncomfortable with this order that was based on the assumption of a close blockade. The contention that Kleinkrieg could lead to equality of strength was a new one and had not previously been seriously considered in the Admiralstab.[9] On 6 August the fleet was ordered to avoid battle in the short term, and to confine itself to mines, submarine, and torpedo boat operations. Pohl told Tirpitz that Chancellor Bethmann wanted to save the fleet as security for a peace settlement.[10] This order must have brought back for Tirpitz bitter memories of idleness and makework in Wilhelmshaven during the Franco-Prussian War. If the British did not send major fleet units into Helgoland Bight, the High Seas Fleet would have to seek them out far to the north near their Scottish bases. Even if they came close to Helgoland, Ingenohl would need timely intelligence to sortie, although some still hoped that enraged British public opinion would force the Royal Navy to attack.[11]

In the first month of the war, when the Grand Fleet was hovering to the south to screen delivery of the British Expeditionary Force (BEF) to France, came the first significant surface action in the North Sea. On 28 August, in a very confused action near Helgoland, there was an engagement of light forces. German light cruisers held their own against their British counterparts until Admiral David Beatty and his battlecruisers came up unexpectedly in support. Three German light cruisers were sent to the bottom, including *Mainz*, that had junior officer Wolfgang von Tirpitz aboard.[12] Ingenohl had not supported the light forces with the High Seas Fleet, and the sand bar problem kept him from sallying against Beatty in a timely manner. The Helgoland encounter was unfortunate for the navy's confidence. Also discomfiting for the navy and for the Emperor was that German light cruisers with 10.5-cm guns had to fight British ones with 15-cm guns. German torpedo boats had two 8.8-cm guns vs. British destroyers with 10.2-cm guns.[13] The encounter prompted Ingenohl to avoid a major battle and to seek engagements with light forces only, even though the German light forces were qualitatively inferior. The decision was in accord with William II's inclination to limit the fleet's license to engage, even though, on 10 September, the Grand Fleet briefly came close to Helgoland, still masking transports to France.[14]

Tirpitz pushed Müller hard to get the Emperor to accept "action." With the army rolling through Belgium and into France, he was afraid that the war would be won without the navy. He wanted to wait until the (obsolete) IV and V (Reserve) Squadrons were ready and then to proceed aggressively.[15] In his marginal notes to Tirpitz's memo, Müller warned of too hasty a sortie for "prestige considerations." Tirpitz himself, on several occasions, felt ambivalent about the degree to which the fleet should be used "offensively."[16] It is evident that, despite his later protestations to the contrary, Tirpitz did not favor an early fleet offensive. On 19 August he approached General Moritz von Lyckner, Chief of the Military Cabinet:

> Tirpitz considers it necessary to justify to me the passive posture of the fleet, that this deployment is really justified for purely military reasons. Also, it would be desirable that in future peace negotiations we should possess at least a portion of the fleet.[17]

To withhold the fleet for diplomatic reasons was an argument that Tirpitz later bitterly opposed. According to Michaelis, Tirpitz's pressure for offensive action early in the war was ambiguous. He did not realize, for example, that it would take about three months to mobilize the obsolete IV and V Squadrons, a condition Tirpitz insisted on for offensive action. He had also advised that battle should wait until the situation in Turkey was clarified.[18]

Tirpitz also pressed for the formation of a Marine Corps to defend the far right wing of the army in Flanders. From the beginning of the war, the army had refused to dispatch troops to execute the navy's goal of securing the Belgian coast and harbors. From there, small craft, submarines, and airplanes could harry traffic in the Channel. The project was a particular favorite of Tirpitz. He obtained command of the mixed force for Admiral Ludwig von Schröder, recalled from retirement. A Cabinet Order of 29 August gave Schröder substantial autonomy.[19] Tirpitz initially provided most of the men, reservists from the North Sea and Baltic Stations, and fought to secure support for the Flanders force from both the army and navy leadership. With small U-boats and torpedo craft, shipped there by canal, and some coastal artillery, this little-known sector of the Western Front made a substantial contribution to the war effort.[20]

From Asia came news on 15 August of a Japanese ultimatum to surrender Tsingtau, Tirpitz's one contribution to Weltpolitik. The Emperor ordered that it be defended to the last man. Outnumbered fifteen to one, the German garrison fought bravely until compelled to surrender on 7 November.[21]

On 31 August Tirpitz wrote to Vice Admiral Wilhelm von Lans to argue against piecemeal attacks like the Battle of Helgoland Bight and for a concentration of forces to seek a decisive battle in the North Sea, even if further out from Helgoland. In a passage omitted from his published documents, Tirpitz justified aggressive use of the fleet with the assertion, reeking of *Ressorteifer,* that the navy had to contribute to the war effort if it were to get its future share of money in competition with the army. The navy would not need a victory; it would be enough to have fought gloriously, because then "the opinion would prevail that we must have a fleet as strong as England's."[22] This statement curiously echoes both the absurdly aggressive operations plans of the 1890s and the October 1918 plan for a fleet death ride. Commenting on a similar letter from Tirpitz to Pohl on 16 September 1914, Salewski has called it "a blatant expression of a politically blind, morally regrettable *Ressort* egoism that had as its goal not the welfare of the whole, but his own self-interest."[23]

OPERATIONS: 1914–SPRING 1915

The question of "what to do if they do not come" came to the fore after the disaster of Helgoland Bight. The British immediately seized control of the sea lanes, secured their own communications, and cut Germany's underwater cables, which forced the Germans to rely on wireless. The German Asiatic Squadron, under Rear Admiral Maximilian von Spee, was harried across the Pacific. Spee defeated a valiant but obsolete British squadron off the west coast of South America on 1 November. An enraged Churchill trumped Spee's victory by the dispatch to the South Atlantic of two Dreadnought battlecruisers. With some luck, they methodically destroyed Spee's force off the Falklands at the beginning of December. German raiders, most notably the spectacular *Emden,* were hunted down.[24]

The German merchant fleet, except in the Baltic, was either captured or interned in neutral ports. Eight BEF divisions successfully crossed to France without incident. The enormous British merchant marine continued to deliver food and raw materials. Seaborne commerce, the lifeblood of the British Empire, flowed worldwide, subject to only minor harassment.

Arguably the Imperial Navy's most significant contribution in the entire war occurred in the Mediterranean. At the outbreak of the war the battlecruiser *Goeben* and the light cruiser *Breslau,* under the command of Rear Admiral Wilhelm Souchon, were at the Austrian base of Pola in the Adriatic.[25] Instead of heading west for home, likely a suicide mission, Pohl and Tirpitz, without the Emperor's knowledge, flummoxed the British and French with an order to Souchon to head for Constantinople.[26] On 11 August Souchon arrived at the Dardanelles with the Royal Navy in pursuit. A week earlier, to the outrage of the Turks, Churchill had confiscated two almost completed Turkish Dreadnoughts from British yards and integrated them into the British fleet. *Goeben* and *Breslau* were "sold" to the Turks, and Souchon subsequently became commander of the Turkish fleet. The German sailor exchanged his cap for a fez. In response, the British had to station two Dreadnoughts in the Aegean. Tirpitz was exultant.[27] Later in October Souchon exceeded the orders of the Germanophile Turkish government and sailed from the Bosphorus to attack Sevastopol. On 31 October Russia declared war on the Ottoman Empire. The British followed suit a few days later. For the price of two ships, Germany had closed off Russian access to the Mediterranean, added an important ally, and vastly complicated the strategic problems of the Entente.

In the North Sea the submarine bogie first appeared on 5 September, when U-21 sank a small cruiser. More spectacular, on 22 September, the old U-9 sank three British armored cruisers off the Dutch coast.[28] Jellicoe was so spooked that he secretly withdrew the Grand Fleet to the Irish northern coast while the defenses of Scapa Flow were strengthened. Purely by chance, the new Dreadnought *Audacious* struck a German mine off Lough Swilly and sank on 27 October.

A British coup in the autumn of 1914 was the acquisition, partly by luck and partly by design, of the main German naval codebooks. The most important of these came from the Russians, who salvaged the signal book from the light cruiser *Magdeburg* that had run aground in the

Gulf of Finland. Bureaucratic inefficiency in the Admiralty meant that this windfall was not used to full effect; however, by late 1914 the British usually had ready access, for example, to the crucial information of when the High Seas Fleet sallied from the Jade.[29] German ignorance (until 1917) of this security breach had far-reaching consequences for the war in the North Sea.

Lack of similar intelligence for the German side encouraged passivity.[30] At the start of the war Britain had about a 3:2 advantage in Dreadnoughts. For a period late in 1914 detachments, a few collisions, and normal maintenance needs, along with the loss of *Audacious*, whittled down British superiority in Dreadnoughts to 17:15, and to 5:4 in battlecruisers, although, of course, the Germans were not fully aware of the situation.

They decided to stick to the Kleinkrieg strategy and avoid a sortie of the fleet. One gambit that might lure the Grand Fleet near Helgoland was a "tip and run" raid on the British coast. On 3 November, partly for morale reasons, Ingenohl sent Hipper and the battlecruisers to bombard and mine Yarmouth, while the rest of the fleet lingered at sea near Helgoland. The main result of the raid was to enrage British opinion because of civilian casualties. The raid accomplished nothing significant.[31]

With an idea that eerily foreshadowed the demise of the *Bismarck* in 1941, on 12 November Hipper proposed to send the battlecruisers via the Shetlands into the Atlantic[32] to wreak havoc on British trade. Despite some imaginative but unrealistic ideas to solve the insuperable coaling problem, the potentially suicidal raid was never attempted. Some of the rationale for the raid was vintage Tirpitz: "Carrying out a cruiser war with the battlecruisers in the Atlantic remains the one way in which our High Sea fighting force can damage the enemy and thereby justify their existence."

William II was first elated by Spee's victory at Coronel but then thirsty for revenge after his defeat in the Falklands, so he approved a second raid. Ingenohl agreed, partly for psychological and morale reasons, and partly because he knew that two British battlecruisers were in the South Atlantic. He accepted Hipper's plan to raid Scarborough and Hartlepool. The strategic purpose was to lure the Grand Fleet south across newly laid minefields and onto a U-boat screen. Wireless intercepts tipped off the British that the four German battlecruisers and the weaker armored cruiser *Blücher* were coming out. Intercepts did not reveal that, this time,

Ingenohl was behind Hipper as close as the south end of Dogger Bank. Ingenohl did not tell William II how far out to sea the battlefleet was going, lest he forbid it.[33]

The ensuing engagement was one of the great might-have-beens of the war. Beatty's battlecruisers, plus six of the most modern Dreadnoughts under Vice Admiral Sir George Warrendon, lay in wait to pounce on Hipper on his return voyage. The Admiralty had refused permission to send out the whole fleet. Fourteen German Dreadnoughts and eight pre-Dreadnoughts were about thirty nautical miles from the planned British rendezvous on the southeast corner of Dogger Bank. When Ingenohl's light forces clashed with Warrendon's, the former mistakenly believed that the whole Grand Fleet was out. Ingenohl, unknowingly, had the great opportunity to attack part of it with his entire fleet, a lucky break that German admirals had dreamed of. This might have been the "partial success" that would have equalized the two great fleets. Instead, Ingenohl, while acting beyond the Emperor's orders, chose not to risk fighting the whole Grand Fleet. It would have taken a far more daring, imaginative, and, indeed, insubordinate admiral than Ingenohl to take such a risk. By turning toward home, he left Hipper to face Beatty's whole battlecruiser fleet. This, in turn, was the great opportunity the British had long sought; however, a combination of sloppy signaling and bad weather allowed the nimble Hipper to slip away. Both sides were disappointed at opportunities lost. It would be hard to find a better example of the "fog of war."

The last great surface engagement of the early phase of the war came on 24 January 1915. Hipper hoped he might ambush British light forces at the Dogger Bank. This time the Emperor refused to let the main fleet sail beyond waters near Helgoland. Ingenohl took the calculated risk of allowing Hipper's three battlecruisers plus *Blücher* (*Von der Tann* was under repair) to sail without the High Seas Fleet. Once again the Admiralty knew of the raid. Luckily for Hipper, the Admiralty again bungled its order to Jellicoe so that the Grand Fleet was slow off the mark and was 140 miles away when Beatty jumped Hipper. Even with overwhelming superiority, Beatty's orders and signaling were botched again. *Blücher*, at the rear of Hipper's line as he turned south, took a tremendous pounding and finally sank. Good German gunnery severely damaged Beatty's flagship. Because of the ensuing confusion in the British command, Hipper once more slipped the noose.[34] The sinking of only *Blücher* was a disappointment for the Admiralty.

Arthur Marder has argued that the Germans had one great asset that they never used properly. Instead of using Zeppelins for bombing, these craft should have been employed far more vigorously for fleet reconnaissance:

> The German naval authorities sadly mismanaged this scouting force. True, these craft were of no use in misty weather, but on fine days they were incomparable for scouting, as they could see everything that was afloat in the North Sea. Given good visibility, the German Fleet or units of it could put to sea in the hope of meeting weaker British forces without the slightest fear of running into stronger forces, if the Zeppelins were on patrol. Had the Germans used the Zeppelins for what they were intended—naval scouts—the war might have taken an interesting turn.[35]

TIRPITZ IN THE FALL OF 1914

By mid-September 1914 the Schlieffen Plan, although it had made great tactical gains, had not achieved its strategic goal, namely, the defeat of the French Army and the BEF. The news from the east was as good as that from the west was bad. The partnership of Generals Paul von Hindenburg and Erich Ludendorff had decisively turned back the Russians in two battles in East Prussia.[36] Moltke, a broken man, resigned and was replaced by Erich von Falkenhayn as Chief of the General Staff. General Headquarters (GHQ), which included Tirpitz, Müller, and Pohl for the navy, joined the Emperor's entourage.[37]

Tirpitz tried to make the most of his influence at GHQ. He pushed Pohl, and the Emperor when he had access to him, to use the fleet more aggressively, although William II found him more annoying than persuasive. Tirpitz frequently succumbed to pessimism about how the war was going.[38] On 24 October he visited Ingenohl on his flagship in Wilhelmhaven and got the impression that the Fleet Chief might not have the leadership qualities needed in the navy's difficult situation.[39] Tirpitz's dissatisfaction with Ingenohl may well have been related to Tirpitz's own ambitions to change the navy's command structure more in his own favor. Müller believed that Tirpitz, despite his agreement that Pohl was less suited to be Fleet Chief than Ingenohl,[40] was thinking of pushing Pohl out of GHQ by having him replace Ingenohl. Tirpitz would then seek Pohl's place as Chief of the Admiralstab while retaining control of the RMA.[41]

Tirpitz still fantasized about taking over the whole naval war. He told Hopmann that he had thought about asking the Emperor to give him the fleet but realized that, given his age (sixty-six) and physical condition, and "since he had been away from the Front for seventeen years, he no longer had full mastery of the skills a fleet leader needs."[42]

On 10 November Tirpitz met with General Hans von Plessen, Chief of the GHQ, to complain about the navy's command situation. Plessen noted in his diary: "Tirpitz told me in confidence that he wants to replace Ingenohl as Chief of the High Seas Fleet and himself become Chief of the Admiralstab."[43] According to Hopmann, Plessen told Tirpitz that, if the question came up, he would advise the Emperor against giving Tirpitz command of the fleet, partly because he felt that Tirpitz was an indispensable adviser to the Emperor at GHQ. Somehow Tirpitz got the impression that Plessen considered him a possible candidate for Chancellor. Whether this was vanity or a misunderstanding is not clear. After the war the claim was made that Plessen had offered to go to William II and propose Tirpitz for fleet command but that Tirpitz had declined because he was too old.[44] Plessen told the same story to Michaelis after the war. Müller claimed on 15 July 1915, in a letter to Trotha, that on 16 November 1914 he had asked Tirpitz if he would be prepared to take over the High Seas Fleet from Ingenohl. Müller purportedly told Tirpitz that he thought the Emperor would agree but that Tirpitz had declined for reasons of health.[45] To compound the confusion, after the war William II claimed in a private interview that he had offered the fleet to Tirpitz.[46]

Perhaps Michaelis got it right when he asked the opinion of Captain Waldemar Vollerthun, who knew Tirpitz well but was not uncritical of him. Vollerthun found Plessen's story plausible. He believed that Tirpitz had not wanted to be Fleet Chief but did want to lead the naval war. Tirpitz, he said, had an idiosyncratic tendency not to express himself completely, but he wanted to be asked. This tendency may have hindered him from expressing his real views.[47] This odd combination of aggressiveness and reticence was characteristic of Tirpitz's later years.

The idea of Bethmann and the Emperor that the fleet should be preserved as a possible object of compensation for a separate peace with Britain made Tirpitz increasingly frustrated. In a letter to his retired friend

Ahlefeld, he blamed the war on the "mistaken" policy of Bethmann in seeking an "entente" with the British. Inept wartime leadership of the navy he attributed to the "Cabinet" government that Clausewitz and Boyen, the great Prussian reformers, had decried during the Napoleonic War.[48] In a conversation with Falkenhayn, on 15 November, Tirpitz suggested the possibility of a separate peace with Russia.[49] He proposed an agreement based on the status quo ante bellum between Russia, Austria, and Turkey. Falkenhayn did not see it as much of a possibility. He shared with Tirpitz a lack of optimism about the war situation, particularly because of the situation in the west. From the beginning he had not wanted war with Russia, and the idea of a separate peace with Russia was one he returned to on later occasions. It is hard to see how he, or anyone, could have persuaded ardent annexationists to accept such a policy.

By the turn of 1915 Tirpitz was very discouraged about his situation. He wrote to Marie on 2 January 1915:

> The bastion around the Kaiser is at present more than ever impenetrable. . . . [William II] is reported to have said to Müller several times: "Now the fleet must really do something," but he cannot be induced to resolve what it is to do, and he simply evades me when I tackle and harangue him, which I never lose an opportunity of doing.[50]

Destiny intervened on 24 January 1915 in the form of the Battle of Dogger Bank and the sinking of *Blücher*. This was the last straw for Ingenohl. On 2 February Pohl replaced him as Fleet Commander. The change was a sign that Tirpitz still had some influence, since "little man" Pohl was no longer an obstacle at GHQ; however, Müller refused Tirpitz's request to remove Hipper. As a consolation prize for Tirpitz, the Emperor and Müller appointed Vice Admiral Gustav Bachmann as Pohl's replacement. Bachmann had served under Tirpitz in the Torpedo Arm, the OK, and the RMA. Müller saw Bachmann as calm and experienced but not particularly strong. He lamented that the crop of senior admirals was not blessed with "natural" leaders.[51] One of Bachmann's first acts was to ask Müller to propose Tirpitz as Supreme Commander of the navy. Müller brusquely refused.[52]

Tirpitz, on 25 January, wrote a curious letter to Müller, "which I must say, surprised me in the light of his former utterances." Despite meager results in whittling down British superiority, Tirpitz thought it was still worthwhile to push for further successes through "minor victories."

Surprising to Müller was Tirpitz's advocacy of airship raids on the City
of London, a submarine blockade sensitive to political considerations,
aggressive submarine and destroyer raids from Flanders, and, most astonishing, "the immediate launch of a cruiser war in the Atlantic."[53] Hipper
had previously proposed this idea,[54] but Tirpitz had always dismissed
such Kleinkrieg measures because of tremendous logistical problems,
especially coal supply in a hostile Atlantic. There is no evidence that
Müller carried the suggestion any further.

Pohl's final act as Chief of the Admiralstab was to proclaim an un-
limited submarine war on commerce. Although Tirpitz favored the idea
in principle, both he and Müller were enraged. Müller saw it as an act of
"pirate bravado" at the start of Pohl's new post as Fleet Chief. Pohl had
sold the idea behind his back to the Emperor and the Chancellor. Tirpitz
was angry not just because he was left out of the decision but also because
he had the sensible objection that Germany did not yet have enough U-
boats, trained crewmen, or bases.[55] Tirpitz was also afraid of the effect
of the proclamation on neutrals in a situation where Germany did not
yet have the means to enforce a real blockade. To put the question of a
blockade in context, we must first examine international law and practice
regarding a commercial blockade.

ECONOMIC BLOCKADE AT THE OUTBREAK OF WAR

If the almost universal expectation of a short, decisive land war did not
come to pass, economic blockade would play an increasing role in the
war. Even the British, with the exception of Lord Kitchener, thought that
the war would not last more than six to eight months. In the unlikely
event that an economic blockade was required, the governing principle
of wartime maritime law in 1914 was the Declaration of Paris of 1856.

As summarized by Avner Offer, the main points of the Declaration
were the following:

1. Trade of neutrals should be immune from belligerent capture or
   interference during wartime.
2. Enemy goods transported in neutral ships were immune from
   seizure.
3. Cargoes that belonged to neutrals could not be seized, even if
   captured in enemy ships.

4. A qualification on these points was that neutral immunity did not extend to "contraband."[56]

In a kind of grand bargain, stronger belligerents agreed to respect the immunity of neutral commerce. In exchange, their merchant fleets were given a measure of protection by the abolition of privateering by weaker belligerents. If, in wartime, the stronger belligerent reverted to full belligerent rights, such as the doctrine of continuous voyage (i.e., interdiction of neutral vessels whose cargo was ultimately destined for enemy ports), this was expected to provoke protests from neutrals, the most powerful of which was the United States.[57]

The Declaration did not define "contraband" but divided it into two categories: "absolute contraband" comprised goods only useful for war, such as munitions and uniforms; "conditional contraband" was material useful in either peace or war, and could only be seized if it was clearly intended for an enemy port. Conditional contraband might include food or raw materials, but the category was not clearly defined. For the British, who imported almost two-thirds of their food, and the Germans, who imported one-fifth, and an even higher proportion of protein and fats, whether food for belligerents could be considered conditional contraband was a critical question. For both moral and humanitarian reasons, there was a strong case for the exemption of food.

As German naval power grew, the British Admiralty's Intelligence and Trade Divisions in 1905 began to think ahead about economic warfare in the event of war with Germany. A blockade would surely banish the burgeoning German merchant marine from the high seas, but the Admiralty confidentially admitted that, unless indirect shipments to Germany via neutral ships and ports could be seized, an economic blockade would have significant, but limited, impact.[58] Measures considered, all of them illegal, included, among others, a huge contraband list, including food and raw materials; an unprecedented expansion that included neutral ships with neutral cargoes in trade with neutral ports; a paper (i.e., distant) blockade with no legal status; and a declaration of the entire North Sea as a "military zone" with extensive mining. This proposal contradicted British policy on maritime law during the Russo-Japanese War and also at The Hague (1907)[59] and London (1909) Conferences. The latter established a long free list and exempted food for non-soldiers, prohibited blockade of neutral harbors, forbade belligerents to seize conditional contraband by invoking the doctrine of continuous voyage, and considered only an effective (i.e., close) blockade to be legal.[60]

Amazingly the Admiralty, despite its tentative secret plans, accepted the Declaration of London and its support of neutral trade. Strachan concludes, correctly, that "the only rationalization of the Admiralty's, and of Fisher's, position is hard-headed cynicism: that in the event of being at war, the declaration would be neglected; in the event of neutrality, it would be enforced." Surprisingly again, in the half-decade before the war, the Admiralty stopped planning for an economic war. The exception to this neglect was Maurice Hankey. In the years immediately before the war he was the civil servant secretary of the Committee of Imperial Defence and kept alive the idea of economic warfare.[61]

Only if Britain came into the war *and* if the Schlieffen Plan failed to deliver a quick victory on the continent would Germany face a two-front defensive war and be in a situation where an economic blockade mattered very much. It is necessary to examine the plans Germany prepared to deal with this double contingency, even though it was almost universally believed to be unlikely. Of Imperial Germany's post-Bismarckian Chancellors, the only one who had given serious thought to a blockade and its consequences, albeit in different circumstances, was Leo von Caprivi (1890–94), who worried about a two-front war and the problem of feeding the population.[62] Even Caprivi did not anticipate war with Britain. Tirpitz was one of the few prominent people to publicize the danger of a blockade, but he only used the threat as yet another propaganda tool to build more battleships.[63] The civil service paid little attention to the question of food and even less to potential raw material shortages. Measures such as stockpiling would have brought up complicated issues of politics, federalism, and, above all, money at a time when the Reich's financial situation was under great strain. Also, even the crudest agricultural statistics were lacking.

A few academics and businessmen raised their concerns of a food shortage, but they were ignored. In 1907, in preparation for the Second Hague Conference, the RMA conducted a study that Offer considers "shrewd."[64] Tirpitz noted the importance of neutral ports, especially in Belgium and the Netherlands, and pointed out that if food and raw materials were classified as contraband, even access to neutral ports could not circumvent a British blockade. He correctly observed that a blockade would only begin to pinch after about eighteen months. Even if grain from the east was available, railroads could not carry enough to replace seaborne imports. Despite these insights, he opposed immunity for private property at sea.[65] He took this position because he (rightly as it turned out) did not trust that the British would obey the rules. He wanted to be free to wage commerce war against Britain; to argue otherwise would undermine one of the principal rationales for building a large fleet. In preparation for the 1907 Hague Conference, Tirpitz, against Foreign Office advice, had persuaded the Emperor to retain the right of capture.[66] Although some discussions took place on the food question at the Prussian War Ministry, the General Staff, and the Reich Ministry of the Interior, very little was done. The latter had the peacetime responsibility for such preparations, but the task was marginal to its mission, and so the Interior Ministry virtually ignored it. When it did propose minor measures, the Reich Treasury stymied them.

Another obstacle, which was partly a consequence of the army's organizational behavior, was that stockpiling grain, let alone raw materials, would be an admission that a long war was possible. To posit a possible failure of the Schlieffen Plan would be tantamount to defeatism. Because of the immense cost to amass and store the necessarily huge quantity of grain, a cost the Imperial Treasury would not countenance, Offer expressed the dilemma as follows: "For a short war stockpiling was unnecessary. For a long war it was impossible."[67] As a result, Germany went to war with no coherent plan to counter an economic blockade.

Once Britain entered the war and the Schlieffen Plan failed to produce a quick victory, the key economic question for Germany was whether Britain would observe the limits on belligerent rights as outlined in the Paris and London Treaties; and, if they did not, would neutrals, especially the United States, act to enforce what Hobson has characterized as the maritime "balance of power"?[68]

As early as 12 August 1914 Grey proposed a formal blockade of the German North Sea coast.[69] The Admiralty gagged at this idea because a distant blockade could not keep neutral ships from entering German ports, and a close blockade would, in view of mines and torpedoes, be too dangerous. Despite reluctance on the part of the Admiralty and some Cabinet members, Churchill, Grey, and Asquith persuaded the Cabinet to invoke the principle of continuous voyage and apply it to food as conditional contraband, even though a blockade was never formally declared. In an Order in Council of 20 August 1914 the highly dubious legality of this decision was ignored in the vague hope that the interception of food imports might help defeat Germany. The decision violated the agreements reached in Paris and London, and even Prize Court Proceedings under British law. At war supposedly to save neutral Belgium, the British, on 25 August, threatened the neutral Dutch with starvation unless they limited food imports to peacetime levels. As casualty lists grew and the outcome of the war seemed uncertain, such British ruthlessness won popular support at home. Direct shipments of food and oil to Rotterdam were interdicted. Given the immensity of Britain's seapower, it had the resources to enforce such a cavalier treatment of maritime law.

European neutrals protested loudly but to no avail. Only one country, the United States, had enough naval and economic power to make its protests heard in Britain. The decision rested squarely on the shoulders of President Woodrow Wilson, even though the State Department told him that the blockade was legally indefensible. The instinctively Anglophile President struggled with the need to preserve the appearance of neutrality because, as Coogan and Hobson have pointed out, he saw Germany, like the France of Napoleon, as a hegemonic power. As an historian he saw America's entrance into the War of 1812 as a mistake for that reason. The need to appear neutral prevented him from dealing with the dilemma candidly and publicly. The "compromise" his diplomats negotiated, accepting raw materials such as copper and oil as contraband, plus a Dutch assurance not to re-export food to Germany, amounted to a capitulation to the British in all but name. Even this deal did not satisfy the British, who insisted on retaining their future freedom of action and issued a revised Order in Council to that effect on 29 October. By the end of October 1914 Wilson had persuaded himself and the American people that the United States was neutral; by international law, however, American behavior was in no way neutral. Instead, the United States had become "a partner, and not always a silent partner in the allied campaign to strangle Germany."[70] On 3 November the Admiralty declared the entire North Sea a military zone and strewed it with mines. To be directed through the minefields, neutral ships had to call at British ports and, in effect, be subject to British jurisdiction. The United States protested in individual cases but did not challenge the policy even as it became ever more stringent.

Even though they did not use the word "blockade," the British put increasing pressure on neutrals that bordered Germany by land and sea. They were prevented from re-exporting their imports to Germany. Imports of strategic materials were rationed so as not to exceed normal peacetime domestic needs. Gradually, but inexorably, commodities such as oil, metals, nitrates, and eventually food became much harder for Germany to find on international markets.[71]

ORIGINS OF THE GERMAN U-BOAT WAR

At the beginning of the war the U-boat was seen by all navies as an auxiliary to the battlefleet, not as a weapon in its own right. During the war's first six months German U-boats had impressive success against British warships, though they never sank a Dreadnought. Besides U-9's famous sinking of three armored cruisers, other boats sank a Russian armored cruiser, a British pre-Dreadnought and a seaplane tender, along with some smaller ships.[72] It seemed obvious to extend the submarine war to attacks on merchantmen, but there were significant technological and legal difficulties. Against warships, however, there were no restrictions.

The submarines of that era were hybrids in their propulsion systems. Above water they ran on diesel engines, but when submerged, they had battery motors which needed frequent recharging by the diesels on the surface. Batteries could power them only for a few hours and only at slow speeds. On the surface U-boats were helpless either against warships or even armed merchantmen. One near miss with a relatively small artillery piece could sink them, not to mention the risk of ramming. Early in 1915 only twenty-nine U-boats were available. Most had four torpedo tubes—two fore and two aft—and carried only six torpedoes. Not until May 1915 did all the U-boats have deck guns, and fourteen were dangerous petrol boats, suitable only for short missions. Construction was so slow that by the end of 1915 only fifty-nine boats were available. For reasons of fuel and the endurance of the crews, even the most modern boats could stay at sea only about three weeks.[73] The greatest military effect of the U-boat was more psychological than material. For a while, in 1914, the Grand Fleet was withdrawn from Scapa Flow to Northern Ireland. Submarines were too slow to operate in formation with battlefleets, and, although the British underestimated the point, they had only a small chance of hitting a warship moving at speed. Mines were a much greater threat to battleships than were U-boats. International law, over centuries, had developed rules that applied to the conduct of commerce war, but the rules were designed for surface raiders. For example, an enemy merchantman could only be legally sunk with the crew aboard if it tried to escape warning shots. If it stopped, either the cruiser would send a prize crew aboard, take the ship's crew prisoner, and sail it to a friendly or neutral port; or, if the ship were to be sunk, the crew had to be allowed to board lifeboats. If a neutral ship were stopped, it had to be searched for contraband. If it carried none, it had to be released. Following rules designed for surface raiders was extremely difficult for U-boats. Their crews were too small to allow them to take prizes, and there was no room aboard to rescue merchant crews. To sink a ship without warning was against international law and was thought to be barbaric. U-boats had difficulty determining whether a merchant ship was the enemy or neutral, and, moreover, an enemy ship could (illegally) fly a neutral flag. Restrictions on engagement made commerce raiding both clumsy and dangerous for the U-boat.

Tirpitz's attitude toward submarines had changed since the prewar years when he had objected to their participation in fleet maneuvers. He had gradually raised the budget for them since 1906, but the sum of 15 million marks for the 1914 estimates was only a tiny portion of the overall budget. His objection, based on experience from his torpedo years, was that, until diesel engines were developed for U-boats, a slow approach was best so as not to invest in obsolete technology. As early as 8 August 1914 Tirpitz had informed Pohl of his objections to U-boat warfare.[74]

By November 1914 it was clear that Britain, with American connivance, would run roughshod over international law with a technically illegal blockade. Tirpitz soon became more sympathetic to the use of U-boats in commerce war. On 7 November Pohl gave Bethmann a draft declaring a blockade of the coasts and harbors of Great Britain and Ireland. Neutral ships that approached British ports would be made aware of the danger of sinking without warning. Neutral ships heading for neutral ports would be advised to stay well away from the British coast. Pohl wanted to make the announcement before the end of November.[75] Tirpitz argued sensibly, however, that because a submarine blockade was unprecedented, new questions would emerge about international law still based on rules from the age of sail. Germany should not declare a blockade until there were enough U-boats to enforce it; otherwise the threat could look hollow, a transparent bluff. He suggested, as an alternative, that Admiral Schröder in Flanders declare a blockade of the mouth of the Thames. This would be plausibly enforceable and would not commit the Emperor and the government to a broad and unenforceable blockade. Such a small blockade would also avoid political trouble with American passenger liners, all of which docked at Liverpool.[76] Problems could be dealt with as they arose, and practices could be refined over time. This idea is reminiscent of the solid, methodical Tirpitz of the torpedo years. He dismissed, as even worse politically, Pohl's rejoinder of 15 December suggesting a commerce war without the declaration of a blockade.[77]

In what was perhaps a misguided attempt to reap sympathy in the United States, Tirpitz, at Erzberger's suggestion,[78] granted an interview on 21 November with Karl Henry von Wiegand, a German-born American journalist and war correspondent for the Hearst newspaper chain. Raffael Scheck believes that Tirpitz was testing the American reaction to the prospect of unrestricted submarine warfare.[79] The most controversial part of the interview was that, when asked if Germany was contemplating such a measure, Tirpitz replied: "If pressed to the limit, why not?"[80] After a half-hearted vetting by a junior official in the Foreign Office, permission was granted to publish the interview and it appeared in the American press a few days before Christmas. Contrary to what he had told Pohl a few weeks previously, Tirpitz claimed that Germany had a sufficient number of U-boats to enforce such a blockade. Also provocative was von Wiegand's speculation that Tirpitz was the strongest man in the German government, and possibly the future Chancellor. When published in Germany, the article roused popular enthusiasm but angered Pohl, who saw it as meddling in his sphere as Chief of the Admiralstab as well as a public disclosure of a top-secret contingency still in the planning stage.[81] It is hard to discern what Tirpitz wanted to achieve from this interview. As late as 25 January 1915 he supported a more restrained and nuanced version of commerce warfare than did Pohl. In early January Bethmann found himself in the unaccustomed company of Tirpitz regarding the delay of a U-boat war,[82] but by early February he had changed his mind, influenced by popular pressure and the Emperor's desire.

Once the proclamation on submarine warfare was issued on 4 February, Tirpitz supported it, reluctantly abandoning his more nuanced approach. Müller, too, had misgivings.[83] Tirpitz finally and unreservedly supported unrestricted submarine warfare. He soon became an advocate of assertive diplomacy toward the United States, on the theory that it would deter the U.S. from war. To that end he argued that the remaining restrictions on U-boat warfare be dropped.[84] Tirpitz, with firm resolve, pressed the Chancellor to take a hard line against American protests over the U-boat policy and for declaring the coasts of Britain and France as a war zone.[85]

The addition of five newly completed Dreadnoughts to the Grand Fleet by early February diminished the chances of even a partial victory in the surface war. The passivity of the fleet had a deadening effect on morale in the naval officer corps. Hopmann was a good example:

> When I received my promotion to rear admiral, privately I had not the slightest satisfaction. What does it mean for me. I can no longer believe in the future of our fleet. Under Pohl, even less will be done than under Ingenohl.

On the same day, Tirpitz went for a walk with Hopmann and gave vent to his pessimism:[86]

> To some degree, only a dictator can save us. Hindenburg must become Chancellor. . . . [Tirpitz] said openly that the Emperor must be pressed to the wall, and eventually the Crown Prince must be called upon.

On 27 March, Tirpitz wrote to Marie:

> I see only one way out: the Kaiser must say that he is on the sick list for eight weeks or more, Hindenburg must come and take Bethmann's place, and both the army and the Admiralty should be directed by him *and* the Emperor.[87]

As the nation faced its greatest crisis, the eccentricities and weaknesses of William II, tolerable in peacetime, began to tear at even committed monarchists like Tirpitz. As the Emperor said to Bachmann, "He did not want to lose his beautiful fleet to mines and U-boats."[88] To the Emperor the fleet was the same toy it had been from the beginning. Tirpitz wrestled with the dilemma of what to do. As Epkenhans has pointed out, others high in the Reich had similar private misgivings.[89] To add to Tirpitz's woes, on 16 April Hopmann departed for Kiel to assume command of the reconnaissance force for the Baltic fleet.[90]

In the spring of 1915 Pohl took the fleet out on a few timid probes that came to nothing. On 14 May Tirpitz met with Pohl and his Chief of

Staff Michaelis in Wilhelmshaven. The content of the conversation was so surprising that Michaelis remembered it clearly:[91]

> People say that I [Tirpitz] want the fleet to attack *coûte qui cout* [at all costs]. I have no thought of doing this. I am certainly not stupid enough to want this. Not once did I consider it correct to drive our fleet to the English coast. We must strike within 50 miles of Helgoland in order to use all the ships, including the *Siegfrieds* and the guns of Helgoland. You want to strike 100 miles from Helgoland. To me this is too far, but I will not contest you over these numbers.

He proposed a startling plan to Pohl by which individual groups of ships, in order of their speed (fastest first), would sail about fifty miles northwest of Helgoland. They would be distributed over the North Sea, battlecruisers in the lead. The British would attack with the Grand Fleet. The battlecruisers would retreat onto the III (strongest) Squadron of the High Seas Fleet, and then onto the rest of the fleet, including the *Siegfrieds*, and draw them under the guns of Helgoland.

Not surprisingly Pohl rejected this bizarre plan as a "practical impossibility" and an "irresponsible division of our forces." This proposal, using tactics reminiscent of the 1890s, reveals how very out of touch Tirpitz was with the realities of war in 1915. How, for example, could the British, despite all wartime experience, be persuaded to go so close to Helgoland when the High Seas Fleet was out? Even to think that the obsolete *Siegfried* class of coastal battleships could be of any use at all shows how old-fashioned Tirpitz's idea was. There could be no better proof than this plan that Tirpitz was unfit to be Fleet Chief, let alone Supreme Commander of the navy. There is something pathetic as well as arrogant about the old lion coming up with this absurd idea.

In the summer of 1915 came the first rumblings of open discontent with both the ongoing conduct of the naval war and with Tirpitz's strategic framework for it. The ostensible source of the revisionist view was Vice Admiral Wilhelm von Lans, who had been forced to retire in February 1915 from his command of the First Squadron of the High Seas Fleet. Tirpitz had urged the departure of Lans, an old adversary.[92] Lans signed off on the document, "Reflections on Our Maritime Situation," and it quickly became known throughout the navy as the "First Squadron Memorandum." The real author was a thirty-nine-year-old Lieutenant Commander, Wolfgang Wegener, an Admiralty Staff Officer who had worked under Lans.[93]

The memo described German ships as "inferior," especially in gun caliber, and argued that the best elements of the fleet should concentrate in the Baltic rather than the North Sea. Sorties there were undertaken just to have "something to do," the memo stated, putting the fleet at serious risk of annihilation for no purpose. Such ventures, therefore, should be terminated. Controlling the Baltic with superior ships would ensure supply lines in the Baltic, leaving the older ships for coastal defense in the North Sea. Wegener mentioned Germany's disadvantageous geographic position in the North Sea but did not elaborate.

Over the next seven months Wegener wrote three more memoranda, "Thoughts about Our Maritime Situation" (June 1915), "Can We Improve Our Situation?" (July 1915), and "Naval Bases, Policy, and Fleet" (August 1915)."[94] The geographic and strategic scope of his suggestions was sweeping. He argued that the Helgoland Bight was a dead end, far from the exits of the North Sea and the trade routes beyond. Wegener recognized that battle at sea was not, in itself, decisive. The key goal was to attain command of the sea, which Wegener identified as having dominance over the principal trade routes. Since these were already under British control, there was no point to court battle in the North Sea except under very favorable circumstances.[95] The bold first step would be to occupy Denmark to open the Belts, and establish bases in Jutland to gain control of the Kattegat and Skaggerak. Wegener even speculated on an occupation of the Faroe Islands and basing the fleet in Norwegian fjords. To further outflank the British Isles, he advocated the seizure of Cherbourg, and maybe Brest. His fantasies extended to bases in the Azores. Implicitly such grandiose ambitions would require a gigantic and unrealistic fleet expansion. The memoranda combined a sober and correct assessment of Germany's geographic embarrassment versus Britain, an analysis Tirpitz had never seriously undertaken, with an expansion plan of staggering range that contained within it seeds of the 1940 invasions of Denmark and Norway. Wegener's scheme was a complete repudiation of Tirpitz's essentially defensive strategy. To implement it would have required a fleet far greater than any Tirpitz had ever imagined.

Tirpitz was furious when he heard of Wegener's work. He even commissioned Hopmann and Captain Friedrich Boedicker to draft a refutation, which turned out to be feeble, and told them to ignore Wegener's powerful and compelling geographic analysis. Scholars have failed to

find any contemporary response by Tirpitz, but after the war he termed
Wegener's notions "poison for the fleet."[96]

THE FIRST U-BOAT OFFENSIVE

On 18 February 1915, with only a handful of submarines, the German
Navy began its U-boat offensive. Its ostensible purpose was retaliation
for British violations of international law and for the resultant "hunger"
blockade. President Wilson protested even before any ships were sunk. In
London Churchill reacted with glee, openly hoping that American ships
would be sunk and ultimately bring the United States into the war. The
Admiralty, aware of the paucity of German submarines, regarded the
proclamation as a nuisance rather than a real threat.[97]

Wilson tried to mediate between Britain and Germany. On 21 February he proposed that Germany discontinue the U-boat war if Britain
abandoned the blockade of food to be delivered to German ports. On 28
February the Germans accepted. Britain rejected the proposal in desul-
tory fashion on 15 March, but Wilson let the British off with a flaccid
protest.[98]

In March and April sinkings totaled 116,000 tons, and after that they
averaged about 130,000 tons per month. During 1915 six passenger ships
were sunk, killing citizens from neutral countries. The largest and most
famous of these was the British liner *Lusitania* that went down on 7 May
off the southern coast of Ireland with a loss of about 1,200 passengers,
128 Americans among them. Despite that the German Embassy had
published warnings before it sailed, that it had munitions in its cargo, and
that it was listed by the Admiralty as an auxiliary cruiser, the outcry was
enormous, especially in the United States. Even though Americans were
providing credits and munitions to the Entente powers, Germany did not
dare court a war declaration from the United States.[99]

The U-boat offensive was popular among Germans, but Bethmann
feared American intervention and, with Müller's support, persuaded the
Emperor to order the U-boats not to attack any sizable passenger liners,
even if sailing under enemy flags. Commanders were sternly warned
against attacking any ship before discovering it was not neutral. Falkenhayn, also fearful of U.S. intervention, supported Bethmann. Tirpitz
and Bachmann argued that such restrictions would make U-boat warfare

much more difficult and dangerous. They refused to accept responsibility for the policy and submitted their resignations on 6 June. William II refused angrily, insisting they remain.[100]

Mainly omitted from Tirpitz's postwar writings, but unearthed by Scheck, is a meeting Tirpitz had in August 1915 with Hindenburg and Ludendorff at Libau. Tirpitz hoped that the generals would pressure the Emperor to accept Bülow as Chancellor, Hindenburg as head of the army, and Tirpitz himself as chief of the navy. To Tirpitz's satisfaction, the meetings were cordial. Hindenburg and Ludendorff shared his dislike of Bethmann and those around him; but at that time they were mostly miffed at Falkenhayn's refusal to give the Eastern Front a higher priority. They also disagreed with Tirpitz's desire for a moderate peace with Russia.[101]

Tirpitz continued to believe that the majority of the Reichstag, including Conservatives, National Liberals, and the Center, was with him in favor of a more vigorous prosecution of the U-boat war. Despite the Emperor's restrictions, matters came to a head with the U-24's sinking of the mixed freighter/liner *Arabic* off the southern coast of Ireland. Though it flew no flag, it was a British ship of the White Star line. Eight passengers drowned, among them three Americans.[102]

After *Arabic*, Tirpitz wanted to head off further German concessions in the U-boat war. To avoid conflict with the United States, he proposed to move the U-boats to the Mediterranean to attack commerce and to harry Entente efforts in the Dardanelles, in the hope that their removal from the British Isles would be enough to satisfy the Americans. The Emperor refused.[103] As Bachmann put it to Tirpitz, "The orders remain the same. We are not permitted to irritate [*reizen*] Uncle Sam."[104] Bethmann also ignored Tirpitz's idea and did not consult him when he agreed to more restrictions. Once again, on 27 August, both Tirpitz and Bachmann offered their resignations.[105] Bachmann's was accepted, but the Emperor angrily refused Tirpitz's resignation. He ordered him to stay in office during the national crisis, but he removed him from his theoretical advisory role. For Tirpitz, that the Emperor had expressly forbidden him to resign again seemed like the crowning humiliation. The British press had a field day with the Germans backing down under American pressure. The *Daily Mail*, on 28 August, reprised the famous 1890 Punch cartoon "Dropping the Pilot," when William II had fired Bismarck, with an article that referred to Tirpitz with the remark "Dropping the Pirate."[106]

Another American protest note arrived on 30 August, resulting, on 18 September, in what amounted to a cancellation of unrestricted U-boat warfare. On 13 September Tirpitz met with William II. Scheck is probably correct that it was on this occasion that the Emperor lost whatever remained of Tirpitz's respect when he said: "If I must kowtow to Wilson, I will."[107] Bachmann's replacement was Tirpitz's old rival Henning von Holtzendorff, called out of retirement partly because he agreed to accept Bethmann's line on the U-boat war.

THE RMA CONTEMPLATES THE FUTURE, 1914–1915

The outbreak of the war weakened the already waning feeling in Germany that its future was on the ocean. The life-and-death struggles of the army in Belgium, France, and Poland, combined with the navy's initial inactivity, reinforced Tirpitz's pessimism for the future of his life's work. He did not worry about being defeated in the war—in 1914 no one thought that possible—but what would happen to the navy in the event of a compromise peace, or even if Germany won a convincing victory?

The RMA, with Capelle effectively in charge, grappled with how to support the war effort. The normal prewar budget negotiations with the parties were no longer really necessary.[108] For the first time the limiting factor was not money; a patriotic Reichstag provided plenty. The army's need to call up reservists threatened to deplete the shipyards of skilled manpower. The prewar priority of keeping a full construction program of new capital ships had to go by the wayside. Only two battlecruisers were added to the fleet after *Derfflinger* in September 1914: *Lützow* in August 1915 and *Hindenburg* in May 1917, the last German Dreadnought to be put into service. The only new battleships to join the fleet after the *König* class in the fall of 1914 were *Bayern* (July 1916) and *Baden* (October 1916), each armed with eight powerful 38-cm guns.[109] They arrived too late, however, to participate in any major battles.

The extraordinary demands of war, which kept ships seaborne far more than in peacetime, escalated the need for maintenance and refits. Lessons learned in the early battles such as the need for even thicker armor in the battlecruisers and the installation of improved range-finding devices on all ships enhanced the demand. Needed, too, was investment in dirigibles, fixed-wing aircraft, mine-laying and minesweeping craft, and replacements for some of the vulnerable and overworked light cruisers and torpedo boats. These competing priorities slowed the rate of U-boat construction. By the time Tirpitz left office in 1916, Germany had only a few dozen oceangoing U-boats.

In Tirpitz's mind the wartime navy had to provide a raison d'être, given the vast resources spent on it. He referred to the danger that, if the navy contributed little, it would get little money from a postwar Reichstag. A large fleet action would, he believed, justify his past efforts and also enhance the navy's future prospects. Even modest success in a great battle would allow a continuation of his grand design after the war. His wartime "hatred for England," manifest in his postwar writings, was a way to justify everything he had done; hence his quest for a "decisive battle" and, later, unrestricted U-boat warfare.

In October 1914 the Chancellor asked Tirpitz's opinion about whether Germany should annex all of Belgium.[110] Tirpitz replied cautiously. He favored annexation of coastal towns to provide bases in the Channel that would threaten Britain; but he also warned that any annexation outside the Flemish parts of Belgium would court trouble. Even so, Tirpitz was cautious about the seizure of the great port of Antwerp, although he saw its economic advantages and believed that taking Antwerp would bring the Netherlands closer to Germany economically. Pohl, too, placed great importance on the occupation of the Flemish and, if possible, the French Channel coast, especially Calais and Boulogne.[111]

In response to Bethmann's request in January 1915 to put his thoughts on paper, Tirpitz replied more definitively.[112] He cited two factors; one was purely military and the other was the effect an annexation would have on Germany's maritime geographical position. The war, he argued, had provided further proof that Germany's position in the southeast corner of the North Sea for an offensive against Britain was extremely unfavorable, an implicit admission that his "Helgoland to the Thames" strategy had not worked. Germany needed a strong base on the Channel. The war presented a one-time opportunity to remedy this disadvantage through the conquest of the Belgian coast. In contrast to his caution of a few months earlier, now he considered the annexation of Antwerp as "urgently desirable." In a more comprehensive memo of October 1915,[113] Tirpitz argued for even wider annexations in Belgium, even though he was well aware that such an action would lead to serious occupation problems.

Dähnhardt, too, had some thoughts on war aims, although it is not clear whether Tirpitz prompted his ideas. Late in 1914 he drafted a thought piece of staggering scope, concerning fleet development after a victorious peace. He proposed a double squadron of battleships in the Mediterranean based in Malta or Cyprus, with additional squadrons based in East and West Africa. He envisioned vast annexations for Germany and the Ottomans.[114] A diligent search in the archives failed to uncover any reaction by Tirpitz to the memo, which was filed away in March 1915, although Holtzendorff resurrected some of its ideas in 1916 and 1917.[115]

THE RETURN OF HOLTZENDORFF

On 5 September 1915 the Emperor called Tirpitz's old adversary, Admiral Henning von Holtzendorff, out of retirement to replace Bachmann as Admiralstab Chief. He got the job not because he was a distant relative of Müller, as some alleged, but rather because he accepted Bethmann's line on the U-boat war. He entered office with the comment, "Believe me gentlemen, you will not scratch the whale's (Britain's) skin with your U-Boat war."[116] Hubatsch has characterized him as "a vigorous spirit, restless and often volatile, personally undemanding, and clever at handling the Emperor."[117] Tirpitz and his allies "feared in Holtzendorff's comeback a danger to themselves—a strong man with good connections." Captain Walter Freiherr von Keyserlingk, noted that the choice between the active admirals was a "sadly limited" (*bedenklich gering*) one.[118] Upon receiving the news Hopmann, in command of the Baltic Fleet's cruisers in Libau, wrote to his wife: "Tirpitz is already at his wake, or at least put out in the cold."[119]

According to Müller, Tirpitz was "foaming with rage" at the news. Only with much difficulty was Tirpitz dissuaded from attempting to resign once again, something the Emperor had only recently forbidden on 30 August. William II was livid upon receiving letters from two of his sons, including the Crown Prince, in favor of Tirpitz's position on the U-boat war and against the appointment of Holtzendorff. Tirpitz's wounded vanity made his anger hard to contain. Müller's strenuous efforts at mediation, encouraged by Löhlein and Erzberger of the Center Party, brought Tirpitz and the Emperor together on 13 September. Tirpitz was in a tense mood, angry with Bethmann and Holtzendorff, and thought it might be his last audience with the Emperor. To avoid any awkwardness in public opinion both at home and abroad, Müller persuaded both men to cool off. Tirpitz accepted the Emperor's assurance that he would be consulted on future naval policies,[120] but he was not optimistic. As he noted to Trotha: "They will naturally try to undermine me further and then, when the moment is right, they will get rid of me."[121]

Another disruptive event for Tirpitz occurred almost at the same time. His deputy, Capelle, reported sick late in August 1915. Though Tirpitz still considered him his designated successor, Capelle, genuinely ill and very tired, insisted on resigning and retiring, but he agreed to carry on until 1 November.[122] Büchsel came out of retirement to assume the position of Under State Secretary.[123] Tirpitz still hoped that Capelle would return. Capelle clearly did not expect to return and saw his position as redundant, given the RMA's reduced workload, much smaller than before the war. He wrote privately to Müller:

> I was very happy that the last great Tirpitz crisis was satisfactorily resolved . . . a departed Tirpitz would be used as a battering ram against the Emperor and the Chancellor. As things stand now, Tirpitz will, and must, stay until peace is concluded.[124]

New Admiralstab Chief Holtzendorff saw Pohl as "a tired Fleet Chief, hemmed in by the fleet operations order and the failure to use U-boats broadly. He could do little in the larger questions due to the Emperor's opinions.[125]

The loyal Bachmann was concerned about Tirpitz's judgment in basing his resignation attempt more on his conflict with Bethmann than on questioning the Emperor's decision to curtail the U-boat war. Bachmann wrote to Trotha: "In my opinion, the State Secretary is a finished [abgetaner] man." "The Chancellor has defeated him and rejoices in his victory." He noted that the British press was already speculating on Tirpitz's departure.[126]

After the resignation attempt blew over, Tirpitz worked on his memo about the necessity of including Belgian harbors among German war aims.[127] Trotha wrote to his wife: "I fear they have only thrown him a bone to keep him occupied."[128]

Büchsel, shortly after replacing Capelle, sized up Tirpitz's position cannily:

Doubtless, as far as I can see, the RMA's influence has weakened over the groups that the State Secretary rightly dominated in peacetime in order to develop the navy, and in such wartime circumstances the RMA's influence would naturally decline; but the greater problem is that the State Secretary's personal influence, especially with His Majesty, is gone.[129]

By early 1915, when the initial euphoria of the Burgfrieden and the prospect of early victory had faded, dissention about the conduct of the war rose among wide circles of the public, including among the nationalist Right, to whom rumors of a compromise peace were anathema. Groups such as the Pan-German League suspected that Bethmann, who had suppressed public discussion of war aims early in the war, might be conspiring with the Social Democrats for a moderate peace.[130]

Büchsel was right that Tirpitz's influence with the Emperor and the highest ranks of the navy had declined, but few among the public were aware of it. He was still the unquestioned public face of the navy and had many friends and supporters in the Reichstag, in the Bundesrat, and with the industrial barons and related interest groups, many of whom had contractual dealings with the RMA over the years since 1897.[131] Despite his many conflicts with the Emperor, he retained friendly relations with the imperial family, including the Empress and the Crown Prince. It was therefore natural that right-wing interest groups should look to him for leadership. His hard-line position on the war was publicly well known, not least because of his interview with the American journalist von Wiegand.

The Emperor was certainly no pacifist, but he was cautious and, in hindsight, sensible in his opposition to unrestricted submarine warfare. He and Bethmann had a healthy appreciation that to provoke the United States into war would be a fiasco, but they feared foreign and domestic repercussions were Tirpitz to be dismissed. Until March 1916 a kind of cold war festered between Tirpitz and the opposing Emperor and Bethmann.

In his anger, frustration, and even desperation, Tirpitz flirted with ideas that should have been unthinkable for a lifelong monarchist. At least until the end of April 1915, with a singular lack of discretion, he bruited about the idea to get the Emperor to report sick for eight weeks and temporarily cede his political and military powers to Hindenburg, with the Crown Prince playing a role. Luckily for Tirpitz, the discreet Müller kept this idea from the Emperor's ears.[132]

The weaker Tirpitz's position became with the Emperor, the greater the support he received from interest groups. Rumors of his departure created an outcry. Even the Empress implored him not to leave.[133] Moderates like Albert Ballin and the Center leader Matthias Erzberger pressed him to stay. In what Scheck called an "unprecedented event in Prussian and German history,"[134] William II felt the need to *order* the naval officer corps, roiled by rumors of Tirpitz's resignation, to obey both his personnel choices and support his decision to restrict U-boat warfare.[135]

By the fall of 1915, as his old idea of a decisive surface battle appeared less and less likely, Tirpitz's energies became increasingly devoted to unrestricted U-boat warfare and, backed by the nationalist press, to conflict with Bethmann over it.[136] Tirpitz nevertheless persevered in renewed attempts to become the Fleet Commander. For example, when he met with Müller on 3 December, the latter noted that the discussion was "barren as usual":

> The old refrain that the fleet must be engaged or otherwise the Kaiser's life work would be destroyed was repeated with the rider that Tirpitz was ready to take over the fleet himself. Admittedly he cannot constantly remain onboard; he also needed a subordinate commander to take care of the technical side and be given control of the Baltic forces.[137]

His conversation with Pohl the prior spring demonstrated how utterly out of date Tirpitz was about the requirements of commanding the fleet. His tactical ideas, such as they were, dated back to the 1890s.

At the end of 1915 Tirpitz won Holtzendorff to his side for unrestricted U-boat warfare and persuaded Falkenhayn to agree.[138] Tirpitz summarized his argument in a memo to Falkenhayn of 2 January 1916.[139] He wanted to start the offensive by 1 March, although Holtzendorff favored 1 April.[140] He pointed out that the prior year's offensive had begun with twenty-one boats and ultimately averaged thirty-five, with about one-third on station at any particular time. Tirpitz argued that, despite the restrictions and their small numbers, their effect had been large and had a steadily growing impact on British commerce. He estimated that, on 1 January, thirty-seven boats were available for service against Britain, increasing to fifty-three by 1 April and by an average of ten more per month thereafter. Assuming losses of three or four boats a month, he estimated that the successes of 1915 could be doubled or tripled.

Tirpitz acknowledged that unrestricted U-boat warfare would create "difficulties of a serious nature with the United States." Germany must nevertheless be willing to risk active American participation, since the United States was already supplying Britain to such a degree that formal belligerence would make little difference. The target would not only have to be British ships but Britain's entire maritime trade, including neutrals. "The sharper the pressure, the greater the prospect that Britain would be forced to make concessions [*nachgeben*]." In an irrationally sanguine moment Tirpitz, on 10 January, told Erzberger that it was "his unshakable belief that a ruthlessly conducted U-boat war could force England to its knees in six weeks." A few weeks later Holtzendorff told Erzberger that it would take six months. The disagreement reinforced Erzberger's skepticism on the whole question.[141]

Both Tirpitz and Holtzendorff were far too optimistic. Although Germany had sunk 748,000 tons of British shipping in 1915, in Britain and its Empire alone new construction had amounted to 1.3 million tons.[142] He and Holtzendorff also grossly underestimated the economic strength of the United States. American credits would feed the Allies and allay their economic problems, even though the United States had, in the short term, only a small army. Politicians like Bethmann, Erzberger, and the Social Democrats had a clearer understanding that to antagonize the United States into belligerency would reap the whirlwind.

On 9 January 1916 Pohl, in the final throes of liver cancer, was replaced as Fleet Chief by the vigorous Vice Admiral Reinhard Scheer. U-boat warfare resumed on 23 February, but not in the way that Tirpitz had hoped. Only armed freighters, and no passenger ships, could be torpedoed without warning. The Emperor wanted at all costs to avoid a repetition of the fallout from *Lusitania*. Only the small submarines of the Flanders squadron and the boats based in the Adriatic were allowed to attack without warning. The decision was a crushing disappointment to Tirpitz.[143] On 24 March some Americans drowned when U-29 sank the French liner *Sussex*. A strong American protest on 20 April persuaded the Emperor to suspend the U-boat offensive. Scheer realized that it was futile to continue under prize rules that required U-boats to surface before they attacked, as it would be both ineffective and dangerous to the crews. He recalled all the oceangoing boats. This marked, for all practical purposes, the end of submarine warfare except in Flanders and the Mediterranean.[144]

After the turn of 1916 a fresh wave of pessimism assailed Tirpitz. He confided to Trotha:

> It is becoming very hard, and you and I had discussed it before, how little it is possible to work under the double regime of M [Müller] and H [Holtzendorff]. I would still do it because Germany and the Germans are in such great peril. The probability lies ahead that we will succumb in a war of exhaustion.
> After the war, M will make me the scapegoat.[145]

Bethmann had long been working up the nerve to get rid of Tirpitz, whose disposition, connections, and ruthless intensity had nettled him since he became Chancellor in 1909. Bethmann knew that truly unrestricted U-boat warfare would be a catastrophe despite its attractiveness to many in the public, including some rank-and-file Social Democrats. With the Emperor's support, he had staved off Tirpitz's latest effort in that direction.[146] Bethmann claimed that Captain Heinrich Löhlein, Chief of the Etatsabteilung, had presented inflated numbers to the Bundesrat about the status of U-boat construction. Actually Löhlein's numbers were correct. On 1 March 1916 Germany had 54 boats at the Front, with another 149 in construction, trials, or refit. Some naïve Bundesrat members conflated the numbers to believe that the navy had more than 200 boats ready for service, an enormous number.[147]

The final straw for Tirpitz was a meeting convened by the Emperor on 4 March 1916 about the U-boat question. Present were William II, Bethmann, Falkenhayn, and Holtzendorff, but, by a prior decision by the Emperor, not Tirpitz[148]—a deliberate attempt to provoke Tirpitz to leave. Since, technically, Tirpitz had been forbidden to resign by the Emperor's order of August 1915, Tirpitz reported sick in a letter to the Emperor of 8 March. The next day the Emperor gave him permission to resign, and on 12 March Tirpitz did so. William II noted on Tirpitz's letter, "he is leaving the sinking ship" but mustered some appearance of graciousness when he accepted the resignation on 15 March. Tirpitz, after fifty-one years of service, was once again a civilian.

The keen-eyed William Michaelis, by then back in the RMA as a Department Chief, summed up Tirpitz's departure well:

> It was questionable for me whether Tirpitz could have remained effective in office. Doubtless he had rendered great service by building up the fleet, but after 20 years away from the Front, he had nothing more to contribute in a military sense, and during the war he could only be a fruitless critic with nothing he could do about it. . . . Of course, Tirpitz's departure was a loss of prestige, and it might have been better to put him in cold storage until the war ended.[149]

16
UNCOMMON RECESSIONAL,
1916–1930

Tirpitz, upon leaving the RMA, moved from his grand official residence with his wife Marie and daughter Margot to a large flat in Berlin at von der Heydt Strasse 15. His salary as State Secretary had been 45,000 marks, plus 15,000 for office expenses. His pension would be half his salary (22,500 marks).[1] His family's financial situation appeared reasonably secure. The status of his holdings in Alghero, Sardinia, San Remo on the Italian Riviera, and a Paris apartment was uncertain. He also had invested a substantial amount in war bonds,[2] and he retained the house at St. Blasien.

Tirpitz's son, Wolfgang, was a prisoner of war in Britain and was later interned in Holland. Ulrich von Hassell, the husband of daughter Ilse, slowly recovered from the bullet in the heart he had received at the Marne in 1914. His convalescence took place at the Tirpitz home. Unable to resume his diplomatic career for health reasons, in January 1916 he took an administrative position for the government of Prussia at Stettin.[3] From then on Hassell served Tirpitz as a political agent and surrogate in dealing with nationalist opposition figures, particularly Wolfgang Kapp.[4]

After his resignation Tirpitz was inundated with letters, telegrams, and newspaper columns from hundreds of well-wishers.[5] The British, who, along with most Germans, mistakenly believed that Tirpitz had played a major role in the naval war, were completely baffled by his departure, and even suspected that it was a diabolical trick.

On 19 March Admiral Eduard von Capelle came out of retirement to become State Secretary. Tirpitz later learned, to his chagrin, that Capelle had quietly accepted Bethmann's U-boat policy.[6] The very fact of

Capelle's selection should have made that obvious. Michaelis, who joined the RMA just before Tirpitz's departure, noted that Tirpitz felt Capelle had campaigned for the post. Their decades-long friendship was shattered. Thereafter Tirpitz worked to diminish Capelle's reputation within the navy.[7] Tirpitz's resentment is probably why, in his memoirs, he minimized Capelle's contributions to the navy.

After his dismissal Tirpitz was exhausted and dispirited. On 29 March he wrote to Trotha: "My nature and thought are foreign to those who now rule Germany. . . . After my departure, the official circle is completely closed." He noted Capelle's admission in the Budget Commission that unrestricted U-boat warfare could not force the British to peace within six months.[8] For the moment Tirpitz himself remained passive, although his allies continued to agitate, within the limits of the wartime censorship laws, for more vigorous U-boat warfare.

Despite his discomfort with Capelle, he visited the RMA occasionally. He retained support at court from the Crown Prince and the Empress. The active officer to whom he was closest was Trotha, by then Scheer's Chief of Staff. Trotha, who had worked in the MK before the war, still enjoyed a friendly relationship with Müller.

Although cut off from genuine influence, Tirpitz tried, through a letter to William II, to affect the U-boat debate and the diplomacy of the war.[9] He argued that keeping Flanders would undermine the British in the long run, while a robust U-boat war would threaten them in the shorter run. Two main British war goals were to prevent those eventualities. He conceded that "the [economic] connection [between Britain and the United States] is so close that America has a direct interest in the victory of England." American threats about the U-boat war were blackmail. He argued that the more Germany acquiesced, the more American demands would escalate. He even rhetorically asserted that if Germany doubted that the U-boat war could achieve a decisive victory over England, it should completely abandon the U-boat war on commerce, a policy that would be better than the half-measures then in progress, which annoyed the United States as much as an unrestricted campaign. The only way a dilatory campaign would make sense would be in the context of an attempt to achieve an understanding with Russia, an idea Tirpitz had favored since the beginning of the war. He concluded with a passionate appeal that now was the time to launch an unrestricted U-boat war, "which would be a decisive success against England in a series [*Reihe*] of months." Tirpitz's naiveté about the United States is also shown in a letter to his old friend Eisendecher: "The Yankee [*sic*] fleet is without meaning for us with respect to the loss of the tonnage needed to transport troops. For their merchant ships to use convoys would be futile against U-boat attacks."[10] Tirpitz requested an audience with William II on the matter. The Emperor wrote gruffly that he would refer the issue to his advisers.

The nationalist opposition continued to push the limits of wartime censorship that forbade criticism of the government. Although Tirpitz's personal role in the matter is unclear, on 20 May 1916 Wolfgang Kapp published a pamphlet titled "The National Circles and the Imperial Chancellor." Ulrich von Hassell wrote an early draft but kept his own role secret, lest Tirpitz suffer embarrassment. Kapp made the case that Bethmann's weakness had led to the abandonment of a vigorous U-boat offensive, and had inadvertently focused public attention on the effort of the Left to achieve Prussian suffrage reform in the midst of war.[11]

While domestic turmoil festered, Scheer, the aggressive new commander of the High Seas Fleet, took steps to sharpen the North Sea cat-and-mouse game. He sallied the whole fleet on 5 March without results; but on 24/25 April he sent Rear Admiral Friedrich Boedicker's cruiser force (Hipper was ill) to shell Lowestoft and Yarmouth. Boedicker, with Scheer in support, returned home. On 4 May Jellicoe, using two seaplane carriers as a lure, approached the Skagerrak, but when Scheer arrived in the afternoon Jellicoe had departed.[12]

Aggressive and persistent, Scheer took advantage of the withdrawal of U-boats from commerce war to set up screens offshore from the main British bases. Bad weather prevented the use of Zepplins for reconnaissance. The original plan had been a coastal bombardment by Hipper to winkle out Beatty's battlecruisers and to draw them onto the High Seas Fleet; but because of delays that taxed the endurance of the U-boats, Scheer decided on a sweep to the Skagerrak, with Hipper leading the way. Radio intercepts told Jellicoe that the German cruisers were out, but until they met at sea he did not know that Scheer had sailed with the main body. Jellicoe nevertheless was at sea with the Grand Fleet several hours before Hipper left port at 1:00 AM on 31 May, with Scheer closely following.

Space limitations prevent any detailed account of the battle, and so only a summary is given here.[13] All told, at sea there were 37 British and

21 German Dreadnoughts and battlecruisers, plus six slower German pre-Dreadnoughts. British light forces outnumbered German by 113 to 72. Beatty, in *Lion*, had 6 battlecruisers to Hipper's 5, but ten miles behind Beatty were 4 fast battleships of the *Queen Elizabeth* class, the most powerful and modern British Dreadnoughts, with a 38-cm main armament.

At 3.30 PM, when Hipper spotted Beatty's force, he immediately turned south to draw the ships onto Scheer. Decades of German gunnery training paid off. Beatty's flagship was hammered, and only heroic damage control kept it afloat. *Indefatigable* and *Queen Mary* sank within minutes because of inadequate flash protection. Beatty famously remarked: "There is something wrong with our bloody ships today." As the *Queen Elizabeth*s closed, the German battlecruisers took a battering as well, but superior armor and flash protection saved them from crippling damage.

The situation changed dramatically when Scheer and the High Seas Fleet arrived. Beatty turned back to the north. Hipper and Scheer pursued into the unknown. They might have guessed what lay beyond the horizon. After another British battlecruiser, *Invincible*, blew up at about 7:00 PM Hipper remarked: "Something lurks in that soup. We would do well not to thrust into it too deeply."[14] He was right. Within a half-hour the Grand Fleet arrived, and Hipper, in the van, began to take a terrible pounding. Even worse, Jellicoe had maneuvered to cross the "T" of the German single line formation and could bring full broadsides to bear. A desperate struggle ensued for the High Seas Fleet. Scheer ordered Hipper to cover as he made a simultaneous 180-degree "battle turn away." Peacetime exercises paid off, as Scheer's fleet formed single-line ahead in the opposite direction. After another hour of hair-raising conflict and evasion, darkness descended. With a large dose of good fortune, Scheer managed to get his battered fleet home. Battlecruisers had suffered the most. *Lützow* had to be scuttled. The butcher's bill made it seem a German victory. The British lost three battlecruisers, the Germans one, plus the pre-Dreadnought *Pommern*. Three British armored cruisers and four German light cruisers went down, along with eight British and five German destroyers. About six thousand British sailors and twenty-five hundred German sailors died.

The ecstatic Emperor visited Wilhelmshaven on 5 June and promoted both Scheer and Hipper. The British were disappointed that the "quarry" had escaped. German admirals outwardly supported Scheer, but Trotha, his Chief of Staff, said jokingly to the Austrian Naval Attaché that if an admiral had gotten into such a dicey situation in peacetime maneuvers, he would never have gotten another command.[15] Publicly Scheer was hailed as a German Nelson.

Scheer himself was more sober. On 4 July 1916 he reported to the Emperor that, despite the courage of the crews and the aggressiveness and efficiency of his subordinates, "not even the most successful result from a high seas battle will compel England to make peace."[16] He pointed out Germany's geographic disadvantages and the vast British numerical superiority that made it impossible to break the blockade. The only remedy was "the crushing of English economic life through U-boat action against English commerce." He proposed the resumption of unrestricted submarine warfare, and, in so doing, tolled the death knell *sans phrase* for Tirpitz's strategy of a decisive battle in the North Sea.

Tirpitz felt vindicated by the "victory" of Skagerrak. Against Front complaints that German Dreadnoughts were inferior, he argued that the battle proved that individual German ships were, overall, equal, and in some cases superior to British ships of comparable vintage.[17] He was certainly right on the points of durability, armor, and watertight integrity. Only a few hits each sank three British battlecruisers. It took a prolonged battering to sink *Lützow*. German gunnery was marginally superior in the number of hits, and German shells were better, but the largest German guns in the battle were 30.5-cm, markedly inferior in throw-weight to British 35-cm and 38-cm artillery in Britain's newer ships. The Germans had nothing to match the *Queen Elizabeths*. Privately Tirpitz was bitter about the weakening of his political influence after 1908. The consequent lack of money had made it impossible to improve ship types to match the most modern British battleships.[18]

Tirpitz lamented that the fleet had not been used more aggressively earlier in the war, when the 37:21 British margin of superiority in modern ships was considerably less. "The idea that the German fleet would be annihilated in a sea battle and could achieve nothing decisive against the English fleet was a sick underestimation, a lack of confidence in our own ships that we had to atone for terribly."[19] Though an earlier battle would still have been fought with inferior force, the odds would have been somewhat better. There is no guarantee that the outcome would have been better. In his analysis Tirpitz concealed his own ambivalence about risking a major battle in 1914–15. The obligatory telegram of congratulations from the Emperor on 5 June provided Tirpitz cold comfort.[20]

Despite the partial rehabilitation of his reputation, Tirpitz was still convinced that Bethmann, if given the opportunity, would try to reach an understanding with Britain at the expense of the navy. He feared that a combination of the Emperor, the army leadership (Falkenhayn), and "Anglophiles" in high places would be inclined to accommodate Britain.[21] Though pessimistic overall, Tirpitz thought that the battle had justified the Navy Law. In a letter to Trotha, he omitted the following awkward expectation from the published version:

> Even if we are victorious in war, the monstrous financial pressure will make it extremely difficult to move the Reichstag to approve a new Navy Law for large ships. The present Navy Law in fact exists, and need only be changed by expanding certain small types, which could be easily done outside the law.[22]

Tirpitz privately tried to court Hindenburg to his side in favoring U-boats but hoped at the same time to keep a low public profile, lest he be accused of conducting a vendetta against Bethmann.[23] The latter's position became weaker when, on 28 August, in the wake of the Rumanian declaration of war, the Emperor finally dismissed Falkenhayn and replaced him with Hindenburg and Ludendorff. The latter pair eventually undermined both Bethmann and ultimately the Emperor himself. Kapp energetically lobbied Hindenburg and Ludendorff to replace Bethmann with Tirpitz, although it was not obvious that Tirpitz himself had any interest in the position. Kapp had little success with this gambit, but Trotha learned in September that OHL (Army High Command) was at least willing to consider support for unconditional submarine warfare. A Tirpitz Chancellorship was impossible as long as Tirpitz remained toxic to the Emperor.[24]

In the fall of 1916 Tirpitz engaged in a double-edged game with the Emperor. First through Hassell,[25] and then directly, he approached Count August von Eulenburg, a minister of the Imperial House and personally close to William II. Tirpitz suggested a Cabinet comprised of the elderly Eulenburg as Chancellor, Tirpitz as Naval Minister, and Kapp as Interior Minister.[26] This bizarre plan, though unrealistic at the time, shows that Tirpitz was still interested in a position lesser than Chancellor and that he wanted to hitch his wagon to Hindenburg and Ludendorff's star.

Tirpitz, in response to a hint from Trotha, once again (as he had in January 1915 in a letter to his wife) broached the possibility of having the Emperor temporarily replaced, even though he admitted that there was no suitable regent among the princes to fill that role. It would also have to be done with William II's consent. Tirpitz was thinking of preserving the monarchy by temporarily deposing the monarch with a regent from outside the immediate Prussian imperial family.[27] Not surprisingly, Tirpitz omitted this letter from his postwar publications. The Emperor would have considered such thoughts treasonous. Tirpitz's nationalism and monarchism, once united in his mind, were bifurcating under the terrible stress of war.

Tirpitz's relatively Russophile view was directly contrary to the view of Hindenburg and Ludendorff. Before the latter ascended to OHL, they both had demanded more resources from Falkenhayn to defeat Russia. On this fundamental question of war aims Tirpitz was at odds with OHL, as he felt that the retention of Flanders should be the top priority.[28] Bethmann's proclamation in November 1916 in favor of an independent Polish state, with the support of OHL which hoped for Polish volunteers for the army, ended any chance of a rapprochement with Russia, and dealt a death-blow to Tirpitz's Russian hopes.

Even though the Emperor was unwilling to dismiss Bethmann, Kapp continued to lobby OHL to support unrestricted submarine warfare. By 8 December 1916 Hindenburg, with the defeat of Rumania imminent, wanted the submarine war to resume by the end of January 1917. OHL and Holtzendorff demanded that William II begin submarine warfare by 1 February and that he fire Bethmann if he refused. The Emperor finally gave his consent, and Bethmann, unwilling to resign and with no other choice, capitulated.[29] Despite all the good objective reasons not to provoke the United States into the war, the psychological dimension was compelling to the decision makers. It was not just Tirpitz and the German Right who saw the U-boats as a possible panacea; many others in the country did as well. The army was stressed beyond endurance, with no clear scenario for military victory; the navy was impotent to affect the war's outcome; and the civilian population was frustrated and hungry. Given this scenario, it would be very difficult if not impossible to turn away from a plan that could plausibly break the deadlock. Tirpitz played a major, albeit veiled, public role in making it appear that a successful U-boat war was feasible; however, even had he, uncharacteristically, remained passive on the matter, it is hard to argue, given all the pressures, that events would have played out much differently.[30]

The final decision was made on 9 January 1917. Holtzendorff "guaranteed" that the U-boats could sink 500,000 tons per month and that, by October, the British war economy would be strangled. OHL hoped that the submarine warfare would substantially interdict delivery of supplies and munitions from America, and though he anticipated U.S. intervention in the war, he was prepared to take the risk. Along with Tirpitz, OHL believed that the U-boats could win the war before the Americans could arm, train, and deliver enough troops to be decisive. The historian can only wonder whether it would have affected their decision had they known that, within a few weeks (12 March), Imperial Russia would collapse amid revolution. The U-boat campaign began on 1 February. Wilson's reluctance to fully grasp the nettle was overcome by a major German blunder. In January 1917 British cryptographers deciphered a telegram from German Foreign Minister Arthur Zimmermann to the German Minister to Mexico, von Eckhardt, offering U.S. territory to Mexico in return for joining the German cause. The American press published news of the "Zimmerman Telegram" on 1 March, and on 6 April the U. S. Congress formally declared war on Germany and its allies.

Hindsight tells us that the German decision regarding unrestricted submarine warfare ignored important political factors, such as the huge boost to the Allies' morale from American entry into the war, even though OHL was correct to anticipate that it would take a year or more for U.S. troops to make a military difference. They grossly underestimated the extent to which American shipbuilding, economic credits, and grain supplies could affect the war despite serious losses in merchant shipping.[31]

After the U-boat decision was made, Tirpitz wrote to his former adjutant Mann:

> Now we are late, not too late I hope, to direct our war effort against
> England. In any case it is the last hour. One can only guess how our foes
> have used the time to prepare countermeasures against our U-boats. But the
> bad world harvest has given us another chance and, despite our leadership,
> I hope our brave U-boat men will give us a good war outcome. At that point
> I can rest easy and no longer regret that I was not at the helm at the fateful
> hour for our people.[32]

With the U-boat war under way, many rightists felt that Tirpitz should replace the embattled Bethmann. Late in February Hindenburg and

Ludendorff made a concerted effort to persuade William II to accept Tirpitz as Chancellor.[33] The Emperor's rage at Tirpitz boiled over again, and he adamantly refused.[34] Tirpitz and his allies had achieved unrestricted submarine war; but the stubbornness of William II, wounded by decades of real and imagined slights and manipulation at Tirpitz's hands, refused, unsurprisingly, to consider Tirpitz for Chancellor. Tirpitz's own ambivalence may also have come into play, considering the staggering amount of responsibility he would have had to assume. His age and fragile health, compounded by his tendency toward hypochondria, might have stood in the way. At times he favored, instead, a return of Bülow; but the latter, because of the Emperor's past embarrassments at his hands, was also unacceptable.

The U-boat war began even better than its advocates could have hoped. The target was 600,000 tons per month. Holtzendorff had foolishly given an October deadline for the collapse of British trade. Sinkings rose from 540,000 tons in February to 600,000 tons in March and to 841,000 tons in April, the highest of any month in the war.[35] Panic reigned among British admirals, who could think of no effective countermeasures. In May the Prime Minister, David Lloyd George, intervened decisively and forced the Admiralty to institute convoys, the same tactic that had worked in the Napoleonic Wars. The admirals' excuses were many: escorting convoys would remove destroyers from the Grand Fleet's screen; lubberly merchant captains could not sail in convoy; and congestion in the ports would be intolerable. The Admiralty reluctantly consented to convoy practices. In May losses dropped to 600,000 tons, rose again to 700,000 tons in June, and were 550,000 tons in July. By then the convoys had taken effect, and sinkings dropped to an average of about 350,000 tons for a number of months. These losses were serious but not catastrophic, and the ships could be replaced.

Technological improvements reflected Tirpitz's prediction of anticipated countermeasures. Depth charges, nets with mines, a primitive form of sonar and other innovations gradually phased in. Losses of twenty U-boats in the first six months of 1917 more than doubled in the second half of the year.[36] Although U-boats did serious damage, by the late summer of 1917 it became clear that they could break neither the war economy nor the will of the British.[37]

THE FATHERLAND PARTY

As the war dragged on to 1917, the endless casualty lists, domestic food shortages, and receding hopes for victory sharpened unrest among civilians.[38] The Emperor and Bethmann, in desperation, reached out to the Center and even to left-wing parties. On Easter 1917 William II actually promised a major revision in the Bismarckian Constitution: the abolition of the three-class suffrage system in Prussia. He did not fully specify what would replace it or when, but clearly its blatant favoritism toward the wealthy and the powerful landlords would diminish significantly.

Popular unrest found expression early in July 1917, when the Center and the leftist parties offered a Reichstag resolution for a peace without annexations and reparations, a direct repudiation of the rightists' large territorial demands. Tirpitz, from St. Blasien, wrote to his old friends in the Reichstag to oppose the resolution.[39] The peace resolution passed on 19 July but found rejection in the Reich government and did not impress the Allies. In an attempt to stop the resolution, a strange combination of its supporters and OHL, who had other reasons to get rid of Bethmann, finally succeeded. The Emperor rejected both Bülow and Tirpitz for Chancellor. Georg Michaelis, a politically unknown Prussian bureaucrat, became William II's next Chancellor.[40] Tirpitz rejoiced in Bethmann's dismissal.[41]

On 1 August 1916 the pan-German leader Heinrich Claß visited Tirpitz at St. Blasien to persuade him to chair a nationalist umbrella group he was trying to organize. Tirpitz refused, partly because he felt that a retired officer should not engage in partisan politics and partly because he did not want to be seen publicly as taking revenge on Bethmann.[42] In August 1917, consistent with this belief, he refused Stresemann's offer of a safe Reichstag seat.[43]

By August 1917 the situation had changed, and Bethmann was gone. Perhaps because of his dismay about the course of the war and the peace resolution, and perhaps also because he had given up hope of a recall from the government, Tirpitz was receptive to Kapp's suggestion that he chair a mass popular movement under the name of the German Fatherland Party. It was explicitly *not* to be a political party in the usual sense, because it would not run or support candidates. Its purpose was to raise civilian effort and commitment to carry on the war until a favorable peace might be achieved.[44] The army passively supported it by allowing the group to distribute its message to soldiers. The government cooperated by not applying wartime censorship laws to the party. Although led by old elites, it was an attempt to rally the masses. This approach appealed to Tirpitz's patriotism and old fighting spirit. Finally happy to do what he saw as meaningful work,[45] Tirpitz accepted the honorary co-chairmanship with the Duke of Mecklenburg. Kapp apparently expected actually to run the organization himself, while Tirpitz and the Duke functioned as figureheads. Tirpitz, instead, threw himself into the campaign with his old ferocious energy. As Scheck aptly puts it:

> He acted as a public speaker, a fundraiser, a safeguard of the party's domes-
> tic neutrality, a secretary, and a liaison to the OHL and the government.
> It was he who mainly built up the party's central office in Berlin. That the
> Fatherland Party declared—however shakily—a neutrality in domestic
> politics, and that it remained friendly toward Catholic and Jewish support-
> ers, was largely his doing and cost him struggles with the Pan Germans and
> conservatives in the party.[46]

The campaign had its public debut with an array of speakers at a large meeting hall in Berlin on 24 September 1917.[47] Tirpitz began with a "fatherland in danger" theme and made visionary comments about the importance of German seapower and the Navy Law. He boasted that England's plan to starve Germany by blockade had failed. He angrily proclaimed that a peace without annexations and reparations for Germany, as the Reichstag resolution proposed, would set the German economy back for decades. To give back Belgium would amount to having lost the war. With Germany's huge economic losses, the status quo ante bellum would be disastrous. To fortify the party's "non-political" status, the party, contrary to Tirpitz's own strong personal feelings, took no position on the prospect of Prussian electoral reform.

Tirpitz's commitment to the cause was so strong that he was willing to speak at public meetings. Except occasionally in the Reichstag, surrounded by his own experts, Tirpitz had little experience as a public speaker before large groups. As heard in a rare recording,[48] he spoke without inflection, simply reading a speech in a squeaky voice and a monotone.[49] Nevertheless, because his message mirrored the fears and hopes of many Germans, he usually received an enthusiastic welcome. In an age before the marketing of politicians via the mass media, a visit from the creator of the High Seas Fleet lent an air of celebrity to the occasion. To fight his more overt political battles, he enlisted prominent academics to defend him against accusations by Reichstag opponents such as the Progressive Dr. Peter Struve that, as State Secretary, Tirpitz had paid too much attention to large ships and not enough to U-boats.[50]

Tirpitz tapped friends and acquaintances in heavy industry for contributions to the Fatherland Party. Finances were a major problem.[51] There was never enough money for a well-funded central office, despite Tirpitz's best efforts. Local offices often had their own agendas. Friction within the party was constant, especially from the Pan-German faction. Without a well-trained staff, as Tirpitz had enjoyed in the RMA, he and his colleagues were often at wit's end to make the organization run productively.

Tirpitz strove hard to keep the party "neutral" in its domestic policy. Anti-Semitic and anti-Catholic groups, such as the Pan-German League, bitterly resented that Tirpitz encouraged Jewish and Catholic membership. Kapp and the Duke of Mecklenburg took the Pan-German side. They wanted huge conquests at the expense of Russia, whereas Tirpitz saw war with Britain and the possession of Flanders as paramount.[52] The Treaty of Brest-Litovsk of March 1918 resulted in gigantic, albeit ultimately temporary, gains in the east.

Tirpitz's chairmanship of the party gave him a semi-official position that freed him from his previous pariah status in official circles. William II was still unable to tolerate his proximity, but Tirpitz did have easier access to Hindenburg and Ludendorff, and to Chancellors Michaelis and Georg von Hertling, the former's successor in October 1917. Tirpitz tried to convince OHL to hold onto Belgium at all costs. He argued that, even in the face of their declining success, the U-boats could defeat Britain soon enough to ward off OHL's fears of a leftist revolution in Germany.[53]

Ulrich von Hassell later summed up the Fatherland Party's problems from its birth.[54] First, that the Duke of Mecklenburg, Kapp, and Tirpitz were temperamentally incompatible and, second, the party had fragmented goals. Most party members wanted an advocacy organization pushing for far-reaching war aims. Many wanted the party to act as a bulwark against domestic insurrection. Only a few, like Hassell and

Tirpitz, saw it as an instrument to mobilize national power to wage the war. Although Hassell underplayed Tirpitz's obsession with Belgium, his observation of the latter's fixation was dead-on.

By the summer of 1918 Tirpitz's energy had flagged and his frustration had grown. The failure of Ludendorff's spring offensive cast a pall over the popular enthusiasm the Fatherland Party had roused the previous year. In July 1918, without officially resigning his chairmanship, Tirpitz retreated to St. Blasien and turned his attention to writing his memoirs. He thought he had done all he could for the war, and he wanted to defend his reputation from the waves of recrimination that were likely to come from enemies of all sorts. The Fatherland Party limped along on sheer momentum for a few more months. Its propaganda, along with that of the army, concealed from the population how truly desperate the German military situation had become.

TIRPITZ AT THE END OF THE WAR

One attack on Tirpitz came from a familiar direction. His old prewar opponent, retired navy captain Lothar Persius, wrote a slashing pamphlet against Tirpitz's life's work. The navy failed to ban its publication.[55] Persius criticized everything, from Tirpitz's choice of battleship type to his neglect of U-boats before the war to a late conversion to submarine warfare during the war. He blamed Tirpitz's fleet for the creation of enmity with Britain that resulted in a coalition that put Germany in mortal danger. These accusations, many of them justified in hindsight, seriously rankled Tirpitz.

All was not well with the fleet. There had been no major sorties since October 1916. The most energetic young officers volunteered for the U-boat service, which commanded the nation's attention and affection.[56] Idleness, combined with the abominable food served to enlisted men, sapped the morale of the High Sea Fleet's crews. The relatively well-fed officer corps responded with martinet emphasis on dress and disciplinary regulations. Capelle tried, as the army had done long since, to give the sailors at least some influence over food preparation. Scheer and the officer corps refused any attempts at even marginal improvements as outside interference. Sailors resorted to unavailing passive resistance. Events culminated in August 1917 when the crew of the battleship *Prinzregent Luitpold* went on strike, and two of their leaders were shot.

To lift navy morale late in 1917, part of the High Seas Fleet conducted aggressive, almost overkill, operations in the Baltic. Even beforehand Hopmann, then commander of cruiser forces in the Baltic, wrote to Tirpitz that such a diversion from the North Sea gave the navy a psychological boost, but that he failed to understand its purpose in the overall context of the war.[57] The modest prize was control of the Gulf of Riga at a time when the Russian war effort was on its last legs.

After another fruitless sally into the Skagerrak in April 1918, crew morale again began to sink. Exposure to right-wing literature (including that of the Fatherland Party) and speeches was no palliative for ordinary sailors, especially in view of the rigid discipline of life aboard idled ships in Wilhelmshaven. Morale was better in smaller ships and U-boats because these craft saw action more frequently, even, as 1918 went on, U-boat casualties rose and sinkings fell. U-boat men faced a gigantic British mine barrier between the Orkneys and the Norwegian leads, and effective convoy practices that were buttressed by increasing numbers of escorts, many of them American. By 1918 losses of ships in Atlantic convoys slipped below 1 percent.

In the desperate hours of August 1918 Scheer bullied the thoroughly enervated William II to establish a Supreme Naval Command (*Seekriegsleitung*). Scheer became its Chief. Holtzendorff and Capelle retired. Hipper succeeded Scheer as Fleet Chief. Trotha became the heir-apparent of Müller at the Naval Cabinet. Tirpitz, who had witnessed the demolition of the Admiralty in 1889, and who, to preserve and expand his own power, had engineered the splintering of the Oberkommando in 1899, now saw the wheel come full circle. From the beginning of the war he had pushed for a de facto restoration of the Admiralty, hoping that he would be named its wartime head. Instead, he had to be content with a letter of congratulations to Scheer.[58]

Scheer proposed a gigantic program of 450 U-boats and two additional battleships. Since materials, workers, and even crews were lacking, the plan amounted to a pipe dream. Equally fantastic was the navy's retention of Holtzendorff's grandiloquent war aims that included Flanders, Constantinople, more colonies in Africa, and much else.[59]

While the navy was vainly reorganizing itself, the army finally cracked. On 8 August, a date Ludendorff called "the black day of the German Army," Allied troops broke through German lines on the Somme. By early September German forces had to retreat to where they had started their great offensive in March. On 29 September Ludendorff asked the Emperor to seek an armistice. On 2 October William II appointed as Chancellor the liberal Prince Max of Baden, who applied to Wilson for an armistice. To appease Wilson, submarine warfare ended on 22 October.

This kaleidoscopic turn of events moved Tirpitz to leave St. Blasien and attempt, quixotically, to resuscitate the propaganda campaign of the Fatherland Party. In a speech in Königsberg, on 9 October, he called for resistance and perseverance.[60] In such a situation, propaganda was not much of a weapon. In Berlin he met with Eulenburg on 20 and 26 October to see if the latter could persuade the Emperor to abdicate in favor of the Crown Prince, who would not be bound by his father's commitment to suffrage reform. That this should be one of Tirpitz's top priorities in such a desperate situation is strange. He hoped that the Crown Prince would appoint a dictator to mobilize the whole population for last-ditch resistance.[61] Tirpitz completely misjudged the war weariness of the country. Casualties, hunger, hardship, and the appealing prospect of an armistice had irretrievably broken morale in Germany. By then even the optimistic Trotha was despairing.[62] By mid-October Hindenburg was frustrated by the Fatherland Party's calls to fight to the end: "Does nobody at home know that we have been fighting to the last man for weeks already?" Despite his later claims of a "stab in the back," Hindenburg wrote in December that, in modern war, a universal mobilization would not have worked.[63]

Unknown to Tirpitz at the time, Hipper, for honor's sake and with an eye to justifying the navy's future, planned a suicide charge of the High Seas Fleet into the North Sea. Neither the Emperor nor General Wilhelm Groener, the new head of OHL, was informed. The operation was scheduled for 30 October.[64]

A few days before the operation rumors spread among nervous crews that they were about to be sacrificed to save the honor of the officer corps.[65] On 29 October some men failed to return from shore leave in Kiel and Wilhelmshaven. Insubordination on an unprecedented scale soon spread through the large ships. There was broad antiwar sentiment and hopes for Wilson's idea of an armistice. Rebellious sailors found support in the civilian population. By 30 October even Hipper conceded that the operation was off. The naval officer corps tried to blame the mutiny on leftist agitation among the sailors. Although there was some such contact, political agitation was marginal compared to other factors. Of much greater significance was the war-weariness pervasive in the bulk of the population and the expectation of an armistice that came with the appointment of Prince Max of Baden as Chancellor.[66]

The armistice of 11 November brought humiliating news for the navy and the nation. The ten most modern battleships, six battlecruisers, eight light cruisers, most of the modern destroyers, and all the U-boats were to be interned in British ports. Germany could only retain six pre-Dreadnought battleships and a few of the smaller ships, and was banned from building any new capital ships or U-boats.

On 21 November the sad procession, led by Vice Admiral Ludwig von Reuter, defiantly flew the imperial battle ensign as it departed Wilhelmshaven for the last time, to sail to Scapa Flow under British guard.[67] The ecstatic Admiralty put on an extravagant show to receive them and forced the late imperial navy to drink the last dregs of humiliation. Beatty, Chief of the Grand Fleet, could not resist a touch of pity as he saw his great antagonists forced to suffer such an ordeal. Thus, to all appearances, the fruit of Tirpitz's life's labor to harness the energy, treasure, and skills of the German nation for more than two decades passed from history. Its story, however, was not quite over.

By 9 November the imperial superstructure had collapsed amid revolution and the abdication of William II. The short tradition of the Bismarckian Empire, along with the centuries-long tradition of the Prussian monarchy, ended forever.

TIRPITZ AS MEMOIRIST

When the revolution came a fearful Tirpitz fled to a friend's hunting lodge in Pomerania to work on his memoirs. He stayed in hiding for months. The newly founded German Communist Party declared him a war criminal for his advocacy of unrestricted submarine warfare and because of his leading role in the Fatherland Party.[68]

Before leaving office Tirpitz had assembled some of his wartime papers.[69] After his departure he shared these papers with Professor Fritz Kern, of Bonn University, to prepare them to use for a polemic against

Bethmann.[70] Tirpitz hesitated to attack Bethmann publicly and personally at the time, because he did not want to be accused of conducting a
vendetta. In August 1918 Kern persuaded Tirpitz that he needed to write
his memoirs for the sake of the future of the fleet. He began, with Tirpitz's
permission, to prepare a first draft. Leftist attacks on Tirpitz intensified
his efforts.

Kern was not a ghostwriter; the ideas and prose bear the unmistak-
able stamp of Tirpitz's views, character, and rhetoric. Not surprisingly the
memoir is replete with examples of bureaucratic thinking. Tirpitz rejected
the accusation, mainly from the Left, that his fleet-building policy had
driven Britain into an alliance with France and Russia, despite Tirpitz's
assertion that the fleet would make Germany *bündnisfähig* (attractive as
an ally) to the British. Tirpitz, instead, saw the Anglo-German enmity as
driven mainly by economic rivalry. The only way to avoid war was energetic fleet building to deter British attack. The war came not because the
fleet had failed as a deterrent but because of weakness, miscalculation,
and blunders by the government, mainly Bethmann, during the July
1914 crisis. Implicitly this argument also reflected badly on the Emperor,
which annoyed fellow nationalists, who saw Tirpitz's view as inimical to
the struggle against the war-guilt clause of the Treaty of Versailles.

Tirpitz also accused Bethmann and the government of mismanaging
wartime diplomacy. Bethmann was too soft with Britain and too hard on
Russia. He knuckled under to blackmail from Wilson to cripple and delay
the U-boat war. In each instance Tirpitz was right and Bethmann wrong.

On the conduct of the war, he criticized Pohl, Ingenohl, Holtzendorff, and Müller for holding back the fleet in 1914–15, even though Tirpitz himself at the time was not nearly as aggressive as he later claimed
in his memoirs. He accused the government and the Emperor of keeping
the fleet as a bargaining chip for peace negotiations with Britain. Both the
fleet and the submarines should have been used much sooner and more
resolutely. He feared that if the fleet did not fight, it would be impossible
to muster public support to continue its development after a victorious
war. Perhaps here he also remembered the navy's frustrating inaction
during the Franco-Prussian War.

The perceived success at Jutland quieted those inside and outside
the navy who had argued that German capital ships were inferior. Tirpitz
attacked critics who said he had not pushed U-boat development fast
enough. He evaded discussion of the embarrassing mutinies, essentially

because they had not occurred on his watch. In short, everything he did was right. Others would have to bear the responsibility for losing the war and for the collapse of the monarchy. In the final words in his memoirs, Tirpitz claimed that their publication was his last political act.

As early as January 1919 Trotha, Chief of the Naval Personnel Office (successor to the Naval Cabinet), sent Tirpitz a draft memorandum that blamed the mutinies on the government's morale-crushing armistice request which, he claimed, the Socialists had seized upon to subvert the soldiers' and sailors' loyalty to the monarchy.[71] Tirpitz's encouraging reply showed that he anticipated a postwar conflict for resources between the army and navy, precisely the reaction one would expect from a bureaucratic warrior.[72]

After reading almost the entire manuscript, Trotha gave Tirpitz some perceptive advice:

> If you put personal feelings and *Ressort* battles in the foreground, I fear the mass of readers will say: "If the navy was in such mixed-up circumstances, nothing could be expected of the navy than the disaster that finally occurred." But I also very much fear that all the navy people and groups who are attacked will be provoked to reply in self-defense; it will also raise a storm of attacks on Your Excellency.[73]

Tirpitz agreed to tone down his manuscript a bit,[74] but he noted, in true bureaucratic fashion, that if the seapower idea were to be rehabilitated, it could not be done without demolishing Bethmann's reputation and manipulating the historical narrative. Tirpitz acknowledged that it might be better to publish the book posthumously; nevertheless, he felt that he needed to publish it now in order to succor the navy (i.e., himself) against the attacks of its enemies.

On 21 June 1919 the High Seas Fleet entered the spotlight for the last time in a most dramatic way. Admiral Reuter ordered watertight doors and seacocks open on the ten Dreadnoughts, five battlecruisers, and smaller ships in British captivity in Scapa Flow. As the British harbor patrol watched in helpless astonishment, the whole fleet, German ensigns flying, was beached or slipped below the waves. Most Germans rejoiced at the sheer audacity of it. When the crews, in January 1920, returned home after internment they were received as heroes.[75] Bands played, flags flew proudly, and the press responded ecstatically. In its suicide, the fleet redeemed itself in the eyes of the nation. The mutinies were soon forgotten. The scuttling provided a new narrative and a fresh start for the fledgling *Reichsmarine*, limited by treaty to 1,500 officers and deck officers and 13,500 men.

Tirpitz had mixed feelings about the Scapa episode, as evinced in the letter he wrote to his former adjutant Mann:

> For myself, it is drinking the cup to the dregs. Our people have sunk so deeply that they have lost their sense of honor, and do not understand that, for the coming century, no material loss will make our recovery as difficult as the moral catastrophe of our nation now does. . . . That Admiral Reuter and our officers have saved somewhat the honor of our flag has deeply touched all of us here and quietly reawakens our hope for the future.[76]

The Treaty of Versailles, reluctantly signed at the end of June 1919, ratified the armistice clauses that left Germany with a skeletal navy. An army of one hundred thousand was, in a Central European context, derisory. The loss of Alsace Lorraine to France and parts of West Prussia and Silesia to Poland were serious blows, although Germany's industrial infrastructure was largely intact. In 1919 reparations and the war-guilt question loomed large, both materially and psychologically.

On the eve of the publication of his memoirs, in October 1919, Tirpitz shared with Admiralty Chief Trotha his hopes and fears for Germany's future.[77] He did not see how a parliamentary government, especially one run by the Left, could solve Germany's problems. He wanted a dictator, with the values and strengths of a Bismarck, who could break the chains of disarmament. The small army could be used as a school for officers and noncommissioned officers. Although the navy's situation was bleak, he wanted to gather all the country's maritime interests under the Admiralty, including surveys, fisheries, pilots, and so on, the same idea he had proposed, without success, to William II in January 1896. At that time he wanted to consolidate all these duties, except for the military command function, under the RMA. In foreign policy, the only hope he saw was in an understanding with Russia, a course the Republic pursued in 1922 with the Treaty of Rapallo.

Between 1919 and 1922 his financial situation deteriorated. When Italy entered the war in 1915 its government seized the family property in Sardinia.[78] The new government cut Tirpitz's relatively generous pension, and the gradual inflation of the first few postwar years eroded his economic security.[79]

After the memoirs were published Scheer privately gave Trotha his candid opinion. He agreed with Tirpitz about Bethmann but criticized him for his failure to prevail over the Bethmann clique. On the other hand, he praised the book and told Trotha, in a refrain that would become common among German nationalists and naval officers in the 1920s, that he would follow the Tirpitz line in his own memoirs.[80]

The imperial family had a different response. Prinz Heinrich, the Emperor's brother and himself a Grand Admiral, was furious.[81] The Prince accused Tirpitz of disloyalty and regretted that he no longer considered him a "comrade." Tirpitz's petulant reply denied that he had buffed his reputation by blackening the Emperor's.[82] Tirpitz conceded that portions of the memoir may have seemed to reflect personal bitterness, but he lamely explained that intended corrections could not be made because of a threatened printer's strike. He argued that the Emperor did not understand that, with limited funds, Germany had created the maximum degree of seapower possible. To credibly counter Bethmann's partisans, he had to include the Emperor's "occasional temperamental expressions and marginalia" that the Foreign Office had preserved in the documents. To justify the monarchy, he asserted, he had to reveal some of the monarch's missteps. His convoluted reply failed to pacify loyal monarchists and only reinforced the accusation that Tirpitz had schemed against the Emperor during the war. The Crown Prince, whose fecklessness exceeded even that of his father, viewed the memoirs as "excellent."[83]

Early in 1920 Ella von Pohl, widow of the former Fleet Chief, published a selection of papers and letters in her husband's defense that was unflattering to Tirpitz.[84] Other prominent people, such as Houston Stewart Chamberlain, chimed in with praise for Tirpitz.[85]

A central player in constructing the interwar narrative was the Marinearchiv.[86] Since 1916 its chief was Captain, later Vice Admiral, Eberhard von Mantey. Too young (b.1869) to be a part of the Torpedo Gang, Mantey, with the help of the Weimar navy leadership, pursued an undeviating pro-Tirpitz line. As early as 1920 the multivolume series *Der Krieg zur See* (The war at sea) began to appear with startling rapidity. Edited by Captain Otto Groos, the purpose of the series was to foster the rebirth of the navy and to propagate a narrative to that end.

Mantey consulted Tirpitz every step of the way. The official history took Tirpitz's line and was therefore critical of Ingenohl, Pohl, and Müller. The books discreetly ignored Tirpitz's silence about the aggressive use of the fleet in the first few weeks of the war. Erich Raeder, later head of Hitler's navy, wrote the volumes on the cruiser war abroad and followed the same refrain, despite private reservations on some points.[87] When Müller and Ingenohl later tried to contest the pro-Tirpitz view, they made little headway against what was by then conventional opinion.[88]

"QUIET" YEARS, 1920–1924

With his historical legacy in safe hands, but with a leftist government in power, Tirpitz believed that his political life was at an end in 1920. The German National People's Party (DNVP), which succeeded the right wing of the imperial National Liberal Party, offered him a Reichstag seat in Charlottenburg (Berlin). Tirpitz turned it down. He believed that a democratically elected Reichstag with proportional representation was incapable of putting Germany in order and would lead to the election of people who would only cater to the masses.[89] The egalitarian Weimar system offended his more traditional and hierarchical view of government.

Tirpitz's reluctance to become actively involved in politics at that time proved to be wise. On 13 March 1920 his old collaborator/adversary from the Fatherland Party, Wolfgang Kapp, attempted a putsch. Admiralty Chief Trotha foolishly offered Kapp the support of the navy. Tirpitz wanted nothing to do with the improvised coup. After just a few days the putsch collapsed in the face of a general strike. On 23 March Trotha was sacked as Chief of Admiralty and was temporarily replaced by the more moderate William Michaelis, who had to fight to avoid the navy's abolition.[90] The putsch and the brutal assassinations of Finance Minister Erzberger and Foreign Secretary Rathenau, which Tirpitz condemned, were blows to the popularity of the Right in the country.

Tirpitz had some leftover business from the war. The victorious powers had spotlighted him as a candidate for war crime accusations, especially concerning the submarine warfare. The Treaty of Versailles referred the case to the high court in Leipzig. Based on the RMA's constitutional position in the Empire, it was easily demonstrated that Tirpitz had no command authority in military matters. The decision of December 1920 freed Tirpitz of any fear of prosecution.[91]

For the next several years Tirpitz, by then in his early seventies, played no active public role in politics. His long-range hope was to foster unity among squabbling groups on the right and, in the long run, to undermine the Republic.[92] He was not attracted to the mass politics approach of the fledgling National Socialist Party. For example, in September 1921 he declined to reply to an invitation from Rudolf Hess to join the party.[93]

Tirpitz envisioned a type of authoritarian government not possible, in his opinion, under a democratic constitution. His main goals were to gain independence from the Versailles Treaty, to cast off the shackles of disarmament, and to restore Germany to its accustomed place in Europe.[94] Gustav von Kahr, who as Prime Minister of Bavaria in 1920–21 had upheld rightist rule, became a good friend of Tirpitz and shared many of his views.

As Tirpitz's interest in active politics was rekindled, his financial situation continued to slide. Inflation, by then large but not yet catastrophic, ate into the value of his pension and of government bonds he had purchased during the war. Late in 1922 the possibility of a French incursion into the Ruhr started to drive inflation faster. Even Tirpitz's book royalties were affected. Originally linked to inflation, the publisher unilaterally reduced the royalties to 2.5 marks for a book whose price had risen as high as 750 marks.[95]

Until his election to the Reichstag in 1924, with its regular salary, Tirpitz even had to worry about the price of a train ticket. Some of his navy and industrialist friends tried to help quietly in ways that would avoid embarrassment.[96] In July 1922 he wrote to Mann, by then an associate of Alfred Hugenberg of the DNVP, "after the inflation, I do not know how I can maintain my household without help."[97]

Notwithstanding financial woes and authoritarian political views, Tirpitz, unlike some right-wing politicians, never succumbed to the growing anti-Semitism of the time. His former subordinate, Waldemar Vollerthun, foreign policy editor of the *Münchner Neueste Nachrichten*, had become friendly with Hess and other Nazis. When Vollerthun raised the question, Tirpitz replied:

> Regarding the Jewish question, I would readily talk with you further. In general I believe that our type of anti-Semitism is not advisable [*zweckmässig*] because it strives for unachievable goals. I regard it necessary and achievable to try to limit the inflow of Jews from the east, and I believe we must limit ourselves to, and concentrate on, this goal.[98]

It was not widely known, even within the family, that the father of Tirpitz's wife Marie was a convert from Judaism. Tirpitz's opinion is objectionable

432 TIRPITZ AND THE IMPERIAL GERMAN NAVY

to the modern eye but was relatively enlightened among people of his class and politics.

Tirpitz was invited to a rightist conference in Munich in early November 1922. Despite the expense, he made the trip and stayed at Kahr's residence.[99] A German default on reparations heightened the anticipation of French and Belgian intervention to collect the debt. At the conference Tirpitz renewed his acquaintance with Ludendorff and shared his concern about what the French might do. He saw the situation as a possible opportunity for political gain.[100]

> For us it is no doubt correct to . . . inflame hatred against France. If that were successful, it would also indirectly strengthen national feeling among the working masses, and it would suppress their internationalist sympathies.

On 11 January 1923 French President Raymond Poincaré ordered the French Army to occupy the Ruhr Valley, the center of German coal, iron, and steel production, to collect defaulted German reparations. The workers of the Ruhr, with government encouragement, responded with passive resistance. At first German national unity surged enormously, but the consequences included massive unemployment and inflation on an unprecedented scale.[101]

As Scheck has unearthed, Tirpitz spent much of late 1922 and 1923 plotting, in view of the crisis, to foster the idea of a nationalist dictatorship.[102] Others had similar ideas, many of them inspired by Mussolini's success in Italy. Tirpitz collaborated with Ulrich Wille Jr., a high-ranking Swiss officer and a relative of Tirpitz's wife. It is quite remarkable that a notable of neutral, democratic Switzerland would be so readily prepared to meddle in the internal affairs of Germany. The two drew up a plan to stir up a massive anti-French propaganda battle that would also damage the German Left. A coordinated group of business leaders, rightist parties, and patriotic organizations, including the small Nazi Party, would ratchet up agitation. Kahr, whose national popularity Tirpitz and Wille overestimated, would emerge, Mussolini-like, as the people's savior. This utopian plan foundered on, among other things, the aroused patriotism of the Ruhr workers.

In August 1923 the new Chancellor, Gustav Stresemann of the moderately rightist German People's Party (DVP), believed that the only way out of the employment/inflation crisis was to cease passive resistance in the Ruhr. When Tirpitz returned to Munich early in September he had lunch with Hitler, who made a poor impression. From this meeting Tirpitz observed the following: "This man may have a noble turn of mind; to me he seems inaccessible to reason: a fanatic inclined to craziness who pampering has made unrestrained."[103] On only a quick take, Tirpitz had perceptively read Hitler's narcissistic nature. He did not see Hitler as a credible national leader and retained his faith in Kahr.

By mid-September the situation appeared so bad that Tirpitz wrote in great alarm to Hugenberg: "Very likely we are on the brink of catastrophe." He doubted that Stresemann's plans would succeed, and feared, if they failed, that a dictatorship of the Left would replace it. He was also apprehensive that, with a French-sponsored secession of the Rhineland, regional separatism would spread throughout the country and national unity would collapse.[104] Tirpitz's own financial situation deteriorated further because of the hyperinflation. He told Trotha that his daughter, Margot, had left her work in a children's home in Lübeck to take a bank position at a higher salary. "Life has become quite hard for us."[105]

On 26 September Stresemann called off passive resistance and declared a national emergency, granting the government special powers. The Catholic Center Party announced a state of emergency within Bavaria and appointed Kahr dictator, hoping to contain the anticipated turmoil. Through Vollerthun, Kahr hinted that he expected that Tirpitz would soon play a national role during the crisis. Vollerthun was disappointed that General Hans von Seeckt, head of the army, had been unwilling to seize power in Berlin.[106]

On 8 November Hitler, Ludendorff, and their allies mounted a coup against Kahr and the Bavarian government with the optimistic intention of leading a march on Berlin, akin to what Mussolini had done in Italy. The details need not be addressed here, but in the short run it turned out to be a fiasco for Hitler. The so-called Beer Hall Putsch surprised Tirpitz. Afterwards it seemed to many that any possibility of a rapid national takeover from the Right was beyond achievement. Some, like Vollerthun, still believed that Tirpitz had a major role to play in the future, especially in foreign policy.[107]

Stresemann used the government's powers to good effect on the inflation question. On 15 November 1923, by an act of economic sleight-of-hand, he abolished the old mark and introduced a new one, the rentenmark. This resolved the inflation overnight, although other basic economic problems remained.

REICHSTAG DEPUTY, 1924–1928

The hopes and fears of radicals on both sides foundered during the state of emergency, although Seeckt's special powers expired at the end of February 1924. In November 1923 a new coalition government formed with the Center's Wilhelm Marx as Chancellor and Stresemann as Foreign Minister. Early in 1924 Tirpitz kept a low public profile. He was untainted by association with the Beer Hall Putsch. He remained in St. Blasien, hit hard by the aftermath of the inflation. "It has been bitter cold here. We have no coal."[108] He kept in close touch with Trotha and Vollerthun, who conspired with rightist groups on Tirpitz's behalf. The conflicted and cautious Seeckt was the focus of rightists who still hoped he would lead a kind of Fronde. Tirpitz's agents advertised his willingness to participate in some vaguely defined role. He was attractive to many, because he had credibility and support in both north and south Germany. Kahr's equivocal role in the Putsch had lowered his stock.[109]

On 5 April 1924 Tirpitz had a sobering meeting with Seeckt. It was clear that, in the short run at least, Seeckt had no interest in the deposition of President Ebert. Such an act might lead to chaos.[110] Tirpitz had earlier flirted with a belligerent stance against France in the event that Ebert was successfully overthrown. He found Seeckt's realism in foreign affairs convincing and agreed with his policy of developing the army gradually and surreptitiously with Soviet cooperation, beyond the limits of the armaments clauses of the Versailles Treaty. Tirpitz saw that, for a time, it was impossible for the Right to take power extra-constitutionally.

A few days after the meeting with Seeckt, Tirpitz received an invitation to run for the Reichstag from Oberpfalz-Niederbayern, as the leader of the DNVP ticket in Bavaria. After a few days Tirpitz replied, his feelings obviously mixed. He cited his age and the disorganization of the Reich, and felt that his contribution would be modest; nevertheless he accepted in the hope that he could help bridge the gaps between the parties. He insisted that he be placed in a high position on the DNVP national list in case he lost in Bavaria. Nostalgically he noted: "I am ready to enter into the ranks of the Reichstag, where in past years I found many understanding collaborators in the development of the German fleet of the past."[111] Getting such a well-known figure to lead its list in Bavaria, where in the past it had had small success, was a major coup for the DNVP.

Tirpitz engaged in little personal campaigning,[112] something he regarded with distaste. Mann secured financing for his campaign from Hugenberg. The DNVP presented him as a man above party, and he did not spell out specifically what he stood for. He talked vaguely of the advantages of Bismarckian-style federalism. The most important issue facing Germany in 1924 was whether to accept the Dawes Plan. The plan offered reduced reparation payments over the next four years, with a payment schedule after 1928 based, to some degree, on Germany's ability to pay. After a short interval the Allies would end their occupation of the Ruhr and respect German territorial integrity.

The offer posed a dilemma for the DNVP. Some nationalists saw the plan as a continued violation of German sovereignty, but almost all agreed that Germany had to make serious economic adjustments. Foreigners had to be persuaded to lend money and to invest in the country. Consistent with Tirpitz's desire to keep his candidacy on an elevated plane, he took no public position on the Dawes Plan, although his party, at least on paper, opposed it.[113]

On 4 May the DNVP had an excellent national electoral result. They won 19.5 percent of seats and became the second-largest party in the Reichstag, just 1 percent behind the Social Democrats. Tirpitz won his race convincingly, and the DNVP vote in Bavaria increased substantially from 7 percent to 11.6 percent. The relatively favorable outcome contributed to the party's overall success in the country. Its electoral good fortune posed a Hobson's choice for the DNVP. If it led or joined a governing coalition with more leftist parties, that would mean implicit acceptance of the Weimar system. It would have to swallow some variation of the Dawes Plan. In the first weeks after the election, Tirpitz did what he could to get the other right-wing parties to work in concert with the DNVP.[114]

After the election, during the jockeying among the parties, Tirpitz received a surprise: the leadership of the DNVP wanted to propose him for Chancellor.[115] Not surprisingly, given Tirpitz's past reluctance to assume responsibility in a sphere larger than the navy, he hesitated. How he was ultimately persuaded is unclear, but on 21 May the DNVP announced his candidacy for the Chancellorship. Anticipating a hostile foreign reaction, partly out of revulsion to the U-boat war, the Center and the liberal German Democratic Party (DDP) rejected his candidacy.

With delicate negotiations expected over the Dawes Plan, Foreign Secretary Stresemann asked German diplomats to ascertain foreign attitudes toward Tirpitz as Chancellor. The reports showed that a DNVP-led coalition would undermine the confidence that Stresemann's diplomacy had built up. A coalition led by the middle parties would be acceptable but only if the DNVP were willing to accept the Dawes Plan. The negative reaction to Tirpitz as Chancellor was widespread, with the express belief that his appointment would imperil international loans to Germany. Negotiations with the DNVP failed, and on 8 June 1924 the former coalition of the middle parties and the Social Democrats returned, with Marx again as Chancellor.

Although Tirpitz still believed that some form of dictatorship was necessary, he recognized that, had he become Chancellor, the need to juggle a multiparty coalition would have made forceful initiatives impossible.[116] This calculation reinforced his timidity about taking on large, non-naval responsibilities. Given Germany's precarious situation, with foreign loans the only realistic solution to economic recovery, an activist foreign policy would only have aggravated the situation. Tirpitz's vast experience in dealing with the Imperial Reichstag stood him in good stead as a member of the more powerful and democratic Reichstag of the 1920s. As he entered the new Reichstag, it remained to be seen how he could function as an individual member of the DNVP under the Weimar Constitution. Publicly he presented himself as a senior statesman, dedicated to the restoration of Germany to a position which he and many others saw as its rightful position in Europe.

It soon became clear, as Scheck has noted, that Tirpitz "was as tough a practitioner of power politics as he had always been."[117] Tirpitz saw Stresemann as his chief adversary and, in some ways, the heir of Bethmann, though the analogy was weak. Stresemann was a far more capable statesman than Bethmann. Like Tirpitz, he wanted to maneuver Germany into a more powerful position, but his methods were subtle and in tune with the diplomatic realities of the 1920s, so very different from the prewar years. Tirpitz and the DNVP thought that Allied concessions to Stresemann were a cynical ploy to bolster a German democracy that was internationally weak.

The central point was whether and on what terms to accept the Dawes Plan. The middle and leftist parties supported it, but a consensus, including at least some DNVP votes, was needed to give foreign bankers enough confidence to invest in Germany. Tirpitz and the DNVP publicly opposed the plan. Their stubbornness, if not carried too far, was useful to Stresemann in his negotiations with the Allies. To attain marginally better terms, he could argue that he had to satisfy at least part of the DNVP. The French, for domestic political reasons, could not withdraw their occupation troops immediately. Negotiations in London led to a tempting offer of a French and Belgian withdrawal from the right bank of the Rhine within a year.

Tirpitz understood that the offer was appealing to some moderates within the DNVP. During September 1924 the main clauses of the Dawes Plan passed the Reichstag by a majority, without DNVP support. One crucial point, on a railroad issue, was treated as a constitutional question that required a two-thirds majority. Without its passage, the Dawes Plan would fail. Large economic interests, desperately dependent on foreign loans, pressured the DNVP to vote yes; wounded national sensibilities favored a negative vote.

In secret party councils, amid many intrigues, Tirpitz bit the bullet and, along with the party moderates, decided to vote yes. In a tumultuous meeting Tirpitz's faction managed to divide the DNVP vote in a secret caucus.[118] In the end the DNVP vote was split, with 48 in favor—including agrarians and industrialists—and 52 opposed. The split was enough to pass the bill by 71 percent, just over the two-thirds required. Tirpitz took some heat for his reluctant vote; nevertheless, he was chosen honorary party chairman.[119] While DNVP deputies argued among themselves over whether to join a governing coalition, Ebert dissolved the Reichstag on 20 October. The elections of December 1924 would be the second within seven months. Tirpitz's initial take on the party's electoral prospects was optimistic.[120]

As Tirpitz prepared to run in the election of 7 December 1924, he became embroiled in a public uproar over the publication, early in November, of his first volume of annotated documents. The volume, titled *Der Aufbau der deutschen Weltmacht. Politische Dokumente I* (The rise of German world power. Political documents I), was published by the prestigious Stuttgart publishing house Cotta. The book covered the period from 1906 to the outbreak of war in 1914. Tirpitz's enemies accused him of stealing documents from the Marinearchiv. Evidence suggests, according to Scheck, that Stresemann successfully used the scandal to disqualify Tirpitz from the Chancellorship and from running for President in an election scheduled for June 1925.[121]

The genesis of the volume, which Scheck skillfully tracked,[122] was rooted largely in Tirpitz's desire to refute the critics of his memoirs who accused him of lies and manipulation. As with his memoirs, Tirpitz intended *Aufbau* to be a preemptive strike against his detractors. He was in a hurry to publish the book because he knew that the Foreign Office was poised to publish the naval/diplomatic volumes of the massive series Die Große Politik der europäischen Kabinette, 1871–1914 (Diplomacy of the European powers, 1871–1914), under the editorship of the Bethmann-friendly Friedrich Thimme, one of his own prior critics. Under fierce pressure of time, and to the chagrin of Cotta, in the late summer Tirpitz and his editor, Kern, submitted a sloppily edited set of documents that only covered the years 1906 to 1914, not through 1918 as they had promised. Kern angrily demanded a second volume, but Cotta passed on the opportunity.

The publication created a scandal. The Foreign Office had both a "good" and a "real" reason to attack it. The "good" reason was that Tirpitz had used official materials in the book that the Foreign Office claimed he had taken with him when he retired in 1916. Leftists who had done something similar in Bavaria had been prosecuted. It later emerged that Widenmann, in 1918, had indeed walked into the RMA and removed documents from the RMA files that a left-wing government might have used to embarrass the navy. Tirpitz apparently returned most of the documents to the navy but, had the Foreign Office brought legal charges, Tirpitz may well have had cause for distress.

The "real" reason for the dismay of the Foreign Office, and of some others on the right, was that Tirpitz published many documents which contained the Emperor's often belligerent, arrogant, and fantasy-driven marginalia. The Foreign Office feared that such disclosures could hamper the official effort to counter the war-guilt clause of the Versailles Treaty. The problem was not that Tirpitz was dishonest, though he was deceptive in some of his editing, but rather that he was *too* honest in the book, and this threatened to undermine the official policy of "patriotic self-censorship."[123]

In his campaign for the 7 December 1924 election Tirpitz, because he only spoke before friendly crowds, managed to ignore the fracas publicly.[124] He recruited former naval officers with access to the nationalist press to try to reframe the controversy. Personal attacks on Thimme's character and competence as a historian followed.[125] After the election the controversy died down. The second volume, *Deutsche Ohnmachtspolitik im Weltkrieg* (The impotence of German power in the war) was published by a small right-wing press in 1926. The publication uproar, though it did not hinder Tirpitz's election, demonstrated that he was willing to throw the Emperor overboard,[126] and, indirectly, it weakened the argument against the war-guilt clause by reinforcing his contention that his naval policy had been both beneficial and necessary.

Even though he ignored the archival theft accusation, Tirpitz campaigned vigorously throughout much of the country, as he had done seven years earlier for the Fatherland Party.[127] He was still a reluctant public warrior, however.[128] His burst of energy was related to the anticipated presidential election, when Ebert's term expired in June 1925. Tirpitz spoke as a man with barely concealed presidential aspirations, urging unity among the DNVP, the DVP, and the BVP, and even reaching out to the more conservative elements of the Center.

The December election provided what, in hindsight, would be the DNVP's greatest success. It won 20.5 percent of the national vote, a full percentage point higher than in May 1924. The Social Democrats remained the largest party, at 26 percent, up 5.5 percent from the previous vote. In Bavaria the DNVP's national vote increased from 11.6 percent to 14.4 percent. Stresemann's DVP vote rose to 10%, a reward for his artful diplomacy. The Communist Party (Kommunistische Partei Deutschland, or KPD) dropped substantially to 9%. With foreign loans again available, the Dawes Plan in place, and the economy in recovery, extremism on both the left and the right seemed to be receding.

Tirpitz became the party's honorary chairman and represented the DNVP on the Reichstag's Defense and Foreign Affairs Committees.[129] Tirpitz had his eye on the presidential election and approached Seeckt for support that was not forthcoming. Seeckt noted in his diary about the meeting: "He wants to become Reich president, but he will not succeed. He suffers from senile vanity and the need to boast."[130]

The election was expedited by Ebert's unexpected death on 28 February 1925. The first ballot was at the end of March. The leadership of the DNVP and the DVP tried to form a rightist alliance behind one candidate. Opposition from the DVP, Stresemann's party, the BVP, and even some in the DNVP doomed Tirpitz's presidential hopes,[131] partly because a Tirpitz presidency would have undesirable foreign policy consequences. The Center nominated the former Chancellor Marx. The Social Democrats' decision to support Marx on the second ballot apparently doomed all hope among the Right for the presidency.

This conundrum prompted the DNVP to try to persuade the reluctant Hindenburg to run on the second ballot. He was well aware of his age and weariness. In reply to entreaties, he stressed his monarchist feelings and political inexperience. As a last throw of the dice, the DNVP sent Tirpitz to Hindenburg as an emissary. Tirpitz appealed strongly to Hindenburg's Prussian sense of duty, arguing that only the old soldier had any chance to defeat Marx, who had socialist support. Finally Hindenburg, feeling hard-pressed, consented, contingent on the Emperor's permission, which was forthcoming. If Tirpitz made a difference in Hindenburg's decision, it was probably his most significant political act during his Weimar years. The final vote, on 26 April, was close. Hindenburg, with 48.3 percent of the vote, beat Marx by only 3 percent. Had the Communist Thälmann (winning 6.4%) not been in the race, the outcome might have been different.

For Tirpitz, the result was too close for comfort. Hindenburg won "only by a horse's length." Much would depend, he realized, on who controlled the President's entourage, and he feared that the old *Feldmarschall* "cannot be won over to the policy of an iron fist in a velvet glove."[132] Tirpitz and his comrades lost that battle, as Hindenburg made no attempt to change the constitution and supported Stresemann's gradualist foreign policy.[133] Despite Tirpitz's early hopes, he could not manipulate Hindenburg as he had William II.

Stresemann's success in getting DNVP moderates to accept the Locarno Treaty was a crushing blow for Tirpitz's ambition for a return to the Bismarckian system. The treaty guaranteed Germany's western borders and paved the way for entry into the League of Nations. On 25 October

DNVP hard-liners, by a majority within the party caucus, forced DNVP ministers to resign from the Cabinet.

Tirpitz fought back the best he could, both within and outside the party.[134] He correctly sensed some ambivalence about the treaty on Hindenburg's part. In a memo to the President, unvetted by his party, Tirpitz argued that the treaty was tantamount to "a legalization of the *Diktat* of Versailles." He called "unbearable" the demilitarization of the Rhineland that forbade even a single German soldier from setting foot in that part of Germany. To join the League would be to voluntarily acquiesce in the enforcement of the treaty.[135] Hindenburg's indifferent reply disheartened Tirpitz. He felt that his efforts had all been in vain.

After his failed interventions with Hindenburg, Tirpitz became further disenchanted with his DNVP colleagues' willingness to lean in a moderate direction by accepting Stresemann's foreign policy. On 23 March 1926 Tirpitz gave his last, defiant Reichstag speech. To the hoots and catcalls of the Left, he passionately argued for a withdrawal of the government's application for League of Nations membership.[136] A few days later Tirpitz visited Hindenburg in a vain attempt to stiffen his resistance to League entry.[137]

By 1926 Tirpitz was seventy-seven years old. Hindenburg's indifference to his ideas seemed to sap his zest for combat. He spent more time away from Berlin and took long cures. His Reichstag salary and improved economic situation allowed such amenities once again.

By the fall of 1926, once Germany had entered the League, Tirpitz began to see some advantages to German participation. He felt that, over time, the League could help lift some of the burdens of Versailles and strengthen Germany's international position.[138] The new Chancellor, again Marx, tried and failed to put together a governing coalition that included the Social Democrats. The door was open once more for the DNVP. Once it agreed to accept Stresemann's foreign policy, it could join the new coalition. On 29 January 1927 it joined the BVP, the DVP, and the Center, and received several important Cabinet posts. Tirpitz took no major initiatives in his final year in the Reichstag. He limited himself to making further calls for unity among German nationalists.[139]

By January 1928 Tirpitz was already planning to move from the pleasant house that overlooked the Black Forest town of St. Blasien to Feldafing, on a scenic lake near Munich. He regretted leaving behind friends of thirty years, but the political environment there had turned unfriendly for a man of his beliefs, and he felt more at home in Bavaria.[140] On 6 February Tirpitz informed the party leadership that he would not run in the May Reichstag elections.[141] Jost Dülffer aptly summed up Tirpitz's parliamentary career:

> Despite his disinclination towards party engagement, he believed he would be able, at least, to be involved in the leadership of a right-wing convergence in the Republic's politics; but he achieved this effect neither within the DNVP nor in wider circles. He failed to successfully promote his candidacy for Reich President.[142]

LAST DAYS, 1928–1930

By September 1928 Tirpitz and Marie had moved to Feldafing, not far from the Ebenhausen home of the Hassell family. By late 1928, in anticipation of William II's seventieth birthday on 27 January, efforts were afoot to reconcile the former Emperor with Tirpitz. Retired Admiral Magnus von Levetzow reached out to Trotha as a possible middleman. Trotha gingerly wrote to Tirpitz on 9 October with Levetzow's suggestion that Tirpitz, on the occasion of the birthday, visit Doorn, Holland, where William II was in exile.[143] Trotha's reply to Levetzow was pessimistic, offering, as excuses, Tirpitz's health and his difficult relations with Prinz Heinrich, strained since the publication of Tirpitz's memoirs.[144] Tirpitz wavered about accepting the invitation, worried, too, that Müller might be there, which would add to the awkwardness. In physical pain that disturbed his sleep (very likely from atherosclerosis), such a trip would be difficult.[145] On 5 November, however, Tirpitz decided that he must "bite the sour apple" and go to Doorn.[146]

The Empress Hermine (Augusta Victoria had died in 1921) handled the negotiations from Doorn and did not inform her imperial husband until very late in the game.[147] She wanted an apology from Tirpitz, which he stubbornly resisted. Finally Tirpitz avoided an invitation to the birthday celebration and, instead, sent a noncommittal but gracious telegram that in one sentence recalled their collaboration. Though Tirpitz did not know it, the Emperor was just as glad as he to avoid a personal meeting.[148] William II sent an equally brief but cordial telegram for Tirpitz's eightieth birthday on 19 March 1929.

Tirpitz's final political act was to sign a petition and join a rally in protest of the Young Plan, which reduced, but continued payments, of reparations.[149] On his way home from Berlin to Feldafing he suffered a heart attack. He died on 6 March 1930, just short of his eighty-first birthday. He lies at rest today at the Waldfriedhof in Munich with his wife Marie and daughter Margot. He received a state funeral, with politicians and military leaders, active and retired, in attendance. Present also, though uninvited by the family, were rightist marchers including members of Hitler's private army, the Sturm Abteilung.[150] A few days later a quiet memorial service took place in the Old Garrison Church in Berlin, where Alfred and Marie had married forty-six years ago.[151]

In what, in hindsight, was a remarkably ironic event, on 1 April 1939, in the presence of Hitler, Ilse von Hassell christened the mighty battleship *Tirpitz* at the government yards in Wilhelmshaven. The elderly Trotha gave the dedication.[152] A little more than five years later Ulrich von Hassell was executed for his participation in the plot to assassinate Hitler. In the Norwegian leads, a few miles south of the small city of Tromsø, the remains of the *Tirpitz*, sister ship of the *Bismarck*, lie underwater in a small inlet, sunk on 12 November 1944 by a gigantic British bomb.

17
CONCLUSION

Tirpitz entered the navy in 1865 as a gangly adolescent. From the outset he showed elements of the intelligence, diligence, and sheer determination that marked his entire career. His father, jokingly but prophetically, predicted he would be a Grand Admiral. As he matured into a junior officer and suffered the frustrating experience of serving through two wars without firing a shot, he demonstrated a talent, rare among his contemporaries, for working out on paper ideas that were logical, empirical, and creative. This talent attracted the attention of both peers and superiors and helped him obtain enviable career assignments, first (1877) as a junior officer in the mint-new Torpedo Arm, and later (1892) as Chief of Staff of the Oberkommando. Except for royalty, there was no early promotion within the navy's iron-hard seniority system, and he was never promoted ahead of his own seniority (fifth within the "crew" of 1865).

Luck, too, played a role, even before he entered the navy. When the training ship *Amazone* sank with all hands in 1861, six senior officers and nineteen ensigns and sea cadets were among the crew, and each would have preceded him on the seniority list. Good fortune also spared him from the accidents and exposure to disease that cut short many careers. A lifelong hypochondriac, in 1876 he dreaded a posting to China. When he briefly went to China in 1896–97 he did become ill. Instead of service abroad, in 1877 he was assigned to the Torpedo Arm. He served there for twelve years with an unusual degree of autonomy and rose from Lt. Commander to Captain, with increasing levels of responsibility, taking a giant step toward the creation of a formidable reputation.

Like most successful officers in any navy, Tirpitz had a gift for cultivating his superiors. Rear Admiral Carl Batsch, in 1876 Chief of Staff of the Admiralty, very likely chose him to enter the recently founded Torpedo Arm. While there, Tirpitz's driving energy and leadership qualities won him the merited patronage of Stosch and Caprivi, the two soldiers who led the navy between 1873 and 1888. Later, despite Tirpitz's prickly personality, Senden and William II advanced his career in the Oberkommando and the RMA.

While at the Torpedo Arm he attracted and trained some of the most capable young naval officers. Many of them followed him into the Oberkommando and the RMA. This group, the "Torpedo Gang," is documented in detail for the first time in this work (see the appendix). The group became a cadre that Tirpitz could mobilize in official and unofficial ways during his many power struggles within the navy. Some, such as Ahlefeld, Dähnhardt, Heeringen, and Hopmann, remained consistently loyal to him; others, such as Fischel, Pohl, and Müller, became his adversaries after about 1908. The role of the Torpedo Gang, and cadre formation in the navy more generally, deserve more attention than they have so far received from historians.[1] Carl-Axel Gemzell has addressed this question but solely in the realm of strategic planning.

What made Tirpitz such a major figure in the history of Wilhelmian Germany?

STRATEGY AND GEOGRAPHY

The risk theory and its flaws (see chapter 10) need not be recapitulated here. If it was sincerely meant, it was a disastrous conception. Its premises were demolished with the formation of the Triple Entente. By 1914 German isolation was so complete that the High Seas Fleet, despite Tirpitz's Herculean efforts, was nearly as inferior to the Allied fleets as the German fleet had been to the Royal Navy in 1898. Numbers alone do not tell the whole story. If one ignores the role of Tirpitz's policies in tying Britain to France, in some respects Germany's naval position had improved considerably since 1898. Assuming that the German Army would have invaded Belgium in a war against France, and that Britain would have fought Germany anyway, Tirpitz's policy was a limited success. Marder details his view of what would likely have been the results of a decisive British victory at Jutland. He therefore inadvertently points out what the naval situation might have been if Germany had fought the Entente without a respectable fleet.[2] A negligible German fleet would have allowed British light forces to penetrate Helgoland Bight and seal up German U-boats. The Royal Navy could have forced entry into the Baltic and opened supply lines to beleaguered Russia. Swedish iron ore imports, vital to war industry, would have stopped. Defense of the Pomeranian coast would have required an army presence there, even if the British were not rash enough to attempt an actual landing.

Tirpitz's achievements were more than countered by his geographic and strategic blindness. The idea that a decisive battle would, even must, be fought between Helgoland and the Thames was deeply flawed. A German attack on the Thames estuary, 300 nautical miles west-southwest of Wilhemshaven, would have been dangerous, possibly suicidal. A glance at a map shows how vulnerable the High Seas Fleet would have been to a flanking attack by the Grand Fleet. Tirpitz's famous statement about a battle "from Helgoland to the Thames" really only meant a battle near Helgoland. The most crucial British seaports were on the southern and western coasts, far from the North Sea. The Helgoland Bight was a strategic dead end, as Wegener recognized in 1915.

Tirpitz's idea of deterrence failed as soon as Britain entered the war. Against his expectations in 1900, British governments, Conservative and Liberal, showed their willingness to compete in both construction and fleet redistribution when they thought their vital interests were threatened. British wealth and patriotism, plus Fisher's scrapping of many obsolete ships, solved the manning problem that Tirpitz had believed was insurmountable for a volunteer navy. In only one narrow sense did deterrence work, but it was in a way that went against Tirpitz's interests. The High Seas Fleet was strong enough by 1914 to keep the Grand Fleet from storming into Helgoland Bight. This fact made Tirpitz the victim of his own success, because it removed even the small chance of a major success if Jellicoe acted rashly. Tirpitz's fleet was not large enough to seek decisive battle any substantial distance north or west of Helgoland, but it was too large and politically important to risk in a reckless attack. The unique geographical circumstances that permitted a wide blockade proved to be the final determinant to frustrate Tirpitz's design for a battle near Helgoland.

On several occasions before the war Tirpitz acknowledged the possibility of a wide blockade. As early as 1894, in Dienstschrift IX, when he criticized defensive use of the fleet, he argued that the defense could not assume that the enemy would come to them. The attacker need not come close to the German coast but could keep its large units far out to sea. A German defensive fleet would then have to choose between demoralizing inactivity and a fight in the open sea with inferior numbers.[3] He later forgot or ignored this insightful premonition.

In 1909 Tirpitz told the Budget Commission: "Today a close blockade in the old sense is no longer possible." The enemy's battlefleet could stand off several hundred miles.[4] In May 1914 Tirpitz asked Fleet Chief Ingenohl: "What would you do if, in the event of war, the English do not come to our coasts?"[5] Büchsel in 1902, and Heeringen in 1911–13, raised the same question, when, as Admiralstab Chiefs, they wrestled with the impossible task of planning for naval war with Britain. The canny Heeringen recognized, as did Tirpitz to some degree, that unrealistic offensive scenarios were not seriously meant but were a sop to the Emperor and a boost to the fleet's morale.

Why was Tirpitz, who had great influence over war planning, not more attuned to the possibility of a wide blockade, even though he was obviously aware of it? The precise reason for such self-deception is hard to ascertain. Tirpitz had successfully squelched any independent views on the matter either inside or outside the navy. Perhaps this blindness came from his uncritical attachment to a Social Darwinist worldview; whatever the case, it was another example of the narrowness of view entailed by his adherence to the Navy Law and all its consequences, such as designing a whole fleet of capital ships and escorts to fight in concert solely near Helgoland. This was a result of his bureaucratic politics mentality. He was unable to take seriously any contingencies that were at variance with his preconceptions.

Looked at purely from the perspective of German national interest, the navy should have been the greatest advocate of friendly relations with Britain, although for a variety of reasons an alliance would probably not have been wise. Just as the Pentagon needed a strong Soviet military during the Cold War to justify its huge appropriations, Tirpitz needed the Royal Navy as a yardstick and an "enemy" to justify the creation of his power base. To actually fight the British, let alone wage an offensive against them, was a highly dubious proposition, even as the High Seas Fleet grew. Without positing the "strongest seapower" as an enemy, a prophecy that became self-fulfilling, Tirpitz could have built a more than respectable navy even without the "threat." Because of the dismal position of the German fleet relative to France and Russia in 1898, Tirpitz's brilliantly systematic approach could very likely have resulted in passing a law like that of 1898, which was readily defensible on national security grounds since the other secondary naval powers already had building plans in place. If, beyond that, he could ultimately replace a few cruisers and the *Siegfried* class of coastal defense battleships with real ones, Germany could at least safeguard Baltic lines of communication even if the British entered the war. Against just France and Russia, such a fleet would reinforce Germany's splendid interior lines. With Britain in the war, Germany would have been scarcely worse off than it was in 1914, even with smaller forces. The decision to use Britain as a measuring rod had fateful consequences and was, arguably, Tirpitz's greatest mistake.

In 1911 Hopmann confided in his diary that the fleet had grown "like a greenhouse plant." As a result, its branches lacked dynamism. He believed (for the 1912 Novelle) that it would be enough to put a third squadron into service and add a few cruisers. He thought that England would understand this and not venture a renewed arms race. What would Germany do with sixty capital ships? England would see that number as a permanent threat. He felt that Germany could safely get by with a 1:2 ratio, and he saw a ratio of 2:3 as provocative, but he never confided his view to Tirpitz.[6]

An even greater misfortune was the lethal combination of the Schlieffen Plan and a long war. For a short, successful war, the invasion of Belgium and consequent British intervention might not have changed the outcome. A defensive stance against France with an offensive against Russia, the elder Moltke's plan, would have been far less likely to bring Britain into the war. Without Britain in the war, Tirpitz's navy would have been strong enough to prevent an effective French blockade. As Hobson has pointed out, a more moderately sized fleet, combined with a non-hegemonic military defense strategy toward France, would have made it far more difficult for Britain to threaten Germany's worldwide maritime interests.[7] Neutral powers, especially the United States, would have been more likely to uphold neutral rights, to Germany's advantage.

The most dangerous fault line in German defense policy was its complete lack of coordination by the Supreme War Lord, William II. Without regard for consequences, he allowed Tirpitz, until 1912, to hijack the defense agenda and make it likely that Germany would have Britain as an enemy as well as France and Russia. In addition, the army and navy had entirely separate war plans. The army wanted to invade Belgium and leave Denmark alone, and the navy wanted the opposite. The Emperor, who until 1912 supported Tirpitz's design, should have taken a wider view of the national interest and had at least a semblance of a sensible grand strategy.

TIRPITZ AND REICH DIPLOMACY

Tirpitz played a surprisingly small direct role in German diplomacy prior to the war. He failed, in November 1897, to delay or even avoid the annexation of land for a naval base in China, even though in his postwar writings he claimed credit for the colony. At that critical time he concentrated solely on preparations for the First Navy Law. He feared annexation might lead to unwelcome foreign or domestic complications that might derail it. Those who were eager to go ahead with the forced lease scorned his nervousness.

In April 1898 Tirpitz dismissed, as too risky, William II's initiative to acquire the Danish Virgin Islands. Such a potential provocation, he argued, should be avoided while the fleet construction program was still in its infancy, at the beginning of the "danger zone." For unclear reasons he briefly changed his mind on this point in the summer of 1899 and supported the Emperor's pressure on the Foreign Office to investigate the purchase of St. John. He even generated some press agitation in favor of it. Bülow and Holstein, not eager to anger the United States, managed to squelch the idea.[8]

In November 1904, in the wake of Anglo-German tension caused by the Dogger Bank fiasco, William II, Bülow, and Holstein suggested an alliance proposal to Russia. Foreign Secretary Richthofen, with Tirpitz's support, opposed it. Tirpitz was afraid of a "Copenhagen"-style attack on the German fleet and thought that a Russian alliance might be dangerously provocative to Britain.[9] Here, too, the preservation of his fleet and the Navy Law was of far greater importance to Tirpitz than the putative "alliance value" corollary to the risk theory.

With one important exception, Tirpitz generally did not meddle in the bureaucratic realm of the Foreign Office, although he fought vigorously against the Foreign Office or any other body that threatened his realm. Tirpitz did not protest when he was not officially informed in advance of the Emperor's descent on Tangier in 1905 or even about the landing of the gunboat *Panther* in Agadir in 1911; nevertheless, he took full advantage of these events to advance his own agenda. This behavior clearly illustrates that Tirpitz had little interest in the diplomatic side of Weltpolitik. His form of Weltpolitik was more concerned with economic development and, to some degree, with his disappointment that Germans living abroad were assimilating into the local culture, especially in the United States.

Tirpitz's life's work of building a navy had, nonetheless, tremendous diplomatic consequences for Germany. At first welcomed or regarded with indifference in Britain, the growth of a rival battlefleet began gradually to awaken fear from about 1902 on. On one level, Tirpitz seemed to understand this. He rued the Emperor's flaunting bombast about the fleet, most conspicuously at Kiel Week. Tirpitz himself contributed to the fear by coordinating agitation when a Novelle was pending. His efforts to tamp down agitation at times inconvenient to him were only partly successful. He tried to make the best of the situation by presenting himself as a "moderate" compared to the Flottenverein. English invasion novels and press sensationalism had real diplomatic consequences, as did the occasional British use of the German fleet to raise fear at times coordinated with annual estimates debates. As usual in arms races, manipulators on both sides played off each other.

Although Fisher's naval reforms, culminating in his Dreadnought and Invincible policies, were not originally directed against Germany, his energetic conduct amplified the background noise that strengthened anti-German aspects of Britain's Entente relationships. Inept German diplomacy was a bigger factor in the Anglo-German estrangement than was Tirpitz's fleet, but the latter was an important reinforcing factor that concealed the advantages of peaceful diplomatic and economic relations between the two countries.

In the last months of his Chancellorship Bülow, and then Bethmann, began to understand the volatile effects of the naval rivalry on Germany's international position. A naval arms agreement would ease financial pressures in both countries and perhaps open a way to better relations.

Conceivably such a measure might have made a difference during the series of crises that led to the war. To carry a counterfactual too far is not a course historians can sanction, but it is hard to see how a naval agreement could have worsened the situation, and it might have created beneficial possibilities.

Tirpitz's negative position against even the feeblest naval agreement, such as information exchange, showed him at his bureaucratically inflexible worst. At every step he fought bitterly against any idea that threatened to undermine in the slightest either the existing edifice of the Navy Law or his ability to increase it still further. The Emperor reinforced Tirpitz's stubbornness. Only with the 1912 Novelle, when the army finally resumed an active role in the struggle for money, did William II agree to a small reduction in the bill. Tirpitz nevertheless kept intact the core of the Navy Law even as it became clear by the end of 1912 that his power was waning. Tirpitz later claimed that his "acceptance" of Churchill's suggestion for a 16:10 capital ship ratio marked the end of the naval race; by then, however, the damage had been done. Only the invasion of Belgium and the concomitant threat of German continental hegemony made it virtually certain that Germany and Britain would be on opposite sides in a war; in any event, Tirpitz's perverse tenacity and ongoing influence over the Emperor certainly set the table for fiasco. Tirpitz was therefore a major contributor to the ineptitude and recklessness of Reich diplomacy. Even though there is no convincing evidence that Tirpitz wanted war in 1914, he did nothing to head it off. His diminished circumstances by then made him a minor player in the crisis of July/August 1914.

TIRPITZ AND THE REICHSTAG'S BUDGET RIGHT

A central question in the assessment of Tirpitz's life is Berghahn's assertion that a principal aspect of the "Tirpitz Plan" was to preserve the Prussian/German monarchical system. The navy would be made financially independent of the Reichstag by the establishment of an "iron budget" that, once fixed, could not be reduced. The aim was to weaken the Reichstag by directly attacking its power of the purse, particularly with an automatic replacement clause for battleships, ultimately set at twenty years by the 1908 Novelle.[10] The fleet was therefore built "against the Reichstag." Tirpitz's ideal situation would have been a fleet of about sixty large ships, each eternally replaced at a tempo of three per year, a goal well launched by the time the war started.

By all appearances Tirpitz had his way with the Reichstag. Only once, in 1900, when he deferred six large cruisers (subsequently added in the 1906 Novelle) was he denied a major construction request. The Reichstag appeared to be committed for all time.

In practice matters were more complicated and, in some respects, contradictory. The "iron budget" was more contingent than it appeared. Only in hindsight, and only because Tirpitz and his chief collaborators, Capelle and Dähnhardt, took enormous pains to woo and court the Reichstag, was the RMA so successful. Berghahn exhaustively documents (as this work does in chapters 9–14) how Tirpitz tried to cajole, manipulate, and reason with deputies of virtually all parties first to establish and then expand and consolidate the Navy Law. As Berghahn argues: "It does not seem correct to consider the State Secretary as the forerunner of a minister responsible to a parliament. He saw himself as a true servant of the crown."[11] At least between 1897 and 1908 Tirpitz was not moving "in the direction of a parliamentary-democratic form of government, but was tending towards a plebiscitary supported authoritarian-conservative power-state."[12]

It would make no sense to argue that Tirpitz was a democrat rather than a committed monarchist, although in 1915 and after, because of the war and disagreements with William II, his monarchist loyalty was severely tried. Discussion of Tirpitz and the budget right should be limited to the prewar era. Berghahn is correct to disagree with Steinberg's view that Tirpitz was a "liberal." On the other hand, Tirpitz functioned in the Reichstag in a manner completely different from the army's approach, which held parliament in utter contempt.

A paradox here needs further explanation. If Tirpitz had had his way in foreign policy, the Reich would have pursued a quiescent foreign policy while construction carried the navy through the "danger zone," only to emerge as a fully fledged world power after fifteen or twenty years. With this policy the Emperor, thirty-eight years old in 1897, would have had to keep his mouth shut until he reached his late fifties. Passivity was necessary now in order to dominate later. Similarly, by this reasoning, Tirpitz would have had to cooperate with the Reichstag in the quasi-parliamentary manner he pursued, until, when the fleet was near completion, the regime could dominate the Reichstag. Parliamentary cooperation now would enable the iron fist later. If one accepts the "Tirpitz Plan" at face value, one would also have to accept a remarkable degree of deferred gratification from an Emperor not noted for his patience. This point alone would make unlikely any long-term conspiratorial "plan" that involved the Emperor.

Even after the 1900 Navy Law brought in automatic replacement and dropped the financial limits of the 1898 law, Tirpitz was enmeshed in a multiple dilemma. He had agreed to a projected table of estimates for construction that did not take into account continuous cost increases. These escalated enormously with the compelling necessity to match *Dreadnought* and, later, *Invincible*. The ramshackle imperial tax system created a budget problem that, in the long term, could only be solved by large increases in direct taxes, a dagger in the heart of any monarchic alliance of agrarians and industrialists. The determined stewardship of Adolf Wermuth as Finance Secretary (1909–12) compounded the financial problem for Tirpitz. He further had to contend with an imperial master and external pressure groups, such as the Flottenverein, all pushing hard for more and bigger ships. In addition, Front officers demanded militarily justified increases in readiness.

His principal weapon to cope with all these challenges was his masterful way of dealing with the Reichstag. "Cow trading," which was Hollmannn's policy, was not enough. Whether he wanted to or not, he had no choice but to function as a quasi-parliamentary minister in order to preserve the Navy Law against all comers. That he did so with surpassing skill and guile is a tribute to his cunning and resourcefulness. If preservation of the Navy Law was his first priority, an indispensable means of doing so was to keep the Reichstag's confidence. In contrast to more bombastic elements in the government, he seldom threatened dissolution. He tried to make his own direct propaganda effort (as opposed to those of the Flottenverein) appear "objective" and backed it by reams of statistical evidence. He made his cost estimate tables appear to be a limit, and went to great lengths, often at the expense of the Front, to keep to it. Their howls, often leaked to the public by Tirpitz's opponents, reinforced the penny-pinching image he tried to project.

Although Tirpitz himself spoke sparingly in the Reichstag, the Bundesrat benches there were filled with knowledgeable RMA experts led by Capelle and Dähnhardt. To the dismay of many officers, Capelle and

Dähnhardt gave selected parliamentarians, such as Center leaders Lieber and Erzberger, access to RMA secret files and cars. Such "insider" treatment, and the feeling of self-importance that came with it, bound key deputies to the RMA. Michaelis noted: "The young men of the RMA had to go arm-in-arm with Social Democratic deputies. This may have been for the greater good, but I did not find this witch's policy to be very congenial."[13] Tirpitz took deputies from many parties on naval inspection trips and, rare for civilians, to dinner with officers.

Apart from Richter and the Social Democrats, few delegates would suggest a return to annual appropriation, even when there were particularly high price hikes after 1906. The financial problem required Tirpitz to introduce another Novelle in 1908, mainly to increase the per ship construction money. The resulting four tempo was partly camouflage to justify going back to the Reichstag so soon after 1906. On these occasions the RMA would move quickly to distract and assuage those deputies when they touched on this most tender of sore points for Tirpitz, that is, to return to annual appropriations.

Tirpitz and Capelle paid particularly close attention to the Center party. Early on they understood the Center's desire for the position of decisive party after so many years in the political wilderness during Bismarck's time. They gave a sympathetic ear to the Center's sectarian concerns, such as the repeal of the Jesuit laws, although they could do little to actually help. They appeared to try to address the Center's wish that taxes not be increased on those with "weaker shoulders." During the "Hottentot" election of 1907, when Bülow led the charge against the Center, Tirpitz personally refrained from attacks on the Center. When the government anathematized the Center Party, Tirpitz quietly kept open lines of communications with its leaders. When he finally decided on a four tempo Novelle in the fall of 1907, he claimed, as an argument within the anti-Center government, that the other parties would see the three tempo Novelle as a "concession" to the Center. Even with that, the majority of the Center voted for the four tempo. Deist, who accepts the Berghahn thesis, concedes:

> Since the goal of the Äternat could only be achieved by the passage of the Navy Laws and the Novelles, the cooperation of the Reichstag was therefore an indispensable necessity. Tirpitz and his aides, in the scope of their intense cooperation with the deputies and the parties, went far beyond the practice accepted at the time.[14]

If one looks at Tirpitz's relations with the Reichstag through the lens of bureaucratic politics, the situation becomes clearer. Berghahn argues that Tirpitz's dealings with the Reichstag were merely "tactical" accommodations. On the contrary, a relatively strong Reichstag was to Tirpitz's advantage. It made him able to maneuver against the Emperor's sporadic and overblown demands with the claim that the Reichstag would not provide the money. He used the same maneuver against the Front's pleas for more money to pay for everything from preparedness to increased meal allowances. If his most central agenda was to expand and preserve the Navy Law as his own power base, it partially explains why a relatively strong Reichstag would help him achieve his own ends and not, as Berghahn contends, be a dragon to be slain.

In many respects Tirpitz indeed functioned as a parliamentary minister. His multiple resignation threats were, if not "democratic," inconsistent with the behavior of a State Secretary under the Bismarckian Constitution, especially since he held high military rank. Less well known, but also significant, is that on several occasions he threatened Reichstag members that he might resign if they did not do things his way. His personal feelings toward the monarch and the Reichstag matter less than how he actually *dealt* with the Reichstag. To preserve his power base, the Navy Law, he was willing to act in what may readily be described as a quasi-parliamentary manner. Success in the Reichstag made him indispensable until 1914, when the mission of the navy shifted from construction to war.

In evaluating Tirpitz's work, sincerity should not be an issue. As Capelle confided to Michaelis when he explained that the risk theory was only meant as a shield against accusations of limitless fleet plans: "The Reichstag does not want the truth from us, but a suitable formula with which the sensible ones can guide those who are stupid."[15]

Tirpitz's awareness of his potentially precarious position in the Reichstag is evident in the speech he gave in April 1910 in Kiel to higher officers and cadets. The speech was a response to complaints from fellow officers that Tirpitz was too close to the Reichstag. In this semi-private meeting, he disclosed that the parliament's obligation to fund new construction was moral and political, not ironclad. Hence the navy needed to maintain the Reichstag's confidence. In a draft in Dähnhardt's hand, but crossed out and presumably not delivered, is a hair-raising remark about the Reichstag's relationship to the replacement clause. The Reichstag, the text stated, was bound to approve the ships but not necessarily the full amount of payment that the navy wanted in a given year. Depending on the amount provided, the Reichstag could string out ship construction over ten years or more, instead of the customary four.[16] This unusual speech, combined with Tirpitz's management of the Reichstag, illustrate that the "iron budget" was more of an aspiration than a reality.

The conclusion that Tirpitz was more dependent on the Reichstag than was previously thought will no doubt cause controversy; it is explicable, however, in terms of bureaucratic thinking. Tirpitz the monarchist was willing to use any means necessary, even parliamentary methods, to enhance his own power. Virtually all historians agree that the attempt to build a fleet large enough to deter the Royal Navy was an irrational decision, with weighty and deleterious consequences for Germany. Paradoxically Tirpitz's pragmatic and skillful quasi-parliamentary approach was, by and large, a good example of a rational actor in pursuit of a bureaucratic political goal.

THE ALLISON CATEGORIES AS APPLIED TO TIRPITZ

The Allison categories for governmental decision making are summarized in chapter 1 of this volume.[17] Most historical analysis is based upon Model 1, the Rational Actor Model. What are the rational goals and objectives of a government trying to serve the national interest? An event is explained in this manner when Tirpitz's policies were, in the context of his times, reasonable and in the national interest, even if the outcome, in the end, did not meet the desired goal.

In many ways Tirpitz did function as a rational actor. In his work on the Torpedo Arm, up to 1889, he started almost from scratch. By dogged and methodical work, and a willingness to experiment, he created a weapon that, for its time, was perhaps the best and most efficient in the world. While still in the Torpedo Arm he empirically developed a set of tactical plans that he successfully carried over when he became Chief of Staff of the Oberkommando in 1892. Though subsequent technological developments and experiments by others made much of his early tactical work obsolete, as State Secretary he accepted, albeit grudgingly at times, the tactical changes that made the High Seas Fleet a formidable opponent amid the chaos of Jutland.

At the end of his OK service (late 1895), he belatedly understood Stosch's 1892 advice that, instead of fighting the RMA, he should try to become a strong State Secretary himself.[18] Probably he came to this realization when he finally understood that the key to power in the navy was having control of the money.[19] In 1898 he wrote to a friend: "It is comical that I had worked hard to make the Oberkommando the center of all war directives and naval staffs."[20]

Perhaps his greatest triumph as a rational actor was his organized, skillful, and generally moderate way of dealing with the Reichstag. He went to great lengths to preserve the Reichstag's confidence. Until 1907 he resisted pressures and temptations to build more than the three tempo, which he thought was the maximum the foreign and domestic situations would bear.

Another example where Tirpitz clearly acted rationally in the national interest was the cleverness with which he handled the shipbuilding industry.[21] He played off private yards against the imperial yards and created the necessary infrastructure without overly burdening the imperial treasury. He had somewhat less success with Krupp, who had a near monopoly on guns and armor; but by appealing to patriotism and comparing prices of armor to international armor prices, he limited Krupp to high, but not exorbitant, profits.

When war came Tirpitz, at first, had some well-conceived, rational ideas about the use of U-boats in commerce warfare. He wanted to blockade only the Thames estuary. This could be plausibly enforced and would keep U-boats away from Liverpool and the south coast, where politically sensitive passenger liners docked. He also wanted to avoid provoking the neutral United States. For the same reason he favored a more aggressive commerce war in the Mediterranean. Only in the spring of 1915, when avoiding a more broadly based U-boat war would spark criticism of his overall fleet policy, did he loudly advocate all-out submarine warfare. One could cite other examples of Tirpitz's behavior as a rational actor, but to look at Tirpitz solely through a rational lens leaves much unexplained.

A second way to view Tirpitz is as a member of the Seaofficer Corps, a group that had many ideas and values in common. This approach is considered in Allison's Organizational Behavior Model (Model 2). Gemzell has done pioneering work on this aspect of the navy.[22] Tirpitz had indispensable, though inadvertent, help from the organizational behavior of the army. From 1897 to 1911 the army, for reasons of its own, had little desire to expand. This behavior allowed Tirpitz to increase the navy's share of the defense budget to about half that of the far larger army. Until the army reasserted itself in irresistible fashion in 1912, Tirpitz had a clear field.

One of the navy's obvious organizational interests was to develop a bigger fleet, with better prospects for promotion. The appeal of a naval career was, for this reason, strong under Stosch, waned under Caprivi, and rose again when Tirpitz resumed fleet expansion. Chancellor Hohenlohe understood this institutional motivation when he told Lieber, in 1897: "If the navy takes up the mission, they carry it to excess, and find reasons everywhere to support their convictions in science and experience."[23]

Another common organizational experience/memory was the navy's passivity during the Franco-Prussian War, after which the navy, at first, was given no medals for its participation in the war, whereas the army covered itself with glory. This shameful experience, which Tirpitz painfully expressed in his memoirs, was partly responsible for the hallucinatory series of naval war plans that called for a blockade of French Channel ports. The plans were based on heroic assumptions that defied reality—first, that the French Channel Fleet would attack the blockaders without waiting for reinforcement from the Mediterranean and, second, that neutral Britain would provide coal and repairs to the blockading German fleet. Until the eve of war in 1914, all plans against Britain presupposed that the Grand Fleet would, at the outbreak of war, charge into the minefields off Helgoland and meet defeat by a counterattacking German fleet. As Heeringen admitted, in 1911, the navy, to sustain morale in the officer corps, needed to pretend that it had a militarily feasible chance of victory against Britain.[24]

Hobson provides a further explanation for this offensive bias; he relates it to a misapplication of Clausewitz to naval war that did not acknowledge the advantages of the strategic defensive.[25] In 1911 Maltzahn saw the exaggeration of the offensive as a counterweight to resigning to the inevitable in a war with Britain. Aggressive rhetoric was the product of this kind of thinking.

Even Tirpitz recognized that prewar plans "only had educational and morale value" and that it was always better to emphasize the offensive. He told Heeringen that a real war plan, as opposed to one on paper, would have to await the actual circumstances upon the outbreak of war.[26] Tirpitz, in his postwar writings, never acknowledged this uncomfortable truth. Tirpitz and the navy were no exceptions to the organizational

aphorism that where you stand often depends on where you sit. The institutional interests of the non-RMA parts of the navy sometimes reinforced,
sometimes contested, Tirpitz's vision of what the navy should be.

Allison's Governmental, or Bureaucratic, Politics Model (Model 3)
emphasizes outcomes that are not rational choices focused as such on the
national interest, nor as organizational outputs, but on policy as the outcome of bargaining games among players within a national government.
Readers familiar with U.S. history will recognize the names of Admiral
Hyman Rickover, father of the nuclear navy, and J. Edgar Hoover, longtime director of the Federal Bureau of Investigation.[27] Both men greatly
expanded powerful public organizations; both followed strategies that led
to undisputed domination over their respective organizations; and both
achieved a remarkable degree of autonomy from the normal practices
of political life. Both men influenced their national agendas to a degree
far greater than their nominal positions would normally allow. A Tirpitz
biography is not the place to judge the achievements or foibles of either
man. Their names are invoked to make more comprehensible the meaning of the bureaucratic politics aspect of Tirpitz's career.

Even before he became State Secretary of the RMA in 1897, Tirpitz
displayed a hearty appetite for the accumulation of personal power. As a
lowly Commander in 1886, he gained practical autonomy for the Torpedo
Arm. In that instance, a good case can be made that he acted in the interests of the service and the nation; afterward, however, when his priority
became the construction of capital ships, his interest in torpedo boats and
destroyers slackened. Germany entered the war with destroyers that were
under-gunned and had range sufficient only for the southern North Sea.

As a Captain and Chief of Staff of the Oberkommando in 1892, he
initiated tactical improvements that others later refined, but he personally was locked into the tactics of the 1890s. In May 1915 he offered an
astonishing plan to Pohl to scatter the fleet in the North Sea, expecting
that it would draw the Grand Fleet to Helgoland. It was also in the OK
that he acquired his first major taste for bitter bureaucratic infighting with
the RMA. When he left the OK in 1895 as a Junior Rear Admiral, he had
an epiphany that real power in the navy belonged to the State Secretary
because he controlled the money. For a brief moment, early in 1896, it
appeared that he would get the job. In a much-cited memo of December
1895/January 1896, he argued that the RMA, presumably with him as

leader, should control not only all non-command functions of the navy but also the maritime interests of the state as a whole. Hollmann's brief success with the Reichstag in the spring of 1896 aborted the idea. Little noticed in the memo is that, if implemented, it would have wreaked havoc on the sacred seniority system in the navy. Many senior admirals would have had to retire. No wonder Senden and the Emperor backed off from naming Tirpitz State Secretary in 1896.

Once Tirpitz actually assumed the office in 1897, with lesser powers than he had asked for the previous year, he began his brilliant work to pass the 1898 Navy Law. One of his most effective initiatives was to assemble statistics that incontestably illustrated Germany's dramatic growth in maritime commerce over the prior decade. He used growth to justify the expansion of the fleet. Though fleet expansion was perhaps justifiable in military terms, Tirpitz's approach reveals his intoxication with Mahan's bogus link of seapower to peacetime maritime trade. In fact, the statistics actually showed that the German economy had grown *without* an appreciable fleet. Few noticed this piece of Orwellian doublethink.

The bureaucratic politics (*Ressorteifer*) side of Tirpitz came into full bloom after the 1898 law was safely passed. In 1898–99, partly by appealing to the Emperor's vanity and partly because his unprecedented success with the Reichstag had made him indispensable, Tirpitz systematically demolished the OK and left the fleet without a coherent top command except for the Emperor himself. Seven or eight individual offices, with the RMA by far the most powerful, reported directly to the Emperor. This institutional arrangement left Tirpitz with no formidable rival within the navy.

He worked hard to keep it that way, but an important question remained: Who would command the seagoing battlefleet in time of war? That a navy should have such a commander is blatantly obvious; if one were named, however, the fleet leader might become a rival power. Tirpitz fought a long and successful battle to avoid the peacetime designation of a wartime commander. His excuse was that the Emperor had to retain the flexibility to choose the best admiral and not necessarily the most senior one. This attitude made some sense because, from 1906 to 1909, the Fleet Chief (title finally conferred in 1907) was the mediocre Prinz Heinrich. Still, rational planning was greatly hindered by not knowing for certain who would command in wartime. Heinrich's successors,

Holtzendorff (1909–13) and Ingenohl (1913–15) had no prior certitude that they would remain in command in wartime.

The Admiralstab survived the OK's breakup but was left with the task of designing war plans that commanders ignored unless the plans suited their own purposes. When Chiefs Diedrichs and Büchsel tried to increase the Admiralstab's handful of officers, and establish an Admiralty Staff Officer Corps, Tirpitz, with Front support, quashed the idea. He similarly averted efforts to raise the status of the Engineering Officer Corps and took naval education away from the Admiralstab. When Admiralstab Chiefs like Baudissin and Fischel tried to propose alternatives to Tirpitz's ideas, they were both removed in short order. He persecuted his old friends, Oldekop and Maltzahn, for minor deviations from his viewpoint.

Tirpitz also exerted control indirectly. For example, he rarely consulted the Fleet Command, the Admiralstab, or the Front on ship design. One result was that German battleships had cramped quarters and a short cruising radius that would have made combat outside the southern North Sea difficult.

Control of the purse also gave him power over the Front. The Front wanted more reserves activated, and more ships kept manned and in commission year-round. Front officers argued that wars could start at any time. But the more ships in the active fleet, the higher the cost at a time when Tirpitz needed every available pfennig for construction. Similar conflicts occurred over salaries, workload, and mess allowances. Under pressure from the Emperor, Tirpitz finally addressed some of the readiness issues in the 1912 Novelle. By then it was clear that readiness could not wait until the fleet was "complete."

All these conflicts reflected the reality that Tirpitz would go to any extreme to protect his power base, the Navy Law. He was indispensable to the ever more grudging Emperor until the war began and the navy's mission changed. One reason why Tirpitz thought it essential that he exert dominance within the navy was because he expected, if war came, that something like the old Admiralty would be reconstituted, with him at its head. Tirpitz, in 1914, did not realize that the Emperor would not permit it, nor would many of those in the fleet whom he had bullied. They, correctly, saw him as out of touch, as he had not commanded at sea since 1897.

Tirpitz's *Ressorteifer* had serious negative consequences. When his bureaucratic politics reached into the wider world of politics and diplomacy, it had substantial adverse effects on the national interest. Tirpitz's decision, taken in 1897 but only publicly announced in 1900, to use the "strongest seapower" as a rationale for expanded German seapower, was ultimately disastrous. In the 1900 law he effectively doubled the projected size of the fleet. Since it was then preposterous to assume that Germany could actually fight the Royal Navy, he invented the idea of a "risk fleet" that would also have "alliance value." Capelle believed that these were only slogans to give Reichstag plausibility to a larger fleet.

The concomitant requirement to "build and keep quiet," at least when no Novelle was pending, put Tirpitz in a peculiar position. Theoretically the fleet was meant to support Weltpolitik, but Tirpitz rarely meddled directly in diplomatic matters. He opposed the seizure of Tsingtau in November 1897, an obvious act of Weltpolitik, because he thought it would complicate his campaign in the Reichstag to pass the 1898 Navy Law. Later, in 1904–1905, when, consistent with the "alliance value" idea, William II tried to make an alliance with Russia, Tirpitz opposed it, believing that it might provoke the British to engage in a "Copenhagen"-style attack on the fledgling German Navy. He was never very clear as to when the day would come when *completion* of a navy, supposedly built to support Weltpolitik, would finally allow Germany to *practice* Weltpolitik. This conundrum is another reason to view *Ressorteifer* as a far greater motivator for Tirpitz than was Weltpolitik.

Despite Tirpitz's very limited direct involvement in diplomacy, the fleet had important indirect diplomatic effects. Even though Fisher, initially, neither laid down *Dreadnought* nor began fleet reform and redistribution because of the German fleet, the arms race that began in earnest in 1905 played a huge role in the Anglo-German estrangement.

The escalation in ship type that *Dreadnought* brought with it posed a terrible dilemma for Tirpitz's bureaucratic empire. Its central buttresses were the Navy Law and the need to retain the Reichstag's confidence. The unwelcome news meant that to build ships of comparable dimensions, ship costs would skyrocket to an unprecedented height and the Kaiser Wilhelm Canal would have to be widened. Although he managed to finesse the canal problem, the financial demands, not to mention the

Emperor's desire for even greater type escalation, put Tirpitz's empire at risk. In this context it was fortunate that, in 1900, he had already revealed the likelihood of a cruiser Novelle in 1906. His hard-won pool of goodwill proved sufficient to persuade the Reichstag to increase the per ship appropriations high enough to build first-generation Dreadnoughts.

A deeper quandary threatened the Navy Law as soon as 1907. Fisher's type escalation expanded to cruisers. To compete in this category as well would escalate costs even more. Were the navy to go to the Reichstag solely with another request for higher per ship appropriations, now including cruisers, only a year after it had gotten a large raise, Reichstag sentiment might want to go back to the pre-1898 system of annual construction appropriations. The only plausible excuse to return to the Reichstag in 1907–1908 was to shorten the lifespan of battleships from twenty-five to twenty years.; but since the 1906 law had assured the three tempo through 1911, a four tempo had to be introduced to make a change sufficient to amend the Navy Law. Otherwise, Tirpitz could not counter the argument that, were prices to rise every year, why not go back to annual appropriations? Such a change would have left Tirpitz's bureaucratic empire, and therefore his power base, at mortal risk. An unintended but foreseeable consequence of the four tempo was a severe acceleration of the arms race. Only in 1908, when the type escalation was a fait accompli, did Tirpitz console himself with the thought that, after *Dreadnought*, both sides were starting from scratch. The arms race was a financial and diplomatic catastrophe for Germany. To preserve his own power base, and without a wise Emperor to say no to the four tempo, Germany's international position was placed at serious risk.

By 1910, when the futility of his policy became more apparent, and when he was meeting effective opposition from Bethmann and Wermuth, Tirpitz was reduced to the bureaucratic politician's argument of last resort. On 24 October 1910 he met with William II and presented the argument he would make with increasing frequency until his resignation in 1916:

> If the English fleet can be made permanently strong enough so that an attack on Germany is no risk, German naval development, from the historical standpoint, would have been a failure and the naval policy of Your Majesty a historical fiasco.[28]

This "sunk costs" argument is a variation of what politicians use to urge the continuation of failed or futile wars. "Our fallen soldiers cannot be made to have died in vain." Tirpitz's need to defend his bureaucratic empire made him persist in a policy that actually became "a historical fiasco." He therefore refused to countenance any reasonable mutual arms reduction with Britain.

One of Tirpitz's greatest fears, even after the war began and he was effectively out of power, was that the navy would become a scapegoat for the war. If the fleet was not used aggressively, after the war the navy would have a hard time getting enough money to carry on the Navy Law.

The Bureaucratic Politics Model explains much of Tirpitz's behavior that would be difficult to account for with the historians' usual default model, the rational actor. Clearly many of Tirpitz's actions were not rationally grounded in the national interest. Looking at Tirpitz through this lens, there is no need to posit a massive conspiracy designed to stabilize the monarchical system. One of the greatest factors in destabilizing the monarchy was the monarch himself.

The analytical underpinning of this work, supported by archival sources, addresses in a substantially new way some of the many apparent contradictions of Tirpitz's life. Even given the Social Darwinist flavor of his thought after the mid-1890s, Tirpitz clearly had no serious intention of matching or exceeding the size of the British Navy, despite his blustering in his postwar writings. The consistent thread of *Ressorteifer*, though not omnipresent in his life's work, provides an underestimated key to his thoughts and actions. Tirpitz's important role in the Wilhelmian Reich cannot be adequately understood without sufficient attention to its bureaucratic politics aspects.

AFTERMATH

The Treaty of Versailles drastically limited the size of the postwar navy to six pre-Dreadnoughts, six light cruisers, twelve destroyers, and no U-boats or aircraft. Replacement battleships could not exceed 10,000 tons. Personnel were limited in proportion. For active and retired naval officers, the scuttling in Scapa Flow on 21 June 1919 satisfied the honor of the officer corps, and the defiant gesture was viewed as a sign that the spirit of the navy still lived. The mutinies were dismissed as a manifestation of the "stab in the back."

Nationalist naval circles, in eclipse during the Weimar era until the Depression and the rise of Hitler, struggled to create a narrative crafted to demonstrate that Tirpitz's fleet-building policy had not been an "historical fiasco," despite the surface fleet's passivity during the war. Such a narrative was their only hope for a navy reborn.

As considered in chapters 15 and 16, Tirpitz himself, with the cooperation of adherents such as Scheer, Trotha, Raeder, and the Marinearchiv, as well as friendly historians like Hallmann, recast the narrative to blame the navy's passivity on Bethmann, Müller, Pohl, and Ingenohl. Tirpitz was practically alone among rightists in placing part of the blame on William II.[29]

Tirpitz's most perceptive contemporary critic, Wolfgang Wegener, recognized important flaws in Tirpitz's thought, such as his scant appreciation of Germany's disastrous geographic position with respect to Britain and his lack of strategic insight as seen, for example, in his willful dismissal of a wide blockade. However, Wegener essentially ignored the fact that Germany could not contest the sea lanes with a numerically inferior fleet.[30]

Admiral Eric Raeder, Navy Chief from 1928 to 1943, although he had some private misgivings, invoked Tirpitz's legacy to persuade Hitler to build the mighty battleships *Bismarck* and *Tirpitz*, and to entertain his Z-Plan to contest Britain's naval supremacy on a grand scale. Without the Nazis, Tirpitz's historical reputation would likely be different.

Some more recent historians[31] see a strong ideological continuity between Tirpitz's "fleet against England" of 1897 and Raeder's eventually grandiose naval ambitions. Gerhard Schreiber argues that the Admiralstab's overblown war plans from the Tirpitz era, even including some against the United States, demonstrate a continuity of goals over the entire period.

A work of this scope cannot review the exhaustive naval literature of the period from 1919 to 1945. It is true that Tirpitz's wartime and postwar writings display the distortions and exaggerations which fed the myth that later proved useful to Raeder and the Nazis. Tirpitz, like most of those involved in the war from many nations, was swept up in the war's passions, even as his own power greatly diminished at its outbreak. Tirpitz cannot be blamed for the Nazis— in fact, he found Hitler personally distasteful—but his perceived "legacy" proved useful to them. Nationalism and the phenomenon of patriotic self-censorship provided many with the will to believe.

Tirpitz's actual legacy, as opposed to the constructed version, namely the significance of his prewar life and work at a time when he did have power, deserves a reexamination independent of how the Nazis construed it. Viewed in this light, ideas such as "risk theory," "alliance value," and even "Weltpolitik" were, for Tirpitz, slogans more than reality, despite what he said about these notions in public. He wanted a strong fleet for Germany in an era when virtually all great powers wanted stronger fleets. He knew he could never match Britain, but he was more skillful than his non-British counterparts in turning paper programs into ships. Weltpolitik, for Tirpitz, could wait until the distant future, lest its consequences impede building a fleet—in his way and under his control. He believed he knew how to do it better than his imperial master, his naval colleagues, and the Reichstag. His master plan was not to preserve the Prusso-German monarchy but rather to enhance and retain his own power. Except to steer them in his own favor, he had little interest in war plans which, in his more lucid moments, he realized were mainly to palliate the Emperor and to keep spirits up in a naval officer corps that would be demoralized if confronted with an actual war with Britain. Deterrence was his only hope, and actual war was a sign of its, and his, failure.

Tirpitz's real legacy is to demonstrate to others how an unlikely success, building a German battlefleet against great odds, could be accomplished with determination, luck, cunning, and trickery. The 1900 Navy Law, which doubled the size of the fleet, was clearly an overreach, and he lacked the wisdom or vision to countermand it, even as its doleful consequences unfolded into a catastrophic naval arms race. A wiser Emperor, perhaps William II's father, might have presided over a better outcome. Tirpitz, like most leaders, was not equal to the challenge of untrammeled power. His success at bureaucratic politics was both his triumph and his downfall.

APPENDIX

The semi-tabular form used below lists each officer's name; year of birth; years in the Torpedo Arm while Tirpitz was there (1877–89); years in the Oberkommando der Marine (OKM) when Tirpitz was Chief of Staff (1892–95); and years in the Reichsmarineamt (RMA) while Tirpitz was there (1897–1916). Listed last is each officer's final service rank and the most important position he ever held. A few of them also served with Tirpitz when he was Chief of the East Asian Cruiser Squadron (1896–97). These are noted where applicable. Almost all the data below are from Hans Hildebrand, ed., *Deutschlands Admirale, 1849–1945*. Names listed as "von" indicate hereditary nobility; names listed as "(von)" indicate non-nobles by birth but enobled during their lifetime for their services.

Hunold von Ahlefeld (1851): Torpedo Arm, 1880–91; OKM, 1893–96; RMA, 1902–1907; Vice Admiral and Chief of the Baltic Station, 1907–1908.

Otto Braun (1864?): Torpedo Arm, 1885–87; OKM, 1892–95; died in a ty-phoon on 23 July 1896 as Lieutenant Commander and Commander of the gunboat *Iltis*, part of Tirpitz's East Asian Cruiser Squadron.

Gustav Bachmann (1860): Torpedo Arm, May–August 1884; OKM, 1892–94; RMA, 1897, 1907–1910; Admiral, Chief of the Admiralstab, 1915.

Wilhelm Büchsel (1848): Torpedo Arm, summer 1881; RMA, 1895–99, 1900–1902; Admiral, Chief of the Admiralstab, 1902–1908.

Carl von Coerper (1854): Torpedo Arm, 1881–83; RMA, 1897–98; Naval Attaché in London, 1898–1903, 1904–1907; Admiral, Chief of Baltic Station, 1912–14.

Harald Dähnhardt (1863): Torpedo Arm, 1887–88; RMA, 1895–99, 1899–1900, 1904–1916; Vice Admiral, Head of Estimates Department at RMA, 1904–1916

Karl Dick (1858): Torpedo Arm, 1885; OKM, 1893–96; RMA, 1910–1916; Admiral, RMA Dockyard Director, 1910–1916.

Max (von) Fischel (1850): Torpedo Arm, 1879–80, 1881–84, 1887–89; OKM, 1889–92; RMA, 1895–1900; Admiral, Chief of the Admiralstab, 1909–1911.

August von Heeringen (1855): Torpedo Arm, 1884, 1886–89; OKM, 1893–96;

RMA, 1897–99, 1899–1900, 1903–1907; Admiral, Chief of the Admiralstab, 1911–13.

Heinrich, Prince of Prussia (1862): Torpedo Arm, April–September 1887; no other service under Tirpitz; Grand Admiral, Chief of Baltic Forces, 1914–18.

Albert Hopmann (1865): Torpedo Arm, 1888–89; OKM, 1895–97; RMA, 1911–15; Vice Admiral, Chief of Staff, Baltic Station, 1915–1916.

Paul Jaeschke (1851): Torpedo Arm, 1880–86; Captain, Governor of Kiaochou, 1899–1901.

Friedrich (von) Ingenohl (1857): Torpedo Arm, 1888; OKM, 1892–94; RMA, 1897–1901; Admiral, Chief of the High Sea Fleet, 1913–15.

Günther von Krosigk (1860): Torpedo Arm, 1884, 1887–89; RMA, 1913–14; Admiral, Chief of Baltic Station, 1915–18.

Georg Alexander (von) Müller (1854): Torpedo Arm, 1879–82, 1884–85; OKM, 1892–95; Admiral, Chief of the Naval Cabinet, 1906–1918.

Hugo (von) Pohl (1855): Torpedo Arm, 1882–85; RMA, 1895–98, 1901–1903; Admiral, Chief of the High Seas Fleet, 1915–16.

Max Rollmann (1857): Torpedo Arm, 1883–89; RMA, 1901–1904, 1907–1910;

Vice Admiral, Chief of III Squadron, 1910–1912.

Wilhelm Schack (1860): Torpedo Arm, 1885–86, 1887; RMA, 1896–99, 1901–1904; Vice Admiral, Inspector of Coast Artillery, 1911–13.

Reinhard Scheer (1863): Torpedo Arm January– May 1888; RMA, 1897–1900, 1903–1907, 1911–13; Admiral, Chief of High Seas Fleet, 1916–18.

Ludwig (von) Schröder (1854): Torpedo Arm, 1885–88; OKM, 1895–98; Admiral, Chief of Marine Corps in Flanders, 1914–18.

Rudolf Siegel (1852): Torpedo Arm, 1879; OKM, 1889–94; Captain, Naval Attaché in Paris, 1895–1907.

Oskar (von) Truppel (1854): Torpedo Arm, 1887–88; OKM, 1894–97; RMA. 1899–1901; Admiral, Governor of Kiaochou, 1901–1911.

Raimund Winkler (1855): Torpedo Arm, 1887–89; OKM, 1892–95; RMA, 1906–1911; Vice Admiral, Department Head in RMA, 1911–1915.

Hugo Zeye (1852): Torpedo Arm, 1885, 1886–88; Commander of *Kaiser,*Tirpitz's flagship in East Asia, 1896–98; RMA, 1901–1903; Vice Admiral, Inspector of Torpedo Forces, 1903–1909.

NOTES

1. INTRODUCTION

1. The German version of Chinese place names of the time are used throughout this book.

2. He was made a member of the hereditary nobility by the Emperor in 1900. From then on he was von Tirpitz.

3. J. A. R. Marriott and C. G. Robertson, *The Evolution of Prussia*, 370ff. See also Jonathan Steinberg, *Yesterday's Deterrent* chap. 1 (cited as Steinberg).

4. Alfred von Tirpitz, *My Memoirs*, 2 vols. (cited as Tirpitz, *Memoirs*); *Der Aufbau der deutschen Weltmacht* (cited as Tirpitz, *Aufbau*); and *Deutsche Ohnmachtspolitik im Weltkrieg* (cited as Tirpitz, *Ohnmachtspolitik*).

5. See, e.g., Hans Hallmann, *Der Weg zum deutschen Schlachtflottenbau* (cited as Hallmann); Walther Hubatsch, *Die Ära Tirpitz* (cited as Hubatsch, *Ära*); and *Der Admiralstab und die obersten Marinebehörden 1848–1945* (cited as Hubatsch, *Admiralstab*).

6. Hubatsch, *Ära*, 83, 18.

7. Gerhard Ritter, *Staatskunst und Kriegshandwerk*, 2:201 (cited as Ritter).

8. See, e.g., Carl Galster, *England, Deutsche Flotte, und Weltkrieg* (cited as Galster, 1925), and Wolfgang Wegener, *The Naval Strategy of the World War* (cited as Wegener). Their critiques, and others from Tirpitz's in-service critics, are dealt with below, as is the trenchant analysis of Rolf Hobson, *Imperialism at Sea: Naval Strategic Thought, the Ideology of Sea Power, and the Tirpitz Plan, 1875–1914* (cited as Hobson).

9. Holger Herwig, "Clio Deceived, Patriotic Self-Censorship in Germany after the Great War," 87–127 (cited as "Clio Deceived"); and Michael Epkenhans, "Clio, Tirpitz, und die Marine," 466–485 (cited as Epkenhans, "Clio").

10. Nachlass Capelle, N 170/3, 11–14, Hollweg to Capelle, January 1926.

11. See Eckart Kehr, *Schlachtflottenbau und Parteipolitik 1894–1901* (cited as Kehr) (English translation: *Battleship Building and Party Politics, 1894–1901*, ed. and trans. Pauline R. Anderson and Eugene N. Anderson); and Kehr, *Economic Interests, Militarism, and Foreign Policy: Essays on German History*.

12. Volker Berghahn, *Der Tirpitz Plan, Genesis und Verfall einer innenpolitischen Krisenstrategie* (cited as Berghahn). Also see his *Germany and the Approach of War in 1914*(cited as Berghahn, *War 1914*); and *Imperial Germany 1871–1914: Economy, Society and Politics* (cited as Berghahn, *Imperial Germany*).

13. Wilhelm Deist, *Flottenpolitik und Flottenpropaganda: Das Nach-richtenbüro des Reichsmarineamts, 1897–1914* (cited as Deist); Michael Epkenhans, *Die Wilhelmische Flotten-rüstung, 1908–1914: Weltmachtstreben, industrieller Fortschritt, soziale Integra-tion* (cited as Epkenhans). Just before this work was completed, Epkenhans published *Tirpitz: Architect of the Ger-man High Seas Fleet.* This is the first English-language Tirpitz biography. Al-though only eighty-seven pages of text, it is easily better than the existing short German language biographies. Epken-hans's interpretation sticks closely to the existing Berghahn/Deist view of Tirpitz, and thereby differs substantial-ly from this work. Its brief scope does not permit an in-depth look at many of the issues that surrounded Tirpitz.

14. From a review article of Berghahn's book by Jonathan Stein-berg, *Historical Journal*, 196–204.

15. Hajo Holborn, *A History of Modern Germany: 1840–1945*, 308.

16. Carl-Axel Gemzell, *Organiza-tion, Conflict, and Innovation: A Study of German Naval Strategic Planning, 1888–1940* (cited as Gemzell).

17. Graham Allison and Philip Zelikow, *Essence of Decision: Explain-ing the Cuban Missile Crisis* (cited as Allison). The title is somewhat mislead-ing because the book goes far beyond a single crisis. The author reviewed a number of other political science models, but most are jargon-filled and too purely theoretical to suit empiri-cally based historical study. The Allison model, though not perfect, is both flexible and fact-oriented, and therefore seemed the best instrument available to explore many of Tirpitz's deviations from rational behavior. The default model for most historians is the rational actor one, and sometimes historians

can fall into the trap of assuming their subjects are as rational as they are. Such is the case, in my opinion, of some of the work of otherwise excel-lent historians such as Berghahn and Paul Kennedy, when they write about Tirpitz.

18. Allison, 15.

19. Ibid., 18.

20. Ibid., 255–56.

21. Tirpitz, *Memoirs*, 1:128–29.

22. Nachlass Capelle, N 170/3, 6, Capelle to Hollweg, 9 November 1925. Capelle was Tirpitz's chief subordi-nate in the RMA until 1915, when he resigned for reasons of health. Tirpitz later resented him for succeeding him at the RMA in 1916 when he was forced out. This estrangement saddened Ca-pelle, who held no personal grudge against Tirpitz.

23. Ibid., 9–10, Hollweg to Capelle, 12 December 1925.

24. Ibid., 14, Capelle to Georg Alexander von Müller, 26 November 1925. Müller had been a close associate of Tirpitz during the torpedo years and after, but Tirpitz disowned Müller for his support of Chancellor Bethmann-Hollweg during the war. Müller was Chief of the Naval Cabinet from 1906 to 1918.

2. TIRPITZ'S EARLY LIFE

1. The most thorough extant description of family history is in a rambling but coherent letter written by Tirpitz's sister, Olga, dated 1 May 1916, to her son Erich-Edgar Schulze. I am grateful to Agostino von Hassell, who made this letter available to me. The best two published accounts of family background are in Ulrich von Hassell, *Tirpitz*, 66–70 (cited as Hassell); and Franz Uhle-Wettler, *Alfred von Tirpitz in seiner Zeit*, 15–17 (cited as Uhle-

Wettler). What follows is based on an amalgam of these sources.

2. For information on Rudolf's legal career, I am indebted to Peter Schmidt-Spaeth, Rechtsanwalt, who provided me with nineteenth-century Prussian legal registers that document Rudolf's career.

3. For Malwine's letters, see N 253/164.

4. The fullest description of Rudolf Tirpitz is in a letter of Wolfgang von Tirpitz (his grandson), written in 1918. See N 253/114.

5. See the massive collection of letters that Rudolf wrote to Alfred from 1865 on in N 253/326 and 327.

6. Descriptions of Tirpitz's youth are from Hassell, 65–75. Hassell interviewed Tirpitz in 1918.

7. Tirpitz, *Memoirs*, 1:1–2.

8. The full curriculum is in N 253/317.

9. Tirpitz, *Memoirs*, 1:2.

10. On the decision to enter the navy, see ibid., 2ff.; and Hassell, 73ff.

11. On the *Amazone*, see Hans Hildebrand, Albert Röhr, and Hans-Otto Steinmetz, *Die deutschen Kriegsschiffe*, 1:92 (cited as Hildebrand).

12. Baldur Kaulisch, *Alfred von Tirpitz und die imperialistische deutsche Flottenrüstung. Eine politische Biographie.*, 13 (cited as Kaulisch).

13. Tirpitz, *Memoirs*, 1:2.

14. A selection of histories of the pre-1870 Prussian Navy include the relevant sections of Lawrence Sondhaus, *Preparing for Weltpolitik: German Sea Power before the Tirpitz Era*, a lucid account and the best available in English (cited as Sondhaus); Eberhard von Mantey, *Deutsche Marinegeschichte* (cited as Mantey); Walther Hubatsch, *Die Erste Deutsche Flotte, 1848–1853*; Wolfgang Petter, "Deutsche Flottenrüstung von Wallenstein bis Tirpitz,"

13–262 (cited as Petter); and Hans-Georg Steltzer, *Die deutsche Flotte: Ein historiker Überblick von 1640 bis 1918*. This section is based on an amalgam of these sources.

15. See, e.g., James F. Baxter, *The Rise of the Ironclad Warship*.

16. For details on the *Stralsund*, see Hildebrand, 5:138.

17. Tirpitz, *Memoirs*, 1:4.

18. On these ships, see Hildebrand, 1:96–100, 2:128–131.

19. On the Prussian fleet abroad, see Willi Boelcke, *So Kam das Meer zu uns: Die preussische-deutsche Kriegsmarine in Übersee 1822 bis 1914* (cited as Boelcke).

3. THE ASPIRANT, 1865–1870

1. Hassell, 76–77.

2. For details on *Niobe*, see Hildebrand, 5:14ff.

3. The best source by far on the 1865–1866 cruise of the *Niobe* is the personal diary kept by Diedrichs, which was generously made available to me by Terrell Gottschall. See also Terrell Gottschall, *By Order of the Kaiser: Otto von Diedrichs and the Rise of the Imperial German Navy, 1865–1902*, 16–25 (cited as Gottschall).

4. Gottschall, 17. Tirpitz to parents, 27 June 1865, N 253/384, 5–6.

5. Report of *Niobe* to Admiralty, Berlin, 1 September 1865, RM 1/2460.

6. Diedrichs Diary, N 255/46.

7. See Knorr and Senden articles in Hans Hildebrand, *Deutschlands Admirale, 1849–1945* (cited as Hildebrand, *Admirale*). Knorr, in 1894, became Tirpitz's superior when he was Chief of Staff of the Oberkommando der Marine (OK). Senden, as Chief of the Naval Cabinet in the 1890s, had great influence on Tirpitz's career

8. Tirpitz, *Memoirs*, 1:13, 15.

9. Ibid., 1:15.

10. See Jörg Duppler, *Der Junior Partner: England und die Entwicklung der deutschen Marine, 1848–1890*, passim.

11. Diedrichs Diary, N 255/43, entries for 6–10 October 1865.

12. On the training of both officers and men, see Herbert Graubohm, *Die Ausbildung in der deutschen Marine von ihrer Gründung bis zum Jahre 1914* (cited as Graubohm).

13. Gottschall, 19–20; Diedrichs Diary, N 255/43, entries for 10 October–4 November 1865; see also Hassell, 78.

14. Hassell, 79.

15. Diedrichs Diary, N 255/43, entries for 4 November–31 December 1865.

16. Batsch to Admiralty, 20 November and 21 December 1865, RM 1/2406, 414–415.

17. On the Cadiz visit, see Batsch to Admiralty, 22 February–3 April 1866, RM 1/2461, 29–35; Diedrichs Diary, N 255/43, entries for 22 February–3 April 1866.

18. Hassell, 80.

19. Gottschall, 23.

20. Tirpitz, *Memoirs*, 1:6.

21. Ibid.

22. Gottschall, 24–25.

23. *Gazelle* was built in 1859 in Danzig as a sister ship to *Arcona*. It was armed with six 68-pound and twenty 36-pound muzzleloaders.

24. Hildebrand, 2:123–131.

25. Tirpitz, *Memoirs*, 1:7.

26. Fritz Hellwig to parents, 25 July 1866, N 253/251, 119–120. This letter was sent to Tirpitz in the 1920s by Fritz Hellwig's son. Thanks to Raffael Scheck for bringing this to my attention. See also Hassell, 80–81, where the story is told more melodramatically.

27. Tirpitz to parents, 28 August 1866, N 253/384, 9–10.

28. The exact date is uncertain. The official record (N 253/10, 32) says 1 August. A letter to his parents (N 253/384, 9–10) indicates that it was a few weeks later

29. Hildebrand, 4:141ff.

30. The voyage is described in a letter, Tirpitz to parents, late October 1866, N 253/384, 16–21.

31. Hassell, 31. See also Tirpitz to parents, N 253/384, 23ff.; and Adolf Mensing to Tirpitz, 9 May 1921, and Tirpitz's reply, N 253/258.

32. Tirpitz to parents, diary/letter, October–December 1866, N 253/384, 22–31.

33. Tirpitz to parents, 30 December 1866 and 7 January 1867, N 253/384, 32–34 and 35–38.

34. Hassell, 82.

35. Tirpitz to parents, letters of 7 and 22 February 1867, N 253/384, 43–50. For *Musquito*'s full itinerary, see RM 1/2461, 165–366.

36. Tirpitz to parents, letters of 26 April and 10 May 1867, N 253/384, 54–58.

37. Hildebrand, 2:133ff. To accommodate cadets and ship's boys its armament was cut down to eighteen 36 pounders, six 24 pounders, and two 12 pounders on a hull of 1,800 tons, with a crew of 420.

38. Tirpitz to parents, 6 July 1867, N 253/384, 65–66.

39. Ibid., 2 August 1867, 69–70.

40. Ibid., 15 August 1867, 71–72.

41. Rudolf Tirpitz to Alfred, 22 August 1867, N 253/165, 20.

42. Hildebrand, 5:145–46.

43. Tirpitz to parents, 14 October 1867, N 253/384, 81–82.

44. Ibid., 30 January 1868, 100–101.

45. Ibid., 1 March 1868, 106–107.

46. Nachlass Knorr, N 578/7, 133–136.

47. Organization der Marineschule, January 1868–December 1869,
RM 1/206, 35–38.

48. On the curriculum and individual students' results, see RM 1/722,
78–81; and RM 1/214, 327–328, 380–401.

49. Tirpitz to parents, 11 August
1868, N 253/384, 140ff.

50. Ibid., 3 November 1868, 161–162.

51. Ibid., 28 November 1868,
164–165f.

52. Ibid., 7 February 1869, 3–4.

53. Ibid., 9 June 1869, 24–25.

54. See RM 1/722, 17–18; RM 1/214,
402.

55. Tirpitz, *Memoirs*, 1:15; Tirpitz
to parents, 19 October 1869, N 253/385,
36–37.

56. Ibid., 2 September 1869, 34–35.

57. Sondhaus, 84–85.

4. THE YOUNG OFFICER, 1870–1877

1. Sondhaus, 86.

2. Petter, 83. On parliamentary
relations during the whole period,
see Thomas Brysch, *Marinepolitik im
preussischen Abgeornetenhaus und
Deutscher Reichstag 1850–1888.*

3. Sondhaus, 87.

4. Petter, 98–99.

5. Hildebrand, 4:28–39.

6. Tirpitz, *Memoirs*, 1:8.

7. Ibid., 17 July 1870, 70–71; and
Tirpitz, *Memoirs*, 1:8.

8. Ibid., 9.

9. Tirpitz to parents, July 1870, N
253/385, 72–73. See also RM 1/2531.

10. See Knorr's own account in
Nachlass Knorr, N 578/8, 24–50.

11. Hildebrand, 1:114–115.

12. Ibid., November 1870, 90ff.

13. Ibid., 22 December1870, 96–97;
and Tirpitz, *Memoirs*, 1:11–12.

14. Tirpitz to parents, 10 September
1870, N 253/385, 85.

15. Ibid., 29 January 1871, 100–101.

16. Hildebrand, 1:146–147.

17. On the normal daily duties of a
ship in this period, see N 253/391, 17–22.
See also Tirpitz to parents, 21 July 1871,
N 253/385, 102–103.

18. Tirpitz to parents, 27 July 1871,
104.

19. Ibid., 8 August 1871, 108–109;
see also 111–113.

20. For this remarkable letter, see
ibid., 11 September 1871, 123–134.

21. Uhle-Wettler, 36.

22. See letters to parents from the
fall of 1871 and the winter of 1872, N
253/385 and 386.

23. See RM 1/ 233 and 2523 on the
inspection of *Blitz* and its consequences. See also Tirpitz, *Memoirs*, 1:18.

24. On the fisheries, see N 253/386,
July letters; Tirpitz, *Memoirs*, 1:19ff.;
Hassell, 84–85.

25. Tirpitz to parents, 17 August
1872, N 253/386, 24.

26. Ibid., 7 September 1872, 29.

27. Sondhaus, 101–108. On Stosch,
see Frederick Hollyday, *Bismarck's
Rival: A Political Biography of General
and Admiral Albrecht von Stosch* (cited
as Hollyday). See also Petter, 103–129;
and Hubatsch, *Admiralstab*, chap. 3.

28. See Hobson, esp. chap. 3. See
also Sondhaus, 105–106 and Tirpitz,
Memoirs, 1:31ff.

29. Tirpitz, *Memoirs*, 1:21, 24–28,
31–35.See also Henk to Stosch, 7
October 1874, N 253/391, 7–10. Henk
complained that if *Kronprinz* had to
meet the enemy seven days after going
into service the result would be very
unsatisfactory.

30. Petter, 109–110.

31. Sondhaus, 108–115, provides a
good summary of the 1873 program.

32. Hildebrand, 2:97–101. *Friedrich
Carl* carried sixteen 21-cm and five 35-
cm guns, had a crew of 531, and a top
speed of twelve knots.

33. Tirpitz to parents, 5 October 1872, N 253/386, 33–34.

34. Ibid., 23 October–2 November 1872, 41–42.

35. Ibid., 20 November 1872, 43–46.

36. Ibid., 16 December 1872 and 12 January 1873, 47–55.

37. Ibid., 6 February 1873, 56–63.

38. Ibid., 9 and 13 March 1873, 64–67.

39. Ibid., 15 July 1873, 87–90.

40. Ibid., 1–9 August 1873, 93–97.

41. Tirpitz, *Memoirs*, 1:21–23.

42. Petter, 106; RM 1/2405 and 2406. See also Duppler, 252ff.

43. Tirpitz, *Memoirs*, 1:22–23.

44. Hildebrand, 2:99–100.

45. Tirpitz to parents, 29 August 1873, N 253/386, 98–104.

46. Quoted in Uhle-Wettler, 42.

47. RM 1/2479, 59–68.

48. Tirpitz to parents, 20 April 1874, N 253/387, 10–11.

49. Ibid., 1 May 1874, 12–13.

50. Hildebrand, 5:25ff. *Nymphe* had a top speed of twelve knots, and mounted ten 36-pounders and six 12-pounders.

51. Tirpitz to parents, 3 June 1874, N 253/387, 16.

52. Ibid., 19–23 August 1874, 23–26.

53. On the Naval Academy, see Stosch's memorandum of 3 March 1872, RM 1/215, 109–113.

54. For the application form of 3 February 1874, see ibid., 152–154.

55. Tirpitz to parents, 23 October 1874, N 253/387, 31–32.

56. Ibid., Tirpitz to Olga, 26 May 1875, 64.

57. Ibid., Tirpitz to parents, 28 March 1875, 51–52.

58. Hildebrand, 3:52ff. See also Tirpitz's gunnery report in N 253/391, 93–94. *Hansa* had a top speed of twelve knots, and carried eight 21-cm guns.

59. Tirpitz to parents, August–September 1875, N 253/387, 65–75.

60. Ibid., 3 December 1875, 92.

61. Ibid., 13 February 1876, N 253/388, 5–8. On Stenzel, see Hobson, 136–147.

62. See, e.g., Maltzahn to Tirpitz, 11 March 1876, N 253/408, 27–28.

63. Theodore Ropp, *The Development of a Modern Navy: French Naval Policy 1871–1904*, 44 (cited as Ropp).

64. Hildebrand, 4:52ff.; see also RM 1/2541. It had a top speed of 13.5 knots and mounted sixteen 21-cm guns.

65. Tirpitz to parents, 11 May 1876, N 253/388, 17–18.

66. Ibid., 2 July 1876, 24.

67. Ibid., 6 July 1876, 25–26.

68. Ibid., 15 August 1876, 33–34.

69. Hildebrand, 4:115.

70. Tirpitz to parents, 27 August 1876, N 253/388, 35ff.

71. Hildebrand, 4:114–123. *Kaiser* had a top speed of 14 knots, and was armed with eight 26-cm guns and one 21-cm gun.

72. Letters to parents, 6 and 29 October 1876, N 253/388, 42–45.

5. THE CREATION OF THE GERMAN TORPEDO ARM, 1877–1889

1. On the early history of the torpedo, see, e.g., Edwyn Gray, *The Devil's Device: Robert Whitehead and the History of the Torpedo*, passim; Eberhard Rössler, *Die Torpedos der deutschen U-Boote*, chap. 1; Gottschall, 47–56; Albert Röhr, "Vorgeschichte und Chronik des Torpedowesens der deutschen Marine bis zum Ende des 19 Jahrhunderts," *Schiff und Zeit* 7, 47–48; Hildebrand, 7:81–85; Elmer Potter, Chester Nimitz, and Jürgen Rohwer, eds., *Seemacht* (German edition), 241ff. (cited as Potter and Rohwer); Hallmann, 22; and Ropp, 110ff.

2. On Stosch's appointment
and work at the Admiralty, see Petter, 101–128; Hollyday, chaps. 4–6; and
Sondhaus, chaps. 5–6.

3. Röhr, 49; Hildebrand, 6:71.

4. For details on torpedo development during Diedrich's tenure (1873–
1878), see Gottschall, 47–56.

5. N 253/14, 3, Stosch to Tirpitz, 16
May 1877; Hildebrand, 6:71.

6. Biographical information on
Tirpitz's years in the Torpedo Arm has
hitherto been based almost solely on
two sources: his *Memoirs*, 1:46ff.; and
Hassell, 94ff. Biographies of Tirpitz
with some substantial, though largely
derivative, treatment of those years
include Michael Salewski, *Tirpitz.
Aufstieg—Macht—Scheitern*, 17ff. (cited
as Salewski); Kaulisch, 27ff., which is
surprisingly good if one ignores its ideological overlay; and Hallmann, 22ff.,
103ff.

7. Tirpitz to parents, 29 April 1877,
N 253/388, 51.

8. Ibid., 20 May 1877, 56–57.

9. Ibid., 22 June 1877, 65.

10. Ibid., 27 July 1877, 72.

11. Ibid., 29 August 1877, 76.

12. See Hildebrand, 6:71.

13. Hassell, 94ff.; N 253 330, 1–10.
Tirpitz to Stosch, 12 October 1877:
"Opinions about the Fish Torpedo and
about the present status of the Torpedo
Question." All quotations below are
from this document.

14. See, e.g., Potter, chap. 16.

15. This was done in 1879. See RM
1 2839, Cabinet Order of 8 July 1879;
and Röhr, 50. See also the personal recollections of Torpedo Engineer Voigt
in RM 8/76, 128ff.

16. Potter, 243ff.

17. For the correspondence on this
trip, see N 255/2 (Diedrichs Nachlass),
Tirpitz to Diedrichs, 12 February 1878;
N 253/14, 6–31; and Tirpitz's letters to

parents, N 253/388, 89–96. Tirpitz's
later relationships with contractors is
controversial. See Epkenhans; and
Weir, *Building the Kaiser's Navy: The
Imperial German Naval Office in the
von Tirpitz Era, 1890–1918* (cited as
Weir).

18. Tirpitz, *Memoirs*, 1:46.

19. N 253/14, 32–35. Tirpitz to Baltic Command, 8 November 1878.

20. RM 31/453. Stosch to Baltic
Command [Admiral Kinderling] 29
July 1878. See also Stosch's letter of
commendation to Tirpitz, 1 May 1879,
N 253 10, 43.

21. On this episode, see Hildebrand, 5:57ff. and 6:71. An eyewitness
account of this by Torpedo Engineer
Voigt may be found in RM 8 76, 121–
122, on which this narration is based.

22. Hallmann, 18. See also N 253/
40, 14–15, Graf Schack to Tirpitz, 12
November 1879; and Gemzell, 58. On
29 May 1878 *König Wilhelm*, squadron
flagship, collided with and sank, with
great loss of life, the armored frigate
Grosser Kürfurst in the English Channel. Squadron Commander Batsch, a
protégé of Stosch, was on the bridge.
The helmsman was directed by Tirpitz's old friend and classmate, watch
officer Oskar Klausa. The affair led to
a series of courts-martial of Batsch, and
an imbroglio between Stosch and Bismarck. In the end the Emperor sided
with Stosch, and Batsch got a reprieve
for his career. See Sondhaus, chap. 6,
for a detailed account.
Tirpitz, in private, defended Klausa
but, along with many others in the
navy, attributed the catastrophe to
Stosch's rigidity and inability to distin-
guish the complex and technological
needs of the navy from the robotic,
drill-oriented methods of the army.
See Tirpitz to parents, 8 July 1878, N
253/388, 107–109.

23. Röhr, 50; Hallmann, 23.

24. See RM 1/24 for a description of the attack and the referees' comments. See also A. Tesdorpf, *Geschichte der kaiserlichen deutschen Kriegsmarine,* 212ff. For a similar attack tried the following year, see Credner's report of an attack on 9 August 1882 in RM 1 327, 262–263.

25. Testorpf, 214; Hildebrand, 1:123, 6:71; for Voigt's account, see RM 8/76, 123; and Hallmann, 22, 103.

26. The first two large ships to be armed with torpedoes were the corvettes *Prinz Adalbert* and *Ariadne* in 1881 (Röhr, p. 50).

27. N 253/40, 16–17, Schack to Tirpitz, 1 August 1880. Schack had succeeded Heusner at the Admiralty in 1879. Stosch could not be present because to be greeted publicly by the Crown Prince would have been regarded as an insult by Bismarck, who was feuding with Stosch at the time. See Hollyday, chaps. 5 and 6.

28. See Hildebrand, 1:150ff. For one year's example of the role of *Blücher* in training the officers of the fleet, see Tirpitz's notes, probably from April 1881, in RM 31/39.

29. Hildebrand, 6:20.

30. Ahlefeld later worked closely with Tirpitz in the Reichsmarineamt. Despite his obvious competence he had some bizarre ideas. Until the 1890s he was an ardent advocate of the ram. See, e.g., NS SA Dep. 18 Nachlass Trotha (cited as Trotha Papers), Trotha's notes on Ahlefeld. Müller became Chief of the Naval Cabinet in 1906.

31. Space considerations do not permit a detailed discussion here of the technical aspects of torpedoes. For a sample, see RM 31/39, "Torpedo and Exercise Plan for May to July 1881."

32. Nachlass Knorr N 578/9, 94.

33. The best account, Voigt's, is in RM 8/76, 86–87 and 124. See also Testdorpf, 224; Hildebrand, 1:151; and Hallmann, 23. For the program of the torpedo firing, see RM 31/183, "Program for the Fleet Maneuvers," 17 September 1881, appendix 12. See also Nachlass Knorr N 578/9, 104.

34. Röhr, 50.

35. Hildebrand, 7:83ff.

36. See N 253/15, "Concerning the Development of the Torpedo Arm," written by Tirpitz in April 1889. This is a very important document for understanding how torpedo boat types evolved.

37. For the plan, see RM 1/327, 108–124, Batsch to Stosch, 27 August 1882.

38. Later Governor of Kiaochou. See Hildebrand, 3:119.

39. Knorr, for one, did not regard Wickede highly: "He was from the Austrian Navy and not enough of a seaman. . . . He was an enormous windbag and saw his main mission to be the exercise of 'Turks' for the inspections" (N 578/9, 94–95).

40. See Tirpitz's Report of 11 September 1882 in RM 1/327, 154f. The map, in Tirpitz's hand, is also in this document.

41. For Pohl's account, see RM 1 327, 168–169.

42. For reports of two of the torpedo boat commanders, see RM 1/327, 170–174.

43. See RM 1/2862, 49–68, "Stosch's Report on the Fall Maneuvers of 10–11 September," dated 23 September 1882.

44. Hallmann, 24, 104. See also Tirpitz's retrospective memo of April 1889 in N 253/3.

45. Hollyday, chap. 6. An interesting and little known insight into the origins of the feud comes from the

Nachlass Knorr, N 578/9, 123ff. Knorr claimed Stosch told him that the conflict began during the Franco-Prussian War, when Stosch arrested one of Bismarck's adjutants for insubordination. Bismarck took it as an attack on his authority.

46. See, e.g., Nachlass Knorr N 578/9, 127–134. Knorr concluded, after a conversation with the Emperor, that Caprivi had received the position because the army wanted to get rid of him. Tirpitz was distantly related to Caprivi. He and Rudolf were both cousins of Köpke, an official of the Cultus Ministerium (N 253/ 327, 100–101). Rudolf Tirpitz to Marie Tirpitz, 25 August 1897. On Tirpitz's close unofficial connection to Caprivi, see his letters to his wife in this period. See N 253/389 and 390. Additional letters in the Hassell family archive show the same.

47. Tirpitz to Marie, 5 May 1885, N 253/389, 7–8.

48. For an overall view of Caprivi's stewardship of the navy, see Petter, 128–138; Hildebrand, 1:31ff.; and Ivo N. Lambi, *The Navy and German Power Politics, 1862–1914*, chap. 2 (cited as Lambi). Hobson, chap. 2, makes a plausible case that Caprivi's was the first genuinely systematic strategy the German navy had up to this time. Even Tirpitz, who was very critical of Caprivi for building no real armored ships, admitted that Caprivi had a clear set of priorities and a coherent program (*Memoirs*, 1:37–38). He intended to construct large ships once the short-term coastal defense problem was solved.

49. Tirpitz, *Memoirs*, 1:54, Hassell, 51.

50. Tirpitz, *Memoirs*, 1:49–50. See also Röhr, 50; and Hildebrand, 7:82. See also Tirpitz's "Notes about the Self-Fabrication of Torpedos," n.d., but almost certainly 1888–1889, in N 253/14, 302ff.

51. Tirpitz, *Memoirs*, 1:51–52.

52. See ibid.; and Caprivi to Wickede, 16 November 1883, in the same file.

53. For this memorandum, including the torpedo part, see Reichstag, V Leg. Per., IV Sess., 1884, Anlage 26, 430–436. See also Lambi, 6–7. The text of the torpedo memorandum, the style of which reeks of Tirpitz, is also in Curt von Maltzahn, *Geschichte unserer taktischen Entwicklung*, 1:117–123 (cited as Maltzahn).

54. Tirpitz, *Memoirs*, 1:144.

55. On the Jeune École, see the latest, and probably the best account to date, Arne Røksund, "The Jeune École: The Strategy of the Weak," chap. 6 in Rolf Hobson and Tom Kristiansen, eds., *Navies in Northern Waters*; see also Røksund's consequent book of the same title. Also see Hobson, chap. 2; and Jöst Dülffer, "The German Reich and the Jeune École," in *Marine et technique au XIXe siècle*, 499–516; David H. Olivier, "Staatskaperei: The German Navy and Commerce Warfare," chap. 7; Volkmar Bueb, *Die junge Schule der französischen Marine: Strategie und Politik, 1875–1900*, passim; Ropp, chaps. 9–10; Potter, 249–250; and Petter, 131–132. The starkest statement of the Jeune École's ideas came in a series of articles by Admiral Aube's unofficial publicist, Gabriel Charmes, in *Revue des deux Mondes*: La réforme de la marine I: "Torpilleurs et cannoniéres" (15 December 1884), 872–906; La réforme de la marine II: "La guerre maritime et l'organisation de la force navale" (1 March 1885), 127–168; and La réforme de la marine, III: "Défense des côtes" (15 April 1885), 770–806. See also Tirpitz's evaluation of their ideas

in N 253/3, 23–28. What follows is the author's synthesis of these sources.

56. Ropp, 48.

57. In a test voyage across the Bay of Biscay in February 1886, accounted a "success," after twenty days at sea, "the crews were so worn out from seasickness and the lack of warm food that there could be no question of their inability to fight at the end of the trip" (ibid., 176). The conclusion was that they could never be used on the high seas for any extended period.

58. See Røksund, passim.

59. Hallmann, 25. See also Ekkard Verchau, "Von Jachmann über Stosch und Caprivi zu den Anfängen der Ära Tirpitz," in Herbert Schottelius and Wilhelm Deist, eds., Marine und Marinepolitik, 1871–1914, 54–72, quote at 67 (cited as Schottelius/Deist).

60. See Petter, 132ff.; and Hallmann, 25ff. Tirpitz's role in drafting this program is unclear, because contemporary evidence is lacking. It would be very surprising if Caprivi did not consult him, but, because of his low seniority among other things, it is unlikely that he was the major force behind this initiative. In his draft of Tirpitz's biography, Michaelis claims that, much later, officials in the RMA told him that Tirpitz had been its driving spirit. See Nachlass Michaelis N 164/2. Caprivi, already a "true believer" in torpedo boats, would not have needed more than technical advice from Tirpitz to put together such a proposal.

61. The analysis that follows is based on part of the memo Tirpitz wrote in April 1889, "On the Development of the Torpedo Arm," N 253/3, 1–18. The contemporary documents agree with his analysis.

62. For construction data, see Eric Gröner et al., German Warships, 1815–1945, Vol. 1, Major Surface Vessels,

152–155 (cited as Gröner); and Harald Fock, Fast Fighting Boats, 1870–1945: Their Design and Use, 1:13ff.

63. Sources on the cruise are in RM 31/237; N 253/15, 9ff.; and Hassell, 99ff. The fullest and most vivid account is Voigt's. He was aboard Blücher. See RM 8/76, 136–137.

64. Heeringen later became one of Tirpitz's closest collaborators in the Reichmarineamt and elsewhere.

65. In a letter to his wife, Tirpitz referred to Pohl with the affectionate diminutive "Pöhlchen" (Tirpitz to Marie, 12 July 1885, N 253/389, 11–12).

66. Tirpitz to Marie, 24 September 1885, ibid., 46–47.

67. N 253/14, 123–124.

68. N 253/15, 7–13.

69. On this point, see Epkenhans; and Weir.

70. Tirpitz, Memoirs, 1:54, 64ff.; Ropp, 30; Hallmann, 104–109.

71. RM 1/337, 12–17, Caprivi to Monts, 20 March 1884.

72. For the extensive March to November correspondence on these points between Caprivi and Tirpitz, see RM 1/337, RM 31/465, and RM 31/237, which contain the order to officially establish the experimental torpedo boat division on 1 August.

73. See, e.g., RM 31/308.

74. On 18 November 1884, Tirpitz married Marie Lipke.

75. See, e.g., N 253/408, 68–69, von Reichenbach to Tirpitz, 19 November 1884; N 253/197, 17–18, Ahlefeld to Tirpitz, 2 January 1885; and N 253/14, 116–121.

76. See, e.g., N 253 197, 15–16, Ahlefeld to Tirpitz, 15 January 1885; N253/14, 175, Tirpitz to Ahlefeld, 3 September 1885; ibid., 187, Tirpitz to Schichau, 2 September 1885; and N 253/15, 7–8.

77. N 253/408, 50–51., Oldekop [in effect, the Naval Attaché in London] to

NOTES TO PAGES 60–65

NOTES TO PAGES 60–65

Tirpitz, 13 October 1884. That Oldekop had to ask for basic information seems significant.

78. N 253/408, 52, Tirpitz to Oldekop, 3 April 1885; See also N 253/15, 9.

79. N 253/197, 15–16, Ahlefeld to Tirpitz, 15 January 1885.

80. N 253/408, 7–8, Jaeschke to Tirpitz, 11 March 1885; and N 253 15/, 34–35.

81. See RM 31/237, Goltz to Caprivi, 27 March 1885. For the most detailed description of the technical aspects of 1885-vintage torpedo boats, see RM 31/465, "Draft of Instructions for Military Personnel of Torpedo Boats," 19 April 1885.

82. N 253/14, 210–220, Tirpitz to Caprivi, 18 December 1885.

83. N 253/14, 271. Tirpitz's notes on reorganization, n.d., but between 9 February and 15 March 1886. On the work of the Inspectorate, see RM 27/III 16; RM 1/2674; N 253/14, 276ff.; N 253/15, 39–41; Hildebrand, 7:84; Hallmann, 104; Petter, 133; and Graubohm, 96, 187.

84. For technical specifications, see Hildebrand, 7:86f; Gröner, I, 152–158; and N 253/15, 13ff.

85. On these boats, see Potter, 244; Hildebrand, 7:85; Gröner, 1:166–167; and RM 253/15, 35–39. When he left the Torpedo Inspectorate in 1889, Tirpitz was trying to acquire an even bigger boat for a flotilla leader. See, e.g., Tirpitz's correspondence with Rear Admiral Friedrich Hollmann in late 1887 in N 253/204.

86. Ropp, 30; Hallmann, 107ff.

87. N 253/258, Captain Adolf Mensing [ret.] to Tirpitz, 9 May 1921. Mensing specifically wrote that the quote was verbatim. On the 1886 maneuvers, see RM 1/253 and RM 1/338, 36–39, Caprivi's observations about the

fall maneuvers, 11 October 1886. See also Hildebrand, 1:116–117.

88. See, e.g., Tirpitz to Marie, 9 September 1887, N 253/390, 80.

89. Hallmann, 109; N 253/14, 321–334; N 253/16, 33–34, Caprivi to Tirpitz, 14 December 1887. For the 1888 maneuvers, see RM 1/339.

90. Lambi, chap. 2; Petter, 137ff.

91. Nachlass Knorr, N 578/11, 123ff.

92. For a summary of the answers of all the respondents, see N 253/35, "Report of the Ship Examination Commission," 13 March 1888.

93. The response is in N 253/35 and N 253/58.

94. N 253/58, 129–137.

95. Ibid., 131.

96. See diagrams and discussion of tactical formations in chapter 7, this volume.

97. See Maltzahn, 1:226, 2:33, and summaries of the various responses to the questions in N 253/35.

98. Hildebrand, 1:151.

99. Kaulisch, 40.

100. On this trip, see Hildebrand, 1:149; RM 1 2717, 71–90; and N 253/ 14, 52. See also Tirpitz's later account of this in N 253/104.

101. See Caprivi to Tirpitz, 26 June 1888, in Hassell, 53. For Tirpitz's personal account, see Tirpitz to Marie, 19 June 1887, N 253/390, 32–33.

102. See, e.g., Tirpitz to Marie, 30 August 1887, N 253/390, 73.

103. Tirpitz, *Memoirs*, 1:57; and Petter, 144.

104. Nachlass Senden, N 160/4, "Denkschrift betreffend Neuorganisation," October 1890. See also Berghahn, 28–33.

105. See N 253/14, 295–299, 341–342, and especially his valedictory memorandum of 21 February 1889, in ibid., 350–360; Tirpitz, *Memoirs*, 1:57.

106. RM 2/827, 14, 1 January 1889. In a letter to Caprivi on 26 December 1888, Tirpitz shared his fears for the future of the navy. He favored its gradual and controlled expansion rather than the rapid one William II wanted. He also opposed the tripartite division of the navy. Hassell Family Archive.

107. Salewski, 22; Hallmann, 107; Gemzell, 59; Petter, 129; and Berghahn, 60ff.

108. Ropp, chap. 10 and 236.

109. For a rough numerical comparison, see Potter, 244. For more detailed comparative information, see Robert Gardiner, ed., Conway's All the World's Fighting Ships, 1860–1905 (cited as Gardiner). Perhaps the best existing comparative analysis for that particular point in time is one Tirpitz himself did in 1889. See N 253/15, 18–30 and 49–56.

110. " Über die Entwicklung des Torpedowesens, N 253/15, with additional written comments by Tirpitz in RM 3/11957.

111. For a fascinating clue to the answer to this question, see Nachlass William Michaelis, N 164/4, 29–40. Michaelis was a department head in the Admiral Staff, 1910–1913. He wrote that Tirpitz simply refused to believe unimpeachable evidence that, by then, British torpedos were better than German ones. Fred T. Jane, ed., Jane's Fighting Ships, 1914 (cited as Jane, 1914), demonstrates the superiority of comparable classes of British destroyers to German ones, particularly regarding speed, range, and armament.

112. RM 8/1233, Michaelis's recollections.

113. Tirpitz, Memoirs, 1:67.

114. Trotha Papers, L 40. Trotha's notes on Tirpitz's life, 16 March 1937.

115. Nachlass Michaelis N 164/4, 29–40, demonstrates how submissive Heeringen had to be to Tirpitz to stay in the latter's good graces.

116. It is possible that Scheer also should be on the short list. Walter Freiherr von Keyserlingk, a battleship commander in the wartime High Seas Fleet, noted in the 1930s: "[Scheer] was in on the early development of the torpedo weapon under Tirpitz and was one of those young officers on whom their experience with this weapon had a decisive influence. From then came his close relationship with Tirpitz." Nachlass Keyserlingk, N 161/9, 39ff.

117. Berghahn, 58.

118. See their 1892–1896 correspondence in N 253/320, 321.

119. Salewski, 23.

6. INTERIM, 1889–1891

1. Tirpitz (Kiel) to Marie (Berlin), 7 September 1884; Marie to Tirpitz, 31 April [sic] 1884. Hassell Family Archive.

2. Tirpitz to Marie, 19 October 1884, Hassell Family Archive.

3. See N 253/408, 52, Tirpitz to Iwan Oldekop, 3 April 1885.

4. Holger Herwig, The German Naval Officer Corps: A Social and Political History, 1890–1918, 80ff. (cited as Herwig, Officer Corps).

5. The standard genealogical guides contain no hint that Marie's father was born Jewish. See, e.g., Walter von Hueck, ed., Genealogisches Handbuch der Adelingen Häuser Adelige Häuser B, 17:473ff. Apparently, during the Nazi years, Ulrich von Hassell, Tirpitz's son-in-law, had friends in the Foreign Office conduct a secret investigation on Gustav Lipke's pedigree. One might speculate that Marie, a widow since 1930, alerted daughter Ilse, who had her husband quietly investigate. Nazi law (though not Jewish law, which is matriarchal) would have considered Marie, by then in her seventies, a half-

Jew, with potentially dire consequences for the family. One wonders today whether the Nazis would have had the nerve to persecute the Tirpitz family for this reason, as he was still highly revered in the navy. I am grateful to Agostino von Hassell for bringing these facts to my attention, and for supplying additional information on Gustav Lipke.

When Tirpitz was raised to the hereditary nobility in 1900, the Royal Prussian Herald Office vetted Tirpitz's background but did not pursue Marie's heritage. Königliche Heraldamt, Rep. 176 VI T nr 147 (this file was in the Merseburg Archive).

6. See N 253/390, 3–4, 13–14, 9–10, Tirpitz to Marie, 8, 14, and 18 January 1887.

7. Kaulisch, 39.

8. Interview with Ambassador Wolfgang-Ulrich von Hassell, 18 April 1990.

9. Ibid., and Hassell, 220–221.

10. Hassell, 219. Much of the information on Alghero comes from Ilse von Hassell's Bilderbuch (picture book), Hassell Family Archive.

11. Ilse's Bilderbuch, Hassell, 217; some details are from Ambassador von Hassell interview.

12. Hassell, 214; Ilse's Bilderbuch.

13. On the whole question of naval displays, see Jan Rüger, The Great Naval Game: Britain and Germany in the Age of Empire (cited as Rüger).

14. Ilse's Bilderbuch.

15. N 253/114, Wolfgang von Tirpitz to Kolshorn, 20 February 1918.

16. See, e.g., Herwig, Officer Corps, 85–86.

17. See, e.g., N 253/390, 19–20, Tirpitz to Marie, 15 March 1887. The letter also infers that he was unaware of Marie's Jewish heritage or considered her Protestant by birth.

18. N 252/327, 118, Rudolf to Marie, 29 June 1898.

19. Hassell, 235.

20. Ibid., 216–217; Ambassador von Hassell interview.

21. Paul G. Halpern, A Naval History of World War I, 31–32 (cited as Halpern); Hildebrand, 4:102.

22. For Ulrich's own account, see Ulrich von Hassell, Der Kreis Schliesst Sich, 199–200.

23. April 1889, " Über die Entwicklung des Torpedowesens." N 253/15, with additional written comments by Tirpitz in RM 3/11957.

24. Hildebrand, 5:54–55.

25. Ibid.; and Sondhaus, 179.

26. Hildebrand, 6:64–66.

27. Tirpitz, Memoirs, 1:65.

28. N 164/2, 9. William Michaelis in Nachlass Michaelis.

29. See, e.g., N 253/16.

30. See Tirpitz's notes in N 253/104.

31. Hallmann, 100.

32. On Bismarck's diplomacy, see, e.g., Klaus Hildebrand, Das vergangene Reich, 1–149.

33. Albert Hopmann, Das Logbuch eines deutschen Seeoffiziers, 223 (cited as Hopmann, Logbuch).

34. Nachlass Knorr, N 578/11, 136.

35. N 253/42, 29–48, "Gründe, welche für Beibehaltung eines Oberkommandos mit kräftigen Befügnisse sprechen," with Knorr's comments. Knorr had further comments in the version of the document in N253/39.

36. Hubatsch, Admiralstab, chap. 4; Hallmann, 111ff.

37. Aptly summarized in Hobson, 194ff. See also Berghahn, 68–69.

38. RM 3/32, 115–139, " Über unsere Maritime-militärische Fortentwicklung," with mostly positive appended notes by Büchsel, then in the RMA, 140–144. An earlier draft is in N 253/42,

53–76. Knorr's generally compatible view is in N 253/3, 27–28. Partly published in Volker R. Berghahn and Wilhelm Deist, eds., *Rüstung im Zeichen der wilhelmischen Weltpolitik: Grundlegende Dokumente, 1890–1914*, 82–87 (cited as Berghahn/Deist).

39. For example, Tirpitz's old friend and subordinate in the Torpedo Arm, Hunold von Ahlefeld, pointed out that Tirpitz's putative "consensus" was somewhat mythical. Ahlefeld believed that such a view should be pressed on the officer corps. Hallmann, 113.

40. N 253/3, 15–57, "Denkschrift über die Neuorganisation unserer Panzerflotte." See Hallmann, 117–120; and Hobson, 198–199.

41. Ibid., 198–199.

42. See, e.g., his letter to Marie, 29 July 1889, Hassell Family Archive.

43. See Senden and Tirpitz articles in Hildebrand, *Admirale*.

44. For more details on Senden's life, see Hans-Otto Steinmetz, "Admiral Freiherr von Senden-Bibran: Erster Chef des Marine-Kabinetts von 1889 bis 1906," ca. 1971, typed ms. in the MGFA Library, Potsdam.

45. See Lambi, 36; Hallmann, 54ff.; and Isabel Hull, *The Entourage of Kaiser Wilhelm II, 1888–1918*, 178ff.

46. Fürst Chlodwig zu Hohenlohe-Schillingsfürst, *Denkwürdigkeiten der Reichskanzlerzeit*, 289–290 (cited as Hohenlohe).

47. Hopmann, *Logbuch*, 85. In the light of later events, Hopmann's assessment may have been too optimistic.

48. See, e.g., N 253/228.

49. Tirpitz to Marie, 28 July1889, Hassell Family Archive.

50. Hallmann, 115–116.

51. See Tirpitz, *Memoirs*, 1:62. For a fuller account by Tirpitz, see N 253/104, 217–220. See also Hallmann, 116.

52. Hallmann, 117–118.

7. OBERKOMMANDO DER MARINE, 1892–1895

1. Part of this chapter is based on Patrick J. Kelly, "Strategy, Tactic and Turf Wars: Tirpitz and the Oberkommando der Marine, 1892–1895," *Journal of Military History* 66 (October 2002): 1033–1066.

2. On Lissa, see Lawrence Sondhaus, *The Habsburg Empire and the Sea: Austrian Naval Policy 1797–1866*, 252ff.

3. See Hildebrand, 5:124–125.

4. On the Jeune École and naval conditions in general in the 1880s, see Bueb, passim; Røksund; Hobson, 96–109; and chap. 5 in this volume. See, too, Arthur J. Marder, *The Anatomy of British Sea Power, 1880–1905*, pts. 1 and 3 (cited as Marder, *Anatomy*); Petter, 139; Ropp, chap. 13; Sondhaus, 177ff. See also Nachlass Michaelis, N 164/2, 15.

5. See, e.g., Tirpitz, *Memoirs*, vol. 1, chap. 1.

6. On William II's interest in the navy, see Lambi, chap. 3; Petter, 139ff.; and Sondhaus, chaps. 8 and 9.

7. Hildebrand, 1:156ff.

8. Most astonishing, in January/February 1896, when the OK finally believed he had opted for a battleship navy, he suddenly shifted back to cruisers. See Berghahn, 90ff.; and Steinberg, chap. 2. See also Chapter 8 in this volume.

9. On the reorganization, see Hubatsch, chap. 4; Berghahn, 23ff.; and Nachlass Michaelis, N 164/ 2, 7f. See also below.

10. On tactical exercises in the 1880s see Maltzahn, 1:passim. It covers German tactical development encyclopedically and generally very objectively. It is indispensable for any serious study of German tactics in that era. Michaelis notes in his papers (N 164/2, 1–31)

that in 1911, when he was a department head in the Admiralstab, Maltzahn wrote this work. Heeringen, then its Chief, buried it in the files for fear of offending the Emperor or Tirpitz.

11. Nachlass Michaelis, N/164/2, 17.

12. The following summary is based on Ropp, 105ff.; Hallmann, 107ff.; Maltzahn, 1:passim; and Hopmann, *Logbuch*, 45ff.

13. One of Tirpitz's closest collaborators, Hunold von Ahlefeld, believed in the ram well into the twentieth century. See N 253/31, 17; see also Admiral Adolf von Trotha's recollections of Ahlefeld in Trotha Papers, Ahlefeld.

14. Maltzahn, 1:220, 2:28.

15. The following information comes mainly from a careful perusal of Hildebrand, *Admirale*. Members of the Torpedo Gang who followed Tirpitz into the OK include Hunold von Ahlefeld, a close collaborator; Otto Braun, who died in a typhoon while serving under Tirpitz in Asia in 1896 (hewas Tirpitz's protégé and is widely believed to have had a major hand in writing the famous Dienstschrift IX in 1894); Gustav Bachmann, later a wartime Chief of the Admiralstab; Karl Dick; August von Heeringen, also a Chief of the Admiralstab and Tirpitz's propaganda wizard in 1897; Albert Hopmann, whose log book is an important source; Friedrich Ingenohl, commander of the High Seas Fleet in 1914; Georg Müller, Senden's successor as Chief of the MK; Ludwig Schröder; Rudolf Siegel, later naval attaché in Paris; and Raimond Winkler. A glance at the OK's office list in 1895 (RM 4/7, pp.145ff.) reveals how pervasive the Torpedo Gang was in the OK. See the original list of the Torpedo Gang in the appendix.

16. For a good characterization of Tirpitz, see Berghahn, 58.

17. Maltzahn, 2:42.

18. Ibid., 2:44; Sondhaus, 194ff.

19. Hopmann, 189. On the 1892 maneuvers, see also N 253/2, passim.

20. Maltzahn, 2:45ff. See also the note by Goltz of 28 April 1894 in N 253/2.

21. Kaulisch, 52.

22. Quoted in Sondhaus, 196.

23. The following discussion of tactical questions is based principally on Maltzahn, 2:50ff. See also Hopmann, *Logbuch*, 182–186.

24. On Thomsen, see Hildebrand, 4:106–107.

25. "Tactical and Strategic Memorandum of the OKM VI," 15 February 1894, signed by Goltz, RM 4/176, 145–152. On Otto Braun's important role in writing tactical memoranda, see Hopmann, *Logbuch*, 181.

26. Hopmann, Logbuch, 181. See also Maltzahn, 2:73ff.

27. "Tactical and Strategic Memorandum of the OKM IX," 16 June 1894, RM 4/176, 219–245.

28. Hildebrand, 3:140ff.

29. N 253/ 177, Tirpitz to Blanca Amsler, 25 March 1895. See also Nachlass Michaelis, N 164/2, 18.

30. On the 1895 maneuvers, see Maltzahn, 2:77ff; Sondhaus, 199–200. On Goltz's departure and the question of ship type, see Hallmann, 139ff., and esp.,Hopmann, 216.

31. Maltzahn, 2:15 and 103.

32. In this consideration, the word "strategy" is used in its 1890s sense. Anything beyond pure tactics was regarded as "strategy." The only published attempt to definitively study German operation plans is Lambi, who heroically spent years plowing through the turgid files of the Admiralstab. A new, clear-sighted, and, in my judgment, persuasive look at the roots of German strategy in this period is Hobson.

33. Lambi, chap. 2.

34. Ibid., 16–17.

35. N 253/365, 123–124. See also Hassell, 88–91.

36. See chapter 5, this volume.

37. These three memos are insightfully discussed in Hobson, chap. 5, upon which the summary below is largely based.

38. Hallmann, 114.

39. Büchsel's comments are in RM 3/32, 140; Knorr's are in N 253/3, 27.

40. Hobson, 264.

41. Ibid., chaps. 3–5.

42. Such humiliation was a common feeling in the navy, which smarted keenly about this for decades. There is no better example than Tirpitz, *Memoirs*, 1: chap. 1. See also Lambi, 201.

43. See again Tirpitz's April memo of 1891 in chapter 6 of this volume. On the Emperor, see Hallmann, 101.

44. RM 4/176, 219–245, "Taktische und Strategische Dienstschriften des Oberkommando der Marine Nr. IX: Allgemeine Erfahrungen aus den Manövern der Herstübungs-Flotte, June 16, 1894." The document is internally paginated and those page numbers are used in the citations below. It is excerpted in Berghahn/Deist, 87–99.

45. See RM 4/6, 179–180, 184–185. Hopmann, Braun's close friend, noted that the tactical and strategic memoranda of the OK were largely drafted by Braun. *Logbuch*, 181.

46. See N 253/390, 78f, Tirpitz to Marie, 8 September 1887.

47. Dienstschrift IX, 3.

48. Ibid.

49. Ibid.

50. See Hobson, chaps. 6–7. See also Tirpitz's correspondence with Maltzahn in N 253/408.

51. Julian Corbett, *Some Principles of Maritime Strategy* (cited as Corbett); B. Mitchell Simpson III, ed., *The Development of Naval Thought: Essays by Herbert Rosinski* (cited as Simpson, ed., Rosinski); Azar Gat, *The Development of Military Thought: The Nineteenth Century* (cited as Gat).

52. On these points, see, esp, Hobson, 200–212; quote at 190.

53. See, e.g., N253/320, Stosch to Tirpitz, 20 July 1894, wherein Stosch, after reading Dienstschrift IX, complimented Tirpitz on his acceptance of Clausewitz's principles.

54. Dienstschrift IX, 3.

55. Ibid., 5–6.

56. Ibid., 6–7.

57. Ibid., 4–5.

58. Ibid., appendix.

59. Unfortunately for Tirpitz and the Emperor, Hollmann at the RMA paid little attention. For example, the Emperor favored a medium class of cruisers, later constructed as the five-ship *Hertha* class and referred to by the British as "ten-minute cruisers," because that was how long they would have lasted in battle against a serious enemy. See Hildebrand, 3:73–77; and Lambi, 78.

60. "Memorandum of an Operations Plan for an Attack on the (English) Channel in Case of a War with France," signed by Goltz, though written by Tirpitz and drafted by Heeringen, and given to William II on 19 February 1895. RM 8/78, 5–17. See also Hallmann, 129; and Lambi, 79–86. There was, of course, a plan against Russia alone. Hopmann, responsible for preparing it, thought of it as a joke. Ironically, in 1915, as a commander, he put it into operation. Hopmann, *Logbuch*, 217–218. See also Lambi, 78–84.

61. Hallmann, 101.

62. Knorr memorandum for William II, 28 November 1895, N 253/3, 82–92.

63. Space does not permit a comprehensive account of all aspects of the OK vs. RMA turf battles up to 1895, and this part of the story is already fairly well known. See Berghahn, 23ff., 90ff.; Steinberg, chap. 2; Hallmann, passim; Hubatsch, chap. 4; and Gemzell, 92ff.

64. Hubatsch, 54.

65. Hallmann, 56, 69.

66. Tirpitz to Hollmann, 14 September 1888, N 253/14, 295–299. But, in his memoirs, he presented a different view; see *Memoirs*, 1:61–62. After he succeeded Hollmann in 1897, Tirpitz became friendly toward him again and often asked his advice.

67. Hallmann, 111.

68. Senden Nachlass, N 160/5, 1–4, Tirpitz to Senden, 30 December 1892.

69. For example, the whole N 253/2 file is filled with scores of such exchanges on a wide variety of matters.

70. On this first propaganda campaign, only summarized here, see RM 3/ 9785, passim; Deist, 32–50; and Kehr, 33ff.

71. Tirpitz, *Memoirs*, 1:76.

72. Deist, 50.

73. Trotha Papers, Trotha's notes on Ahlefeld, 2 April 1937.

74. See some of the correspondence in N253/2, and Hallmann, 84–85.

75. For an overview of this conflict, see Steinberg, *Yesterday's Deterrent*, chap. 2; or Hallmann, 138ff.

76. A good example, among countless many, is in his letter to Goltz of 19 February 1895. RM 8/78, 14–17.

77. Stosch to Tirpitz, 6 June 1892, N 253/320, 8–11.

78. There are many examples of this point in N 253/2.

79. Tirpitz to Senden, 30 December 1892; Nachlass Senden, N 160/5, 1–4.

8. ON THE VERGE OF POWER, 1895–1897

1. On Germany's population and industrial growth, as well as related phenomena, see the very useful tables in Berghahn, *Imperial Germany*.

2. See, e.g., Paul Kennedy, *The Rise of the Anglo-German Antagonism 1860–1914*, esp. chaps. 3 and 15 (cited as Kennedy, *Antagonism*).

3. Cf. Boelcke, passim.

4. Holger Herwig, *"Luxury Fleet," The Imperial German Navy, 1888–1918*, 98 (cited as Herwig).

5. On Caprivi's appointment, see J. C. G. Röhl, *Germany without Bismarck: The Crisis of Government in the Second Reich, 1890–1900*, esp. 56–70 (cited as Röhl, *Bismarck*).

6. Ibid., 60ff.

7. See Hobson, 116–131; Kehr, 251–257. The following analysis is based mainly on these sources.

8. Berghahn/Deist, 37, illustrates these fears in a memo of 27 August 1891.

9. See Hobson, 124–128; and Kehr, 251–257.

10. Röhl, *Bismarck*, 118ff.

11. See the articles on *Brandenburg, Kurfürst Friedrich Wilhelm, Weissenburg,* and *Wörth* in Hildebrand.

12. See Kehr, 31–49, for a more detailed rendition of these battles, which included some humorous moments.

13. Hildebrand, 3:126–133.

14. For Reichstag battles in the early 1890s, see Sondhaus, 177–199.

15. See Hallmann, 200–201.

16. N 255/8, Nachlass Diedrichs, Tirpitz to Diedrichs, 17 November 1895.

17. Ibid., Tirpitz to Diedrichs, 4 December 1895.

18. Sondhaus, 201. The maneuvers are documented in RM 4/65.

19. Hallmann, 154–158.

20. N 253/3, 82–92. See also the table in Lambi, 85.

21. N 253/3, 131–132, Hollmann Memo on the Z Commission, 18 December 1895.

22. N 253/3, 128–129, includes both the order of 16 December 1895 and Senden's accompanying letter to Tirpitz of the following day. See also RM 3/2525, 2–3.

23. See, e.g., his irritated letter to Senden of 30 December 1892. Nachlass Senden, N 160/5. 1–4.

24. N 253/320, 8–11, Stosch to Tirpitz, 6 June 1892.

25. See Kennedy, *Antagonism*, 220–221; Steinberg, 82–83.

26. N 253/321, 10–13, Tirpitz to Stosch, 21 December 1895. See also Hobson, 222–226. The letter is reproduced in Berghahn/Deist, 103–105.

27. N 253/321, 14–20, Stosch to Tirpitz, 25 December 1895. Note that Stosch wrote this *before* the Jameson Raid.

28. N 253/3, 102–111, Tirpitz Memo to William II about OK Report of 28 November 1895; sent 3 January 1896. There is a marginal note on the original in William II's hand, "read with great interest." Also printed in Berghahn/Deist, 105–108, 195–198. For a thorough analysis of the document, see Hobson, 223–227; and Berghahn, 90–95.

29. See William II's letter of 8 January 1896 in Hohenlohe, 153ff.

30. See Senden Diary, entry of 12 January 1896, in Kehr, 464.

31. Steinberg, 85–86; Hallmann, 177–179.

32. Senden Diary, entry of 14 January 1896, in Kehr, 464.

33. N 253/3, 275–278, Tirpitz's "Notes from the Meeting with William II on the Political Side of the Fleet Proposal," 28 January 1896. Printed in

Berghahn/Deist, 109–111, See also Hallmann, 182–189. Tirpitz had heard from Senden on 20 January that the Emperor intended to name him State Secretary after Hollmann completed that year's estimates negotiations. Hallmann, 183.

34. See, e.g., N 253/40, 28–36, correspondence with Schuncke, January–March, 1896. Schunke was an old friend and comrade of Tirpitz from the torpedo days. Tirpitz was reluctant to employ him in the RMA Construction Department, despite their friendship. See N 160/5, 8–11, Tirpitz to Senden, 15 February 1896.

35. N 253/321, 21–24, Stosch to Tirpitz, 12 February 1896.

36. N 253/321, 25–31, Tirpitz to Stosch, 13 February 1896. The mention of Madrid is an allusion to Schiller's drama, *Don Carlos*. The latter was the alienated son of Spanish King Philip II, who wanted to leave Madrid to escape the intrigues of the Royal Court.

37. N 253/3, 273–274, Senden to Tirpitz, 13 February 1896.

38. N 160/5, 8–11, Tirpitz to Senden, 15 February 1896.

39. N 160/11, Senden Memo, dated March 1896.

40. The draft speech is not in the archives but is published in Hans Hallmann, *Krügerdepesche und Flottenfrage*, 79–87. See also the clear analysis of it in Hobson, 224–228.

41. Steinberg, 94–95.

42. N 160/5, 12–13, Tirpitz to Senden, 20 March 1896.

43. N 253/3, 275–276. Senden to Tirpitz, 31 March 1896.

44. See Knorr's unusually warm letter to Tirpitz in N 253/408, 15–16, 4 April 1896.

45. Gottschall, 134.

46. See John E. Schrecker, *Imperialism and German Nationalism: Germany in Shantung*, 11–14 (cited as

NOTES TO PAGES 118–123

Schrecker). See also Ferdinand von Richthofen, *China: Ergebnisse eigener Reisen*, 2:1882.

47. Gottschall, 135–136. The force consisted of the new cruiser *Irene* and three older cruisers, *Alexandrine*, *Arcona*, and *Marie*. Early in 1895 the armored cruiser *Kaiser* and *Prinzess Wilhelm*, sister ship of *Irene*, replaced *Alexandrine* and *Marie*.

48. Gottschall, 137–138.

49. RM 38/28, Knorr's notes for IV, 8 November 1895.

50. The following account of his journey comes from a series of letters that Tirpitz wrote to his wife, Marie, which are in N 253/167.

51. On these ships, see the relevant articles in Hildebrand.

52. N 255/8, Nachlass Diedrichs, Tirpitz to Diedrichs, 17 November 1895.

53. RM 38/28, Knorr to Tirpitz, 21 May 1896.

54. See Gottschall, 141; Tirpitz, *Memoirs*, vol. 1, chap. 8; See also N253/237, Alfred Gwinner to Tirpitz, 25 July 1896. Gwinner ran the Deutsche Bank and described to Tirpitz some of the bank's many interests in China.

55. Tirpitz, *Memoirs*, 1:94.

56. See the account of one of the survivors in RM 93/2253, dated 3 August 1896.

57. For full reports on the disaster, see RM 3/2536.

58. N 253/197, 141–142, Ahlefeld to Tirpitz, 2 August 1896.

59. RM 3/2536.

60. RM 38/28, Tirpitz to Knorr, 2 August 1896; Tirpitz, *Memoirs*, 1:94.

61. N 253/45, Notes in Tirpitz's hand of a meeting with Heyking, 6 August 1896. See also RM 3/3155, 162–166, Tirpitz to Knorr, 8 August 1896.

62. Ibid., 168–170, Tirpitz (Hakodate) to Knorr, 24 August 1896.

63. See Foreign Office R 18163, *Beabsichtigte Erwerbung der Grossmächte aus Anlass des chinesisch-japonischen Krieges*, Vol. 8.

64. N 253/45, 22–32, Tirpitz to Knorr, 5 September 1896. A draft copy is in RM 38/28.

65. Tirpitz's reports on Vladivostok are in RM 92/2732 and RM 3/3155, 178–179, 211–215. See also his letters to Marie in N 253/167.

66. Most of his descriptions of Japan come from his letters to Marie in N 253/167. Some are published in Hassell, 132–147. For his official report, see RM 3/3155, 240–244, Tirpitz to Knorr, 10 November 1896.

67. Tirpitz, *Memoirs*, 1:97. See also Heyking's telegram in N 253/45, 49.

68. RM 3/3155, 219–222, Tirpitz to Knorr, October 15, 1896; and RM 3/3108, 109–111, Tirpitz to Knorr, 5 November 1896.

69. N253/167, letters to Marie from that period.

70. RM 38/29, Tirpitz to Knorr, 21 November 1896.

71. See PG 65990, OK Memo for IV about Kiaochou Bay, 5 November 1896.

72. RM 3/6693, Knorr's Memo for IV, 24 November 1896.

73. Gottschall, 143.

74. N 253/45, 72–73, Senden to Tirpitz, 22 November 1896.

75. N 253/167, Tirpitz to Marie, 2 December 1896.

76. N 253/45, 56–58, 70–71 (printed version); RM 38/28 (handwritten version), Tirpitz to Knorr, 7 December 1896.

77. Gottschall, 144.

78. See RM 4/170, 11–14, personal letter to Knorr, 8 December 1896. Tirpitz asked Knorr not to share it with the Foreign Office.

79. See ibid., and letter to Müller, 11 December 1896, in Wolfgang von Tirpitz, "Tirpitzs letztes Frontkommando," *Marine Rundschau* 62 (1965): 321–335, 325–326; and N 253/45, 74–77, Jaeschke (Berlin) to Tirpitz, 19 December 1896.

80. N 253/167, 47–49, Tirpitz to Marie, 24 December 1896.

81. Ibid., 38–41, 1 January 1897. For his report to Berlin, see RM 3/3155. See also OK Note for IV, 4 January 1897, PG 65990.

82. N 253/167, 34–37, Tirpitz to Marie, 10 January 1897.

83. PG 65990, OK Memo about seizing a base in China, 9 January 1897. See also Knorr's orders to Tirpitz, 12 January 1897 (arrived 19 February) in RM 38/28.

84. N 253/45, 78–79, Tirpitz (Hongkong) to Senden, 10 January 1897. He repeated this argument in a more elaborate form in N 160/5, 16–19, Nachlass Tirpitz (Mirsbay) to Senden, 20 January 1897. Only the letter of 20 January may have been sent.

85. See Gottschall, chaps. 5 and 6.

86. Hallmann, 204–237, Steinberg, chap. 3; and Kehr, chap. 2 Most of the account below is synthesized from these sources.

87. For the full text, see RM 3/32, 218–227.

88. RM 3/32, 237, Lieber to Hollmann, 20 November 1896.

89. See, e.g., the clippings in N253/278.

90. RM 4/170, 15–16, Tirpitz (Samsah) to Knorr, 22 November 1896.

91. See ibid., Knorr to Hollmann, January 1897, and Hollmann's reply, N 253/3, 281, 6 January 1897.

92. Ibid., 282, Knorr to Tirpitz, 7 January 1897, and Tirpitz's reply, 290–291, 16 February 1897.

93. N 253/45, 78f, Tirpitz to Senden, 10 January 1897. A similar letter also went to Senden on 20 January, Nachlass Senden, N 160/5, 16–19.

94. N 253/40, 123, Müller to Tirpitz, 9 February 1897. See also Steinberg, 108; and Hallmann, 217.

95. Steinberg, 109–114; Berghahn, 99–103.

96. N 253/167, 19–21, Tirpitz to Marie, 1 March 1897.

97. Ibid., Tirpitz to Marie, 8 March 1897.

98. Steinberg, 114–115.

99. N 253/167, 2–3, Tirpitz to Marie, 14 April 1897.

100. PG 65990, OK Memo for IV, 9 April 1897; and ibid., Senden to Knorr 20 April 1897.

101. Steinberg, 119–123.

9. TIRPITZ ASCENDANT, 1897–1898

1. Hopmann, *Logbuch*, 240.

2. N 253/321. Partially printed in Berghahn/Deist, 103ff.

3. On public reaction to Tirpitz's appointment, see Kehr, 73–78.

4. N 253/166, Tirpitz to Blanca Amsler, 18 July 1897.

5. N 253/407, 22–25, Bendemann to Tirpitz, 6 October 1897.

6. Gottschall, 225–229.

7. On this complex situation, see, e.g., Wilhelm Deist, "Die Armee in Staat und Gesellschaft, 1890–1914" in Michael Stürmer, ed., *Das Kaiserliche Deutschland*,312–339; and Stig Förster, *Der doppelte Militarismus. Die Deutsche Heeresrüstungpolitik zwischen Status-quo Sicherung und Aggression, 1890–1913* (cited as Förster).

8. He officially assumed office on 18 June.

9. N 253/4, 1–2. Notes re Immediatvortrag, 15 June 1897.

10. Tirpitz, *Memoirs*, 1:121–122.

11. The printed proposal, "General Considerations on the Constitution of the German Fleet according to Ship Classes and Sizes," is in PG 66712.

12. N 253/4, 1–2.

13. Trotha Papers, L 68, Adolf von Trotha's biographical notes on Capelle, April 1937. Contrary to some authors, Capelle was never a member of the Torpedo Gang.

14. Tirpitz, *Memoirs*, 1:122.

15. Trotha Papers, L 68. An excellent example of the Tirpitz-Capelle collaboration can be seen in N 253/4, 148–149, Capelle/Tirpitz notes for a meeting with Chancellor Hohenlohe, which contains a written dialogue regarding the strategy and tactics of the Navy Bill.

16. Tirpitz, *Memoirs*, 1:123.

17. PG 66017, 97, 19 June 1897.

18. See Hans Hildebrand, *Deutschlands Admirale V, Marinebeamte*, 131–132 and 84–85. See also N 253/100, Tirpitz's notes sent to Hollmann years later, n.d. The document provides Tirpitz's own summary of the estimates process and the politics of the 1898 law.

19. For most of these exchanges, see PG 66017, 66712, N 253/4. Nachlass Tirpitz, and N 168/11, Nachlass Büchsel. See also Hallmann, 257ff., and Steinberg, 134ff.

20. Deist, 135–136.

21. Ibid., 71.

22. See his letters to Tirpitz in the summer and fall of 1897 in N 253/407 and /4. See also Deist, 88–98.

23. Kehr, 90–119, provides an extensive treatment of the propaganda campaign for the 1898 law; on paying for the campaign, see Tirpitz, *Memoirs*, 1:146.

24. On this seminal article, which Tirpitz later referred to repeatedly, see E. L. Woodward, *Great Britain and the German Navy, 1898–1914*, 42–43 (cited as Woodward). Oron J. Hale, *Publicity and Diplomacy*, 42–43 (cited as Hale). Steinberg, 143.

25. On the "Flottenprofessoren," see Wolfgang Marienfeld, *Wissenschaft und Schlachtflottenbau in Deutschland, 1897 bis 1906*, (cited as Marienfeld).

26. On Halle, see Kehr, 101–102.

27. Beghahn, 124; Steinberg, 143.

28. Hopmann, *Logbuch*, 240.

29. Hallmann, 308–309.

30. See Berghahn, 123; Steinberg, 147, 222; and Petter, 196.

31. See, e.g., BA Koblenz, Nachlass Hohenlohe NL 7/1678; and Tirpitz's correspondence with Miquel and Thielmann, with the involvement of Heeringen and Capelle, N 253/4. Miquel's *Sammlungspolitik* was an attempt to reconstitute a common front between the right-wing liberal industrialists and conservatives, many of whom were agrarians, against democratic and socialist groups. A centerpiece of Miquel's policy was to raise tariffs on imports, which Caprivi had reduced in the 1890s, in order to protect domestic manufacturing and agriculture. This policy penalized consumers by, among other things, raising the price of bread. For a good summary of *Sammlungspolitik*, see Petter, 188.

32. See N 253/4, 22–23, Tirpitz to Thielmann, 8 August 1897. See also N 253/100, Tirpitz's later note to Hollmann.

33. N 253/4, 46–47, Tirpitz to Miquel, 5 August 1897.

34. Ibid., 49–59, 59–64, Capelle to Tirpitz, 6 and 7 August 1897.

35. Ibid., 105–106. Tirpitz's notes of meeting with William II, 19 August 1897.

36. See Hohenlohe, 377; Kehr, 115–116; and Tirpitz, *Memoirs*, 1:142ff.

37. N 253/4, 88–91, Heeringen letter, 13 August 1897.

38. N 253/100, Tirpitz's notes given to Hollmann, n.d.

39. On preparations for this meeting, see Tirpitz's correspondence with Senden, Heeringen, and Bülow in N 253/4. See also Nachlass Eisendecher, T 291, Tirpitz to Eisendecher, 31 August 1897.

40. Tirpitz, *Memoirs*, vol. 1, chap. 10. The quotation is from Kehr, 92. See also Hallmann, 293–294. Bismarck's letter to Tirpitz of 4 December 1897 is in N 253/4, 184. See also John Röhl, *Wilhelm II: The Kaiser's Personal Monarchy, 1888–1900*, 868–869 (cited as Röhl, *Wilhelm II*, vol. 2).

41. The peculiarities of the German tax system and their impact on the navy are addressed in the following chapter.

42. See Berghahn, 126ff.

43. The text is in PG 66019.

44. The entire public record of the Reichstag and Budget Commission hearings on the Navy Bill is in RM 3/11720. The best accounts of the Navy Bill in the Reichstag and the Budget Commission are in Kehr, 121ff.; Steinberg, 36ff. and chap. 5; Hallmann, 279ff.; Karl Bachem, *Vorgeschichte, Geschichte, und Politik der deutschen Zentrumspartei*, 5:469ff. (cited as Bachem); Hjalmar Grimm, "German Naval Legislation, 1898–1914," 57ff. The best account of the Center Party during this period is John K. Zeender, *The German Center Party, 1890–1906* (cited as Zeender). Dr. Zeender generously made available to the author unpublished materials from the Lieber Papers, Wroclaw Diocesan Archive.

45. See Hallmann, 276.

46. N 253/4, 77–78, Miquel to Tirpitz, 11 August 1897.

47. Ibid., 100, Heeringen to Tirpitz, 16 August 1897.

48. Lieber Papers (Wroclaw) File 59, Capelle to Lieber, 13 October 1897.

49. Ibid., Lieber to Capelle, 15 October 1897.

50. See Hohenlohe, 397. On the factions within the Center, see Zeender, esp. chaps. 4 and 5.

51. Lieber Papers (Wroclaw), File 59, Capelle to Lieber, 16 October 1897.

52. Ibid., 24 October 1897. Lieber's notes on the draft law and Begründung.

53. Ibid., Capelle to Lieber, 24 October 1897.

54. Hohenlohe, 397.

55. Lieber's notes on the reverse side of the first law draft, and notes on Hohenlohe to Lieber, 27 October 1897, Lieber Papers (Wroclaw). Lieber's rendition of part of Hohenlohe's remarks is undated but, from the context, it is almost certain that Hohenlohe made them at the 27 October meeting.

56. On the seizure of Kiaochou and its diplomatic repercussions, see GP, XIV, pt. 1, chap. 90, and Foreign Office Archives, Bonn, R 18166, vols. 12 and 13, and PG 65990a. On Diedrichs's role, see Gottschall, chap. 6.

57. Quote is from Hohenlohe, 412; see also 415. Tirpitz omits any mention of these hesitations in *Memoirs*, vol. 1, chap. 7.

58. Foreign Office, R 18166, vol. 12, Tirpitz to Bülow, 11 November 1897.

59. Norman Rich and M. H. Fisher, eds., *The Holstein Papers*, 383 n. 2 (cited as *Holstein Papers*).

60. N 253/4, 173ff.

61. Michael Epkenhans, ed., *Albert Hopmann, Das ereignisreiche Leben eines Wilhelminer*, 120–121 (cited as Epkenhans, *Hopmann*).

62. Petter, 170–171; Schrecker, chap. 6. See also Herwig, 103–106.

63. N 253/4, 173ff., Tirpitz to Grand Duke of Baden, 14 November 1897.

64. On the military penal reform, see Röhl, 224, 243–244; and Hull, 220–221.

65. N 253/4, 179f, Tirpitz to Crailsheim, 16 November 1897. The draft is in Capelle's hand.

66. Ibid., 164–165, Prinz Heinrich to Tirpitz, 17 October 1897.

67. Hohenlohe, 422; See also Hallmann, 310ff.

68. For the draft law and the Begründung, see PG 66712. Other preparation documents are in PG 66023 and 66024.

69. For "Die Seeinteressen des deutschen Reiches" see PG 66712.

70. Ropp, 335.

71. 1 December 1897, Hohenlohe, 422–423.

72. The debate can only be summarized here. For the official account, see *Stenographische Berichte über die Verhandlungen des Reichstages*, Berlin, Norddeutsche Buchdruckerei, 1867–1933, 9 Legislative Period, 5 Session, 4–7 Sittings (cited as Reichstag). The complete text for 6–9 December is also in PG 66712. The best detailed analysis is in Steinberg, 162ff. See also Kehr, 120ff.

73. Tirpitz later claimed (*Memoirs*, 1:150) that Capelle had persuaded him to accept financial limits; it is clear from materials in the Lieber Papers noted above that it was Lieber who won the point.

74. On the propaganda campaign, see Deist, 71–146; and Kehr, 93ff. A short summary is in Steinberg, 179ff.

75. Zeender, 69–70.

76. Miquel Memorandum, 14 February 1898, PG 66712 and PG 66023, 226–239; also discussed in Steinberg, 175–176. The overall and crucial question of the budget right, and whether the Navy Law provided, as Tirpitz claimed, an "iron budget" for the navy is discussed in the next chapter.

77. Transcripts of the Budget Commission Hearing are in PG 66712. Newspaper clippings and Capelle's preparation are in PG 66024. See also Kehr, 150ff., and Steinberg, 178ff.

78. Steinberg, 184–185.

79. See his euphoric telegram to the Emperor on 5 March 1898 in PG 66712.

80. Zeender, 71.

81. Even without the Fritzen amendment, there may have been a way for the Reichstag to sabotage automatic replacement, at least Dähnhardt thought so. See the next chapter.

82. PG 66712, Tirpitz to Senden, 9 March 1898.

83. For this analysis, somewhat overstated, see Steinberg, 191–192.

84. On the final debate, see Reichstag, 9 Leg. Per., V Sess., 68–69 Sittings. See also Kehr, 160ff.; and Steinberg, 193ff.

85. A Tirpitz biography is not the place for a detailed treatment of the broader aspects of the relationship between economic interests and the navy. This controversy is the core of Kehr's and Berghahn's arguments, which are addressed on a narrower scale in this biography. On the agrarians, see also Hans Puhle, *Agrarische Interessenpolitik und preussischen Konservatismus im wilhelmischen Reich*, 240ff. (cited as Puhle).

86. Lieber Papers (Wroclaw), Hertling to Lieber, 25 November 1897.

87. N 253/4, Tirpitz to Lieber, 23 April 1898.

88. Röhl, *Bismarck*, 250–251.

89. An excellent discussion of the Sammlung question, and of Kehr's and Berghahn's ideas as applied to the 1898 Navy Law is in Geoff Eley, "Sammlungspolitik, Social Darwinism, and

the Navy Law of 1898," 110–153 (cited as
Eley, "Sammlungspolitik").

90. William II to Hohenlohe, 27
March 1898, Hohenlohe, 436–437.

91. Tirpitz, *Memoirs*, 1:151–152.

92. N 253/4, 42–43, Tirpitz to Senden, 11 August 1897.

93. Lambi, 149.

94. Steinberg, 197.

95. On the "alliance value" canard,
see chapter 10 in this volume.

96. See chapters 6–8 in this volume; and Hubatsch, *Admiralstab*, chap.
4.

97. Deist, 86.

98. PG 66110, Tirpitz to Knorr, 26
December 1897.

99. RM 4/170, 27ff., and 31–32.

100. N 253/39, 17ff., Tirpitz to Knorr,
3 January 1898, and 20–24, Knorr to
Tirpitz, 13 January 1898.

101. Ibid., Tirpitz to William II, 3
February 1898; William II's reply of
February 7 is in PG 66110, 24.

102. Cited in Hubatsch, *Admiralstab*,
78.

103. N 160/11, 51–52, Tirpitz to William II, 24 April 1898. Bendemann had
pleaded for restraint in his letter of 6
April. See N 253/39, 43–44. See also
Gottschall, 227; and Hubatsch, *Admiralstab*, 79.

104. PG 66110, Tirpitz to Senden, 28
April 1898.

105. Tirpitz's notes, N 253/39, 37–42.

106. Ibid., 45, Tirpitz to Bülow, 25
April 1898.

107. Ibid., 56–57, Senden to Tirpitz,
29 April 1898.

108. N 160/11, 46, Senden note,
March 1896.

109. N 253/39, 60f, Tirpitz to Senden, 1 May 1898.

110. PG 66110, 47. See draft AKO,
tentatively signed by William II, 5 May
1898; and N 253/39, 115–116, Tirpitz to
William II, 28 May 1898.

111. Tirpitz's copy of Knorr's letter
of 21 May 1898 is in N 253/39, 75–93,
including Tirpitz's sarcastic marginal
notes.

112. Ibid., 94–115.

113. See, e. g., RM 4/170, 25–26,
Bendemann to Knorr, 28 May 1898.

114. PG 66110, 89, William II to Tirpitz, 1 June 1898.

115. PG 66110, 100, Tirpitz to William II, 6 June 1898; and William II's
reply in ibid., 101, 14 June 1898.

116. N 253/39, 124–128, Tirpitz to
Hohenlohe, 14 June 1898.

117. PG 66110, William II to Tirpitz,
20 June 1898.

118. Letters in N 253/200.

119. N 253/39, 134–135, Pohl to Tirpitz, 11 July 1898.

120. N 160/4, 12–15, Prinz Heinrich
to Senden, 25 July 1898.

121. N 160/11, 50, Senden's notes on
a meeting with William II, 27 July 1898.

122. Nachlass Büchsel, N 168/11, 19–
25, Tirpitz to Büchsel, 7 August 1898.

123. See Hohenlohe's note, quoted
in Berghahn, 166 n. 37.

124. N 253/39, 140–143, Prinz Heinrich (Shanghai) to Tirpitz, 7 September
1898.

125. N 253/39, 144–153. Tirpitz to
Prinz Heinrich, 15 November 1898.

126. Nachlass Michaelis, N 164/1.

127. RM 3/2, Cabinet Order of 19
December 1898; also in PG 66110.

128. PG 66108, Protocol of RMA
meeting, 14 February 1899.

129. Printed in Hubatsch, *Admiralstab*, 237–238.

130. N 253/39, 157–160. Tirpitz to
William II, 10 March 1899. Quoted
in Hubatsch, *Admiralstab*, 81–82. For
Tirpitz's rationalization of the dissolu-
tion, distorted in hindsight, see Tirpitz,
Memoirs, 1:83–91.

131. N 253/39, Prinz Heinrich
(Shanghai) to Tirpitz, 21 April 1899.

132. Gottschall, 227–228.

133. Ibid., 230, and Tirpitz's notes on Maltzahn, 1899, N253/345.

134. Gottschall, 230–231.

135. Well summarized in Michael Epkenhans, "William II and 'His' Navy, 1888–1918," 12–36.

10. THE SECOND NAVY LAW, 1899–1900

1. On the origins and first two years of the Flottenverein, see Deist, 147–162: Geoff Eley, *Reshaping the German Right: Radical Nationalism and Political Change after Bismarck*, 68–85 (cited as Eley, *Reshaping*); Pauline Anderson, *The Background of anti-English Feeling in Germany, 1890–1902* (cited as Anderson); Kehr, esp. 168ff.; and Marienfeld, 83ff.

2. Quote from Anderson, 167 n.; originally from the Flottenverein's monthly, *Die Flotte*, no. 1 (January 1900): 15.

3. Kehr, 168.

4. Ibid., 169.

5. Eley, *Reshaping*, 70; Deist, 147–148.

6. Deist, 153–158; Eley, *Reshaping*, 83–86.

7. Anderson, 167–168; Marienfeld, 83.

8. Kehr, 101; Anderson, 168–169.

9. Archibald Hurd and Henry Castle, *German Sea Power*, 207ff.

10. Anderson, 107–108; Marienfeld, 85–86; Deist, 102–110.

11. Cited in Kehr, 175–176.

12. This section is an amalgamation from the following: Peter-Christian Witt, *Die Finanzpolitik des Deutschen Reiches von 1903 bis 1913*, 17–23, 37–54 (cited as Witt); Berghahn, *Imperial Germany*, 197–201; Berghahn, *War 1914*, 73–79.

13. See, e.g., Lambi, 150–151; and chapters 11 and 12 in this volume.

14. N 253/39, Tirpitz's notes for organizational change. Though the notes are undated, it is clear from the context that it is the summer of 1898.

15. Tirpitz, *Memoirs*, 1:151–152.

16. PG 66084, Protocol of the Meeting of 29 October 1898.

17. N 253/19, 111–115, n.d. Another purpose of the memo seems to have been to avoid being squeezed by contractors. See, e.g., N 253/197, Ahlefeld (the Dockyard Director in Kiel) to Tirpitz, 11 November 1898.

18. PG 66075, Tirpitz's notes for a meeting with Willam II on 28 November 1898. Also printed in Berghahn/Deist, 154ff. See also Berghahn, 160–163.

19. Tirpitz here may already have been thinking of a deal with the agrarians to raise tariffs in exchange for their support of a Novelle.

20. The AKO is in PG 66105.

21. The text of Tirpitz's declaration is in PG 66041.

22. PG 66084, Protocol of a meeting of RMA department heads.

23. Berghahn, 163. Berghahn is probably incorrect when he refers to these early contracts as an "acceleration."

24. See Capelle's notes of February 1899 in PG 66105 and 66084, and Tirpitz's notes in N 253/4.

25. See Tirpitz's notes in N 253/4, PG 66105, 65990c, and RM 3/68.

26. N 253/4, Tirpitz's notes to meeting of 2 May 1899.

27. On the canal and the agrarians, see Kehr 173–174; and Röhl, *Bismarck*, 264–265.

28. Geoff Eley, *From Unification to Nazism*, 120.

29. On the Samoa crisis, see GP, XIV, pt. 2, 565ff.; and Paul M. Kennedy, *The Samoan Tangle*, chaps. 4–6.

30. Hohenlohe, 464.

31. Hohenlohe's version of this conversation is that Tirpitz had said, "until we have a fleet as strong as England's." This was almost certainly a misunderstanding by the elderly Hohenlohe, as even Tirpitz's highest ambitions never soared to this extent.

32. Ibid., 497–498.

33. N 253/197, 51–52. Ahlefeld to Tirpitz, July 1899.

34. Halle to Tirpitz, with memorandum attached, 7 July 1899, PG 66074, 1–11. See also E memo (summer 1899) in RM 3/6655, 17–21, printed in Berghahn/Deist, 156–159.

35. Tirpitz, *Memoirs*, 1:151ff.

36. For a good example, see N 253/197, 53f, Ahlefeld to Tirpitz, 8 August 1899. Ahlefeld grumbled about an international iron cartel, which drove up prices. He also relayed his discovery that Halle was Jewish and wondered how to deal with him. This awkward remark is proof positive that Ahlefeld, whose wife and children were close to Tirpitz's family, had no idea that Marie Tirpitz was the daughter of a converted Jew.

37. N 253/200, 45f, Tirpitz to Büchsel, 23 August 1899.

38. The text is in PG 66074, 12–14, and is printed in Berghahn/Deist, 159–162.

39. Tirpitz lied in his memoirs when he claimed that he had only asked for thirty-eight battleships at this meeting. Tirpitz, *Memoirs*, 1:161.

40. Ibid., 156–157.

41. PG 66075, 114–115. Memo for an Immediatvortrag on Maltzahn, 26 September 1899. See also Tirpitz to Bülow, 8 October 1899, PG 66075, 109.

42. Speech draft in RM 3/1, 21–22. Also published in Berghahn/Deist, 162ff. Original draft is in N 253/5, 9–12.

43. On Samoa, see Kennedy, *The Samoan Tangle*, 329ff.

44. PG 66074, Tirpitz to Koester, 21 October 1899, and Koester's reply of 23 October.

45. On the press, see Kehr, 178ff.

46. Tirpitz's notes are in N 253/5, 18; and PG 66074, 27.

47. PG 66037, 27, 24 October 1899.

48. PG 66074, 20, Hohenlohe to Tirpitz, 26 October 1899, and Tirpitz's reply of 28 October; Hohenlohe, 533ff. See also Tirpitz's travel diary for October and November in PG 66712.

49. Tirpitz's travel diary, entry of 2 November 1899, PG 66712. For the princes' replies, see PG 66074, 43ff.

50. Berghahn, 215–216.

51. PG 66030, Hohenlohe to the Federal Princes, 6 November 1899. Replies are in PG 66028, 110–111.

52. Monts to Hohenlohe, PG 66030, 3 November 1899.

53. On these preparations, see, esp., PG 66029–66034.

54. First Novelle draft (n.d., probably late October 1899), PG 66038, 6ff.

55. Tirpitz to all Departments, 8 November 1899, PG 66028, 15ff.

56. Dähnhardt's notes, 8 November 1899, PG 66028, 1–2; and PG 66038, 32–33. Dähnhardt was right that there would be opposition to the "one-sided binding" of such a law. On 10 and 11 November the *Kölnische Volkszeitung*, an organ of the Rhineland faction of the Center, published articles sharply critical on this point. See PG 66037, 20–21.

57. Tirpitz to Naval Attaché, London, 16 November 1899, PG 66028, 56.

58. Tirpitz notes this point in *Memoirs*, 1:158ff.

59. PG 66028, Thielemann to Tirpitz, 30 November 1899.

60. N 253/5, 30, William II to Hohenlohe, 29 November 1899. Reproduced in Berghahn/Deist, 164.

61. See PG 66074, 27; and PG 66028, 145.

62. PG 66074, 72.

63. Tirpitz to Krupp, 2 December 1899, PG 66074, 98–99. See also Deist, 156ff.

64. Zeender, 82.

65. RM 3/11679, Capelle to Hollweg, 3 September 1925.

66. Tirpitz to Lieber, 6 December 1899.

67. Tirpitz to Lucanus, 8 December 1899, PG 66074, 86. Tirpitz had previously spoken in this vein to Hohenlohe and other Cabinet members. See Hohenlohe, 537–538.

68. The debates are in Reichstag, X Leg. Per., 1 Sess., 119–122 Sittings. Copies of the speeches of Tirpitz, Bülow, and Hohenlohe are in PG 66074, 90ff.

69. For details, see GP, XV, chap. 102.

70. Quoted in Röhl, *William II*, 1036.

71. See Ekkehard Böhm, *Überseehandel und Flottenbau: Hanseatische Kaufmannschaft und deutsche Seerüstung 1879–1902*, 214–215.

72. Hohenlohe, 555ff. Reproduced, with Tirpitz's notes, in PG 66074, 100. See also Röhl, *William II*, II, 1057.

73. The drafts, with explanatory tables for the last two, are arranged in chronological order in PG 66038, 40ff. The comparisons given below are drawn from that same material. Along with the 15 January draft was a massive economic compilation titled, "The Growth of German Sea Interests between 1896 and 1898." A few weeks later came economic data broken down by region. See Deist, 114. This document was an update of "The Sea Interests of the German Reich," published in support of the 1898 Navy Law. See PG 66712.

74. Omitted in the 15 January and subsequent drafts was the expression "under the assumption that a standstill in the naval armaments of these powers is not to be counted upon." Tirpitz had a notion that the Novelle might promote an arms race, but he did not want to admit it or even mention the possibility in the Reichstag. Only Richter and the Social Democrats attacked the Navy Law on the basis that it would start an arms race. The Center and the other parties seem not to have realized this possibility until much later, and then used the arms race as an excuse for still faster building.

75. This is the author's calculation from the tables that give only individual totals for the three categories. They were not totaled in the material that went to the Reichstag. See PG 66038, 71, of the Berechnung to the draft of 23 January.

76. Just like today, private firms were reluctant to make large investments for government purposes without a guaranteed market.

77. This is exactly what transpired, especially after 1905. The true but tame reply given below indicates that the law could easily be changed if circumstances changed. But the momentum of the law became so great, and Tirpitz was so successful in his *Ressorteifer*, that the law changed only in an upward direction. See below on the budget right.

78. Tirpitz's diary notes for mid-January 1900, PG 66712. See also notes for a meeting with the Emperor, 31 January 1900, where Tirpitz outlined his Reichstag strategy, PG 66074, 109a and N 253/5, 38.

79. Because the debate was far less tempestuous than for the 1898 bill, it is not analyzed here in detail. See Kehr, 194ff. The complete texts and the Budget Commission debates are all in PG

66041. For a report to Tirpitz about the Commission debates on 7 May, see N 253/5, 39–42.

80. Deist, 97.

81. Ibid., 143.

82. Oliver Stein, *Die deutsche Heeresrüstungspolitik 1890–1914: Das Militär und der Primat der Politik,* 213–214.

83. Zeender, 83.

84. Kehr, 202.

85. RM 3/11679 Capelle to Hollweg, 3 September 1925. It is unfortunate that Capelle was so discreet that he left almost nothing behind in personal papers. Historians would give much to see his notes on the hundreds of meetings he and Dähnhardt had with parliamentarians.

86. This report, which includes transcripts of all the debates in the Budget Commission, is in PG 66712.

87. See Böhm, 248–251; and Petter, 214.

88. Tirpitz, *Memoirs,* 1:162–163.

89. The document is in both PG 66029 and 66031. See also Lambi, 151.

90. See Kehr, 259ff. The agrarians by then were confident that they would get compensation in the realm of tariffs.

91. Bachem, 6:35ff.

92. The French naval program proposed a fleet of twenty-eight battleships, twenty-four cruisers, and large numbers of torpedo boats and submarines. This program was conceived independently of the German one, toward which the French were favorably disposed in view of their rivalry with the British. The announcement of the French program on 30 January 1900 was another stroke of luck for Tirpitz. On the French program, see PG 66034, Nos. 5, 7–10a, 20–24, 36. See also Ropp, chap. 18; and Fischel's comparison in N 253/9, 151–154.

93. Bachem, 6:28ff.

94. Tirpitz, *Memoirs,* 1:164. Paragraph 2 of the Jesuit Law was finally repealed in 1904.

95. See Zeender, 82ff.

96. For the French reaction, see PG 66034; for the Russian reaction, see, e.g., Radolin to Hohenlohe, 11 February 1900, PG 66037, 41a.

97. Quoted in Woodward, 48–49.

98. Hale, chaps. 8 and 9.

99. Nachlass Capelle N 170/1, 1.

100. Merseberg, Königliches Heraldsamt, Rep. 176, VI, T nr. 141. Along with the title, he received a bill from the Heraldsamt for 530 marks and 50 pfennig for calligraphy, family crest, diploma, and seal.

101. Nachlass Capelle, N 170/1, 1, Tirpitz to Capelle, 15 June 1900. Tirpitz took great pains to keep the nonpareil Capelle in the RMA. The MK for years tried to hijack the physically frail Capelle back to sea duty as early as 1898 (PG 68847).

102. Kehr, 205ff.

103. Tirpitz, *Memoirs,* 1:164.

104. Brett Fairbairn, "Interpreting Wilhelmine Elections: National Issues, Fairness Issues, an Electoral Mobilization," 17–48, esp. 32ff. See also Fairbairn, *Democracy in the Undemocratic State: The German Reichstag Elections of 1898 and 1903,* esp. chaps. 4 and 7 (cited as Fairbairn).

105. Notes are in RM 3/11690, 1–89.

106. Ibid., 24. The draft is in Dähnhardt's hand.

107. Ibid., 44.

108. Ibid., 44–45.

109. Eckart Kehr, "The German Fleet in the Eighteen Nineties and the Politico-Military Dualism in the Empire," 11–21, quote at 18.

110. Manfred Rauh, *Föderalismus und Parlamentismus im Wilhelmischen Reich,* 222 (cited as Rauh).

111. Thomas Nipperdey, *Deutsche Geschichte*, 2: 208 (cited as Nipperdey).

112. Ibid., 246–247. For discussion of the controversy between "constitutional" and "parliamentary" government in a broader context, see Mark Hewitson, "The Kaiserreich in Question: Constitutional Crisis in Germany before the First World War," 725–780.

113. Nipperdey, 247. Tirpitz's method of dealing with the Reichstag may reinforce the argument that Margaret Lavinia Anderson advances in *Practicing Democracy: Elections and Political Culture in Imperial Germany,* esp. chaps. 1 and 12. She makes the case that the practice of years of elections gradually made Germany move not to democracy but in a clearly democratic direction. Tirpitz's respect for and consideration of the Reichstag, in contrast to his opinion of the army, is an example of Anderson's view.

114. Nachlass Michaelis, N 164/2, 23–24.

115. See Paul Kennedy, "Tirpitz, England, and the Second Navy Law of 1900: A Strategical Critique," 33–57; Kennedy, "Maritime Strategieprobleme der deutsch-englischen Flottenrivalität," 178–210; and Hobson, esp. 257–273.

116. Kennedy, "Maritime Strategieprobleme," 180–181. What follows is a summary of Kennedy's argument from this article.

117. Hallmann, 24–25.

118. This point receives further consideration in chaps. 15 and 16 in this volume.

119. From Michaelis's statement in RM 8/1233, 21.

120. See, esp., Kennedy, "Maritime Strategieprobleme," 202–210.

121. This will be examined in chapter 11 in this volume.

122. See Hobson, esp. chaps. 5 and 6.

123. From Tirpitz's famous memo to William II of July 1897, reprinted in Steinberg, 208ff. See also Lambi, 141–142.

124. Hobson, 257–273, addresses this question painstakingly and convincingly.

125. See chaps. 7 and 8 in this volume.

126. The historians I refer to are Steinberg, Berghahn, Kennedy, Lambi, and Hobson. Kennedy is a partial exception in his speculations about Tirpitz's long-term plan.

127. Hobson, 260–271.

128. Ibid., 267–270.

129. See chapter 8 in this volume.

130. Salewski, 63–64.

131. See, e.g., Deist, 17–18; and Franz Huberti, "Tirpitz als Verschleierungs-Politiker?" 535–554, 550–551. Hobson effectively demolished the "palliative" idea. See Hobson, 315, 318. Even Kehr, in his masterwork, as Hobson points out, used the term only in his analysis of the risk theory.

132. RM 8/1233, 20.

133. Ibid., 22.

134. Quoted in Petter, 218.

11. THE "QUIET" YEARS, 1900–1906

1. Tirpitz was deeply concerned to about keeping the Center's support even in relatively small matters. For example, in the summer of 1900 he wrote to Senden:

The Center expects compensation for their approval of the Navy Law, which I will not be able to get for them [this presumably refers to the repeal of the anti-Jesuit law that only occurred in 1904]. On the day after the passage of the Navy Law, two deputies saw me and accompanied their requests with threats. Obviously, I was not intimidated, but I made them promises. Otherwise, the visit was typical. . . . This year our initiatives will be mixed in with the China affair. Whether comfortable or not, we need the Center all the more for this. . . . Every step that upsets the Center is therefore undesirable for us.

Nachlass Senden, N/160/5, Tirpitz to Senden, 30 August 1900.

2. Deist, 10–17.

3. See relevant articles in Hildebrand.

4. For details on the construction of the pre-1906 ships, see Weir, chaps. 2 and 3.

5. Jane, 1914, 50–51.

6. See ship articles in Hildebrand.

7. Jane, 1914, 47ff.

8. See descriptions in Hildebrand.

9. Jane, 1914, 46–47.

10. On German cruisers in 1898–1906, see the ship biographies in Hildebrand.

11. Biographical notes on Michaelis are in Werner Rahn, ed., *Deutsche Marinen im Wandel*, 397–398. During the 1930s, at the request of the Chief of the Naval Archives Rear Admiral (ret.) Kurt Assmann, Michaelis wrote several pieces about his career and his relationships with other officers he had served with and under, particularly Tirpitz, whom, by turns, he admired and criticized. Though not completely objective, his writings, some of which are summarized below, provide the clearest and perhaps the fairest picture of the hothouse atmosphere in the RMA during the period from 1903 to 1906.

12. For life in the Naval Academy, see Nachlass Michaelis, N 164/4, 7–9.

13. Michaelis, N 164/2, 20.

14. The above account, including all quotations except where otherwise noted, is drawn from Michaelis, N 164/2, 11–17.

15. On Bürkner, see Hildebrand, Vol. 4, *Marinebeamte im Admiralsrang*, 26–27.

16. Trotha Papers, L 40, Trotha's notes on Tirpitz's life.

17. *Hamburger Correspondent*, July 23, 1901, quoted in Böhm, 259.

18. Peter Winzen, *Bernhard Fürst von Bülow: Weltmachtstrategie ohne Fortune; Wegbereiter der grossen Katastrophe*, chap. 4 (cited as Winzen).

19. For the diplomatic background of the Boxer Rebellion and its effects in East Asia and Europe, see Friedrich Thimme et al., eds., *Die Grosse Politik des Europäischen Kabinettes*, Vol. 16 (cited as GP); G. P. Gooch and Harold Temperley, eds., *British Documents on the Origins of the War, 1898–1914*, 2:1ff. (cited as BD). For a brilliant summary of the rebellion and the Anglo-German negotiations that accompanied it, see William L. Langer, *The Diplomacy of Imperialism, 1890–1902*, 2:692ff. (cited as Langer). The German Navy's part is summarized in Hubatsch, *Ära*, 41ff.; and Boelcke, 235ff.

20. Röhl, *Bismarck*, 268.

21. From Waldersee's *Memoirs*, as quoted in Hubatsch, *Ära*, 56. For a recent examination of Germany and the Boxer Rebellion, see Annika Mombauer, "Wilhelm, Waldersee, and the Boxer Rebellion," in Annika Mombauer and Wilhelm Deist, eds., *The Kaiser: New Researches on William II's Role in Imperial Germany*, 91–118 (volume cited as Mombauer and Deist).

22. Hopmann, *Logbuch*, 256ff.; Berghahn, 296ff.

23. N 253/20, 2 a–b, Tirpitz to Prince Henry, 14 July 1900. Also in PG 66075, 163ff.

24. Nachlass Senden, N 160/5 20–21, Tirpitz to Senden, 15 July 1900.

25. See the exchange between Co-erper and Tirpitz, PG 69122, 31 October 1901, and 3 February 1902. See also Kennedy, *Antagonism*, 257.

26. N 253/16, 203–206, Prinz Hein-rich to Tirpitz, 5 October 1903; Kennedy, *Antagonism*, 257–258.

27. RM 3/11679, 12 October 1902; Berghahn/Deist. 211ff. See also Deist, 170–171; and Kennedy, *Antagonism*, 258.

28. For Anglo-German cooperation in Venezuela, see GP, chap. 112; *BD*, ii, 153ff. For a short summary of the German role, see Hubatch, *Ära*, 46ff.; and *Admiralstab*, 111ff. On planning German operations off the Venezuelan coast, see PG 66075, 241ff.; and PG 67434, passim.

29. Rich, Holstein Papers, IV, 245, diary entry, 11 January 1902. For Tir-pitz's views, see Protocol of General Naval Meeting, 3 November 1902, PG 66075, 241ff.; and Tirpitz to Rich-thofen, 13 January 1903, ibid., 250–251. See also Holger Herwig, *Politics of Frustration: The United States in German Naval Planning, 1889–1914*, 76ff. (cited as Herwig, *Politics of Frustration*). The Venezuela episode evoked a bi-zarre series of plans in the Admiralstab for war with the United States.

30. Trotha Papers, L 40, Trotha's notes on Tirpitz's life, 6 March 1937. Trotha accompanied Tirpitz on the journey.

31. As noted in chapter 8, Tirpitz's letters home to his wife while he was in Asia provide his interesting impressions of the United States. Unfortunately I have been unable to locate similar let-ters from 1902, assuming they still exist.

32. For the full entourage, see RM 3/2368, 203.

33. MK reports of the visit, written by Müller, are in RM 2/404, 405, 406,

415, and PG 68084a. An abbreviated version of his report is in Walther Gör-litz, *Der Kaiser . . . Aufzeichnungen des Chefs des Marinekabinettes Admiral Georg Alexander von Müller über die Ära Wilhelms II*, 53–58 (cited as Müller, *Der Kaiser*).

34. RM 2/405, 112–117, 7 March 1902.

35. RM 3/9951, 73–93, Heeringen Memo on the reorganization of N, 28 September 1900. Also published in Berghahn/Deist, 201–211. On organiza-tion in general, see Hubatsch, *Admi-ralstab*, appendices 17 and 18; and PG 66075, 241–242.

36. Cabinet Order of 14 March 1899, printed in Hubatsch, *Admiralstab*, appendix 16.

37. Gottschall, 253–254.

38. Ibid., 244–245; on the contro-versy with Diedrichs, see PG 66074, passim; and PG 66075, 234ff.

39. Joachim Lehment, *Kriegsma-rine und politische Führung*, 53.

40. Hubatsch, *Admiralstab*, 100–101.

41. See, e.g., N 253/20 33–34, Prinz Heinrich to Tirpitz, 8 June 1901; and Tirpitz's note for a meeting with the Emperor, 12 February 1901, in ibid., 7–8.

42. Berghahn, 291.

43. Nachlass Büchsel, N168/8 IV on Operations Plan 1903. The best analy-sis of the war plan with France is in Lambi, 193–209.

44. On operations plans against England in the period 1899–1905, see Lambi, 209–226. A more readable and analytical view is in Paul Kennedy, "The Development of German Naval Operations Plans against England 1896–1914," 48–76. See also Hobson's insightful treatment of the question, 274ff.

45. Hopmann, *Logbuch*, 222.

46. Well summarized in Petter, 232–233.

47. Ibid., 312ff.; Berghahn, 346ff.; and PG 66075, Tirpitz's IV notes, 16 September 1902 (not held).

48. Well described in John Röhl, *Wilhelm II: Der Weg in dem Abgrund, 1900–1941* 512ff. (cited as Röhl, *Wilhelm II*).

49. Hopmann to his wife, 17 May 1905, in Epkenhans, *Hopmann*, 134–135.

50. Berghahn, 199.

51. Such as the letter from Prince Otto von Salm, President of the FV to Tirpitz, 3 December 1901, RM 3/6659. Also printed in Berghahn/Deist, 289–290. Tirpitz politely demurred on financial grounds, Tirpitz to Senden, 14 December 1901, PG 66042.

52. Berghahn, 272–285.

53. For the particulars, see Witt, pt. 2.

54. See memo in Capelle's hand, 6 November 1901, and Tirpitz's memo to Department Heads, 6 January 1902, PG 66046. The latter is in Berghahn/Deist, 168–169.

55. Documentation on this episode and the public reaction are in PG 66042. See also PG 66075, 239; and RM 3/2368, 285–286. Tirpitz's final speech draft is in N 253/19, 165–172. He tried unsuccessfully to track down the leak. See Tirpitz memo, RMA III, 2, 7, 32a, vol. 6, 29 January 1902.

56. Marder, *Anatomy*, 460.

57. RM 3/6659, Tirpitz memo on preparations for future fleet development, 6 January 1902. Printed in Berghahn/Deist, 165–166.

58. Hubatsch, *Admiralstab*, 103.

59. E (Capelle) to Tirpitz, 12 December 1902, PG 66045.

60. E to Tirpitz, 24 December 1902, ibid.

61. Novelle draft in Dähnhardt's hand, 7 May 1903, and a printed version dated June 1903, ibid.

62. The 1900 Navy Law established a fleet of thirty-eight battleships in two double squadrons. There were to be sixteen ships and one flagship in each double squadron, with a total of thirty-four ships. Each squadron had one material reserve ship, a total of four, and a grand total of thirty-eight. By adding two ships and converting the flagships to material reserve, this would leave two double squadrons, a total of thirty-two ships, plus eight material reserves, a total of forty battleships in all or, in effect, *five* squadrons instead of four. Tirpitz used the same gimmick to try to acquire a fifth squadron out of the 1912 Novelle. Only the conversion to Dreadnought-type ships and the consequent need to build homogeneous squadrons over again kept him from doing this sooner.

63. This important memo, Capelle to Tirpitz, 9 July 1903, is in PG 66046; printed in Berghahn/Deist, 167–171. Berghahn, 607–617, contains an extremely useful set of thirty-three tables that show all the various fleet building plans for 1898 to 1908.

64. Berghahn, 315–316.

65. Memo, July 1903, PG 66046. Drafted to share with the Budget Commission, but clearly it never was.

66. See Dähnhardt's memos of 20 October and 2 November 1903 in PG 66046.

67. Tirpitz's diary note in Trotha's hand, 12 September 1903, PG 66074, 299.

68. On the 1903 elections, see Fairbairn, esp. 33 and n. 111. See also Jonathan Sperber, *The Kaiser's Voters: Electors and Elections in Imperial Germany* (cited as Sperber).

69. Notes for IV, 10 October 1903; and William II to Tirpitz, 23 October 1903, PG 66076, 1–2.

70. See E's notes for IV, 11 November 1903, PG 66076, 23ff.

71. See PG 66076, 67ff.; and Protocols of RMA meetings of 30 January and 4 February 1904, PG 66086. See also Grand Admiral Erich Raeder, *My Life*, 30. N 253/2, 263ff., has notes in Tirpitz's hand about the sequence of events of October 1903–January 1904 on the question of ship type, which does not lack some comical aspects. The *Moreno* was not built as originally planned but instead became a full-fledged Dreadnought that was not completed until 1914. See Jane, *1914*, 424. On the private meeting, see Trotha Papers, L 40, Trotha's notes on Tirpitz, 16 March 1937.

72. On the effects of this expedition on domestic politics, see W. H. Dawson, *The German Empire, 1867–1914*, 2:330ff. For the war itself, see Isabel Hull's remarkable book, *Absolute Destruction: Military Culture and the Practices of War in Imperial Germany*, pt. 1.

73. Draft of Law Expansion I, 8 February 1904, PG 66046.

74. Dähnhardt archival note, 15 February 1904, PG 66047. Notes on the cover of Ergänzunggesetz I, May–June 1904, PG 66046. There is no specific indication of which deputies were involved. See Spahn's comments in the Reichstag on 13 April 1904, PG 66047.

75. See Dähnhardt, Novelle 1904, n.d. but probably February 1904; Capelle to Z, 18 February 1904. An alternating 3:4 tempo was also suggested. See Capelle to Z, 27 February 1904. All in PG 66047.

76. See, e.g., William II to Tirpitz, 23 February 1904, PG 66076, 99ff.

77. Tirpitz's memo on the development of large cruisers, 8 March 1904, ibid., 91ff.

78. William II to K, 27 February 1904, ibid., 111.

79. William II's observations of the Italian Fleet, 30 March, and his letter to Tirpitz, 11 April 1904, ibid., 124, 140–141.

80. Protocol of the 25 April 1904 meeting, ibid., 163–164; and PG 66086.

81. Tirpitz to Prinz Heinrich, 6 May 1904, PG 66076, 173. See also N 253/20, 248ff. Tirpitz could raid RMA funds to pay for shipbuilding, armor, and artillery cost overruns. For example, in 1904 he took 6.5 million marks from munitions for that purpose. He could do this for as long as he juggled the accounts to make it appear to the Reichstag that he stayed within the original overall budget. See meeting of RMA department heads, 25 May 1904, ibid., 25ff. Because most of the raids were at the expense of something the Front wanted, in this case more reserve munitions, Front resentment was constant. This method would only cover small deficits. Changes in basic ship type required much more and needed a new table of cost per ship projections than only a Novelle could cloak.

82. Capelle to Tirpitz, 30 June 1904, PG 66047, with Capelle's marginal notes.

83. On the shift in plans, see the draft Begründung in Tirpitz's hand, 9 October 1904; Dähnhardt archival note and Capelle to Tirpitz, 12 October 1909; Dähnhardt note, 3 November 1904, and archival note, 15 December 1904. All in PG 66047.

84. On renewed consideration of a third double squadron, see RMA memo on Novelle possibilities, January 1905, PG 66077, 118–119. On the possibility

of deferral to 1907, see E to Tirpitz, 4 January 1905, PG 66047.

85. Kennedy, *Antagonism*, chap. 13, esp. 233. For an overall summary of the Anglo-German arms race, see Peter Padfield, *The Great Naval Race: Anglo-German Naval Rivalry, 1900–1914*. A well-written popular history, with some factual errors on the German side, is Robert K. Massie, *Dreadnought: Britain, Germany, and the Coming of the Great War*. More recent efforts on the subject by younger German scholars are Christian Rödel, *Alfred von Tirpitz und das Seekriegsbild vor dem Ersten Weltkrieg*; and Eva Besteck, *Die trügerische "First Line of Defence":Zum deutsh-britischen Wettrusten vor dem Ersten Weltkrieg*. Interesting and informative on the British side is Matthew S. Seligmann, ed., *Naval Intelligence from Germany: The Reports of the British Naval Attachés in Berlin 1906–1914* (cited as Seligmann). Many of these reports have been published previously, for example, in the British Documents on the Origins of the War, but some are new. Seligmann's introduction catalogues the various British intelligence sources on the German Navy, apart from the obvious attaché reports. Noteworthy is his conclusion that many prewar naval attaché reports, intended for the Naval Intelligence Division, were destroyed by the 1950s or before.

86. Ibid., 247–248.

87. Quoted in Marder, *Anatomy*, 462.

88. Quoted in ibid., 464.

89. On this narrative, see Jonathan Steinberg, "The Copenhagen Complex," 23–46.

90. Tirpitz, *Memoirs*, 1:249ff.

91. Ibid., 262–263. Jan Rüger, *The Great Naval Game: Britain and Europe in the Age of Empire* (cited as Rüger).

Rüger's book provides an engaging social history of the mass media aspects of naval display. Tirpitz, though not the Emperor, tried to discourage such public events, except in the carefully controlled circumstances preceding a Novelle (see 67–76). Rüger has far more to say about Britain than about Germany.

92. Marder, *Anatomy*, 491, 496.

93. See Jonathan Steinberg, "Germany and the Russo-Japanese War," 1965–1986.

94. See GP XIX, pt. 1, 247ff.; and Bernhard Huldermann, *Albert Ballin*, 145ff.

95. On the Dogger Bank incident, see GP XIX, pt. 1, 279ff.

96. See Tirpitz to Richthofen, 1 November 1904, N 253/21. Also in PG 66077, 32–33, and printed in Tirpitz, *Memoirs*, 1:219ff. See also Memo of the R-Commission of the RMA and Tirpitz's notes on it, PG 66077, 71ff.; and Tirpitz's notes on contacts with the Foreign Office, 21 December–2 January 1905 N 253/21, 45–46.

97. On these discussions, see GP XIX, pt. 1, 301ff.; and Tirpitz, *Memoirs*, 1:217ff. On Russo-German relations, see Roderick R. McClean, "Dreams of a German Empire: William II and the Treaty of Björkö of 1905," 119–142.

98. Carl Coerper (Naval Attaché in London) to Tirpitz, with the Emperor's marginalia, 28 November 1904, PG 69122. See also Arthur J. Marder, *From the Dreadnought to Scapa Flow*, 1:27, 40ff. (cited as Marder, *Dreadnought*).

99. On the naval scare, which reached its height in November–December 1904 and was rekindled by Lee's speech, see GP XIX, pt. 2, 84ff.; and Tirpitz, *Aufbau*, 14ff. See also Kennedy, *Antagonism*, 273ff. A more detailed account is in Ilse Metz, *Die deutsche Flotte in der englischen Presse: der Navy*

Scare vom Winter 1904–1905. On Lee's speech, see 85ff.

100. Hale, 272.

101. See memo of the Admiralstab on war with England 1905, January–February 1905, PG 66077, 89ff.; Hubatsch, *Admiralstab*, 118ff.; and Lambi, chap. 12.

102. Büchsel to Tirpitz, 18 February 1905, PG 66077, 117.

103. Coerper to Tirpitz, 5 and 21 January and 20 February 1905, PG 68925. The 20 February letter was the first hint anyone in Germany had about an all-big-gun ship. Fisher, amid deep security, seemed to encourage the rumors. Coerper reported that a well-connected Englishman had characterized Fisher's policy as "professed secrecy, tempered by periodical advertisement." Coerper to Tirpitz, 12 February 1908, PG 68928.

104. See draft letter, not sent, Tirpitz to Bülow, 10 February 1905, PG 66077, 123.

105. The real controversy among British naval historians is not about Germany. Marder, the doyen of the field, who emphasized Fisher's development of Dreadnought battleships, was deceased before two younger historians argued that Fisher's real intention was a battlecruiser/submarine method of naval domination. See Jon Sumida, *In Defence of Naval Supremacy: Fisher, Technology, and British Naval Policy, 1889–1914*; and Nicholas Lambert, *Sir John Fisher's Naval Revolution*. The battlecruiser/submarine proposal did not receive serious consideration by the Board of Admiralty, and Tirpitz, let alone Marder, never heard of it; therefore the ensuing controversy among historians is not discussed here.

106. See, e.g., Tirpitz, *Aufbau*, 40, 69, 74, 145 n., 175. See also Holger Herwig, "The German Reaction to the *Dreadnought* Revolution," 273–283

(cited as Herwig, *Dreadnought*). For a more general view, see Herwig, *Luxury Fleet*, 44, 56ff. For William II's reaction, see Röhl, *Wilhelm II*, 3:525ff.

107. Müller to Tirpitz, 8 February 1905, in Tirpitz, *Aufbau*, 15. The original, in Müller's hand is in PG 66077, 87–88.

108. Draft and note for IV, 10 February 1905, PG 66077.

109. See Tirpitz, *Memoirs*, 1:chap. 15; Herwig, *Dreadnought*, 276–277; and Marder, *Dreadnough*, 1:67.

110. Tirpitz's note of 22 February 1905, in Tirpitz, *Aufbau*, 16ff.

111. For the text of the declaration, see Dähnhardt's note, 22 February 1905, PG 66047.

112. Hansgeorg Fernis, *Die Flottennovellen im Reichstag, 1906–1912*, 7–8.

113. See Waffen Abteilung memo of 9 March 1905, PG 66048; Müller to Krupp, 21 March 1905 and reply on 28 March, PG 66077, 141, 144ff.

114. Discussed briefly below. There is no evidence that the Moroccan Crisis of 1905–6 much affected either Tirpitz's Novelle plans, which were essentially complete by the end of March 1905, or the decision to build Dreadnoughts.

115. William II to Tirpitz, 28 April 1905 and reply on 6 May, PG 66078, 8ff. See also Müller, *Der Kaiser*, 62–63; and Tirpitz's notes of 9 May 1905, PG 66078, 30–31.

116. K Memo of 9 May 1905, ibid., 19.

117. For the discussions between Tirpitz and K, in May–June 1905, see PG 66049.

118. E to Tirpitz, with law draft attached, 6 May 1905, PG 66049.

119. E to Tirpitz, 31 May 1905, ibid. During early summer 1905, Tirpitz secretly tried to bolster Flottenverein moderates against more radical de-

mands. Despite the Emperor's comically inept intervention, Tirpitz was successful but only for a few months. See Deist, 179–183.

120. Even these higher estimates for battleships (first 31 million and then 36 million for battleships) and large cruisers (24 million) proved woefully insufficient when Germany began to build real Dreadnoughts. Cost was a paramount factor in the need for another Novelle in 1908. See chapter 12 in this volume.

121. See Capelle to Treasury, 29 July 1905, PG 66050 5ff.; and PG 66079, 4ff.

122. There is a summary of Tipitz's views on U-boats in Hassell, chap. 11. See also Gemzell, 60ff. On Tirpitz's early attitude toward U-boats, see Weir, chap. 4.

123. Coerper to Tirpitz, 29 April, 21 May, and 9 June 1905, PG 68926.

124. William II to Tirpitz, 20 July 1905 and reply on 30 July, PG 66078, 94ff., 110ff.

125. Senden to Tirpitz, 3 September 1905, PG 66078, 134. In the context of spending 1,500 million marks on inland navigation between 1890 and 1918, 60 million was not a huge amount. See David Blackbourne, *The Conquest of Nature: Water, Landscape, and the Making of Modern Germany*, 215 (cited as Blackbourne).

126. See, e.g., Tirpitz to Scheer, 3 September 1905, RM 3/5. Printed in Berghahn/Deist, 321–322.

127. Tirpitz to Senden, 6 September, and Capelle to Tirpitz, 8 September 1905, PG 66078, 136, 142; Tirpitz to Reich Treasury, 8 September 1905, PG 66050. See also RMA Meeting Protocol, 22 September 1905, PG 66078, 190ff.

128. Dähnhardt Note, 22 September 1905, PG 66050 and N 253/22.

129. Tirpitz and Capelle notes on the IV, 4 October 1905, PG 66079, 10ff.

130. Capelle to Tirpitz, 19 September 1905, PG 66050, 88–89.

131. Tirpitz's note on secrecy, 2 October 1905, 21, and Senden to Tirpitz, 8 October 1905, PG 66078, 250. In 1905 Germany laid down the last ships of the *Deutschland* class. Because of technical difficulties, the first two Dreadnoughts were not laid down until the spring and summer of 1907.

132. On agitation during this period, see Fernis, 5–6; and Marienfeld, 5ff., 95ff. On Tirpitz's relations with the Flottenverein in 1903–6, see Deist, 173–186; and RM 3/ 9914, passim.

133. Tirpitz, *Aufbau*, 19–20. Reventlow's letter is in PG 66079, 74.

134. N 253/6 71–76, Tirpitz to Bülow, 8 November 1905. See also Berghahn, 493ff.; and Tirpitz, *Aufbau*, 10ff.

135. Trotha Papers, L 40, Trotha's notes on Tirpitz's life, 16 March 1937.

136. Tirpitz, *Aufbau*, 22ff.; Tirpitz to Bülow, 8 November 1905, PG 66079, 76ff.; and Senden to Capelle, 10 April 1906, PG 66713, for an account of the conversation. A memorandum of it is in N 253/6, 54–57. Partially printed in Berghahn/Deist. 216ff. On Bülow's tortuous efforts at financial reform, see Witt, 94–132. On the Flottenverein's role, see Deist, 187–191.

137. The complete text is in PG 66050, 187ff. Its initial treatment in the Reichstag and the press are not considered here in detail, as Fernis, chaps. 1–3, has already done this. Only the major points are treated below.

138. The document is in PG 66079, 73.

139. Marinevorlag 1906, PG 66713. For further information on final preparations for the Novelle, see N 253/7.

140. See Witt, 132ff.

141. Deist, 188.

142. Fernis, 22ff.

143. Tirpitz, *Aufbau*, 24; Bachem, 6:301.

144. A faction within the Social Democrats supported German arms against Britain. But these "red imperialists" were a tiny minority. Fernis, 25.

145. Ibid., 30ff.

146. Capelle to Tirpitz, 22 December, and E calculations, 28 December 1905, PG 66053, 206ff, 222.

147. Tirpitz, *Aufbau*, 24.

148. In October 1905 Delcassé published this in the event that France and Germany went to war. Berghahn, 495 n. 81.

149. Ibid., 20–21, 25ff. The originals of these documents are in PG 66713 and PG 66079, 99ff.

150. See E memo about shortening battleship lifespan, February 1906, PG 66079, 105–106.

151. Tirpitz to Senden, 13 February 1906, ibid., 108ff.; and PG 66713. See also Tirpitz, *Aufbau*, 27ff.

152. Tirpitz, *Aufbau*, 29. The ship diagram, with the Emperor's signature, is in PG 66078, 258.

153. On the Budget Commision and Reichstag debate, see Fernis, 37ff. On the tax question, see Witt, 132–143. The tax proposals included an inheritance tax on distant relatives, which made the Right very unhappy, as well as tariffs on certain luxury goods. These formed the bases of Bülow's finance reform that very soon proved insufficient. The Center favored the inheritance tax, a reversal of its position in 1900. For an example of the cordiality of relations between Tirpitz and the Center, see his exchange of letters with Spahn in late March 1906, N 253/6, 203–204.

154. On the article and Tirpitz's subsequent resignation attempt, see PG 66079, 113–114; and Tirpitz, *Aufbau*, 30ff.

155. Müller to Tirpitz, 11 July 1906.

156. Willy Becker, *Fürst Bülow und England, 1897–1909*, passim.

157. Fernis, 2ff.

12. SOW THE WIND, 1906–1908

1. Roster of navy departments in N 253/158.

2. See, e.g., N253/169, 408; and Trotha Papers, L 40.

3. Nachlass Keyserlingk, N/161, 42–45.

4. See chapter 11, this volume.

5. Trotha Papers, L 40.

6. Ibid.

7. Sir Edward Grey, *Twenty-Five Years*, vol. 1, chap. 6 (cited as Grey).

8. On the Cawdor Program and its subsequent history, see Marder, *Dreadnought*, 1:126ff. See also *A Statement of Admiralty Policy Presented to Parliament*, in PG 66056, 2.

9. A. J. Marder, ed., *Fear God and Dread Nought: The Correspondence of Admiral of the Fleet Lord Fisher of Kilverstone*, 2:91–92 (cited as Marder, *Fisher*). See also Disarmament Resolution in the House of Commons, 9 May 1906, PG 66056, 3ff.

10. A. J. P. Taylor, *The Struggle for Mastery in Europe 1848–1918*, 439.

11. Büchsel's memos for IVs, 26 March and 2 April 1906, PG 65966.

12. Berghahn, 506.

13. Flottenverein pamphlet, 19 April 1906, PG 66052.

14. Dähnhardt to Capelle, 11 April 1906, PG 66060.

15. Novelle II: Vorziehen 1907, n.d., but late April or early May 1906, ibid.

16. Novelle III: Vorziehen 1912, ibid.

17. See ibid., appendices.

18. See Tirpitz, *Aufbau*, 34–35. See also Trotha's notes on the conversation, Trotha Papers, B4.

19. Capelle to Tirpitz, 15 May 1906. PG 66060; also in N253/9. See also Dähnhardt to Capelle, 7 July 1906, PG 66060.

20. Dähnhardt to Capelle, 15 May 1906, with appendices seen by Tirpitz, 18 May 1906.

21. On Tirpitz's decisions, see Dähnhardt's memo of 17 May, ca. 18 May, and 21 May 1906, PG 66060. See also Tirpitz to "a friend," 18 June 1906, in Hassell, 173. Tirpitz wrote, "A new proposal cannot be introduced before the fall of 1909." Dähnhardt later suggested that the winter of 1908–9 would be a good time because the campaign coffers of the parties would be empty, and the threat of dissolution would be a strong one. See Dähnhardt's sketch for further fleet development, late May or early June 1906, PG 66060.

22. See the Disarmament Resolution in the House of Commons, 9 May 1906, PG 66060.

23. See notes to Estimates Memorandum for Tirpitz, 16 May 1906, PG 66056, 13. Capelle warned on 22 June that, in fact, the four tempo was relatively low for England, unless the government was really determined to economize. This would be impossible to ascertain until after the Hague Conference. Ibid., 23ff.

24. Coerper to Tirpitz, 23 May 1906, PG 68929. See also Tirpitz's memo, 12 August, and Coerper to Tirpitz, 18 August 1905, PG 66080, 59–60.

25. Coerper to Tirpitz, 31 May 1906, PG 68929.

26. Tirpitz to Coerper, 5 July 1906, ibid.

27. See Herwig, *Luxury Fleet*, 59–60.

28. The discussion included increasing the price of the large cruisers to 36 million marks, and about the cost of *Von der Tann*, the 1907 cruiser project.

29. N 253/23, 26f, Capelle's notes of May 1906 on political assumptions for a new Novelle. Published in Berghahn/Deist, 250–251.

30. Dähnhardt to Capelle, 7 July 1906, PG 66060. Discussed with Tirpitz at St. Blasien, 14 July 1906.

31. Dähnhardt to Reymann, 14 July 1906, PG 66060, and Tirpitz to Capelle, 18 July 1906, PG 66080, 29; also in N253/23, 120.

32. N 253, 23, 135–136, Tirpitz to Capelle, 24 July 1906.

33. Tirpitz to Trotha, 21 July 1906, PG 66060, 41. Capelle wanted to go ahead with 30.5-cm guns for the large cruiser. Capelle to Tirpitz, 4 August 1906, ibid., 49; see also 56ff.

34. N 253/23, 136, Capelle to Tirpitz, 27 July 1906, and Tirpitz to Trotha, same day, ibid., 157ff.

35. Tirpitz to Capelle, 10 August 1906, ibid., 53. Scheer wanted to increase the size of large cruisers only if the British did so first. To do otherwise would leave a bad impression of Germany at the upcoming Hague Conference. He believed that German restraint would expose the falsely "humanitarian" British purpose in supporting the Conference. He felt that Britain's real reasons were more about the economy and propaganda. Scheer to Tirpitz, 22 August 1906, PG 66080, 63–64. See also Boy-Ed to Tirpitz, 18 August 1906, PG 94061.

36. The article is in PG 66056, 66. See also Marder, *Dreadnought*, 1:126–127.

37. Seligman, 10–59, esp. 44–50.

38. See exchange of letters, Müller to Tirpitz, 11 July 1906, and the reply, 22 July 1906, in PG 66060.

39. Boy-Ed to Tirpitz, 30 July 1906, PG 66080, 50–51.

40. Capelle to Tirpitz, 4 and 12 August 1906, N 253/17, 155ff. and 183–184.

41. Tirpitz to Capelle, 6 August 1906, N 253/23, 168–169.

42. PG 65967, Büchsel's notes on French fleet redistribution on operations plans.

43. Siegel to Tirpitz, 12 October 1906, PG 66056, 76ff.

44. Jane, *1914*. France built 257; Japan, 218; the United States, 170; Italy, 295; Russia, 339; and Austria, 319.

45. Berghahn, 517ff.

46. The Protocol for this meeting, dated 1 October 1906 in its final form, is in RMA M VI. 2. 1–12 b. *Large Cruiser Proposal 1907*, Vol. I. Also in PG 94261.

47. Notes on the IV, 28 September 1906, N 253/9, 1–2. Also in PG 66080, 68ff.

48. Cabinet Order of 28 November 1906, RMA A VI.1.1.23.

49. See article on *Von der Tann* in Hildebrand.

50. Bülow to Tirpitz, 22 February 1906, PG 69453.

51. On the army and its hair-raising atrocities, see Hull, *Destruction*, pt. 1.

52. On the Center's position on the Herero Uprising, the election campaign, and the formation of the Bülow bloc, see Bachem, vols. 6–7; and Dawson, 331ff. See also Zeender, 99ff.

53. The Social Democrats went from 81 (out of 397) seats to 43. The Center actually gained 5 seats. The biggest winners were the Progressives, who went from 26 to 49 seats. Berghahn, *Imperial Germany*, 336. On the campaign in general, see Sperber, 240ff.; and George Crothers, *The German Elections of 1907*.

54. For a detailed account of Tirpitz's attitude toward dissolution, see Berghahn, 553ff. For the financial dimension, see Witt, 153ff.

55. Eley, *Reshaping*, 257ff.

56. Quoted in Witt, 162.

57. Eley, *Reshaping*, 263.

58. Deist, 199ff.

59. On the Flottenverein, Keim, the election campaign of 1907 and after, see German Foreign Ministry, "Flottenverein," vol. 2, reel T-149, 387ff. U.S. National Archives. See also RMA Zentralabteilung, Flottenvereinsangelegenheiten Krisis 1907–8, F 2049/3.

60. Most of the above is drawn from Deist, 200ff. For a more detailed treatment, see Eley, *Reshaping*, chap. 8.

61. N 253/8, 30, Tirpitz to Müller. 13 July 1908. Also in PG 67693, 221–222.

62. On the preliminaries to the conference, see GP XXIII, pt. 1, chap. 167; and BD VIII, and RM 2/82. Other accounts of the conference as it affected the naval question are in Marder, *Dreadnought*, 1:130ff.; Woodward, chap. 6; and, esp., Hobson, 274ff.

63. Marder, *Dreadnought*, 1:131.

64. Memo, 29 January 1907, quoted in ibid., 1:132–133.

65. Hobson, 278ff., discusses this point in detail.

66. The points below are further developed in Hobson, 280ff.

67. Lothar Burchardt, *Friedenswirtschaft und Kriegsvorsorge: Deutschlands wirtschaftliche Rüstungsbestreben vor 1914*, 184–185.

68. Jost Dülffer, "Limitations on Naval Warfare and Germany's Future as a World Power: A German Debate 1904–1906," 23–43, 35.

69. Barbara Tuchman, *The Proud Tower*, 304. Siegel's statement is in GP XV, 4274.

70. BD VIII, 261–262.

71. Marschall to Bülow, 28 October 1907, GP XXIII pt. 1, 282–283.

72. On Anglo-Russian negotiations, see BD IV, passim; GP XXV, pt. 1, 183–184. See also Woodward, chap. 7.

73. Tirpitz to Prinz Heinrich, 28 January 1907, N253/16, also in N 253/9.

74. On this renewed consideration of costs, see Capelle to Tirpitz, 24 January 1907, and Dähnhardt to Capelle, 4 February 1907, PG 66060.

75. Dähnhardt to Capelle, ibid.

76. Capelle to Tirpitz, 17 February 1907, PG 66080, 81f; also in N 253/9, 34–35.

77. Draft Novelle, 23 February 1907, PG 66060.

78. E to Tirpitz, 1 March 1907, ibid. Later this would be reduced to 47 and 44 million marks, respectively.

79. Tirpitz note, 9 March 1907, PG 66080, 84–85.

80. Tirpitz to A, B, K, and W, 20 April 1907, PG 66058.

81. K reply to Novelle and Estimates Exemplars, May 1907, ibid.

82. B to Tirpitz, 10 May 1907, ibid.

83. Heeringen (A) to Tirpitz, 15 May 1907, ibid., See also Stengel (Head of the Reich Treasury) to Tirpitz, 13 May 1907, PG 66080, 96.

84. Heeringen to Tirpitz, 18 April 1907, RMA A VI.1.1.23. Vol. 1.

85. Protocol of RMA meeting, 17 May 1907, PG 66087. See also Tirpitz to Bülow, same date, PG 66058; and Berghahn, 566–567.

86. Tirpitz memo of 27 May 1907, PG 66080, 100.

87. Novelle and estimates drafts of June and July 1907 and Tirpitz to Reich Treasury, 28 July 1907, PG 66058.

88. Deist, 210–211.

89. Capelle to Tirpitz, 4 August 1907, N 253/9, 168–169. Printed in Berghahn/Deist, 255ff.

90. Dähnhardt's letter about this meeting to Tirpitz on 23 July 1907 is in N 253/9, 148ff. Published in Berghahn/Deist, 251ff. See Berghahn, 571–572. A summary of Dähnhardt's parliamentary contacts during the campaign for the

1908 Novelle is in his memo of 4 January 1908, in PG 66080, 149ff. See also Jonathan Steinberg, "The Novelle of 1908: Necessities and Choices in the Anglo-German Naval Race," 23–43.

91. Hopmann, who was there, told the story in his diary; see Epkenhans, *Hopmann*, 143–144.

92. Published in *Germania*, 13 August 1907; cited in Fernis, 56. On 13 September Dähnhardt specifically assured Müller-Meinigen that the navy had not inspired the speech, PG 66080, 114.

93. Tirpitz to Bülow, 14 August 1907, N 253/9, 173–174; and PG 66080, 106; Berghahn/Deist, 257–258. The reply of 16 August is in Tirpitz, *Aufbau*, 55–56. The note to this reply indicates that Bülow approved the four tempo on 16 August. As far as the author can determine, the four tempo was not sent to Bülow until 21 September.

94. Capelle to Tirpitz, 17/18 August, 1907, N 253/9, 175–176.

95. Capelle to Tirpitz, 1 September 1907, PG 66080, 108–109. Berghahn/Deist, 260ff.

96. Tirpitz to Capelle, 4 and 13 September 1907, and Dähnhardt's reports of the conversations, ibid., 111ff.

97. Tirpitz, *Memoirs*, 1:266.

98. Tirpitz, *Aufbau*, 46ff.

99. Berghahn, 581ff. Despite his clear analysis of Tirpitz's dilemma, Berghahn sticks to his thesis that Tirpitz created something very close to an "iron budget."

100. See, e.g., notes for a conversation with Bassermann, ca. 25 September 1907, PG 66080, 123–124. Bassermann actually proposed a four tempo from 1908 through 1911, and then, instead of sinking to a two tempo in 1912, to continue a three tempo for four more years, from 1912 to 1916, and only then subside to a two tempo for 1917 and

1918. See also Theodore Eschenburg, *Das Kaiserreich am Scheideweg: Bassermann, Bülow, und der Block.*

101. Holstein to Bülow, 29 August 1907, Holstein Papers, IV, 487ff.

102. Capelle to Tirpitz, 1 September 1907, PG 66080, 108–109.

103. Tirpitz to N and notes for interview with Bülow, 21 September 1907, ibid., 117–118, 138ff. See also Berghahn's keen analysis, 583ff.

104. Bülow to Holstein, 22 September 1907, Holstein papers, IV, 494–495.

105. N 253/9, Capelle to Tirpitz, 4 August 1907. Witt, 143, has a useful table of how battleship costs rose from 25 million marks in 1905 to 49 million in 1913, while the cost of cruisers rose from 21.3 million marks in 1905 to 49 million in 1913.

106. Memo for IV, 29 September 1907, PG 66060, 142ff, and PG 66058.

107. Tirpitz's post factum notes for IV, 29 September 1907, N 253/9.

108. See Capelle's notes for meeting with Stengel, PG 66080, 130ff., n.d., but clearly late September or early October 1907. See also Tirpitz to Reich Treasury, 3 October 1907, PG 66058.

109. See Tirpitz to Bülow, 29 October 1907. For a much more detailed analysis of the estimated tables, see Fernis, 61ff.

110. See Stumm to Bülow, 18 November 1907, and Widenmann to Tirpitz, 23 November 1907, PG 66059.

111. On the debate over the 1908–9 British estimates, see Marder, *Dreadnought*, 1:135ff.

112. On press reaction, see Fernis, 65ff; and Dähnhardt's memo of 4 January 1908, PG 66080, 149ff.

113. Carl Galster, *Welche Seekriegsrüstung braucht Deutschland?* passim; Thimme, 179; Boy-Ed to Tirpitz, 7 October 1907, RM/3 9757, 6–7; Hubatsch, *Admiralstab*, 122–123.

114. Fernis, 69ff. The summary below is mainly taken from Fernis. On Bassermann's speech, see also Capelle to Tirpitz, 1 December 1907, PG 66080, 147ff. On Bassermann's ideas, see notes for IV, 19 February 1908, PG 66059, 118ff.

115. Deist, 210ff.

116. Tirpitz to Müller, 5/6 December 1907, PG 66713, has Tirpitz's handwritten version. Also in N 253/9, 202–203. Berghahn/Deist, 269ff.

117. Fernis, 82–83; Reichstag Proceedings are in PG 66059.

118. RM 8/1233, 20.

119. On the second and third readings and final acceptance, see Fernis, 83ff.; and PG 66059.

120. Fernis, 90–91; and PG 66059.

121. On the Tweedmouth letter, see GP XXIV, 32ff.; Tirpitz, *Aufbau*, 58ff.; and Woodward, 157ff.

122. Müller, *Der Kaiser*, 65–66.

123. Marder, *Dreadnought*, 1:142–143.

124. See, e.g., notes on IV about organization of the Admiralstab, 30 December 1907, N 253/8, 9ff. Also, Hubatsch, *Admiralstab*, 125ff.

13. THE WHIRLWIND RISES, 1908–1911

1. On the parliamentary trip, see RM 3/2364. Tirpitz's speech is in N 253/8, 36ff.

2. Berghahn, *War 1914*, 66ff.

3. On the early actions of the Admiralty and the Cabinet on the 1909 estimates, see Marder, *Dreadnought*, 1:142–143; and David Lloyd George, *War Memoirs*, 1:8–9 (cited as Lloyd George, *Memoirs*).

4. Crowe's memo is in BD III, 397ff.

5. These negotiations are discussed in detail in Woodward, chap. 8. The documents are in GP XXIV, 23ff.;

and BD VI, 108ff. See also PG 66081; and Lamar Cecil, *Albert Ballin: Business and Politics in Imperial Germany, 1888–1918*, 168–169 (cited as Cecil). See also Huldermann, 208ff.

6. Wilhelm Widenmann, *Marine-Attaché an der kaiserlich-deutschen Botschaft in London, 1907–1912*, passim. Even more venom toward Metternich and Bethmann is pervasive in his papers, N 158 (cited as Widenmann).

7. Metternich to Bülow, 16 July and 1 August 1908, GP XXIV, 99ff. and 109ff. See also Tirpitz, *Aufbau*, 75ff.; and Lloyd George, *Memoirs*, 1:11ff.

8. Bülow to Metternich, 8 August 1908, GP XXIV, 117ff.

9. Metternich to Bülow, 12 August 1908, ibid., 132–133.

10. Tirpitz to Müller, 17 July 1908; Tirpitz, *Aufbau*, 84. Tirpitz's notes on the English press, St. Blasien, summer 1908, PG 66081, 70ff.

11. BD VI, 173ff.

12. Epkenhans, 34.

13. Tirpitz, *Aufbau*, 85–86.

14. On the Daily Telegraph Affair and its effects, see Wilhelm Schlüssler, *Die Daily Telegraph Affäire*, passim. The documents are in GP XXIV, 165ff.; BD VI, 201ff.; and Holstein papers, I chap. 10. See also Rudolf von Valentini, *Kaiser und Kabinettschef*, 99ff. On press reaction, see Marder, *Dreadnought*, 1:144ff.; and Hale, 314ff.

15. Marder, *Dreadnought*, 1:144ff.

16. On the Tirpitz-Bülow negotiations, see Tirpitz, *Aufbau*, 93ff.; GP XXVIII, 3ff.; Bülow, *Memoirs*, 2:355–356, 465ff., 474ff.; Woodward, 195ff., 253ff. There is also material on the question in PG 67473. Almost all of it is published in GP XXVIII or *Aufbau*, or both.

17. GP XXVIII, 21ff.; Tirpitz, *Aufbau*, 94ff. On November 25 Tirpitz again used the canard of sending

Bülow the *Saturday Review* article of September 1897 that concluded with an attack on German trade by asserting that if Germany were extinguished tomorrow, every Englishman would be richer for it. Tirpitz invoked the article to refute Metternich's contention that bad Anglo-German relations were principally a result of German naval policy. GP XXVIII, 13.

18. Tirpitz to Bülow, 17 December 1908, GP XXVIII, 13; *Aufbau*, 97ff.

19. Bülow to Tirpitz, 25 December 1908, GP XXVIII, 38ff.; and Tirpitz, *Aufbau*, 100ff. See also PG 66743.

20. Lambi, 295.

21. Tirpitz to Bülow, 4 January1909, GP XXVIII, 51ff.; Tirpitz, *Aufbau*, 104ff.

22. Tirpitz to Bülow, 20 January 1909, GP XXVIII, 67ff.; Tirpitz, *Aufbau*, 116–117.

23. Grey to Goshen, 18 March, BD VI, 244–245; Metternich to Bülow. 12 March 1909; Tirpitz, *Aufbau*, 131ff.

24. GP XXVIII, 148ff., 156ff.

25. See Notes for IV, 3 April 1909, PG 67473, 22ff.; printed in Tirpitz, *Aufbau*, 145ff., and in a slightly different version in GP XXVIII, 145ff. See also Tirpitz to Müller, 25 April and 6 May1909, PG 67473, 49ff. Part of the letter is printed in Tirpitz, *Aufbau*, 150ff. Müller agreed with Tirpitz.

26. BD VI, 265–266.

27. Bülow's proposal is published in GP XXVIII, 168ff. Müller's version, somewhat sharper, is in Tirpitz, *Aufbau*, 157ff. The latter version is also in PG 67473.

28. On the naval scare, see Hale, chap. 12; and Marder, *Dreadnought*, 1:chap. 7. Woodward, chaps. 10–12, deals with it in great detail, but in this author's opinion and that of the above two, Woodward is biased against the German side and tends to suspect, de-

spite decisive evidence to the contrary, that only the naval scare kept Tirpitz from going ahead with a "planned" acceleration of battleship building. The German viewpoint is in Tirpitz, *Aufbau*, 120ff., and, even more vigorously, in Widenmann, 149ff. For an objective view, see Epkenhans, 43ff. The published documents on the naval scare are in GP, XXVIII, 83ff.; and BD VI, 237ff.

29. Epkenhans, 44; Winston Churchill, *The World Crisis*, 1:23ff. (cited as Churchill).

30. Widenmann to Tirpitz, 27 March 1909; Tirpitz, *Aufbau*, 143.

31. Hale, 331ff. shows how British naval budgets were put together and the role of annual scare-mongering.

32. Marder, *Dreadnought*, 1:151–152.

33. GP XXVIII, 33ff.

34. Construction of a German Dreadnought usually took thirty-two to thirty-six months, with six additional months for sea trials. Only in an extreme crisis would a ship join the fleet before sea trials were completed. See Construction Department Memo, 2 December 1908, PG 66056, 124ff. These times were always stated in the contracts.

35. Marder, *Dreadnought*, 1:152.

36. On the evidence of German acceleration, see ibid., 1:152ff.; Hale, 342ff.; and Woodward, 204ff. Woodward puts a sinister connotation on everything and represented the British navalist point of view. The idea that the naval scare was a plot of the arms manufacturers and the navalist Conservatives is put forth in Philip Noel-Baker, *The Private Manufacture of Armaments*, 1:449ff.

37. Widenmann to Tirpitz, 16 December 1908, GP XXVIII, 30ff.

38. Grey to Goschen, 18 March 1908, BD VI, 244ff. For Tirpitz's speech

on 17 March, denying acceleration, see Goschen to Grey, enclosure, ibid., pp. 250–251.

39. Lennoxlove Ms, 15 (?) January 1909, quoted in Marder, *Dreadnought*, 1:154ff.

40. Hale, 345 n.

41. Churchill, 1:33.

42. Woodward, chap. 12.

43. See K memo of 24 January 1906, and E's deliberations on it in PG66065. See also protocol of RMA meeting, 11 December 1905, PG 66057.

44. Reymann to Capelle, 17 April 1906, PG 66055; and Tirpitz's memo to Siegel, 12 October 1906, PG 66056. On 29 October the Emperor agreed.

45. Krupp's letter of 23 October is cited in E to Waffenabteilung (W), 21 December 1905, PG 66055. See also Tirpitz's draft speech to the Reichstag on accelerating building time, PG 66053, 118ff. Draft dated 6 December 1905. Tirpitz detailed technical and financial disadvantages of acceleration. Unlike British yards, Tirpitz pointed out, German yards were not geared for building large ships fast; faster work would lead to poorer quality and carelessness; and the expense of working at night would be considerable. In the same speech he acknowledged the need, were acceleration planned, to have Reichstag approval to increase sums in the installments.

46. K reply to estimates exemplar, May 1907, PG 66058.

47. See draft Novelle and 1908 estimates, n.d., but almost certainly May 1907, ibid.

48. Harms (B) to Tirpitz, 10 May 1907. The Imperial Dockyards took four to six months longer than private yards to build large ships.

49. See Memo for IV, 23 September 1907, ibid.; and 29 September 1907, PG 66060, 142ff.

50. Ziese to Tirpitz, 19 June 1908, PG 66056, 128–129.

51. Construction Department memo on the shortening of building time, 2 December 1908, ibid., 124ff.

52. Tirpitz's Reichstag speech, 29 March 1909, PG 67473. See also his draft speech, 12 March PG 66056, 135ff. On the two later ships, see Tirpitz to Müller, 24 July 1909, PG 66081, 187–188.

53. Müller to Tirpitz, 25 March 1909, PG 66081, 177ff.

54. Müller to Tirpitz and reply, 4 August 1909, ibid., 207ff.

55. See Seligmann, *Naval Intelligence*, chap. 3.

56. Churchill, 1:37–38.

57. Marder, *Dreadnought*, 1:178ff.

58. For details on the tedious tax question that broke up the bloc, see Witt, 230ff.; for a more concise version, see Förster, 178ff.

59. The story of Bethmann's attempts at a naval agreement and Tirpitz's opposition to it has been told many times and need not be treated in more than summary form here. Neither side budged from the positions that both had already adopted. The published documents are in GP XXVIII, 143ff.; and BD VI, chaps. 40, 42, 43. See also Tirpitz, *Aufbau*, 163ff. The documents on the naval agreement question, in PG 67473, have almost all been published in the above. The most thorough account using published documents is Woodward, chaps. 14–16. The best fairly recent account is Epkenhans, 52ff. See also Marder, *Dreadnought*, 1:171ff., 221ff. Most significant for a Tirpitz biography are the negotiations *within* the German government, which are emphasized below.

60. Epkenhans, 54, quoting the letter draft Tirpitz to Müller, 15 July 1909,

RM 3/11710. See also Tirpitz to Müller, 17 July 1909, PG 67473, 91–92.

61. Tirpitz to Eisendecher, 23 April 1909, Nachlass Eisendecher, T 291, reel 8.

62. Bethmann's Memorandum, 13 August 1909, GP XXVIII, 211ff.; Tirpitz, *Aufbau*, 165ff., summarizes Tirpitz's 11 August and 1 September plans.

63. Goschen to Grey, 15 October 1909, BD VI, 293ff.; GP XXXVIII, 239ff. Tirpitz, in *Aufbau*, 165, claims that Bethmann did not advance his naval proposal because the German Foreign Office wanted a political agreement first but that Bethmann's actions were in accord with the Emperor's priorities.

64. BD VI, 303f, 304ff., 312.

65. Marder, *Dreadnought*, 1:214ff.

66. BD VI, 406–407.

67. Ibid., 501–502.

68. Ibid., 521ff.

69. Tirpitz to Bethmann, 17 March 1911, N 253/24.

70. Reported in full in Woodward, chaps. 15, 16; Tirpitz, *Aufbau*, 193ff.; PG 67473; and Epkenhans, 72ff.

71. BD VI 598ff.

72. For this interview, see Tirpitz, *Aufbau*, 184–185 (emphasis in original). See Capelle's notes for this meeting, N 253/24.

73. Notes in Capelle's hand with annotations by Tirpitz, 23 September 1910, N 253/24.

74. See the discussion of the 3:4 and 2:3 ratios in Hobson, 255ff.

75. Tirpitz to Bethmann, 4 November 1909, ibid., 168–169.

76. See ibid., 188ff.; Widenmann, 180ff.; and Widenmann to Tirpitz, 14 March 1911, GP XXVIII, 396ff., esp. editor's note, 399–400.

77. Epkenhans, 68ff.

78. Memo of a Conversation between Tirpitz and Bethmann on the

Agreement Question, 4 May 1911, PG 67473, 122–123; also in N 253/24. There is a hint of the content of the conversation in the editors' notes to the German aide-memoire, 9 May 1911, GP XXVIII, 409ff. Quotations are from the former.

79. BD VI, 621ff.; and GP XXVIII, 409ff.

80. See Müller, Personal Version of the Agreement Question, 15 May 1911, PG 67473, 146–147.

81. Hale, 379; Marder, *Dreadnought*, 1:232–233.

82. See, e.g., Watson's Naval Attaché report of 2 May 1911, Seligmann, *Naval Intelligence*, no. 126.

83. See tables in Witt, 380–381; Epkenhans, 84–85; and RM/3.

84. Reichstag debates November/December 1908, cited in Epkenhans, 85–86.

85. N 253/408, Tirpitz to Trotha, 18 March 1909.

86. Transcript of the Budget Commission, 17 March 1909, in RM 3/9757, 97–100.

87. An important exception to this inattention is Hobson. One of the most original insights in Hobson's work is his extensive discussion of this very point, although he only carries it through 1907. See Hobson, esp. 273ff.

88. See Förster, 179–180.

89. See Wermuth's letter on financial planning, 26 August 1909, cited in Berghahn/Deist, 352ff. See also Witt, 316ff.

90. Capelle to Tirpitz, 9 September 1909, N 253/8. Briefly discussed in Epkenhans, 88.

91. Dähnhardt's handwritten draft for the 4 April 1910 speech is in RM 3/11690. See also Epkenhans, 89, whose conclusions about this document are somewhat different from the author's. The parliamentary dimension of the speech is discussed in chapter 10, this volume.

92. See *Zentralabteilung Daily Report*, 8 April 1910, RM 3/11516.

93. See, e.g., RM 3/11621, passim.

94. Capelle to Tirpitz, 24 June 1910, N 253/24.

95. Hildebrand article on *Kurfürst Friedrich Wilhelm*.

96. Capelle to Tirpitz, 29 July 1910, N 253/24.

97. Epkenhans, 91.

98. Memo from early May 1911, N 253/24.

99. Nachlass Keyserlingk N 161/9, 20, on Büchsel as Chief of the Admiralstab.

100. On this conflict, see Hubatsch, *Admiralstab*, 112ff.

101. Nachlass Keyserlingk N 161/9, 24–25.

102. Nachlass Michaelis N 164/4, 27.

103. Gemzell, 99–100; and Hubatsch, *Admiralstab*, 134.

104. See the cordial tone of Büchsel to Tirpitz, just after the former's retirement, 29 September 1908, N 253/200, 57–58.

105. Hopmann, *Logbuch*, 312.

106. Ibid., 313–314.

107. See Hildebrand, *Admirale*, article on Prinz Heinrich.

108. See Bachmann to Trotha, 17 and 21 January, 1909, Trotha Papers.

109. Hopmann, *Logbuch*, 319–320.

110. Nachlass Michaelis, N 164/4. 23ff. See also Thomas Scheerer, "Die Marineoffiziere der Kaiserlichen Marine: Sozialisation und Konflicte," 285–286.

111. Hildebrand articles on *Nassau* and *Westfalen*.

112. The most cogent account is Paul Kennedy's EHR article on German operations plans against England. For details, see Lambi, chaps. 12, 13, 16;

Gemzell, 69ff.; and Hubatsch, *Admiral-stab*, 109ff.

113. Lambi, 221. The close versus wide blockade question is discussed in detail in chapter 14, this volume.

114. See, e.g., Kennedy EHR, German operations plans, 63.

115. See, e.g., Hopmann, *Logbuch*, 316.

116. See ibid., 65–66; Lambi, 341ff.; Hubatsch, *Admiralstab*, 140ff; and Nachlass Michaelis, N 164/4. 29ff.

117. See Michaelis's notes on Tirpitz, RM 8/1233, 26.

118. Nachlass Michaelis, N 164/4, 30. See also Tirpitz's comments on Baudissin's operations plan, 22 May 1909, PG 66081.

119. Hopmann described Fischel as "a man of sharp, cool-headed understanding, gifted with a cold-blooded [i.e., rigorously rational], healthily phlegmatic nature, which is an excellent characteristic of a leader." *Logbuch*, 316.

120. See Kennedy, EHR, German operations plans, 66–67.

121. RM 8/1233, Michaelis's notes on Tirpitz, 27.

122. Nachlass Michaelis, N 164/4, 30–31.

123. Trotha Papers, Trotha's notes on Holtzendorff, 20 February 1937.

124. Müller, *Der Kaiser*, 132.

125. See Lambi, 353ff.

126. N 253/24, Tirpitz to William II, 11 June 1911.

127. On ship types in this period, see PG 66087; PG 66088; and relevant articles in Hildebrand. See also N 253/24.

14. DENOUEMENT, 1911–1914

1. Hubatsch, *Admiralstab*, 147 n. 108. See also Hildebrand article on *Panther*.

2. Nachlass Michaelis N 164/4, 37.

3. Hopmann, *Logbuch*, 370.

4. Diplomatic aspects of this affair need only be summarized here. The documents are in GP XXIX and BD VII. See Woodward, chap. 17; Emily Oncken, *Panthersprung nach Agadir: Die deutsche Politik während der zweiten Marokkokrise 1911*; Tirpitz, *Memoirs*, 1:275ff.; Tirpitz, *Aufbau*, 197ff.; Förster, 208ff.; Fritz Fischer, *Krieg der Illusionen: Die deutsche Politik 1911–1914*, 117ff.; Wilhelm Widenmann, *Marine-Attaché an der kaiserlich-deutschen Botschaft in London 1907–1912*, 182ff.; David Stevenson, *Armaments and the Coming of the War: Europe 1904–1914*, 180ff.; Hale, 380ff.; Epkenhans, 93ff.; and Marder, *Dreadnought*, 1:239ff. The summary below is drawn from these accounts.

5. Müller, *Der Kaiser*, 86; Hubatsch, *Admiralstab*, 147.

6. Tirpitz, *Memoirs*, 1:276.

7. GP XXIX, 164ff; BD VII, 334, 342.

8. On the press, see Hale, 384–385.

9. Quoted in Woodward, 312 n.

10. Tirpitz, *Memoirs*, 1:276–277; Tirpitz, *Aufbau*, 199. See also Z Daily Report to Tirpitz, 2 August 1911, N 253/25, 2.

11. Görlitz, *Der Kaiser*, 86ff.

12. On the Admiralty crisis, see Marder, *Dreadnought*, 1:242ff.

13. On these negotiations, see GP XXIX.

14. See Marder's account from the Asquith ms. of the historic meeting of the CIGS on 23 August 1911. Marder, *Dreadnought*, 1:389ff. Even at this late date the Admiralty plan against Germany was still predicated on a close blockade near Helgoland.

15. Tirpitz, *Aufbau*, 199ff.

16. See notes for Immediatvortrag, 18 February 1908 (not held), PG 66059, 118ff.

17. See the previous chapter in this volume.

18. On the 4 May 1911 meeting and Tirpitz's thoughts on the negotiations and a Novelle, see PG 67473, 122ff.

19. Deist, 264–265.

20. See Tirpitz, *Aufbau*, 200ff., and Deist, 268–269.

21. Capelle to Tirpitz, 12 August 1911, in Tirpitz, *Aufbau*, 203.

22. Tirpitz to Capelle, 12 August 1911, in ibid.

23. Tirpitz to Capelle, 14 August 1911, in ibid.

24. RM 3/11678, Hollweg to Tirpitz, 24 September 1911.

25. Tirpitz to Bethmann 30 August 1911, PG 66082, 1ff. Reproduced in Tirpitz, *Aufbau*, 207–208.

26. The Tirpitz-Bethmann conversations are in Tirpitz, *Aufbau*, 209.

27. Müller, *Der Kaiser*, 88ff.

28. See Epkenhans, *Hopmann*, 159 and n. 23; Hopmann Diary, entry of 2 October 1911, in Epkenhans, *Hopmann*, 159.

29. Hopmann Diary, entry of 2 October 1911, in Epkenhans, *Hopmann*, 159.

30. Müller, *Der Kaiser*, 91–92; Tirpitz, *Aufbau*, 212–2143.

31. Capelle to Tirpitz, 14 September 1911, N 253/25. See also Epkenhans, 95.

32. On preparations for Rominten, see Conversations among RMA Departments, 7 and 13 September 1911, PG 66064; PG 66082; and Tirpitz, *Aufbau*, 209ff. If the Emperor rejected the Novelle, Tirpitz planned to ask for increased manpower in the 1912 estimates. See also Hopmann, *Logbuch*, 379ff. Tirpitz's anxiety was sharpened by the report that even the navalist Count Reventlow showed little enthusiasm for a Novelle. N to Tirpitz, 15 September 1911, PG 66082, 7–8.

33. Tirpitz, *Aufbau*, 213.

34. Accounts of the audience, which differ only slightly, are in PG 66082, 2ff., 12ff.; and Tirpitz, *Aufbau*, 213ff. See also N253/25, 57.

35. Tirpitz, *Aufbau*, 216ff. The complete version of the September 30 letter is in PG 66082, 17ff.; and PG 66061.

36. William II to Koester, 29 September 1911, PG 67474. Koester was very upset, but, like a good soldier, he complied immediately. Müller to William II, 30 September 1911, PG 67474. Dähnhardt prepared the RMA's version of what the propaganda campaign should be if the agreement were proposed before the Novelle. See "Argument for Press Agitation (in Dähnhardt's hand, n.d. but probably late October 1911), PG 66064.

37. See Bethmann to Tirpitz, 4 October 1911, PG 66082, 30ff.; and Tirpitz, *Aufbau*, 218ff.; Tirpitz to Bethmann, 5 and 7 October 1911, PG66061, 23ff.; and Tirpitz, *Aufbau*, 222ff.

38. The memo is in N 253/25. See Epkenhans, 100.

39. Tirpitz, *Aufbau*, 225–226. The tendentious conversation between Tirpitz and Wermuth on 9 October 1911 is in PG 66082, partly published in Tirpitz, *Aufbau*, 226–227.

40. Hopmann Diary, entry of 16 October 1911, in Epkenhans, *Hopmann*, 163.

41. The Novelle draft of 16 October 1911 is in PG 66064. See also Disposition for a Conversation with Schmoller and Erzberger, same date, PG 66061.

42. Dähnhardt's notes on conversations with Center deputies on 18 October 1911 is in RM 3/6678; also in PG 66061. See also Epkenhans, *Hopmann*, 163, 165; and Deist, 287.

43. Tirpitz, *Aufbau*, 226, 228. Müller to Tirpitz. 15 October 1911, PG

66082, 45; and Müller to Bethmann, 16 October 1911, PG 67474.

44. On the government's dilemma in the Reichstag, see Oncken, 351ff.

45. Holtzendorff memo of 25 October 1911, PG 66082; Lambi, 367.

46. Hopmann Diary, entry of 16 November 1911, in Epkenhans, *Hopmann*, 172.

47. Dähnhardt's notes of 2 and 3 November 1911, PG 66065, 77, 84, 94, 97; and "Novelle Zusammenstellung" dated 22 May 1914, PG 66063.

48. Novelle draft of 21 November 1911, PG 66082, 62ff. See also Widenmann, 220ff.

49. Müller to Tirpitz, 15 November 1911, PG 67474; and Tirpitz, *Aufbau*, 257–258.

50. Tirpitz to Bethmann, 27 November 1911, PG 66082, 106–107.

51. Wermuth to Tirpitz, 28 November and 8 December 1911, PG 66082, 111ff. and 142ff. Also printed in GP XXXI, 35ff. For Tirpitz's comments, see Tirpitz, *Aufbau*, 258–259. For Wermuth's view, see Adolf Wermuth, *Ein Beamtenleben*, 280–281, 305ff.

52. Hopmann Diary, note of 28 November 1911, in Epkenhans, *Hopmann*, 175.

53. For calculations, see Herwig, 61.

54. "Notes for a Survey of the 1912 Budget," Bundesrat Publication #137, 28 November 1911; and "Memorandum of a Conversation between Dähnhardt and Wahnschaffe (Reichkanzlei)," 1 December 1911, PG 66061.

55. On the origins of what would become a sea change in German defense policy, see, e.g., Förster, 218ff.; and Roger Chickering, *We Men Who Feel Most German: A Cultural Study of the Pan-German League, 1886–1914*, 264ff. (cited as Chickering). Chickering gives a particularly lucid account of the

growth of radical nationalism in the wake of the Agadir crisis.

56. Bethmann to Josias von Heeringen, 28 November 1911, PG 66061. Printed in Tirpitz, *Aufbau*, 265; and 4 December 1911, PG 66082, 125. See also Hopmann Diary, note of 30 November 1911, in Epkenhans, *Hopmann*, 176–177; Deist, 273–274; and Fischer, *Krieg der Illusionen*, 174ff.

57. The conversations between the Heeringen brothers are in PG 66082, 124, 139. They are printed with Tirpitz's comments, in Tirpitz, *Aufbau*, 266–267. See also Lambi, 368. Bethmann's maneuver made Tirpitz very angry, but Hopmann was hopeful for some kind of compromise. Hopmann Diary, note of 9 December 1912, in Epkenhans, *Hopmann*, 179.

58. See Bethmann's Bundesrat Declaration of 9 December 1911, in PG 66082, 138. The Emperor called this a "betrayal." William II to Müller, 9 December 1911, PG 66082, 126. He also said that if Bethmann would not accept the Novelle he would be dismissed. Müller, *Der Kaiser*, 101.

59. Müller, *Der Kaiser*, 102ff; Tirpitz, *Aufbau*, 267–268. See also Epkenhans, *Hopmann*, 181.

60. Tirpitz, *Aufbau*, 268; Hopmann Diary, note of 16 December 1911, in Epkenhans, *Hopmann*, 182.

61. See, e.g., Valentini to Müller, 1 December 1911, PG 67474.

62. Müller to Tirpitz, 23 December 1911, PG 66082, 149; and Müller's Memo of the Immediatvortrag of the same date, PG 66061. A short summary is in Tirpitz, *Aufbau*, 268. The new draft Novelle had a tempo from 1912 to 1917 of 3:3:2:3:2:3. PG 66067, 80.

63. Müller to William II, 2 December 1911, PG 66082, 150.

64. Tirpitz, *Aufbau*, 268ff, 275ff. The correspondence on this point is in

RM 2/1764. See also Epkenhans, *Hopmann*, 191 n. 10.

65. See Müller note, and Tirpitz to William II, both dated 12 January 1912, PG 67474; Tirpitz, *Aufbau*, 275ff.; and Müller, *Der Kaiser*, 107ff.

66. Hopmann Diary, entries of 13 and 26 January 1912, in Epkenhans, *Hopmann*, 192–193.

67. Fernis, 121.

68. Tirpitz to Bethmann, 26 January 1912, PG 66082, 188. See also Tirpitz's notes, N 253/26, 35.

69. Wermuth, 305ff.; Tirpitz, *Aufbau*, 277ff.

70. Fernis, 101.

71. The literature on the Haldane Mission is immense. The published documents are in BD VI, chap. 49; GP XXXI, chap. 243; and unpublished material in N 253/26. Also important are Tirpitz, *Aufbau*, 279ff., and *Memoirs*, 1:282ff.; Widenmann, 235ff.; Müller, *Der Kaiser*, 110ff.; Theodore von Bethmann-Hollweg, *Reflections on the World War*, 1:50ff.; Richard Haldane, *Before the War*, 55ff.; and Haldane, *An Autobiography*, 238ff.; Churchill, 1:94; and Grey, 1:241ff. The best summaries are Marder, *Dreadnought*, 1:275ff.; and Woodward, chap. 18. New material is in Epkenhans, *Hopmann*, 198ff. The summary below is based on these materials.

72. See Cassel to Ballin, 9 January 1912, PG 67473. Ballin's original letter has been lost. Since it came from the German side, the Cabinet believed that Germany initiated events. Because the first diplomatic feelers came from the British, the Germans believed it was a British initiative. This misperception raised false hopes on both sides.

73. Both letters are in GP XXXI, 98; but see also 99 n.; and Churchill, 1:95.

74. Metternich to Foreign Office, 31 January 1912, GP XXXI, 102.

75. Bethmann to Metternich, 4 February 1912, ibid., GP XXXI, 105–106.

76. Churchill, 1:98.

77. Quoted in Jonathan Steinberg, "Diplomatie als Wille und Vorstellung: Die Berliner Mission Lord Haldanes im Februar 1912," 263–282, in Schottelius and Deist, 269 (cited as Steinberg, "Haldane").

78. See Müller to William II, 3 February 1912, PG 67474. The preliminaries of Tirpitz's conversation with Haldane are in RM 2/1764–65. Some of this (substantially abridged) is in Tirpitz, *Aufbau*, 282ff.; and Müller, 111ff. Tirpitz and Müller wanted to use the original Novelle as a basis for negotiations, even though the Emperor and Bethmann had already informed Cassel of the alternating two-three tempo. Churchill, 1:95ff; and GP XXXI 99 n.

79. Epkenhans, 115.

80. Marder, *Dreadnought*, 1:277. Note the title of Herwig's book, *Luxury Fleet*.

81. Watson to Admiralty, 12 April 1912, Seligmann, *Naval Intelligence*, 418.

82. On the 8 February conversation, see PG 66063; BD VI 676ff; GP XXXI, 109ff., including notes. Tirpitz, in *Aufbau*, 286, claimed that Haldane had the latest copy of the Novelle at that meeting and that it was Bethmann's fault that the original three tempo Novelle was not the basis for negotiations;as noted above, however, Cassel had already given it to the Cabinet.

83. N 253/26, 79, copy of a letter from William II to Müller, 9 February 1912. Trotha was then Müller's deputy. The Emperor encouraged Müller to show the letter to Tirpitz but not to Bethmann or Kiderlen.

84. Haldane, BD VI, 710, stated that he was given the Novelle at the

February 9 meeting [even though Cassel had previously shared it with the Cabinet]. On the contents of this conversation, see GP XXXI, 112ff., 221ff.; BD VI, 679ff. See Tirpitz, *Aufbau*, 286ff., which leaves out some details that are in N 253/420; and RM 2/1795. See also Müller, *Der Kaiser*, 112–113. Tirpitz claimed, in *Aufbau*, 286, that Haldane said he was speaking in the name of the Cabinet, and Tirpitz thereby thought that he was speaking officially, despite his protestations to the contrary. For a good summary, see Steinberg, "Haldane," 277ff.

85. Hopmann Diary, entry of 9 February 1912, in Epkenhans, *Hopmann*, 196–197.

86. Summarized in Woodward, 332ff.

87. Hopmann Diary, entry of 10 February 1912, in Epkenhans, *Hopmann*, 198–199. See also Epkenhans, 121–122.

88. Hopmann Diary, entry of 12 February 1912, in Epkenhans, *Hopmann*, 199.

89. Epkenhans, *Hopmann*, 197ff.

90. Tirpitz, *Aufbau*, 290–291.

91. Müller to William II, 23 February 1912, PG 67475. A slightly less accurate version is in Tirpitz, *Aufbau*, 292.

92. Tirpitz, *Aufbau*, 300; PG 66082, 209ff.; and PG 67475.

93. See Zara Steiner, *Britain and the Origins of the First World War*, 138ff.

94. Tirpitz, *Aufbau*, 307–308.

95. Marder, *Dreadnought*, 1:279ff.; BD VI, 697ff.; and GP XXXI, 132ff. See also Hopmann Diary, entry of 26 February 1912, in Epkenhans, *Hopmann*, 202–203.

96. Tirpitz to Müller, 26 February 1912, in Tirpitz, *Aufbau*, 299–300; Tirpitz to Bethmann 27 February 1912, with Novelle draft attached, PG 66082, 212–213. This draft, with only minute

changes, went to the Reichstag late in March. For the full correspondence, see RM 2/1765.

97. Hubatsch, *Ära*, 105.

98. Müller to William II, 1 March 1912, PG 67475.

99. Hopmann Diary, entry of 18 March 1912, in Epkenhans, *Hopmann*, 213.

100. Tirpitz, *Aufbau*, 315ff.; GP XXXI, 150ff., 158ff.; BD VI, 704ff.; and Marder, *Dreadnought*, 1:280ff.

101. Marder, *Dreadnought*, 1:280.

102. Tirpitz, *Aufbau*, 318ff., includes an account of his struggle to get the Novelle published before the British reply of 18 March. Tirpitz's post mortem on the Haldane Mission is in his notes of a conversation with William II, 18 March 1912, N 253/26, 207–208.

103. Fernis, 102ff. On the publicity campaign, see Deist, 305ff.

104. Josias von Heeringen to Tirpitz, 21 February 1912, and Reich Treasury to Tirpitz, 13 March 1912, PG 66062. Wermuth resigned three days later. In his diary Hopmann privately noted about Wermuth: "In many ways I regret his departure. There is no doubt that he was a very capable and energetic man, who also had a backbone." Entry of 1 March 1912, in Epkenhans, *Hopmann*, 211–212.

105. This draft is in PG 66082, 213ff. The Novelle is described at length in Fernis, 108ff. The RMA's expectations about the Reichstag are in N 253/26, 16ff.

106. For a detailed treatment of the debates, see Fernis, 121ff. Budget Commission and Plenary debates are in RM 3/11678.

107. See Tirpitz's notes for Immediatvortrag, 22 May 1912, PG 66063.

108. Tirpitz, *Aufbau*, 345.

109. Hopmann Diary, entry of 10 May 1912, in Epkenhans, *Hopmann*, 223.

110. Marder, *Dreadnought*, 1:276; and Churchill, 1:95ff.

111. Marder, *Dreadnought*, 1:287ff.; Woodward, chap. 21.

112. Quoted in Marder, *Dreadnought*, 1:293.

113. On the Grey-Cambon exchange, see BD X, pt. 2, 614–615. See also Grey, 1:96ff. On the "moral" obligation, see Marder, *Dreadnought*, 1:308–309.

114. Churchill's several attempts to suggest a "naval holiday" roused fear in Tirpitz that the Chancellor would be interpellated about it in the Reichstag. He had Capelle craft arguments to counter it. See, e.g., Capelle's notes of early April 1913, N 253/28, 71–72; and Capelle to Tirpitz, 7 April 1913, N 253/28, 73–74.

115. Woodward, chaps. 20–24, covers the topic exhaustively, and this exchange need only be summarized in a Tirpitz biography. On Tirpitz's views, see Tirpitz, *Aufbau*, 380ff., 395ff., 402ff., and 407. See also, e.g., Referat über Budgetkommission," 9 November 1912, PG 66083; Dähnhardt to Tirpitz, 13 May 1913, PG 66057, 67–68; and Tirpitz to Bethmann (not sent), 21 November 1913, PG 66057, 83ff.

116. Epkenhans, 338 PG 66057,339; and N253/28, Tirpitz's notes for an Immediatvortrag (held the next day), 22 February 1913.

117. Deist, 306–307. See also Förster, 238ff., 275ff.; Roger Chickering, "Der deutsche Wehrverein: die Reform der deutschen Armee 1912–1914," 7–33.

118. See relevant material in Jane; Hildebrand; and Siegfried Breyer, *Schlachtschiffe und Schlachtkreuzer 1905–1970*.

119. See, e.g., RMA meeting on the battlecruiser type on 6 November 1913, N 253/29, 38ff.

120. PG 66080.

121. PG 66082, 243ff. Memo by William II.

122. N 253/27, Tirpitz to William II, 5 May 1912.

123. PG 67858, Tirpitz to Müller, 2 and 5 August 1912. See also Lambi, 374.

124. Lambi, 374–375.

125. Epkenhans, 323–324.

126. On the manning question, see notes of an RMA meetings of 18 and 19 December 1912, N 253/28, 87ff.

127. N 253/28, Tirpitz to Capelle, 17 August 1912. Tirpitz bared his troubles in a memo to Hopmann in late August 1912, in ibid.

128. Ibid., Capelle to Tirpitz, 20 August 1912.

129. Ibid., Capelle to Tirpitz, probably 24 August 1912.

130. Ibid., dated September 1912. Hopmann also noted that Tirpitz was pessimistic at the time. See Hopmann Diary, entry of 9 September 1912, in Epkenhans, *Hopmann*, 238.

131. On the army, see Förster, 247ff.; and Berghahn/Deist, 372, 388ff.

132. Epkenhans, 325ff.

133. Hopmann Diary, entry of 24 November 1912, in Epkenhans, *Hopmann*, 262ff.

134. GP XXXIX, 123ff. On these exchanges, see John Röhl, "Dress Rehearsal in December: Military Decision-Making in Germany on the Eve of the First World War," 162–189 (cited as Röhl, "Military Decision Making").

135. This meeting has generated much interest among historians. Röhl, in "Military Decision Making," cites thirty-three books and articles by eighteen different authors. The documents for the actual meeting are in Nachlass Müller N 159/4, 8 December 1912; a

useful secondhand account is Hopmann Diary, entry of 9 December 1912, in Epkenhans, *Hopmann*, 268ff. Most of the documents are also collected in John C. G. Röhl, "An der Schwelle zum Weltkrieg: Eine Dokumentation über den 'Kriegsrat' von 8 Dezember 1912," 77–135 (cited as Röhl, "An der Schwelle"). Fischer, *Krieg der Illusione*, 232ff., and Röhl, in the works cited above, see the "war council" as a kind of dress rehearsal for the 1914 crisis. Wolfgang Mommsen, in "Domestic Factors in German Foreign Policy before 1914," 3–43, and elsewhere, argues, as do other historians, that it was not nearly so significant for 1914. See also Lambi, 382ff.

136. Berghahn, *War 1914*, 180.

137. Hopmann Diary, entry of 11 December 1912, in Epkenhans, *Hopmann*, 270–271.

138. Ibid., entries of 13 and 14 December 1912, 271–272.

139. Ibid., entry of 16 December 1912, 272; Tirpitz, *Aufbau*, 369.

140. RM 3/11624, 42ff., notes in Tirpitz's hand dated 17 December 1912.

141. RM 3/11624, Capelle's comments on E estimates, 11 January 1913.

142. Epkenhans, 333.

143. Tirpitz, *Aufbau*, 370, 19 December 1912.

144. Hopmann Diary, entry of 2 January 1913, in Epkenhans, *Hopmann*, 279.

145. PG 66083, Müller to Tirpitz, 4 January 1913, and notes by Tirpitz and Capelle, with draft Novelle of 5 January 1913. Documentation on the 1913 Novelle is also in N253/28.

146. Hopmann Diary, entries of 4 and 6 January 1913, in Epkenhans, *Hopmann*, 280ff.

147. PG 66713, Müller to Tirpitz, 6 January 1913, printed in Tirpitz,

Aufbau, 370ff. See also Müller, *Der Kaiser*, 127.

148. Hopmann Diary, entry of 6 January 1913, in Epkenhans, *Hopmann*, 282.

149. See, e.g., Eley, *Reshaping*, pt. IV.

150. Förster, 272–273.

151. Summarized in Berghahn, *War 1914*, 167–168. For Capelle's and Tirpitz's take on this method of finance, see N253/28, 39–40. Capelle thought that an inheritance tax would be more rational, but he recognized that a one-time wealth tax was more politically palatable in the Reichstag.

152. Memo of 9 October 1913 meeting, N 253/423.

153. See the ship articles in Hildebrand. Epkenhans, in *Hopmann*, 337 n. 238, mentions this trip but misidentifies *König Albert* as *König*. See also Boelcke, 132–133.

154. Hopmann Diary, entry of 31 December 1913, in Epkenhans, *Hopmann*, 348.

155. Epkenhans, 358–359.

156. Tirpitz's notes, mid-May 1914, N 253/29, 108.

157. N 253/29, 125–126, Capelle's notes, 17 May 1914.

158. N 253/29, 117ff., Tirpitz to Bethmann, 22 May 1914. Also in PG 66083; and PG 67474.

159. PG 66083, Bethmann to Tirpitz, 3 June 1914.

160. Ibid., Kühn to Tirpitz, 13 June 1914.

161. See the chart in Weir, 85.

162. See Weir, Tirpitz and U-Boats, 179–180.

163. Lambert, *Sir John Fisher's Naval Revolution*, esp. chaps. 2 and 6.

164. A good summary of Tirpitz's position on prewar U-boats is in Hassell, 181ff.

165. RM 3/11603, Handakten Göhren, "U-Boatsdebatten in der Budget Kommission von 1900–1903," an appendix to "U-Bootsdebatten im Plenum und in der Budget Kommission von 1904–1914."

166. Ibid., 1ff.

167. See his statements of 7 December 1905 and 6 March 1906, in ibid., 5–6.

168. For a history of German U-boat construction, see Eberhard Rössler, *Geschichte des deutschen U-Bootbaus*.

169. RM 3/11603, 8–9.

170. Ibid., 30 January 1908, 14, 15–16.

171. Ibid., 17 March 1909, 20–21.

172. See, e.g., ibid., 38–39, Erzberger's remarks in Plenum, 1 March 1913.

173. Ibid., 41, Budget Commission Session, 11 February 1914.

174. See PG 69522 (also stamped PG 65314) and PG 69523, passim.

175. Nachlass Michaelis, N 164/4, 32.

176. See, esp., Nachlass Michaelis N 164/4. Part of Michaelis's papers has finally reached printed form in Werner Rahn, ed., *Deutsche Marinen*, 397–426.

177. See Hopmann, *Logbuch* and *Kriegstagebuch*;, and Epkenhans, *Hopmann*.

178. Nachlass Michaelis N 164/4.

179. See, e.g., Heeringen to Capelle, 10 August 1911, N253/24.

180. Nachlass Michaelis, N 164/4, 31.

181. Ibid. Maltzahn's book on tactics was indispensable in earlier chapters of this book.

182. Ibid., 32.

183. Hopmann, *Logbuch*, 378.

184. Epkenhans, *Hopmann*, 280.

185. On the conversation with Scheer and Hopmann's comments above, see Hopmann Diary, entry of 16 November 1911, in Epkenhans, *Hopmann*, 172–173.

186. Hopmann, *Logbuch*, 385. See also Hopmann Diary, entry of 4 January 1912, in Epkenhans, *Hopmann*, 189–190.

187. Hopmann Diary, entry of 28 June 1912, in ibid., 229.

188. See, e.g., ibid., 22 August 1912, 235.

189. Ibid., 23 August 1912, 235–236.

190. Ibid., 12 September 1912 237–238; and 4 January 1913, 280.

191. Ibid., 21 March 1912, 205.

192. Ibid., 30 June 1913, 332. For rumors of a possible Tirpitz Chancellorship, see N's report of 8 August 1913, N 253/28. Also cited in Epkenhans, *Hopmann*, 332 n. 217.

193. See, e.g., Hubatsch, *Admiralstab*, 150ff.

194. On these deliberations, see Lambi, 310ff.

195. Holtzendorff to Tirpitz, 2 and 11 December 1911; and Müller to Holtzendorff, 18 January 1912, PG 67472.

196. Ibid., Tirpitz to William II, 2 February 1912.

197. Nachlass Müller N 159/4, 114.

198. PG 66709, Tirpitz to William II, 22 March 1912.

199. Holtzendorff botched the fall 1912 maneuvers and was sharply criticized by the Emperor. See Gemzell, 85–86.

200. Leonidas E, Hill, ed., *Die Weizsäcker Papiere 1907–1932*, entry of 15 February 1910, 120. On the scarcity of good senior admirals in 1914, see Wulf Diercks, "Der Einfluss der Personalsteuerung auf die deutsche Seekriegsführung 1914–1918," 1–19 (cited as Diercks). Werner Rahn kindly brought this to my attention. Diercks convincingly advances the idea that the wartime cadre of admirals entered the navy between 1869 and 1882, during the Stosch era, when the navy, then devoid of snob appeal, had a hard time recruiting and keeping capable men.

201. PG 65975 Draft of an Operations Plan for a War against England, 28 November 1912; approved by the Emperor on 3 December.

202. See the notable comments on this point in Diercks, 14.

203. On the token and futile attempts to collaborate with the army to disrupt the anticipated British troop transports to France in the event of war, which were rejected in favor of U-boat interdiction, see Lambi, 392–393.

204. Nachlass Michaelis N 164/4, 35. See also Michaelis's notes on Tirpitz in RM 8/1233, 26ff.

205. N 253/28, 63ff., Notes for Immediatvortrag, 22 February 1913.

206. The following analysis is synthesized from Marder, *Dreadnought*, 1:367–377. On the early history of the shift from the close blockade, see M. S. Partridge, "The Royal Navy and the End of the Close Blockade, 1885–1905: A Revolution in Naval Strategy?" 119–136. A good analysis of the geographic side of the question is in Wolgang Michalka, ed., *Der erste Weltkrieg: Wirkung, Wahrnehmung, Analyse* (cited as Michalka, ed.). See, too, Werner Rahn, "Strategische Probleme der deutsche Seekriegsrüstung 1914–1918," 345–346, 348–365.

207. Nachlass Michaelis, N 164/4, 39.

208. Paul M. Kennedy, "Strategic Aspects of the Anglo-German Naval Race," 149ff.

209. On Büchsel, see Lambi, 221; on Tirpitz's comment, see transcript of the 121st Session of the Budget Commission, 17 March 1909, in RM 3/9757, 97–100.

210. RM 8/1233.

211. For a characterization of Pohl, see Nachlass Michaelis N 164/4, 27. Michaelis believed that Pohl was selected partly because Tirpitz felt he could

easily be removed if a serious situation developed. RM 8/1233, 28.

212. Considered in detail in Lambi, 401ff.

213. RM 3/11679, undated note by Hollweg dating Tirpitz's remark as May 1914.

214. Hopmann Diary, entry of 4 June 1914, in Epkenhans, *Hopmann*, 372. Heeringen left no Nachlass and thereby left many stories untold. He died in 1927. See the touching farewell letter that he wrote to Tirpitz on 28 June 1914, N 253/18.

215. Hopmann Diary, entry of 11 June 1914, in Epkenhans, *Hopmann*, 375. On the conversations that became moot with the outbreak of the war, see Manfred Rauh, "Die englisch-russische Marinekonvention von 1914 und der Ausbruch des Ersten Weltkrieges," 37–62.

216. N 253/29. Mid-May 1914 memo of Tirpitz, and note on an IV memo of Capelle, 17 May 1914. See also Michalka, ed., Michael Epkenhans, "Die kaiserliche Marine im ersten Weltkrieg," 319–346 (cited as Michalka, ed., Epkenhans).

217. Hopmann Diary, entry of 15 June 1914, in Epkenhans, *Hopmann*, 377.

218. See, e.g., Müller, *Der Kaiser*, 139. For a detailed picture of the frivolity of William II during this critical time, see Walter Görlitz, ed., *The Kaiser and His Court: The Diaries, Notebooks, and Letters of Admiral Georg Alexander von Müller, Chief of the Naval Cabinet 1914–1918*, chap. 1 (cited as Müller, 1914–1918).

219. Hopmann Diary, entry of 28 June 1914, in Epkenhans, *Hopmann*, 380.

220. Ibid., 29 June 1914, 382.

221. The most recent extensive examination of the literature on the origins of the war is a review article by

Samuel R. Williamson and Ernest R. May, "An Identity of Opinion: Historians and July 1914," 335–387. No attempt is made in this Tirpitz biography to comprehensively reexamine this whole vast question.

222. The principal primary sources for Tirpitz in July 1914 are Epkenhans, *Hopmann*; Volker Berghahn and Wilhelm Deist, "Kaiserliche Marine und Kriegsausbruch 1914: Neue Dokumente zur Juli-Krise," 37–58 (cited as Berghahn/Deist, "Dokumente"). This article contains the daily reports from Hopmann to Tirpitz and has slightly different versions from contemporaneous material in Hopmann's diary. Tirpitz's own two volumes of documents, *Aufbau* and *Ohnmachtspolitik*, say surprisingly little about the period from July 6 to July 27. The diary of Captain Johann-Bernhard Mann for this period, N 568/1, who worked under Hopmann, seems almost entirely based on Hopmann's work and is of little original value. Material from the latter in the war is of some use.

223. Hopmann to Tirpitz, 6 July 1914, Berghahn/Deist, "Dokumente," 45.

224. Hopmann Diary, entries of 6 and 7 July, in Epkenhans, *Hopmann*, 384–385. Tirpitz, and other leading figures on leave, including Moltke and Pohl, were ordered not to interrupt their leaves.

225. Tirpitz to Hopmann, likely 10 or 11 July 1914, Berghahn/Deist, "Dokumente," 46.

226. Hopmann to Tirpitz, 13 July 1914, ibid., 49ff.

227. Hopmann Diary, entry of 16 July 1914, in Epkenhans, *Hopmann*, 389–390.

228. Hopmann to Tirpitz, 16 July 1914, Berghahn/Deist, "Dokumente," 51–52.

229. Marder, *Dreadnought*, 1:432–433.

230. Berghahn/Deist, "Dokumente," Behncke's memo of conversations with Jagow, 20 July 1914, 53–54; Hopmann Diary, entry of 21 July 1914, in Epkenhans, *Hopmann*, 391–392. See also Lambi, 420ff.

231. Hopmann Diary, entry of 22 July 1914, in Epkenhans, *Hopmann*, 392–393; Hopmann to Tirpitz, entry of 22 July 1914, Berghahn/Deist, "Dokumente," 56–57.

232. Hopmann Diary, entry of 25 and 26 July 1914, in Epkenhans, *Hopmann*, 396ff.; Berghahn/Deist, "Dokumente," 25 July 1914, 58.

233. Tirpitz, *Memoirs*, 1:227.

234. Hopmann Diary, entry of 27 July 1914, in Epkenhans, *Hopmann*, 399f. See also Epkenhans, 405.

235. Epkenhans, 404.

236. Hopmann Diary, entry of 28 July 1914, in Epkenhans, *Hopmann*, 401ff.

237. Epkenhans, 405 n. 41.

238. On this conference of 29 July 1914, see Tirpitz, *Ohnmachtspolitik*, 2ff.

239. Hopmann Diary, entry of 30 July 1914, in Epkenhans, *Hopmann*, 405ff. On the thorny question of Tirpitz's wartime portfolio, see chapter 15, this volume. On Tirpitz's remark to Ingenohl in May 1914, see Hollweg's note in RM 3/11679.

240. Tirpitz, *Memoirs*, 2:119.

241. Ibid., 118–119.

242. Müller, *1914–1918*, 15–16.

243. Tirpitz, *Ohnmachtspolitik*, 11–12.

244. Ibid. See also Tirpitz, *Memoirs*, 1:361–362.

245. Notes Tirpitz dictated about the meeting on 1 and 2 August, N253/104; printed, in part, in Tirpitz, *Ohnmachtspolitik*, 20ff. The last, astonishing, sentence from this dictation is omitted

from the printed version: "[Moltke] told me, in greatest secrecy, that he had prepared for signing an agreement draft with the Swiss military commander Spraher von Bruegg but had not dared to take this matter up with the diplomats."

246. Here is not the place for an extended critique of the Schlieffen Plan. Just as the Imperial Navy formed wildly optimistic offensive plans for most of its history, so, too, did Germany, France, and Russia for their army plans. On this discussion, see, e.g., Jack Snyder, *The Ideology of the Offensive: Military Decision Making and the Disaster of 1914*; and Stephen Miller, Stephen van Evera, and Sean M. Lynn-Jones, eds., *Military Strategy and the Origins of the First World War*.

15. TIRPITZ AT WAR, AUGUST 1914–MARCH 1916

1. For a summary of ship specs, see Marder, *Dreadnought*, 1:appendix, 439ff.: and Paul G. Halpern, *A Naval History of the First World War*, 7ff. (cited as Halpern).

2. Halpern, 79–80.

3. Müller, *1914–1918*, 15; Gemzell, 198.

4. Nachlass Michaelis N 164/1, 2.

5. Nachlass Delbrück, N 17, 55, Müller to Parliamentary Investigating Subcommittee, 27 March 1926.

6. Ingenohl had served only briefly in the Torpedo Arm, but was in the OK for two years under Tirpitz.

7. Müller, *1914–1918*, 18.

8. The text is in *Der Krieg in der Nordsee*, 1:54; Gerhard Granier, ed., *Die deutsche Seekriegsleitung im Ersten Weltkrieg-Dokumentation*, 1:67–68 (cited as Granier, *Dokumentation*); Tirpitz, *Ohnmachtspolitik*, 35–36.

9. Hubatsch, *Admiralstab*, 164.

10. On the correspondence of 6 and 7 August, see Tirpitz, *Ohnmacht-spolitik*, 41ff.; and Müller, *1914–1918*, 17.

11. Hubatsch, *Admiralstab*, 165.

12. For the battle, see Eric W. Osborne, *The Battle of Helgoland Bight*. Wolfgang was rescued, and, in a chivalrous gesture, after a few anxious days for the family, Churchill telegraphed Tirpitz the good news via the U.S. Embassy (see chaper 6, this volume).

13. See Pohl's memo of 29 August 1914 in Admiral Hugo von Pohl, *Aus Aufzeichnungen und Briefen während der Kriegszeit*, 24 (cited as Pohl); published posthumously by his wife.

14. Herwig, 149.

15. See Tirpitz's memo of 15 August 1914. Tirpitz, *Ohnmachtspolitik*, 53ff.

16. See Granier, *Documentation*, 19 and n. 49; Hopmann, *Kriegstagebuch*, 94ff.; Pohl, note of 18 September 1914, 67

17. Lyckner's diary, 19 August 1914. Published in Holger Afflerbach, ed., *Kaiser Wilhelm als Oberster Kriegsherr im Ersten Weltkrieg: Quellen aus der militärischen Umgebung des Kaisers 1914–1918*, 137 (cited as Afflerbach, *Kaiser Wilhelm*). Afflerbach provides a nuanced argument that William II, overwhelmed by his responsibilities, did not function effectively as Supreme Commander except, to some degree, in personnel matters. With the exception of decisions on the U-boat war, in which Afflerbach concedes that William II played a major role (see 23ff.), he ignores the navy almost entirely. Clearly the Emperor played a major role for most of the war in virtually all important decisions that affected the navy. For a good summary, see Afflerbach, "Wilhelm II as Supreme Warlord in the First World War," 195–216.

18. RM 8/1233, 31f. See also Kurt Assmann, *Deutsche Seestrategie in zwei Weltkriegen*, 57 n. 22.

19. Hubatsch, *Admiralstab*, 165.

20. Memo of conversations with the Chancellor, 27 and 28 August 1914, Tirpitz, *Ohnmachtspolitik*, 63. For more on this theater, see Mark D. Kalau, *"Wielding the Dagger": The MarineKorps Flandern and the German War Effort, 1914–1918*.

21. Charles B. Burdick, *The Japanese Siege of Tsingtau*.

22. Tirpitz to Lans, 31 August 1914, Tirpitz, *Ohnmachtspolitik*. 81ff. The omitted part was originally discovered by Gemzell, 193 n. 84, in the Levetzow Nachlass. See N 253/354 for the complete version.

23. Salewski, 97. For notes on this letter, see RM 3/11679, 16 September 1914.

24. Nachlass Eisendecher, T 291, reel 10, Tirpitz to Eisendecher, 20 December 1914.

25. On this important event, see Halperin, 57ff.

26. Tirpitz claimed, in a postwar letter to Souchon, that the breakout to Constantinople was his idea alone and that he had greatly pressured Pohl, who weakly acquiesced. Nachlass Souchon, N 156/2, 32, Tirpitz to Souchon, 15 June 1921.

27. Nachlass Souchon, N 156/2, 1. Tirpitz to Souchon, 14 August 1914.

28. *Der Krieg in der Nordsee*, 2:48ff.

29. Halpern, 36–37.

30. The following section is from ibid., 38ff.; Herwig, 149ff.; and *Der Krieg in der Nordsee*, vols. 1–3.

31. Herwig, 149–150; Halpern, 40–41; for a fuller account of the raid, see Tobias R. Philbin, *Admiral von Hipper: The Inconvenient Hero*, 88ff.

32. Analyzed in Philbin, 92ff.; quote at 93.

33. On the Scarborough raid and its aftermath, see Philbin, 97ff.; and Marder, *Dreadnought*, 2:134ff. For an analysis of Ingenohl as Fleet Chief and Pohl as both Chief of the Admiralstab and Fleet Chief, see Diercks, 13–19.

34. Philbin, 103ff.

35. Marder, *Dreadnought*, 2:46.

36. For the mood at GHQ, see Müller, *1914–1918*, 29–30.

37. For the day-to-day activities in GHQ in 1914, see RM 3/ 2620.

38. For one of many possible examples, see Hopmann Diary, Hopmann to Capelle, 3 October 1914, in Epkenhans, *Hopmann*, 457ff.; and Hopmann to Trotha Papers, 135, 3. Tirpitz feared, among other things, a separate peace with Britain at the expense of Germany's world position.

39. Tirpitz, *Ohnmachtspolitik*, 152.

40. Ibid., 153; see also Hopmann Diary, entry of 8 November 1914, Epkenhans, *Hopmann*, 489–490.

41. Müller, *1914–1918*, 43.

42. Hopmann Diary, entry of 7 November 1914, in Epkenhans, *Hopmann*, 486ff.

43. Plessen diary note, 11 November 1914, Afflerbach, *Kaiser Wilhelm*, 693.

44. See Nachlass Levetzow, N 239/44, 139ff., for Lt. Col. Niemann's comments in 1927; Tirpitz to Plessen, 15 March 1927, NSSA Tr Dep 18 A 362/72.

45. Müller, *1914–1918*, 93–94. Letter to Trotha of 19 July 1915.

46. Nachlass Levetzow N 239/44, 52–68. Notes dated 1 December 1926 of an interview of William II by Lt. Col. Niemann, 66.

47. Michaelis' notes on Tirpitz, RM 8/1233, 34.

48. N 253/197, 80f, Tirpitz to Ahlefeld, 13 November 1914.

49. See RM 3/2620 (RMA diary entry of 15 November 1914), appendix 37; and Tirpitz, *Ohnmachtspolitik*, 166ff.

50. Tirpitz, *Memoirs*, 2:282f.

51. Müller, *1914–1918*, 61.

52. Bachmann Diary, 2 February 1915. Cited in Tirpitz, *Memoirs*, 2:120ff.

53. Ibid., 58ff.; Tirpitz, *Ohnmachtspolitik*, 198ff.

54. Philbin, 92ff.

55. Tirpitz, *Ohnmachtspolitik*, 306ff.

56. Avner Offer, *The First World War: An Agrarian Interpretation*, 127–128 (cited as Offer). On the entire question, see John W. Coogan, *The End of Neutrality: The United States, Britain, and Maritime Rights, 1899–1915* (cited as Coogan).

57. Hobson, 72–73.

58. Offer, 226–227, 230–231.

59. For an exhaustive review of both Hague Conferences, see Jost Dülffer, *Regeln gegen den Krieg: Die Haager Friedenskonferenzen von 1899 und 1907 in der internationalen Politik*.

60. See Hobson, 73–74; Coogan, chaps. 4–7; and Strachan, 410–411.

61. Strachan, 401.

62. See Hobson, 121ff.

63. The following discussion is based mainly on Offer, chap. 23.

64. Ibid., 348.

65. See his memos on this point to Bülow, 20 and 29 April 1907, in GP XXIII, pt. 2, 359ff.

66. See chapter 12, this volume.

67. Offer, 344–345. For a more extended treatment, see Burchardt, passim.

68. Hobson, 64–65.

69. The following is based mainly on Coogan, chaps. 8–10.

70. Ibid., 193.

71. For a good summary of the whole problem, see Lance E. Davis and Stanley L. Engerman, *Naval Blockades in Peace and War: An Economic History since 1750*, esp. chap. 5; for a statistical

overview of the decline in German imports, see Table 5.2, 166ff.

72. For a summary, see Herwig, 162.

73. Ibid., 163–164.

74. Tirpitz, *Ohnmachtspolitik*, 48.

75. Pohl to Bethmann, 7 November 1914, Tirpitz, *Ohnmachtspolitik*, 283ff.

76. Ibid., 285–286. Tirpitz, *Memoirs*, 2:139–140.

77. Ibid., 140ff.

78. NL 97 Erzberger 44, Tirpitz to Erzberger, 15 November 1914.

79. Raffael Scheck, *Alfred von Tirpitz and German Right-Wing Politics, 1914–1930*, 26 (cited as Scheck).

80. Tirpitz, *Ohnmachtspolitik*, 623ff.

81. Gemzell, 186. See also Pohl to his wife, 22 and 23 December 1914, in Pohl, 93–94.

82. Report of Mann, 3 January 1915, in Tirpitz, *Ohnmachtspolitik*, 295.

83. Tirpitz, *Memoirs*, 2:144ff.

84. Scheck, 27; see also Arno Spindler, ed., *Der Handelskrieg mit U-Booten*, 1:37–38, 62. No neutrals were to be sunk, but the British soon began more extensive use of neutral flags. Tirpitz, *Memoirs*, 2:151.

85. See, e.g., Tirpitz, *Ohnmachtspolitik*, 309ff., 322ff.; Hopmann Diary, entries of 15 February and 3 March 1915, in Epkenhans, *Hopmann*, 566, 571.

86. Ibid., 22 March 1915, 582.

87. Tirpitz to Marie, 27 March 1915, in Tirpitz, *Memoirs*, 2:321–322.

88. Hopmann Diary, entry of 30 March 1915, in Epkenhans, *Hopmann*, 589.

89. Ibid., 582 n. 159.

90. Ibid., 16 April 1915, 598.

91. Michaelis's notes, RM 8/1233, 38–39.

92. Wegener, xxii–xxiii.

93. The text of this memorandum is in Wegener, Appendix A. See also Jost Dülffer, *Weimar, Hitler, und die*

Marine, 185–189 (cited as Dülffer, *Hitler*).

94. Wegener, Appendix B.

95. On this point see also Gemzell, 215ff.; and Hobson, 293ff.

96. Tirpitz, *Ohnmachtspolitik*, 208; for Hopmann and Boedicker's responses, see 213ff.

97. Coogan, 222–223.

98. Ibid., 225–226.

99. Summarized in Scheck, 26ff.

100. Müller, *1914–1918*, 83–84.

101. Scheck, 40–41.

102. Tirpitz, *Ohnmachtspolitik*, 400–401.

103. Ibid., 399ff.; Scheck, 28.

104. Tirpitz to Trotha, 24 July 1915, N 253/169; cited in Tirpitz, *Ohnmachtspolitik*, 257.

105. Tirpitz, *Ohnmachtspolitik*, 409–410.

106. RM 3/47 contains press clippings from the incident. The "Pirate" reference is on 267.

107. Tirpitz, *Ohnmachtspolitik*, 430–431; Scheck, 28.

108. For examples of this change, see the RMA's GHQ War Diary entries for 14 September 1914 and 23 January 1915.

109. See relevant ship articles in Hildebrand.

110. RM 3/11961, 19 October 1915. Printed in Granier, *Dokumentation*, 1:402ff. An overall view of the army's and navy's war aims is in Holger Herwig, "Admirals vs. Generals: The War Aims of the Imperial German Navy, 1914–1918," 208–233 (cited as Herwig, "War Aims").

111. See Pohl's letter to his wife, 20 August 1914, in Pohl, 21.

112. Tirpitz to Bethmann, 19 January 1915, in Granier, *Dokumentation*, 1:405–406.

113. Memo, Tirpitz to Bethmann, 17 October 1915, N 253/231, 2–20. Also

printed in Granier, *Dokumentation*, 1:409ff.

114. Dähnhardt to Tirpitz, 26 January 1915, RM 3/11624, 87–148. The document is a handwritten draft with corrections. Presumably a printed version went to Tirpitz. It is partly analyzed in Michalka, ed.; and Epkenhans, 330ff.

115. Granier, *Dokumentation*, 1:425ff.

116. Quoted in Herwig, 165.

117. Hubatsch, *Admiralstab*, 170.

118. Nachlass Keyserlingk, N 161/9, 11–19. Notes on Holtzendorff. Written in April 1937.

119. Hopmann to his wife, 5 September 1915, in Epkenhans, *Hopmann*, 690–691.

120. Diary entries of 5–13 September 1915, N 159/5, published with a few elisions in Müller, *1914–1918*, 104ff. See also NL 97/44 Nachlass Erzberger, notes on Tirpitz and the Chancellor, 1915; and Tirpitz to Trotha, mid-September 1915, N253/169, 39–40; and Tirpitz, *Ohnmachtspolitik*, 437ff.

121. Tirpitz to Trotha, September 1915, N 253/169, 30ff.

122. Granier, ed., *Dokumentation*, 1:76 n. 13. Capelle wrote the following to Trotha on 26 November 1915, Trotha Papers, A 48 1:

The fact that I had to leave in the middle of a war presses on me, but it is the right thing to do. My health was and is so bad that I am not up to the demands of office, and I was at the breaking point. It was very hard to leave with the State Secretary hard-pressed and abandoned on all sides. I am afraid that he thinks me ungrateful, but nowhere was I more straightforward to him than at the moment when I asked to leave. I cannot fail to say that in great fundamental questions certain differences have arisen between us; for I told him I had the idea that I even had the ambition to become State Secretary myself. He is not right about it, but such thoughts are in-eradicable [*unausrottbar*] to Tirpitz. The result was that our confidential relationship suffered very much and cast a shadow despite our mutual cooperation in our work.

This hostility would arise again when Capelle later replaced Tirpitz.

123. Büchsel was chafing in retire-ment. Büchsel to Tirpitz, 19 March 1915, N 253/200.

124. Capelle to Müller, October 1915, Nachlass Capelle, N 170/2, 1ff.

125. Keyserlingk on Holtzendorff, Nachlass Keyserlingk, N 161/9.

126. Trotha Papers, A 8 4, Bach-mann to Trotha, 26 September 1915.

127. Granier, *Dokumentation*, 1:409ff.

128. 14 November 1915, Trotha Pa-pers, N 20 bd 3, 223.

129. Büchsel's notes, late 1915, Nach-lass Büchsel, N 168/8, 163.

130. See Heinz Hagenlücke, *Deutsche Vaterlandspartei: Die natio-nale Rechte am Ende des Kaiserreiches*, chaps. 1 and 2.

131. See Bruno Thoß, "Nationale Rechte, militärische Führung und Dik-taturfrage in Deutschland von 1913–1923," 27–76. See also Scheck, 39ff.

132. These convoluted intrigues are well presented in Scheck, 36ff. See also Müller, *1914–1918*, 72–73, entry of 18 April 1915.

133. Empress to Tirpitz, 31 August 1915; Tirpitz, *Ohnmachtspolitik*, 416.

134. Scheck, 41.

135. This remarkable document of 7 September 1915 is printed in Tirpitz, *Ohnmachtspolitik*, 420.

136. See Gemzell, 211–212.

137. Müller, *1914–1918*, 121.

138. Ibid., 124–125, entries of 30 January 1915 and 6 January 1916.

139. Tirpitz, *Ohnmachtspolitik*, 450ff.

140. For Holtzendorff's view, see his memo of 13 January 1916, RM 5/902; and his memo to Bethmann of 21 Janu-ary, ibid.

141. Nachlass Erzberger NL 97/44, notes by Erzberger dated 20 March 1916.

142. Herwig, 165.

143. On the Emperor's decision about the restrictions, see Tirpitz, *Ohn-machtspolitik*, 450–485.

144. Herwig, 165.

145. Original in Trotha Papers, 362/12. Also in N 253/169, 41. Published in Tirpitz, *Ohnmachtspolitik* (with the last sentence omitted).

146. See, e.g., Müller, *1914–1918*, en-try of 9 February 1916, 155; and Scheck, 30.

147. Tirpitz, *Ohnmachtspolitik*, 494ff, 634ff.

148. On this meeting, see Müller, *1914–1918*, diary entry, 141ff.

149. Nachlass Michaelis N 164/5, 20, Michaelis had lost his post as Pohl's Chief of Staff when Scheer took over the fleet.

16. UNCOMMON RECESSIONAL, 1916–1930

1. N 253/405, Capelle to Tirpitz, 30 March 1916. The pension was sched-uled to rise to 24,524 marks in 1920, and, from 1 July 1921 to 36,261 marks.

2. Private communication from Agostino von Hassell.

3. Gregor Schöllgen, *Ulrich von Hassell: Ein Konservativer in der Oppo-sition*, 26–27.

4. Scheck, 48.

5. N 253/72, 73. Tirpitz printed some of these letters in *Ohnmachtspolitik*, 511ff.

6. Scheck, 31.

7. Nachlass Michaelis, N 164/5, 20.

8. The letter is in N 253/64; and Trotha Papers, A 362/15. Printed with only minor changes in *Ohnmachtspolitik*, 524–525. Capelle's speech is summarized in ibid., 525–526.

9. Tirpitz to William II, 27 April, and reply, 28 April 1916, N 253/192. Printed in *Ohnmachtspolitik*, 531ff.

10. Nachlass Eisendecher T 291 Reel 10, Tirpitz to Eisendecher, 11 July 1916.

11. See Nachlass Kapp (Merseburg), Hassell to Kapp, 17 April 1916, 714; and Scheck, 49.

12. On the pre-Jutland/Skagerrak sparring, see Herwig, 173ff.

13. On Jutland, see Marder, *Dreadnought* 3; N. J. M. Campbell, *Jutland: An Analysis of the Fighting*; Herwig, chap. 9; *Krieg in der Nordsee*, 5:444ff. For an excellent short summary, see Halperin, 310–329. For Tirpitz's take on the battle, see *Ohnmachtspolitik*, 549ff.; and his letter to Trotha, 24 June 1916, N253/178, 43ff.

14. Quoted in Herwig, 183.

15. Marder, *Dreadnought*, 3:128 n. 50.

16. Quoted in Halpern, 328–329.

17. Tirpitz, *Ohnmachtspolitik*, 550ff. See also his letter to Trotha, 24 June 1916, N 253/169, 49ff.

18. See, esp., N 253/220, Tirpitz to Dähnhardt, 10 October 1916.

19. Tirpitz, *Ohnmachtspolitik*, 551. William II to Tirpitz, 5 June 1916, RM 2/1191. The exchange is printed in Tirpitz, *Ohnmachtspolitik*, 552.

20. RM 2/1991, William II to Tirpitz, 5 June 1916. The exchange is printed in Tirpitz, *Ohnmachtspolitik*, 552.

21. Tirpitz to Trotha, 24 June 1916, N 253/178, 43ff.

22. Tirpitz to Trotha, 22 July 1916, N 253/169, 60ff. The published version, without the quote, is in Tirpitz, *Ohnmachtspolitik*, 567ff.

23. Tirpitz to Hindenburg, 16 July 1916, in Tirpitz, *Ohnmachtspolitik*, 562ff.

24. Scheck, 49ff.

25. Trotha Papers, A 120, 2, Hassell to Tirpitz, 13 September 1916; and ibid., A 120 3, 2 October 1916.

26. See Tirpitz's notes on these September 1916 meetings in N253/203.

27. Trotha Papers, A 362/24, Tirpitz to Trotha, sometime between 10 and 18 September 1916.

28. See, e.g., N 253/169, 91ff. Tirpitz to Trotha, 16 October 1916. Printed in Tirpitz, *Ohnmachtspolitik* (with significant elisions). 577–581.

29. Scheck, 56–57.

30. For Tirpitz's intervention with Hindenburg, see N 253/176, Tirpitz to Hindenburg, 14 January 1917. Although he warned Hindenburg that success would take time, and lamented that the most opportune time would have been the previous spring, he felt there was still time to prevail. The next day he summarized the letter for Trotha. The letter is in N 253/169, and is printed, in part, with significant elisions, in Tirpitz, *Ohnmachtspolitik*, 580.

31. For a clear summary of the U-boat decision and its consequences, see Herwig, 197–198. Herwig also provides an excellent analysis of Holtzendorff's assumptions and misjudgments in his "Total Rhetoric, Limited War: Germany's U-Boat Campaign, 1917–1918." See also Matthew Stibbe, "Germany's 'Last Card': Wilhelm II and the Decision in Favor of Unrestricted Submarine Warfare in January 1917," 217–234.

32. Nachlass Mann, N 586/6, Tirpitz to Mann, 31 January 1917.

33. On the convoluted intrigues that led to this attempt, see Scheck, 54ff.

34. See Ludendorff's postwar account of this meeting to Tirpitz's son. N 253/175, Ludendorff to Wolfgang von Tirpitz, 8 February 1921.

35. For research on World War I U-boats, a guide to the microfilmed records is published by the U.S. National Archives, *National Archives Guide to Microfilmed Records, U-Boats and T-Boats, 1914–1918.*

36. On the U-boat war in this period, see Halpern, chap. 11; and Herwig, 226–227.

37. See N 253/199, 11ff.; Ballin to Tirpitz, 19 July 1917. Partially printed in Tirpitz, *Ohnmachtspolitik*, 604ff. Ballin clearly understood both the economic power of the United States and the great effectiveness of convoy in the deterrence of U-boat attacks.

38. The most comprehensive work on the Fatherland Party is Hagenlücke. He, in contrast to previous historians, does not see the Fatherland Party as a fascist forerunner but as a last gasp of Wilhelmian *Sammlungspolitik,* with an unprecedented twist: it was *against* the state. The historiography on this question is summarized in Hagenlücke, introduction and chap. 1. See also Scheck, 65ff. On this point both Scheck's work and this volume on Tirpitz are in general agreement with Hagenlücke.

39. See his letters to Basserman (National Liberal) and Peter Spahn (Center) on 1 July 1917, Tirpitz, *Ohnmachtspolitik*, 604.

40. Events of the summer of 1917 are summarized in Scheck, 65ff.

41. For Tirpitz's take on the dismissal, see N 253/169, 141ff.; Tirpitz to Trotha, 2 August 1917. Partly published in Tirpitz, *Ohnmachtspolitik*, 609ff.

42. Hagenlücke, 100–101.

43. Ibid., 154.

44. See Nachlass Kapp, 557, Kapp to Hassell, 19 August 1917. Scheck 66–67. There is a copy of the party's constitution in N 253/106.

45. Trotha Papers, N 20, 4, 299, Trotha to his wife, 9 September 1917.

46. Scheck, 68.

47. Text in N253/216.

48. Generously made available to the author by Raffael Scheck.

49. Drafts of some speeches are in N 253/216.

50. See, e.g., an article on the U-boat war by Prof. Georg von Below in the right-wing periodical *Grössere Deutschland* of 9 March 1918, in N 253/106.

51. On finances, see Hagenlücke, 188ff.

52. See Scheck, 69ff.

53. Ibid., 73.

54. Hassell, *Der Kreis*, 199.

55. Lothar Persius, *Die Tirpitz-legende.* On the navy's efforts to stifle the pamphlet in May 1918, see RM 3/9754, 46ff., 77f. For other examples of press sniping early in 1918, see N 253/123.

56. On these first major fleet disruptions, see Herwig, 230ff.

57. See Epkenhans, *Hopmann,* 1028ff.; Hopmann to Tirpitz, 4 October 1917. Also see his letter to his wife of 27 September 1917, 1023ff. The letter to Tirpitz is also in N 253/172.

58. Trotha Papers, A/362, 37, Tirpitz to Scheer, 4 September 1918.

59. Summarized in Herwig, 245ff.

60. The speech is in N 253/215.

61. Accounts of these conversations are in N 253/203. See also Scheck, 74–75.

62. N 253/169, 171–172., Trotha to Tirpitz, 27 October 1918.

63. Quoted in Scheck, 76.

64. On the "death ride," see Philbin, 154ff.

65. On the mutinies, see Daniel Horn, *The German Naval Mutinies of World War I.*

66. Wilhelm Deist, "Die Politik der Seekriegsleitung und die Rebellion der Flotte Ende Oktober 1918," 362–363.

67. The scene is memorably described in Herwig, 254–255.

68. See Scheck, 76–77. One of the great contributions of Scheck's work is that he deciphered hundreds of arcane letters in the Tirpitz Nachlass that pertain to the period from 1918 to 1928. Since Tirpitz was afraid that his correspondence might be intercepted by the Prussian police, many of the letters contain veiled references to individuals involved in some of his intrigues during that time.

69. See N 253/100.

70. On the publishing history of Tirpitz's memoirs, and the consequent polemics, see the essay by Epkenhans, "Clio," 466–485, esp. 473ff. On the wider question of Germany's systematic postwar manipulation of the history of World War I, see the seminal essay by Holger Herwig, "Clio Deceived."

71. N 253/342. Trotha's "Ideas about the Collapse of the Navy," 10 January 1919.

72. Trotha Papers, A 362/41, Tirpitz to Trotha, 16 February 1919.

73. N 253/64, 113ff. Trotha to Tirpitz, part dated 13 March 1919. On 26 March 1919 Trotha was appointed Admiralty Chief of the greatly reduced navy.

74. Ibid., 117ff.; Tirpitz to Trotha, 20 March 1919.

75. On their reception, see Herwig, 257.

76. Nachlass Mann, N 568/6, Tirpitz to Mann, 27 June 1916.

77. Trotha Papers, A 362/46, Tirpitz to Trotha, 29 September 1919. Tirpitz was then at St. Blasien.

78. Ibid.

79. Scheck, 85.

80. Trotha Papers, A 304/20, Scheer to Trotha, 3 October 1919. See also Epkenhans, "Clio," 474.

81. N 253/194, Prinz Heinrich to Tirpitz, 29 October 1919. Also in N 253/183.

82. Trotha Papers, A 362/54, Tirpitz to Prinz Heinrich, drafted November 1919, sent before 6 January 1920.

83. Ibid., A 362/49, Tirpitz to Trotha, 17 November 1919.

84. See Pohl, passim; and Trotha Papers, A 365/55, Tirpitz to Trotha, 6 January 1920.

85. N 253/177, Tirpitz to Chamberlain, 9 January 1920.

86. Well summarized in Epkenhans, "Clio," 476ff. See also Keith Bird, *Raeder: Admiral of the Third Reich*, 49ff. (cited as Bird, *Raeder*). See also N 253/257 for some of the Mantey/Tirpitz correspondence.

87. See Bird, *Raeder*, 52–53.

88. Epkenhans, "Clio," 479–480.

89. Trotha Papers, A 362/56, Tirpitz to Trotha, 14 January 1920.

90. Scheck, 56. On the effect of the putsch on the navy, see Keith Bird, *Weimar, the German Naval Officer Corps, and the Rise of National Socialism*, chaps. 3, 4. See also Werner Rahn, *Reichsmarine und Landesverteidigung, 1919–1928*, chap. 3.

91. For the navy's files on the case, see RM 20/860, 861.

92. Tirpitz's views in 1921–23 are aptly summarized in Scheck, 87ff.

93. N 253/251, Hess to Tirpitz, 12 September 1921.

94. See, e.g., Trotha Papers, A 362/56, Tirpitz (St. Blasien) to Trotha, 13 January 1921.

95. N 253/175, Tirpitz to Ludendorff, 2 December 1922.

96. On his finances at the time, see Scheck, 86.

97. N 568/6, Tirpitz to Mann, 11 July 1922. The comment is in Tirpitz's handwritten version only. Perhaps he did not want his daughter Margot, his secretary, to see it.

98. N 253/309, 20, Tirpitz to Vollerthun, 13 January 1922.

99. Ibid., Tirpitz to Mann, 5 and 30 October 1922.

100. N 253/175, Tirpitz to Ludendorff, 2 December 1922.

101. Conan Fischer, *The Ruhr Crisis, 1923–1924*.

102. The following summarizes the research, much of it new, in Scheck, chap. 7.

103. Hassell family source, quoted by Scheck, 103.

104. N 253/192, Tirpitz to Hugenberg, 14, and reply 22 September 1923.

105. Trotha Papers, A 362/63, Tirpitz (St. Blasien) to Trotha, 21 September 1923.

106. N 253/309, 48ff., Vollerthun to Tirpitz, 1 and 7 September 1923.

107. N 253/309, 53–54. Vollerthun to Tirpitz, 20 November 1923.

108. N253/64, Tirpitz to Trotha, 26 February 1924.

109. Much of Tirpitz's correspondence during this period is in N 253/64, 309. See also Scheck, chap. 8.

110. See Tirpitz's notes on this meeting in N 253/242.

111. N 253/60, Tirpitz to Hergt, 11 April 1924.

112. Scheck, 148.

113. On the election, see ibid., 147ff.

114. For Tirpitz's election result, see N 253/60, 212, 13 May 1924. The DNVP was very glad, almost obsequiously so, to have Tirpitz run. See N 253/60, 363, 14 April 1924.

115. On the controversy over Tirpitz as Chancellor, See Scheck, 153ff.

116. See, e.g., N 253/242, Tirpitz to Arnim, 24 July 1924.

117. Scheck, 168. Comments below are partly based on Scheck, chap. 10.

118. For some of this correspondence, see N 253/60, 278.

119. For a detailed view of Tirpitz's feelings about the parliamentary negotiations that he contended were conducted in bad faith by the middle parties and Ebert, see his memo to Hergt, 24 August 1924, N 253/60, 197–200.

120. N 253/296, 31ff., Tirpitz to Carl von Hassell (Ulrich's East Prussian Cousin), 27 October 1924.

121. Scheck, 182.

122. Ibid., 182ff.

123. See Nachlass Thimme, NL 58, 32, 41, for some of Thimme's criticisms. See also Herwig, "Clio Deceived." On the 1925 controversy over this in the Reichstag, see N 253/61.

124. See his speech at Bad Homburg, 12 November 1924, N 253/214, 8ff.

125. A good example is in RM 3/11679, an anonymous article in "Roland," 25 December 1924.

126. See Scheck, 186.

127. For his speeches, see N 253/214, 216, 240. For the campaign, see Scheck, 192–193.

128. N 253/309, 97, Tirpitz to Vollerthun, 3 November 1924.

129. N 253/60, 146–147. DNVP party assignments, 6 February 1925.

130. Quoted in Scheck, 194.

131. On the presidential election, see ibid., 195ff.

132. N 253/309, 109, Tirpitz to Vollerthun, 1 May 1925.

133. Scheck, 200–201.

134. See N 253/309, 115–116, Tirpitz to Vollerthun, 21 September 1925.

135. N 253/211, 30ff., Tirpitz Memo to Hindenburg, 5 November 1925.

136. The text is in N 253/61, 159–160, 23 March 1925, Tirpitz's drafts are in N 253/145.

137. See N 253/188, Tirpitz to the Duke of Oldenburg, 27 March 1926; Scheck, 205.

138. See his speech in Stuttgart, 22 October 1926, N 253/238. Draft in N 253/214, 124ff.

139. On Tirpitz's last year in the Reichstag, see Scheck, 205ff.

140. Personal communication from Wolfgang-Ulrich von Hassell.

141. N 253/60, 10, Tirpitz to Hans Hilpert, 6 February 1928.

142. Dülffer, *Hitler*, 45.

143. Trotha Papers, A 192, 26, Trotha to Levetzow, 9 October 1928.

144. Ibid., Trotha to Levetzow, 10 October 1928.

145. Ibid., Trotha to Levetzow, 31 October 1928.

146. N 263/408, 159, Tirpitz to Trotha, 5 November 1928.

147. See Nachlass Levetzow N 239/50, 8ff.; and Trotha Papers, A 362, letters of December 1928 and January 1929.

148. N 239/50, 44 Sell (Doorn) to Levetzow, 28 January 1929.

149. Scheck, 208.

150. Personal comment from Wolfgang-Ulrich von Hassell, who was at the funeral.

151. Program is in N 253/67, 13 March 1930.

152. See Dülffer, *Hitler*, 540.

17. CONCLUSION

1. A notable exception to this inattention is Eric C. Rust's *Naval Officers under Hitler: The Story of Crew* 34, a pioneering longitudinal study.

2. Marder, *Dreadnought*, 3:209ff.

3. Dienstschrift IX, 3.

4. RM 3/9757, 97–100, Tirpitz's statement in the Budget Commission, 17 March 1909.

5. RM 3/11679, undated note by Hollweg.

6. Epkenhans, *Hopmann*, 172–173, 16 November 1911.

7. See Hobson, 326ff.

8. Röhl, *William II*, 3:265–266.

9. See Tirpitz to Richthofen, 1 November 1904, N 253/21. Printed in Tirpitz, *Memoirs*, 1:219ff.

10. Berghahn, 531–556, presents his main argument on this point.

11. Ibid., 538.

12. Ibid., 532–533.

13. Nachlass Michaelis, N 164/2, 11–17.

14. Deist, 330.

15. RM 8/1233, 20.

16. RM 3/11690, 44–45.

17. For Allison's short version, see his chap. 1.

18. N 253/320, 8–11, Stosch to Tirpitz, 6 June 1892.

19. Nachlass Senden N 160/5, 1–4, Tirpitz to Senden, 30 December 1892.

20. Hassell, 171–172.

21. Well summarized in Epkenhans, 414–417.

22. See Gemzell, esp. chaps. 1–2. Another interesting example of type 2 behavior is documented by Perry McCoy Smith, *The Air Force Plans for Peace*, *1943–1945*. Smith examines the struggle that the U.S. Army Air Force waged to secure its independence from the U.S. Army. Its main argument was the need to retain a strong postwar strategic bombing force. To justify that idea, the Soviet Union had to be posited as a future enemy, even as early as 1943.

23. Lieber's notes on a conversation with Hohenlohe, 27 October 1897, Lieber Papers (Wroclaw). John Zeender kindly made this available to me.

24. See Michaelis's account, RM 3 1233, 21.

25. Discussed in Hobson, chaps. 3–5.

26. Nachlass Michaelis, N 164/4, 35; and Michaelis's notes, RM 8/1233, 26ff.

27. For an insightful discussion of the phenomenon these men represented, see Eugene Lewis, *Public Entrepreneurship: Toward a Theory of Political Power; The Organizational Lives of Hyman Rickover, J. Edgar Hoover, and Robert Moses.*

28. Tirpitz, *Aufbau,* 184–185.

29. A good summary of these controversies is in Epkenhans, "Clio."

30. See Rosinski's critique of Tirpitz and Wegener in Simpson, ed., *Rosinski,* esp. 78–87.

31. Most especially Gerhard Schrieber, "Thesen zur ideologischen Kontinuität in den machtpolitischen Zielsetzungen der Deutschen Marineführung 1897 bis 1945," in Manfred Messerschmidt et al., eds., *Marinegeschichte: Probleme—Thesen—Wege,* 260–280.

BIBLIOGRAPHY

The starting point for serious research on German naval history is Keith Bird's massive bibliographic essay on the subject (see listing below). Published in 1985, it is an indispensable guide to both printed and archival material. The largest holding by far on the Tirpitz era in the Imperial German Navy is at the Bundesarchiv-Militärarchive in Freiburg im Breisgau. Much of the official naval archive was microfilmed after World War II and is available at the U.S. National Archives. Each file of the filmed materials was given an accession number, preceded by the initials PG, which legend has it means "pinched from the Germans." Of the multiple classification systems for these documents, the PG number is the one universally cross-referenced among the many naval finding aids. The PG number is used for citation in this work wherever possible. The vast numbers of official documents from the Marinearchiv that are not available at the U.S. National Archives are cited in the most recent classification system used by the Bundesarchiv. The letters RM precede an archival number that indicates the specific naval branch where the document originated, although duplicates are present in recipients' files as well.

In addition to the official documents, the Bundesarchiv-Militärarchiv Freiburg has a large collection of private papers (Nachlässe), acquired by various means over the years. The single most important of these for this work is the huge Tirpitz Nachlass (N 253), purchased from the Tirpitz family in the late 1960s.

German Foreign Office documents for the period are available in original form at the Foreign Office Archive in Bonn, but they are also available on microfiche at the U.S. National Archives.

The thousands of files for this work, among the official naval and diplomatic documents, are too many to list individually. Nachlässe and other collections the author perused are listed individually below.

ARCHIVAL MATERIALS

Bundsarchiv-Militärarchiv Freiburg

Marinearchiv
RM 2 Naval Cabinet (MK)
RM 3 Imperial Naval Office (RMA)
RM 4 Naval High Command (OK)
RM 5 Admiralty Staff
RM 8 Naval Department of War Study
RM 31 Baltic Naval Station

RM 38 Cruiser Squadrons
RM 92–93 Ships' Logbooks

Private Papers
N 173 Behncke
N 168 Büchsel
N 170 Capelle
N 255 Diedrichs
N 536 Hintze
N 326 Hopmann
N 161 Keyserlingk
N 578 Knorr
N 239 Levetzow
N 568 Mann
N 164 Michaelis
N 159 Müller
N 391 Raeder
N 43 Schlieffen
N 160 Senden
N 156 Souchon
N 588 Thomsen
N 253 Tirpitz
N 158 Widenmann

Bundesarchiv Koblenz
R 43 F Reichskanzlei

Private Papers
NL 16 Bülow
NL 17 Delbrück
NL 97 Erzberger
NL 36 Hertling
NL 7 Hohenlohe
NL 231 Hugenburg
NL 183 Stadelmann
NL 58 Thimme

**Deutsches Zentralarchiv
Merseburg (now at Potsdam)**
Civil Cabinet
Prussian State Ministry
Königliche Heraldamt: Familie von
   Tirpitz
Journals of Flügel Adjutants of
   William II
Papers of Kapp and Kiderlen-Wächter

Bundesarchiv Potsdam
R 43 F Reichskanzlei
Colonial Office
Imperial Interior Ministry
Pan-German League
Papers of Westarp

Foreign Office Bonn
Archives of the German Foreign
   Ministry

United States National Archives
German Foreign Office Archive
Tambach Collection of German Naval
   Archives
Eisendecher Papers T 291

**Niedersächsisches
Staatsarchiv Bückeburg**
Trotha Papers

Landesarchiv Speyer
Lieber Papers (portions also at Arch-
   diocesan Archiv, Wroclaw, Poland,
   made available courtesy of Professor
   John K. Zeender)

Hassell Family Archive
Family correspondence, photographs,
   and so on (made available courtesy of
   Agostino von Hassell)

BOOKS, ARTICLES, AND
PUBLISHED DOCUMENTS

Afflerbach, Holger, ed. *Kaiser Wilhelm als Oberster Kriegsherr im
   Ersten Weltkrieg: Quellen aus der
   militärischen Umgebung des Kaisers
   1914–1918.* Munich: Oldenbourg Verlag, 2005.
Afflerbach, Holger. "Wilhelm II as
   Supreme Warlord in the First World
   War." In *The Kaiser: New Research
   on Wilhelm II's Role in Imperial Germany,* ed. Annika Mombauer and
   Wilhelm Deist, 195–216. Cambridge:
   Cambridge University Press, 2003.

Allison, Graham, and Philip Zelikow. *Essence of Decision: Explaining the Cuban Missile Crisis.* 2nd ed. New York: Longmans, 1999.

Anderson, Margaret Lavinia. *Practicing Democracy: Elections and Political Culture in Imperial Germany.* Princeton, N.J.: Princeton University Press, 2000.

Anderson, Pauline. *The Background of Anti-English Feeling in Germany, 1890–1902.* Washington, D.C.: American University Press, 1939.

Arnauld de Periere, G. *Prinz Heinrich von Preussen: Admiral und Flieger.* Herford: Koehler, 1983.

Art, Robert J. *The Influence of Foreign Policy on Sea Power: New Weapons and Weltpolitik in Wilhelmian Germany.* Beverly Hills, Calif.: Sage, 1973.

Assmann, Kurt. *Deutsche Seestrategie in zwei Weltkriege.* Heidelberg: Vomackel, 1957.

Bachem, Karl. *Vorgeschichte, Geschichte, und Politik der deutschen Zentrumspartei.* 9 vols. Cologne: Bachem, 1929–32.

Balfour, Michael. *The Kaiser and His Times.* New York: Norton, 1972.

Batsch, Carl. "Albrecht von Stosch [Obituary]." *Marine Rundschau* (1896): 223–228.

———. "Zur Vorgeschichte des Flottes." *Marine Rundschau* (1897): 1–12, 103–116, 167–179, 289–299, 385–407, 475–487, 591–603, 677–689, 779–795, 871–886, 947–960.

Baxter, James F. *The Rise of the Ironclad Warship.* Hamden, Conn.: Archon Books, 1968.

Becker, Willy. *Fürst Bülow und England, 1897–1909.* Bamberg: Greifswald, 1929.

Berghahn, Volker R. "Der Bericht der Preussischen Oberrechnungskammer. 'Wehlers' Kaiserreich und seine Kritik." *Geschichte und Gesellschaft* 2 (1976): 125–135.

———. *Der Tirpitz-Plan. Genesis und Verfall einer innenpolitischen Krisenstrategie unter Wilhelm II.* Düsseldorf: Droste, 1971.

———. *Germany and the Approach of War in 1914.* 2nd ed. New York: St. Martin's, 1993.

———. *Imperial Germany, 1871–1914: Economy, Society, and Politics.* Providence, R.I.: Berghahn Books, 1994.

———. *Rüstung und Machtpolitik: zur Anatomie des "Kalten Krieges" vor 1914.* Düsseldorf: Droste, 1973.

———. "Zu den Zielen des Deutschen Flottenbaus unter Wilhelm I." *Historische Zeitschrift* 210, no. 1 (February 1970): 34–100.

Berghahn, Volker R., and Wilhelm Deist. "Kaiserliche Marine und Kriegsausbruch 1914." *Militärgeschichtliche Mitteilungen* 7 (1970): 37–58.

———, eds. *Rüstung im Zeichen der Wilhelmischen Weltpolitik: Grundlegende Dokumente, 1890–1914.* Düsseldorf: Droste, 1988.

Besteck, Eva. *Die trügerische "First Line of Defence": Zum Deutschenglischen Wettrüsten vor dem Ersten Weltkrieg.* Freiburg im Breisgau: Rombach, 2006.

Bethmann-Hollweg, Theobald von. *Reflections on the World War.* 2 vols. London: Butterworth, 1920.

Biddness, Michael D. "From Illusion to Destruction: The German Bid for World Power, 1897–1945." *British Journal of International Studies* 2 (1976): 173–185.

Bidlingmaier, Gerhard. *Seegeltung in der deutschen Geschichte.* Darmstadt: Wehr und Wissen, 1967.

Bird, Keith. *German Naval History: An Annotated Bibliography.* Amsterdam: Grüner, 1985.

———. *Raeder: Admiral of the Third Reich.* Annapolis, Md.: Naval Institute Press, 2006.

———. *Weimar, The German Naval Officer Corps, and the Rise of National Socialism.* Amsterdam: Grüner, 1977.

Blackbourne, David. *The Conquest of Nature: Water, Landscape, and the Making of Modern Germany.* New York: Norton, 2006.

Bley, Helmut. *Bebel und die Strategie der Kriegeverhütung 1904–1913: Eine Studie über Bebels Geheimkontakte mit der britischen Regierung Dokumente.* Göttingen: Vandenhoeck and Ruprecht, 1975.

Boelcke, Willi. *So Kam das Meer zu uns: Die preussische-deutsche Kriegsmarine in Übersee 1822 bis 1914.* Frankfurt: Ullstein, 1981.

Böhm, Ekkehard. *Überseehandel und Flottenbau: Hanseatische Kaufmannschaft und deutsche Seerüstung 1879–1902.* Düsseldorf: Bertelsmann Universitätsvelag, 1972.

Bolen, C. Waldron. "Kiderlen's Policy on Anglo-German Naval Conventions, 1909–1912." *Journal of Central European Affairs* 9, no. 2 (July 1949): 131–149.

Breyer, Siegfried. *Schlachtschiffe und Schlachtkreuzer 1905–1970.* Munich: Lehmann's, 1970.

Brézet, François-Emmanuel. *Le Plan Tirpitz (1897–1914): Une flotte de combat allemande contre l'Angleterre.* Paris: Librare de L'inde, 1998.

Brysch, Thomas. *Marinepolitik im preussischen Abgeordnetenhaus und Deutscher Reichstag 1850–1888.* Hamburg: Mittler, 1996.

Bueb, Volkmar. *Die junge Schule der französischen Marine: Strategie und Politik 1875–1900.* Boppard am Rhein: Harald Boldt, 1971.

Burchardt, Lothar. *Friedenswirtschaft und Kriegsvorsorge: Deutschlands wirtschaftliche Rüstungsbestrebungen vor 1914.* Boppard: Boldt, 1968.

Burdick, Charles B. *The Japanese Siege of Tsingtau.* Hamden: Archon, 1976.

Calthorpe, Somerset A. G. "Welche Taktik gestattet die beste Ausnutzung der Kräfte?" *Marine Rundschau* 6 (January– December 1895): 11–29.

Campbell, N. J. M. *Jutland: An Analysis of the Fighting.* London: Conway Maritime Press, 1986.

Castex, Raoul. *Strategic Theories.* Trans. and ed. Eugenia C. Kiesing. Annapolis, Md.: Naval Institute, Press. 1994.

Cecil, Lamar. *Albert Ballin: Business and Politics in Imperial Germany, 1888–1918.* Princeton, N.J.: Princeton University Press, 1967.

———. *The German Diplomatic Service, 1871–1914.* Princeton, N.J.: Princeton University Press, 1976.

———. *Wilhelm II: Prince and Emperor, 1859–1908.* Chapel Hill: University of North Carolina Press, 1989.

Challener, Richard. *Admirals, Generals, and American Foreign Policy, 1898–1914.* Princeton, N.J.: Princeton University Press, 1973.

Charmes, Gabriel. La réforme de la marine I: "Torpilleurs et cannoniéres." *Revue des deux Mondes* (15 December 1884): 872–906.

———. La réforme de la marine II: "La guerre maritime et l'organisation de la force navale." *Revue des deux Mondes* (1 March 1885): 127–168.

———. La réforme de la marine, III: "Défense des côtes." *Revue des deux Mondes* (15 April 1885): 770–806.

Chickering, Roger. "Der deutsche Wehrverein: die Reform der deutschen Armee 1912–1914." *Militärgeschichliche Mitteilungen* 25 (1979): 7–33.

———. *We Men Who Feel Most German: A Cultural Study of the Pan-*

German League, 1886–1914. Boston: Allen and Unwin, 1984.

Churchill, Winston S. *The World Crisis*. Vol. 1. New York: Scribner's, 1923.

Clark, Christopher. *Iron Kingdom: The Rise and Fall of Prussia, 1600–1947*. London: Allen Lane, 2006.

Clark, John J. "Merchant Marine and the Navy: A Note on the Mahan Hypothesis." *Journal of the Royal United Services Institute* 112, no. 648 (November 1967): 162–164.

Coetzee, Marilyn S. *The German Army League: Popular Nationalism in Wilhelmine Germany*. New York: Oxford, 1990.

Coler, Christfried. "Der Konflikt Bismarck–Stosch Marz/April 1877." *Wehrwissenschaftliche Rundschau* 17 (1967): 578–593.

———. "Der Sturz Albrecht von Stosch März 1883." *Wehrwissenschaftliche Rundschau* 17 (1967): 692–704.

———. "Palastrevolte in der Marine 1878/9." *Wehrwissenschaftliche Rundschau* 17 (1967): 638–656.

Coogan, John W. *The End of Neutrality: The United States, Britain, and Maritime Rights, 1899–1915*. Ithaca, N.Y.: Cornell University Press, 1981.

Corbett, Julian S. *Some Principles of Maritime Strategy*. Reprint. Annapolis, Md.: Naval Institute Publishing, 1988 [1911].

Cowpe, Arthur. "The Royal Navy and the Whitehead Torpedo." In *Technical Change and British Naval Policy*, ed. Bryan Ranft, 23–36. London: Hodder and Stoughton, 1977.

Craig, Gordon. *The Politics of the Prussian Army, 1640–1928*. New York: Oxford University Press, 1964.

Crothers, George. *The German Elections of 1907*. New York: AMS Press, 1968.

Crozier, Michael. *The Bureaucratic Phenomenon*. Chicago: University of Chicago Press, 1964.

———. *The Stalled Society*. New York: Viking, 1973.

Davis, Lance E., and Stanley L. Engerman. *Naval Blockades in Peace and War: An Economic History since 1750*. New York: Cambridge University Press, 2006.

Davis, Vincent. *The Politics of Innovation in Naval Cases*. Denver: University of Denver Press, 1967.

Deist, Wilhelm. "Die Armee in Staat und Gesellschaft, 1890–1914." In *Das Kaiserliche Deutschland*, ed. Michael Stürmer, 312–339. Düsseldorf: Droste, 1970.

———. *Flottenproganda und Flottenpolitik: Das Nachrichtenbüro des Reichsmarineamtes 1897–1914*. Stuttgart: Deutsche Verlags-Anstalt, 1976.

———, ed. *Militär und Innenpolitik im Weltkrieg 1914–1918*. 2 vols. Düsseldorf: Droste, 1970.

———. *Militär, Staat und Gesellschaft. Studien zur preußisch-deutschen Militärgeschichte*. Munich: Oldenbourg, 1991.

———. "Die Politik der Seekriegsleitung und die Rebellion der Flotte Ende Oktober 1918." *Vierteljahresheft für Zeitgeschichte* 14 (October 1966).

Diercks, Wulf. "Der Einfluss der Personalsteurung auf die deutsche Seekriegsführung 1914–1918." *Militärgeschichliches Beiheft zur Europäischen Wehrkunde/Wehrwissenschaftlichen Rundschau*, 1–19. Herford. Verlag Europäische Wehrkunde.

Dülffer, Jost, ed. *Bereit zum Krieg; Kriegsmentalität in Wilhelmischen Deutschland 1890–1914*. Göttingen: Vandenhoeck, 1986.

———. "The German Reich and the Jeune École." In *Marine et technique au XIXe siecle*, Actes du colloque international Paris, ecole militaire, les 10, 11, 12 Juin 1987, Paris, 1988.

———. "Limitations on Naval Warfare and Germany's Future as a World Power: A German Debate, 1904–1906." *War and Society* 3 (1985): 23–43.

———. *Regeln gegen den Krieg: Die Haager Friedenskonferenzen von 1899 und 1907 in der internationalen Politik.* Berlin: Ullstein, 1981.

———. *Weimar, Hitler, und die Marine.* Düsseldorf: Droste, 1973.

Duppler, Jörg. *Der Junior Partner: England und die Entwicklung der Deutschen Marine, 1848–1890.* Herford: Mittler, 1985.

Ehlert, Hans. "Marine- und Heeres—Etat im deutschen Rüstungs—Budget 1898–1912." *Marine Rundschau* 75 (1978): 311–323.

Eley, Geoff. "Defining Social Imperialism: Use and Abuse of an Idea." *Social History* (October 1976): 265–290.

———. *From Unification to Nazism: Reinterpreting the German Past.* Boston: Allen and Unwin, 1986.

———. "Die 'Kehrites' und das Kaiserreich: Bemerkungen zu einer aktuellen Kontroverse." *Geschichte und Gesellschaft* 4 (1978): 91–107.

———. *Reshaping the German Right: Radical Nationalism and Political Change after Bismarck.* New Haven, Conn.: Yale University Press, 1980.

———. "Sammlungspolitik, Social Darwinism, and the Navy Law of 1898." In Geoff Eley, *From Unification to Nazism: Reinterpreting the German Past,* 110–153. Boston: Allen and Unwin, 1986.

———. "Shaping the Right: Radical Nationalism and the German Navy League." *Historical Journal* 21, no. 2 (1978): 327–354.

Epkenhans, Michael, ed. *Albert Hopmann, Das ereignisreiche Leben eines Wilhelminers.* Munich: Oldenbourg, 2004.

———. "Clio, Tirpitz, und die Marine." In *Geschichtsbilder: Festschrift für Michael Salewski zum 65. Geburtstag,* ed. Jürgen Elvert et al., 465–485. Hamburg: Franz Steiner, 2003.

———. *Tirpitz: Architect of the German High Seas Fleet.* Washington, D.C.: Potomac Books, 2008.

———. *Die Wilhelminische Flottenrüstung, 1908–1914: Weltmachtstreben, industrieller Fortschritt, soziale Integration.* Munich: Oldenbourg, 1991.

———. "William II and 'His' Navy, 1888–1918." In *The Kaiser: New Research on Wilhelm II's Role in Imperial Germany,* ed. Annika Mombauer and Wilhelm Deist, 12–36. Cambridge: Cambridge University Press, 2003.

———. "Zwischen Patriotismus und Geschäftsinteresse. F. A. Krupp und die Anfänge des deutschen Schlachtflottenbaus 1897–1902." *Geschichte und Gesellschaft* 15 (1989): 196–226.

Eschenburg, Theodore. *Das Kaisereich am Scheidweg-Bassermann, Bülow, und der Bloc.* Berlin: Verlag für Kulturpolitik, 1929.

Fairbairn, Brett. *Democracy in the Undemocratic State: The German Reichstag Elections of 1898 and 1903.* Toronto: University of Toronto Press, 1997.

———. "Interpreting Wilhelmine Elections: National Issues, Fairness Issues, An Electoral Mobilization." In *Mass Politics and Social Change in Modern Germany: New Perspectives,* ed. Larry Jones and James Retallack, 17–48. New York: Cambridge University Press, 1992.

Fairbanks, Charles. "Choosing among Technologies in the Anglo-German Naval Arms Competition, 1898–1915." In *Naval History: The Seventh Symposium of the U.S. Naval Academy,* ed. William B. Cogar,

127–142. Wilmington, Del.: Scholarly Resources, 1988.

———. "The Origins of the Dreadnought Revolution: An Historical Essay." *International History Review* 13, no. 2 (May 1991): 246–283.

Fernis, Hansgeorg. *Die Flottennovellen im Reichstag 1906–1912.* Stuttgart: Kohlhammer, 1934.

Fioravanzo, Giuseppe. *A History of Naval Tactical Thought.* Trans. Arthur W. Holst. Annapolis, Md.: Naval Institute Press, 1979.

Fischer, Conan. *The Ruhr Crisis, 1923–1924.* New York: Oxford University Press, 2003.

Fischer, Fritz. *Krieg der Illusionen: Die deutsche Politik 1911–1914.* 2nd ed. Kronberg: Athenäum, 1978.

———. "Recent Works on German Naval Policy." *European Studies Review* 5 (1975): 443–461.

———. *War of Illusions: German Politics from 1911 to 1914.* Trans. Marian Jackson. New York: Norton, 1975.

———. *World Power or Decline: The Controversy over Germany's Aims in the First World War.* New York: Norton, 1974.

Fock, Harald. *Fast Fighting Boats, 1870–1945: Their Design and Use.* Annapolis, Md.: Naval Institute Press, 1974.

———. "Das Kaisers Preisauschreiben." *Marine Rundschau* 74 (1977): 112–118, 183–188, 299–303, 384–389, 585–588.

Förster, Stig. *Der Doppelte Militarismus: Die deutsche Heeresrüstungspolitik zwischen Status—Quo—Sicherung und Aggression 1890–1913.* Stuttgart: Steiner, 1985.

———. *Moltke. Vom Kabinettskrieg zum Volkskrieg, Eine Werkauswahl.* Bonn: Bouvier, 1992.

Fricke, Dieter, ed. *Die bürgerlichen Parteien in Deutschland.* Vol. 1 (1830–1945).* Berlin (East): Militärverlag der DDR, 1968.

Galster, Karl. *England, Deutsche Flotte, und Weltkrieg.* Kiel: Scheible, 1925.

———. *Welche Seekriegsrüstung braucht Deutschland?* Berlin, 1907.

Ganz, A. Harding. "Colonial Policy and the Imperial German Navy." *Militärgeschtliche Mitteilungen* 1 (1977): 35–52.

Gardiner, Robert, ed. *Conway's All the World's Fighting Ships, 1860–1905.* London: Conway Maritime Press, 1979.

Gat, Azar. *The Development of Military Thought: The Nineteenth Century.* New York: Oxford University Press, 1992.

Geiss, Imanuel. *German Foreign Policy, 1871–1914.* Boston: Routledge and Kegan Paul, 1976.

Gemzell, Carl-Axel. *Organization, Conflict, and Innovation: A Study of German Naval Strategic Planning, 1888–1940.* Stockholm: Lund, 1973.

———. *Raeder, Hitler und Skandanavien: Der Kampf fur einen maritimen Operationsplan.* Stockholm: Lund, 1965.

Geyer, Michael. *Rüstungspolitik 1860–1980.* Frankfurt: Suhrkamp, 1984.

Goltz, Colmar von der. *Denkwürdigkeiten.* Berlin: Mittler, 1932.

Gooch, G. P., and Harold Temperley, eds. *British Documents on the Origins of the War, 1898–1914.* 11 vols. London: HM Stationery Office, 1926–1938.

Görlitz, Walter. *Auzeichnungen des Chefs des Marinekabinettes Admiral Georg Alexander von Müller über die Ära Wilhelms II.* Göttingen: Musterschmidt, 1965.

———, ed. *The Kaiser and His Court: The Diaries, Notebooks, and Letters of Admiral Georg Alexander von Müller, Chief of the Naval Cabinet,*

1914–1918. Trans. Mervyn Savill. New York: Harcourt, Brace and World, 1961.

Gottschall, Terrell. *By Order of the Kaiser: Otto von Diedrichs and the Rise of the Imperial German Navy, 1865–1902*. Annapolis, Md.: Naval Institute Press, 2003.

Granier, Gerhard, ed. *Die deutsche Seekriegsleitung im Ersten Weltkrieg-Dokumentation*. 3 vols. Koblenz: Bundesarchiv, 1999.

———. *Magnus von Levetzow: Seeoffizier, Monarchist, und Wegbereiter Hitlers*. Boppard: Boldt, 1982.

Graubohm, Herbert. *Die Ausbildung in der deutschen Marine von ihrer Gründung bis zum Jahre 1914*. Düsseldorf: Droste, 1977.

———. "Historische Würzeln der Ausbildung in der Marine." In *Die Deutsche Marine*, ed. Wolfgang Petter, 131–142. Herford: Mittler, 1983.

Gray, Sir Edward. *Twenty-Five Years*. 2 vols. New York: Stokes, 1925.

Gray, Edwyn. *The Devil's Device: Robert Whitehead and the History of the Torpedo*. Rev. and exp. ed. Annapolis, Md.: Naval Institute Press, 1991.

Grimm, Hjalmar. "German Naval Legislation, 1898–1914." Ph.D. diss., Ohio State University, 1949.

Gröner, Erich. *German Warships, 1815–1945*. Rev. and exp. ed. Vol. 1, *Major Surface Vessels*. Vol. 2, *U-Boats and Mine Warfare Vessels*. Annapolis, Md.: Naval Institute Press, 1982, 1983.

Groos, Otto, and Walther Gladisch. *Der Krieg in der Nordsee*. 7 vols. Berlin: Mittler, 1920–65.

Guth, Rolf. "Die Organization der deutschen Marine in Krieg und Frieden 1913–1933." In *Die Deutsche Marine*, ed. Wolfgang Petter, 263–336. Herford: Mittler, 1983.

Haferkorn, Joachim. *Kampf um das Reichskanzleramt im Jahre 1906*. Würzburg: Triltsch, 1937.

Hagenlücke, Heinz. *Deutsche Vaterlandspartei: Die nationale Rechte am Ende des Kaiserreiches*. Düsseldorf: Droste, 1997.

Haldane, Richard. *An Autobiography*, London: Hodder and Stoughton, 1929.

———. *Before the War*. London: Cassel, 1920.

Hall, Alex. *Scandal, Sensation, and Social Democracy: The SPD Press and Wilhelmine Germany, 1890–1914*. New York: Cambridge University Press, 1977.

Hallmann, Hans. *Krugerdespesche und Flottenfrage*. Stuttgart: Kohlhammer, 1927.

———. *Der Weg zum deutschen Schlachtflottenbau*. Stuttgart: Kohlhammer, 1938.

Halperin, Morten. *Bureaucratic Politics and Foreign Policy*. Washington, D.C.: Brookings, 1974.

Halpern, Paul G. *The Mediterranean Naval Situation, 1908–1914*. Cambridge, Mass.: Harvard University Press, 1971.

———. *A Naval History of World War I*. Annapolis, Md.: Naval Institute Press, 1994.

———. *The Naval Situation in the Mediterranean, 1914–1918*. Annapolis, Md.: Naval Institute Press, 1987.

Hansen, Hans Jürgen. *The Ships of the German Fleets, 1848–1945*. New York: Hamlyn, 1974.

Hassel, Fey von. *Hostage of the Third Reich*. New York: Scribner's, 1989.

Hassell, Ulrich von. *—. Tirpitz*. Stuttgart: Belsersche, 1920.

Hassell, Ulrich von, Jr. *Im Wandel der Aussenpolitik. Von der französischen Revolution bis zum Weltkrieg*. Munich: Bruckmann, 1939.

———. *Der Kreis Schliesst Sich: Aufzeichnungen in der Haft 1944*. Ed. Malwe von Hassel. Berlin: Propylaen, 1994.

Hattendorf, John B. "Alfred Thayer Mahan and His Strategic Thought." In *Maritime Strategy and the Balance of Power: Britain and America in the Twentieth Century*, ed. John B. Hattendorf and Robert S. Jordan, 83–94. New York: St. Martin's, 1989.

———, ed. *The Influence of History on Mahan*. Newport, R.I.: Naval War College Press, 1991.

———. "Recent Thinking on the Theory of Naval Strategy." In *Maritime Strategy and the Balance of Power: Britain and America in the Twentieth Century*, ed. John B. Hattendorf and Robert S. Jordan, 136–161. New York: St. Martin's, 1989.

Hattendorf, John B., and James Goldrich, eds. *Mahan Is Not Enough: The Proceedings of a Conference on the Works of Sir Julian Corbett and Admiral Sir Herbert Richmond*. Newport, R.I.: Naval War College Press, 1993.

Hattendorf, John B., and Robert S. Jordan. "Conclusions: Maritime Strategy and National Policy: Historical Accident or Purposeful Planning?" In *Maritime Strategy and the Balance of Power: Britain and America in the Twentieth Century*, ed. John B. Hattendorf and Robert S. Jordan, 347–355. New York: St. Martin's, 1989.

———, eds. *Maritime Strategy and the Balance of Power: Britain and America in the Twentieth Century*. New York: St. Martin's, 1989.

Heckart, Beverly. *From Bassermann to Bebel: The Grand Bloc's Quest for Reform in the Kaiserreich, 1900–1914*. New Haven, Conn.: Yale University Press, 1974.

Herwig, Holger H. "Admirals vs. Generals: The War Aims of the Imperial German Navy, 1914–1918." *Central European History* 5 (1972): 203–228.

———. "Clio Deceived, Patriotic Self-Censorship in Germany after the Great War." In *Forging the Collective Memory*, ed. Wilson Keith, 87–127. Providence, R.I.: Berghahn Books, 1996.

———. "German Imperialism and South America before the First World War: The Venezuela Case 1902/03." *Frankfurter Historische Abhandlungen* 17 (1978): 117–130.

———. *The German Naval Officer Corps: A Social and Political History, 1890–1918*. Oxford: Clarendon, 1973.

———. "The German Reaction to the *Dreadnought* Revolution." *International Historical Review* 13, no. 2 (May 1991): 273–283.

———. *"Luxury Fleet": The Imperial German Navy, 1888–1918*. Boston: Allen and Unwin, 1980.

———. *Politics of Frustration: The United States in German Naval Planning, 1889–1941*. Boston: Little, Brown, 1976.

———. "Total Rhetoric, Limited War: Germany's U-Boat Campaign, 1917–1918." *Journal of Military and Strategic Studies* 1, no. 1 (1998): 1–8.

Hewitson, Mark. "The Kaiserreich in Question: Constitutional Crisis in Germany before the First World War." *Journal of Modern History* 73 (December 2001): 725–780.

Hildebrand, Hans. *Deutschlands Admirale, 1849–1945*. 3 vols. Osnabruck: Biblio, 1988–90.

———. *Deutschlands Admirale V, Marinebeamte*. Osnabruck: Biblio, 1996.

Hildebrand, Hans, Albert Rohr, and Hans-Otto Steinmetz. *Die deutschen Kriegschiffe*. 7 vols. Heford: Koehler, 1979–83.

Hildebrand, Klaus. *Das vergangene Reich*. Stuttgart: Deutsche Verlags-Anstalt, 1995.

Hill, Leonidas E., ed. *Die Weizsäcker-Papiere 1900–32*. Berlin: Ullstein, 1972.

Hobson, Rolf. *Imperialism at Sea: Naval Strategic Thought, the Ideology of Sea Power, and the Tirpitz Plan, 1875–1914*. Boston: Brill, 2002.

Hohenlohe-Schillingsfürst, Chlodwig von. *Denkwürdigkeiten*. Stuttgart: Deutsche Verlagsanstalt, 1907.

Holborn, Hajo. *A History of Modern Germany, 1840–1945*. New York: Knopf, 1969.

Hollyday, Frederic. *Bismarck's Rival: A Political Biography of General and Admiral Albrecht von Stosch*. Durham, N.C.: Duke University Press, 1960.

Hopmann, Albert. *Das Kriegstagebuch eines deutschen Seeoffiziers*. Berlin: Scherl, 1925.

———. *Das Logbuch eines deutschen Seeoffiziers*. Berlin: Scherl, 1924.

Horn, Daniel. *The German Naval Mutinies of World War I*. New Brunswick, N.J.: Rutgers University Press, 1969.

Hubatsch, Walter. *Der Admiralstab and die obersten Marinebehörden*. Göttingen: Musterschmidt, 1955.

———. *Die Ära Tirpitz*. Göttingen: Musterschmidt, 1955.

———. *Die Erste Deutsche Flotte 1848–1853*. Herford: Mittler, 1981.

———. *Kaiserliche Marine*. Munich: Lehmann, 1975.

Huberti, Franz. "Tirpitz als Verschleierungs-Politiker?" *Marine Rundschau* 71 (1974): 535–554.

Hueck, Walter von, ed. *Genealogisches Handbuch der Adelingen Häuser B*. Vol. 17. Limburg: Starke , 1986.

Hull, Isabel V. *Absolute Destruction: Military Culture and the Practices of War in Imperial Germany*. Ithaca, N.Y.: Cornell University Press, 2005.

———. *The Entourage of Kaiser Wilhelm II, 1888–1918*. Cambridge: Cambridge University Press, 1982.

Hunt, Barry D. "The Strategic Thought of Sir Julian S. Corbett." In *Maritime Strategy and the Balance of Power: Britain and America in the Twentieth Century*, ed. John B. Hattendorf and Robert S. Jordan, 110–135. New York: St. Martin's, 1989.

Hurd, Archibald. *The German Fleet*. New York: Hodder and Storighton, 1915.

Hurd, Archibald, and Henry Castle. *German Sea Power*. London: Murray, 1913.

Jäckh, Ernst, ed. *Kiderlen-Wächter, der Staatsmann und der Mensch*. Vol. 2. Berlin: Deutsche Verlags-Anstalt, 1924.

Jane, Fred T., ed. *Jane's Fighting Ships, 1914*. Repr. New York: ARCO, 1969.

Jaques, Elliot. *A General Theory of Bureaucracy*. New York: Wiley, 1976.

Jarausch, Konrad. *The Enigmatic Chancellor: Bethmann-Hollweg and the Hubris of Imperial Germany*. New Haven, Conn.: Yale University Press, 1973.

Kalau, Mark D. "*Wielding the Dagger*": *The MarineKorps Flandern and the German War Effort, 1914–1918*. Westport, Conn.: Praeger, 2003.

Kalau vom Hofe, K. A. *Unsere Flotte im Welkrieg: Die Ereignisse zur See 1914/16 dem deutschen Flotte geschildert*. Berlin: Mittler, 1917.

Kaulisch, Baldur. *Alfred von Tirpitz und die imperialistische deutsche Flottenrüstung. Eine politische Biographie. Kleine Militärgeschichte Biographien*. Berlin (East): Militärverlag der DDR, 1982.

Kehr, Eckart. *Battleship Building and Party Politics in Germany, 1894–1901*. Ed. and trans. Pauline R. Anderson and Eugene N. Anderson. Chicago: University of Chicago Press, 1973.

———. *Economic Interest, Militarism, and Foreign Policy: Essays on Ger-*

man History. Ed. Gordon A. Craig. Trans. Grete Heinz. Berkeley: University of California Press, 1970.

——. "The German Fleet in the Eighteen Nineties and the Politico-Military Dualism in the Empire." In Kehr, *Economic Interests, Militarism, and Foreign Policy: Essays in German History*, ed. Gordon A. Craig, trans. Grete Heinz, 11–21. Berkeley: University of California Press, 1977.

——. *Schlachtflottenbau und Parteipolitik 1894–1901*. Repr. Vaduz: Kraus Reprint, 1965 [1930].

Kelly, Patrick J. "Strategy, Tactics, and Turf Wars: Tirpitz and the Oberkommando der Marine, 1892–1895." *Journal of Military History* 66 (October 2002): 1033–1066.

Kennedy, Paul M. "The Development of German Naval Operations Plans against England, 1896–1914." *English Historical Review* 89 (January 1974): 48–76.

——. "Fisher and Tirpitz Compared." In Kennedy, *Strategy and Diplomacy, 1870–1945: Eight Studies*, 109–128. London: Allen and Unwin, 1983.

——, ed. *Germany in the Pacific and Far East, 1870–1914*. Australia: University of Queensland Press, 1977.

——, ed. *Grand Strategies in War and Peace*. New Haven, Conn.: Yale University Press, 1991.

——. "Mahan versus Mackinder: Two Interpretations of British Sea Power." In Kennedy, *Strategy and Diplomacy, 1870–1945: Eight Studies*, 41–85. London: Allen and Unwin, 1983.

——. "Maritime Strategieprobleme der deutsch-englischen Flottenrivalität." In *Marine und Marinepolitik 1871–1914*, ed. Herbert Schottelius and Wilhelm Deist, 178–210. Düsseldorf: Droste, 1972.

——, ed. *The Realities behind Diplomacy: Background Influences on British External Policy, 1865–1890*. London: Allen and Unwin, 1981.

——. "The Relevance of the Prewar British and American Maritime Strategies to the First World War and Its Aftermath, 1898–1930." In *Maritime Strategy and the Balance of Power: Britain and America in the Twentieth Century*, ed. John B. Hattendorf and Robert S. Jordan, 165–188. New York: St. Martin's, 1989.

——. *The Rise and Fall of British Naval Mastery*. New York: Scribner's, 1976.

——. *The Rise of the Anglo-German Antagonism, 1860–1914*. London: Allen and Unwin, 1980.

——. *The Samoan Tangle: A Study in Anglo-German-American Relations, 1878–1908*. New York: Barnes and Noble, 1974.

——. "Strategic Aspects of the Anglo-German Naval Race," In Kennedy, *Strategy and Diplomacy, 1870–1945: Eight Studies*, 127–160. London: Allen and Unwin, 1983.

——. *Strategy and Diplomacy, 1870–1945: Eight Studies*. London: Allen and Unwin, 1983.

——. "Tirpitz, England, and the Second Navy Law of 1900: A Strategical Critique." *Militärgeschichliche Mitteilungen* 2 (1970): 33–57.

——, ed. *The War Plans of the Great Powers 1880–1914*. London: Allen and Unwin, 1979.

Klein, D. von. "Vize Admiral z. D. Wilhelm von Wickede." *Marine Rundschau* (1896): 1–7.

Koch, Paul. "Admiral von Knorr." *Marine Rundschau* (1904): 864–865.

——. "Aus der Zeit des Admirals von Stosch. Skizzen aus den Akten des Geh. Admiraliatsrat Koch. [Final] Part V." *Marine Rundschau* (1903): 826–847.

——. "Aus der Zeit des Admirals von Stosch. Skizzen aus den Akten von Geh. Admiralitätsrat Koch. Part I." *Marine Rundschau* (1902): 1271–1287.

——. "Aus der Zeit des Admirals von Stosch. Skizzen aus den Akten von Geh. Admiralitätsrat Koch. Parts II–IV." *Marine Rundschau* (1903): 21–35, 585–598, 682–698.

——. "S. M. Kannonenboot 'Iltis.'" *Marine Rundschau* (1896): 793–807.

Kohut, Thomas A. *Wilhelm II and the Germans: A Study in Leadership.* New York: Oxford University Press, 1991.

Langer, William L. *The Diplomacy of Imperialism, 1890–1902.* New York: Knopf, 1935.

Lambert, Nicholas. *Sir John Fisher's Naval Revolution.* Columbia: University of South Carolina Press, 1999.

Lambi, Ivo N. *The Navy and German Power Politics, 1862–1914.* Boston: Allen and Unwin, 1984.

Lauren, Paul. *Diplomats and Bureaucrats: The First Institutional Responses to Twentieth-Century Diplomacy in France and Germany.* Stanford, Calif.: Hoover Institute, 1976.

Lehment, Joachim. *Kriegsmarine and Politische Führung.* Berlin: Junker and Dünnhaupt, 1937.

Leopold, John A. *Alfred Hugenberg. The Radical Nationalist Campaign against the Weimar Republic.* New Haven, Conn.: Yale University Press, 1977.

Lerman, Katherine Anne. *The Chancellor as Courtier: Bernhard von Bülow and the Governance of Germany, 1900–1909.* Cambridge: Cambridge University Press, 1990.

Lewis, Eugene. *Public Entrepreneurship: Toward a Theory of Political Power; The Organizational Lives of Hyman Rickover, J. Edgar Hoover, and Robert Moses.* Bloomington: Indiana University Press, 1980.

Lloyd George, David. *War Memoirs.* 6 vols. Boston: Little, Brown, 1933–37.

Lohmann, Korvetten Kapitän. "SMS Meteor bei Havana." *Marine Rundschau* 35, no. 2 (1930): 509–517.

Maehl, William. "German Socialist Opposition to the Tirpitz Plan: Bebel and the Naval Law of 1900." *The Historian* 40 (August 1978): 704–728.

Mahan, Alfred Thayer. "Die Blockade in ihrer Beziehung zur Seestrategie." *Marine Rundschau* (1896): 65–76.

——. *Letters and Papers of Alfred Thayer Mahan.* 3 vols. Ed. Robert Seager II and Doris D. Maguire. Annapolis, Md.: Naval Institute Press, 1975.

Maltzahn, Curt Freiherr von. "Ein Brief des Generals von Stosch aus dem Jahr 1877 und seine Stellung in der Entwicklungsgeschichte moderner Seetaktik." *Marine Rundschau* (1904): 1187–1204.

——. *Geschichte unserer taktischen Entwicklung.* 2 vols. Berlin: Admiralstab, 1910–11.

——. "Was lehrt das Buch des Generals v. Clausewitz 'Vom Kriege' dem Seeoffizier?" *Marine Rundschau* (1905): 683–702.

——. "Das Meer als Operationsfeld und als Kampffeld." Lecture given in January 1904 at the Institut für Meereskunde of the University of Berlin. *Marine Rundschau* (1904): 273–290, 412–426.

——. *Naval Warfare.* London: Longmans, 1908.

Mantey, Eberhard von. *Deutsche Marinegeschichte.* Charlottenburg: Offene Worte, 1926.

Marder, Arthur J. *The Anatomy of British Sea Power, 1880–1905.* New York: Knopf, 1940.

——, ed. *Fear God and Dread Nought: The Correspondence of Admiral of the Fleet Lord Fisher of Kilverstone.* 3 vols. London: Jonathan Cape, 1952–1959.

——. *From the Dreadnought to Scapa Flow.* 4 vols. Vol. 1, *The Road to War, 1904–1914.* London: Oxford, 1961.

Marienfeld, Wolfgang. *Wissenschaft und Schlachtflottenbau in Deutschland 1897–1906.* Berlin: Mittler, 1957.

Marriott, J. A. R., and C. G. Robertson. *The Evolution of Prussia.* Oxford: Oxford University Press, 1937.

Massie, Robert K. *Dreadnought: Britain, Germany, and the Coming of the Great War.* New York: Random House, 1991.

McClean, Roderick R. "Dreams of a German Empire: William II and the Treaty of Björkö of 1905." In *The Kaiser: New Research on Wilhelm II's Role in Imperial Germany,* ed. Annika Mombauer and Wilhelm Deist, 119–142. Cambridge: Cambridge University Press, 2003.

Metz, Ilse. *Die deutsche Flotte in der englischen Presse, der Navy scare vom Winter 1904/05.* Berlin: Ebering, 1936.

Michalka, Wolfgang, ed. *Der erste Weltkrieg: Wirkung, Wahrnehmung, Analyse.* Munich: Piper, 1994. Werner Rahn, "Strategische Probleme der deutsche Seekriegsrüstung 1914–1918," 348–365.

Miller, Stephen, Stephen van Evera, and Sean M. Lynn-Jones, eds. *Military Strategy and the Origins of the First World War.* Rev. and exp. ed. Princeton, N.J.: Princeton University Press, 1991.

Mittelmann, Fritz, ed. *Ernst Bassermann, Sein Politisches Wirken.* Vol. 1. Berlin: Curtius, 1914.

Mombauer, Annika. "Wilhelm, Waldersee, and the Boxer Rebellion."

In *The Kaiser: New Researches on William II's Role in Imperial Germany,* ed. Annika Mombauer and Wilhelm Deist, 91–118. Cambridge: Cambridge University Press, 2003.

Mombauer, Annika, and Wilhelm Deist, eds. *The Kaiser: New Research on Wilhelm II's Role in Imperial Germany.* Cambridge: Cambridge University Press, 2003.

Mommsen, Wolfgang J. *Der autoritäre Nationalstaat: Verfassung, Gesellschaft, und Kultur des deutschen Kaiserreichs.* Frankfurt: Fischer Taschenbuch, 1991.

——. "Domestic Factors in German Foreign Policy before 1914." *Central European History* 6 (1973): 3–43.

Morgan, Patrick. *Deterrence, A Conceptual Analysis.* London: Sage, 1977.

Müller-Meiningen, Ernst. *Parlamentismus.* Berlin: de Gruyter, 1926.

Nauticus. *Jahrbuch fur Deutschlands Seeinteressen.* Berlin: Mittler, 1899, 1900, 1906.

Nipperdey, Thomas. *Deutsche Geschichte.* Vol. 2. 2nd ed. Munich: Beck, 1993.

Noel-Baker, Philip. *The Private Manufacture of Armaments.* 2 vols. London: Gollancz, 1936.

Offer, Avner. *The First World War: An Agrarian Interpretation.* Oxford: Clarendon, 1989.

Olivier, David H. "Staatskaperei: The German Navy and Commerce Warfare." Ph.D. diss., University of Saskatchewan, 2001.

Oncken, Emily. *Pantherspung nach Agadir: die deutsche Politik während der zweiten Marokkokrise 1911.* Düsseldorf: Droste, 1981.

Osborne, Eric W. *The Battle of Helgoland Bight.* Bloomington: Indiana University Press, 2006.

Padfield, Peter. *The Great Naval Race: Anglo-German Naval Rivalry, 1900–1914.* New York: McKay, 1974.

Peck, Abraham J. *Radicals and Reactionaries: The Focus of Conservatism in Wilhelmine Germany*. Washington, D.C.: University Press of America, 1978.

Persius, Lothar. *Die Tirpitz-legende*. Berlin: Engelmann, 1918.

Petter, Wolfgang. "Deutsche Flottenrüstung von Wallenstein bis Tirpitz." In Manfred Messerschmidt, ed., *Handbuch zur Deutschen Militärgeschichte. VIII Deutsche Marinegeschichte der Neuzeit*. Munich, 1977. 13–262.

———. "'Enemies' and 'Reich Enemies': An Analysis of Threat Perceptions and Political Strategy in Imperial Germany, 1871–1914." In *The German Military in the Age of Total War*, ed. Wilhelm Deist, 22–20. Dover, N.H.: Berg, 1985.

———. *Seemacht*. German ed. Munich: Bernard and Craefe, 1974.

———. "Systemkrise und Marinekonzeption im Wilhelmischen Deutschland." In *Die Deutsche Marine*, ed. Wolfgang Petter, 35–52. Herford: Mittler, 1983.

Philbin, Tobias R. *Admiral von Hipper: The Inconvenient Hero*. Amsterdam: Grüner, 1982.

Pohl, Hugo von. *Aus Aufzeichnungen und Briefen während der Kriegszeit*. Berlin: Siegesmund, 1920

—-. "Die Thätigkeit S.M.S. Irene in den Gewässern der Philippinen 1896 bis 1899." *Marine Rundschau* (1902): 759–776.

Pollard, Sidney, and Paul Robertson. *The British Shipbuilding Industry, 1870–1914*. Cambridge, Mass.: Harvard University Press, 1979.

Potter, Elmer, Chester Nimitz, and Jürgen Rohwer, eds. *Seemacht*. German ed. Munich: Bernard und Graefe, 1974.

Pühle, Hans. *Agrarische Interessenpolitik und preußischer Konservatismus im Wilhelminischen Reich 1893–1914*. Hannover: Verlag für Literatur und Zeitgeschen, 1967.

Raeder, Erich. *My Life*. Annapolis, Md.: Naval Institute Press, 1960.

Rahn, Werner. "Die Ausbildung zum Marineoffizier und der Marineschule Mürwik 1910 bis 1980." In *Die Deutsche Marine*, ed. Wolfgang Petter, 143–169. Herford: Mittler, 1983.

———, ed. *Deutsche Marinen im Wandel*. Munich: Oldenbourg, 2005.

———. "Führungsprobleme und Zusammenbruch der Kaiserlichen Marine." In *Die Deutsche Marine*, ed. Wolfgang Petter, 171–187. Herford: Mittler, 1983.

———. "Marinerüstung und Innenpolitik einer parlamentarischen Demokratie—das Beispiel des Panzerschiffes A 1928." In *Die Deutsche Marine*, ed. Wolfgang Petter, 53–72. Herford: Mittler, 1983.

———. *Reichsmarine und Landesverteidigung 1919–1928*. Munich: Bernard and Graefe, 1976.

Rauh, Manfred. "Die englisch-russische Marinekonvention von 1914 und der Ausbruch des Ersten Weltkrieges." *Militärgeschichtliche Mitteilungen* 41 (1987): 37–62.

———. *Föderalismus und Parlamentismus im Wilhelmischen Reich*. Düsseldorf: Droste, 1973.

Raulff, Heiner. *Zwischen Machtpoltik und Imperialismus: Die deutsche Frankreichpolitik 1904–1905*. Düsseldorf: Droste, 1976.

Rich, Norman, and M. H. Fisher, eds. *The Holstein Papers*. Vol. 4, *Correspondence, 1897–1909*. Cambridge: Cambridge University Press, 1963.

Ritter, Gerhard. *Staatskunst und Kriegshandwerk*. Vol. 2. Munich: Oldenbourg, 1960.

Rödel, Christian. *Alfred von Tirpitz und das Seekriegsbild vor dem Ersten Weltkrieg*. Stuttgart: Steiner, 2003.

Röhl, John C. G. "Admiral von Müller and the Approach of War, 1911–1914." *Historical Journal* 12, no. 4 (1969): 651–673.

———. "Dress Rehearsal in December: Military Decision-Making in Germany on the Eve of the First World War." In *The Kaiser and His Court*, ed. John C. G. Röhl, 162–189. Cambridge: Cambridge University Press, 1994.

———. "Die Generalprobe. Zur Geschichte und Bedeutung des 'Kriegsrats' vom 8 Dezember 1912." *Industrielle Gesellschaft und politisches System*, ed. Dirk Stegman. Bonn: Herford, 1978.

———. *Germany without Bismarck: The Crisis of Government in the Second Reich, 1890–1900.* Berkeley: University of California Press, 1967.

———. *Kaiser, Hof, und Staat: Wilhelm II und die deutsche Politik.* Munich: Beck'schen,1987.

———. "An der Schwelle zum Weltkrieg: Eine Dokumentation uber den 'Kriegsrat' vom 8 Dezember 1912." *Militärgeschichtliche Mitteilungen* 21, no. 1 (1977): 77–84.

———. *Wilhelm II, Vol. 1, Die Jugend des Kaisers.* Munich: Beck, 1993.

———. *Wilhelm II: The Kaiser's Personal Monarchy, 1888–1900.* New York: Cambridge University Press, 2004.

———. *Wilhelm II: Der Weg in dem Abgrund, 1900–1941.* Munich: Beck, 2008.

Röhl, John C. G., and Nicolaus Sombart, eds. *Kaiser Wilhelm II: New Interpretations; The Corfu Papers.* Cambridge: Cambridge University Press, 1982.

Röhr, Albert. Handbuch der deutschen Marinegeschichte. Hamburg: Stalling, 1987.

———. "Vorgeschichte und Chronik des Torpedowesens der deutschen Marine bis zum Ende des 19, Jahrhunderts." *Schiff und Zeit*, 7, 47–51.

Röhrkramer, Thomas. *Der Militarismus der "kleinen Leute": Die Kriegervereine im Deutschen Kaiserreich 1871–1914.* Beiträge zur Militärgeschichte, Band 29, ed. Militärgeschichtliches Forschungsamt. Munich: Oldenbourg, 1990.

Røksund, Arne. "The Jeune École: The Strategy of the Weak." In *Navies in Northern Waters*, ed. Rolf Hobson and Tom Kristiansen, chap. 6. London: Cass, 2004.

———. *The Jeune École: The Strategy of the Weak.* Boston: Brill, 2007.

Ropp, Theodore. *The Development of a Modern Navy: French Naval Policy, 1871–1904.* Annapolis, Md.: Naval Institute Press, 1987.

Rössler, Eberhard. *Geschichte des deutschen U-Bootbaus.* Munich: Lehmann, 1975.

———. *Die Torpedos der deutschen U-Boote.* Herford: Koehler, 1984.

Rüger, Jan. *The Great Naval Game: Britain and Germany in the Age of Empire.* Cambridge: Cambridge University Press, 2007.

Rust, Eric C. *Naval Officers under Hitler: The Story of Crew 34.* New York: Praeger, 1991.

Salewski, Michael. *Tirpitz. Aufstieg—Macht—Scheitern.* Persönlichkeit und Geschichte 12/12a, Göttingen: Musterschmidt, 1979.

———, ed. Kiel, *Die Deutschen und die See.* Stuttgart: Steiner, 1992.

Scheibe, Albert. *Tirpitz.* Lubeck: Coleman, 1934.

Schöllgen, Gregor. *Ulrich von Hassell 1881–1944. Ein Konservativer in der Opposition.* Munich: Beck, 1990.

Schrader, Ernst. *Albrecht von Stosch: der General-Admiral Kaiser Wilhelms I: Eine Biographie.* Berlin: Ebering, 1939.

Scheck, Raffael. *Alfred von Tirpitz and German Right-Wing Politics, 1914–1930.* Atlantic Highlands, N.J.: Humanities Press, 1998.

Scheerer, Thomas. "Die Marineoffiziere der Kaiserlichen Marine: Sozialisation und Konflikte." Ph.D. diss., University of Hamburg, 1993.

Schottelius, Herbert, and Wilhelm Deist, eds. *Marine und Marinepolitik 1871–1914.* Düsseldorf: Droste, 1972.

Schrecker, John E. *Imperialism and German Nationalism: Germany in Shantung.* Cambridge, Mass.: Harvard University Press, 1971.

Schrieber, Gerhard. "Thesen zur ideologischen Kontinuität in den machtpolitischen Zielsetzungen der Deutschen Marineführung 1897 bis 1945. In *Marinegeschichte: Probleme—Thesen—Wege,* ed. Manfred Messerschmidt et al., 260–280. Stuttgart: Deutsche Verlags-Anstalt, 1982.

Schubert, Helmuth. "Admiral Alfred von Trotha 1868–1940: Ein Versuch zur historisch-physchologischen Biographie." Ph.D. diss., Freiburg University, 1976.

Schurman, Donald M. *The Education of a Navy: The Development of British Naval Strategic Thought, 1867–1914.* Malabar, Fla.: Krieger, 1984.

———. "Mahan Revisited." In *Maritime Strategy and the Balance of Power: Britain and America in the Twentieth Century,* ed. John B. Hattendorf and Robert S. Jordan, 95–109. New York: St. Martin's, 1989.

Schwengler, Walter. *Völkerrecht, Versailler Vertrag und Auslieferungsfrage. Die Strafverfolgung wegen Kriegsverbrechen als Problem des Friedensschlusses 1919/1920. Schriftenreihe des Militärgeschichtlichen Forschungsamtes 34.* Stuttgart: Deutsche Verlags-Anstalt, 1982.

Seager, Robert. "Alfred Thayer Mahan: Christian Expansionist, Navalist, and Historian." In *Admirals of the New Steel Navy: Makers of the American Naval Tradition, 1880–1930,* ed. James C. Bradford, 24–72. Annapolis, Md.: Naval Institute Press, 1990.

———. *Alfred Thayer Mahan: The Man and His Letters.* Annapolis, Md.: Naval Institute Press, 1977.

Seligmann, Matthew S., ed. *Naval Intelligence from Germany: The Reports of the British Naval Attachés in Berlin, 1906–1914.* London: Naval Records Society, 2007.

Sheehan, James J., ed. *Imperial Germany.* New York: Watts, 1976.

Shimshoni, Jonathan. "Technology, Military Advantage, and World War I: A Case for Military Entrepreneurship." *International Security* 15, no. 3 (winter 1990–91): 187–215.

Simpson, B. Mitchell, III, ed. *The Development of Naval Thought: Essays by Herbert Rosinski.* Newport, R.I.: Naval War College, 1977.

Smith, Jeffrey R. *A People's War: Germany's Political Revolution, 1913–1918.* New York: University Press of America, 2007.

Smith, Percy McCoy. *The Air Force Plans for Peace, 1943–1945.* Baltimore, Md.: Johns Hopkins University Press, 1970.

Snyder, Jack. *The Ideology of the Offensive: Military Decision Making and the Results of 1914.* Ithaca, N.Y.: Cornell University Press, 1984.

———. *Myths of Empire: Domestic Politics and International Ambition.* Ithaca, N.Y.: Cornell University Press, 1991.

Sondhaus, Lawrence. *The Habsburg Empire and the Sea: Austrian Naval Policy, 1797–1866.* West Lafayette, Ind.: Purdue University Press, 1989.

———. *The Naval Policy of Austria-Hungary, 1867–1918: Navalism, Industrial Development, and the Politics of Dualism.* West Lafayette, Ind.: Purdue University Press, 1994.

———. *Preparing for Weltpolitik: German Sea Power before the Tirpitz Era.* Annapolis, Md.: Naval Institute Press, 1997.

Sperber, Jonathan. *The Kaiser's Voters: Electors and Elections in Imperial Germany.* New York: Cambridge University Press, 1997.

Spindler, Arno, ed. *Der Handelskrieg mit U-Booten.* 5 vols. Berlin: Mittler, 1932–66.

Stadelmann, Rudolf. *"Die Epoche der deutsch-englischen Flottenrivalität."* Deutschland und Westeuropa Schoss Laupheim, 1948, 85–146.

Stein, Oliver. *Die deutsche Heeresrüstungspolitik 1890–1914: Das Militär und der Primat der politik.* Paderborn: Schöningh, 2007.

Steinberg, Jonathan. "The Copenhagen Complex." *Journal of Contemporary History* 1, no. 3 (July 1966): 23–46.

———. "Diplomatie als Wille und Vorstellung: Die Berliner Mission Lord Haldanes im Februar 1912." In *Marine und Marinepolitik 1871–1914,* ed. Herbert Schottelius and Wilhelm Deist, 263–282. Düsseldorf: Droste, 1972.

———. "The Novelle of 1908: Necessities and Choices in the Anglo-German Arms Race." Transactions of the Royal Historical Society Series 5, 21 (1971): 25–45.

———. "Review of 'Der Tirpitz Plan.'" *Historical Journal* 16, no. 1 (1973): 196–204.

———. *Yesterday's Deterrent: Tirpitz and the Birth of the German Battle Fleet.* New York: MacMillan, 1965.

Steiner, Barry. *Arms Races, Diplomacy, and Recurring Behavior: Lessons from Two Cases.* Beverly Hills, Calif.: Sage, 1973.

Steiner, Zara. *Britain and the Origins of the First World War.* New York: St. Martin's, 1977.

Steinmetz, Hans-Otto. "Admiral Freiherr von Senden-Bibran: Erster Chef des Marine-Kabinetts von 1889 bis 1906." Typed ms. in the MGFA Library, Potsdam, ca. 1971.

———. "Im Schatten der Armee und der grossen Politik: Eine Betrachtung zum Einsatz der preussisch-deutschen Marine im Krieg 1870/71." *Marine Rundschau* 70 (1973): 212–229.

———. "Noch einmal: Bismarck-Stosch." *Wehrwissenschaftliche Rundschau* 19 (1969): 703–713.

Steltzer, Hans-Georg. *Die deutsche Flotte: Ein historiker Überblick von 1640 bis 1918.* Frankfurt am Main: Societäs, 1989.

Stenographische Berichte über die Verhandlungen des Reichstages. Norddeutsche Buchdruckerei, 1867–1933

Stevenson, David. *Armaments and the Coming of the War: Europe, 1904–1914.* Oxford: Clarendon, 1996.

Stibbe, Matthew. "Germany's 'Last Card': Wilhelm II and the Decision in Favour of Unrestricted Submarine Warfare in January 1917." In *The Kaiser: New Research on Wilhelm II's Role in Imperial Germany,* ed. Annika Mombauer and Wilhelm Deist, 217–234. Cambridge: Cambridge University Press, 2003.

Stürmer, Michael, ed. *Das Kaiserliche Deutschland: Politik und Gesellschaft 1870–1918.* Düsseldorf: Droste, 1970.

Sumida, Jon Tetsuro. *In Defense of Naval Supremacy: Finance, Technology, and British Naval Policy, 1889–1914.* Boston: Unwin Hyman, 1989.

———. "The Historian as Contemporary Analyst: Sir Julian Corbett and Admiral Sir John Fisher." In *Maritime Strategy and the Balance of Pow-*

er: *Britain and America in the Twentieth Century*, ed. John B. Hattendorf and Robert S. Jordan, 125–140. New York: St. Martin's, 1989.

Taylor, A. J. P. *The Struggle for Mastery in Europe, 1848–1918.* Oxford: Oxford University Press, 1954.

Tesdorpf, A. *Geschichte der kaiserliche deutschen Kriegsmarine.* Kiel: Lipsius, 1889.

Thimme, Frederich. *Front Wider Bülow.* Munich: Bruckmann, 1931.

Thimme, Friedrich, et al., eds. *Die Grosse Politik des Europäischen Kabinette*, 40 vols. in 53, Vols. 16 ands 24. Berlin: Deutsche Verlagsanstalt, 1922–27.

Thomas, Charles S. *The German Navy in the Nazi Era.* Annapolis, Md.: Naval Institute Press, 1990.

Thoß, Bruno. "Nationale Rechte, militärische Führung und Diktaturfrage in Deutschland von 1913–1923." *Militärgeschichliche Mitteilungen* 42 (1987): 27–76.

Tirpitz, Alfred von. "Flottenpläne und Flottenbau." In *Unsere Marine im Weltkrieg*, ed. Eberhard von Mantey, 1–6. Berlin: Vaterländische /Weller, 1928.

———. *Memoirs.* 2 vols. New York: AMS Press, 1970 [1919].

———. *Politische Dokumente I. Der Aufbau der deutschen Weltmacht.* Berlin: Cotta'sche Nachfolger, 1924.

———. *Politische Dokumente II. Deutsche Ohnmachtspolitik im Weltkriege.* Berlin: Hanseatische Verlagsanstalt, 1926.

Tirpitz, Wolfgang von. "Tirpitz's letztes Frontkommando." *Marine Rundschau* 62 (1965): 321–335.

Trotha, Adolf von. Grossadmiral von Tirpitz. *Flottenbau und Reichsgedanke.* Breslau: Korn, 1933.

Tuchman, Barbara. *The Proud Tower.* New York: MacMillan, 1966.

Uhle-Wettler, Franz. *Alfred von Tirpitz in seiner Zeit.* Hamburg: Mittler, 1998.

U.S. National Archives. *National Archives Guide to Microfilmed Records, U-Boats, and T-Boats, 1914–1918.* Washington, D.C.: U.S. General Services Administration, 1984.

Usedom, Guido von. "Nelsons Taktik in der Trafalger Schlacht." *Marine Rundschau* (1905): 1467–1486.

Valentini, Rudolf von. *Kaiser und Kabinettschef.* Oldenbourg: Stallings, 1931.

Verchau, Ekkehard. "Von Jachmann über Stosch und Caprivi: Zu den Anfängen der Ära Tirpitz." In *Marine and Marinepolitik 1871–1914*, ed. Wilhelm Deist, 54–73. Düsseldorf: Droste Verlag, 1972.

Waldersee, Graf von. *Denkwürdigkeiten* II. Berlin: Deutsche Verlagsanstalt, 1923.

Walser, Roy. *France's Search for a Battle Fleet: Naval Policy and Naval Power, 1898–1914.* New York: Garland, 1992

Wegener, Wolfgang. *The Naval Strategy of the World War.* Trans. and ed. Holger Herwig. Annapolis, Md.: Naval Institute Press, 1989 [1929].

Wehler, Hans Ulrich. *Das Deutsche Kaiserreich 1871–1918.* Göttingen: Vandenhoek and Ruprecht, 1975.

Weir, Gary E. *Building the Kaiser's Navy: The Imperial German Naval Office in the von Tirpitz Era, 1890–1918.* Annapolis, Md.: Naval Institute Press, 1992.

———. "Naval Strategy and Industrial Mobilization at the Twelfth Hour: The Scheer Program of 1918." *Mariners' Mirror* 77, no. 3 (August 1991): 275–287.

———. "Tirpitz: Architect of Modern German Naval Power." In *Naval History: The Seventh Symposium of the U.S. Naval Academy*, ed. William B.

Cogar, 117–126. Wilmington, Del.:
Scholarly Resources, 1988.
———. "Tirpitz, Technology, and Build-
ing U-Boats, 1897–1916." *Interna-
tional History Review*, 6, no. 3 (May
1984): 174–190.
Wermuth, Adolf . *Ein Beamtenleben.*
Berlin: Scherl Verlag, 1922.
Werner, B von. *Die Kriegsmarine, Ihre
Personal und ihre Organization.*
Leipzig: Fredrich, 1894.
Wichmann, Ulrich. *Der ewige Tirpitz.
Weltmachtstreben, Ressortegoismus,
Egoismus.* Self-Published—MGFA
Library.
Widenmann, Wilhelm. *Marine Attaché
an der kaiserlich-deutschen Botschaft
in Londen 1907–1912.* Göttingen:
Musterschmidt, 1952.
Williams, Rhodri. *Defending the Em-
pire: The Conservative Party and
British Defense Policy, 1899–1915.*
New Haven, Conn.: Yale University
Press, 1991.

Williamson, John D. Karl *Helfferich,
1872–1924: Economist, Financier,
Politician.* Princeton, N.J.: Princeton
University Press, 1971.
Williamson, Samuel R., and Ernest R.
May. "An Identity of Opinion: Histo-
rians and July 1914." *Journal of Mod-
ern History* 79 (2007): 335–387.
Winzen, Peter. Bernhard Fürst von
Bülow: Weltmachtstrategie ohne
Fortune; Wegbereiter der grossen
Katastrophe. Göttingen: Muster-
schmidt, 2003.
———. Bülows Weltmachtkonzept.
*Untersuchungen zur Frühphase seiner
Aussenpolitik 1897–1901.* Boppard:
Boldt, 1977.
Witt, Peter-Christian. *Die Finanzpolitik
des Deutschen Reiches 1903 bis 1913.*
Hamburg: Matthieson, 1970.
Zeender, John K. *The German Center
Party, 1890–1906.* Philadelphia:
American Philosophical Society,
1976.

INDEX

Page numbers in italics refer to illustrations.

A (Allgemeine Marine Department), 359

Adalbert, Prinz, 20–21, 31, 33, 34, 36, 39, 226

Admiralstab: creation of, 163; formal meetings of, 165; Front and, 237, 317; officer corps, 263, 292, 317; peacetime duties of, 236–38, 317–18; strategic planning, 1902–1911, 319–22; Tirpitz's conflicts with, 316–19, 357–61, 378, 461; war games of 1901–1902, 242

Afflerbach, Holger, 524n17

Agadir Crisis (Second Moroccan Crisis; 1911), 309, 322, 323–26, 327, 328, 330–31, 347, 361, 450

agrarian interests: aristocratic interests, linked with, 3, 8, 351; canal bill of 1899, 174–75; on Dawes Plan, 437; direct taxation, resistance to, 351, 453; grain tariffs, 105, 169–70; industrialists versus, 166; Navy Law of 1898 and, 138, 139, 140, 147, 151, 152, 153, 489n31; Navy Law of 1900 and, 166, 167, 174–75, 176, 180, 183, 184, 187–88, 493n19, 496n90; Navy Law amendment of 1906 and, 256; Sammlung between industrialists and, 138, 152, 489n31; Weltpolitik, lack of interest in, 231

Ahlefeld, Hunold von: Navy Law amendment if 1908 and, 273; in OK, 483n15; photograph of, 207; ram, advocacy of, 476n30, 483n13; at RMA, 263; on Tirpitz's memorandum on fleet development, 481n39; in Torpedo Arm, 52, 58–59, 67, 445, 467; in WWI, 387

Albatross, 40

Alexandrine, 487n47

Alexiev, Russian Admiral, 121

Algeciras Act (1906), 323, 324

Algeciras Conference (1906), 264, 265–66, 269

Alghero, Sardinia, Tirpitz family's estate at, 71, 205, 410, 428

Allgemeine Marine Departement (A), 359

"alliance value," 95, 114, 115, 133, 196, 252, 279, 286, 449, 462, 466

Allison, Graham, 10, 11, 12, 68, 91–92, 132, 225, 456–64, 470n17

Almansa (Spanish frigate), 41

Alsace-Lorraine, 5, 200, 307, 352, 428

Amazone, 17, 20, 22, 24, 444

Anderson, Margaret Lavinia, 497n113

Anna, Anna-Luise (Tirpitz's grandmother), 15

annihilation, naval battles of, 88–89

annual appropriations, 98, 131, 230, 283, 294, 315, 454, 463

anti-British feeling in Germany: German Imperial War Council on,

348; Navy Law of 1898 and, 155; Navy Law of 1900 and, 175, 182, 194; Navy Law amendment of 1906 and, 225, 231–32, 249–50, 262; Navy Law amendment of 1912 and, 327; propaganda campaigns making use of, 114–15, 249–50, 262, 324; Second Moroccan Crisis and, 324

anti-Catholicism, 72, 106, 141–42, 276, 420, 421

anti-Jesuit laws, 142, 143, 147, 150, 175, 176, 180, 184, 189, 454, 496n94, 497n1

anti-Semitism, 72, 420, 421, 431

Arabic, 400

Arcona, 17, 22, 24, 119, 120, 122, 123, 472n23, 487n47

Ariadne, 476n26

arms limitation/reduction, 265, 269, 276–78, 284, 298, 352, 428, 431, 464. *See also* diplomatic efforts to reach naval agreement with Britain

arms race: diplomacy with Britain failing to curb, 306, 312, 314, 462; *Dreadnought*-type battleships and, 262, 462–63; historical analysis of, 6, 448, 450, 462, 463, 466; Navy Law of 1900 and, 187, 195, 495n74; Navy Law amendment of 1906 and, 253, 255, 257, 259, 262; Navy Law amendment of 1908 and, 278, 280, 286, 290; Navy Law amendment of 1912 and, 335; ships' gun calibers, 346

Armstrong (artillery company), 32

Army. *See* German Army

artillery: accuracy of, 84, 86, 88; ramming incompatible with use of, 84; ships' gun calibers, 345–46, 359–60, 379; Yalu, Battle of the (1894), 87

artillery test commission, Tirpitz on, 32

Asquith, Herbert, 265, 293, 296, 302, 304, 391

Aube, Théophile, 56–57, 65, 68

Audacious, 382, 383

Aufbau, publication of, 437–39

Augusta, 35

Augusta Victoria (Empress), 405, 406, 411, 442

Australian contributions to British battleship construction, 305, 306

Austria: Balkan War of 1912 and, 3, 347; Bosnia-Herzegovina, annexation of (1908), 296; *Dreadnought*-type battleships, 344; German 1879 defensive alliance with, 74–75; Lissa, Battle of (1866), 27–28, 43, 81, 84, 88; Schleswig, acquisition of, 22; in summer of 1914 leading up to WWI, 367, 368, 369, 370

Austro-Prussian war (1866), 22, 27

Bachem, Karl, 151, 189

Bachmann, Gustav, 67, 387, 396, 399–401, 403, 404, 467, 483n15

Baden, 401

Baden, Grand Duke and Duchess of, 70, 138, 143

Balfour, Lord, 304

Balkans: Austria-Hungary, Germany's defensive alliance of 1879 with, 75; Ottoman Empire, Balkan coalition's defeat of, 347–48

Ballin, Albert, 334–35, 406

Baltic Sea: geography of, 377; map, *xv*; naval and trade dominance of, 18, 19, 23; operations of 1917 in, 423; torpedoes in, 49

Baltic Station, Tirpitz as Chief of Staff at (1890–91), 74–80

Barandon, Carol, 156

Barbarossa (barracks ship), 52

Barth, Wilhelm, 193

Bassermann, Ernst, 289, 290, 326, 508–509n100

Batsch, Carl, 24–27, 39, 44–46, 53, 55, 444–45, 475n22

battles: Dogger Bank (1915), 384–85, 387; Falkland Islands (1914), *219*, 381, 383; Fehman Sound (1882), 53–54, 54; Jutland (1916), 412–15, 426; Lissa (1866), 27–28, 43, 81, 84, 88; the Nile (1798), 88; Somme, German retreat from (1918), 424; Trafalgar (1805), 88; the Yalu (1894), 87

battleships. *See Dreadnought*-type battleships; entries at ship; *specific ships and ship classes by name*

Baudissin, Friedrich Graf von, 296, 320–21, 322, 361, 362, 461

Bauernbund (Peasant League), 141, 151

Bayern, 401

Beatty, David, 379, 384, 412–13, 425

Bebel, August, 151, 155, 242, 259, 289

Becker, Gottlieb, 119

Becker, Willy, 261

Beer Hall Putsch, 433, 434

BEF (British Expeditionary Force), 326, 379, 382

Behncke, Paul, 368–69, 371

Belgium: German naval front on Flanders coast, 380–81, 395; in German operational plans, 94, 116, 252, 320, 368, 370, 390; Ruhr, occupation of, 432, 437; Tirpitz on annexation of, 402, 404, 420, 421–22; WWI German invasion of, 1, 372–73, 380, 392, 448, 451

belligerents' rights, at Hague Peace Conference (1907), 277

Bendemann, Felix (von), 131, 157, 160, 232, 236

Bennigsen, Rudolph von, 149, 150

Berger, Adolph, 28

Berghahn, Volker, 7–9, 12, 67, 111, 152–54, 191, 194, 201, 240–41, 244, 288, 342, 348, 451–52, 454–55, 470n16, 508n99

Bethmann-Hollweg, Theobald von: army increase approved by, 351; in diplomatic talks with Britain, 298, 299, 306–12, 316, 330, 335–40, 450, 512n63; dismissal as Chancellor, 419; on financial conditions at end of 1913, 353; Haldane Mission and, 335–40; Müller's support for, 470n24; Navy Law amendment of 1912 and, 328–34, 340, 341, 463; Second Moroccan Crisis and, 323, 324, 328,

347; Stresemann compared, 436; in summer of 1914 leading up to WWI, 367–73; Tirpitz as possible replacement for, 360–61; Tirpitz's fears of putsch involving, 346; in Tirpitz's memoirs, 6, 425–27, 428–29, 465; in WWI, 378, 379, 386, 387, 394–96, 399–408, 410, 412, 415–17, 419

Bismarck, 383, 443, 465

Bismarck, Otto von: Elbe, order for watch ship on, 37; fall of, 74, 75, 82, 104, 400; Franco-Prussian War and, 33–34; German Constitution put into place by, 3, 169, 343, 350, 419, 455; Lipke opposition to, 70; Navy Law of 1898 and, 139; naval upgrade of 1873, approval of, 40; Navy under, 4, 39; Salonika, assassination of German consuls in, 45; on Social Democrats and Catholic Center, 104, 150; Spanish civil war (1873), court martial of Werner during, 42; Stosch and, 39, 55, 476n27, 477–78n45; Tirpitz compared, 2; Tirpitz's father as schoolmate of, 14, 139; Tirpitz's meeting with, 139; wars of unification, 18, 22; worldview of, 74–75, 82, 104

Black Prince, 269

Blanc, Louis, 57

"blank check" meeting, 367

Blitz, 35–38

Blohm & Voss, 304

Blücher (armored cruiser), 221, 256, 259, 269, 272, 300, 303, 383, 384–85, 387

Blücher (corvette), 52–54, 56, 58, 64

Boedicker, Friedrich, 398, 412

Boer Republic, Jameson Raid into (1895–96), 110, 113, 114

Boer War (1899–1903), 177, 179, 181, 182, 184, 190, 249, 295

Boeter, Oscar, 24

Bosnian Crisis (1908), 296

Bothwell, Arthur von, 30–31

Bouvet (French ship), 34–35

Boxer Rebellion (1900), 197, 232–33, 241

Boyen, Hermann von, 387

Brandenburg class, 85, 87, 88, 105–107

Brandenburg-Prussia, rise of, 18

Braun, Otto: drowning of, 120–21, 124, 467, 483n15; in East Asia with Tirpitz, 107, 120–21, 483n15; at OK, 92, 97, 107, 483n15; in "Torpedo Gang," 66, 67, 120, 467, 483n15; as writer of tactical memoranda, 92, 483n15, 483n25, 484n45

Braunschweig class, 226

Breslau, 382

Brest-Litovsk, Treaty of (1918), 421

Brinkmann, Alfred, 120

Britain: Anglo-French Entente of 1904, 201, 250–51, 262, 266, 308, 340; Anglo-Russian Entente of 1907, 279, 287, 366; on arms limitation/reduction, 265, 269, 276–77; Balkan war of 1912 and, 348; "benevolent neutrality," policy of, 63, 97, 115–16; Bismarck's relationship with, 75; Boer Republic, Jameson Raid into (1895–96), 110; Boer War (1899–1903), 177, 179, 181, 182, 184, 190, 249, 295; Fashoda Affair (1898), 171, 177, 327; German alliance, possible repercussions of, 249; German fleet expansion plans, view of, 154–55, 190, 233, 250, 251, 266, 271, 288, 291, 293–99; German operational plans against and hypothetical war scenarios involving, 114–15, 116, 133, 175, 178, 233–34, 238, 252–53, 319–22, 361–66; Hamburg, treaties with, 19; Hong Kong, acquisition of, 117; Japan, defensive alliance with, 251; Liberal party in, 264–65, 269, 299, 307; "little navy" wing of Liberal Party, 265, 299; Moroccan Crises and, 261, 324–26; Navy Law of 1898 and, 136–37; neutrality in WWI, failure of, 370, 372–73, 458; operational plans for war with Germany, 1911, 326; in potential war be-

tween Germany and France/Russia, 115–16; risk theory regarding (*See* risk theory); Samoan controversy, 175; in summer of 1914 leading up to WWI, 367–74; Tirpitz's first visit to Plymouth, 25–26; in Tirpitz's memo of 1896 on fleet development, 111, 112; Tirpitz's resignation, reaction to, 410; trade and naval dominance of, 18. *See also* anti-British feeling in Germany; British Navy; diplomatic efforts to reach naval agreement with Britain; World War I

British Expeditionary Force (BEF), 326, 379, 382

British Navy: at beginning of WWI, 1; building program aimed at Germany, 339–40; close blockade strategy, abandonment of, 313, 343, 355, 364–65; close blockade strategy employed by, 196, 200, 320, 362, 363–64, 514n14; fleet redistributions, 251–53, 320, 343–45; France, naval conversations with, 343, 344–45; German "fleet against England," 343; German ships compared, 226, 227, 230; herring fisheries, German impotence in, 38; Imperial Fleet, beginning of, 305; interpretation of Tirpitz's intentions regarding, 5, 8–9; "luxury fleet," Churchill's description of German Navy as, 336; Navy Law amendment of 1912, repercussions of, 343–46; ships of German Navy compared to British, 226, 227, 230, 376–77, 383, 414; Spanish civil war (1873), cooperation with Germans in, 41–42; in summer of 1914 leading up to WWI, 368, 370; torpedo fleet of, 65, 480n111; U-boats, 256, 354. *See also* World War I

Brommy, Rudolf, 20

Bruegg, Spraher von, 524n245

Buchholz, Glomsda von, 36, 38

Büchsel, Wilhelm: Admiralstab, as head of, 237, 263, 272, 317–18, 320, 447, 461; Navy Law of 1898 and,

129; OK dissolution and, 160, 161; photograph of, *213*; retirement of, 296, 320;; strategic thought of, 90; in "Torpedo Gang," 67, 467; in training with Tirpitz, 24, 27, 28; as Under State Secretary in place of Capelle, 404–405

budget right: historical analysis of concept of, 4, 451–56; "iron budget," concept of, 6, 8, 191, 193, 230, 286, 342, 451–52, 456, 508n99; Navy Law of 1898 and, 130, 131, 145, 148, 491n76; Navy Law of 1900 and, 177, 191–95; Navy Law amendment of 1906 and, 244

Bulgaria, in Balkan War of 1912, 347

Bülow, Bernhard von: diplomacy with Britain, 295–99, 305–306, 311, 316, 450; elections of 1907, 274–75, 454; fall of, 305–306, 307, 312; heart attack in early 1906, 266; Navy Law of 1898 and, 129–30, 132, 133, 147, 152; Navy Law of 1900 and, 177, 179, 180, 189, 197; Navy Law amendment of 1906 and, 258, 260, 262; Navy Law amendment of 1908 and, 266, 274–76, 279, 282, 284, 286–88, 292; OK, dissolution of, 158; rejected as possible Chancellor in 1917, 419; Russia, proposed German alliance with, 251, 449; Tirpitz on, 6; Weltpolitik and, 231, 232, 234, 306; on widening Kaiser Wilhelm Canal, 256

Bundesrat, 3–4; on naval takeover of commercial activities, 115; Navy Law of 1898 and, 130, 132, 138–40, 143–45, 150, 293; Navy Law of 1900 and, 168, 181, 183, 187; Navy Law amendment of 1906 and, 258; Navy Law amendment of 1908 and, 271, 282, 288; Navy Law amendment of 1912 and, 332–33, 342; Tirpitz's relationship with, 342, 453; in WWI, 405, 408

Bundesrath affair, 184, 188, 189, 197, 324

Burchardt, Lothar, 277

Bureaucratic or Governmental Politics Model *(Ressorteifer)* or Model 3 behavior: Admiralstab, Tirpitz's ability to defeat, 317; collapse of institutional edifice supporting, 373–74, 377–78; historical analysis of, 459–64; naval operations plans, 1911–1914, and, 363, 365; Navy Law amendment of 1906, 261–62; Navy Law amendment of 1908, 286; Navy Laws of 1898 and 1900, 155, 158, 164, 175, 195, 495n77; at OK, 102, 459; Reichstag, Tirpitz's relationship, 455; at RMA, 225, 228, 229–30, 459–64; "sunk costs" fallacy, use of, 309; theory of, 10, 11–12; at Torpedo Arm, 67–68, 459; U-boats, 357; in WWI, 381

Burgfrieden, 405

Bürkner, Hans von, 231, 269, 282

Butterlin, Adolph, 30–31

BVP, 439, 440, 441

Campbell-Bannerman, Sir Henry, 265, 293

Canadian contributions to British battleship construction, 306

canal bill of 1899, 174–75, 180

Capelle, Eduard von: on diplomatic talks with Britain, 309–10, 337–38; Heeringen and, 358; importance on Tirpitz's staff, 223; Michaelis and, 230; Navy Law of 1898 and, 134–35, 137, 138, 141, 142, 148, 152; Navy Law of 1900 and, 176, 178, 181, 183, 187, 188, 191, 201; Navy Law amendment of 1906 and, 241, 243, 245, 249, 255, 256; Navy Law amendment of 1908 and, 266–67, 270–73, 279, 280, 283, 284, 287–90; Navy Law amendment of 1912 and, 327–30, 332, 359, 520n151; Navy Law amendment of 1913–14, consideration of, 349, 352; on navy prospects at end of 1913, 353; OK, dissolution of, 162; personal and professional relationship with Tirpitz, 470n22; photograph of, *210*; Reichstag, relationship with, 452,

453–54, 455; retirement as RMA State Secretary, 423; retirement as RMA Under State Secretary, 404, 527–28n122; on risk theory, 455, 462; as RMA department head, 240, 263; RMA in WWI, effectively in charge of, 401; as RMA State Secretary after Tirpitz, 410–11, 422; in summer of 1914 leading up to WWI, 360, 366–70; on Tirpitz, 7, 12–13; Tirpitz's fears of putsch in 1912, counsel regarding, 346–47; on Treasury under Wermuth, 314–16; U-boats, 356

Caprivi, Leo Graf von: Army bill of 1893, 132; as Chancellor, 74, 75, 76, 79, 99, 104–105, 106; on economic blockade, 116, 390; as head of navy, 477n48; immediate preparedness, emphasis on, 82; strategic thought of, 89–90, 116; tariff reductions by, 105, 169–70; Tirpitz's history of Torpedo Arm sent to, 73; Tirpitz's relationship to, 55, 445, 477n46; Torpedo Arm under, 55–64, 67, 68, 478n60; trade treaties, expiration of, 177; Weltpolitik and, 231

capture, right to, 277–78, 388, 391

Cassel, Sir Ernest, 335, 518n84

Catholic Center Party: anti-Jesuit laws, 142, 143, 147, 150, 175, 176, 180, 184, 189, 454, 496n94, 497n1; in coalition of 1926, 441; in coalition to block Social Democrats, 8; Conservative alliance, 1909, 305; declaration of state of emergency (1923), 433; diplomatic efforts to reach naval agreement with Britain and, 312, 316, 345; elections of 1907, 274–75; elections of 1912, 334; factions within, 4, 141–42, 151; Flottenverein and, 167; German Southwest Africa (Namibia), tribal rebellion in (1903–1907), 247; grain tariffs, 170; naval funding, 1890–1897, 106, 113, 128; Navy Law of 1898 and, 130, 140–42, 144, 147–53; Navy Law of 1900 and, 173, 175, 176, 180, 183–84, 187–90, 192, 194, 195; Navy Law amendment of 1906 and, 244, 246, 266; Navy Law amendment of 1908 and, 266, 274–75, 282–83, 284, 285, 289–91; Navy Law amendment of 1912 and, 340, 341, 342; peace resolution of 1917, 419; stability of representation in Reichstag, 103; Tirpitz and, 72, 497–98n1

Catholic membership in Fatherland Party, 420, 421

Catholicism, German prejudice against, 72, 106, 141–42, 276, 420, 421

Cato, 137

Cawdor Memorandum, 264–65

Center Party. See Catholic Center Party

Chancellor, office of, 4

Chancellorship, Tirpitz proposed for, 360–61, 415, 417–18, 419, 435–36

Cheltenham Lady's College, 71

Childers, Erskine, 266

China, 119

China: Boxer Rebellion (1900), 197, 232–33, 241; Sino-Japanese War (1894–1895), 87, 106, 118; Tirpitz in East Asia (1896–97) (See East Asia, Tirpitz in); Tsingtau, German base at, 1, 122, 232, 313, 361, 381, 462. See also Kiachou Bay, China

Churchill, Winston: diplomatic efforts at naval agreement with Germany, 293, 294, 299, 300, 302, 305, 335, 336, 339–40, 451; fleet redistributions under, 344; Haldane Mission and, 335, 336, 339, 340; at Kiel Week, 71; in "little navy" wing of British Liberal Party, 265, 299; "luxury fleet" remark, 336; "naval holiday" proposals, 340, 345, 519n114; observational blockade, dislike of, 364; operational plans for war with Germany and, 326; risk theory and, 344; telegram to Tirpitz reporting son's safety, 72, 524n12; in WWI, 381, 382, 391, 399

ciphers, 358, 382–83

Civil War, U.S., 18, 43, 235

Claß, Heinrich, 419

Clausewitz, Carl von, 32, 72, 77, 81, 91, 93–94, 228, 383n53, 387, 458

close blockade: British abandonment of strategy of, 313, 343, 355, 364–65; as British strategy, 196, 200, 320, 362, 363–64, 514n14; German defense planning against, 105, 314, 320; Tirpitz on modern impossibility of, 447; WWI and, 379, 390, 391

coalition (Sammlung or Sammling-spolitik), 8, 138, 151–53, 174, 274–75, 289–91, 306, 441, 489n31, 530n38

codes and codebooks, 358, 382–83

Coerper, Carl (von), 233, 253, 256, 268, 271, 273, 279, 294, 467, 503n103

Colbert, Jean-Baptiste, 111

Colonial Society, 136, 168, 176

commercial blockade, 116, 388–93, 394–95, 399

Communist Party in Germany (Kommunistische Partei Deutschland, or KPD), 425, 439, 440

compressed air torpedoes, 358

Congress of Berlin (1884), 104

Congress of Vienna (1815), 19

Conservative Party: Center alliance, 1909, 305; collapse of coalition of 1907, 305; concerns over growth of Social Democrats and Catholic Center, 103–104; diplomatic efforts to reach naval agreement with Britain, repercussions of, 313; elections of 1907, 274; elections of 1912, 334; naval funding, 1890–1896, 106, 113; Navy Law of 1898 and, 140, 147, 148, 151; Navy Law of 1900 and, 176, 184, 189, 192; Navy Law amendment of 1906 and, 259; Navy Law amendment of 1908 and, 274, 283, 290; Navy Law amendment of 1912 and, 340, 341; U-boat war, Tirpitz's beliefs about support for, 400

Constitution: of German Empire, 3–4, 38–39, 132, 169, 343, 350, 419, 455; of Weimar Republic, 436

contractors, Tirpitz's dealings with, 50, 52, 55–56, 59, 303–304, 457

Coogan, John W., 392

"Copenhagen," 250, 252, 258, 260, 266, 273, 293, 369, 462

Corbett, Julian, 93

Cormoran, 119–20, 122

Cotta (publishing house), 437, 438

Courbet, 272

Crailsheim, Krafft von, 144–45

crew training issues, 229

Crimean War, 18

Crowe, Sir Eyre, 294

D-1, 216

Dähnhardt, Harald: on diplomatic talks with Britain, 337, 338; at E, 240; importance on Tirpitz's staff, 223, 263; Michaelis and, 228; Navy Law of 1898 and, 134–35; Navy Law of 1900 and, 182, 189, 494n56; Navy Law amendment of 1906 and, 243, 245, 246, 247, 256; Navy Law amendment of 1908 and, 266–68, 270, 279, 280, 283, 284, 290; Navy Law amendment of 1912 and, 327, 330–31, 332, 338, 359; Navy Law amendment of 1913–14, consideration of, 349; Reichstag, relationship with, 452, 453–54, 455; in summer of 1914 leading up to WWI, 368, 370; in "Torpedo Gang," 263, 445, 467; war aims, thought piece on, 403

Danish Virgin Islands, 449

Dawes Plan, 435, 436, 437, 439

Declaration of London (1909), 389–90

Declaration of Paris (1856), 105, 388–89

deep line ahead, 86, 87

Deist, Wilhelm, 8, 100, 454

Delcassé, Theophile, 251, 252, 505n148

Delphin, 41

Denmark: assumed as potential German enemy, 82, 89; Danish Virgin Islands, 449; in German operational plans, 94, 253, 277, 320; German wars of unification, 17–18, 22; Na-

poleonic Wars, British seizure of
Danish fleet during, 250; Schleswig-
Holstein, efforts to incorporate,
20–21, 22; tolls for Atlantic-directed
trade charged by, 19; WWI, neutrality in, 377

Derfflinger, 376, 401

deterrence. *See* risk theory; strategy

Deutscher Flottenverein. *See*
  Flottenverein

Deutscher Reichsmarine Verein, 166

Deutschland class, 226, 504n131

Dewey, George, 124, 177, 234

Dick, Karl, 467, 483n15

dictatorship, Tirpitz's support for, 396,
424, 428, 432, 433, 434, 436

Diedrichs, Otto von: Admiralstab, as
head of, 236–37, 461; German base
in East Asia and, 118, 124, 128, 143;
Michaelis and, 228; Navy Law of
1898 and, 131; photograph of, 213; retirement of, 317; at Torpedo Arm, 48;
in training with Tirpitz, 24, 27

Diedrichsen, Otto, 228

Dienstschrift VI (1893), 86

Dienstschrift IX (1894), 87, 91, 92–98,
107, 200, 446–47

Diercks, Wulf, 521n200

diplomacy: Anglo-French Entente
(1904), 201, 250–51, 262, 266; Anglo-
German alliance, possible repercussions of, 249; Anglo-Russian Entente
(1907), 279, 287; Hague Peace Conference (1907), 276–78, 284, 389–91;
Navy Law amendment of 1906 affected by, 249–53; Russo-German
alliance, proposal for, 251–52, 362,
449; Tirpitz's minor role in, 449–51

diplomatic efforts to reach naval agreement with Britain, 293–316; arms
race, failure to curb, 306, 312, 314,
462; Bethman-Hollweg's efforts, 298,
299, 306–312, 316, 512n63; Bülow's
attempts, 295–99, 305–306; effective
end of, 345; Haldane Mission, 334–
40, 345; naval scare of 1909, 291, 297,

299–306, 312; Navy Law amendment
of 1908, reaction to, 293–99; Navy
Law amendment of 1912 and, 307,
309–310, 326, 328, 330, 334–40, 367;
Reichstag and Treasury repercussions, 312–16, 511n45

disarmament. *See* arms limitation/
  reduction

distant blockade, 134, 314, 362–65, 376,
389, 391, 414, 446–47

DNVP (German National People's
Party), 430, 434–37, 439–42

Dogger Bank, Battle of (1915), 384–85,
387

Dogger Bank incident (1904), 251–52,
319, 449

double-screw torpedoes, 49

doubling system proposed by Hollmann, 77–78, 80, 100

Dreadnought, 87, 217, 253–54, 256, 354,
454, 463

Dreadnought-type battleships: arms
race started by, 262, 462–63; Austrian, 344; British construction of,
253–57, 265, 282, 288, 300, 302, 306,
307, 396; cost increases required for
construction of, 140, 170, 191–92,
230, 259, 275, 332, 462–63, 504n120;
Fisher's intentions regarding, 253,
254, 257, 262, 462–63, 503nn103,104;
in French Navy, 272; German construction of, 256–57, 268, 271, 272,
300, 307, 511n34; German interior
line advantage lost due to size of,
319–20, 361; *Invincible* class, relationship to, 269; Italian, 254–55, 344;
Japanese construction of, 253, 282;
last German and British pre-*Dreadnought* ship types, 226; "material reserve" trick and, 500n62; risk theory
and, 197, 199, 200; Russian, 377; U.S.
construction of, 253, 282, 283; WWI,
in British and German Navies at beginning of, 1, 376–77

"Dropping the Pirate" cartoon, *Punch*,
400

DuBois, Commander, 119
Dülffer, Jost, 278, 442
Dumas, Philip, 271
Duncan class, 226
Duppler, Jörg, 25
DVP (German People's Party), 432, 439–41

E (Etatsabteilung), 181, 229, 240, 242, 246, 248, 249, 255, 268, 280, 282, 330, 331, 342, 408
East Asia, Tirpitz in (1896–97), 117–28; base scouting, 119–24; German base, plan to establish, 117–19, 449; recall, events leading to, 124–28
Ebert, President, 434, 437, 439, 440
economic blockade, 116, 388–93, 394–95, 399
economics: belligerents' rights and, 278; Navy Laws and amendments, arguments for, 146, 258, 350–51; Tirpitz's reductionist view of, 93–94, 278, 510n17
Edward VII (king of England), 251, 283, 291
Eickstedt, Rudolf von, 230–31, 255, 272, 273, 282
Elbe, 53
Eley, Geoff, 152, 175
Elisabeth, 40, 41, 42
Emden, 381
Emden (port), Prussian loss of, 18, 19
Emperor, King of Prussia as, 3, 38
Ems dispatch (14 July, 1870), 33–34
England. *See* Britain
Enigma machine, 358
Epkenhans, Michael, 8, 346, 357, 370, 396, 470n13, 513n91
Erzberger, Matthias, 229, 274, 312, 313, 314, 330, 351, 366, 395, 403, 406, 407, 430, 454
Erzherzog Friedrich, 25, 27
Etatsabteilung (E), 181, 229, 240, 242, 246, 248, 249, 255, 268, 280, 282, 330, 331, 342, 408
Eulenburg, Count August von, 415, 424

Fairbairn, Brett, 192
Falkenhayn, Erich von, 369, 370, 372, 385, 387, 399, 406, 408, 415, 416
Falkland Islands, Battle of (1914), *219*, 381, 383
Fashoda Affair (1898), 171, 177, 327
Fatherland Party, 418–22, 424, 439, 530n38
Fehman Sound, Battle of (1882), 53–54, *54*
Feldafing, Tirpitz's move to, 441–42
Fernis, Hansgeorg, 261
Fichte, Johann Gottlieb, 15
Firma Stabilimento Tecnico, Fiume, 47–48, 50
First Moroccan Crisis (1905), 254, 260, 261, 262, 265–66
First Navy Law. *See* Navy Law, 1898
First World War. *See* World War I
Fischel, Max (von): at Admiralstab, 321–22, 323, 361, 362, 461; description of, 514n119; OK, dissolution of, 162; OK-RMA naval bill draft, 128; photograph of, *213*; in Torpedo Arm, 56, 67, 445, 467
fish torpedoes, 47
Fisher, Sir John: close blockage strategy, abandonment of, 364; First Sea Lord, appointed as, 251; fleet expansion efforts, 291, 294, 307; Liberal majority of 1906 and, 265; naval scare of 1909 and, 299–302; on old ships, 244, 245–46; redistribution of British Navy and, 252, 253, 320; Tirpitz's indiscreet remark about, 283; torpedo boats designed by, 62; type escalations, intentions regarding, 253, 254, 257, 262, 462–63, 503nn103,104; U-boats, 354
Flanders. *See* Belgium
Fleet Command: absence of Fleet Chief, prior to 1903, 163, 238–40, 264, 318, 460; Admiralstab and, 321; conflict between naval staffs, 357–61, 461; creation of Office of Fleet Commander, 318–19; Koester's struggles

with Tirpitz over, 238–40, 264, 318–
19; Prinz Heinrich as Fleet Chief,
264, 319; Tirpitz's efforts to become
Fleet Chief, 386, 406
Flottenverein (Navy League): crisis in,
168–69, 183, 276, 289; decreasing
public support for, 353; formation
of, 166–67; Navy Law of 1900 and,
166–69, 176, 183; Navy Law amendment of 1906 and, 240, 254, 257, 259,
266, 503n119; Navy Law amendment
of 1908 and, 266, 270, 275–76, 289;
Navy Law amendment of 1912 and,
327, 330, 340; Tirpitz and, 167, 450;
Wehrverein and, 345
flying squadron, 172, 176, 242, 243,
268, 353
food shortages, 116, 238, 390–93, 419,
422–23
France: Alsace-Lorraine, 5, 200, 307,
352, 428; Anglo-French Entente of
1904, 201, 250–51, 262, 266, 308,
340; on arms limitation/reduction,
277; Balkan war of 1912 and, 348; in
Bismarck's worldview, 74–75; British naval conversations with, 343,
344–45; Fashoda Affair (1898), 171,
177, 327; First Moroccan Crisis, 254,
260, 261, 262; fleet redistribution,
272; German ships compared to
French, 227; Great Britain, projected
German war with, 115; interpretation
of Tirpitz's intentions regarding, 5;
Jeune École, 56, 82, 354, 477n55; naval program of, 496n92; Navy Law,
1900, reaction to, 190; operational
plans against, 55, 57, 62–63, 75, 82,
89–90, 96–98, 104–105, 108, 112,
115–16, 134, 237, 242, 272; Revolution of 1848, 20; risk theory regarding
(see risk theory); Ruhr, occupation
of, 431–33, 435, 437; Second Moroccan Crisis (Agadir Crisis), 309, 322,
323–26; torpedo boats of, 56–57, 65;
U-boats, 256, 354
Franckenstein Clause, 169–70
Franco-Prussian War (1870–71), 5, 10,
15, 22, 33–35, 36, 82, 91, 379, 426

Franz Ferdinand, assassination of, 367
Franzius, Georg, 122, 123, 124
Frederick II the Great (king of Prus-
sia), 18
Frederick (Crown Prince, later Em-
peror Frederick III), 38, 39, 51
Frederick VII (king of Denmark), 20
Frederick William, Great Elector of
Brandenburg, 18
Frederick William IV (king of Prussia),
19, 20
Freie Vereinigung fur Flottenvortrage,
168
Freisinnige Volkspartei, 140. See also
Richter, Eugen
French Congo, 326
French Revolution (1789–99), 2
Friedrich Carl, 33, 38, 40–42, 44, 45,
46, 226, 473n32
Friedrich Carl, Prinz, 36, 43
Friedrichsort, Torpedo Depot at, 56
Fritzen, Alois, 150, 187
Front: Admiralstab and, 237, 317; crew
training issues, 229; Navy Law
amendment of 1912, emphasis on
readiness in, 341; officer shortages,
complaints about, 131, 137, 159, 317;
postponement of interests of, 174,
189, 224, 241; on ships' gun calibers,
346; Tirpitz's conflicts with, 161, 163,
190, 227, 228–29, 264, 271, 378, 461;
torpedoes and, 49, 66. See also Fleet
Command
Fürst Bismarck, 226

Galster, Carl, 6, 289, 295, 313, 343,
354–56
Gat, Azar, 93
Gazelle, 22, 27–28, 472n23
Gefion, 29–30
Geissler, Richard, 24
Gemzell, Carl-Axel, 10, 445, 457
George V (king of England), 370
German Army: ability of empire to feed
army in wartime, 105; Army Bill of
1913, 347–53; Bethmann and Wer-
muth's requests for budget increases
from, 332–33; Fatherland Party and,

420; "luxury fleet," Army reaction to Churchill's description of German Navy as, 336; naval propaganda directed at, 187; Navy, lack of coordinated planning with, 373; Navy Law amendment of 1912 and, 332–33, 341; OHL, 415–17, 419, 420, 421, 424; operational plans compared to Navy, 253; organization of, in German Empire, 3; postponement of Army Bill, 341; propaganda campaigns for, 351; quiescence in budget matters, 1897–1911, 131–32, 332; Schlieffen Plan, 6, 96, 370, 373, 385, 390–91, 448; Somme, retreat from (1918), 424; Wehrverein, 345, 347, 351

German Cameroons, 326

German Colonial Society, 136, 168, 176

German Communist Party (Kommunistische Partei Deutschland, or KPD), 425

German Confederation, 19–22

German Emperor, King of Prussia as, 3, 38

German Empire: Balkan war of 1912 and, 348; colonies, acquisition of, 104; Constitution of, 3–4, 38–39, 132, 169, 343; inception of, 38–39; naval fleet plans intended as stabilization of, 8–9; official name of, 3; population and economic growth, 1871–1910, 103–104; Revolution and collapse of (1918), 425. *See also* anti-British feeling in Germany; Bundesrat; Imperial Reichstag; World War I

German Fatherland Party, 418–22, 424, 439, 530n38

German Imperial War Council, 348, 352, 377, 519n135

German merchant marine. *See* merchant marine, German

German National People's Party (DNVP), 430, 434–37, 439–42

German Navy: annual appropriations for, 98, 131, 230, 283, 294, 315, 454, 463; armored ship program, Caprivi's desire to abandon, 57; Army, lack

of coordinated planning with, 373; at beginning of WWI, 1–2; British bases, early dependence on, 25; as developed by Tirpitz, 1–3; entry of Tirpitz into Prussian Navy, 17–18, 22–23, 24; "fog of peace" due to technological change, 81–84; in Franco-Prussian War, 33–35; herring fisheries and need to expand, 37–38; historical background, 17–23; interpretation of Tirpitz's intentions regarding, 5–13; leadership in event of war, 371–72, 377–78, 460–61; "luxury fleet," Churchill's description of German Navy as, 336; morale in WWI, 396, 401, 422–23, 424–25, 427; North German Confederation, Federal Navy of, 28, 33–34; officer corps, creation and training of, 21–22, 39, 43–45, 131; operational plans, 1911–1914, 361–66; postwar limitation on size of, 428, 464; Reichstag funding, 1890–1895, 105–107; scuttling of, 427–28, 464–65; ship construction, 1898–1905, 225–27; ships of German Navy compared to British, 226, 227, 230, 376–77, 383, 414; Stosch regime, 38–40; suicide charge, collapse of, 424–25; training of Tirpitz in Prussian Navy, 17–18, 22–23, 24; William II's reorganization of, 4–5, 63–65, 76–77, 82, 98, 371, 480n160; young officer in, Tirpitz as, 33–46. *See also* Admiralstab; Fleet Command; Front; Marinekabinett or MK; Oberkommando or OK; Reichsmarineamt or RMA; seniority system in German Navy; Supreme Naval Command; Torpedo Arm; World War I

German People's Party (DVP), 432, 439–41

German Republic: Beer Hall Putsch, 433, 434; inflation problem, 428, 431, 432–34; Kapp Putsch, 264, 430; political turmoil in Reichstag (1920–1924), 434–42; Ruhr Crisis (1923–1924), 431–33, 435; Russia, Treaty

of Rapallo with (1922), 428; Tirpitz
as Reichstag deputy (1924–1928),
434–42; Tirpitz's dislike of egalitar-
ian government of, 428, 430–31
German Southwest Africa (Namibia),
rebellion in (1903–1907), 247, 274–75,
305
Germania (naval yard), 60, 301
Gneisenau, August Neidhardt von, 15
Gneisnau, 227
Goeben, 1, *218*, 322, 376, 382
Goltz, Max Freiherr von der: Hol-
lmann at RMA, friction with, 74; on
Kaiser, 46; photograph of, *213*; on
Thetis, 30, 31; Tirpitz as OK Chief
of Staff under, 81, 84, 86, 88, 92, 98,
99, 101, 102
Goschen, British Ambassador, 307
Gottschall, Terrell, 123, 124
Governmental Politics Model. *See* Bu-
reaucratic or Governmental Politics
Model
grain tariffs, 105, 169–70
Great Britain. *See* Britain
Great War. *See* World War I
Greece, in Balkan War of 1912, 347
Grey-Cambon letters, 343, 344
Grey, Sir Edward: diplomatic talks with
Germany, 1909–1911, 294, 297, 300,
307, 308, 309, 311, 312, 335, 339;
Navy Law amendment of 1908 and,
264, 277, 291; Second Moroccan
Crisis and, 325; in summer of 1914
leading up to WWI, 369, 370; in
WWI, 391
Gröber, Adolf, 187, 330
Groener, Wilhelm, 424
Groos, Otto, 429
Grosser Kurfürst, 62, 475n22
gun calibers on ships, 345–46, 359–60,
379

Habsburg Empire, 19
Hague Peace Conference (1907), 276–
78, 284, 389–91
Haldane, Richard, and Haldane Mission, 334–40, 345, 348

Halle, Ernst von, 137, 146, 176, 178,
494n36
Hallmann, Hans, 6, 125, 151, 465
Hamburg: British attack, ability to re-
sist, 175; England, treaties with, 19;
in North German Confederation, 33
Hamburg-Amerika shipping line
(HAPAG), 251
Hankey, Maurice, 390
Hannover, 18, 21, 27, 28, 37
Hansa, 44, 474n58
Hanseatic League, 18, 94
HAPAG (Hamburg-Amerika shipping
line), 251
Harms, Theodor, 304
Hartmann, Malwine (Tirpitz's mother),
14–15, 24, 70
Hartmann, Peter Emmanuel (Tirpitz's
uncle), 15
Hartmann, Peter Immanuel (Tirpitz's
grandfather), 15
Harvey tow torpedoes, 47, 48
Hassell, Ilse von (née Tirpitz), 70,
71–72, 73, *206*, 410, 443
Hassell, Ulrich von (Tirpitz's son-in-
law), 71–73, 410, 412, 415, 421–22,
443, 480n5
Heath, British Naval Attaché, 304–305
Heeringen, August von: at Admiralstab,
323, 358, 447; Flottenverein and,
167, 168; at Imperial War Council,
348; Michaelis and, 230; on naval
operations plans, 1911–1914, 361–63,
364, 365; Navy Law of 1898 and,
136–37, 141, 148, 153; Navy Law
of 1900 and, 187, 199; Navy Law
amendment of 1908 and, 273, 281;
Navy Law amendment of 1912 and,
332; on need to sustain feasibility of
victory, 447, 458; at OK, 100, 107,
483n15, 484n60; OK, dissolution of,
162; photograph of, *211*; retirement
of, 366; at RMA, 263; as Tirpitz collaborator, 478n64; in Torpedo Arm,
58–59, 66–67, 445, 467–68
Heeringen, Josias von, 332–33, 341, 347,
348, 351

Heinrich (prince): as boy, 38; as Fleet Chief, 264, 319, 460; in Great Britain, 64, 233, 250; Navy Law of 1898 and, 145, 160, 161–62, 164; Navy Law of 1900 and, 168; photograph of, *207*; in ships' gun calibers disagreement, 346; in summer of 1914 leading up to WWI, 370, 371; on Tirpitz's memoirs, 429, 442; in "Torpedo Gang," 468; in U.S., 235

Helgoland: in British hands, 20–21, 37; exchanged for Zanzibar, 75, 104; German fortification of, 328; in WWI, 1, 371, 379, 381, 383, 398

"Helgoland and the Thames" argument, 133, 196, 198, 364, 446

Helgoland class, 322, 332

Henk, Wilhelm (von), 39, 473n29

Herero insurrection, German Southwest Africa (Namibia; 1903–1907), 247, 274–75

Hermine (Empress), 442

herring fisheries, 37–38

Hertha class, 107, 133, 337, 348

Hertling, Georg von, 151, 152, 330, 421

Hess, Rudolf, 431

Heusner, Eduard von, 48, 50

Heyking, Eduard von, 121–24

Hindenburg, Paul von, 385, 396, 400, 401, 405, 415–17, 421, 424, 440–41, 529n30

Hipper, Franz Ritter von, 383–84, 387–88, 412–13, 423, 424, 425

Hitler, Adolf, 429, 433, 443, 465–66

Hobson, Rolf, 44, 78, 90, 91, 93, 154, 197, 199, 200, 225, 391, 392, 448, 458, 513n87

Hohenlohe-Schillingsfürst, Prince Chlodwig: as Chancellor, 105, 112, 127; East Asia, support for German base in, 118; Navy Law of 1898 and, 129, 138, 143, 146; Navy Law of 1900 and, 175, 178, 180–81, 183, 185, 494n31; on Senden, 78

Hohenzollern (imperial yacht), 73, 74, 106

Holland. *See* Netherlands

Holland, John, 353–54

Hollmann, Friedrich (von): as commander of II Division, 73; dismissal from RMA, 127, 129, 130, 140; doubling system proposed by, 77–78, 80, 100; East Asia, support for German base in, 118; Emperor, friendship with, 315; fleet development plan and, 107, 109, 125–27, 146; at Kiel Naval School, 31; OK dissolution and, 160; OK, turf war with, 73, 98–101, 107, 108, 125–27, 161; as RMA State Secretary, 74, 76, 82, 96, 105–107, 113, 115, 116–17, 125–27, 138, 140, 460

Hollweg, Carl, 7, 12–13, 328, 330–31, 365

Holstein, Friedrich von, 104, 118, 127, 234, 251, 266, 286, 287, 449

Holtzendorff, Henning von: as Admiralstab head during WWI, 401, 403–404, 406–407, 461; as Fleet Chief, 315, 319, 321–22, 357; Hopmann on, 360; naval operations plans, 1911–1914, 361, 362, 363; Navy Law amendment of 1912 and, 329, 331; on OK-RMA turf war, 156; photographs of, *213, 214*; retirement of, 423; Tirpitz's fears of putsch involving, 346, 360; in Tirpitz's memoirs, 426; on U-boats, 403, 406–407, 416, 417, 418

Holy Roman Empire, 19

Hong Kong: British acquisition of, 117; Tirpitz in, 122, 123, 124, 127

Hoover, J. Edgar, 459

Hopmann, Albert: on conflicts between naval staffs, 1911–1914, 357, 359–61; on Fischel, 514n119; on "fleet against England," 343; on Fleet Command, 318; gloominess at end of 1913, 352; on Kiaochou Bay, 144; on Koester, 238; Michaelis and, 358; on Navy Law of 1898, 129; Navy Law amendment of 1912 and, 329, 331, 332, 333, 334, 338, 359, 448; Navy Law amendment of 1913–14, consideration of, 349–50; at OK, 483n15; on plan for attack on English Channel in case of war with France, 484n60; on Second Moroccan Crisis, 324; on Senden, 79; in summer of 1914 leading up to WWI, 366–70; on tactical exercises, 85; in "Torpedo Gang," 445, 468; on war-readiness, 240; William II's anonymous article on cruisers (1904), response to, 247; in WWI, 386, 396, 398, 403, 423

Hubatsch, Walther, 6, 403

Hugenberg, Alfred, 431, 433, 435

hyperinflation, postwar, 428, 431, 432–34

Iltis, 107, 120–21, 122, 124, 232

Imperial Chancellor, office of, 4

Imperial Chancellorship, Tirpitz proposed for, 360–61, 415, 417–18, 419

Imperial Naval Office. *See* Reichsmarineamt or RMA

Imperial Navy. *See* German Navy

Imperial Reichstag: annual appropriations from, 98, 131, 230, 283, 294, 315, 454, 463; budget right and (*see* budget right); diplomatic efforts to reach naval agreement with Britain, repercussions of, 312–14, 511n45; elections of 1907, shift in power after, 274–75, 279, 507n53; elections of 1912, 334; Franckenstein Clause, 169–70; Hollman's bungling of fleet expansion plan presented to, 125–27; naval funding, 1890–1895, 105–107; naval upgrade of 1873, approval of, 40; Navy Law of 1898 and (*see under* Navy Law, 1898); Navy Law of 1900 and, 173–74, 176–77, 183–84, 187–89, 191–92; Navy Law amendment of 1906 and, 244, 246, 248, 249, 253, 254, 255, 257–61; Navy Law amendment of 1908 and, 270–71, 274–75, 282–85, 289–91; Navy Law amendment of 1912 and, 330–31, 334, 340–43; peace resolution of 1917, 419; powers and responsibilities of, 4, 39; on Second Moroccan Crisis, 330–31;

State Secretary of RMA as negotiator of naval budget with, 4; Tirpitz's father-in-law in, 70; Tirpitz's relationship with, 224–25, 229–30, 233, 241, 275, 282–83, 451–56, 457, 497n113; U-boat war, Tirpitz's beliefs about support for, 400. *See also* specific political parties

imperial tax system, 169–70. *See also* taxes

Imperial War Council, 348, 352, 377, 519n135

Indefatigable, 413

industrialists: agrarian interests versus, 166; on Dawes Plan, 437; direct taxation, opposition to, 453; in Flottenverein, 166–69, 176; Navy Law of 1898 and, 138, 153, 154, 489n31; Navy Law of 1900 and, 166, 175; Sammlung between agrarian interests and, 138, 152, 489n31; Tirpitz's connections with, 405, 421, 431

inflation, postwar, 428, 431, 432–34

The Influence of Sea Power Upon History (Mahan; 1890). *See* Mahan, Alfred Thayer

Ingenohl, Friedrich (von): as Fleet Chief, 362, 365–66, 378, 387, 447, 461; at OK, 100, 483n15; in Tirpitz's memoirs, 426, 429–30, 465; in "Torpedo Gang," 66, 67, 468; in WWI, 378–79, 383–87, 396

inheritance tax, 259, 305, 329, 341, 505n153, 520n151

The Invasion of 1910 (Le Queux, 1906), 266

Invincible, 257, 269, 271, 413, 453

Invincible class, 253, 259, 265, 269–74, 450

Irene, 119, 122, 123, 487n47

Irish Home Rule, 308, 311

"iron budget," concept of, 6, 8, 191, 193, 230, 286, 342, 451–52, 456, 508n99

Italy: on arms limitation/reduction, 276–77; Austria-Hungary, Germany's defensive alliance with, 75; *Dread-*

nought-style battleship plans, 254–55, 344; Lissa, Battle of (1866), 27–28, 43, 81, 84, 88; Mussolini in, 432, 433

Jachmann, Eduard (von), 20, 32, 33, 39
Jaeschke, Paul, 53–54, 67, 468
Jagow, Gottlieb von, 368
Jameson, Leander Starr, and Jameson Raid (1895–96), 110
Japan: British defensive alliance with, 251; *Dreadnought*-style battleship, plans to construct, 253, 282; Russo-Japanese War (1904–1905), 144, 239, 240, 251–52, 265, 389; Sino-Japanese War (1894–1895), 87, 106, 118; Tirpitz in, 119, 121–22; Tirpitz on hypothetical war with, 174; in WWI, 381
Jellicoe, John, 71, 301, 366, 382, 384, 412, 413, 446
Jesuit laws, 142, 143, 147, 150, 175, 176, 180, 184, 189, 454, 496n94, 497n1
Jeune École (France), 56, 82, 354, 477n55
Jews and Judaism: anti-Semitism, 72, 420, 421, 431; Cassel, Sir Ernest, 335; in Curaçao, 41; Fatherland Party, 420, 421; Halle, Ernst von, 137, 494n36; Lipke, Gustav (Tirpitz's father-in-law), 69–70, 72, 431, 480–81n5, 481n17, 494n36; Tirpitz's views on, 72, 420, 421, 431–32
Jutland, Battle of (1916), 412–15, 426

K (Konstruktionsabteilung), 230–31, 248, 255, 257, 281, 303
Kahr, Gustav von, 431–34
Kaiser (battleship), 352
Kaiser (frigate), 45, 46, 487n47
Kaiser (Tirpitz's flagship in East Asia), 119, 121, 122
Kaiser class, 322, 332
Kaiser Friedrich III class, 87–88, 106–107, 225
Kaiser Wilhelm Canal: ability of ships to pass through, 227, 254, 256, 320, 361; eastern terminus, map, *xvi*; geography of, 376; RMA, expansion of,

112; strategic advantage provided by, 97, 319; widening of, 254, 256, 257, 320, 328, 331, 362, 367, 463
Kant, Immanuel, 15, 72
Kapp, Wolfgang, 264, 410, 412, 415, 416, 419, 420, 421, 430
Karcher, Guido, 131, 164
Kardorff, Wilhelm von, 271, 354
Karl der Grosse, 179
Kehr, Eckart, 7, 8, 10, 111, 152, 191, 194
Keim, August, 168, 276, 345
Kennedy, Paul, 197, 199, 364, 470n16
Kern, Fritz, 425–26, 438
Keyserlingk, Walter Freiherr von, 317, 403, 480n116
Kiachou Bay, China: additional bases, need for, 174; German seizure of, 143–44, 198; RMA, under aegis of, 156; Russian interest in, 121, 123, 143; scouted as potential German base, 118–24
Kiderlen-Wächter, Alfred von, 310, 323–25, 330, 333, 337, 338, 340
Kiel: dockyard shipbuilding capacity and costs, 225; map, *xvi*; Naval Academy, 39, 43–45, 228, 315; Naval School, 31–32; Prussian acquisition of, 1; Tirpitz known as *Kossachenhetmann* in, 59; Tirpitz slated as Dockyards Director, 74, 79
Kiel Week, 71, 251, 323, 360, 366–67, 450
Kinderling, Franz, 51
King Edward class, 226
king of Prussia, as German emperor, 3, 38
Kitchener, Herbert Horatio, Lord, 171, 388
Klausa, Oscar, 24, 27, 46, 475n22
Kleinkrieg, 289, 313, 354, 355, 362, 379, 383, 388
Kleist, Heinrich von, 15
Knorr, Eduard von: armored ship program, Caprivi's desire to abandon, 57; at Baltic Station, 73, 74, 75–76, 90; on Caprivi, 63, 477n46; description of, 75; East Asia, support for

German base in, 118, 120; on feud
between Stosch and Bismarck,
477n45; fleet development plan,
107–109, 128; in Franco-Prussian
War, 34–35; on Helgoland, 75; Maltzahn on, 358; Navy Law of 1898 and,
128, 129; OK, dissolution of, 156,
158–61, 164; OK, Tirpitz's departure
from, 88; on *Rover*, 25; strategic plans
at OK, Tirpitz's influence on, 97–98;
on *Thetis*, 30–31; Tirpitz's plan to expand RMA and, 117, 126, 156; as Tirpitz's superior at OK, 471n7; Torpedo
Arm officers' independence, resentment of, 64; on Wickede, 476n39
Koester, Hans von: Fleet Command,
struggle with Tirpitz over, 238–40,
264, 318–19; at Flottenverein, 276,
327, 330, 340, 515n36; *Kaiser Friedrich III* class, backing of, 87–88, 106;
Navy Law of 1898 and, 131; photograph of, *213*; tactical expertise of,
87, 88, 101
Kommunistische Partei Deutschland or
KPD (German Communist Party),
425
König Albert, 352
König class, 376, 401
König Wilhelm, 33, 34–35, 49, 62, 125,
475n22
Konstruktionsabteilung (K), 230–31,
248, 255, 257, 281, 303
Kopp, Georg Cardinal, 142, 143
KPD (Kommunistische Partei Deutsch-
land or German Communist Party),
425
Kronprinz, 33, 45–46, 473n29
Krosigk, Günther von, 468
Kruger, Paul, and Kruger telegram,
110, 155, 250
Krupp (artillery company), 32, 59,
166–67, 183, 232, 301, 303, 457
Kühn, Hermann, 341, 353
Kulturkampf, 141–42, 151

Lambert, Nicholas, 354
Lambi, Ivo N., 90, 154, 320

Landtag (Prussian Parliament), 3–4, 22
Lans, Wilhelm (von), 319, 381, 397
Le Queux, William, 266
League of Heavy Industry, 176
League of Nations, 440–41
Lee, Arthur, 252, 256
Leibe, C. A., 31–32, 43
Levetzow, Magnus von, 442
Liberal party in Britain, 264–65, 269,
299, 307
Liberal party in Germany. *See* National
Liberal Party
Lichnowsky, Karl (prince), 348, 370
Lieber, Ernst: as Center Party leader,
106, 130, 454; on fleet expansion
prior to Tirpitz at RMA, 116, 126;
Navy Law of 1898 and, 141–43, 145,
147–52; Navy Law of 1900 and, 173,
183–84, 187, 190
line abreast, 81, 85–86, 89, 101–102
line ahead, 85–86, 87, 88, 89, 102
Lion class, 346
Lipke, Gustav (Tirpitz's father-in-law),
69, 70, 431, 480n5, 494n36
Lipke, Marie (Tirpitz's wife), 69–71,
204–205, 432, 442, 443, 480n5,
494n36
Lissa, Battle of (1866), 27–28, 43, 81,
84, 88
List, Friedrich, 20
"little navy" wing of British Liberal
Party, 265, 299
Livonius, Otto, 45, 233
Lloyd George, David, 265, 293, 294,
299, 300, 302, 305, 310, 325, 327, 335,
418
Locarno Treaty (1925), 440
logistical implications of Tirpitzian
strategy, 94–95
Löhlein, Heinrich, 403, 408
London class, 226
London Conference and Declaration
of London (1909), 389–90
Lord Nelson class, 226
Louis XIV (king of France), 94, 111
Lucanus, Hermann von, 115, 180, 184,
189

Ludendorff, Erich, 347, 385, 400, 415–16, 418, 421, 422, 424, 432, 433
Luitpold of Bavaria, Prince Regent, 138
Lusitania, 399, 407
Luther, Martin, 145
Lützow, 401, 413, 414
Luxemburg, German invasion of, 1, 373
"luxury fleet," Churchill's description of German Navy as, 336
Lyckner, Moritz Freiherr von, 380

M II, 136, 137, 146
machine ciphers, 358
Magdeburg, 382
Mahan, Alfred Thayer, *The Influence of Sea Power Upon History* (1890): belligerents' rights, expansion of, 277–78; Navy Law amendment of 1906 and, 258; Navy Law of 1898 and, 136, 146, 149, 154; Social Darwinism of, 111, 199, 328; tactical development and, 85, 89; Tirpitz's 1891 memos not indicating awareness of, 78; Tirpitz's 1896 memo on fleet development influenced by, 111, 112; Tirpitz's meeting with, 236–37; Tirpitz's risk theory influenced by, 199; Tirpitz's strategic thought at OK influenced by, 93–94, 102; William II's reading of, 107
Mainz, 72, 379
Maltzahn, Curt von: army, consideration of leaving navy for, 44–45; on Dienstschrift IX, 91; enjoinment of publication of, 164, 179, 358; on *Friedrich Carl*, 40; Mahan, influence of, 93; at Naval Academy, 228; removed from Naval Academy, 358, 461; on tactics, 88; Tirpitz influenced to enter navy by, 17
Manila, 122, 123–24, 177
Mann, Johann-Bernhard, 417, 428, 431, 435, 523n222
Mansion House speech (David Lloyd George; 1911), 325, 327
Mantey, Eberhard con, *213*, 429
Marchand, Captain, 171

Marder, Arthur J., 65, 254, 385, 445, 503n103
Marie, 487n47
Marine Rundschau, 99, 159, 236, 247
Marinekabinett or MK (Naval Cabinet): conflict between naval staffs, 1911–1914, 357–61; establishment of, 5, 64; marriage advertisements by naval officers censured by, 69; Senden as Chief of, 78–79
marriage: of Alfred von Tirpitz and Marie Lipke, 69–70; of Ilse von Tirpitz and Ulrich von Hassell, 71–72
Marschall von Bieberstein, Adolf Freiherr, 118, 127, 130, 278
Marx, Wilhelm, 434, 436, 440, 441
material reserve: Navy Law of 1898 and, 112, 135; Navy Law of 1900 and, 181, 185, 500n62; Navy Law amendment of 1906 and, 243, 255, 500n62; Navy Law amendment of 1908 and, 266–68, 281; Navy Law amendment of 1912 and, 328, 329, 341
Max of Baden (prince), 424, 425
McKenna, Reginald, 291, 293, 300, 301, 311, 325
Mecklenburg, Duke of, 420, 421
memoirs of Tirpitz, 5–6, 425–30, 465
merchant marine, British, 382
merchant marine, German: North German Confederation, 33; Prussian Navy's recruitment of officers from, 21; in WWI, 382
merchant marine, U.S., 33, 412
Meteor (German gunboat), 34–35, 75
Meteor (Prinz Heinrich's racing yacht), 235
Metternich (Prince Klemens Wenzel von Metternich), 20
Metternich (Paul Graf von Wolff-Metternich), 294–95, 298, 300, 301, 308, 310, 335, 339, 348, 510n17
Michaelis, Georg, 419, 421
Michaelis, William: at Admiralstab, 321, 357–58; as Admiralty Chief after WWI, 430; biographical information, 227–28; on daily work life at

Tirpitz's RMA, 227–30; on Holtzendorff, 319; Hopmann and, 358;
Naval Archives request to write about
career, 498n11; on naval operations
plans, 363, 364, 365; on Navy Law of
1900, 195; OK dissolution and, 162;
on Reichstag and RMA, 454; on risk
theory, 201–202, 455; on Second Moroccan Crisis, 323–24; on Tirpitz's
resignation, 409; on torpedoes and
Tirpitz, 358, 480n11; on U-boats,
356; in WWI, 380, 386, 397, 409, 411
Militär-Wochenblatt, 187
military penal code reform, 141, 143,
144, 147
minelayers and minesweepers, 365, 401
mines, 35, 47, 198, 362, 364, 376, 377,
379, 382, 383, 391, 392, 394, 396,
418, 423, 458
Miquel, Johannes von, 104, 113, 132,
138–42, 148–53, 174, 489n31
MK. *See* Marinekabinett or MK
Moltke, 282, 322
Moltke-Harden trial, 289
Moltke, Helmuth von (the elder), 79,
448
Moltke, Helmuth von (the younger),
298, 320, 321, 347–48, 367, 369–72,
377, 385, 523n224, 524n245
monarchist, Tirpitz as, 396, 405, 416,
429, 440, 452, 456
Monroe Doctrine, 234
Monts, Alexander Graf von, 47–48, 57,
59, 64
Moreno, 247, 501n71
Morgan, J. P., 235
Morocco: First Moroccan Crisis (1905),
254, 260, 261, 262, 265–66; Second
Moroccan Crisis (Agadir Crisis), 309,
322, 323–26, 327, 328, 330–31, 347,
361, 450
motherships, torpedo fleet's use of, 52,
60
Müller, Georg Alexander (von): diplomatic efforts to reach naval agreement with Britain and, 304, 306, 312;
on Emperor's mistrust of Tirpitz,

378; on Hollmann, 127; Holtzendorff's relationship to, 319, 322, 360,
403; at Imperial War Council, 348;
at MK, 264, 271–72, 357, 378; Navy
Law amendment of 1908 and, 267,
273, 276, 290, 291; Navy Law amendment of 1912 and, 329, 333, 338; at
OK, 483n15; personal and professional relationship with Tirpitz, 261,
470n24; in reconciliation efforts
between William II and Tirpitz, 442;
on Second Moroccan Crisis, 325;
in ships' gun calibers disagreement,
346; in summer of 1914 leading up
to WWI, 370, 372; in Tirpitz's memoirs, 426, 429–30, 465; in Torpedo
Arm, 52, 66, 67, 445, 468; Trotha
and, 263–64; in U.S. with Tirpitz,
235; in WWI, 378, 380, 385–88, 396,
399, 403–406, 408, 411, 423
Müller, Richard, 141, 149–50, 151, 188
Müller-Meiningen, Ernst, 283, 285
Musquito, 28–29, 42
Mussolini, Benito, 432, 433

Nachrichtenbüro/Nachrichtenab-
teilung (N), 136, 167, 168, 176, 181,
233, 236, 266, 321, 328, 348, 357,
365, 431
Namibia (then German Southwest
Africa), rebellion in (1903–1907), 247,
274–75, 305
Napoleon, 19, 392
Napoleon III, 34
Napoleonic Wars, 250, 355, 387, 418
Nassau and *Nassau* class, 218, 256–57,
260, 269–70, 273, 301, 303, 315, 319,
321, 322, 332, 345, 367
National Liberal Party: collapse of
coalition of 1907, 305; cruiser funding, 1896, 113; elections of 1907, 274;
elections of 1912, 334; Navy Law of
1898 and, 140, 148, 149, 151; Navy
Law of 1900 and, 176, 184, 189, 192;
Navy Law amendment of 1906 and,
246, 259, 271, 283–85, 289; Navy
Law amendment of 1912 and, 326,

328, 340; succeeded by DNVP, 430; U-boat war, Tirpitz's beliefs about support for, 400

National Socialist Party (Nazis), 70, 264, 431, 432, 465–66, 480n5

Nauticus, 236

Naval Academy, Kiel, 39, 43–45, 228, 315

naval agreement with Britain, diplomatic efforts to reach. *See* diplomatic efforts to reach naval agreement with Britain

Naval Cabinet. *See* Marinekabinett or MK

Naval High Command. *See* Oberkommando or OK

"naval holiday" proposals, 340, 345, 351, 519n114

naval scare of 1909, 291, 297, 299–306, 312

Navy. *See* British Navy; German Navy

Navy Law, 1896 consideration of, 113–17

Navy Law of 1898, 2, 129–55, 460; argument of, 145–46; budget right, 130, 131, 145, 148, 491n76; Bundesrat on, 130, 132, 138–40, 143–45, 150; challenges faced by Tirpitz in orchestrating, 129–32; cost estimates in, 134, 139–40; economic document in support of, 146; effect on Tirpitz's career, 68; imperial tax system and, 169; July 1897 draft, 133; Kiaochou, annexation of, 143–44; OK/RMA draft, 128, 129, 133, 137; rationale of, 145–46; Reichstag, analysis of motives and intentions of parties in, 151–53; Reichstag, Budget Commission, 148–50; Reichstag, debates in, 147–48, 150–52; Reichstag, passage in, 152; Reichstag, preliminary negotiations with, 140–43; Reichstag, presentation of documents to, 145–47; Tirpitz's care in staying within financial limits of, 172, 181, 224; Tirpitz's intentions regarding, 153–55; Tirpitz's memoirs on, 11–12;

Tirpitz's preparations for presentation of, 132–40

Navy Law of 1900, 2, 166–202, 466; Battle of Jutland (1916) regarded as vindication of, 415; in Budget Commission, 187–88; budget right, 177, 191–95; domestic and foreign events affecting, 174–76, 177, 181; drafts and supporting documents, 179–85, 495n73; Emperor's statement precipitating, 179–80; European reaction to, 190; Flottenverein and, 166–69, 176, 183; imperial tax system and, 169–70; "iron budget" supposedly established by, 6, 8, 191, 193, 230, 286, 342, 451–52, 456, 508n99; officer corps, Tirpitz seeking support of, 179–80; rationale of, 185–87; Reichstag and, 173–74, 176–77, 183–84, 187–89; risk theory and, 179, 182, 185–86, 189, 190, 195–202; Samoan crisis and, 175; significance in Tirpitz's career, 190; Tirpitz's care in staying within financial limits of, 191–92, 241, 501n81; Tirpitz's initial planning for amendments to 1898 law, 170–74; Tirpitz's planning for 1901 or 1902 amendment, 176–78

Navy Law amendment of 1906, 2, 192, 229, 240–62; analysis of Tirpitz and, 261–62; diplomatic issues affecting, 249–53; Emperor's ship design efforts, 246–49; HMS *Dreadnought* and, 253–57; initial proposals for, 240–48; Reichstag and, 244, 246, 248, 249, 253, 254, 255, 257–61

Navy Law amendment of 1908, 2, 263–92; Anglo-Russian Entente (1907), 279, 287; British Liberal majority of 1906 and, 264–65, 269; cost table and draft preparation, 279–82; diplomacy following, 293–99; early planning for, 265–69; elections of 1907 and, 274–75, 279; four tempo, switch from three tempo to, 280, 284–89, 292, 303; Hague Peace Conference (1907), 276–78, 284; *Invincible* class

and, 269–74; Reichstag and, 270–71,
274–75, 282–85, 289–91
Navy Law amendment of 1912, 2, 249,
289, 307, 326–47; diplomatic relations with Britain and, 307, 309–10,
326, 328, 330, 334–40, 367; doubts
about, 359; drafts, 330, 331; early
preparations for, 326–34, 515n32;
Haldane Mission, 334–40; propaganda campaigns, 230, 324, 515n36;
Reichstag and, 330–31, 334, 340–43;
repercussions of, 343–47; Second
Moroccan Crisis and, 324, 325, 326,
328, 330–31; as Tirpitz's last great
parliamentary success, 342–43; Treasury economies and, 316
Navy Law amendment of 1913–14, consideration of, 347–53
Navy League. See Flottenverein
Nazis (National Socialist Party), 70,
264, 431, 432, 465–66, 480n5
Netherlands: in German operational
plans, 94, 116, 252–53, 277, 368;
Stosch on seizure of, 111; trade and
naval dominance, loss of, 18, 94; in
WWI, 392
neutrality: of Belgium, Netherlands,
and Denmark in German operational plans, 252–53, 277; British neutrality in WWI, failure of, 370, 372–73,
458; British policy of "benevolent
neutrality," 63, 97, 115–16; Danish
neutrality, 250, 377; diplomatic talks
with Britain and, 295, 297, 307, 310,
313, 319; economic blockade on neutrals in WWI, 388–94; of Fatherland
Party, 420, 421; of Germany in Russo-Japanese War, 251; Hague Peace
Conference (1907), neutral rights at,
277, 390; Haldane Mission, 335–39;
in strategic outlook, 92, 94; of U.S.,
115–16, 277, 392, 448, 457; WWI
U-boat war and, 399, 407, 457,
526n84
New Zealand's contributions to British
battleship construction, 305, 306
Nicholas II (czar), 234, 252, 283, 367
Nile, Battle of the (1798), 88

Niobe, 24–27, 28, 48
Nipperdey, Thomas, 194–95
North German Confederation, 28,
33–34
North Sea: geography of, 375–76; her-
ring fisheries, 37–38; map, xiii; naval
and trade dominance of, 18, 19, 23,
28
Novelles (amendments) to Navy Laws.
See entries at Navy Law amendment
Nymphe, 42–43

Oberkommando or OK (Naval High
Command): dissolution of, 12; establishment of, 4, 21, 64; fleet development plan of 1895, 107–109; principle
responsibility for fleet development,
struggle with RMA for, 76–77; RMA,
turf war with, 73, 98–101, 107, 108,
125–27, 155–56; Tirpitz's volte-face
on RMA versus, 109–110, 112, 117,
456–57
Oberkommando or OK (Naval High
Command), Tirpitz as Chief of Staff
of (1892–95), 81–102; circumstances
leading to appointment, 79–80;
conclusions regarding, 101–102; departure from, 88, 97, 102, 107; "fog
of peace" regarding response to technological change, 81–84; interpretation of Tirpitz's intentions, 5, 10,
12; propaganda campaign, 99–100;
RMA, turf war with, 98–101; strategic thought, 89–98, 102; tactical
development, 84–89, 87, 101–102;
Torpedo Arm years, advantages from,
83–84
Oberste Heeresleitung (Army High
Command or OHL), 415–17, 419,
420, 421, 424
observational blockade, 364
offensive dominance of Tirpitz's strategic thought at OK, 89–98
Offer, Avner, 388
OHL (Oberste Heeresleitung or Army
High Command), 415–17, 419, 420,
421, 424
OK. See Oberkommando or OK

Oldekop, Iwan F. J., 24, 27, 60, 131, 164, 213, 461
Oldenburg, 322
Olympia, 124
Organizational Behavior Model (Model 2 behavior), 10, 91–92, 132, 225, 457–59, 533n22
Ottoman Empire: Balkan coalition's defeat of, 347–48; Russo-Turkish War, 50; in WWI, 382

palliative, concept of, 45, 111, 112, 201, 423, 497n131
Pan-German League, 136, 168, 176, 340, 405, 420, 421
Panther, 322, 323, 324, 450
Paris, Declaration of (1856), 105, 388–89
Paschen, Carl, 58, 62
peace resolution of 1917, 419
penal code, military, reform of, 141, 143, 144, 147
Persius, Lothar, 422
Petter, Wolfgang, 144
Plessen, Hans von, 386
Pohl, Ella von, 429
Pohl, Hugo (von): Admiralstab, as head of, 365, 372, 378; in Boxer Rebellion (1900), 232; as Fleet Commander, 387, 407, 459; as leader of navy in WWI, 372, 522n211; Navy Law of 1898 and, 136; OK, dissolution of, 160; in summer of 1914 leading up to WWI, 368–72; in Tirpitz's memoirs, 426, 429, 465; in Torpedo Arm, 54, 58, 66–67, 445, 468; widow's publications defending, 429; in WWI, 378–79, 381, 382, 385–88, 394–97, 402, 404, 406, 407
Poincaré, Raymond, 368, 369, 432
Poland: First Partition of, 18; postwar German losses to, 428
political science models used in interpreting Tirpitz, 10–13, 456–64, 470n17
Pommern, 413
Preussen, 54, 65, 73–74
Preussischer Adler, 51
Prinz Adalbert, 226, 227, 476n26

Prinz Heinrich, 226
Prinzess Wilhelm, 119, 487n47
Prinzregent Luitpold, 423
Progressive Party: collapse of coalition of 1907, 305; diplomatic efforts to reach naval agreement with Britain, repercussions of, 312–13; elections of 1907, 274, 275; elections of 1912, 334; Navy Law of 1900 and, 183; Navy Law amendment of 1906 and, 261; Navy Law amendment of 1908 and, 261, 274, 275, 283–85, 289; ship construction, money for, 106
propaganda campaigns: anti-British feeling, use of, 114–15, 249–50, 262, 324; for Army, 351; Fatherland Party, 424; flag-showing cruise of 1913, 352; on fleet development and expansion, 112, 125, 130; Flottenverein and, 167, 259; M II, 136, 137, 146; N, 136, 167, 168, 176, 181, 233, 236, 266, 321, 328, 348, 357, 365, 431; on Navy Law of 1900, 187; for Navy Law amendment of 1908, 275–76; for Navy Law amendment of 1912, 230, 324, 515n36; OK, Tirpitz as Chief of Staff at, 99–100; Tirpitz's postwar dictatorship schemes, 432
Prussia: German Confederation and, 19; Holstein, acquisition of, 22; king as German emperor, 3, 38; Navy at time of Tirpitz's entry, 17–23; place in German Empire and Constitution, 3
Prussian Navy. *See* German Navy
Przewisinski, Hermann, 42
Punch "Dropping the Pirate" cartoon, 400

Queen class, 226
Queen Elizabeth class, 332, 343, 346, 413, 414
Queen Mary, 413
Le Queux, William, 266

Raeder, Erich, 429, 465
ramming, use and advocacy of, 81, 83, 84, 476n30, 483n13

Rapallo, Treaty of (1922), 428
Rathenau, Foreign Secretary, assassination of, 430
Rational Actor Model (Model 1 behavior), 10–11, 101, 155, 164, 456–57
Rauh, Manfred, 194
recruits, Tirpitz's idea to man reserve ships with, 346–47
Reichsmarineamt or RMA (Imperial Naval Office): establishment of, 4–5, 64; OK, turf war with, 73, 98–101, 107, 108, 125–27, 155–56; principle responsibility for fleet development, struggle with OK for, 76–77; Tirpitz's *volte-face* on OK versus, 109–10, 112, 117, 456–57 (*See also* specific departments and divisions)
Reichsmarineamt or RMA (Imperial Naval Office), Tirpitz as State Secretary at (1897–1916), 2–3; conflict between naval staffs, 1911–1914, 357–61; daily work life at, 227–31, 263–64; interpretation of Tirpitz's intentions at, 5, 12; Navy Laws and amendments under stewardship of (*See* entries at Navy Law); official appointment of 1897, 127–28; organization of, 1900–1906, 236–40; potential appointment in 1896, 113–17, 460; Tirpitz's 1896 memo as application for, 110, 112, 113–14; Tirpitz's resignation from, 408–409; in WWI, 401–403, 405
Reichstag, German Empire. *See* Imperial Reichstag
Reichstag, German Republic: political turmoil in (1920–1924), 434–42; Tirpitz as deputy (1924–1928), 434–42
Reinsurance Treaty with Russia, 75, 104
reparations, 432, 435, 443
Repington, Colonel, 291
resignation of Tirpitz from RMA, 408–409
resignation, Tirpitz's threats of, 12, 150, 158–60, 223, 239, 260, 261, 297, 333, 339, 340, 342–43, 347, 349, 378, 400, 403, 404, 406, 455

Ressorteifer behavior. *See* Bureaucratic or Governmental Politics Model
Reuter, Ludwig von, 425, 427, 428
Reventlow, Ernst von, 257, 272, 515n32
Revolution of 1848, 15, 20, 131
Revolution of 1918 in Germany, 425
Richter, Eugen: annual appropriations, support for, 454; death of, 274, 283; elections of 1907, followers in, 274; Navy Law of 1898 and, 137, 140, 144, 147, 149, 151; Navy Law amendment of 1906 and, 242; Navy Law of 1900 and, 176, 184, 187, 188, 189, 193, 495n74; Tirpitz echoing, 350; on U-boats, 354
Richthofen, Oscar Freiherr von, 251–52, 449
Rickover, Hyman, 459
The Riddle of the Sands (Childers, 1903), 266
right to capture, 277–78, 388, 391
"risk fleet," 8, 197, 198, 200, 250, 319, 373, 462
risk theory, 195–202; "alliance value," 95, 114, 115, 133, 196, 252, 279, 286, 449, 462, 466; analysis of significance of, 445, 449, 455, 462, 466; collapse of, 344–45, 364, 373, 445; defined, 5; diplomatic talks with Britain and, 309; *Dreadnought* revolution lending credibility to, 262; early stages in development of, 112, 115, 116; first public declaration of, 185–86; "Helgoland and the Thames" argument, 133, 196, 198, 446; Michaelis on, 230; Naval bill of 1898, draft of, 134; Navy Law amendment of 1908 and, 268, 279, 286; Navy Law of 1900 and, 179, 182, 185–86, 189, 190, 195–202; Russian alliance, Tirpitz's arguments against, 252
Ritter, Gerhard, 6
RMA. *See* Reichsmarineamt or RMA
Rockefeller, John D., 235
Röhl, J. C. G., 152
Rohleder, Ulrika (Tirpitz's grandmother), 14

Rollmann, Max, 468

Roon, 227

Roon, Albrecht Graf von, 21, 33, 39, 139, 142

Roosevelt, Alice, 235

Roosevelt, Theodore, 234, 235

Ropp, Theodore, 45, 65, 146

Rosinski, Herbert, 93

Rothpletz, Karoline (Tirpitz's mother-in-law), 70

Rover, 25, 28

Rügen, Prussian acquisition of, 19

Rüger, Jan, 502n91

Ruhr Crisis (1923–1924), 431–33, 435

Rumania: in Balkan War of 1912, 347; in WWI, 415, 416

Rupprecht of Bavaria (prince), 276, 289

Russia: Anglo-German alliance, possible repercussions of, 249; Anglo-Russian Entente of 1907, 279, 287, 366; on arms limitation/reduction, 276–77; Balkan war of 1912 and, 348; in Bismarck's worldview, 74–75; *Dreadnought*-type battleships, 377; Fatherland Party on, 421; fleet expansion in 1913, concern over, 352; German alliance with, proposal for, 251–52, 362, 449; German ships compared to Russian, 227; Great Britain, projected German war with, 115; Kiachou Bay, interest in, 121, 123, 143; Navy Law, 1900, reaction to, 190; operational plans against, 53, 55, 57, 75, 82, 89, 96–98, 104–105, 108, 112, 115–16, 237–38, 242; Rapallo, Treaty of (1922), 428; Reinsurance Treaty with, 75, 104; risk theory regarding (*See* risk theory); in summer of 1914 leading up to WWI, 367, 368, 369, 370, 372; Tirpitz ordered by Emperor to show battleship plans to Czar, 234; torpedo boats of, 65; in WWI, 382, 385, 387, 416, 417

Russian Revolution (1917), 417

Russo-Japanese War (1904–1905), 144, 239, 240, 251–52, 265, 389

Russo-Turkish War, 50

S-boats, 58, 59, 60, 61, 64

Sachsen class, 248

Salewski, Michael, 67, 201, 381

Salm, Otto Prince von, 258

Sammlung or *Sammlingspolitik* (coalition), 8, 138, 151–53, 174, 274–75, 289–91, 306, 441, 489n31, 530n38

Samoa, German colonial troubles in, 168, 175, 177, 179

Scapa Flow, scuttling of German Navy in, 427–28, 464–65

Schack, Wilhelm, 468

Schack-Wittenau, Arthur Graf von, 52, 60, 476n27

Schädler, Franz, 187

Scharnhorst, 227

Scharnhorst, Garhard von, 15

Schau, Aneker, 27

Scheck, Raffael, 395, 400, 401, 406, 420, 432, 436, 438

Scheer, Reinhard: as Fleet Chief in WWI, 407, 412–14, 422; historical narrative, role in recasting of, 465; Navy Law amendment of 1906 and, 256; Navy Law amendment of 1908 and, 506n35; Navy Law amendment of 1912 and, 331, 359; recasting of historical narrative by, 465; at RMA, 263; Supreme Naval Command, creation of, 423; on Tirpitz's memoirs, 428–29; in "Torpedo Gang," 66, 468, 480n116; Trotha and, 263–64

Schichau Yard, 58–61, 64, 303–304

Schiller, Friedrich, 15, 72, 486n36

Schlesien, 365

Schleswig-Holstein: Danish efforts to incorporate, 20–21, 22; *Gefion* captured by rebels of, 29; Prussian annexation of, 28; Prussian-Austrian conflict over, 27

Schlieffen, Alfred von, 6, 96, 238, 253, 320

Schlieffen Plan, 6, 96, 370, 373, 385, 390–91, 448

Schmoller, Gustav, 137, 167

Schoen, Wilhelm Freiherr von, 208

Schrader, Progressive Deputy, 313

Schreiber, Gerhard, 465
Schröder, Jan, 20
Schröder, Ludwig (von), 380, 395, 468, 483n15
Schütze-class torpedo boats, 53, 54
Schwarzkopff (torpedo manufacturers), 52, 55–56
Schweinburg, Viktor, 166–68, 183
Second Moroccan Crisis (Agadir Crisis; 1911), 309, 322, 323–26, 327, 328, 330–31, 347, 361, 450
Second Navy Law. *See* Navy Law of 1900
Second World War, Tirpitz's legacy in, 465–66
Seeckt, Hans von, 433, 434, 439–40
Seewehr Schlachtflotte, 243, 244
Selborne, Earl of, 250
Seligman, Matthew S., 502n85
Senden-Bibran, Gustav von: background and characterization of, 78–79; Diedrichs at Admiralstab, support for, 237; East Asia, German base in, 124; influence on Tirpitz's career, 78–79, 84, 445, 471n7; Koester, support for, 239; Navy Law of 1898 and, 128, 129, 154; Navy Law of 1900 and, 178; OK dissolution and, 157, 158, 160, 161, 164, 460; OK fleet development plan and, 109, 125–28; photograph of, 213; retirement of, 271; Tirpitz's history of Torpedo Arm sent to, 73; in training with Tirpitz, 25; in turf wars between OK and RMA, 98, 99, 101, 155
seniority system in German Navy: Fleet Chief, selection of, 239, 318, 319, 322; Michaelis and, 228; OK, dissolution of, 157, 163, 164, 460; Prinz Heinrich and, 319; Tirpitz and, 17, 29, 32, 68, 79, 102, 129, 223, 444; Tirpitz's offer to serve under Pohl in defiance of, 372
Serbia: in Balkan War of 1912, 347, 348; in summer of 1914 leading up to WWI, 367, 368, 369, 370
Seydlitz, 322

Seymour, Edward, 232
Shimonoseki, Treaty of (1895), 118
ship construction, 1898–1905, 225–27
ship design, Emperor's efforts regarding, 246–49, 254–55
ship lifespans, 68, 145, 185, 242–44, 248, 253, 257, 259–60, 266–67, 280–81, 284–85, 288, 355, 463
ship type escalations, Fisher's intentions regarding, 253, 254, 257, 262, 462–63, 503nn103,104
ship types, Tirpitz on, 95–96, 100, 102, 107, 243, 247
shipbuilding industry, Tirpitz's dealings with, 50, 52, 55–56, 59, 303–304, 457
ships' gun calibers, 345–46, 359–60, 379
ships of German Navy compared to British, 226, 227, 230, 376–77, 383, 414
Siegel, Rudolf, 278, 468, 483n15
Siegfried class, 55, 81, 85, 96, 98, 102, 106, 109, 112, 172, 178, 181, 185, 217, 242, 248, 397, 448
single-screw torpedoes, 49
Sino-Japanese War (1894–1895), 87, 106, 118
size of fleet, Tirpitz's formula for determining, 96
Skagerrak, Battle of Jutland in (1916), 412–15, 426
Smith, Perry McCoy, 533n22
Social Darwinism, 12, 93, 111, 199, 225, 328, 447, 464
Social Democrats: annual appropriations, support for, 454; in coalition of 1926, 441; elections of 1907, 274, 279; elections of 1912, 334; elections of 1924, 435, 436, 439; German naval development plans and, 8; grain tariffs, 170; growth of, 1871–1910, 103; Navy Law of 1898 and, 140, 147, 151, 152, 155; Navy Law of 1900 and, 176, 183, 184, 187, 189, 192, 195, 201, 495n74; Navy Law amendment of 1906 and, 242, 246, 259, 261; Navy

Law amendment of 1908 and, 289, 290, 291; Navy Law amendment of 1912 and, 340, 342; ship construction, money for, 106; Tirpitz's 1896 fleet development memo and, 111; on U-boat warfare, 408; Weltpolitik, lack of interest in, 231

socialism and socialists: on economics and naval power, 146; Galster and, 289; German naval development plans and, 7, 8; growth in German Empire, 1871–1910, 103; low morale at end of war blamed on, 427; National Socialist Party, 431; Tirpitz in Reichstag and, 440

Somme, German retreat from (1918), 424

sortie fleet, 89–90

Souchon, Wilhelm, 382, 525n26

South Africa: Boer War (1899–1903), 177, 179, 181, 182, 184, 190, 249, 295; Jameson Raid into Boer Republic (1895–96), 110, 113, 114

Southwest Africa (Namibia), rebellion in (1903–1907), 247, 274–75, 305

Spahn, Peter, 275, 283–85, 289

Spanish-American War (1898), 168, 171, 181

Spanish civil war (1873), 41–42

spar torpedoes, 47, 48

Spee, Maximilian Graf von, 219, 227, 381, 383

St. Blasien, Tirpitz's country home at, 70–71, 135, 170, 243, 261, 266, 271, 284, 327, 367, 368, 370, 410, 419, 422, 424, 434, 441–42

Staffel line ahead, 86, 87

Stein, August, 284

Steinberg, Jonathan, 7, 8–9, 136, 150, 154, 340, 342, 452

Stengel, Hermann von, 241, 288

Stenzel, Alfred, 40, 44

Stosch, Albrecht von: Bismarck, feud with, 476n27; *Blitz*, reassignment of, 37; on Great Britain, 111, 114; *Grosser Kurfürst* and *König Wilhelm*, collision of (1878), 475n22; influence on Tirpitz's career, 445, 456–57; Navy Law of 1898 and, 142; OK fleet development plan of 1895, Tirpitz's response to, 109–112; reorganization of German Navy under, 38–40; strategic thought of, 89–90, 105; Tirpitz's history of Torpedo Arm sent to, 73; Torpedo Arm under, 47–55, 67; on turf war between OK and RMA, 100–101, 156, 456–57

Strachan, Hew, 390

Stralsund, 19

Strassburg, 352

strategy: analysis of Tirpitz's significance regarding, 445–49; changing situation requiring development of, 1902–1911, 319–22; collapse at beginning of WWI, 373; defined, 483n32; naval operations plans, 1911–1914, 361–66; OK, Tirpitz's strategic thought developed at, 89–98, 102; Schlieffen Plan, 6, 96, 370, 373, 385, 390–91, 448; Wegener memoranda, 396–99. *See also* risk theory

Stresemann, Gustav, 419, 432–34, 436–41

Stroschein, J. E., 166

Struve, Peter, 421

Stumm, Wilhelm von, 372

Sturm Abteilung, 443

submarines. *See* U-boats

suicide charge of High Seas Fleet at end of WWI, collapse of, 424–25

"sunk costs" fallacy, 309, 362, 464

Supreme Naval Command: Emperor's failure to function as, 448–49, 524n17; finally established in 1918, 423; Tirpitz's expectations regarding, 378, 387, 397

Sussex, 407

Swedish Pomerania, Prussian acquisition of, 19

Swiftsure, 41

T formation, 86–87, 87, 89, 102, 413

tactical development of Tirpitz at OK, 84–89, 87, 101–102

Taku, allied forces at, Boxer Rebellion (1900), 232

tariff reductions under Caprivi, 105, 169–70

taxes: direct taxation, resistance to, 149, 169, 170, 259, 305, 351, 453; general tax increase, 279–80; grain tariffs, 105, 169–70; imperial tax system and Navy Law of 1900, 169–70; inheritance tax, 259, 305, 329, 341, 505n153; Navy Law amendment of 1906 and canal widening, increases for, 259, 505n153; Navy Law amendment of 1908 and, 270, 279–80, 283

Technische Abteilung (B), 303, 304

technological change: Dreadnought-type battleships, 191, 197; "fog of peace" and, 81–84; Navy Law of 1898, claim of slowing technological change to pass, 139–40, 142, 170; Tirpitz's wariness regarding, 354; torpedo boats, development of, 48, 49–50, 52, 53, 54–55, 57–62; torpedo technology, 47–49, 50, 52, 67–68, 358; U-boat countermeasures, 418; U-boats, development of, 353–55. See also U-boats

Tegetthoff, Wilhelm Freiherr von, 22, 27–28, 81

ten-minute cruisers, 484n59

Thetis, 30–31

Thiele, Adolf, 119

Thielmann, Max von, 132, 138, 139, 147, 182–83, 188, 241

Thimme, Friedrich, 438

Thomsen, August (von), 86, 258

Thorneycroft torpedo boats, 58, 59, 60

Tiger, 376

Tirpitz, 443, 465

Tirpitz, Alfred (von): Baltic Station, as Chief of Staff at (1890–1891), 74–80; birth of (1849), 14; Chancellorship, proposed for, 360–61, 415, 417–18, 419, 435–36; combined talent and luck of, 444–45; death of (1930), 443; decline of power in WWI, 373–74, 377–78, 403–404; dictatorship, support for, 396, 424, 428, 432, 433, 434, 436; diplomatic efforts, minor role in, 449–51 (see also diplomacy); diplomatic talks with Britain (1908–1912) and (see diplomatic efforts to reach naval agreement with Britain); in East Asia (1896–1897) (see East Asia, Tirpitz in); economics, reductionist view of, 93–94; entry into Prussian Navy (1865), 17–18, 22–23, 24; family heritage, childhood, and education, 2, 14–17; Fatherland Party, 418–22, 424, 439, 530n38; financial situation of, 410, 428, 431, 433, 434; in Franco-Prussian War (1870–71), 33–35; hypochondria of, 48, 72, 161, 175, 343, 418, 444; Imperial Reichstag, relationship with, 224–25, 229–30, 233, 241, 275, 282–83, 451–56, 457, 497n113; at Imperial War Council, 348, 377; interpretation of naval career of, 5–13; legacy of, 464–66; marriage, children, and family life, 69–73, 204–206; memoirs of, 5–6, 425–30, 465; as monarchist, 396, 405, 416, 429, 440, 452, 456; at Naval Academy (1874–76), 43–45; Navy Laws and amendments under stewardship of (See entries at Navy Law); nicknames for, 59, 83–84; as OK Chief of staff (1892–95) (see Oberkommando or OK (Naval High Command), Tirpitz as Chief of Staff of); Organizational Behavior Model applied to, 10, 91–92, 132, 225, 457–59; personal motto of, 10; photographs of, 204–209, 213, 214, 222; political interests postwar, rekindling of (1920–1924), 430–34; publication of annotated documents by, 437–39; as Rational Actor, 10–11, 101, 155, 164, 456–57; reconciliation with Emperor, efforts to engineer, 442; as Reichstag deputy (1924–1928), 434–42; resignation from RMA (1916),

408–409; resignation threats of, 12, 150, 158–60, 223, 239, 260, 261, 297, 333, 339, 340, 342–43, 347, 349, 378, 400, 403, 404, 406, 455; as *Ressorteifer* (See Bureaucratic or Governmental Politics Model *(Ressorteifer)* or Model 3 behavior); as RMA State Secretary (1897–1916) (See Reichsmarineamt or RMA (Imperial Naval Office), Tirpitz as State Secretary at); sex life as young naval officer, 32; as ship commander (1889–1890), 73–74; strategic thought of (See strategy); in Torpedo Arm (1877–89) (see Torpedo Arm); training in Prussian Navy (1865–70), 24–32; U-boat construction and, 353–57 (see also U-boats); *volte-face* on OK versus RMA, 109–110; von, enoblement leading to addition of, 191, 469n2; war crimes, accused of, 425, 430; Weltpolitik and (see Weltpolitik); on William II's reorganization of navy, 480n160; in WWI (see World War I); as young officer (1870–77), 33–46

Tirpitz, Alfred (von), naval memoranda of: Baltic Station, written while Chief of Staff at, 76–80, 90; Braun's role in, 483n15, 483n25, 484n45; Dienstschrift VI (1893), 86; Dienstschrift IX (1894), 87, 91, 92–98, 107, 200, 446–47; OK fleet development plan of 1895, evaluation of, 109–117; on torpedoes and torpedo boats, 48–51, 56, 61, 63, 65–66; Werner pamphlet, letter on, 36–37

Tirpitz, Christian Ferdinand (great-great-grandfather), 14

Tirpitz, Friedrich Wilhelm (grandfather), 14

Tirpitz, Ilse von (daughter), 70, 71–72, 73, 206, 410, 443

Tirpitz, Jacob Friedrich (great-grandfather), 14

Tirpitz, Malwine (née Hartmann; Tirpitz's mother), 14–15, 24, 70

Tirpitz, Margot von (daughter), 70, 71, 433, 443

Tirpitz, Marie von (née Lipke; Tirpitz's wife), 69–71, *204–205*, 432, 442, 443, 480n5, 494n36

Tirpitz, Max (brother), 15, 16, 30, 35, 44, 70

Tirpitz, Max von (son), 70

Tirpitz, Olga (sister), 15

Tirpitz, Paul (brother), 15

Tirpitz, Rudolf Friedrich (father), 14–17, 30–31, 32, 36, 70, 139, 203

Tirpitz, Wolfgang von (son), 70, 72, 379, 410, 524n12

Tirpitz Nachlass, 8

"Tirpitz Plan," existence of, 8, 9, 153, 154, 224–25, 234, 258, 287, 288, 350, 451, 453

Torpedo Arm, 47–68; assignment of Tirpitz to, 46, 48; under Caprivi, 55–64, 67, 68; contractors, Tirpitz's dealings with, 50, 52, 55–56, 59; departure of Tirpitz from, 64–65; development of torpedo boats, 48, 49–50, 52, 53, 54–55, 57–62; Fehman Sound, Battle of (1882), 53–54, *54*; fleet tactics, development of, 59–63; "fog of peace," dispelling, 83–84; later development of, 66; motherships, use of, 52, 60; Rational Actor model of interpreting Tirpitz and, 10, 456; significance of Tirpitz's time in, 67–68; under Stosch, 47–55, 67; in summer of 1914 leading up to WWI, 368; superiority of German torpedo fleet, 65–66, 480n111; Tirpitz's history of, 73; tonnage arguments, 360; torpedo technology, 47–49, 50, 52, 67–68, 358; U-boats initially placed under, 356; William II's naval plans and, 63–65

"Torpedo Gang," 52, 66–67, 263, 378, 445, 467–68, 483n15

torpedo warfare in WWI, 380

torpedoes in U-boats, 393

tow torpedoes, 47, 48

Trafalgar, Battle of (1805), 88
Transvaal: Boer War (1899–1903), 177, 179, 181, 182, 184, 190, 249, 295; Jameson Raid into Boer Republic (1895–96), 110, 113, 114
Treasury Department under Wermuth (1909–1912), 308, 314–16, 353
treaties: Brest-Litovsk (1918), 421; Caprivi trade treaties, expiration of, 177; Hamburg and Britain, treaties between, 19; Locarno (1925), 440; Rapallo (1922), 428; Reinsurance Treaty between Germany and Russia, 75, 104; Shimonoseki (1895), 118; Versailles (1919), 426, 428, 430, 431, 434, 438, 440, 441, 464
Treitschke, Heinrich von, 56, 72
Triple Alliance, 333, 344, 370
Trotha, Adolf von: on anti-navy sentiment in press, 1908–1909, 313; Bürkner, consultations with, 231; on Capelle, 135; on Emperor's battleship designs, 247; on flag-showing cruise of 1913, 352; historical narrative, role in recasting of, 465; Kapp and, 430; Navy Law amendment of 1906 and, 258; personal and professional relationship with Tirpitz, 263–64; post-war political involvement of, 430, 434; recasting of historical narrative by, 465; in reconciliation efforts between William II and Tirpitz, 442; *Tirpitz*, dedication of, 444; Tirpitz's memoirs and, 427, 428–29; on the "Torpedo Gang," 66; in U.S. with Tirpitz, 235; in WWI, 386, 404, 408, 411, 414, 415, 416, 423, 424
Truppel, Oskar (von), 67, 468
Tsingtau, China, German base at, 1, 122, 232, 313, 361, 381, 462
Tuchman, Barbara, 278
Turkey. *See* Ottoman Empire
Twain, Mark, 235
Tweedmouth Letter, 288, 291, 293
two-power standard, 278, 296, 300, 305, 306, 311, 337
II Division, German maneuver fleet, 73

U-boats, 353–57; distant blockade and, 365; Galster's advocacy of, 289; at Imperial War Council, 348; in Navy Law amendment of 1906, 256; in Navy Law amendment of 1908, 280; in Navy Law amendment of 1912, 328, 331, 339, 341; photograph of, 220; in summer of 1914 leading up to WWI, 368; Torpedo Arm, initially placed under, 356; torpedoes carried by, 393. *See also* World War I U-boats war
Ulan (tender), 52, 54
United Kingdom. *See* Britain
United States: on arms limitation/reduction, 276–77; China Trade, 117; Civil War, 18, 43, 235; declaration of war on Germany (1917), 417; *Dreadnought*-style battleship plans, 253, 282, 283; economic blockade in WWI and, 392, 394–95; growing economy of, 103; merchant marine, 33, 412; navy, 94, 235–36, 277; neutrality of, 115–16, 277, 392, 448, 457; in potential war between Germany and France/Russia, 115–16; risk theory and, 201; Samoan controversy and, 175; Spanish-American War (1898), 168, 171, 181; Tirpitz in, 119, 235–36; U-boat warfare in WWI and, 395–96, 399–401, 405, 407–408, 411–12, 416, 457; U-boats of, 256, 353–54; Venezuela, blockade of, 234

V (Verwaltungsabteilung), 240, 263
Valentini, Rudolf von, 333, 338
Valois, Victor, 164
Venezuelan debt crisis (1902) and blockade, 197, 234, 241
Versailles, Treaty of (1919), 426, 428, 430, 431, 434, 438, 440, 441, 464
Verwaltungsabteilung (V), 240, 263
Victoria, 41
Victoria (queen of England), 41, 63, 71, 82, 295
Victory, 26
Voigt, Torpedo Engineer, 51

Vollerthun, Waldemar, 386, 431, 433, 434

Von der Tann, 259, 273, 279, 282, 384

Vulkan torpedo boats, 58, 59

Waldersee, Alfred Graf von, 232–33

war crimes, Tirpitz accused of, 425, 430

war-guilt clause, Treaty of Versailles (1919), 426, 438

War of 1812, 392

Warrendon, Sir George, 384

Watson, British Naval Attaché, 336

Wegener, Wolfgang, 6, 397–99, 446, 465

Wehrverein, 345, 347, 351

Weimar Republic. *See* German Republic

Weizsäcker, Ernst von, 362

Weltpolitik: Bethmann-Hollweg not advocate of, 306; Bülow's efforts at, 231, 232, 234, 306; German colonialism and, 104; Kruger Telegram and calls for, 110; quietist approach to, 1900–1906, 231–34, 249–50, 273, 462; risk theory and, 5; as slogan versus reality, 466; Tirpitz's concept of, 450

Wermuth, Adolf: Navy Law amendment of 1912 and, 330, 331–33, 334; resignation of, 334, 341, 518n104; as Treasury Secretary, 308, 314–16, 353

Werner, Reinhold, 36–37, 40–42, 44

Weser of Bremen (shipbuilders), 53

Westfalen, 256, 319, 321

White Star Line, 400

Whitehead, Robert, and Whitehead torpedoes, 47–49, 50, 55, 67

Wickede, Wilhelm von, 53–54, 57, 62, 476n39

wide (distant) blockade, 134, 314, 362–65, 376, 389, 391, 414, 446–47

Widenmann, Wilhelm, 294, 299, 301, 310, 311, 338, 438

Wiegand, Karl Henry von, 395, 405

Wiemer, Progressive Party delegate, 289, 290

Wilhelmshaven: at beginning of WWI, 1; construction of dockyards, 34; *Dreadnought*-type battleships based

in, 361; in Franco-Prussian War, 34–35; geography of, 375, 376; map, *xiv*; Prussian acquisition from Duke of Oldenburg, 21; shipbuilding capacity and costs, 225; Tirpitz's dislike of, 35, 45

Wille, Ulrich, Jr., 432

William I (emperor), 22, 36, 131, 466

William II (emperor): abdication of, 425; Admiralstab and, 321; *Aufbau* publication and, 438; Boxer Rebellion (1900) and, 232; as boy, 38; characterization of, 2, 3; Constitution, promise to revise, 419; crowned heads of Europe, relationship to, 234, 251, 283, 502n91; diplomatic talks with Britain and, 295–96, 297–98, 304, 307, 309, 311, 335, 336–37; *Dreadnought.*, response to construction of, 253–54, 256, 257; East Asia, interest in, 118; Fleet Commander, Koester appointed as, 318; German Army and, 131; German Navy, reorganization of, 4–5, 63–65, 76–77, 82, 98, 371, 480n160; on government coup against Reichstag, 4; Holtzendorff, Tirpitz's fears of replacement by, 346, 360; Imperial War Council, 348; on *Invincible* class, 269; *Invincible* class, reaction to, 272, 273; Jameson Raid, response to, 110; on Kiachou affair, 143; naval control exercised by, 163, 164–65; naval operations plans, 1911–1914, 361, 362, 363; Navy Law of 1898 and, 128, 129–30, 132, 133, 138, 141, 153; Navy Law of 1900 and, 171–72, 174, 178, 179, 180, 190; Navy Law amendment of 1906 and, 246–47, 260–62; Navy Law amendment of 1908 and, 267, 269, 272, 273, 281, 287–88, 291, 292; Navy Law amendment of 1912 and, 328, 329–30, 332, 333–34, 451, 515n32; Navy Law amendment of 1913–14, consideration of, 348–50; OK Chief of Staff, advancement of Tirpitz to, 79–80; OK, dissolution of,

156–64; OK fleet development plan and, 109, 125–28; photographs of, 212, 214; population and economic growth of empire under, 103–104; reconciliation with Tirpitz, efforts to engineer, 442; Russia, proposed German alliance with, 251, 462; Second Moroccan Crisis and, 323, 325; ship design efforts of, 246–49, 254–55; ship types supported by, 100, 102, 106–107; on ships' gun calibers, 346; in summer of 1914 leading up to WWI, 366–73; Supreme Naval Commander, failure to function as, 448–49, 524n17; tactical development assigned to OK by, 84; Tirpitz family and, 71; Tirpitz's ability to handle, 223, 224–25, 247, 315, 342, 378; Tirpitz's appointment as RMA State Secretary, 113–14, 117; Tirpitz's efforts to replace, 396, 405, 416, 424, 452; in Tirpitz's memoirs, 429; Tirpitz's wariness of, 79; in turf wars between OK and RMA, 98, 100, 156; in WWI, 378–88, 391, 395, 396, 399, 400, 401, 403–408, 413–16, 418, 423, 424

William (Crown Prince, son of William II), 396, 403, 405, 411, 424, 429

Wilson, Arthur, 364

Wilson, Woodrow, 392, 399, 401, 424, 426

Windthorst, Ludwig, 106

Winkler, Raimund, 67, 263, 468, 483n15

Wittelsbach class, 225, 226

Wolff-Metternich, Paul Graf von, 294–95, 298, 300, 301, 308, 310, 335, 339, 348, 510n17

Woodward, E. L., 510–11n28, 511n36

world policy. See Weltpolitik

World War I, 375–409; armistice, 424–25; Dogger Bank, Battle of (1915), 384–85, 387; economic blockade in, 388–93, 394–95, 399; end of, 422–25; Falkland Islands, Battle of (1914), 219, 381, 383; geographic advantages

and disadvantages of Germany and Britain in, 375–77, 414, 445–49; German GHQ in, 378, 385–88; German Revolution at end of, 425; Holtzendorff appointed as head of Admiralstab, repercussions of, 401, 403–408; initial phase, 377–81; Jutland, Battle of (1916), 412–15, 426; leadership of German Navy in, 371–72, 377–78, 460–61; material positions of Germany and Britain at beginning of, 375–77; morale of Navy and, 396, 401, 422–23, 424–25, 427; operations and engagements through spring of 1915, 381–85; position of German Navy at beginning of, 1–3; reparations for, 432, 435, 443; RMA in, 401–403, 405; scuttling of German Navy after, 427–28, 464–65; suicide charge, collapse of, 424–25; summer of 1914 leading up to, 366–74; Tirpitz in retirement during, 410–18; Tirpitz's decline of power with, 373–74, 377–78, 403–404; Tirpitz's resignation from RMA, 408–409; Tirpitz's son and son-in-law in, 72–73; Tirpitz's unawareness of realities of war in, 397, 406, 461; Wegener memoranda, 397–99

World War I U-boats war, 393–96; Capelle's acceptance of restricted policy on, 410–11; construction of U-boats, slowing of, 402, 408; countermeasures in, 418, 423; first offensive, 399–401; Flanders naval front, 380; Holtzendorff's views on, 403, 406–407, 416, 417, 418; morale of U-boat crews, 422, 423; neutrality and, 399, 407, 457, 526n84; in North Sea, 382, 393; resumption of unrestricted use of, 416–18, 423; Tirpitz's championing of unrestricted use of, 388, 395–96, 400, 402, 406–407, 411–12, 415, 416–17, 457; U.S. neutrality and restriction of, 395–96, 399–401, 405, 407–408, 411–12, 416, 457

World War II, Tirpitz's legacy in, 465–66
Württemberg, 73–74

Xerxes, 45

Yalu, Battle of the (1894), 87
Yarrow torpedo boats, 58, 60
Yorck, 227
Young Plan, 443

Z (Zentralabteilung), 235, 236, 256, 357, 359
Zabern affair, 352

Zanzibar exchanged for Helgoland, 75, 104
Zeender, John, 151
Zeiten, 48–52, 60, *215*
Zelikow, Philip, 10
Zentralabteilung (Z), 235, 236, 256, 357, 359
Zeppelins, 331, 341, 385
Zeye, Hugo, 67, 119, *213*, 468
"Ziel erkannt, Kraft gespannt," 10
Ziese, Carl, 303–304
Zimmerman Telegram, 417
Zollverein (tariff union), 20

PATRICK J. KELLY is Professor of History at Adelphi University. His article on the Imperial German Navy, "Strategy, Tactics, and Turf Wars: Tirpitz in the Oberkommando der Marine, 1892–1895," won the *Journal of Military History*'s Moncado Prize in 2003.

This book was designed by Jamison Cockerham and set in type by Tony Brewer at Indiana University Press and printed by Thomson-Shore, Inc.

The text type is Electra, designed by William. A. Dwiggins in 1935, and the display type is ITC Machine, designed by Bonder & Carnase, Inc. in 1970, both issued by Adobe Systems Incorporated.